Human Factors Issues in Complex System Performance

Edited by

D. de Waard
G.R.J. Hockey
P. Nickel
K.A. Brookhuis

2007, Shaker Publishing

Europe Chapter of the Human Factors and Ergonomics Society

europechapter@hfes-europe.org

http://www.hfes-europe.org

© Copyright Shaker Publishing 2007

All rights reserved. No part of this publication may be reproduced, stored in a retrieval system, or transmitted, in any form or by any means, electronic, mechanical, photocopying, recording or otherwise, without the prior permission of the publishers.

Printed in The Netherlands.

D. de Waard, G.R.J. Hockey, P. Nickel, and K.A. Brookhuis (Eds.).

Human Factors Issues in Complex System Performance

ISBN 978-90-423-0325-6

Chapter and cover illustrations by Eva Fabriek (http://www.lelijkepoppetjes.nl)

Cover design by Klaas Woudstra

Shaker Publishing BV
St. Maartenslaan 26
6221 AX Maastricht
Tel.: +31 43 3500424
Fax: +31 43 3255090
http://www.shaker.nl

Contents

Preface 9
   Dick de Waard, Bob Hockey, Peter Nickel, & Karel Brookhuis

The human factors of complex systems: a personal view 11
   Neville Moray

WORKLOAD & WORK ANALYSIS 41

Tactile land navigation for dismounted soldiers 43
   Maaike Duistermaat, Linda R. Elliott, Jan B.F. van Erp,
   & Elizabeth S. Redden

Sleep loss and complex team performance 55
   Jeff Whitmore, Scott Chaiken, Joseph Fischer,
   Richard Harrison, & Donald Harville

The structure of contributing factors of human error in safety-critical industries 67
   Nicki Marquardt & Rainer Höger

Cognitive Work Analysis of a Sensor to Effecter System:
   implications for network structures 73
   Daniel P. Jenkins, Neville A. Stanton, Guy H. Walker,
   Paul M. Salmon, & Mark S. Young

A computer based tool for cognitive workload measurement in marine operations . 85
   David Embrey & Claire Blackett

Short-term heart rate measures as indices of momentary changes in invested
   mental effort 101
   Ben Mulder, Heleanne Rusthoven, Marnel Kuperus,
   Michel de Rivecourt, & Dick de Waard

Concurrent validity of an ocular measure of mental workload 117
   Marco Camilli, Michela Terenzi, & Francesco Di Nocera

Enhanced decision support for train drivers: "Driving a train by the seat of
   your pants" 131
   Anjum Naweed, Richard Bye, & Bob Hockey

Human reliability: analysis of procedure violations on traffic control of a
   light railway network 145
   Pedro Ferreira

Railway infrastructure engineering in the wild 157
   Richard Bye & Anjum Naweed

Biomechanics of securing vehicles for transport 161
   Sandra Anstaett Metzler, Jeffrey Bookwalter, & Nick Eiselstein

TRANSPORTATION 167

'Intuitive' vibrotactile collision warnings for drivers 169
   Cristy Ho, Nick Reed, & Charles Spence

Driver behaviour analysed by image analysis 177
   Gaetano Bosurgi, Antonino D'Andrea, & Orazio Pellegrino
Evaluation of different ergonomic factors in the cabin of drivers
   in public transport 185
   Iva Macku & Alexandr Pesak
Perceived styling and usability in integrated centre panel layouts as a
   function of interaction style and age 193
   Robert Broström, Peter Bengtsson, & Jakob Axelsson
Driver attitudes towards advanced driver assistance systems
   – a cross-cultural study 205
   Anders Lindgren, Robert Broström, Fang Chen, & Peter Bengtsson
Solving communication problems in the transportation sector 217
   Claire Huijnen & Ilse Bakx
Correlates of simulator sickness in a truck driver training programme and the
   development of an effective screening process 221
   Nick Reed & Andrew M. Parkes
Enhanced information design for high speed trains 235
   Anjum Naweed, Richard Bye, & Bob Hockey
Effects of a new railway information system on train driver efficiency
   and subjective performance 241
   Karel Brookhuis, Irene Taroni

SITUATION AWARENESS 251

The use of three-dimensional animations in aircraft maintenance documentation .. 253
   Joël Tapie, Yvonne Barnard, Patrick Mazoyer, Jonathan Devun, & Marie Moal
Shared situational awareness as a systems-level phenomenon: applying
   propositional networks to shared awareness in teams 267
   Chris Baber, Robert J. Houghton, Richard McMaster, & Neville A. Stanton
Representing Distributed Situation Awareness: a case study in
   Multi-National operations 277
   Paul M. Salmon, Neville A. Stanton, Chris Baber, Guy H. Walker,
   Rob Houghton, Daniel P. Jenkins, & Richard McMaster
Users' mental models of infotainment systems 291
   Tanja Schilling

AUTOMATION 305

A comparison of HEART and FMEA risk assessment results in evaluating an
   automated dispensing system in hospital pharmacy 307
   Tabassum Jafri, Melinda Lyons, Shelly Jeffcott, James Ward, & John Clarkson
Making it quantitative: early phases of development of a new taxonomy
   for levels of automation 313
   Michela Terenzi, Marco Camilli, & Francesco Di Nocera
Development of a cyclic loading method for the study of patterns of breakdown
   in complex performance under high load 325
   Peter Nickel, Adam C. Roberts, Michael H. Roberts, & G. Robert J. Hockey

Effects of cyclic loading on complex performance and operator functional state .. 339
    G.E. (Gareth) Conway & G.R.J. (Bob) Hockey
How to develop and use assistance systems efficiently – Using the microworld
    to acquire knowledge for developers and operators... 345
    Barbara Gross & Jens Nachtwei
Do cognitive assistance systems reduce operator workload?................................. 351
    Stefan Röttger, Krisztina Bali, & Dietrich Manzey
Supporting human-centred function allocation through animated formal models . 361
    Hendrik Oberheid, Bernd Lorenz, & Bernd Werther
Design of alarm systems in different complex control settings.............................. 373
    Anna Thunberg & Anna-Lisa Osvalder

INTERFACE ISSUES.. 385

Locating task-objective relevant information in text 387
    Martin Groen & Jan Noyes
Haptic, visual and cross-modal perception of interface information 399
    Annie Rydström & Peter Bengtsson
Control of information flooding and mode confusions: lessons from major
    engineering projects... 411
    W. Ian Hamilton, Joanne Stokes, & Graham Kenyon
Videoconferencing in a collaborative environment: Do partial gaze awareness
    and shared workspace make a difference?... 423
    Marc Arial & Brigitta Danuser

INSPECTION & MONITORING 433

Effects of time pressure on searching for terrorist threats in X-ray air
    passenger luggage images... 435
    Xi Liu & Alastair Gale
Methodological approach to advancing airport screener X-ray threat
    detection skills 443
    Gerald D. Gibb, Bill C. Fischer, & Brett R. Cabeca
Using SWOT and risk analysis in prevention of coal dust emission during its
    transportation in Tallinn ports... 455
    Piia Tint, Henn Tosso, Karin Reinhold, & Kai Aava

TRAINING AND ORGANISATIONAL ISSUES 461

Adaptive training methodology: skills analysis for the design of a Targeting
    Pod training programme 463
    Jelke van der Pal & Machteld van der Vlugt
Cognitive requirements analysis to derive training models for controlling
    complex systems 475
    *Dina Burkolter, Annette Kluge, Kerstin Schüler, Jürgen Sauer, & Sandrina
    Ritzmann*
How should causal knowledge about complex technical systems be trained?........ 485
    Anne Klostermann

Training operators in Micro-World simulations 491
   Michael H. Roberts, Adam C. Roberts, Peter Nickel, & G. Robert J. Hockey
Introducing "medarbetarskap" as a concept facilitating work related
   relationships: theoretical considerations in an airport change process 497
   Johan Jönsson, Curt R. Johansson, Marcus Arvidsson, Roland Akselsson

Acknowledgement to reviewers 511

Preface

Dick de Waard[1,2], Bob Hockey[3], Peter Nickel[3], & Karel Brookhuis[1,2]
[1] University of Groningen, [2] Delft University of Technology
The Netherlands
[3] The University of Sheffield
UK

The 2006 annual conference of the Europe Chapter of the Human Factors and Ergonomics Society was held in Sheffield, England. This publication summarises the content of that meeting, with contributions based on presentations that were given. The book begins with a written version of the keynote address by Neville Moray, who has personally witnessed the history of Human Factors from its beginning, and has managed to condense his detailed "personal view" into 30 pages.

Apart from the keynote, 44 papers are included, grouped into seven chapters. Eva Fabriek has kindly illustrated these chapters and the cover with her "lelijke poppetjes" ("ugly little figures"). A big thanks to Eva, amongst other things, for giving her view on "Bird Strike" (p. 461).

We are indebted to all who made the meeting and the book a success. In particular we would like to thank the external reviewers, who took the trouble to support us editors and evaluate the manuscripts thoroughly, and The University of Sheffield Department of Psychology for hosting us. The conference was also supported by the European Office of Aerospace Research and Development of the USAF, under Award No. FA8655-07-1-5004. We are very grateful for all this support.

In D. de Waard, G.R.J. Hockey, P. Nickel, and K.A. Brookhuis (Eds.) (2007), *Human Factors Issues in Complex System Performance* (pp. 9). Maastricht, the Netherlands: Shaker Publishing.

The human factors of complex systems: a personal view

Neville Moray
Magagnosc
France

Introduction

Exactly 50 years ago I finished my first year as an undergraduate psychology student at Oxford, and the following year the Human Factors Society (now the Human Factors and Ergonomics Society) was founded. Furthermore I recently (Moray, 2005) reviewed ergonomics work over more than a century, and I would like to consider some of the changes that have occurred in that period. I will present a very personal view: I am well aware that there will be exceptions to what I say were I to consider the history of ergonomics in many European, Japanese and other foreign countries. I shall throughout assume that "ergonomics" means the same as "human factors".

It is a particular pleasure to give this, my final talk on human factors, in Sheffield where such a significant part of my professional career took place under the guidance of the late Harry Kay, who was my first psychology tutor at Oxford, and a head of department here in Sheffield who always maintained a firm belief in the importance of psychological research being applicable even if not always applied.

The history of Ergonomics

Table 1 is a summary of the history of our discipline. It is modified from an outstanding review of the history of ergonomics by Zionchenko & Munipov (1989) which is far more thorough than any British or American histories.

In the 1950s the desire to make psychology a science was intense, although with the Applied Psychology Research Unit at Cambridge and several European groups doing ergonomics and applied psychology, I am puzzled that as students we did not hear more about ergonomics and human factors. It is amazing to realise that in 1956 the Human Factors Society had not been founded, and the first volume of Ergonomics had not yet appeared. In those days academic experimental psychology distanced itself both from applied psychology and from "soft" psychology, (clinical, personality, even to some extent social) in pursuit of a scientific status reflecting that of the physical and biological sciences.

Table 1. History of Ergonomics

1857	Jastrzebowski, W.B. "An Essay on Ergonomy, or Science of Labour Based on the Laws of Natural Science"
1898	Bryan, W. L. and Harter, N. Studies on telegraph operators
1900	Sechenov, I. Physiology of work and working conditions
1890-1920	Taylor, F., and Gilbreth, F.B. "Scientific Management"
1915	U.K. Health of Munition Workers Committee
1918	U.K. Industrial Health Board
1918	Soviet Department of Occupational Psychology and Labour Research Department
1920	The Hawthorne Experiments
1921	Tanaka, K. "Human Engineering" published in Japan
1930-	Dobrotvorsky, N. Human Factors Analysis of Aircraft Cockpit
1930s	Development of personnel psychology, motivation and groups dynamics in USA
1937	First volume of "Le Travail Humain"
1939 - 1945	World War II Tavistock industrial psychology, UK Flying Personnel Research Committee, Military human factors research, USA.
1949	U.K. Ergonomics Research Society
1953	U.S.A. First National Symposium on Human Factors
1957	Human Factors Society founded First volume of "Ergonomics"
1961	International Ergonomics Association
1970 - 1980	NATO Science Committee Special Panel on Human Factors
1993	Human Factors Society becomes Human Factors and Ergonomics Society

The methodology of psychology was modelled on physical science. See, for example, the monumental "Psychology: Study of a Science" (Koch, 1963) which aimed to justify psychology as a hard science based on a reductionist laboratory methodology. It is hard to appreciate how little experimental psychology could offer if asked to deal with "real" problems. There were three standard textbooks on experimental psychology; namely those by Osgood (1953), by Woodworth & Schlosberg (1953), and the encyclopaedic "Handbook of Experimental Psychology", edited by S.S. Stevens (1951). Although the last of these had a chapter called "Engineering Psychology" by Paul Fitts, it had little to contribute to human factors of complex systems as we deal with them today. Except for Fitts's (1951a) chapter there was little if any advance over the content of the admirable Woodworth (1938) "Experimental Psychology"[*].

The three chapters in Stevens that one might expect to be most relevant are those on *Learning*, on *Skills*, and the aforementioned *Engineering Psychology*. *Learning* is concerned almost entirely with conditioning, reinforcement theory, maze learning and the rote learning of verbal lists, and *Skills* concentrates on functions relating performance acquisition and practice, with data averaged over many subjects and many trials. There is almost no mention of knowledge of results, nothing on closed loop control, almost no mention of Information Theory (either of discrete or continuous signals), nothing (of course, given the date) about the Theory of Signal Detection, and almost no mention of real time dynamic tasks, even those as simple as single axis tracking. Fitts' chapter is mainly concerned with the design of instruments for cockpits, and while that underlines the claim that often there is less need for ergonomics research than for the application of classic results, there is little about dynamic tasks. There are brief references to the work of Birmingham & Taylor (subsequently published in 1954) on quickening and aiding, although the mathematics used are differential and integral calculus, not the much more powerful Laplace transforms, and there is some treatment of stimulus–response compatibility and stimulus–response stereotypes, including references back to the earlier work in the 1940's by Vince (1944). In no chapter is cognition discussed, nor the importance of a "sociotechnical" approach that would couple ergonomics and human factors as tightly to social science as to engineering. One or two comments that come from a contemporary document are interesting:

> *It is our conclusion, based on what we know about human abilities, that as a rule machines should monitor men* (Fitts, 1951a).
> *Research in human engineering should keep abreast of new engineering techniques, and new equipment developments if it is to foresee human operator problems and provide information in time to influence the design of new items* (Fitts, 1951a).

Although Fitts called for close relations with engineering there is not much evidence of it in the *Handbook*, and it is very striking in the history of the Ergonomics Society (Waterson & Sell, 2006) that there is no mention of any direct links with engineering. The Human Factors and Ergonomics Society (HFES) by contrast has always counted a substantial number of industrial and mechanical engineers among its members.

Looking then at the psychology of the early 1950s, while ergonomists were already asking to be allowed to take part in systems design they had little to contribute. What was the practice of applied experimental psychology like 50 years ago? If one *had*

---

[*] It is still possible to find copies of this text through second hand booksellers, and I strongly urge those who have never seen it to buy a copy. Some material in it has never been bettered and cannot readily be found elsewhere.

wished to investigate "the human factors of complex systems", what techniques were available?

Data logging was primitive, using either pencil and paper or bulky special purpose built electro-mechanical recorders. Photocopying did not exist. Tape recorders had only just become commercially available. (In 1957, Anne Treisman and I had to ask a manufacturer to build us "one–off" tape recorders because we needed independent stereo channels for research on auditory attention). Statistical calculation was done either by pencil and paper or at best by electromechanical machines such as the FACIT®. Digital computers did not exist. (I took the second course that was ever given at Oxford on how to program a computer in 1958, on the main frame Ferranti MERCURY using five-hole punched paper tape as the input medium.) No computer was available on a regular basis for data processing until well into the 1960s. The usual method for scoring manual tracking was to measure manually the amplitude of the signal and of the controlled output, and to compute the RMS error manually. It would be 20 years before a thorough review of mathematical models for the analysis of human–machine systems (HMS) would be available (Sheridan & Ferrell, 1974). More sophisticated mathematical analysis using power spectral analysis and Fourier analysis was used in the USA, but was very limited. John Senders once told one of my students that manually performing Fourier analysis meant that five minutes of tracking data required several months of hand calculation on electromechanical calculators. Faced with such constraints it is not surprising that we tended to adopt a research methodology that oversimplified the situation and concentrated on single variable laboratory tasks. It would have been almost impossible to perform experiments on complex systems.

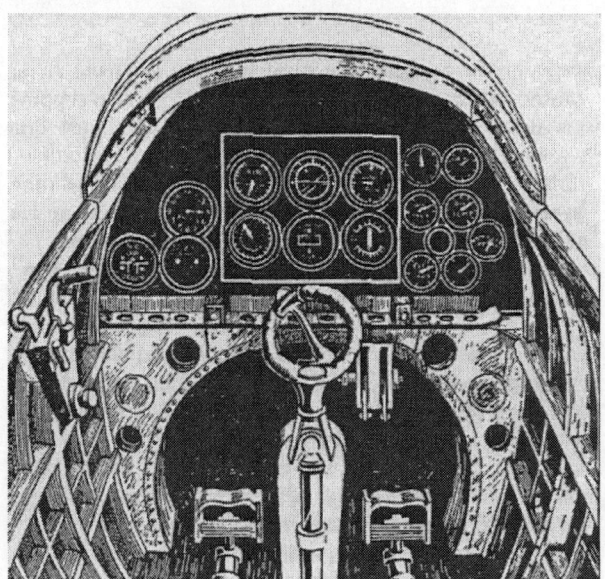

Figure 1. The Cambridge Cockpit

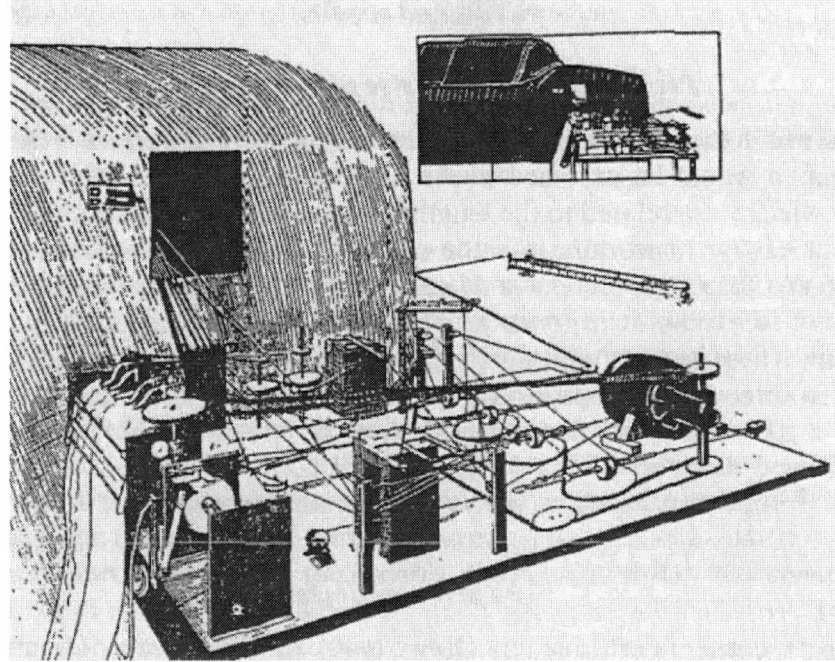

Figure 2. The Cambridge Cockpit mechanism details (Russell Davis, 1948)

There were some places where more realistic work was done, such as APRU in Cambridge (Broadbent, 1958), the Institute for Perception RVO-TNO in the Netherlands, at the Road Research Laboratory in the UK, and in some industrial laboratories, particularly in the British Steel Corporation. There was also a strong tradition of field studies of industrial processes, particularly in Belgium and France, which used methods that have become increasingly common in the 1990s and 2000s. (The approaches favoured by Klein et al. (1993) are really just a renewal of these earlier field studies.)

There were a few very early simulators such as the Link trainer in the USA, and the Cambridge Cockpit in the UK (Russell Davis, 1948). The latter (Figures 1 and 2) was a real example of "string and sealing wax" design, and is to modern simulators what the Swordfish biplanes that attacked the Bismarck are to modern jet fighters. There was I think, particularly in the United Kingdom, a pride in being able to do research on complex systems without a great expenditure of money and hardware, much in the same tradition as the love of veteran and vintage cars still plays a cultural role in the UK: as late as the 1970s Christopher Poulton (Poulton, 1974) would advocate the use of a smoked drum as a suitable way to record dynamic manual skills!

Research was thus constrained by the equipment available, by research funding, and also by a particular philosophy of science. The paradigm was usually to perform experiments that would exclude a major class of possible explanations (for example, in attention, "Does or does not selection occur prior to pattern analysis?"). Occasionally attempts were made to develop and test quantitative models, but following the failure of Hull's learning theory such attempts were rare. The statistical design aimed to establish a causal effect at an acceptable level of statistical significance, which was taken to mean that a variable did or did not have a causal effect. Almost never was the aim to predict behaviour in detail and moment-by-moment, that is in "real time". A highly significant effect was valued even if the size of the effect was negligible in its effect on performance, because it meant that there *really was a cause there!* Almost never was the aim to predict the behaviour of an individual; results were presented as group means, and were implicitly taken to express universal behavioural laws or effects – despite the fact that lip service was paid to the fact that subjects – I shall call them *participants* in the future – were drawn from very constrained populations, students, subject panels, or military "volunteers", and were overwhelmingly from North American and other Anglophone populations. What were being sought were "context-free" psychological laws. (I shall return to the problem of context later.)

That philosophy of science is very different from that of an applied science, particularly one that uses engineering as a paradigm. Engineering models are concerned above all with prediction, not explanation, and magnitude of effects is as important as significance – a highly significant result that explains only 1% of the variance in prediction is of little or no interest. Context, the particular setting in which research is carried out is seen as introducing both constraint and uncertainty. As Jens Rasmussen once said, "The operator completes the design of the system". Useful results are more important than truth. A model that is known to be wrong but that allows prediction to ±10% may well be acceptable. *The aim is to predict in detail* what will happen.

When are Human-Machine Systems "Complex"?

Complexity connotes a system that is difficult to understand and manage, and which has some or all of the following characteristics:

> many variables, many degrees of freedom, rich co-ordination and interaction among the variables (including interaction between human operator and automation if present), tight coupling among variables and usually between the human and the system, high orders of control and complex control laws, "opaque" displays that do not allow the operator to observe the state of the system easily, and poor feedback about the effect of control actions

For a more abstract description of a hierarchy of increasing complexity see Ashby (1956):

> *Deterministic* – systems that are completely and exactly predictable, because the state transition matrix is complete and there is only one transition from any current state to the next state.

Stochastic – systems that are completely but not exactly predictable because the state transition matrix contains all possible states and all possible transitions, but the transition from the current state to the next state is probabilistic.
Self-organising – systems whose components change "spontaneously" from time to time and are therefore neither completely nor exactly predictable. The state transition matrix changes from time to time.

In dynamic systems, whether involving single axis or multi-axis manual control, the feeling of complexity is related to the order of control, the presence of instability, the degree of homogeneity of control, and the physical form of the displays and controls provided. This feeling of complexity can arise even with quite simple systems. For example two-axis tracking is an easy task if both axes require the same order of control, say velocity control (1/s in Laplace form). If the spot moves both up and sideways at equal rates, one simply moves the control stick on the diagonal. But if the movements on the two axes have different control laws, even if one of them is simple, (k on the x-axis, say, and 1/s on the y-axis) the task becomes harder, and it seems that the two control tasks cannot be synthesised into a single task.

To show how quickly a simple task can become complex, consider the skill of scheduling (Sanderson, 1989, 1991) applied to a small scale laboratory study. Moray, Dessouky, Kijowski, & Adapathya (1991) investigated a task devised by Tulga & Sheridan (1980). Subjects were confronted with displays such as that shown in Figure 3.

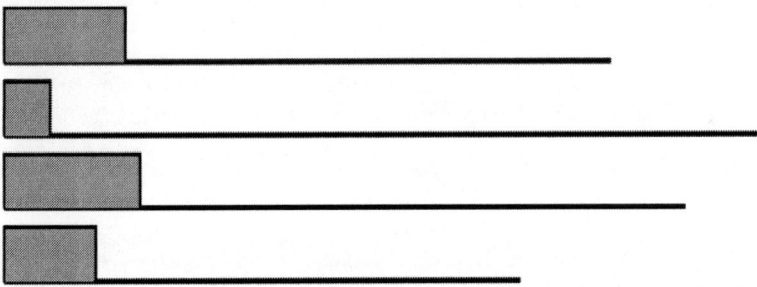

Figure 3. Tulga's Task. The blocks move from left to right. If the cursor is placed over a moving block its size is progressively reduced. The participant must reduce each block to zero before it reaches the deadline at the end of its horizontal line

The boxes moved from left to right at a fixed speed. In some versions all the boxes were initially the same size. In some versions all deadlines were equal. Sometimes, as shown, both block size and deadlines differed. The task was to reduce as many boxes as possible to zero size before each reached its own deadline at the end of its line. Subjects selected boxes with a cursor, and while the cursor pointed to a box its size was continuously reduced. The scheduling question is simple: in what order should one attack the boxes?

The answers to two of the three cases are:

> If all the deadlines are the same date, and just the sizes of the boxes differ, then the boxes should be attacked in the order smallest to largest (shortest task to longest task), and most people intuitively use this rule; If the boxes are identical and only the deadlines differ, then tasks should be performed in the order from earliest deadline to latest deadline, except that any task which cannot be finished by its deadline should not even be started.

The scheduling rule suddenly becomes very complex if we simply combine the two constraints as shown in Figure 3, so that both individual sub-task duration and the deadlines differ. Optimal scheduling now requires a much more elaborate rule – the Moore-Hodgson Algorithm for minimizing tardy jobs:

> Arrange the jobs in order from the earliest to the latest due date. Examine the jobs in sequence. If any job has a completion time less than or equal to its due date (that is, it can be finished in time) then leave it and continue to the next job in the list. If any job *cannot* be finished by its due date, then look back at the items so far considered in the list, and delete the one with the longest processing time (even though it was accepted earlier). Keep doing this until no more jobs remain to be considered. Use the resulting (usually reduced) list as the schedule for the task.

What looks like a trivial change to the task makes it subjectively extremely complex. Since scheduling rules are so often complex it is surprising that humans, interacting with automated schedulers, can produce joint performance that is better than "optimal"[*]. In real industrial situations human schedulers can be amazingly effective, providing that they are highly experienced and are fully conversant with the process, the degrees of freedom, the dynamics, the raw materials, the decision criteria, etc.

Returning to the mid-1950s, several conceptual frameworks were developed for the analysis of complex systems, of which two, Information Theory (Shannon & Weaver, 1947) and Cybernetics (Wiener, 1948) were particularly important. The first provided a common metric over different kinds of variables, based on the Shannon measure of uncertainty:

$$H = -\sum p_i \log_2 p_i$$

The assumptions of ergodicity and fixed channel capacity were soon shown to be incorrect, but the model was a useful approximation and remains so to this day. Sadly, since it has some attractive features as a metric of performance, relatively little use has been made of its application to continuous signals. It is related to cybernetics through the work of Ashby (1956) and Conant (1976) in the context of

---

[*] I always use the word "optimal" in a strong sense. An action is optimal, or a method optimal, if it can be shown by calculation that there is no action or method which can produce a better outcome given a well-defined quantitative performance criterion.

identifying the structure of complex systems[*]. The psychological scope of Information Theory was summarised by Garner (1962).

Models

Engineering is concerned with prediction, which requires a *model*, because one needs to foresee the future. In the 1950s the notion of a *mental* model was unknown; and indeed for several years, although not a philosophical behaviourist, I found it almost embarrassing to introduce the notion of a *mental model* in discussions with psychologists. It was in engineering circles that the notion of mental model first became acceptable, probably because engineers were used to the idea that a system could contain a model, particularly in control theory.

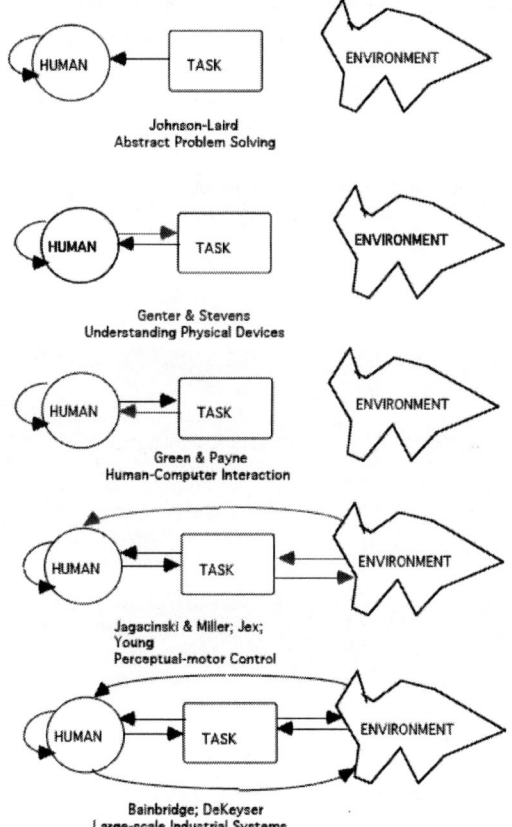

Figure 4. Types of mental model showing flows of information and control (Moray, 1990)

---

[*] The limitations on information theory are summed up in a delightful limerick, which seems to be anonymous, but that I suspect was written by George Miller: *Shannon and Wiener and I, Have found it confusing to try, To measure sagacity, And channel capacity, By $\Sigma p_i log p_i$*
I take this opportunity to pass it on to a future generation.

A fundamental question in modelling concerns the level at which the prediction is to be made, a question that is particularly important when we come to consider complex systems. Experimental psychology often aims at prediction at a very fine scale, reaction times to the nearest millisecond, accuracy to the nearest millimetre. Thus visual reaction time is said to be of the order of 180 ms and the frequency of eye-movements about 4 per second (Grandjean, 1980; Boff & Lincoln, 1988). Seldom are these values correct. Eye movements rarely occur faster than 2 per second in industrial tasks, and RTs may take almost any value, perhaps even several seconds, depending on the task being performed and the design of control rooms. Most constants of psychology and human factors are not really point estimates but asymmetric limits. The reaction time to a light, for example, should really be given as:

$$RT \geq (\mu, \sigma)$$

where μ is some measure of central tendency and σ a measure of expected range.

Context pushes the value of a variable away from equality. Consequently, if someone claims that a new system will ensure RTs below μ such a claim should be regarded with great suspicion unless particularly convincing empirical evidence is provided.

If we want to be able to predict what will happen in human-machine interaction we must choose an appropriate level of analysis. By *level of analysis* I mean something like Rasmussen's *Abstraction Hierarchy* (see Table 2).

Table 2. Rasmussen's Abstraction Hierarchy

Typical Operations	Means-Ends relations	Characteristic modes of thought
Produce and sell electricity to make a profit for the business	GOALS AND CONSTRAINTS	Necessary and sufficient properties to link the performance of the system and its design goals. Language in terms of demands of environment.
Run the plant at high power to follow the real time demands	ABSTRACT FUNCTION	Necessary and sufficient characteristics to prioritise according to design specifications and set points for mass-energy balances. Language in terms of abstract general properties, not specific to a particular plant.
Control local properties such as temperature, energy generation, coolant flows, etc.	GENERAL FUNCTION	Necessary and sufficient properties to identify functions which must be controlled without regard to the particular instantiations of those functions in this particular plant. Language in terms of well-known input-output relations and transfer functions.
Use particular sub-systems to control flows, pressures, core reactivity, etc.. Start a pump, change rod positions.	PHYSICAL PROCESSES AND ACTIVITIES	Necessary and sufficient properties to control particular work activities, choice and use of equipment, predict the results of intervention, diagnose and maintain subsystems. Language related to physical systems and processes.
Open a valve, change the position of a switch.	PHYSICAL FORM AND RELATIONS IN THE CONTROL ROOM	Necessary and sufficient properties to categorise, identify, and operate a particular component, and to physically explore the topology of the system. Language related to the designer's and architect's specification of the system

Consider for example, the well-known time-reliability relations reported by Beare, et al. (1984) shown in Figure 5. These curves allow a strong prediction of the overall performance of a team; but they throw little light or no light on the behaviour of the individuals of the team, or on the moment-to-moment performance of "basic" actions such as RTs or eye movements. But that is irrelevant. What is predicted is the time required to complete the task in relation to the time constants of the whole system, not to any subsystem. It is a model at a grain relevant (fine enough, fast enough) to predict behaviour on a time scale appropriate to the time constants of the hazardous process.

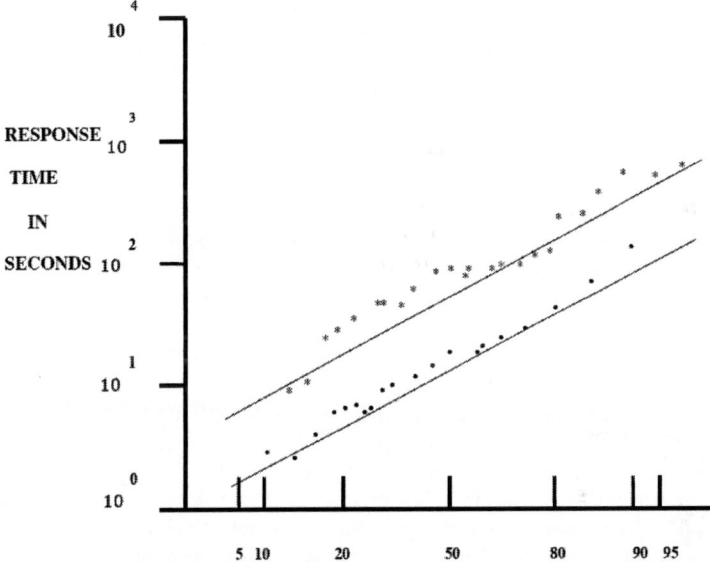

Figure 5. Cumulative probability (x 100) of response related to log(time) since incident (after Beare et al., 1984). The lower curve (•) shows data from performance in a simulator. The upper curve (*) shows data from the same events in real events.

Since human factors is engineering, we are more concerned to predict behaviour than to understand it. The ideal would be a *quantitative* prediction, or at least a *computational* prediction on an interval or ratio scale ("She will use this switch, not that one, at 09.45 not 09.46, to change the temperature to 434°C, not 550°C"), rather than merely an ordinal scale ("Performance will be faster with this control rather than with that, on the average"). One of the first examples of such quantitative prediction was the use of *Classical Control Theory* to describe the quantitative dynamics of human-machine systems (HMS), and to predict gain and phase relations of the input and output of human performance, the margin to stability, and the internal model used by the human to compensate for the properties of the hardware (McRuer & Krendel, 1976). The ability of McRuer and his co-workers to predict stability and performance in real time using the control model called the *Crossover Model* was extremely impressive, and they were able further to model the dynamics of the human muscular motor system, leaving only a small amount of variance unexplained as the *remnant*. They also described how humans can create a series of internal models each of which can compensate for the properties of a particular HMS (see also Young, 1973).

McRuer and his co-workers used Classical Control Theory in an engineering tradition. They assumed linearity, though they acknowledged that human operators are in fact non-linear. Humans can learn the nature of forcing functions and hence can predict the future course of the target. They show non-linear behaviour around perceptual thresholds, and adaptive behaviour of various kinds. Nonetheless, by making an "engineering approximation" of linearity, lumping all the non-linear elements into the remnant term, and assuming that latter can be characterised as white noise, McRuer was able to make predictions of human operator performance in HMS that were more than accurate enough for real applications. The later development of Optimal Control Theory (OCT) was even more powerful, since OCT allows prediction in the time domain for multivariate systems (Kleinman, Baron, & Levison, 1970; Veldhuijzen & Stassen, 1977). Although, as Sheridan once pointed out to me, the application of Classical Control Theory to HMS was perfected just as the rise of automation greatly diminished the importance of manual control; that is not true of the applications of OCT. It is also worth noting that control theory was used in human factors as early as the 1940s by Craik (1947), Tustin (1947), Bates (1947), and by Birmingham & Taylor (1954) a few years later. Most of these references did not appear in psychological or ergonomic journals and went largely unnoticed by psychologists.

By contrast, let us consider a purely psychological strongly predictive model called *GOMS*, or "The Model Human Processor" (Card, Moran, & Newell, 1983, 1986). Whereas control theory is an analytic model with a basis in calculus and Laplace Transform mathematics, GOMS is a "brute force" empirical model based on data from a wide range of experimental psychology, mainly laboratory research. From their vast collection of experimental data Card et al. estimated the mean and range of times for psychological processes such as perception, decision, the size of working memory, the effect of information uncertainty, and so on. Almost all of the model's components are "approximations", and some of them seem very uncertain indeed (for example the length of time a "perception" takes). However, almost everyone who has used GOMS finds that it can predict the time for a task within about ± 10%, which is quite adequate for many system design decisions in real applications. Perhaps its finest hour was the analysis of a proposed workstation design for telephone operators in which Gray, John, & Atwood (1993) predicted a loss of performance that would have cost the company of many millions of dollars. The success of GOMS is probably due to the fact that since most predictions require several estimated values, some will be over-estimated and others under-estimated, giving an overall value approximately correct.

So prediction, even with a purely psychological model, *is* possible. Why is it then there has been little successful application of predictive quantitative models in the last 20 years, despite the enormous rise in the computing power available to ergonomics and human factors? Is it that complex HMS are special in some sense?

Are they perhaps self-organising and open rather than stochastic or deterministic, so that prediction is inherently impossible? Or have we failed to choose suitable levels of abstraction at which to make predictions, and failed to develop a model for switching between levels of abstraction and between models in order to match the dynamics of the processes in which humans work? Even when the physics of a process is fairly simple, large industrial plant is inherently complex, and this emphasises the importance of choosing an appropriate level of analysis. Consider the classic paper by Dutton & Starbuck (1971), who discuss the skill of human schedulers and the cognitive processes which may be involved in a discrete manufacturing process. "Charlie" worked in a factory making cloth, controlling the machine shown in Figure 7, where cloth was formed, and then cut longitudinally ("ripped") and transversely ("cut"). His task was to estimate the time it would take to fill orders.

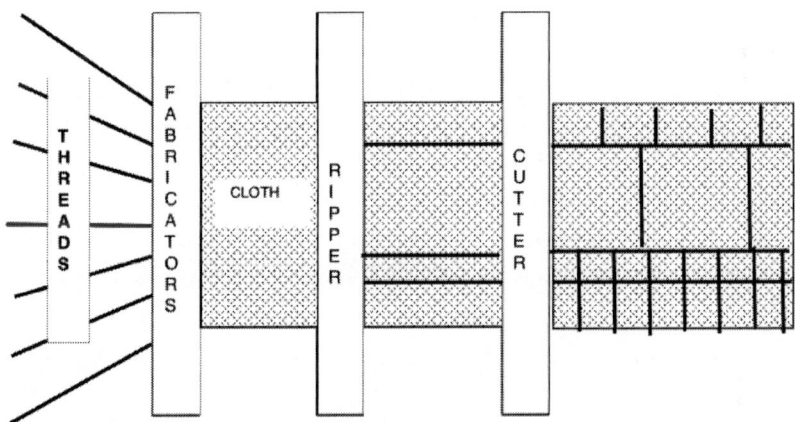

Figure 6. Schematic of "Charlie's" cloth making machine

Table 3. Variables in "Charlie's" scheduling task

Variables	Characteristics	Range of values
Fabricators	1 general, 1 specialised	1 – 2
Measures of schedules	length of material requested in yards	15 – 24000
Types of cloth		1 – 5
Properties of cloth		1 – 500
Width of cloth	number of fibres	1 – 30
Changes of width	number of different fibres	0 - 30
Characteristics of orders from clients		1 – 50
Speed of process	yards per hour	600 – 2400
Duration of run	estimation of remaining material to be cut (hrs)	0.5 – 24

The total number of possibilities is extremely large and yet Charlie was able to perform accurate mental estimates of how long orders would take. After working with "Charlie" for a year Dutton and Starbuck constructed two models of Charlie's behaviour based on objective measures of his behaviour and on interviews and verbal protocols. One was a formal engineering model, based on their observations, and the second was an estimate, based on how Charlie's account of what he was doing.

To predict the production run time, Charlie used his knowledge of the kind of cloth being produced, and the raw material of which the cloth was to be made, the set up of the ripper (which makes the longitudinal cuts), the number of changes of width required, the speed of the machine in yards per hour, the average length of rips, the sum of rip length, the value of this sum divided by the speed, and "several other factors". This involves many thousands of possible values. Dutton and Starbuck developed the following quantitative equation to describe Charlie's behaviour:

$T = aR + (b + gW)L$

where: T = The sum of the times for the segments scheduled, R = The number of "ripper set-ups" used, W = The weight per square yard of the cloth, L = The length in yards of the material to be produced, a = Time required for "set-up", and $(b + gW)$ = time per yard produced.

They also developed a model based on what Charlie told them of how he worked:

$T = L/S$ (1)

where:

$S = f(A, \text{type of cloth, texture, properties of material})$ (2)

and S = speed measured in yards/hour, A = mean length of a "rip".

(Note that $S = 1/(a/A + b + gW)$ even if Charlie was unaware of the fact.)

Dutton & Starbuck comment, "Charlie thus uses two non-linear relations, of which one is quite complex, in order to construct a simple linear relation." This latter is then used to schedule the task. Relation (1) seems to be a description of a mental model rather than a true equation, and (2) is effectively a very large multidimensional look-up table, with between 2000 and 5000 entries. Even very large lookup tables as components of mental models are probably less demanding from the point of view of mental workload than performing mental calculations. Charlie seems to be using a combination of RBB (Rule Base Behaviour, the look-up table) and KBB (Knowledge Based Behaviour, reasoning), and a mental model built up by long experience, to avoid direct complex calculation.

For comparison, nuclear power plants (NPPs) have about 45 degrees of freedom, and are usually managed by teams of two or three control room operators provided with some 1000 displays and controls, or, if computerised, several hundred pages of graphical displays. Even if access to the data displays were instantaneous it is inconceivable that an operator could track the value of such a data vector. The operators *cannot* know the complete state of the system at each moment, so how do they control it? In principle it is necessary and sufficient to monitor only as many variables as there are degrees of freedom, providing they are suitably chosen. But even that can leave an operator with an overwhelmingly large data processing problem.

A mental model of a process can be much smaller providing that the abstraction hierarchy is used to reduce the effective size of the system. Consider a system with the following variables and the number of states indicated: U (2 states), V (4 states), W (3 states), X (2 states), Y (2 states), and Z (3 states). There are about 300 potential system states. But if the operators can model the system appropriately the complexity of the system can be greatly reduced. Operators might discover that U and V are strongly correlated, and that the value of V is caused by the combination of U and Y; that W and Z are closely related, but that the combination of W and X are not connected with the combination of U,V,Y, and that X is independent of all the others. The variables (the "atoms" of which the system is composed), are naturally grouped into "molecules" whose composition are {U,V,W}, {W,Z}, and {X}. For example, U might be a pressure, V a rate, and W the mass of fluid shifted through a pipe, while {U,V,W} can be identified not as a set of variables, but as a "Pump". Similarly W might be a measure of electric current and Z a temperature, and {W,Z} a "Heater". X is the quantity of product manufactured. So operators can think just about "the state of the pump", "the state of the heater", and "productivity". The system then subjectively has only 3 variables, defined at the level of "molecules", rather than 6 variables at the "atomic" level. If the molecules themselves could be combined, {{U,V,W},{W,Z}} would be thought of as a single entity, a "Steam Generator".

What I have described is the subjective construction of a Rasmussen *Abstraction Hierarchy* by highly practised operators form a mental model of the system in their minds. Moray (1987) describes how an operator can reduce the number of states of a simple thermal-hydraulic system that must be considered from 96 to 12. Moray (1990) has developed these ideas into a formalism for mental models, and shows how lattice theory can relate Rasmussen's Abstraction Hierarchy to mental models and the way that operators handle complex HMS. How can people discover the dynamic structure of a system? One possibility was suggested by Roger Conant, who was I believe Ross Ashby's last Ph.D. student (Conant, 1976; Conant & Moray, 1979). His papers are deeply fascinating, and show how an advanced form of Information Theory analysis can identify the natural "molecular structure" of a set of dynamic variables even if one has no information other than the value of all the variables as a function of time.

When variables within a "molecule" are tightly coupled the value of one will give an observer information about the value of others, thus reducing the number of variables whose values need to be sampled to identify the system state. This is a virtue to offset what Perrow (1984) saw as a vice and a source of "normal accidents".

Bainbridge (1974), Iosif (1968), and Moray (1981) each suggested that "intramolecular" correlation should change the pattern of attentional sampling, and could in principle reduce operator workload, and Iosif (1969) recorded sampling behaviour that showed such effects in a power station control room (see Figure 7).

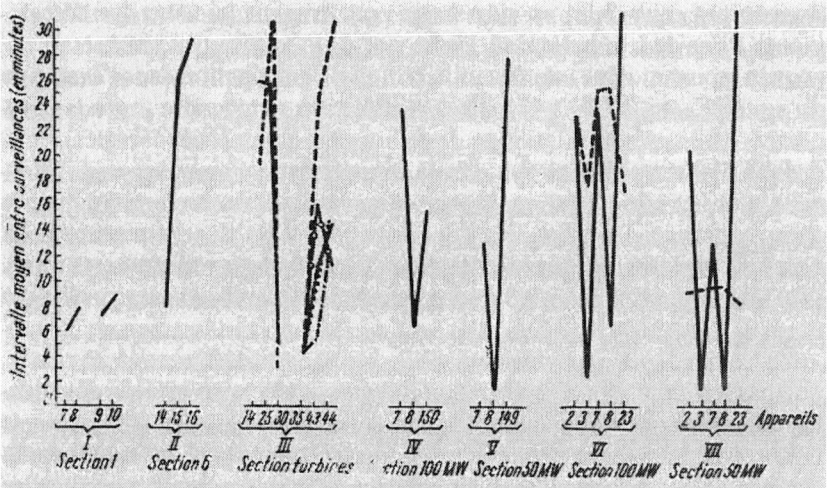

Figure 7. Mean intervals between samples in groups of correlated variables. In this figure each Roman number denotes a subsystem, and within each subsystem the Arabic numerals denote displays relevant to that subsystem. Note that in every case there are one or two variables that are frequently sampled, and several others that are sampled only rarely

Surprisingly, little research seems to have been done on how well can people detect correlation and causality in dynamic systems although it is of great importance, both for economic control and for the management of faults in hazardous systems. What work there is has been done in artificial laboratory tasks, without real-time dynamics, and participants are asked to reason about sets of data to detect correlation. But as Dutton & Starbuck's study of Charlie showed, that is *not* how people handle a complex system. They *live* it; they do not *reason* about it. They come to *embody* the dynamics in their (often unconscious) mental models. A classical experiment is an early paper by Senders (1964, 1983) showing that observers develop a sampling strategy that matches closely that required by the Sampling Theorem in Information Theory. The dynamics of the controlled process copy themselves as a model into the mind of the observer, and then control behaviour appropriately. That is probably why Rasmussen found that people prefer to work at the level of RBB. Lee and Moray (1989) found that people could detect correlations among variables presented as dynamic bar graphs to a limited extent (see Figure 8). I know of *no* research on the detection of negative correlation.

One may think it ironic that while the reductionist approach was adopted by experimental psychology to discover general context-free laws, the greatest progress in understanding complex HMS has come from almost the antithesis of that methodology, namely from field studies. Since the 1960s both quantitative equations and flow chart models of HMS have been proposed for process control industries (Iosif, 1968, 1969a,b; Bainbridge, 1974; De Keyser, 1981).

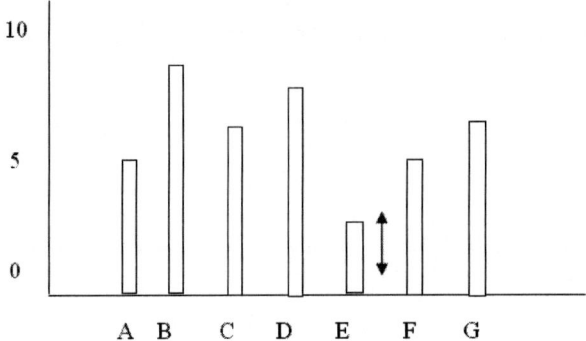

Figure 8. Detection of dynamic correlation. The display used by Lee and Moray. The bars move continuously up and down driven by band-limited white noise. The movements of some of the bars are correlated. People were able easily to detect positive correlations between, say B and D when it existed, but found it much harder to detect the same magnitude of correlation between B and E because their absolute heights differed greatly

A related problem that has often been studied is how theoretical training can help operators to reason about the processes they control during fault management. But it is very difficult to show benefits of theoretical training and experienced operators often claim that theoretical courses are a waste of time. Is this because we have forgotten the classical analysis of causality? Aristotle (*circa* 350 BC) and St. Thomas Aquinas (13th Century AD) distinguished between *efficient* and *material cause*. An example of an efficient cause is, "If I turn this knob to the right the thermometer reading increases."; that is, about *what* to do. A typical material cause is, "If I increase the neutron flux there will be more energy transferred to the coolant."; that is, an account of the underlying physics, *why* to do it. For theoretical training (material causality) to help, the operator must know the correlation between the position of the knob and the position of the control rods, and that the latter controls the neutron flux, and that the energy density is reflected in the thermometer reading. Since traditional hands-on training (efficient causality) and theoretical physics (material causality) are not taught together, how can the operator discover the correlation? Why *should* theoretical training help? The implication of these ideas for training is obvious, and I will leave it as an exercise for the reader.

This is a suitable place to refer to the enormous contribution made by Jens Rasmussen's ideas. It is not too much to say that he caused a paradigm shift in the way that engineers and psychologists view how people think about complex systems. There are three outstanding contributions that Jens has made, his *"ladder"*, the *Abstraction Hierarchy*, and the *Skills, Rules, Knowledge* characterisation of behaviour. If an observer starts from raw data, models it, models the model, and so on, he is unconsciously constructing an Abstraction Hierarchy (Rasmussen, 1986, Rasmussen et al, 1995; see Table 2).

Another property of mental models is that they allow the operator to think about subsystems at different levels of abstraction. It may be that for one of the coolant pumps the operator is concerned with the exact value of the rpm, and thinks about the exact value of a particular gauge, say the pump rpm, asking, "Does meter 27/A read greater than 1530, and is it rising?" But at the same time, because of past monitoring of Pump B, he is thinking of Pump B at a much more abstract level. "Is Pump B still O.K.?" To which the expected answer is simply "Yes" or "No", perhaps based on the colour of the alarm tiles, ignoring details and quantitative information. At any moment the way in which different aspects of the plant are represented in cognition are quite different – some qualitative, some quantitative; some detailed, some general; some material cause, some efficient cause, some even *final cause* (that is, goal orientated: "Will we be able to meet the demand if I hold the pump at 1250 rpm?").

There are important implications for fault management. It may be easy to see that a gauge is abnormal if it is being monitored for its exact value. But if it is being monitored to see whether the schedule or demand can be fulfilled it may be much harder to see that it is abnormal, because what counts as abnormal for a goal may not be what is abnormal in a failing component. Very slow changes (very low bandwidth) may be as hard to detect and understand as very fast changes, and when an abnormal state is detected at some level of abstraction the operator must decide the appropriate Level of Abstraction to use to perform fault diagnosis and fault management.

The fact that mental models contain mixed levels of abstraction suggests how prediction "to a good engineering approximation" can be achieved. We saw that Dutton & Starbuck (1971) found that operators do not identify states by calculating from raw data, but rather use pattern matching against a look-up table in memory to identify the state. There is support for this idea from the work of Beishon (1974) and from field studies (Klein et al. 1993). The efficiency of pattern matching was also shown by Vicente et al. (1996) in the context of ecological interface design in a simulated nuclear power plant steam generation system. When data were presented in the form of 45 gauges, experienced NPP operators could diagnose faults, but mechanical engineering students could not. But when the same data were presented in the form of an "ecological" display, an animated Rankin Cycle graphic, even the novices were quite successful. Ecological Interface Displays (EIDS) provide information at levels of abstraction best suited to an integrated understanding of plant state, but can be configured so that if the operator wants to revert to a more data-heavy display with little abstraction, they can do that easily[*].

Even in situations using more conventional displays strong predictions can be made. I have recently shown that by using detailed data about the psychophysiology of eye movements one can predict the probability that a train driver will perform a SPAD (Signal Passed At Danger) and that one can offer design decisions about the location

---

[*] However, research on EIDS is still at an early stage. Until it is more developed, should one say, parodying Shakespeare in *Julius Caesar*, "Beware the march of EIDS"?

of signals and the choice of speed limits to avoid SPADs at any level of risk one may specify (Moray, 2006).

The social dynamics of groups and teams make it more difficult to make prediction at the level of micro-data. But perhaps here too the question is that of choosing an appropriate level of abstraction. It is not only by choosing a very general level we can make predictions – after all that is what macroergonomics is about. But perhaps we can use a highly abstract level of analysis and description to find a portion of the task or system that can be regarded, for a particular task, as isolated *by* the social interaction from many of the task dimensions. In some situations one or several members of the team may act as filters, preventing external disturbances from acting on the critical operators, whose performance can then be modelled more simply (Conant, 1976). There are examples of this in some SAINT and microSAINT simulations. At its simplest a secretary or a personal assistant acts as a filter and makes it easier to predict the boss's behaviour by reducing the variety and uncertainty in the latter's environment. (Conant & Ashby showed that it takes as much information processing to block information selectively as to transmit it.) An important discovery has been that adding humans to improve system reliability does not have the same effect as adding redundant components. If two pumps each have a probability of failure of $p = 0.001$, then the probability of independent joint failure is clearly $p = 0.00001$. But if a human has a probability of error of $p = 0.01$, then adding a second human may increase this probability if the operator thinks his assistant will catch errors, decrease it if he thinks he will be reported by his colleague if he does not perform perfectly, or leave it unchanged.

Humans and automation

Perhaps the most dramatic change in ergonomics since the 1950s is the rise of automation, together with a vast increase in computational power and a change in function allocation between humans and machines in complex HMS. Here the work of Sheridan (1976, 1987, 1992, 1997) and his co-workers has led the field. The famous "Fitts List" defining what humans do best and machines do best was published in 1951 (Fitts, 1951b). There is doubt as to whether Fitts's list was ever really used in systems design, and in the last 50 years we have reached a situation where, given enough money and enough determination, almost anything that humans can do in a HMS can be performed by machines and computers. Furthermore Fitts's list was a pre-emptive static allocation of function. The contemporary approach to function allocation emphasises the dynamic real-time interaction of human and machine rather than an *a priori* allocation at the design stage (Parasuraman, Sheridan, & Wickens, 2000).

With the changes in allocation of function has come an interest in the social relations between humans and machines, which has developed from the work on trust that began in my laboratory in Toronto (Muir, 1987, 1994; Muir & Moray, 1996; Lee & Moray, 1992, 1994; Tan & Lewandowsky, 1996; Lee & See, 2004; Parasuraman & Riley, 1997). This work has already allowed quantitative prediction of the effect of trust on function allocation, and we can expect the work on trust in machines to give us better ability to predict interaction among the members of teams. The work of

Hutchins (1995), and of Rochlin, Laporte, & Roberts (1987) on the self-organising properties of teams in high reliability systems is also of great importance. In hazardous situations the hierarchy of control in a system such as an aircraft carrier changes spontaneously so that the most experienced and appropriate person informally takes command for the duration of the crisis. I have seen similar behaviour in NPP control rooms, where if an operator has a particularly heavy workload and a possibly hazardous situation develops, members of other teams with less load spontaneously move closer as if to make themselves available should they be needed, signalling to the heavily loaded operator that help is at hand. As the crisis passes they drift back to their stations. Closely related to this is *Resource Management* in teams, particularly the work of Salas and his co-workers, although in a remarkably honest assessment he reports that it is difficult to show that Crew Resource Management training has a marked effect (Salas, Wilson, Burke, & Wightman, 2006).

Increasingly automation means that the task of the human becomes one of supervisory control: compare Sheridan & Ferrell (1974) with Sheridan (1992) and Sheridan (2004). Perhaps those who are currently just starting human factors careers may live to see the time when the human factors of complex systems becomes *primarily* a matter of social dynamics – a far cry from what I would have expected in 1956.

Models for prediction

Three main classes of models have appeared in the last 50 years. First are the very powerful and successful control theory models. In particular in the Optimal Control Theory model (OCT) the Kalman-Bucy filter has many of the properties of estimation and prediction found in humans (Kleinman, Baron, & Levinson, 1970; Veldhuijzen & Stassen, 1977). The Kalman filter can be used independently of control as a state estimator, and hence as part of a fault detection system (Curry & Gai, 1976). Secondly there are some powerful general computational models of cognition, such as SOAR and Anderson's ACT programs. Only very recently have these been applied to real-time problems with dynamic environments, and it is too soon to know how well they handle such problems, even if successful in laboratory cognitive tasks. Thirdly there are some special purpose models developed specifically to model HMS, including Milgram's model of attention (Milgram, 1983), Cacciabue's model of process control (COSIMO), and Hollnagel's model of information processing (CREAM) for modelling human error (Hollnagel, 1998). If I may mention a personal contribution, Sanderson and Moray (Sanderson, 1991) proposed a pseudocode computational version of Rasmussen's "ladder". These models all have attractive characteristics, but they are not fully developed, in the sense that there have been no prolonged study of their properties in the way that SOAR and ACT* have been developed, and the later more elaborate models have seldom been used except by those who developed them. Finally there are number of more or less well developed models of "modules" of psychological processes, such as attention, the Theory of Signal Detection, and scheduling.

the human factors of complex systems 31

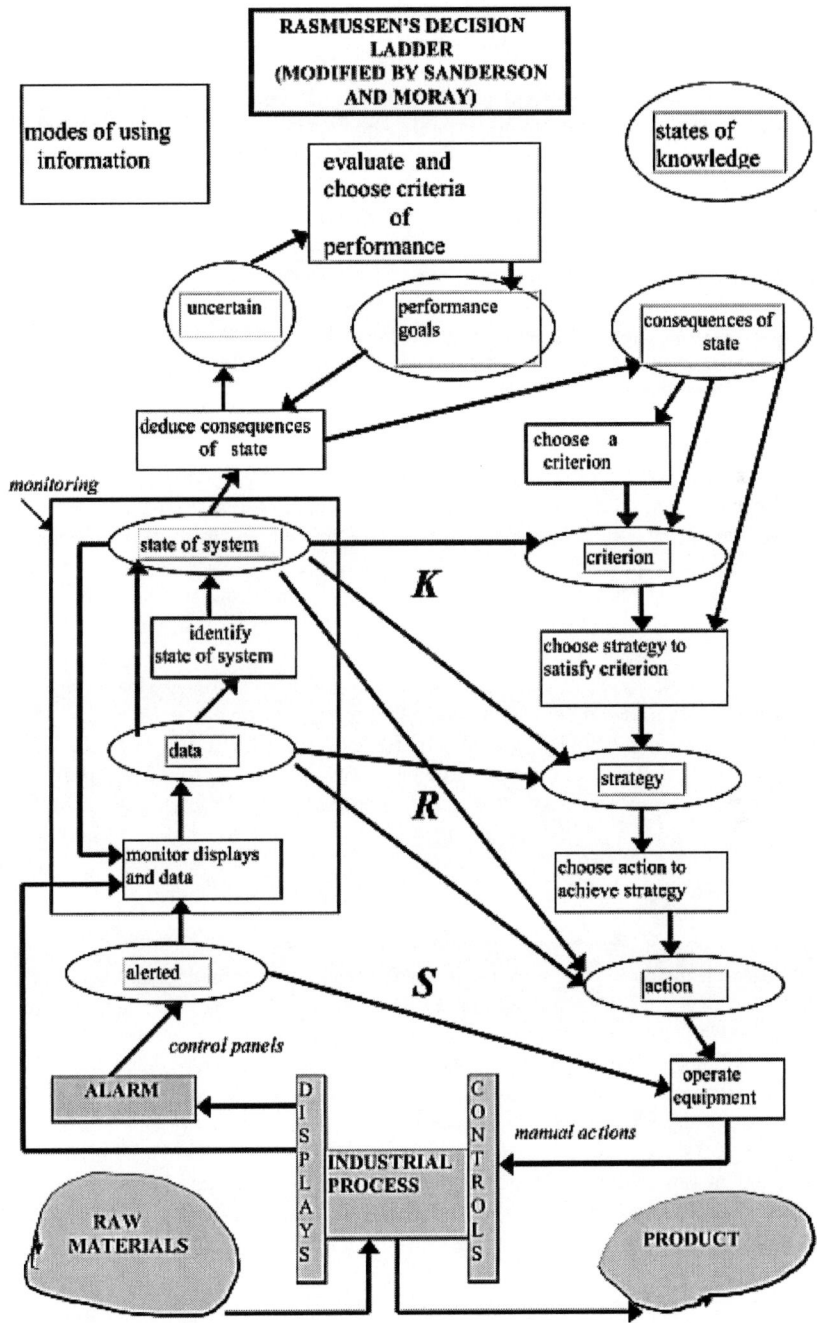

Figure 9. Rasmussen's "Ladder" describing cognition in complex HMS

To my mind the most promising model at present is PROCRU (Baron, Muralidharan, Lancrafty, & Zacharias, 1980), and it is a great pity that its development was halted in the mid-1980s. It was developed to predict behaviour of aircrew on final approach and landing, and later extended to model the behaviour of a NPP operator team. PROCRU uses an OCT front end to model the events in the real time behaviour of the physical plant, and couples the output of that model both to plant dynamics, and to an "expert system" representing the interactions of the human members of the crew. The use of an expert system requires a considerable body of knowledge culled from observation of real operators performing the task in realistic situations, either in a simulator or in the field. Expert systems have rather dropped out of fashion in recent years, (they were another innovation that had to await the increase in computer power that was missing in the 1950s), and one might want to use something more like SOAR, ACT*, or even a computational version of Rasmussen's Ladder rather than an expert system, even though it would probably be more costly to develop.

One problem with PROCRU is that users must know enough control theory to manipulate the OCT elements of the model. It is unlikely that an ergonomist from a psychology background will have such expertise. Indeed, a worrying development of human factors is that there seems to be less knowledge of engineering in today's ergonomists than was the case even ten years ago. For example, few seem to read IEEE journals these days (hence the lack of knowledge of Conant's work and some of Sheridan's quantitative work). This brings out the importance of scale in future ergonomics research. Fifty years ago there was a great deal of applicable research that could be undertaken by a human factors expert working alone, or by a graduate student working for a PhD. If we are aiming for a model that will allow real-time, real task prediction that is no longer the case. We are used to the idea that physics experiments require teams of dozens of researchers. The complexity of human-machine interaction in realistic situations is of a comparable. Future research will require multi-disciplinary teams in human factors, not one or two people. We need research teams that contain psychologists, social scientists, computer scientists, and mechanical engineers.

The research methods that were available 50 years ago are inadequate. It is almost ironic that while the reductionist approach was adopted by experimental psychology to discover general context-free laws, the greatest progress in understanding complex HMS has come from almost the antithesis of that methodology, namely from field studies. Since the 1960s both quantitative equations and flow chart models of HMS have been proposed for process control industries (Iosif, 1968, 1969a,b; Bainbridge, 1974; De Keyser, 1981). One of the most important changes is the rise of high power computation, and with it the development of microworlds and simulations. The implications for experimental design have been shown in Rasmussen's diagrams that illustrate the relation between laboratory studies, simulation, and field studies, and the implications for methodology, choice of "cover stories", etc.. These ideas of Rasmussen deserve to be better known. See Figure 10 a,b,c.

the human factors of complex systems 33

MEANS-ENDS RELATIONS	PROPERTIES OF EXPERI-MENTER'S DOMAIN	SUBJECT'S DOMAIN	SUBJECT'S PRIVATE DOMAIN
GOALS & OBJECTIVES, CONSTRAINTS	Experimental Objectives and Constraints	Subject's Goals	Goals and Constraints of Work and Leisure
PRIORITY MEASURES, MONETARY VALUES, PERSONNEL, MATERIAL	Experimental Evaluation Measures	Subject's Priorities	Subjective Priorities and Performance Criteria
GENERAL FUNCTIONS AND ACTIVITIES	Experiment	Functions involved in Experiment	Functions Of Work and Private Life
PHYSICAL ACTIVITIES AND PROCESSES OF EQUIPMENT		Physical Processes of Experimental Equipment	Processes known from Work and Private Life
APPEARANCE, LOCATION & CON-FIGURATION OF MATERIAL OBJECTS		Configuration of Lab. and Equipment	Familiar Objects, Configurations and Topography

Figure 10 a. Rasmussen's schema for research design

MEANS-ENDS RELATIONS	PROPERTIES OF EXPERI-MENTER'S DOMAIN	SUBJECT'S DOMAIN	SUBJECT'S PRIVATE DOMAIN
GOALS & OBJECTIVES, CONSTRAINTS	Experimental Objectives and Constraints	Subject's Goals	Goals and Constraints of Work and Leisure
PRIORITY MEASURES, MONETARY VALUES, PERSONNEL, MATERIAL	Experimental Evaluation Measures	Subject's Priorities	Subjective Priorities and Performance *(Decoupled by Explicit Instruction)*
GENERAL FUNCTIONS AND ACTIVITIES		Functions involved in Experiment	Functions Of Work and Private Life
PHYSICAL ACTIVITIES AND PROCESSES OF EQUIPMENT		Physical Processes of Experimental *(Constrained by Equipment)*	Processes known from Work and Private Life
APPEARANCE, LOCATION & CON-FIGURATION OF MATERIAL OBJECTS		Configuration of Lab. and Equipment	Familiar Objects, Configurations and Topography

Figure 10b. Schema for laboratory experiments

MEANS-ENDS RELATIONS	PROPERTIES OF EXPERI-MENTER'S DOMAIN	SUBJECT'S DOMAIN	SUBJECT'S PRIVATE DOMAIN
GOALS & OBJECTIVES, CONSTRAINTS	Experimental Objectives and Constraints	Subject's Goals	Goals and Constraints of Work and Leisure
PRIORITY MEASURES, MONETARY VALUES, PERSONNEL, MATERIAL	Experimental Evaluation Measures	**Instructed Priority: Solve the Given Task Effectively**	Priorities and Performance
GENERAL FUNCTIONS AND ACTIVITIES		Functions involved in Experiment, e.g. Trouble-Shooting	Functions Of Work and Private Life *(Analogy Activated by Cover Story)*
PHYSICAL ACTIVITIES AND PROCESSES OF EQUIPMENT		Physical Processes of Experimental Equipment *(Irrelevant to Experimental Function and to Subject)*	Processes known from Private Life
APPEARANCE, LOCATION & CON-FIGURATION OF MATERIAL OBJECTS		Configuration of Lab. and Equipment	Familiar Objects, Configurations and Topography

Figure 10c. Schema for research using micro-world or simulation, with complex cover story to elicit realistic behaviour

Social interaction

I will finish by describing what is perhaps the most surprising development from the viewpoint of the 1950s. This is the striking intrusion of social psychology and social science into human factors and ergonomics. In my case I realised the importance of social factors in the 1980s when preparing a report for the US National Research Council on research needs for the human factors of nuclear safety. I had thought that ergonomics of NPPs was mainly concerned with better control room design and layout, but I came to realise that more important was to understand the role of social interaction and organisational factors. This is hardly a new observation: field studies have long made the same point explicitly or implicitly. Such studies include steel mills, NPPs, civilian aviation, air traffic control, fire-fighting, aircraft carrier operations, and many kinds of continuous process control (DeKeyser, 1981; Bainbridge, 1974; Klein et al., 1996; Rochlin et al., 1987; Salas, 2006.; Ruffle-Smith, 1979; Moray, Sanderson, & Vicente, 1992; Hutchins, 1995). If we are to predict performance in an HMS we must include the social dynamics in the team.

From the point of view of ergonomics as seen in the 1950s this emphasis on social factors is a great surprise. The goal in the 1950s was for context free universal laws, and to admit the importance of social factors is to let in context with a rush and of course if one is searching for universal laws cross-cultural differences are an admission of defeat. One might make the same remark about experimental psychology as a whole. In the early 1960s I investigated the effect of literary context on vocabulary size, and found that for British students the vocabulary size decreased as context became stronger, whereas for US students it was exactly the opposite. (In fact I predicted the British relationship, and an American colleague, James Deese, predicted the US relationship!). Sanderson (personal communication) noted that when students are asked to predict whether people would use cars or buses as a function of the cost of parking and the frequency of buses, the outcome again differed between UK and US students, since to the latter it was almost inconceivable that anyone would want to use a bus. It is striking how little research has been done on cross-cultural ergonomics even now. Yet extensive evidence for strong cultural effects was reported in the work of Hofstede (1984, 1994) and social and organisational factors are also central to *macroergonomics*; see also Kaplan (2004). It seems that prediction of real performance may have to be restricted to cases where either it can be shown that cultural differences are weak, or by including parameters that vary with social and cultural contexts.

. . . and the future?

The development of sophisticated dynamic computational models requires long term investment of money and effort on a scale that has not been common. To obtain funding for efforts on this scale, certainly several millions of euros, will be difficult, and may well require co-operation with large industrial concerns rather than the traditional public (government) research funding sources. Can we make out a convincing case that such an effort would be worthwhile? "Traditional" ergonomics, by which I mean health and safety ergonomics in the industrial workplace will always be needed, and is, in many respects the most socially and economically important. But there is no doubt that a general model of the human operator in complex HMS would be both scientifically extremely interesting and economically extremely valuable. A general model that made predictions of a variety of industrial and commercial performance would show very large returns on the money invested in its development, and the effort should be appropriate to "framework" support in the European Union. The main question is where can the leadership for such an effort come from, leadership that can combine ergonomics, psychology, social science and engineering?

No one, I think, could have foreseen the direction that human factors has taken when I began psychology in 1955-56. And while I have been, I think, a successful experimentalist, my theoretical predictions have not been outstanding. I have to doubt that my prediction of where human factors will go in the next 50 years will be any more accurate.

I leave it to you to see how it works out.

References

Ashby, W.R. (1956). *An Introduction to Cybernetics.* London: Chapman and Hall.
Bainbridge, L. (1974). Analysis of protocols from a process control task. In E. Edwards and F. Lees (Eds), *The Human Operator in Process Control,* London: Taylor and Francis, 146-158.
Baron, S. Muralidharan, R., Lancrafty, R. & Zacharias, G. (1980). *PROCRU: a Model for Analyzing Crew Procedures in Approach to Landing.* Technical Report No. 4374. Cambridge, MA: Bolt, Bernanek and Newman, Inc.
Bates, J.A.V. (1947). Some characteristics of a human operator. *Journal of the Institute of Electrical Engineers, 94,* 298-304.
Beare, A.N., Dorris, R.E., Bovell, C.R., Crowe, D.S., & Kozinsky, E.J. (1984). *A Simulator-Based Study of Human Errors in Nuclear Power Plant Control Room Tasks. NUREG/CR-3309.* U.S. Nuclear Regulatory Commission, Washington, D.C
Beishon, R.J. (1974). An analysis and simulation of an operator's behaviour in controlling continuous baking ovens. In E. Edwards and F. Lees (Eds.), *The Human Operator in Process Control* (pp. 79-90). London: Taylor and Francis.
Birmingham, H.P. & Taylor, F.V. (1954). A design philosophy for man-machine control systems. *Proceedings of the Institute of Radio Engineers, 42,* 1748-1758.
Boff, K. & Lincoln, J. (1988). *Engineering Data Compendium.* Ohio: WPAFB.
Broadbent, D.E. (1958). *Perception and Communication.* Oxford: Pergamon.
Cacciabue, P.C. (1998). *Modelling and Simulation of Human Behaviour in System Control.* Berlin: Springer-Verlag.
Card, S.K., Moran, T.P., & Newell, A. (1983). *The Psychology of Human-Computer Interaction.* Hillsdale, NJ. Lawrence Erlbaum Associates.
Card, S.K., Moran, T.P., & Newell, A. (1986). The model human processor: an engineering model of human Performance. In K.R. Boff, L. Kaufman, and J.P. Thomas (Eds.) *Handbook of perception and Human Performance, Vol 2* (45: pp 1-35). New York: Wiley and Sons.

Conant, R., & Moray, N. (1979). Information Transmission and the Structure of Behavior. *Proceedings IEEE International Conference on Cybernetics and Society*, 13-16.

Conant, R.C. (1976). Laws of information that govern systems, *IEEE Transactions on Systems, Science and Cybernetics, SMC-6*, 240-255.

Craik, K. (1947). Theory of the human operator in control systems I: The operator as an engineering system. *British Journal of Psychology, 38*, 56-61.

Crossman, E.R.F.W. (1959). A theory of the acquisition of speed skill. *Ergonomics, 2*, 153–166. *Reprinted* in N. Moray (Ed.) (2005), *Ergonomics Major Writings*. London: Routledge/Taylor and Francis.

Curry, R.E. & Gai, E.G. (1976). Detection of random failures by human monitors. In T.B. Sheridan and G. Johannsen, (Eds.). *Monitoring Behavior and Supervisory Control*. New York: Plenum Press.

De Keyser, V. (1981). *La fiabilité humaine dans les processus continus, les centrales thermo-éléctriques et nucléaires*. Technical Report 720-ECI-2651-C-(0) Brussels, Belgium: GCE -DGXII, CERI.

Dougherty, E.M. & Fragola, J.R. (1988). *Human Reliability Analysis*. New York: Wiley.

Dutton, J.M. & Starbuck, W. (1971). Finding Charlie's run-time estimator. In J.M. Dutton and W. Starbuck (Eds.). *Computer Simulation of Human Behavior*. NewYork: Wiley.

Edwards, E. & Lees, F. (1976). *The Human Operator in Process Control*. London: Taylor and Francis.

Fitts, P.M. (1951a). Engineering Psychology and Equipment Design. In S.S. Stevens (Ed.*) Handbook of Experimental Psychology and Equipment Design* (pp. 1287-1340). New York: Wiley.

Fitts, P.M. (1951b). *Some Basic Questions in Designing an Air-Navigation and Traffic-Control System*. Washington, DC: National Research Council. 5-11. *Reprinted* in N. Moray (ed.) 2005. *Ergonomics Major Writings*. London: Routledge/Taylor and Francis.

Garner, W. (1962). *Uncertainty and Structure as Psychological Constructs*. New York: Wiley

Grandjean, E. (1980). *Fitting the Task to the Man*. London: Taylor and Francis.

Gray, W.D., John, B.E., & Atwood, M.E. (1993). Project ERNESTINE: Validating a GOMS analysis for predicting and explaining real-world task performance. *Human-Computer Interaction, 8*, 237-309.

Himmelblau, D. (Ed.) (1973). *Decomposition of Large-Scale Systems*. Amsterdam: Elsevier.

Hofstede, G. (1984). *Culture's Consequences*. Newbury Park, California: Sage Publications.

Hofstede, G. (1994). *Cultures and Organizations*. London: HarperCollins.

Hollnagel, E. (1998). *Cognitive Reliability and Error Analysis Method*. Amsterdam: Elsevier.

Hutchins, E. (1995). *Cognition in the Wild*. Cambridge, MA: MIT Press

Iosif, G. (1968). La stratégie dans la surveillance des tableaux de commande. I. Quelques facteurs déterminants de caractère objectif. *Revue Roumanien de Science Social-Psychologique, 12*, 147-161.

Iosif, G. (1969a). La stratégie dans la surveillance des tableaux de commande. I. Quelques facteurs déterminants de caractère subjectif. *Revue Roumanien de Science Social-Psychologique, 13,* 29-41.

Iosif, G. (1969b). Influence de la correlation fonctionelle sur parametres technologiques. *Revue Roumanien de Science Social-Psychologique, 13,* 105-110.

Kaplan, M. (Ed.) (2004). *Cultural Ergonomics.* Elsevier: Amsterdam. 31-60.

Klein, G.A., Orasanu, J., Calderwood, R., & Zsambok, C.E. (1993) *Decision Making in Action: Models and Methods.* Norwood, N.J.: Ablex Publishing Corporation.

Kleinman, D.L., Baron, S., & Levison, W.H. (1970). An optimal control model of human response. Part 1: theory and validation. *Automatica, 6,* 357-369.

Koch, S. (Ed.) (1963). *Psychology: a Study of a Science. Volume* NY: McGraw-Hill.

Kuo, W. & Hsu, J.P. (1990). Update: simultaneous engineering design in Japan. *Industrial Engineering, 22,* 23–28.

Laporte, T.R. & Consolini, P.M. (1991). Working in practice but not in theory: theoretical challenges of high-reliability organizations. *Journal of Public Administration Research and Theory, 1,* 19–47.

Lee, J., & N. Moray, (1989). Making Mental Models Manifest. *Proc. 1989 IEEE International Conference on Systems, Man and Cybernetics* (pp. 56-60). Boston, MA.

Lee, J.D. & Moray, N. (1992). Trust, control strategies and allocation of function in human-machine systems. *Ergonomics, 35,* 1243-1270.

Lee, J.D. & Moray, N. (1994). Trust, self confidence and operators' adaptation to automation. *International Journal of Human-Computer Studies, 40,* 153-184.

Lee, J.D., & See, K.A. (2004). Trust in technology: Designing for appropriate reliance. *Human Factors, 46,* 50-80.

McRuer, D.T. & Krendal, E. (1957). *Dynamic Response of the Human Operator* (WADC TR-56-254) Dayton, OH: Wright-Patterson AFB.

McRuer, D.T. & Krendel, E. (1976). *Mathematical Models of Human Pilot Behavior.* NATO AGARDograph No. 188. Brussels.

Milgram, P. (1983). *A Multivariate Autoregressive Display Monitoring Model.* Report No. NLR MP 83033 U, National Aerospace Laboratory NLR, The Netherlands.

Moray, N. (1966). Cultural differences in statistical approximations to English. *Psychonomic Science, 5,* 467-468.

Moray, N. (1981). The role of attention in the detection of errors and the diagnosis of failures in man-machine systems. In J.Rasmussen and W.B. Rouse (Eds.). *Human Detection and Diagnosis of System Failures.* New York: Plenum Press.

Moray, N. (1987). Intelligent aids, mental models, and the theory of machines. *International Journal of Man-Machine Studies, 27,* 619 – 629.

Moray, N. (1990). A lattice theory approach to the structure of mental models. *Philosophical Transactions of the Royal Society of London, series B. 327,* 577 -583.

Moray, N. (2005). *Ergonomics: Major Writings* London: Routledge/Taylor and Francis

Moray, N. (2006). Real prediction of real performance. In J. Wilson, B. Norris, T. Clarke and A. Mills (Eds.) *People and Rail Systems.* Aldershot: Ashgate Ltd.

Moray, N., Dessouky, M.I., Kijowski, B., & Adapathya, R. (1991). Strategic behavior, workload and performance in task scheduling. *Human Factors, 33,* 607-629.

Moray, N., Sanderson, P.M., & Vicente, K.J. (1992). Cognitive task analysis of a complex work domain: a case study. *Reliability Engineering and Systems Safety, 36,* 207-216.

Muir, B.M. (1987). Trust between humans and machines, and the design of decision aides. *International Journal of Man-machine Studies, 27,* 527-539.

Muir, B.M. (1994). Trust in automation: Part 1 - Theoretical issues in the study of trust and human intervention in automated systems. *Ergonomics,* 37, 1905-1923.

Muir, B.M. & Moray, N. (1996). Trust in automation. Part II. Experimental studies of trust and human intervention in a process control simulation. *Ergonomics, 39,* 429-461.

Osgood, C.E. (1953). *Method and Theory in Experimental Psychology.* New York: Oxford University Press.

Parasuraman, R. & Riley, V. (1997). Humans and automation: use, misuse, disuse, abuse. *Human Factors, 39,* 230 – 253.

Parasuraman, R., Sheridan, T. B., & Wickens, C. D. (2000). A model for types and levels of human interaction with automation. *IEEE Transactions on Systems, Man, and Cybernetics, SMC-30,* 286-297.

Perrow, C. (1984). *Normal Accidents.* New York: Basic Books

Poulton, E.C. (1974). *Tracking Skill and Manual Control.* London: Academic Press.

Rasmussen, J. (1986). *Information Processing and Human-Machine Interaction: an Approach to Cognitive Engineering.* Amsterdam: North-Holland.

Rasmussen, J., Pederesen, A-M., & Goodstein, L. (1995). *Cognitive Engineering: Concepts and Applications.* New York: Wiley.

Rochlin, E., LaPorte, T., & Roberts, K. (1987). The self-designing high reliability organisation: aircraft flight operation at sea. *Naval War College Review* (pp. 76-91) Autumn.

Ruffle-Smith, H.P. (1979). A Simulator Study of the Interaction of Pilot Workload with Errors, Vigilance, and Decisions. Research report. NASA-AMES. 1-39. Reprinted in N. Moray (Ed.). (2005), *Ergonomics Major Writings.* London: Routledge/Taylor and Francis.

Russell Davis, D. (1948). The Role of Laboratory Experiment in the Study of Pilot Error. Air ministry A.P. 3139A. London: HMSO. 1-38.) Reprinted in N. Moray (Ed.) 2005. *Ergonomics Major Writings.* London: Routledge/Taylor and Francis

Salas, E., Wilson, K.A., Burke, C.S., & Wightman, D.C. 2006. Does crew resource management training work? An update, an extension and some critical needs. *Human Factors, 48,* 392 -412.

Sanderson, P.M. (1989). The human planning and scheduling role in advanced manufacturing systems: an emerging human factors role. *Human Factors, 31,* 635-666.

Sanderson, P.M. (1991). Towards the model human scheduler. *International Journal of Human Factors in Manufacturing, 1,* 195-215.

Senders. J.W. (1964). The human operator as a monitor and controller of multi-degree of freedom systems. *IEEE Transactions on Human Factors in Electronics, HFE-5*, 2-5.

Senders, J.W. (1983). *Visual Sampling Processes*. Katholieke Hogeschool, Tilburg, Netherlands.

Shannon, C., & Weaver, W. (1947). *The Mathematical Theory of Communication*. Urbana: University of Illinois Press.

Sheridan, T.B. & Ferrell, W.R. (1974). *Man-Machine Systems*. Cambridge. MIT Press

Sheridan, T.B. (1976). Towards a general model of supervisory control. In. T.B. Sheridan and G. Johannsen (Eds), *Monitoring Behavior and Supervisory Control* (pp. 271-282). New York: Plenum Press.

Sheridan, T.B. (1987). Supervisory control. In G. Salvendy, (Ed). *Handbook of Human Factors*. New York: Wiley.

Sheridan, T.B. (1992). *Telerobotics, Automation and Human Supervisory Control*. Cambridge, MA: MIT Press..

Sheridan, T.B. (1997). Supervisory control. In G. Salvendy (Ed.) *Handbook of Human Factors (2nd Edition)* (pp. 1295-1327). New York: Wiley.

Sheridan, T.B. & Johannsen, G. (Eds.) (1976). *Monitoring Behavior and Supervisory Control*. New York: Plenum.

Stevens, S.S. (Ed.) (1951). *Handbook of Experimental Psychology*. New York: Wiley.

Tan, G. & Lewandowsky, S. (1996). A comparison of operator trust in humans versus machines. Paper presented at the CybErg 96 virtual conference. Retrieved May 16, 2000, from http://www.curtin.edu.au/conferences/cyberg/centre/outline.cgi/frame?dir=tan

Tulga, M.K. and Sheridan, T.B. (1980). Dynamic decisions and workload in multitask supervisory control. *IEEE Transactions on Systems, Man and Cybernetics, SMC-10*, 217-232.

Turksen, I.B., Moray, N., & Kruschelnycky, E. (1988). Acquisition of membership functions in mental workload experiments. In T. Zétény (Ed.) *Fuzzy Sets in Psychology* (pp. 321-343). Amsterdam: North-Holland.

Tustin, A. (1947). The nature of the operator's response in manual control, and its implications for controller design. *Journal of the Institute of Electrical Engineers, 94*, 190-202. Reprinted in N. Moray (Ed.). (2005), *Ergonomics Major Writings*. London: Routledge/Taylor and Francis

Veldhuijzen W. & Stassen, H.G. (1977). The internal model concept: an application to modeling human control of large ships. *Human Factors, 19*, 367-380. Reprinted in N. Moray (Ed.). (2005), *Ergonomics Major Writings*. London: Routledge/Taylor and Francis.

Vicente, K. J., Moray, N., Lee, J. D., Rasmussen, J. D., Jones, B. G., Brock, R., & Djemil, T. (1996). Evaluation of a Rankine cycle display for nuclear power plant monitoring and diagnosis. *Human Factors, 33*, 506-523.

Vierling, A.E. (1990). Machines can only produce as efficiently as the people who operate them. *Industrial Engineering, 22*, 24–26.

Vince, M.A. (1944). *Direction of movement of machine controls.* FPRC 637, APRU, 1-9. Cambridge: Medical Research Council. Reprinted in N. Moray (Ed.). (2005), *Ergonomics Major Writings.* London: Routledge/Taylor and Francis

Waterson, P. & Sell, R. (2006). Recurrent themes and developments in the history of the Ergonomics Society. *Ergonomics, 49,* 743-799.

Wiener, N. (1948). *Cybernetics: Control and Communication in the Animal and the Machine.* New York. Wiley.

Woodworth, R.S. (1938). *Experimental Psychology.* New York: Holt.

Woodworth, R.S. & Schlosberg. H. (1953). *Experimental Psychology.* New York. Holt-Reinhart.

Young, L.R. (1973). Human control capabilities. In J.F. Parker, Jr. and V.R. West. (Eds.), *Bioastronautics Data Book.* Washington, D.C. National Aeronautics and Space Administration.

Yufik, Y.M., Sheridan, T.B., & Venda, V.F. (1992). Knowledge measurement, cognitive complexity, and cybernetics of mutual man-machine adaptation. In C.V. Negoita (Ed.) *Cybernetics and Applied Systems* (pp.187-237). New York: Marcel Decker, Inc.

Zadeh, L., Fu, T., & Shimura, M. (1975). *Fuzzy Sets and their Applications to Cognitive and Decision Processes.* New York: Academic Press.

Zinchenko, V. & Munipov, V. (1989). *Fundamentals of Ergonomics.* Moscow: Progessive publishers.

Workload & Work Analysis

tactile land navigation

In D. de Waard, G.R.J. Hockey, P. Nickel, and K.A. Brookhuis (Eds.) (2007), *Human Factors Issues in Complex System Performance* (pp. 41). Maastricht, the Netherlands: Shaker Publishing.

Tactile land navigation for dismounted soldiers

Maaike Duistermaat[1], Linda R. Elliott[2], Jan B.F. van Erp[1], & Elizabeth S. Redden[2]
[1]TNO Defence, Security and Safety
Soesterberg, the Netherlands
[2]US Army Research Laboratory, USA

Abstract

In land navigation by dismounted soldiers, using a visual display obstructs the use of the soldier's eyes and hands for other tasks. This issue can be resolved by presenting navigation information on a tactile waist belt, which proved to be effective in previous studies. This paper presents an experiment focused on navigation, target detection and situational awareness (SA) in a multitask environment. The performance and subjective ratings for a tactile and two visual navigation systems were compared. 24 Soldiers navigated three densely forested routes at night, with live and silhouette targets along the route. The soldiers found the tactile display easy to use and reached high performance levels: more targets were detected and higher navigation speeds were reached on part of the route. The soldiers rated the tactile system high, and especially appreciated its hands-free and eyes-free aspect. However, the soldiers also indicated that the tactile system was less suited to build up global situational awareness, compared to a map display.

Introduction

Navigation by dismounted soldiers has been identified as having a potential for high workload and stress (Mitchell et al., 2004). The level of multitasking during land navigation will vary in accordance to the task demands in a particular mission. Relevant tasks include navigation in terrain that is unfamiliar and often difficult to manoeuvre, maintaining situation awareness, verbal communication, enemy detection and avoiding obstacles. Many of these tasks rely on visual information processing. In addition, navigation devices also usually require visual attention (e.g., compass, Global Positioning System (GPS) device). According to Wickens' Multiple Resource Theory (Wickens, 2002), competition for the same - in this case visual - modality can produce interference, and can ultimately lead to performance degradation. A possible solution to counteract this threat of visual overload is to present information via other sensory channels, for instance through the sense of touch.

The Multiple Resource Theory states that tactile information can be largely processed simultaneously with visual and auditory information. The goal of using the sense of touch is to present more information than a person could have processed using only eyes and ears (present information both tactilely and visually or auditory), or to offload information from the other channels (present information tactilely, instead of visually or auditory). Several studies have demonstrated the usefulness of tactile information input in multi-task situations (Hopp et al., 2005; Sarter, 2001, 2002; Sklar & Sarter, 1999; Van Erp et al., 2003). Therefore, the interest in the possibilities of applying tactile displays for navigation by dismounted soldiers (see Figure 1) has recently grown.

Figure 1. A dismounted soldier navigates using a tactile display

Tactile orientation and navigation displays

For orientation and navigation, Situation Awareness (SA) is a key issue. Prevett and Wickens (1994) distinguish two navigation sub tasks: a) to perform the actions necessary to get to a location, and b) to understand the spatial structure of the area being traversed. Wickens (1992) termed these sub tasks local guidance and global awareness, respectively. Local guidance has an emphasis on the immediate surrounding environment, focuses on manoeuvring along a route and interacting with objects along that route, and relates to physical challenges. Global awareness focuses on acquiring and maintaining spatial structural information and relates to cognitive challenges, including aspects such as understanding, planning and problem solving. Preferably, the information for global awareness must be presented in a world referenced (north-up) display (Wickens, 1992; Roscoe, 1968). However, local guidance tasks predominantly need correspondence between display and control in terms of left, right, etcetera, which requires an ego-referenced or heading-up display. A tactile display could enhance the local guidance, by providing ego-referenced navigation information without adding visual load.

An important issue for tactile orientation and navigation displays is the choice for the body locus of the display. Gilliland and Shlegel (1994) found limited usefulness of tactile displays on the head for pilot threat warning, while Van Erp (2005) showed that a localized vibration on the waist could easily and accurately be interpreted as a direction in the horizontal plane. Inferring direction from a vibration around the waist or torso, a relatively stable body part, is very intuitive (the 'tap-on-the-shoulder' principle). Using a belt around the waist allows presenting navigation information with a higher resolution than just 'turn left' or 'turn right', and, because of the intuitiveness, with low cognitive load. This concept has been successfully tested in cars, cockpits, speedboats, and the International Space Station (Van Erp & Van Veen, 2003, 2004; Dobbins & Samways, 2002, 2003, Van Erp et al., 2004). The use of a tactile display for land navigation was demonstrated to be successful for navigating short distances on even terrain (Van Erp et al., 2005) and more challenging terrain (Elliott et al., 2006).

Previous studies

Earlier studies were focused on proving the concept of tactile navigation. For instance, Dobbins and Samways (2002) tested the use of a tactile display for navigating with a speed boat. In a more recent study, the use of a tactile display in land navigation was demonstrated (Elliott et al., 2006; Van Erp & Duistermaat, 2005). In that study, navigation performance with a tactile display was compared to performance with visual displays on longer distances, with a main focus on navigation speed. Fifteen soldiers navigated three 1800 meter long routes through a densely forested terrain. Each route consisted of three waypoints, and was navigated using either a compass, a GPS with alphanumerical display, or a navigation system with a tactile display (eight vibrating elements in a waist belt). The results were favourable for the tactile navigation system: little or no training was required, the soldiers had a higher walking speed, reached more waypoints and rated the system higher than the compass and visual GPS system. For more details see Elliott et al. (2006) and Van Erp and Duistermaat (2005).

From these studies we can conclude that (land) navigation using a tactile display is possible, and that navigation performance with a tactile display is as good as, or better than performance using standard visual displays.

Present study

The present experiment examines navigation performance by dismounted soldiers in a multitask environment, with a main focus on night operations, target detection and SA. The effects of visual workload, mental workload and degraded vision on land navigation performance were explored, since these are the issues for which a tactile display is expected to be beneficial. To this end, the trials were performed at night, an off-limits area and object negotiation were added to the routes, and the soldiers had to perform a target detection task. Three navigation systems were compared: the tactile system (which requires little or no training, and has a low cognitive, manual and visual load), a handheld visual system (which requires training and practice, with a high cognitive and manual load and moderate visual load), and a helmet mounted visual system (which requires moderate training, with a moderate cognitive and manual load and high visual load). It was expected that, since a tactile display has no visual load and low cognitive load, performance on the target detection task and local guidance SA would be higher with the tactile navigation system than with the two visual systems.

Method

Participants

Twenty four soldiers participated in the study. Their average age was 27.2 years (SD = 4.37), and their average service time was 4.5 years (SD = 5.36). All soldiers were skilled in land navigation and the use of night vision goggles, and were trained on site on the use of the three navigation systems.

Apparatus

The participants used Night Vision Goggles (AN/PVS-14 monocular system) with each of the three navigation systems (for further details, see Duistermaat, 2005):

- The Army Precision Lightweight GPS Receiver (PLGR) is a hand-held, visual based GPS receiver, with an alphanumeric screen that provided the soldier information on (amongst other) direction, heading, and distance to waypoint.
- The Land Warrior System (LWS) displayed navigational information on a helmet mounted monocular visual display (HMD). It's a GPS based system that provided the soldier with an area map with icons indicating the waypoints and the soldiers own position and heading.
- The Personal Tactile Navigator (PTN) is a GPS and electronic compass based navigation system with a tactile display. An adjustable waist belt consisting of eight vibrating elements (called tactors) displays the navigational information. One tactor is active at a time, and indicates the direction of the waypoint. So to arrive at the waypoint, the user can just "follow the buzz". The PTN system is also described in Van Veen et al. (2004) and Van Erp et al. (2005). See Figure 2.

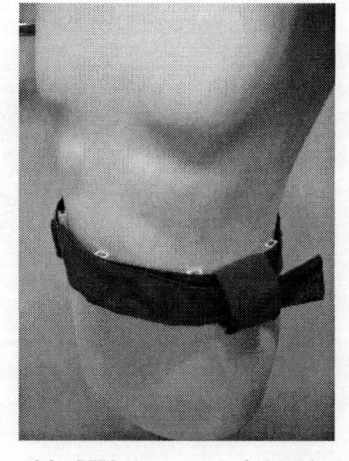

Figure 2. The tactile display of the PTN system (waist belt with eight tactors)

The navigational aspects that were coded on the tactile display were based on several pilot studies, and described in Table 1. The tactile display also provided a warning signal when walking in the off-limits zone.

Table 1. Coding of navigational aspects on the tactile display

	Tactor pattern
Distance to waypoint > 50 m	front tactor: single buzz (200ms) every two seconds other tactors: single buzz (200 ms) every second
15 m < Distance to waypoint < 50 m	front tactor: double buzz (100 ms on, 200 ms off, 100 ms on) every second other tactors: double buzz (100 ms on, 200 ms off, 100 ms on) every half of a second
Distance to waypoint = 15 m = arrival	all tactors: 3 second long buzz

Land navigation course

The experiment was conducted at Fort Benning, Georgia, USA. Three equivalent, triangle-shaped routes (each with three waypoints) were used. Each route included rolling terrain, woodland, open areas, and dense undergrowth, and was about 1500 m long. Each route consisted of three lanes: one obstacle avoidance lane (negotiate around a large obstacle), one lane with three live targets along the lane, and one lane with three live targets and 10 silhouette targets along the lane. The lanes with targets also had an off-limits zone defined on either side of the lane.

Procedure

The experiment was held at night (6 pm – 1 am) over a data collection period of two weeks. Three soldiers participated per night. Each night started with a classroom training session, after which the soldiers were trained on the three navigation systems with hands-on practice. The soldiers completed questionnaires on self-assessment of skill and evaluation of training.

After sunset the soldiers (simultaneously) navigated the routes, each with a different system. The type of navigation system was counterbalanced with route and order. On each lane, the soldiers were instructed to move as quickly as possible, and also to detect as many targets as possible. Navigating a lane ended when the soldier reached the waypoint, moved 50 m beyond the waypoint without detecting it, or failed to reach the waypoint within 30 minutes. If the soldier did not find the waypoint, a data collector led to soldier to the waypoint from which he would start navigating the remaining lane(s). After navigating each route the soldier completed questionnaires on experiences with the navigation devices.

Results

Measures

On each route, a data collector followed the soldier, to record the number of detected targets and navigation time. After navigating all routes, the soldiers completed system evaluation questionnaires.

Performance measures: number of targets detected and time to navigate
The results are based on data of 18 participants (6 soldiers provided incomplete data because of weather conditions and system failure, so were removed from the analyses). The results were analyzed with t-tests for dependent samples, and only significant effects are reported.

Soldiers using the PTN system detected significantly more targets on the complete route (all lanes) than with the LWS system (t(17) = -2.54, p < .025). See Figure 3. With the PTN system soldiers were significantly faster on the lane with 3 (live) targets than with the LWS system (t(17) = 2.89, p < .025). See Figure 4.

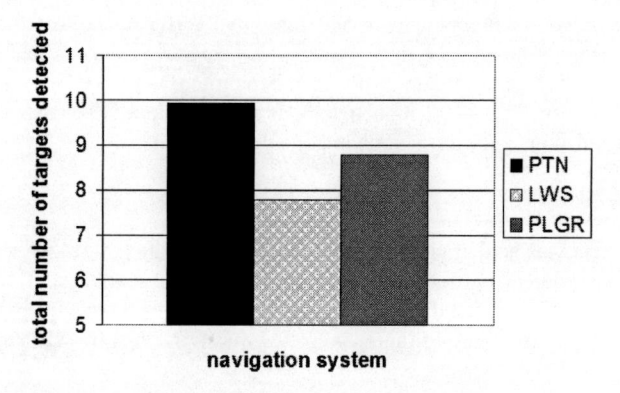

Figure 3. Number of targets detected on all lanes

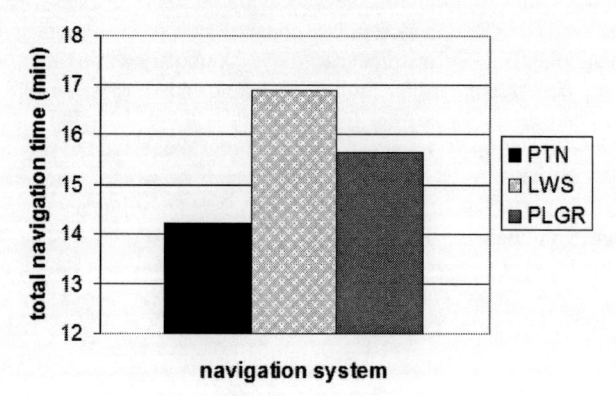

Figure 4. Navigation time on the 3-target lane

Subjective measures: soldiers' evaluation of navigation systems

The results are based on data of 21 participants (weather conditions resulted in incomplete data for 3 soldiers). The soldiers rated the three systems in terms of their expected usefulness for several specific military operations (e.g., night operations, operations in urban territory), assuming that the system works perfectly, on a scale of 1 to 7 (very ineffective to very effective). Figure 5 depicts the differences in rating before and after the soldiers navigated with the systems. Since the differences in rating were equal for all operations, the ratings for the several operations were averaged.

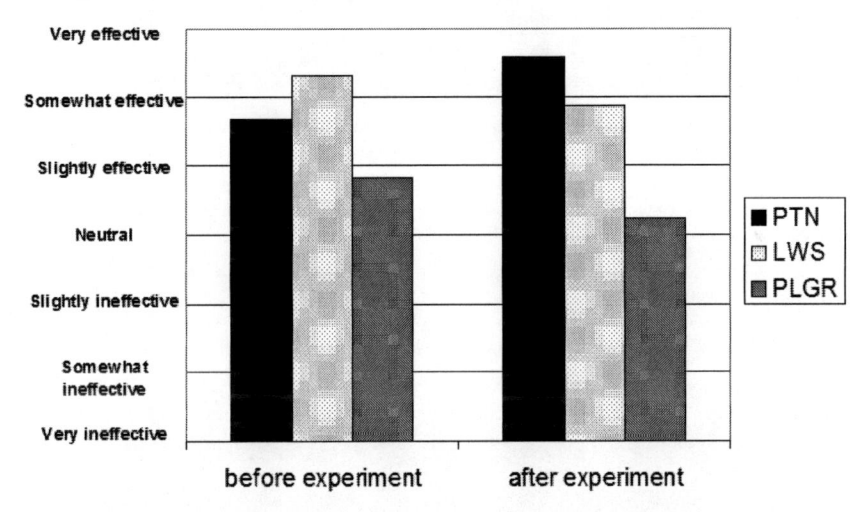

Figure 5. Ratings for military usefulness, before and after navigating with the systems

A significant main effect was found for system type ($F(2,40) = 25.7$, $p < .001$), and a significant interaction effect ($F(2,40) = 9.6$, $p < .001$). Post hoc tests (Holm's Bonferroni: Holm, 1979) revealed that after using the PTN system in the experiment, it was rated significantly more effective than before the experiment ($p < .05$). Also, the PLGR was rated significantly less effective than the PTN and LWS system, both before the experiment ($p < .01$) and after ($p < .001$).

All devices were rated for the effectiveness on several navigation aspects on a scale of 1-7 (very ineffective to very effective). See Figure 6. The ratings for the three systems (as shown in Figure 6) were analyzed per task type. Post-hoc tests (Holm's Bonferroni) revealed that all ratings differ from each other, for at least $p < .025$, except: in rerouting, watching targets, avoiding off-limits, finding waypoints and achieving general SA, the PTN did not differ from LWS, and in watching targets and watching terrain, the LWS did not differ from the PLGR.

All devices were rated for several characteristics of the device on a scale of 1-7 (from very bad to very good). See Figure 7. The ratings for the three systems (as shown in Figure 7) were analyzed per characteristic. Post hoc tests (Holm's Bonferroni) revealed that all ratings differ from each other, for at least $p < .025$, except: for easiness to learn and easiness to use, the LWS and PLGR did not differ from each other, for ease of telling where located the PTN did not differ from the PLGR, and for accuracy of guidance, the PTN did not differ from the LWS.

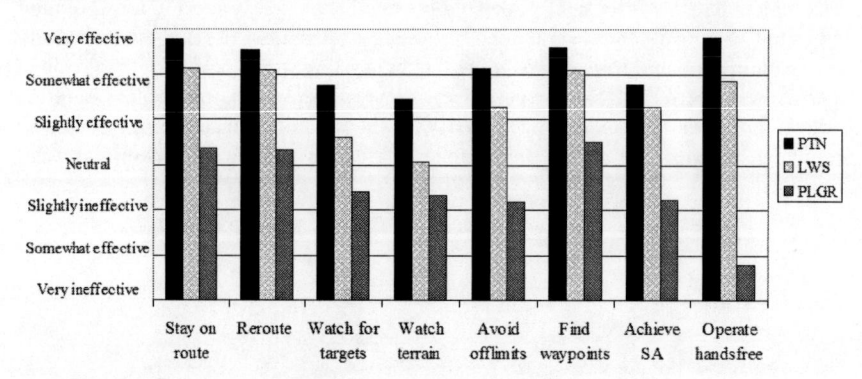

Figure 6. Ratings of effectiveness of the navigation devices

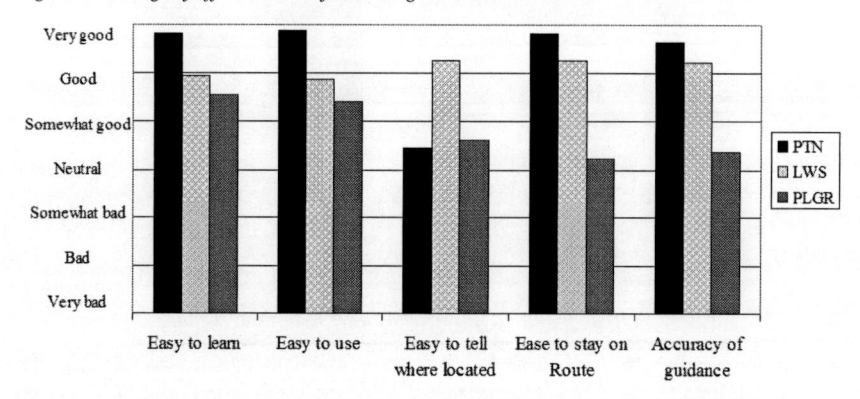

Figure 7. Ratings of device characteristics

Discussion and conclusions

In previous experiments, it was proven that navigation using a tactile display is possible, and that navigation performance (navigation speed) was at least as good as with standard visual navigation systems. The main focus in this experiment was on navigating in a multitask environment. The soldiers had to find waypoints as quickly as possible, but also avoid obstacles and an off-limits area, and they had to detect as many targets as possible. The soldiers detected more targets when using the PTN system (which has no visual load) than with the LWS system (which has a high visual load). At the same time, the soldiers were equally fast in navigating the lanes. In fact, on one lane (the 3-target lane) they navigated faster with the PTN than with the LWS. This indicates that a trade-off between target detection and navigation time does not occur.

The soldiers indicated they especially appreciated the eyes-free aspect of the PTN system. Also, their rating for the expected usefulness for military operations of the

PTN system after using it was remarkably high (6.6 on a scale of 1-7), and significantly higher than before using the system. This could be explained by the fact that soldiers experienced some downsides of the LWS system, such as lenses fogging up, a delay in the image update rate, night blindness, and difficulty to walk while viewing the helmet-mounted display. The PTN system did not give these disadvantages, since the information is presented on a tactile display. This was also reflected by the higher ratings for the PTN system on 'watching targets' and 'watching for terrain'. However, global awareness seems more difficult to accomplish with a tactile display, as is for instance reflected in the lower ratings for 'ease of telling where you are located'. As Wickens (1992) and Roscoe (1968) also state, a map on a visual display (like that of the LWS) is better suited for global awareness information.

The main conclusions are that:

- Presenting navigation information on a tactile display decreases the visual load of the soldier, and seems to enhance the local guidance SA. The tactile display enables the soldiers to use their eyes for other tasks, such as scanning the environment for landmarks and terrain characteristics and looking for targets. As a result, the soldiers detected more targets along the routes;
- The increase in detected targets did not influence the navigation speed of the soldiers: with the tactile system the soldiers navigated as fast, and on one lane even faster than with the visual systems, which also confirms the results of previous studies;
- The soldiers rated the PTN system highly, especially for the hands-free and eyes-free aspect and the intuitive manner in which the information was presented. However, the soldiers experienced difficulty in building up a global SA when using the tactile display, due to the lack of feedback on their position and distance to the waypoint.

This argues for an integration of a visual and a tactile display, in a multi-modal navigation system, to combine the best aspects of both systems. This is expected to show further improved performance, when soldiers can use tactile information to navigate (hands-free, eyes-free, and mind-free), but are also able to check their visual display (on a self-chosen moment) to gain global situational awareness.

Acknowledgement

This effort was conducted as part of the Army Technology Objective (ATO) for Enhanced Unit of Action Maneuver Team Situational Understanding, sponsored by the Army Research Laboratory, and carried out under EOARD grant N62558-05-P-0372.

References

Dobbins, T. & Samways, S. (2002). The use of tactile navigation cues in high speed craft operations. *Proceedings of the RINA conference on high speed craft: technology and operation.* (pp. 13-20). London: The Royal Institution of Naval Architects.

Dobbins, T. & Samways, S. (2003). The Use of Tactile Navigation Displays for the Reduction of Disorientation in Maritime Environments. In "Spatial Disorientation in Military Vehicles: Causes, Consequences and Cures". RTO-Meeting Proceedings 86 (pp.33-1 – 33-6). Neuilly-sur-Seine cedex, France: NATO RTO.

Duistermaat, M. (2005). *Tactile Land Navigation in night operations.* TNO report: TNO-DV3 2005 M065), Soesterberg, NL: TNO Defence, Security and Safety.

Elliott, L.R., Redden, E., Pettitt, R., Carstens, C., van Erp, J., & Duistermaat, M. (2006). *Tactile Guidance for Land Navigation.* Technical Report ARL-TR-3814. Aberdeen Proving Ground: Army Research Laboratory.

Gilliland, K. & Schlegel, R.E. (1994). Tactile stimulation of the human head for information display. *Human Factors, 36,* 700-717.

Holm, S. (1979). A simple sequentially rejective multiple test procedure. *Scandanavian Journal of Statistics, 6,* 65-70.

Hopp, P., Smith, C., Clegg, B., & Heggestad, E. (2005). Interruption management: The use of attention-directing tactile cues. *Human Factors, 47,* 1-11.

Mitchell, D., Samms, C., Glumm, M., Krausman, A., Brelsford, M., & Garrett, L, (2004). *Improved Performance Research Integration Tool (IMPRINT) Model Analyses in Support of the Situational Understanding as an Enabler for Unit of Action Maneuver Team Soldiers Science and Technology Objective (STO) in support of Future Combat Systems (FCS).* Aberdeen Proving Ground, MD: U.S. Army Research Laboratory.

Prevett, T.T., & Wickens, C.D. (1994). *Perspective displays and frame of reference: their interdependence to realize performance advantages over planar displays in a terminal area navigation task.* University of Illinois Institute of Aviation Technical Report (ARL-94-8/NASA-94-3). Savoy, IL: Aviation Research Laboratory.

Roscoe, S.N. (1968). Airborne displays for flight navigation. *Human Factors, 10,* 321- 332.

Sarter, N. (2001). Human technology interface: Multimodal communication in support of coordinative functions in human-machine teams. *Journal of Human Performance in Extreme Environments, 5*(2), 50-54.

Sarter, N. (2002). Multimodal information presentation in support of human automation communication and coordination. In E. Salas (Ed.), *Advances in Human Performance and Cognitive Engineering Research* (pp.13-36). New York: JAI Press.

Sklar, A. & Sarter, N.B. (1999). Good vibrations: Tactile feedback in support of attention allocation and human automation coordination in event-driven domains. *Human Factors, 41,* 543-552.

Van Erp, J.B.F. (2005). Presenting directions with a vibrotactile torso display. *Ergonomics, 48,* 302–313.

Van Erp, J.B.F., Veltman, J.A., Van Veen, H.A.H.C., & Oving, A.B. (2003). Tactile Torso Display as Countermeasure to Reduce Night Vision Goggles Induced Drift. In Spatial Disorientation in Military Vehicles: Causes, Consequences and Cures. *RTO Meeting Proceedings* 86, pp. 49-1 – 49-8. Neuilly-sur-Seine Cedex, France: NATO RTO.

Van Erp, J.B.F. & Van Veen, H.A.H.C. (2003). *A multi-purpose tactile vest for astronauts in the international space station.* Proceedings Eurohaptics 2003 July 6th - 9th 2003, Dublin 2 Ireland (TNO report: 2003 P 139). Soesterberg, NL: TNO Human Factors.

Van Erp, J.B.F. & Van Veen, H.A.H.C. (2004). Vibrotactile in-vehicle navigation system. *Transportation Research Part F, 7*, 247–256.

Van Erp, J.B.F., Jansen, C., Dobbins, T., & Van Veen, H.A.H.C. (2004). Vibrotactile Waypoint Navigation at Sea and in the Air: two Case Studies. Proceedings *Eurohaptics 2004*, June 5 –7. Technische Universität München, Germany

Van Erp, J.B.F. & Duistermaat, M. (2005). *Tactile guidance for land navigation [Tactiele sturing voor landnavigatie]* (TNO Report: TNO-DV3 2005-C 013). Soesterberg, NL: TNO Defence, Security and Safety.

Van Erp, J.B.F., Van Veen, H.A.H.C., Jansen, C., & Dobbins, T. (2005). Waypoint Navigation with a Vibrotactile Waist Belt. *ACM Transactions on Applied Perceptions, 2*(2), 1-12.

Van Veen, H.A.H.C., Spapé, M., & Van Erp, J.B.F. (2004). Waypoint Navigation on Land: Different Ways of Coding Distance to the Next Waypoint. *Proceedings of Eurohaptics 2004* (pp. 160-165). München, Germany: Technische Universität.

Wickens, C.D. (1992). *Engineering psychology and human performance.* (2nd Ed). New York: HarperCollins, Publishers

Wickens, C.D. (2002). Multiple resources and performance prediction. *Theoretical Issues in Ergonomics Science, 3*, 159-177.

Sleep loss and complex team performance

Jeff Whitmore, Scott Chaiken, Joseph Fischer, Richard Harrison,
& Donald Harville
Air Force Research Laboratory, Texas
USA

Abstract

There are few objective assessments of the impact of sleep loss on team performance. The present study was designed to quantify the effects of fatigue on teams performing a complex task and to compare team data with individual data on a similar task. Participants were trained on a complex air battle management task (both in individual and team mode) for one week and then experienced a 36-hr period of sustained wakefulness. Forty-minute scenarios (individual and team) were iteratively completed throughout each experimental period alongside traditional cognitive performance tasks (e.g., simple math processing). Individual data showed the well-established performance reduction resulting from sleep loss and circadian variation at both the simple and complex task levels. Significant decrements were seen for both process measures (e.g., information gathering) and outcome measures (e.g., number of targets attacked) after sleep-loss on the complex task. In contrast, team scores on similar measures after sleep loss, did not degrade, and in some cases showed improvements relative to baseline (indicating a continuing team building process). Individual performance (both simple and complex) was significantly degraded during the early morning hours. Team data did not show the expected performance decrements.

Introduction

Fatigue, due to both sleep loss and circadian variation, and the resultant subjective and performance effects, have been extensively documented at the individual level. For a review, including the impact of fatigue upon decision-making see Harrison & Horne, 2000. However, very few studies have reported objective data regarding the effects of fatigue upon aspects of team performance. The research presented in this paper was designed to address the issue of fatigue on teams by examining complex team performance (using command and control simulations based upon demanding USAF operational tasks) in a sustained operations laboratory environment using USAF military personnel as research participants.

Teams may be defined as, "two or more individuals working toward a common goal in an interdependent fashion" (Salas, Dickinson, Converse, & Tannenbaum, 1992). Teams of individuals perform tasks ranging from the esoteric (e.g., battle management) to the every-day (e.g., administrative functions in offices). Many of these tasks are performed at all times of day or night (e.g., power plant operations) and after extended work periods (e.g., emergency medical surgery). It seems important therefore to be able to describe, quantifiably, how teams respond to fatiguing situations. Unfortunately, there is a definite lack of research literature on teams in sustained operating environments (Weaver, Bowers, & Salas, 2001). Crew resource management addresses fatigue as one of the factors of which crews should be made aware and trained to expect and control (Helmreich, Merritt, & Wilhelm, 1999); however, the specific effects of fatigue due to sleep loss upon team performance do not seem to be provided by this literature. Hollenbeck, Ilgen, Tuttle, & Sego (1995) performed research on sustained attention in a team environment using well-rested volunteers. These researchers found that decrements on vigilance tasks at the team level were similar to those at the individual level. After additional review they postulated that distractions amongst team members were the cause of some performance loss. In summary, while research programs have examined teams under stress (e.g., see the text by (Cannon-Bowers & Salas, 2000), there is currently little known about teams and fatigue.

Generally, complex performance may be divided into two distinct but related categories: process and outcome. Process measures record information on behaviours which must be taken in order to accomplish some goal. For example, a process measure might be the number of times an operator accesses a database to make a decision on the identity of an aircraft. Outcomes are the most commonly thought of types of measures and provide information on the results of a task (e.g., number of targets engaged). By assessing performance from these two perspectives we may understand not only what happened (e.g., did we win?), but also how it happened (e.g., what types of friendly assets were used to engage targets?). Additional metrics, like number of resources shared, become available as teams become the unit of analysis.

The greatest difference between the team and individual task environments is the interaction between any given individual and other humans (by definition of the tasks). This one difference has broad implications. In the team environment there is a potentially significant communication load and dependence upon others to accomplish one's own task. This likely has the effect of pulling attention from being solely focused 'on the screen' to a broader setting. Potentially, this has implications not only for what the operators respond to, but also for how they think (i.e., allows them to solve problems using different methods). Dependence on others creates a need to have awareness of your team mates' resources and status, establish group consensus, plan, and communicate. All of these processes make the team task different from a solo task.

Team performance is broadly composed of two components (Glickman, Zimmer, Montero, Guerette, & Salas, 1987): 1-taskwork (concerning task requirements), and 2-teamwork (concerning co-ordination amongst members). Thus to be an effective team member requires considerable knowledge and skill beyond the individual task level (see Stout, Salas, & Carson, 1994). It may be that a team can function well when its team members are tired, but if so, this continued performance is likely the result of some type of adaptation by the team members (e.g., to some extent the tired team is now composed of a different set of individuals than when it was rested).

The goal of this study was to objectively assess the effects of sleep loss on team performance within a command and control environment (i.e., an applied environment). The teams: were newly formed, were novices to the task, performed an analogue of a real-world task for which they had a professional alignment, were co-located, were non-hierarchical, and had distributed expertise (as a result of assigned roles). They performed a synthetic task that captured the essential function of air battle managers as identified though cognitive task analysis and subject matter expert input. To fully appreciate the potential effect of fatigue upon teams we sought to relate team performance to the vast literature on individual performance. One way to do this is to have a well-understood reference for comparison to the team data. To this end we compared changes on the team task with performance decrements observed on traditional individual tasks (e.g., simple mathematical processing). We selected two well-established individual tasks and collected data on them alongside our team task.

This study extends the work begun in a previous sleep deprivation study performed in our laboratory. In the previous study we observed that both team performance and individual performance declined (Whitmore, 2005). However, the fatigue effect upon teams seemed to be weaker than the effect upon individual performance. We could not solely attribute this difference to the presence of teams as the tasks performed were quite different. While performance on complex tasks has been shown to decrease after sleep deprivation (Harrison & Horne, 2000), it may be that the characteristics of the team task were more motivating than the simple tasks and that this increased motivation allowed for relatively improved performance. To somewhat address this issue, the current study included both an individual and team version of the complex command and control simulation.

Methods

Participants

A total of 30 junior USAF active-duty officers who were on hiatus from receiving Air Battle Management Training at Tyndall AFB, Florida served as the participants. All participants were volunteers and signed an informed consent document which had been approved by the USAF Surgeon General, protocol #F-BR-2004-0041-H. The participants included 22 males and 8 females. Participants were formed into 10, 3-person teams. One team had three females, another team had two females, and three teams had one female. Prior to their arrival at Brooks City-Base, all participants had completed the Aerospace Basics Course. This course gave them background knowledge of doctrine, but no actual field or simulation experience in Air Battle Management. Exclusion criteria consisted of a history of sleep problems, and current use of medications for sleep, depression, or ADHD. The mean age of the participants was 26.1 (±2.6) years. Prior to the experimental session start on Friday morning, participants averaged 6.0 hrs of sleep (range 4.4 – 8.4 hrs). On Tuesday and Wednesday nights they reported 8.3 and 8.1 hrs of sleep respectively. In the 24-

hrs following the experimental session, participants averaged 16.6 hrs of recovery sleep (range 12.0 – 22.1).

Procedure

A total of 70 hours was required of each participant. Each participant went through 32 hours of training the 4 days prior to the experimental session (i.e., Monday through Thursday). Training on the tasks was spaced over the four days and consisted of 10 trials of the simple individual performance tasks, functional training on the synthetic task, 8 trials of the complex individual performance task, and 5 trials as a team on the team task. They then spent 36 hours in the laboratory without sleep (Friday morning to Saturday afternoon). Participants were driven to on-base housing following the experimental session and given 24 hours to rest. They then returned at 1400 hours the following day (Sunday) for a 2-hour recovery session. Scenario administration times in the experimental session were picked using predicted peaks and troughs of performance based upon historical performance patterns (see respective data tables for administration times).

Baseline performance on all measures was captured in the afternoon on the final day of training (Thursday). The experimental session began at 0300 hours (Friday morning) and ended at 1500 hours the following day. Participants experienced iterative testing throughout the session. Participants worked both in isolation and in three person teams to complete 40-min scenarios on the synthetic task described below. They also performed some basic cognitive tests. While participants were generally successful at remaining awake, occasionally proctors would have to encourage wakefulness through conversation or suggesting that a tired participant stand or walk for a while. Three participants (one team) were run during each experimental session.

Apparatus

Automated Neuropsychological Assessment Metrics (ANAM – Reeves, Winter, Kane, Elsmore, & Bleiburg, 2001) – ANAM is a collection of psychomotor and cognitive tasks developed to assess a range of cognitive capabilities. Two tasks were used for this study. *Continuous Processing* - participants determined whether the current number was the same as the previous value and memorized the current number for comparison to the next value. If the two numbers matched the left mouse button was pressed, the right mouse button was pressed if they did not match. *Mathematical Processing* - presented simple addition and subtraction problems containing two operands. Participants summed the three values and determined if the result was greater than (right mouse) less than (left mouse) 5. A number of metrics are supplied by the software for both tests, however; in this paper only throughput (1/mean response time to correct responses x 60 – giving responses per minute) will be reported. Both tests required approximately 3-min to complete.

Activity Log – Participants recorded their work and sleep times for three days prior to each experimental session.

Synthetic Command and Control Task - C^{3}STARS (C^{3}STARS for Command, Control, and Communication Simulation, Training And Research System) represents the roles, responsibilities, and task demands of a team of AWACS air battle managers (ABMs). This job was chosen for the task because it contains the core elements of command and control teams (resource management, resource assignment to tasks, coordination of responses) and could operate in either a hierarchical or flat structure. For this study, individual and team versions of C^{3}STARS were used.

Team C^{3}STARS Task - The team is composed of three individuals each performing a unique and necessary function for the team. The three roles are (1) Strike, (2) Sweep, and (3) Intelligence, Surveillance, and Reconnaissance (ISR). These three roles contain the functions sufficient to accomplish the team goal of destroying hostile ground missile targets (Surface to Air Missile sites – SAMs). The Strike role controls assets which are capable of jamming SAMs (i.e., prevent SAMs from 'seeing' an aircraft in close proximity or behind the jammer) and destroying SAMs (i.e., bombers). The Sweep role directs air-to-air assets (i.e., fighters) which are capable of defeating hostile aircraft. The ISR role controls information gathering aircraft (i.e., UAVs – unmanned aerial vehicles) and "tankers" capable of refuelling other aircraft.

In this version of C^{3}STARS, the ISR role was intentionally constructed to be the least stressed. That is, to have the fewest activities to perform. This was done to allow for asset transfers between the other two roles and ISR. Transfers were the primary mechanism by which the team could reallocate workload. Strike bombers, once having expended their bombs, could be transferred to either Sweep or ISR for use in air-to-air protection. If Sweep was engaged in several areas and having difficulty tracking all the battles, they could transfer the fighters in one fight to ISR and let ISR manage that engagement.

Individual C^{3}STARS Task - While the individual task has the same goal, the same types of controllable resources, and the same types of hostile entities as the team task; there were two major differences. First and most important, all three roles (Strike, Sweep, ISR) were performed by a single person in isolation. Second, the total number of entities in the simulation was reduced by about 60%. In other respects the individual task scenario was similar to the team task scenario. The individual task required increased task knowledge on the part of the operator compared to the team task. However, all the coordinating activities were moved from external behaviours to internal activities. Thus explicit coordinating activities were no longer required. In retrospect, this reduced communication and coordination burden appeared to have resulted in making the individual task "easier" than the team task.

C^{3}STARS generates a host of performance measures. For this report however, for both the team and individual version, the outcome measures will be limited to two outcome measures and two process measures. The outcome measures are the number of friendly aircraft attacked and the number of air targets engaged. The process measures are the number of information windows opened (IWO) and the number of picture changes (PIX). The outcome measures represent two of the core functions required to accomplish the mission, while the process measures indicate behaviours concerned with information gathering and awareness of the battle area. The team measures are aggregated across team members and thus will be larger than the values for the individual measures. Of all the measures presented at the team level, number of friendly aircraft attacked requires the most cooperation amongst team members (resources controlled by two operators are required for this to occur).

Results

Prior to analysis of the experimental data, Student's t-tests were performed on each dependent measure testing for changes from baseline to recovery. Significant improvements were seen for the majority of the dependent measures (see Table 1). Such learning effects will mask, to varying degrees, any fatigue effects. Consequently, the decision was made to adjust the data for the learning trends prior to analysis. For each individual (or team) the difference between baseline and recovery was calculated. Each trial, except for the first and last, was then adjusted by adding the appropriate proportion of that difference (e.g., for the third experimental trial of the team data 3/5 of the difference was added to the original value). While this linear adjustment is conservative according to learning theory, which would predict more learning on earlier trials in a sequence (exponential improvement), it was used to guard against overestimating the effects of learning.

A repeated measures analysis of variance (ANOVA) was performed on the adjusted data of each dependent measure to test for changes over time. When the result was significant, post-hoc comparisons were made between each trial and baseline using simple effects tests. To quantify and compare effect sizes, partial Eta squared (η_p^2) was calculated for each ANOVA and subsequent t-tests. For tables 2 through 4, numbers in each cell represent the mean and standard deviation (in parenthesis); [h] indicates Huynh-Feldt adjustment; * indicates the mean was significantly different from baseline mean (p<.05, post-hoc 1-tailed t-test); η_p^2 = effect size and; data were adjusted for learning effects before analysis following the method mentioned above.

ANAM results / Confirmation of the Fatigue Model

Continuous Processing Task Throughput – A significant time effect was observed. Performance on this task was well maintained through Day 2 23.00hr after which performance decreased significantly and remained depressed for the remainder of the experimental session (see Table 2). For example, η_p^2 for changes in throughput (i.e., baseline to any specific trial) remained below .03 through Day 2 23.00hr and then increased to .35-.53 for the remaining trials.

Mathematical Processing Task – A significant time change was again present for throughput. Unlike Continuous Processing, significant performance decrements began at the first experimental trial. While following the typical circadian variation, performance remained below baseline throughout (Fig 1). η_p^2 was .18 by the first trial (Day 2 05.30) and ranged from .29 to .61 thereafter.

Table 1. Baseline (Day 1, 17.30hr) vs. Recovery (Day 4, 16.00hr)

Test	Variable	Mean (Standard Deviation) Baseline	Recovery	Change	η_p^2	Student's t-test (one-tailed) t (df)	p
Continuous Processing	Throughput	114.2 (19.6)	129.9 (24.0)	15.7 (11.3)	.67	7.52 (28)	<.001
Math	Throughput	39.5 (8.9)	41.5 (11.7)	1.9 (5.7)	.11	1.89 (29)	.035
Individual CSTARS (Outcome Measures)	Friendly Aircraft Attacked	2.0 (1.6)	1.2 (1.1)	-0.8 (1.7)	.16	-2.36 (29)	.013
	Air Targets Engaged (22 possible)	21.1 (3.3)	21.6 (4.7)	0.5 (4.0)	.02	.68 (29)	.252
Individual CSTARS (Process Measures)	IWO	133.5 (55.2)	127.8 (57.5)	-5.7 (30.4)	.04	-1.02 (29)	.158
	PIX	717.5 (285.7)	750.7 (349.0)	33.2 (269.0)	.02	.68 (29)	.252
Team CSTARS (Outcome Measures)	Friendly Aircraft Attacked	12.3 (3.8)	9.7 (4.3)	-2.6 (3.9)	.34	-2.13 (9)	.031
	Air Targets Engaged (42 possible)	31.1 (5.5)	36.9 (3.1)	5.8 (5.7)	.53	3.20 (9)	.006
Team CSTARS (Process Measures)	IWO	380.6 (107.3)	393.1 (125.2)	12.5 (34.4)	.13	1.15 (9)	.140
	PIX	1789.8 (559.8)	2273.1 (879.1)	483.3 (465.0)	.55	3.29 (9)	.005

Table 2. Individual ANAM–Descriptive statistics and ANOVA results

Test/ Variable	Time (day-hour) 1- 14.00	2- 04.00	2- 10.00	2- 16.00	2- 22.00	3- 04.00	3- 11.00	3- 13.00	MSE	ANOVA test of time effect F (df)	p	η_p^2
Continuous Processing (TP)	114.2 (19.6)	119.3 (21.3)	112.9 (23.5)	115.6 (22.9)	115.9 (20.3)	101.7* (21.5)	97.1* (23.2)	100.0* (23.1)	165.7	19.29^h (5,130)	<.001	.41
Math (TP)	39.5 (8.9)	37.6* (8.7)	34.4* (8.2)	36.3* (8.8)	35.6* (8.2)	32.7* (9.0)	34.3* (8.9)	35.2* (8.7)	26.0	8.26^h (4,128)	<.001	.22

Complex individual performance

Significant time effects were seen for both outcome measures and both process measures. For all of the measures, there was a significant reduction in performance at Day-3 06.00hr (see Table 3). Partial Eta squared values for this change were: .50 for IWO, .15 for Pix, .31 for ATE, and .25 for FAA. In addition FAA, and ATE (see Fig 2) showed earlier reductions (Day-2 18.00). Generally, performance rebounded at the final trial (Day-3 13.00).

Math Throughput
(means and standard errors)

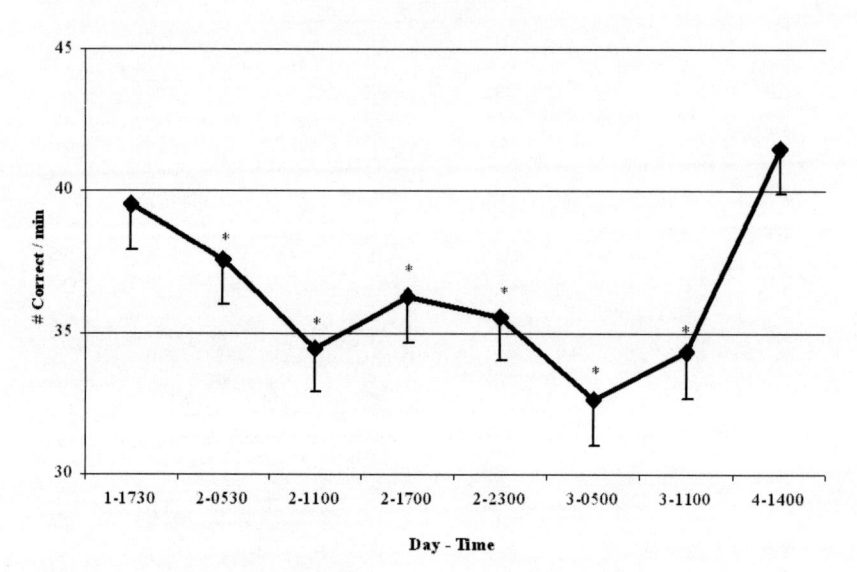

Figure 1. ANAM Math results over time

Table 3. *Individual CSTARS—Descriptive statistics and ANOVA results*

Type of Measure	Variable	Time (day-hour)						ANOVA test of time			
		1-18.00 (baseline)	2-06.00	2-18.00	3-06.00	3-13.00	MSE	F (df)	p	η_p^2	
Outcome	Friendly Aircraft Attacked	1.8 (1.5)	1.4 (1.5)	2.4* (1.8)	2.9* (2.2)	2.2 (2.2)	1.70	4.39 (4,92)	.003	.16	
	Air Targets Engaged	21.5 (3.3)	22.0 (3.3)	19.8* (2.8)	18.7* (4.6)	20.7 (5.4)	13.58	4.60 (3,64)[h]	.007	.17	
Process	IWO	131.0 (55.7)	122.5 (67.3)	125.6 (63.2)	108.2* (67.5)	124.3 (64.7)	624.80	3.72 (3,69)[h]	.015	.14	
	PIX	700.0 (303.1)	746.7 (315.2)	785.8 (325.6)	619.9* (241.9)	692.4 (333.2)	21691.3	4.32 (4,92)	.003	.16	

Complex Team Performance

Few team performance variables appear to be affected by fatigue (see Table 4 & Fig 2). Only one process measure, Pix, showed a significant effect of time. Pix counts decrease significantly at the Day-3 06.00hr trial, $\eta_p^2 = .46$.

Air Targets Successfully Engaged
(means and standard errors)

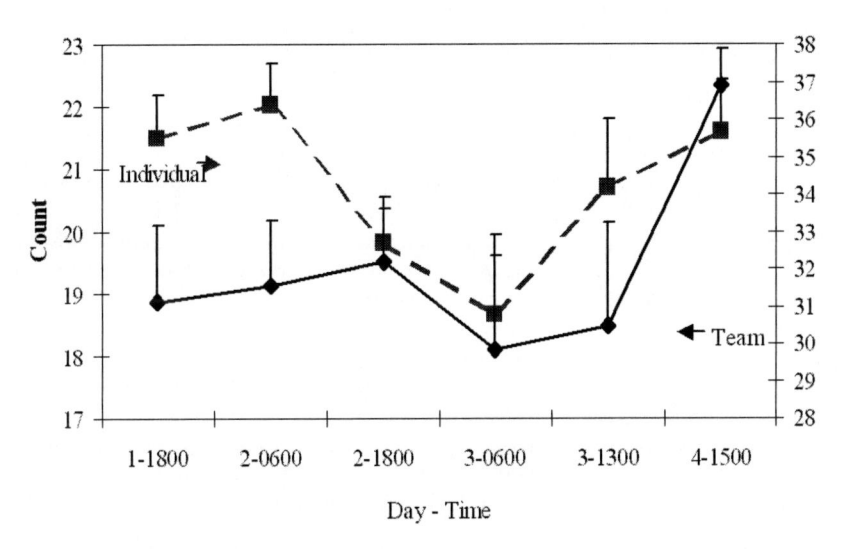

Figure 2. Individual and Team C3STARS

Table 4. Team CSTARS —Descriptive statistics and ANOVA results

Type of Measure	Variable	Time (day-hour)					ANOVA test of time			
		1-16.00 (baseline)	2-04.00	2-16.00	3-04.00	3-10.00	MSE	F (df)	p	η_p^2
Outcome	Friendly Aircraft Attacked	12.3 (4.3)	13.8 (3.1)	12.7 (5.3)	13.6 (5.8)	12.5 (6.3)	14.95	.39 (3,18)[h]	.731	.05
	Air Targets Engaged	31.1 (5.7)	31.5 (5.0)	32.2 (5.0)	29.8 (8.7)	30.5 (7.8)	27.86	.24 (4,28)	.914	.03
Process	IWO	389.3 (111.6)	372.3 (99.4)	387.0 (101.3)	350.1 (109.7)	358.6 (116.1)	1932.40	1.22 (4,28)	.325	.15
	PIX	1846.8 (613.9)	1827.4 (509.2)	1765.6 (590.1)	1615.8* (433.9)	1458.4* (641.6)	72884.91	2.95 (4,28)	**.038**	.30

Discussion

As anticipated, performance on the individual simple cognitive tasks followed the well-established pattern combining circadian and sleep deprivation effects for cognitive metrics (Hockey, 1986). This finding provides support for the efficacy of the experimental manipulation (i.e., keeping people awake for the specified schedule produced negative performance changes). The observed effect sizes for the simple performance data were modest (CPT η_p^2=0.24; Math η_p^2=0.19). Thus, while successful, the experimental manipulation was not overwhelming.

C³STARS individual performance showed the same trends as the more basic tests. All of the dependent measures from this task showed significant changes over time. These findings, support the idea that complex performance can be negatively impacted by fatigue, and proved that C³STARS' is a sensitive measure of fatigue.

Complex team performance generally did not degrade with the level of sleep deprivation used in this study. Of the four measures, only Pix showed a significant time effect. Neither of the outcome measures evinced effect sizes comparable to those seen at the individual level. While power was reduced at the team level relative to the individual level (i.e., team sample size is one third of individual), it is unlikely that significant time effects would have been observed even if the team sample size were increased. It was anticipated that reduced power might lead to non-significant results at the team level but that trends would be present indicating a deleterious impact of fatigue. However, this is not the case for the outcome measures. As can be seen from the data, teams continued to learn throughout the experimental session. One explanation for this is, while they understood the taskwork requirements (as evidenced from their individual performances), they continued to develop teamwork skills (anticipatory behaviours and strategies).

There are several potential explanations operating at different levels which could account for teams performing less poorly under fatiguing conditions than individuals. It is possible that inter-individual communication may produce a stimulating effect which may in turn reduce the amount of perceived effort on the part of team members when compared to individual performance. The debrief and predictive pre-brief may increase a sense of accountability beyond what is experienced in the individual task and reduce social loafing (Latane, Williams, & Harkins, 1979), resulting in increased motivation for the team task. A similar motivational increase may constrain satisficing, maintaining performance expectations and resulting in increased expenditure of effort at the team level. It may be possible that even with a similar level of satisficing and general brain activation (i.e., stimulation) a team is simply more adaptable and better able to cope with the effects of fatigue due to redundancy and mutual assistance capability. Future studies of teams and sleep deprivation should include additional subjective metrics, like estimates of effort and workload, to disentangle these theories.

Many more outcome measures were collected from C³STARS than are reported in this paper. It is intended to present many of these measures in a future publication. As well, it is planned to perform several further analyses of the data. For example, to examine individual participants and teams to determine if there are relationships between baseline performance level, learning, and the impact of fatigue. Finally, analyses will be made relating individual information (e.g., personality traits, amount of pre-session sleep) with their performance in the experimental session.

References

Cannon-Bowers, J.A., & Salas, E. (Eds.). (2000). *Making Decision Under Stress*. Washington, D.C.: American Psychological Association.

Glickman, A.S., Zimmer, S., Montero, R.C., Guerette, P.J., & Salas, E. (1987). *The evolution of team skills: An empirical assessment with implications for training* (No. NTSC 87-016). Orlando, FL: Naval Training Systems Center, Human Factors Division.

Harrison, Y., & Horne, J.A. (2000). The impact of sleep deprivation on decision making: a review. *Journal of Experimental Psychology: Applied, 6*(3), 236-249.

Helmreich, R.L., Merritt, A.C., & Wilhelm, J.A. (1999). The evolution of crew resource management training in commercial aviation. *International Journal of Aviation Psychology, 9*(1), 19-32.

Hockey, G.R.J. (1986). Changes in operator efficiency as a function of environmental stress, fatigue, and circadian rhythms. In *Handbook of perception and human performance. Volume 2.* (pp. 44-41 - 44-49). New York: Wiley-Interscience.

Hollenbeck, J.R., Ilgen, D.R., Tuttle, D.B., & Sego, D.J. (1995). Team performance on monitoring tasks: An examination of decision errors in contexts requiring sustained attention. *Journal of Applied Psychology, 80*, 685-696.

Latane, B., Williams, K., & Harkins, S. (1979). Many hands make light work: The causes and consequences of social loafing. *Journal of Personality and Social Psychology, 37*, 822-832.

Salas, E., Dickinson, T.L., Converse, S.A., & Tannenbaum, S.I. (1992). Toward an understanding of team performance and training. In R.W. Swezey and E. Salas (Eds.), *Teams: Their training and performance* (pp. 3-29). Stamford, CT: Ablex Publishing.

Stout, R.J., Salas, E., & Carson, R. (1994). Inidividual task proficiency and team process behavior: What's important for team functioning? *Military Psychology, 6*(3), 177-192.

Weaver, J.L., Bowers, C.A., & Salas, E. (2001). Stress and Teams: Performance Effects and Interventions. In P.A. Hancock & P.A. Desmond (Eds.), *Stress, workload, and fatigue* (pp. 83-106). Mahwah, NJ: Lawrence Earlbaum Associates.

Whitmore, J.N. (2005). Assessing performance in complex team environments. *Aviation, Space, and Environmental Medicine, 76*(7), C31-C33.

The structure of contributing factors of human error in safety-critical industries

Nicki Marquardt & Rainer Höger
University of Lüneburg
Lüneburg
Germany

Abstract

This paper presents the development of a human factors assessment tool for safety-critical industries. The assessment tool is a questionnaire about human factors issues that can cause human error and accidents in consequence. It is based on the 'Dirty Dozen' human error concept of Dupont (1997, as cited in Safety Regulation Group, 2002). The advantage of this concept is the adaptable nature in the applied field. Moreover, it was intended to search for a latent structure behind the dirty dozen concept. Hence, a questionnaire with 240 items was tested and optimised in two large metal manufacturing companies. In order to find a hidden structure behind the dirty dozen, a factor analysis of all twelve scales was performed. The factor analysis yielded three factors: *Organizational Interaction & Resources, Mental Workload* and *Social Dominance*. Results are discussed in terms of their utility for human error research.

Introduction

Human error can play a significant role in the contribution to incidents and accidents. In most industries more than 70 to 90 percent of factors that cause an accident refer to human error (Hollnagel, 1993). There exist various academic models of human error (Reason, 1990; Rasmussen, 1986). On the contrary, there is only a small number of more practice-oriented concepts. Most of academic models have good explanatory power concerning the cognitive structures and processes underlying human error. However, they often lack their adaptability in the field context. One human error concept which was found very adaptable is the 'Dirty Dozen' concept of Dupont (1997, as cited in Safety Regulation Group, 2002). The dirty dozen have been found to be the 12 most common causes of human error in aviation maintenance. Today, many airlines use this concept in their incident and accident analyses and also for their maintenance human factors training programs (Safety Regulation Group, 2002). The dirty dozen encompass different categories of human factors that contribute to accidents. These categories are individual factors like *lack of awareness, complacency, lack of knowledge, lack of assertiveness, distraction, fatigue, stress,* social factors like *lack of teamwork, lack of communication, social norms,* and contextual conditions like *pressure* and *lack of resources*. Nevertheless,

In D. de Waard, G.R.J. Hockey, P. Nickel, and K.A. Brookhuis (Eds.) (2007), *Human Factors Issues in Complex System Performance* (pp. 67 - 71). Maastricht, the Netherlands: Shaker Publishing.

these categories are not totally independent or exclusive. For example, distraction can be a result of the interaction of individual factors (e.g. lack of awareness, stress or fatigue) and contextual conditions (e.g. pressure). Furthermore, more contributing factors may exist, like leadership, task difficulty or cultural issues.

One goal of this study was to develop a practice-oriented assessment tool for contributing factors of human error. Therefore, this assessment tool was based on Duponts (1997, as cited in Safety Regulation Group, 2002) 'Dirty Dozen' concept, because of its successful application in the field of aviation maintenance. Furthermore, it was tried to test the transferability of this concept to other safety-critical industries. Finally, it was intended to search for a latent structure behind the dirty dozen concept.

Method

Sample

The sample used in this study was drawn from independent worker populations at two different metal manufacturing companies in Germany. Both firms produce vehicles and technical components for the defence industry. Therefore, both companies can be classified into the broad category of safety-critical industries. 90 workers from one company participated in the first survey and 78 workers from the other company joined the second survey. All these participants were shift workers from different departments during one day shift. Due to the precondition of an anonymous survey required by the firms work council, personal data like age, sex and qualification could not be collected.

Instrument

The assessment tool for contributing factors of human error was a questionnaire that comprehended 240 items. The items were developed by the use of academic literature, accidents reports and work experience of human factors practitioners. Each item used in this questionnaire reflected one of the dirty dozen categories. Each of the twelve categories related to 20 items. For all items a five-point Likert scale was applied. Table 1 provides selected examples of items.

Table 1. Examples of items of the assessment tool.

Dirty Dozen Category	Item
Lack of awareness	I always recognise dangers in my work environment on time.
Lack of knowledge	I am well aware of the duties of all those involved in my work process.
Social Norms	I believe safety regulations often disturb an efficient work environment.
Lack of Teamwork	Conflicts within the team often remain unsolved.
Pressure	Due to financial pressure even high risk tasks have to be performed under increasing time demand.

Results

The rate of return of the questionnaires was 100 percent. After data collection of the first survey (90 questionnaires) an item analysis was conducted to all items. Only items with adequate means and item-total correlations above .30 were accepted. Five items of each dirty dozen category which best met these criteria were related to one of twelve dirty dozen scales. The item-total correlations between each of the five items and the specific dirty dozen scale test score ranged from r =.35 to r = .85. The reliabilities of the twelve scales (assessed by Cronbach's α) ranged between α = .69 to α = .90. In order to find a hidden structure behind the dirty dozen, a factor analysis (PCA) of all twelve scales was performed. The factor analysis yielded three factors with eigenvalues greater than 1 for each and explained 77 % of the variance. The rotated factor solutions – only factor loadings of ≥ .5 were accepted – led to the following factors: *Organizational Interaction & Resources* (Factor 1), *Mental Workload* (Factor 2), and *Social Dominance* (Factor 3). Therefore, each of the dirty dozen categories refers to one factor of this new three dimensional human factors model (see Figure 1).

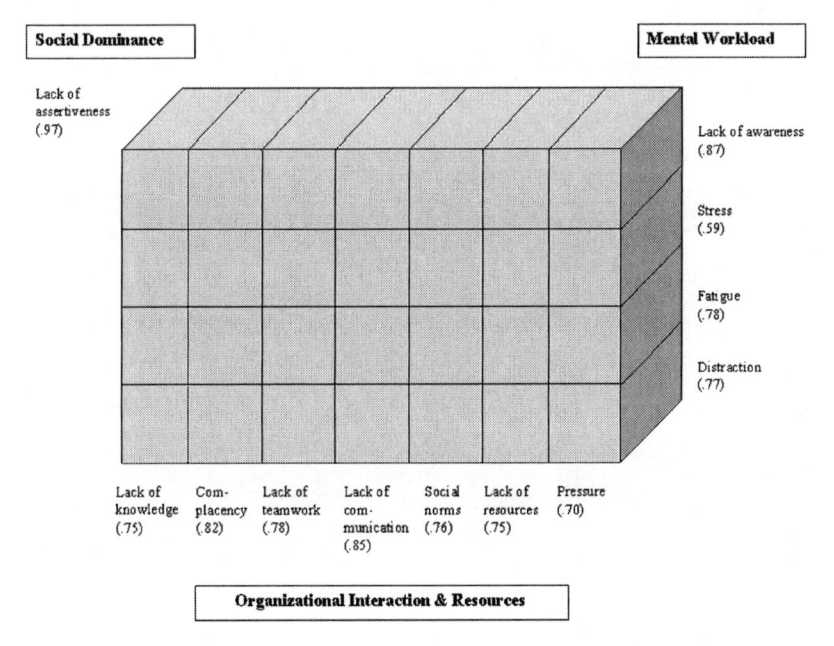

Figure 1. Three dimensional model of contributing factors of human error. The value below each dirty dozen scale indicates the factor loading of each scale on the relevant factor

Moreover, the data of the second survey (78 questionnaires) confirmed this model, including the other mentioned results. Consequently, model based profiles of potential contributors to human error of both companies could be compared.

Figure 2 illustrates the mean differences of the two surveyed companies along the three factors. Both companies were metal manufacturing firms and belong to the

70   Marquardt & Höger

same kind of industry. Thus, there were no big differences between both companies in that global comparison.

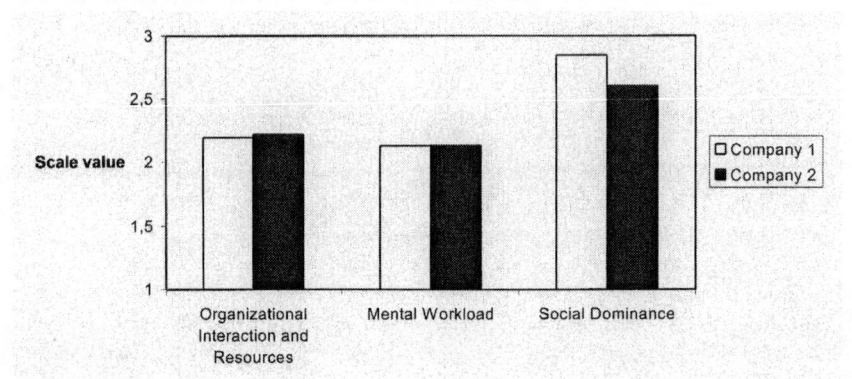

Figure 2. Mean differences of the two surveyed companies along the three factors. The scale values represent a five-point Likert Scale

Figure 3 shows the more detailed profiles of contributors to human error of the two surveyed companies along the dirty dozen scales. Both profiles look similar, but there are significant differences between the two companies in the categories *complacency* ($t_{(166)} = -0.99$; $p < 0.05$), *lack of resources* ($t_{(166)} = -1.25$; $p < 0.05$), *pressure* ($t_{(166)} = 2.05$; $p < 0.001$) and *lack of assertiveness* ($t_{(166)} = 1.23$; $p < 0.05$).

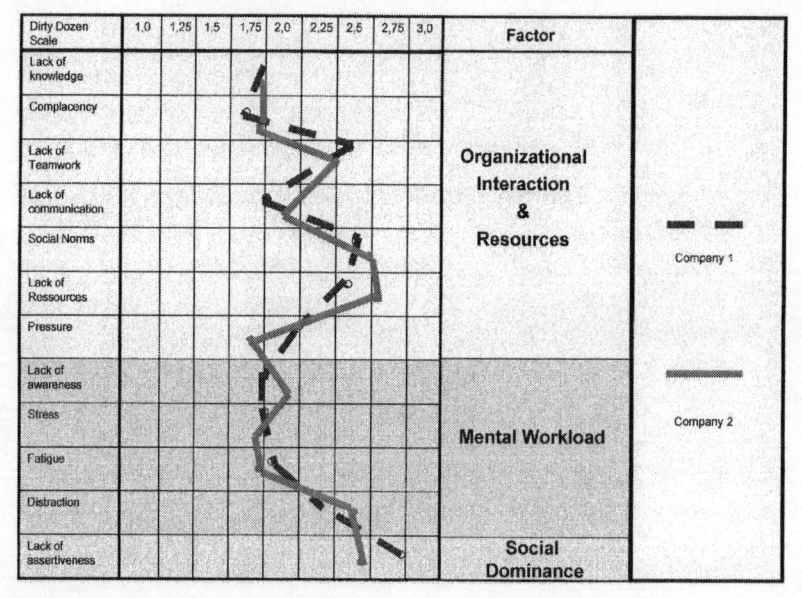

Figure 3. Profiles of contributors to human error of the two surveyed companies. The scale values represent a five-point Likert Scale

Discussion

The main results of this study are the developed model and the questionnaire about contributing factors of human error. This three dimensional human factors model and the related questionnaire are tentative and more research is needed to validate their structure. For example, it is not known what are the cut-offs in the dirty dozen scales to decide whether there is a potential risk or not. Moreover, it is only an assumption on the base of face validity, that each set of five items appropriately covers the relevant dirty dozen category to an equal extend. But this questionnaire was sensitive enough to indicate significant differences between the two companies, though both belong to the same type of industry. Furthermore, it appears to be a sensible approach to combine practice-based human error concepts with research-based models (Stanton et al., 2005). One goal for future studies is to identify unique profiles of contributors to human error in different types of industries by this questionnaire. Finally, based on these profiles specific human error avoidance training programs can be developed.

References

Dupont, G. (1997). The Dirty Dozen Errors in Maintenance. In *Meeting Proceedings Eleventh Federal Aviation Administration Meeting on Human Factors Issues in Aircraft Maintenance and Inspection: Human Error in Aviation Maintenance* (pp. 45-49). Washington, USA: Federal Aviation Administration / Office of Aviation Medicine. (as cited in Safety Regulation Group, 2002, chapter 3, pp. 20-21)

Hollnagel, E. (1993). *Human Reliability Analysis: Context and Control.* London, UK: Academic Press.

Rasmussen, J. (1986). *Information Processing and Human-Machine Interaction: An Approach to Cognitive Engineering.* Amsterdam, the Netherlands: Elsevier Science.

Reason, J. (1990). *Human Error.* New York, USA: Cambridge University Press.

Safety Regulation Group (2002). *An Introduction to Aircraft Maintenance Engineering Human Factors for JAR 66 (Civil Aviation Publication, CAP 715 of the UK Civil Aviation Authority).* Norwich, UK: TSO. (Retrieved on 15/03/2007 from: http://www.caa.co.uk/docs/33/CAP715.pdf.)

Stanton, N.A., Salmon, P.M., Walker, G.H., Baber, C., & Jenkins, D.P. (2005). *Human Factors Methods. A practical guide for engineering and design.* Aldershot, UK: Ashgate.

Cognitive Work Analysis of a Sensor to Effecter System: implications for network structures

Daniel P. Jenkins, Neville A. Stanton, Guy H. Walker,
Paul M. Salmon, & Mark S. Young
Brunel University, Uxbridge, UK

Abstract

This paper presents a Cognitive Work Analysis of a command and control experimental environment. The network facilitates the exchange of information between agents in the field and a series of centrally located commanders. The environment developed allows the manipulation of dependent variables to establish the most efficient network structure for a variety of different scenarios. Cognitive Work Analysis has been used to analyse and model the experimental system and hypothesise the implications of changes to the network structure and the resulting influence this will have on the system and the agents contained within. The analysis uses a *Work Domain Analysis* to capture the purpose of the system. A *Control Task Analysis* outlines the task required to fulfil the purpose of the system. This task is broken down in a *Strategies Analysis*, which explains the possible ways that the system can be configured to enable the same end state. A *Social Organisation and Co-operation Analysis* elucidates which of the actors within the system can perform the tasks required. Finally a *Worker Competencies Analysis* describes the resulting behavioural characteristics the actors will exert depending on the level of tasks they are assigned.

The domain

The system consists of two distributed teams located in an urban environment of approximately 20 hectares. The first team is made up of a number of reconnaissance units known as 'sensors'. Sensors have the ability to sweep a geographic area and identify targets that need to be neutralised. The second team is made up of effecters who are responsible for neutralising identified targets. In this simple experimental model sensors are the only actors that can detect targets and effecters are the only actors who can neutralise previously identified targets.

There are a number of ways that information can be transmitted between the sensors and effectors based on the way the system is configured. The system can be set up to enable information to be sent via the commanders with information travelling up the hierarchy and then back down to the units in the field, alternatively information can be sent peer to peer.

In D. de Waard, G.R.J. Hockey, P. Nickel, and K.A. Brookhuis (Eds.) (2007), *Human Factors Issues in Complex System Performance* (pp. 73 - 84). Maastricht, the Netherlands: Shaker Publishing.

When sending peer to peer the network can be configured so that a sensor can be linked to an effecter. Alternatively the system can be configured so that the sensor has the ability to select the recipient of the information. The system is reconfigurable; the configuration choice will be influenced by a number of variables. These include:

- Number of units – how many sensors
- Ratio of effecters to sensors – how many effecters per sensor
- Ratio of targets to sensors – how many targets per sensor
- Complexity of task – are there a number of conflicting requirements
- Complexity of the target – is interpretation of the target required
- Ambiguity of information – is it clear what the information represents
- Type of information transmitted

Cognitive Work Analysis

Cognitive Work Analysis (CWA) is a structured framework for considering the development and analysis of complex socio-technical systems. The framework leads the analyst to consider the environment the task takes place within and the effect of the imposed constraints on the systems ability to perform its purpose. The framework guides the analyst through the process of answering the question of *why* the system exists; *what* activities are conducted within the domain as well as *how* this activity is achieved and *who* is performing it.

According to Sanderson (2003) CWA does not focus on how human-system interaction should proceed (*normative modelling*) or how human-system interaction currently works (*descriptive modelling*). Instead, it focuses on identifying properties of the work environment and of the workers themselves that define possible boundaries on the ways that human-system interaction might reasonably proceed, without explicitly identifying specific sequences of actions (*formative modelling*).

CWA was originally developed at the Risø National Laboratory in Denmark (Rasmussen et al., 1994). The framework has been developed and applied for a number of purposes including: system modelling (e.g. Hajdukiewicz, 1998); system design (e.g. Bisantz et al., 2003); training needs analysis (e.g. Naikar & Sanderson, 1999), training program evaluation and design (e.g. Naikar & Sanderson, 1999); interface design and evaluation (Vicente, 1999); information requirements specification (e.g. Ahlstrom, 2005); tender evaluation (e.g. Naikar & Sanderson, 2001); team design (Naikar et al., 2003); and error management strategy design (Naikar & Saunders, 2003).

The framework has been applied in a variety of domains including: aviation (e.g., Naikar & Sanderson, 2001); process control (e.g., Vicente, 1999); nuclear power (e.g., Olsson & Lee, 1994); Naval (e.g. Bisantz et al., 2003); military command and control (e.g., Salmon et al., 2004); road transport (e.g., Stoner et al., 2003); health care (e.g., Miller, 2004); air traffic control (e.g., Ahlstrom, 2005); and manufacturing (e.g., Higgins, 1998).

According to Vicente (1999) CWA can be broken down into 5 defined phases.

Phase	Tool
Work Domain Analysis	Abstraction Decomposition Space
Control Task Analysis	Decision Ladder
Strategies Analysis	Information flow map
Social Organisation & Co-operation Analysis	All of the Above
Worker Competencies Analysis	Skills Rules Knowledge

Work Domain Analysis

The first phase work domain analysis (WDA) is used to describe the domain in which the activity takes place independent of any goals or activities. The first stage of this process is to build up an abstraction hierarchy (AH) of the domain.

The AH represents the system domain at a number of levels; at the highest level the AH captures the system's raison d'être; at the lowest level the AH captures the physical objects within the system. In this simple sensor-effecter paradigm the sole reason that the system exists is to detect and neutralise targets within a predefined area. The system is evaluated against its ability to enact its purpose. This can be measured by a number of criteria, including; the time it takes the effecter to receive a target; how quickly all of the targets can be neutralised (this could be achieved by neutralising them based on the targets geographical position); the speed at which threat is reduced (this could be achieved by neutralising the most dangerous targets first); and the number of errors made.

In many circumstances these criteria may be conflicting. An example of this conflict would be units approaching targets in threat priority order; the same effecter prioritising the targets by their geographical position, would approach the targets in a different order; this route is shorter and therefore faster to complete, however the target with the greatest threat may not be neutralised until last. It could also be argued that the speed to complete and error rates are conflicting constraints. The assumption being that; more careful time consuming planning reduces errors.

The bottom level of the AH shows each of the physical objects within the domain, in this case the nodes comprise all of the equipment and all of the actors within the domain. The level above this describes the functions that each of the objects can afford; in many cases an object may perform a number of functions, in the same way a particular function may be afforded by a number of objects.

The generalised functions in the middle of the AH are the functions required to perform the purposes of the system. Each of these levels can be linked by means-ends relationships using the why-what-how relationship. This analysis results in the AH shown in figure 1.

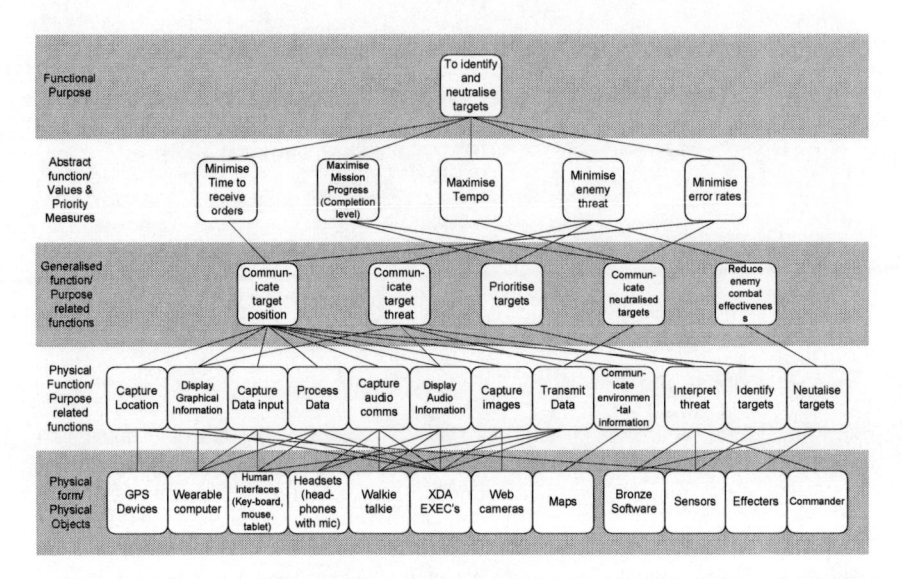

Figure 1. Abstraction Hierarchy for Sensor-Effecter activity

The AH can then be decomposed into a number of categories in this case three categories; system, subsystem and individual components. Once decomposed, the data can be plotted on the Abstraction-Decomposion Space.

Figure 2. Abstraction Decomposition Space for Sensor-Effecter activity

Control Task Analysis

The second stage of the analysis focuses on what has to be achieved independent of how the task is conducted or who will be doing it. The task of identifying a target and neutralising it is shown by following the path up the left hand side and down the right hand side in the decision ladder in figure 3.

The spotting of a target is the activation for the system to start. Once a target is spotted information is recorded on the targets location and type (no inference or calculation is made). Assessment is then made to calculate the threat of the target. Once a threat has been assigned, the target is then considered relative to the task and the environment and a priority is placed. This prioritisation allows the target to be assigned to an effecter. A target is then identified and finally neutralised.

In order to speed up this process it is possible to bypass some of the steps, removing some of the decision making processes allows the transition from spotting the target to neutralisation to be expedited. Figure 3 shows each of the possible leaps (circle to circle) and shunts (circle to square). Figure 3 illustrates that the shortest path for this paradigm is that the target is spotted, information recorded and this information is used to neutralise the target.

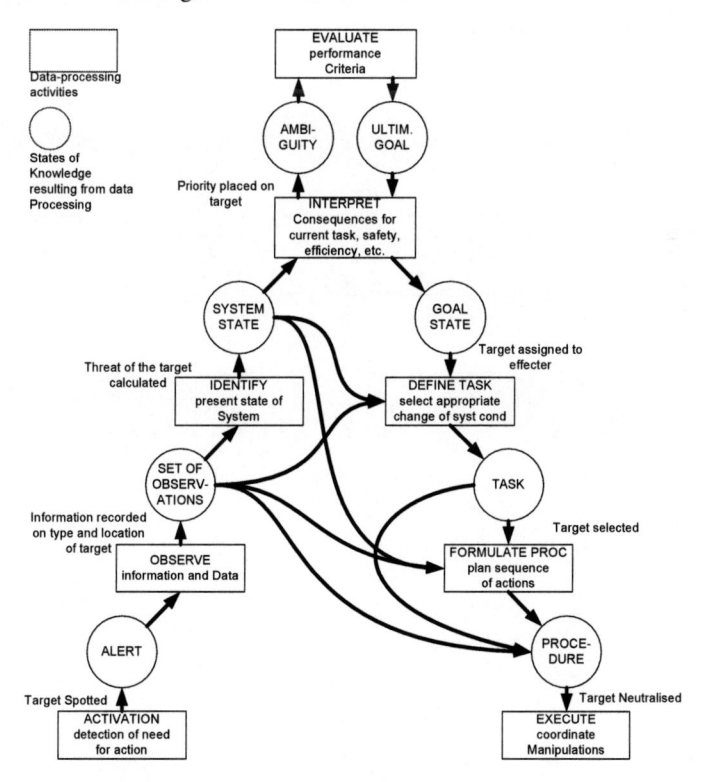

Figure 3. Decision ladder for Sensor-Effecter activity shortened

Naikar et al. (2005) introduce the contextual activity template for use in this phase of the CWA (see figure 4). This template is one way of representing activity in work systems that are characterised by both work situations and work functions. Work situations are situations that can be decomposed based on recurring schedules or specific locations. Rasmussen (1994.) describes work functions as, activity characterised by its content independent of its temporal or spatial characteristics (Rasmussen et al., 1994).

According to Naikar et al. (2005) the work situations are shown along the horizontal axis and the work functions are shown along the vertical axis of the contextual activity template. The circles indicate the work functions and the boxes around each circle indicate all of the work situations in which a work function can occur (as opposed to must occur). The bars within each box indicate those work situations in which a work function will typically occur. This template therefore shows the context, defined by work situations, in which particular work functions can occur.

The work functions are similar to the generalised functions in the WDA (see figure 1). Three distinctly different situations have been selected; in the field searching for targets; in the command centre; in the field neutralising targets. These situations can be considered different due to their geographical variation and their different constraints. Figure 4 shows that the constraints imposed on the system mean that two of the functions are bound by the situations (records information on the type and location; and neutralise the target). The functions of prioritising the targets and of assigning the threat can take place in any situation. Figure 4 illustrates that the function of calculating the threat of the targets is more likely to take place in the field whilst searching for targets.

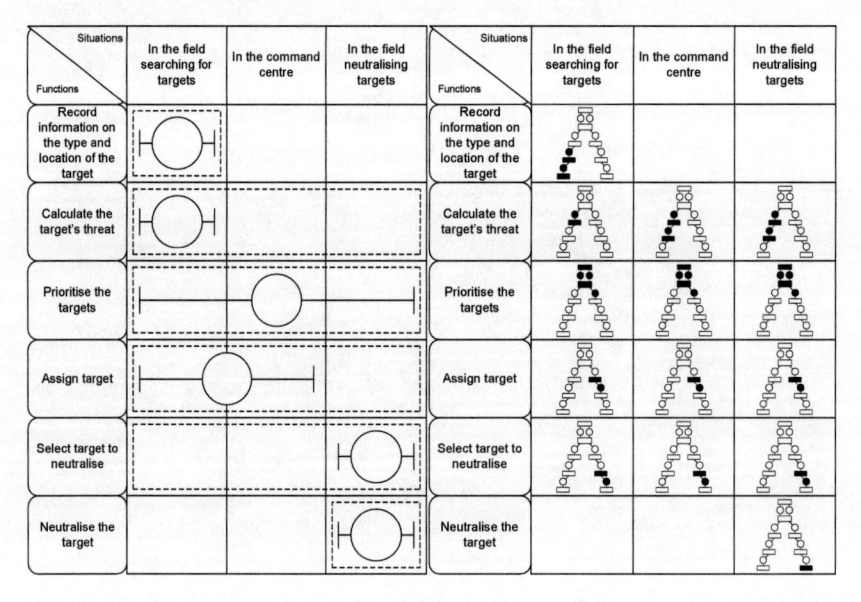

Figure 4. Contextual activity template

CWA of a Sensor to Effecter System 79

The decision ladder introduced in figure 3 can be used to communicate which stage of the task is being completed at any particular mix of work situation or function. The diagram on the right shows the contextual activity template overlaid with this information.

Strategies Analysis

There are a number of ways of achieving the same ends with the system described in the Abstraction Hierarchy. Each of these strategies uses different resources and distributes the workload in different ways.

In this case the start state is that a target is identified and the end state that the target is neutralised. Use of the decision ladder representation in figure 6 illustrates that the strategy chosen affects the way in which the task is completed. The first strategy shows that the task is completed at a simplistic level without threat calculation or prioritisation. This situation requires the targets to be neutralised as they are detected. An example of a more complex situation is situation 6 (shown at the bottom of figure 5), here the target is processed centrally and considered with all other targets, a priority is assigned and the appropriate effecter selected.

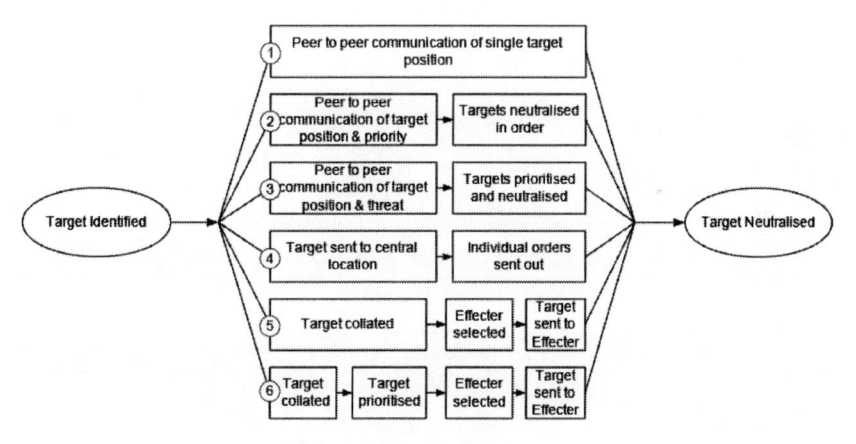

Figure 5. Strategies analysis for Sensor-Effecter activity

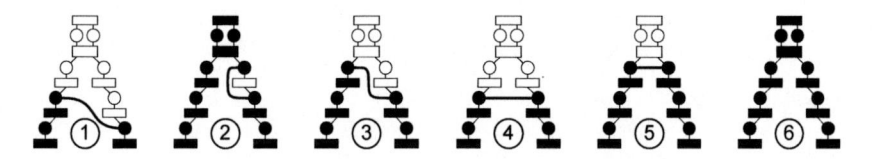

Figure 6. Strategies analysis for Sensor-Effecter activity

Social Organisation & Co-operation Analysis

It is possible to map each of the actor types on to the existing tools in order to show who has the capability of doing what. Using arbitrary colours it is possible to show where each on the actor groups can conduct tasks.

Figure 7. Key of actor type and colour

Figure 8 shows the abstraction-decomposition space (ADS) coloured to show the nodes that can be used by the key actor groups. The total system requirements have been left blank as these are generic and apply to all actors.

Figure 8. ADS showing nodes used by each of the key actor groups

Figure 9 shows the decision ladder introduced in figure 3 coloured to show where each of the actor types can conduct tasks. Due to the limitations of the system sensors are the only actors that can detect targets and effecters are the only actors who can neutralise previously identified targets (highlighted in figure 4). This leads to the 'feet' of the ladder being coloured dark for the sensors and 'medium grey' for the effecters. In these cases they are the only actors physically capable of conducting these tasks. The remaining part of the decision ladder involves taking the basic information from the sensor, interpreting it and making a decision about which

CWA of a Sensor to Effecter System 81

targets to neutralise. In this case this activity can be conducted by the sensor, the commander or the effecter. For this reason the nodes are tri-coloured.

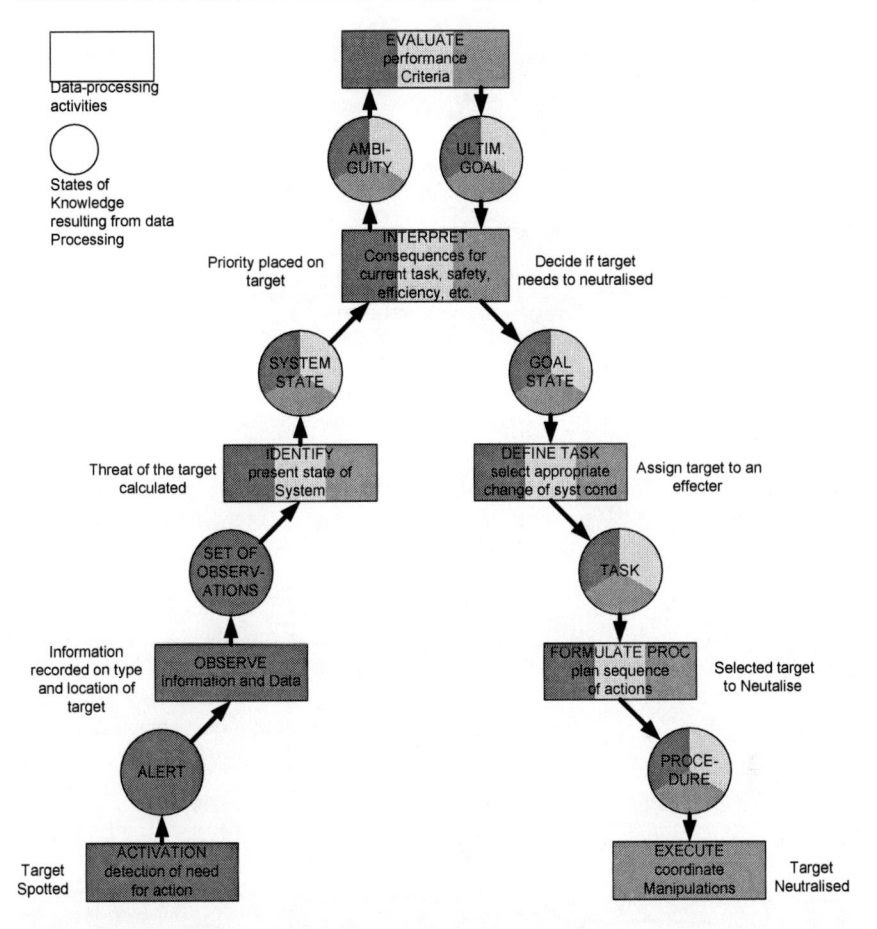

Figure 9. Decision ladder showing tasks that can be conducted by actor types

Figure 10 shows that the strategies analysis diagram introduced in figure 5 can also be coloured to show the actors engaging in the task. Here the initial state must start with the sensor and end with the effecter, however the strategy used in the middle can be enacted by the sensor, the commander or the effecter.

Experimentation is required to decide how the workload should be distributed. The dependant variables listed at the start of this document and the network configuration will affect this decision.

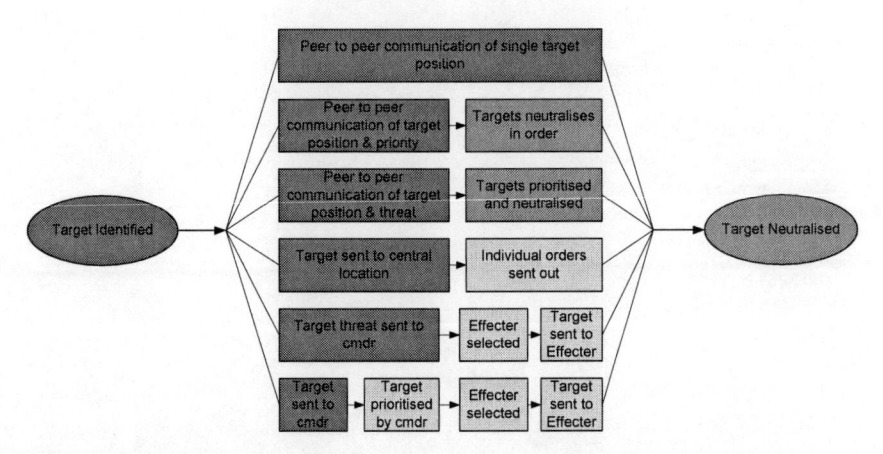

Figure 10. Strategies analysis showing tasks that can be conducted by actor types

Worker Competencies Analysis

According to Vicente (1999) Skill Based Behaviour (SBB) is performed without conscious attention. SBB typically consists of anticipated actions and involves direct coupling with the environment. Rule Based Behaviour (RBB) is based on a set of stored rules that can be learned from experience or from protocol. Individual goals are not considered, the user is merely reacting to an anticipated event using familiar perceptual cues. Unlike SBB, users can verbalise their thoughts as the process is cognitive. When decisions are made that explicitly consider the purpose or goal of the system the behaviour can be considered to be Knowledge Based Behaviour (KBB). KBB is slow, serial and effortful because it requires conscious, focal attention.

Table 1. SRK levels for each of the actors

	Skill based	**Rule based**	**Knowledge based**
Sensor	When an object is spotted send its position	When an object is spotted send its position and a description of its level of threat.	When an object is spotted send its position and its relative priority.
Commander	Send the received information to an effecter.	Match the target to the effecters based on position	Match the targets to effecters considering the position, threat and workload.
Effecter	Neutralise whatever pops up as soon as it pops up regardless of what you were doing	Neutralise the geographically closest object	Neutralise the most dangerous target as long as it will not cause a riot.

The network structure will also be dependant on the behaviour level expected from the actors. The actors can work at three different behaviour levels dependant on the level of processing required to complete the desired activity. Table 1 shows example responsibilities for each of the actors at the three behavioural levels.

Conclusions

This paper has described the sensor to effecter system at each of the five CWA levels. The analysis has described the domain and answered questions on *why* the system exists, *what* it should do, *how* it should do it and *who* should be enacting the various stages of the task.

The CWA demonstrates the flexibility of the network. Due to the physical nature of the sensors, they are essential to the system as they are the only method for capturing target positions. The effectors are also essential to the system as they are the only means of neutralising targets. The commander/command team have no unique role and are therefore are not essential to the system. The physical (skill based) actions of sensing and neutralising are fixed, however the more complicated tasks of interpreting, evaluating and defining the task can be assigned to anyone within the system.

By changing the roles and responsibilities of the groups of actors, it is possible to rapidly reconfigure the network to compensate for environmental changes. By focusing on the constraints the analysis captures every physically possible network configuration.

Acknowledgements

This research from the Human Factors Integration Defence Technology Centre was part-funded by the Human Sciences Domain of the UK Ministry of Defence Scientific Research Programme. Any views expressed are those of the author(s) and do not necessarily represent those of the Ministry of Defence or any other UK government department.

References

Ahlstrom, U. (2005). Work domain analysis for air traffic controller weather displays. *Journal of Safety Research, 36*, 159-169.

Bisantz, A.M., Roth, E., Brickman, B., Gosbee, L.L., Hettinger, L., & McKinney, J. (2003). Integrating cognitive analyses in a large-scale system design process. *International Journal of Human-Computer Studies, 58*, 177-206.

Hajdukiewicz J.R. (1998). *Development of a structured approach for patient monitoring in the operating room.* Masters Thesis. Toronto, Canada: University of Toronto

Higgins, P.G. (1998). Extending cognitive work analysis to manufacturing scheduling. In P. Calder and B. Thomas (Eds.) Proceedings of the 1998 Australasian Computer Human Interaction Conference, OzCHI'98 (pp 236-243). Piscataway, NJ, USA: IEEE.

Miller, A. (2004). A work domain analysis framework for modelling intensive care unit patients. *Cognition, Technology and Work. 6*, 207-222.

Naikar, N. & Sanderson, P.M. (1999). Work domain analysis for training-system definition. *International Journal of Aviation Psychology, 9*, 271-290.

Naikar, N. & Sanderson, P.M. (2001). Evaluating design proposals for complex systems with work domain analysis. *Human Factors, 43*, 529-542.

Naikar, N., Pearce, B., Drumm, D., & Sanderson, P.M. (2003). Technique for designing teams for first-of-a-kind complex systems with cognitive work analysis: Case study. *Human Factors, 45*, 202-217.

Naikar, N. & Saunders, A. (2003). Crossing the boundaries of safe operation: A technical training approach to error management. *Cognition Technology and Work, 5*, 171-180.

Naikar N, Hopcroft R, & Moylan A (2005) Work Domain Analysis: Theoretical Concepts and Methodology. Edinburgh, Australia: DSTO-TR-1665 System Sciences Laboratory.

Olsson, G. & Lee, P.L. (1994). Effective interfaces for process operators. *The Journal of Process Control, 4*, 99–107.

Rasmussen, J., Pejtersen, A., & Goodstein, L.P. (1994). *Cognitive systems engineering*. New York: Wiley.

Salmon, P., Stanton, N., Walker, G., & Green, D. (2004). Future battlefield visualisation: Investigating data representation in a novel C4i system. In V. Puri, D. Filippidis, P. Retter, and J. Kelly (Eds.) Weapons, Webs and Warfighters. Proceedings of the Land Warfare Conference, Melbourne, Australia: DSTO.

Sharp T.D. & Helmicki A.J. (1998). The application of the ecological interface design approach to neonatal intensive care medicine. In Proceedings of the Human Factors and Ergonomics Society 42nd Annual Meeting (pp. 350- 354). Santa Monica, CA: HFES.

Stoner, H.A., Wiese, E.E., & Lee, J.D. (2003). Applying ecological interface design to the driving domain: the results of an abstraction hierarchy analysis. In *Proceedings of the Human Factors and Ergonomics Society 47th Annual Meeting* (pp 444-448). Santa Monica, CA, USA: HFES.

Vicente, K.J. (1999). *Cognitive work analysis: Toward safe, productive, and healthy computer-based work*. Mahwah, NJ, USA: Lawrence Erlbaum Associates

A computer based tool for cognitive workload measurement in marine operations

David Embrey & Claire Blackett
Human Reliability Associates Ltd
Wigan, UK

Abstract

The UK Maritime and Coastguard Agency has commissioned research to develop a tool to assess mental workload in marine operations. This is intended be used proactively, e.g. to determine safe manning levels, and also retrospectively, during accident investigations. A comprehensive literature review was performed and is provided in the full report, which is available on the Maritime and Coastguard Agency website (Embrey et al., 2006). This revealed that few existing tools included factors that are widely recognised by mariners as crucial influences on mental workload in the marine context. The research approach involved eliciting the factors perceived as the main influences on workload from groups of experienced seafarers. Predictive models based on these factors were developed interactively using a computer program developed in earlier research, and then tested by evaluating scenarios that had been experienced by the expert groups. The predictions of the model were compared with those of the groups and the model was then adjusted until a match was achieved between the predictions and the perceived workload of the mariners in the scenarios evaluated. This was repeated with a number of groups, and a combined model was developed. This was encoded as the engine for a computer program called CLIMATE (Cognitive Loading Index Measurement and Assessment TEchnique). CLIMATE assesses the conditions associated with maritime tasks, and calculates the extent to which loading is likely to exceed acceptable levels. CLIMATE also allows 'what if' analyses where the assessments can be manipulated to determine the most cost effective changes to achieve desirable levels of loading.

Introduction

Analyses of shipping and other accidents have indicated that three states of cognitive mental workload may act as precursors or contributory factors. Underload situations, leading to failures to monitor automated navigation systems or maintain effective watchkeeping may arise in the classical vigilance task environment of low demands, unstimulating environments and uncertain signals. Overload situations arise where excessive demands to diagnose or respond may exceed attentional or cognitive resources. Transitional situations arise where there is a rapid change between the between an underload and overload state, e.g. in response to a suddenly identified hazard such as a collision, which may lead to critical delays in assessing a situation and mobilising the resources to take the necessary actions.

The impetus for the study came from an evaluation of shipping incidents in the Marine Accident Investigation Board database, which suggested that underload or overload was a significant contributor to many marine accidents. In order to maximise the applicability of the results of the study, it was decided that the data used to develop the workload measurement tool should be drawn from a number different areas of the shipping industry. The types of shipping activities considered in the project therefore ranged widely from situations where low workload could be expected to arise frequently (e.g. deep sea voyages, sometimes lasting for several weeks, usually with low traffic levels for the majority of the voyage), to high speed ferry operations where there is usually a constant high level of demand on the crew. Even in activities such as deep sea tanker operations, high levels of workload could still arise in situations such as leaving port or berthing. The majority of the accident scenarios examined during the review of accident databases involved outcomes such as collisions or groundings, arising from errors during navigation, manoeuvring and ship control.

Based on the review of the accident databases, it was decided that the primary focus for the workload assessment tool should be on the workload experienced by the Officer of the Watch, in the context of the support provided by other members of the bridge team. During more critical situations such as berthing, the Officer of the Watch would normally be the Ship's Master or First Officer, although this function might sometimes be delegated to other crew members during periods of perceived lower levels of risk.

The UK Maritime and Coastguard Agency commissioned a programme of research to develop a computer based tool that could assess the extent that underload or overload would be likely to arise, by measuring the conditions under which marine tasks are performed. These conditions include those which can be managed, such as manning levels, fatigue and distractions, and environmental variables such as visibility and sea conditions. It was intended that the tool could be used proactively, for example to determine safe manning levels, and also retrospectively, during accident investigations, to gain insights into the contribution of these states to the occurrence of the accident.

In order to develop the workload measurement tool, a research paradigm was deployed which was based on the elicitation, from groups of experienced mariners, of the factors perceived as the main influences on workload under operational conditions. These subjective evaluations, based on operational experience, formed one set of inputs to the workload models developed in this study. These models were also intended to include insights from the research literature into the factors that influence underload and overload. Factors that had been identified in the literature review as being significant influences on overload and underload were therefore included in the models developed for the study, to provide a set of composite models, applicable to different situations (e.g. tankers, high speed ferries) based on discussions within a series of interactive consensus groups. More detailed discussions of the model development process are provided in the methodology section.

This exercise was performed with a number of groups, and the results combined to produce two generic models, one applicable to overload and one to underload situations. This model was encoded as the engine for a computer program called CLIMATE (Cognitive Loading Index for Mariners Assessment TEchnique) which was the primary practical output from this study. CLIMATE provides scales for assessing the conditions associated with underload, and overload, and calculates an index which predicts the extent that these states are likely to exceed acceptable levels. CLIMATE also allows 'what if' analyses where the assessed conditions can be manipulated to determine the most cost effective changes that can be made to achieve safe levels of loading.

In the next section, the findings of a review of current approaches to cognitive underload and overload situations are described, together with a review of measurement tools that have been developed for evaluating workload in particular contexts such as air traffic control and military tasks. The subsequent section describes the methodology called IDEAS (Influence Diagram Modelling and Assessment System) that was used to develop the models of Cognitive Mental Workload that are used within the CLIMATE workload measurement tool. The next section describes the development of the CLIMATE tool itself, and the characteristics of the workload models that drive it. The final section describes the conclusions from the study and discusses the future work required to validate the tool by using data from operational environments.

Background

Review of current literature on cognitive workload

This review attempted to cover the main theoretical models which addressed underload and overload situations (vigilance tasks and mental workload models) together with measurement tools that had been developed in a range of application areas such as Air Traffic Control, aviation, vehicle handling, rail transportation and military operations (Embrey et al., 2006). In general, few theoretical approaches had attempted to address both underload and overload situations within a unified framework, with the exception of De Waard (1996), Meijman and O'Hanlon, (1984), and Teigen (1994).

With regard to workload measurement, the review indicated that although some tools had been developed for measuring workload in a maritime context, e.g. Lee and Sanquist (2000), none of them addressed important contributory factors that were identified in both incident reports and by the subject matter experts in the current study as directly contributing to mental overload or underload on the bridge. Possibly the most significant disadvantage of existing workload measurement tools was that they focussed exclusively on overload situations. This is probably because underload situations such as those represented by vigilance tasks have not been perceived as amenable to the development of predictive tools.

Review of Cognitive Mental Workload Models

The first part of the review focused on the current literature on Cognitive Mental Workload (CMWL). Relatively few treatments of the topic have focused upon consideration of workload error at both the upper and lower limits. The mental workload literature has tended to be mostly concerned with performance problems associated with tasks high in explicit demand (i.e., the overload or cognitive strain scenario). There is, however, a separate major strand of work aimed at exploring/modelling errors at lower levels of the task demand spectrum. In this area, investigators have focused primarily on the performance of tasks requiring vigilance (e.g., target detection, usually in unstimulating situations such as watchkeeping). Predictable falls in performance occurring during such tasks are known collectively as the Vigilance Decrement. Vigilance studies have been carried out extensively in maritime operations where detection of infrequently occurring targets has historically been both problematic and a common feature of the work situation.

The first conclusion that emerges from the review of the research literature is that separate models need to be developed for addressing low demand situations such as watchkeeping on a ship's bridge, compared with the high mental workload that may arise during a complex berthing operation. In the former situation, performance decrements arise from inadequate levels of stimulation to maintain the effectiveness of the basic sensory and cognitive functions required to maintain the effectiveness of detection of infrequently occurring but critical signals (e.g. those which might precede a collision). In the case of overload situations, the consensus that emerges from the literature is that CMWL arises primarily from a mismatch between the demands of the task itself, and the resources available to meet these demands. In the specific context of a ship berthing operation, the demands might arise from the judgements about manoeuvring and monitoring the position of a ship. .. The mental resources available to meet these demands might include the skills and training of the Officer of the Watch (OOW), the supporting bridge team, and technical support systems such as radars and GPS that supplement these human resources, if well designed. The factors contributing to underload or overload in these very different situations cannot easily be accommodated within a single model.

The second important conclusion from the review was that virtually none of the academic research into underload or overload was informed by insights or information from personnel who actually performed real life tasks where overload or underload arises in practice. Although a number of overload measurement tools such as the NASA TLX (Hart & Staveland, 1988) are based on subjective evaluations of a number of pre-specified dimensions, these are usually derived from theoretical view of the generic factors that contribute to overload, rather than the context specific factors that are identified as contributing to underload or overload by subject matter experts or from reviews of incident data. Although there is clearly an issue with regard to the extent to which a person is able to adequately determine the contribution of different stressors to workload, any attempt to develop predictive models of workload is limited unless it takes into account the situation specific knowledge possessed by individuals who have experienced extremes of overload or underload in the areas to which the models will be applied.

In summary, these findings had the following implications for the methodology that was developed in this project. Firstly, it was deemed to be necessary to develop separate models for underload and overload situations. It was regarded as relatively easy to distinguish between such situations, since underload performance decrements were always associated with low levels of demand, which is almost never the case for overload situations. Secondly, the workload models need to combine insights from the research findings regarding the conditions likely to give rise to extremes of workload, together with context specific knowledge that is possessed by experienced practitioners in the domain to which the models will be applied. In other words, the study of workload has to be adequately contextualised, and would appear to be limited if based only on generic models of information processing or cognition.

Review of workload assessment techniques

The second part of the literature review focused on workload assessment techniques. The review indicated five main approaches to workload assessment:

Subjective methods
These are based on the subjective experience of task demands. Data are in the form of beliefs, values, preferences and attitudes and are collected via completion of self report questionnaires. The TLX measurement tool (Hart & Wickens, 1990) described earlier, is typical of this class of tools.

Task performance methods
These provide assessments in the form of either speed/accuracy trade off and/or error rate data for primary tasks and/or measures of cognitive resource availability assessed via completion of secondary tasks. Reviews of these methods are provided in de Waard (1996); Lysaght et al., (1989); and O'Donnell and Eggemeier, (1986).

Physiological monitoring
These methods are based on the recording of the physiological states that are thought to correlate highly with the subjective experience, and possibly the performance decrements, associated with high and low CMWL situations. A comprehensive review of these methods is provided in Andreassi (2000).

Task loading
These approaches provide assessments of psychological load based on explicit measures of task demands coupled with a consideration of the known psychological factors governing the ability to react to those demands. Examples of measurement tools based on this approach are the Task Analysis Workload Methodology (Mitchell, 2000), and the OFM-COG (Lee & Sanquist, 2000)

Influence Diagrams
The Influence Diagram Evaluation System (IDEAS) is an application framework, which allows the insights from theoretical research and from people with extensive

practical experience to be combined in the form of a simple graphical model of causation. The methodology was first developed in the context of human reliability assessment, (Phillips et al., 1990, Embrey, 1992, 1994, 2004), and as a method for accident investigation (Embrey et al., 2000), The IDEAS methodology allows inputs from research, accident investigations and the practical experience of Subject Matter Experts to be combined using a structured consensus based process involving individuals with direct knowledge of the domain being modelled.

The first four of these approaches have been used to develop a wide range of tools for workload assessment, mainly in industries traditionally defined as high risk such as defence, road transportation, railways, aerospace, process control, and power generation. The choice of method is usually based on consideration of the special requirements of the industry concerned. For example, workload assessment for drivers of road vehicles is typically based on performance of a range of secondary test tasks completed concurrently with performance of the primary driving task. Conversely, use of physiological monitoring techniques is frequently used in the defence industry, which has a ready supply of personnel, equipment and high fidelity simulators. Consequently, staff can be recruited to participate in realistic missions using advanced system simulators with performance being monitored using a variety of sensor equipment. IDEAS has been applied in a wide range of industry domains including rail transport, nuclear power generation, aircraft maintenance and healthcare, but not previously to workload measurement.

Identification of factors that influence workload

The CMWL literature review revealed a number of factors called Performance Influencing Factors (PIFs) likely to influence task performance given the presence or absence of task load. In developing final versions of the CMWL models, these factors were supplemented by known PIFs associated with reliability evaluations and other factors specific to shipping operations.

A number of marine accident databases were examined to obtain an overview of the types of accidents in which CMWL overload and underload are contributory factors, and to identify which commonly occurring PIFs may have contributed to workload in these situations.

The PIFs identified were:

- Time of the accident
- The stage of the individual's shift
- Number of individuals on watch
- Type of vessel
- Technology used
- Weather conditions
- The area of the incident
- Fatigue
- Environment

The review of marine accident databases provided some useful insights into the types of scenario that the CMWL measurement tool needed to address and some of the PIFs that affect the level of workload. These and other PIFs also contribute to the likelihood of an error leading to an accident. Examples of incidents where underload, overload and the switch from underload to potentially overloaded situations were identified. However, in common with many accident investigation databases, the nature of the investigation process used tended to focus on the 'what happened' rather than the 'why' of accident causation, and hence the insights into specifically workload related factors are quite limited. Nevertheless, the more general recurrent PIFs that have been identified are useful if the CMWL measurement tool is to be linked with a marine error prediction process.

Methodology

Choosing the methodology

The decision to determine the specific approach for developing the CMWL assessment tool took into account the information gathered from the literature review, the survey of marine accidents, a stakeholder analysis and a task analysis.

The literature review identified a number of criteria for assessing the effectiveness of workload measurement tools (see O'Donnell & Eggemeier, (1986) for a list of such criteria):

Objectivity: The degree to which the measurement tool is independent of the person administering the test and the person analysing the results (i.e., freedom from experimenter effects).
Reliability: The degree to which the measurement tool can be depended upon to provide results that are replicable over time and analysis teams.
Validity: A measure of the degree of provenance a measurement tool provides regarding its accuracy with regard to the items it intends to measure.
Sensitivity: The degree to which obtained measures are responsive to actual changes in task workload.
Diagnosticity: The degree to which the measure is able to discriminate between different kinds, or different sources, of workload.
Generalisability: The extent to which workload measures obtained in particular setting with a particular group of people generalise to a defined universe of situations and/or population of employees.
Usability: The extent to which a technique can be used with accuracy, efficiency and satisfaction of users.

The review of maritime incidents indicated that the CMWL tool needs to be able to include the effects of factors other than those directly related to CMWL under or overload. There were clear indications that CMWL variables interact with other PIFs to give rise to the observed accidents. This is particularly the case in the underload situation, with factors related to fatigue. PIFs identified in the review, such as weather conditions, bridge automation, number of persons on watch and vessel type are typical of the factors that need to be considered. The CMWL assessment tool therefore had to have the capability to include environmental factors of this type.

The stakeholder analysis produced a wide range of information regarding the required capabilities of the tool. In particular, it was clear that there was a requirement that the tool should be usable in several different modes for different application areas and different types of user. For example for on-board applications by pilots or masters, the tool should be simple, rapid to use and require a minimum of expertise. One of the possible applications in the onboard situation would be to use the tool to predict situations of potential overload, for example, arising from deteriorating weather conditions, combined with reduced manning levels on the bridge due to illness. If these conditions were fed into the workload prediction tool, which indicated that loading levels might approach the acceptable limits, then countermeasures could be implemented, such as deferring intensive berthing operations until the weather conditions moderated, or the full complement of the bridge crew became available. For more detailed pre-voyage use, e.g. for the determination of suitable manning levels, in policy-making, the tool could be more comprehensive and detailed.

The results of the task analyses provided a number of insights into the requirements of the CMWL tool. The first was the requirement to be able to apply the tool to whatever level of task decomposition is required. The tool also needed to be applicable to tasks that are predominantly cognitive in nature such as decision-making and problem solving as well as action orientated tasks, information acquisition and communications.

Determination of an appropriate methodology

A requirement in the research specification was to 'identify *safe* maximum and minimum human cognitive workload levels for the maritime industry.....' which implies that CMWL, which is essentially an internal state of a person or group, has to be related to some external measurable parameters such as accident likelihood or error probability. 'Safe' in this context, does not refer to the safe limits of the effects of workload on the well being of the individuals that experience its extremes. Rather, it implies an acceptable level of risk that a negative outcome will occur (e.g. an accident resulting from an error arising from underload or overload). This requires a workload measure that can be mapped on to an externally verifiable dimension such as error or accident probability. Given its essentially subjective nature, there are inevitably likely to be individual differences in susceptibility to workload related performance decrements in extreme conditions. However, in most safety critical situations, competency management systems are deployed to ensure that individual variability affecting skill and hence resource availability is minimized. In addition, in the ship's bridge situation, the overall mental workload experienced by the key person in command, the officer of the watch, is likely to be a function of the capabilities of the overall bridge team, and how this resource is deployed. This should be able to compensate for any individual susceptibility to underload and overload.

Another fundamental requirement arises from the potential use of the CMWL tool as part of a risk based assessment process. This requires that the tool is both able to predict expected workload, and that these predictions are capable of being objectively validated by, for example, incident data collection. A final essential requirement is that the methodology is able to model the effects on CMWL of the PIFs that are identified by mariners as being significant drivers of workload, based on their practical experience.

In order to satisfy these requirements, the Influence Diagram methodology was chosen as the basis for the computer based CMWL assessment tool. The IDEAS methodology had not previously been applied to the measurement of CMWL prior to this project. However, it had a number of unique advantages compare to the other approaches reviewed. Firstly, it was able to combine theoretical insights into the objectively measurable factors influencing workload, derived from the literature survey, with context specific perceptions of people who actually performed the tasks of interest. Secondly the research team had considerable experience in the use of the methodology to elicit information from groups of subject matter experts in interactive sessions called consensus groups. These sessions produce a graphical representation of the factors which influence a particular outcome. In previous applications of IDEAS, this outcome was the likelihood of an error occurring, but in the context of CMWL measurement, an index that measured the likelihood that an individual or team was likely to operate at an unacceptable level of workload could be produced. Finally, the IDEAS methodology could potentially allow the workload index to be mapped on to a scale of predicted error probability. This is a particularly attractive feature, since it would potentially allow workload measurement to be used to estimate risks of accidents. Because of these advantages, the IDEAS approach was selected as the methodology to be applied in the project.

Developing the CMWL tool using the IDEAS approach

Using the insights gained from the research conducted earlier in the project, such as the analysis of shipping incidents, and the review of mental workload literature, a framework model of the factors influencing CMWL was developed which expressed workload as a function of measurable characteristics of tasks, personnel and the context within which marine operations are performed. Separate models were developed for underload and overload situations, since the underlying processes that give rise to these states are very different, based on the research literature considered in the survey. In order to populate the model, data were drawn from the research literature and structured workshops with subject matter experts from the marine industry.

The framework model, including the factors influencing CMWL, was expressed in the form of an Influence Diagram (see Figure 1), using an Influence Diagram modelling software tool called IDEX. This technique provides a modelling environment which allows the insights arising from theory based approaches, together with the knowledge and experience of mariners, to be combined in a form suitable for assessment. Four Influence Diagram (ID) sessions were conducted with groups of officers from three British shipping companies, ranging in rank from master to third officer. Four separate overload models and two separate underload models were created during these sessions.

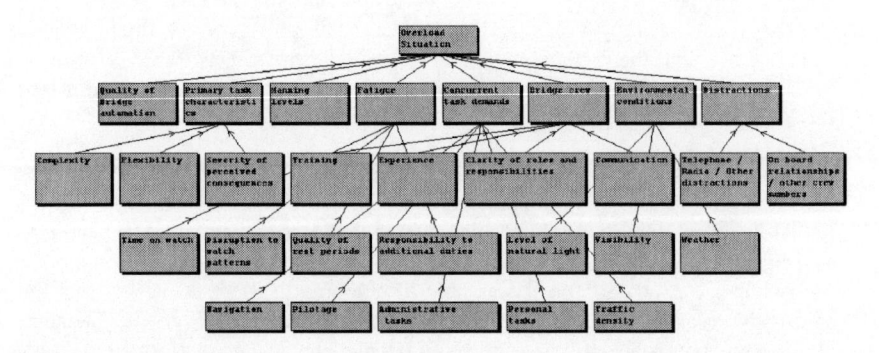

Figure 1. Initial Seed Influence Diagram Model

This framework model was used as the starting point (or Seed model, see Figure 1) for a series of Consensus Groups with subject matter experts from the commercial marine industry, including Masters, First and Second Officers, and recently trained personnel. These sessions were used to develop workload models for different domains of shipping activities from high speed ferries, coasters and deep sea operations such as tankers. Both overload and underload models were developed. These models were then validated by using them to assess scenarios known to the workshop participants.

The main benefit of this approach was that it was pragmatic; evidence based, and did not depend on the accuracy of specific theoretical approaches in order to produce a workable CMWL tool. The use of the IDEAS modelling tool allowed the project to build on an existing tried and tested modelling environment that has been successfully utilized in a wide range of applications over the past ten years. These included human reliability assessment in nuclear power generation, (Phillips et al., 1990) major accident causation modelling (Embrey, 1992), chemical processing (Embrey,1994, 2004) and signals passed at danger in rail operations (Embrey et al., 2000).

Developing the Influence Diagram structure

The first stage of applying the IDEAS process is to develop a model structure for a particular class of scenarios, e.g. overload situations in a specific type of ship operation. This involves identifying the relevant factors, and structuring them using the Influence Diagram format.

The consensus group session required that the participants were able to think about the factors that influenced workload in a hierarchical manner, ranging from those that directly affected workload, e.g. fatigue, to sub-factors influencing the level of fatigue. The ID sessions therefore began with a general discussion about the factors that influence workload, including those that had been identified from the literature survey and the evaluation of marine accident databases. The group was then shown a seed model containing these factors and they were invited to discuss the model, comment upon the factors included, delete factors that they felt were inapplicable, and add factors from their own experience.

These discussions helped determine whether all of the factors were relevant and whether they were in the correct place. Sometimes factors could be expanded upon (by adding additional sub-factors) to more clearly define how they impact upon workload. Other factors were not decomposed any further, as they were self-explanatory, or could be measured directly. The group may also decide that some factors should be removed from the model, as they do not have a significant impact upon cognitive workload in that particular type of situation. At this stage, the group was encouraged to add factors that they felt influenced workload, based on their own experiences, and to expand upon those included in the seed model. Where appropriate, the factors deemed to affect workload directly, e.g. fatigue, team training, were decomposed further to specify their component influences. For example, a direct influence such as fatigue was decomposed in terms of influencing factors such as time on watch, quality of shift management, and quality of rest.

Assigning weights to the factors

The next step is to assign weights to each of the factors in the model. Not all factors influence workload to the same degree, and the differences between the strength of the individual factors is reflected by assigning weights to each factor at each level of the tree. Weights represent the relative strength of influence of each factor at a particular node in the Influence Diagram. In the assessment process, the group is asked to identify the most influential factor in the set of factors at that level in the diagram. The strength of influence of the other factors is then assessed relative to this factor. Weights are intended to be generic across all scenarios of the type being assessed, e.g. underload situations on tankers. This is in contrast to ratings that are scenario specific. The weights and ratings are then combined to give a derived rating for the factor that is influenced by these sub-factors.

Rating the influences

A rating means that a factor at a particular level in the diagram is evaluated on a scale representing the range from the best to the worst case in terms of its current state in the scenario being assessed. Thus, a factor such as time on watch (a sub-factor of fatigue) might be rated as 20 on a scale from 1, (best case, has just arrived on watch), to 100, worst case, (has been on watch continuously for 12 hours). This rating would indicate that for this specific evaluation, the time on watch was near the favourable end of the evaluation range (e.g. the person had been on watch for an hour). A rating is an assessment of a factor on a specific scenario, and is not generic across scenarios. The ratings for all the factors at the same node are then combined with their weights (see below) to calculate a derived rating.

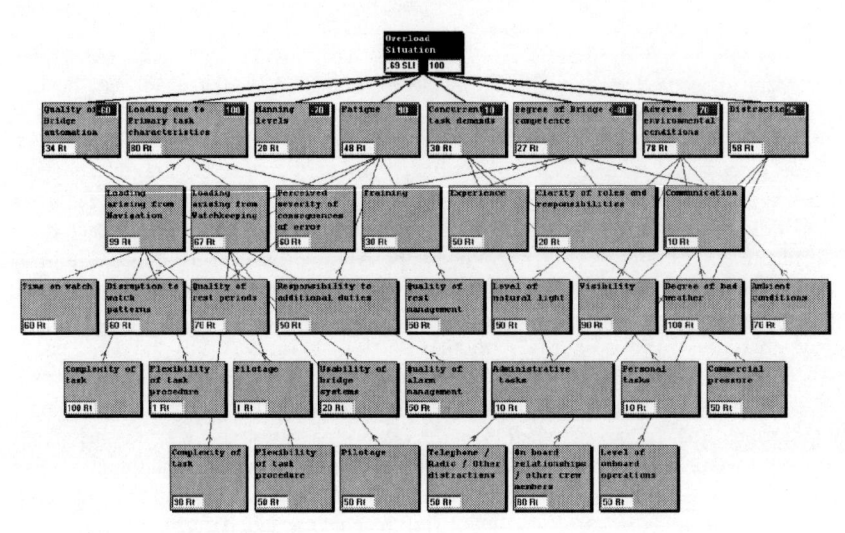

Figure 2. Developed Influence Diagram showing top level weights and ratings

Combining weights and ratings to give a Derived Rating

For example, in Figure 2, the degree of Bridge crew competence is assessed as being influenced by three sub-factors: training, experience, clarity of roles and responsibilities and communication. For illustration, these have been assigned the weights shown in column 1 in Table 1, which indicates that experience and training are the most influential factors, and are assigned a weight of 100. The other factors (clarity of roles and responsibilities, and communication) are then weighted at 50 to reflect their lesser influence relative to the other factors. The next step is to calculate a Normalised weight for each factor, which is the assessed weight divided by the sum of the weights. These are calculated in column 2.

Finally, the normalised weights are multiplied by the ratings for the respective factors to give the derived rating for the top level factor 'Degree of Bridge crew Competence'. These calculations are carried out by the IDEX software for all the assessments in the model to produce an overall Seafarers Loading Index (SLI) at the top of the tree. This is the workload measure which is the primary output of the process. It ranges from 0 to 1, where 0 represents the optimal level of loading, where all factors have been rated at their most favourable levels, to 1 where all factors are at their most unfavourable state in terms of their effects on workload. When all of the assessments have been made, the IDEX software uses the combined ratings and weights for all the factors in the model to show which factors will have the highest impact upon the Seafarers Loading Index if they were to change from their current ratings or states. This is a useful 'what if' exercise, as it allows the consensus group to see how changes in the different factors in the model would impact upon the SLI at the top of the diagram. This provides insights regarding the validity of the model, which can be modified if the results of the 'what if' analysis seem counter intuitive to the group.

Table 1. Calculation of normalised weights and derived rating

Factors influencing Degree of Bridge Crew Competence	Assessed Weights	Normalised weights	Derived rating calculation
Training	100	100/300 = 0.33	0.33 x 30 = 10
Experience	100	100/300 = 0.33	0.33 x 50 = 16.5
Clarity of roles and responsibilities	50	50/300 = 0.16	0.16 x 20 = 3.2
Communication	50	50/300 = 0.16	0.16 x 10 = 1.6
Total	300		Derived rating (Sum of products)=31.3 (=27 with rounding errors)

Evaluating the model

The integrity of the models developed by the process described in previous sections was subjected to an initial evaluation by discussing scenarios which had been experienced by the expert groups. The predictions of the model were then compared with the subjectively experienced workload levels of the individuals who had been involved in these scenarios. Where a good fit was obtained between the model predictions and evaluations by the participants on a subjectively determined scale (e.g. from acceptable to very high perceived workload) the model was adopted on a provisional basis as the starting point for more extensive field evaluations in a later phase of the study. If there was a wide disparity between the predictions and the opinions of the group based on their experiences of the scenario, the model was re-evaluated. This might involve changing the structure of the model by adding or deleting factors, and/or by changing their weights or adjusting the nature of the factors until a reasonable match was achieved between the model predictions and the experience of the loading levels by the subject matter experts. In this context, a 'reasonable' fit between the model's predictions of workload and the consensus group participants opinions was assumed to be achieved if it was within the same interval of a five point subjectively determined workload scale.

It should be emphasised that the process described in the previous sections was not intended to develop a fully validated workload model. Rather, it was regarded as the first stage of a more comprehensive programme of work which will include field studies to validate the predictions of the model in situ. The IDEAS process represents an attempt to combine the research findings on the factors influencing workload with the context specific insights of a group of subject matter experts, using a systematic and structured methodology.

Main results

In this section, an overview of the main results will be presented. A more detailed presentation of the results can be found in Embrey et al. 2006. There were a number of common factors and sub-factors across all of the models that were developed with the separate groups of sea farers. These factors include: quality of the automated bridge systems, manning levels, primary and concurrent task characteristics, distractions, external conditions (e.g. weather, visibility, sea conditions), degree of training and experience of bridge crew, and factors associated with fatigue.

There were also a number of factors that were similarly weighted by each of the individual groups, meaning that, despite differences in vessel types and operations, these factors were largely seen to have the same effect upon the workload of the bridge crew members. These factors include: bridge manning levels; fatigue; degree of restricted visibility; training and experience of the bridge crew); communication; telephone, radio, or other distractions; complexity of the task; disruptions to watch patterns; quality of rest periods; and responsibility for additional duties.

The disparities between the remainder of the factors may be due to the subjective opinions of the individual group members but may also be due to the different trades of the individual groups (i.e., tankers, containers, fast ferries and coastal vessels). The differences in trade mean that groups may have different priorities and goals, and thus the same factor might be of utmost importance to one group, but of relatively little importance to another. Thus, for high speed ferries, interactions with passengers were seen as a significant source of workload. This was not the case in ships where few passengers were carried.

When the Influence Diagram sessions were completed, the various models were compared and a composite model was developed in an attempt to capture all of this knowledge and combine it in a single overload model that was generic enough to be used across all shipping trades, and yet specific enough to include the opinions of all the officers in the Influence Diagram sessions. A composite model was also created for the underload domain.

Conclusions and future work

The research conducted in this study differs from most of the work reported in the workload literature in that it focussed on both the overload and underload domains. It also combined a subjectivist with a theory based approach to the development of the models used to drive the predictive workload assessment tool. It is believed that such a methodology, which has the ability to capture, in a structured manner, the practical experience and tacit knowledge of subject matter experts, has a number of advantages over a purely theoretically based approach. In particular, it allows strategies for optimising workload that are indicated from the application of the tool to be much more specific and practical. The fact that the models are based upon the insights and experiences of mariners also increases the credibility of their predictions to the maritime community, and the likelihood that any proposed improvement strategies will be implemented. Recommendations arising from purely theoretically based models tend to be more general in nature. Although subjective methods for measuring workload have been used in many previous studies of workload (e.g. the TLX method, Hart & Staveland, 1988), the factors measured in these studies have not been tailored to a specific industrial domain such as maritime operations.

The criticism that the models arising from this approach are purely subjective in nature can be answered by pointing out that mental underload and overload is also a subjective phenomenon and hence this approach is entirely appropriate. Of course, this does not preclude the validation of the predictions of the subjectively based models with those obtained from other methods such as physiological data and secondary task performance measures. In fact, the models generated using the IDEAS approach described in this paper are able to include theoretical insights as part of the seed model that is the starting point for the interactive modelling process.

Despite a commitment to the group based subjective modelling process described in this paper, there is an obvious need to validate the predictions of this approach using a large scale field based data collection exercise. To this end, the research team is currently seeking the participation of a number of shipping companies in a diary study involving the recording of the perceptions of Officers of the Watch regarding the workload that they have experienced during their watches. In addition, these personnel will assess the factors included in the workload models with regard to their state during the watch. This exercise will assist in validating the predictions of the models, and will also allow the factors in the models to be reviewed by a much larger sample of experts than those included in the original expert groups. We are also planning to evaluate the relationship between cognitive loading and incidents and near misses, by applying the tool retrospectively as part of the process of investigating maritime incidents.

References

Andreassi, J.L. (2000). *Psychophysiology: Human behaviour and physiological response (4th edition)*. New Jersey, USA: Lawrence Erlbaum Associates.

De Waard, D., (1996). *The Measurement of Drivers' Mental Workload*. PhD Thesis. The Traffic Research Centre VSC, University of Groningen, The Netherlands.

Embrey, D.E. (1992). Incorporating Management and Organisational Factors into Probabilistic Safety Assessment. *Reliability Engineering and Systems Safety, 38*, 199-208

Embrey, D.E. (1994). *Guidelines for reducing Human Error in Process Safety*. New York: Center for Chemical Process Safety, American Institute of Chemical Engineers

Embrey, D.E, Wright, K., & Anderson, M. (2000) Applications of Influence Diagrams to SPAD Investigations and Assessment of 'At-Risk' Sites Rail Professional, September.

Embrey, D.E, (2004) Human Reliability Assessment. In C. Sandom and R.S. Harvey (Eds.). *Human Factors for Engineers*. London: Institute of Electrical Engineers Publishing.

Embrey, D.E., Blackett, C., Marsden P., & Peachey, J. (2006). *Development of a Human Cognitive Workload Assessment Tool*. Research Report 546.Southampton, UK: Maritime & Coastguards Agency, Risk, Analysis & Prevention Branch.

Hart, S.G. & Staveland, L.E. (1988). Development of NASA-TLX (Task Load Index): results of empirical and theoretical research. In P.A. Hancock and N. Meshkati (Eds.), *Human Mental Workload*. Amsterdam: North-Holland.

Hart, S.G. & Wickens, C.D. (1990). Workload assessment and prediction. In H.R. Booher Ed.), *MANPRINT*. An approach to systems integration (pp. 257-296). New York: Van Nostrand Reinhold.

Lee, J.D., & Sanquist, T.F., (2000). Augmenting the Operator Function Model with Cognitive Operations: Assessing the Cognitive Demands of Technological Innovation in Ship Navigation. *IEEE Transactions on Systems, Man and Cybernetics – Part A: Systems and Humans. 30*, 273-285

Lysaght, R.J., Hill, S.G., Dick, A.O., Plamondon, B.D., Linton, P.M., Wierwille, W., Zaklad, A.L., Bittner Jr, A.C., & Wherry, R.J. (1989). *Operator workload: Comprehensive review and evaluation of workload methodologies* (ARI Technical Report 851). Alexandria, VA: U.S. Army Research Institute for the Behavioral and Social Sciences.

Meijman, T.F. & O'Hanlon, J.F. (1984). Workload. An introduction to psychological theories and measurement methods. In P.J.D. Drenth, H. Thierry, P.J. Willems and C.J. de Wolff (Eds.), *Handbook of Work and Organizational Psychology*. (pp. 257-288). New York: Wiley.

Mitchell, D.K. (2000). *Mental Workload and ARL Workload Modeling Tools*. Report No ARL-TN-161. Army Research Laboratory.

O'Donnell, R.D. & Eggemeier, F.T. (1986). Workload assessment methodology. In K.R. Boff, L. Kaufman, and J.P. Thomas (Eds.), *Handbook of perception and human performance. Volume II, cognitive processes and performance* (pp 42/1-42/49). New York: Wiley.

Phillips, L.D., Embrey, D.E., Humphreys, P., & Selby, D.L. (1990) A Socio-Technical Approach to Assessing Human Reliability. In R.M. Oliver and J.A. Smith (Eds.), *Influence Diagrams, Belief Nets and Decision Making: Their Influence on Safety and Reliability*. New York: Wiley.

Teigen, K.H. (1994). Yerkes-Dodson: a law for all seasons. *Theory & Psychology, 4*, 525-547.

Short-term heart rate measures as indices of momentary changes in invested mental effort

Ben Mulder, Heleanne Rusthoven, Marnel Kuperus, Michel de Rivecourt,
& Dick de Waard
University of Groningen
The Netherlands

Abstract

Laboratory research on invested mental effort in demanding mental tasks has given evidence for an increase in heart rate (HR) and decreased heart rate variability (HRV) as a function of task load. In particular the HRV effects are very consistent in short lasting tasks (e.g. 5 minutes) in which working memory is heavily involved. Using this concept in more practical workload situations evokes two types of problems: 1. Generally HRV increases as a function of time due to baroreflex related regulatory processes; 2. workload and mental effort change continuously as a function of time. This latter point is directly related to the reliability of the estimated HRV measures. According to published standards, in many cases time segments of steady workload would be too short to apply spectral techniques for HRV measures.

In this paper a simple time-frequency approach, called spectral profiles, for this type of problems is outlined that is suitable for many (semi-)realistic working conditions. This is illustrated in two studies using two different types of task, i.e. the SON IQ-test for children and a simulated flight for candidate pilots.

The results show that in both experiments HR and HRV effects based on short segment analysis can be related to task demands. It is concluded that the described short segment spectral profile approach is promising for use in (semi-)realistic working situations. The important pre-requisite is that on the basis of simple task analysis relevant segments have to be detected that do not overlap too much (in time or in effect) with respect of the HRV patterns.

Introduction

In several laboratory experiments it has been shown that heart rate variability (HRV) decreases with increasing task demands, while heart increases (Boucsein & Backs, 2000). In general a diminished HRV is interpreted as additional effort invested in the task to be performed (Mulder, 1986). On this basis HRV was proposed to be an index of invested mental effort. Many of these studies, however, can be characterised by short task duration (e.g. 5 minutes), while in most cases working memory load was manipulated specifically. Longer lasting tasks, in general, show a quite different

In D. de Waard, G.R.J. Hockey, P. Nickel, and K.A. Brookhuis (Eds.) (2007), *Human Factors Issues in Complex System Performance* (pp. 101 - 116). Maastricht, the Netherlands: Shaker Publishing.

pattern: after an initial HRV decrease at the start of a task, HRV increases gradually to levels even higher than preceding rest values (Mulder, van Roon, Veldman, Laumann & Burov, 2003) The question arises what the background is of these different patterns and how these can be explained.

The cardiovascular response pattern during short lasting tasks can be described as a defense reaction: compared to preceding rest situations heart rate and blood pressure are increased, while HRV, blood pressure variability (BPV) and baroreflex sensitivity are diminished. In many cases longer lasting tasks start with a similar pattern, but after five or ten minutes this pattern is followed by a distinctive decrease in heart rate in combination with an increase of baroreflex sensitivity and HRV. Mulder et al. (2003) interpret these changes as a response of the short term blood pressure control system (baroreflex) to the increased blood pressure. What happens with the blood pressure level depends on the task situation, but in many cases the initial increase in blood pressure is levelled off or the blood pressure level is even diminished.

It is clear that because of these different response patterns it is difficult to use HRV as a direct index of invested mental effort in long lasting tasks or during normal work in real life or even in simulated working tasks. In the literature it even led to conclusions that HRV is not always a valid index of invested effort during mental work (Boucsein & Backs, 2000, Nickel & Nachreiner, 2003). There are, however, more aspects that make it difficult to use HRV during normal daily work or in simulated workload studies. In normal daily mental loading work such as writing a report, planning, decision-making or car driving mental task load, and therewith required mental effort, is not constant but is varying from moment to moment. Short periods of peak load are interchanged with periods with less effort required. The same holds to a lesser extent for simulated real live situations, such as driving in a driving simulator, the ambulance dispatcher's task, or an air traffic control task. As a matter of fact four problems arise: 1. Is it possible to characterise complexity of specific task segments in terms of simple task analysis methods? 2. Can simple and complex task segments be traced in a simple manner on the basis of such a task analysis? 3. Are the mental loading segments long enough to evoke a distinct cardiovascular response pattern (i.e. increased HR and decreased HRV)? 4. Has an HRV-response on a preceding task event disappeared when a new event occurs, or is overlap between response patterns to be expected?

In the present paper an approach is outlined that tackles these problems. In particular, attention is given to the point of distinguishing short lasting task segments with varying task complexity and how such differences are reflected in HR and HRV patterns. As a matter of fact the question has to be answered whether it is possible to increase reliability of short segment spectral HRV-measures by taking together data of comparable task segments using averaging techniques. After the description of the spectral procedure that is used the results of two studies are described in the remainder of this paper, one related to HRV patterns during an intelligence test with children, the other related to workload in a flight simulator.

Spectral profiles analysis

The basis of the approach is a simple type of time-frequency analysis of HRV. In general in signal processing, time-frequency analysis is a method that delivers spectral distribution measures as a function of time. For instance, the time course of spectral power in a chosen frequency band can be computed or coloured 3-dimensional graphs can be plotted of the spectral power distribution, with time on one axis, frequency on another while the spectral power in a specific time window and specific frequency range is indicated by a colour scale. Sophisticated methods, such as wavelet-analysis procedures, exist in which the time window is adapted to the frequency range at hand: the lower the frequency range, the longer the time window. On this basis Van Steenis (2002) has developed a nice procedure that is suitable for HRV-analysis. For years we have used a simplified method in which the spectral power in a chosen frequency band as a function of time (spectral profile) can be computed (G. Mulder, 1980, L. Mulder, 1992). In this procedure the length of the time window can be adapted to the required frequency range, in such a way that the lower the frequency range of the band, the larger the chosen time window. Theoretically, the time window has to have at least the length of the inverse of the lowest frequency involved. Practically and for reasons of reliability of the computed spectral values, longer lasting time periods are chosen in most situations. For instance, when the power in the frequency band ranging from 0.07 – 0.14 Hz is selected (mid frequency band of HRV) the window length theoretically has to be at least 14 seconds, mostly a window length between 30 and 60 seconds is chosen.

As a matter of fact, such window lengths for computing spectral HRV values are lower than indicated by the guidelines of the committee on HRV spectral analysis headed by Berntson that gives the advice to use at least segment durations of 10 times the target rhythm, which means for instance about 100 seconds for spectral measures from the mid frequency band and between 30 and 60 seconds for the high frequency band (Berntson et al., 1997). There are three aspects with regard to these guidelines. The first has to do with reliability of spectral band values, which increases linearly with window length. The second aspect has to do with the reasoning that for obtaining the same reliability, longer time durations are necessary for lower frequencies than for higher ones. This latter reasoning is theoretically not correct, given the assumption that the data are normally distributed (Bendat & Piersol, 1986). At a given segment length the number of degrees of freedom for each component of the power spectral density function is the same for all frequencies. The third is related to findings that HRV increases with increasing segment lengths. This is probably related to the fact that HRV values are not homogeneous distributed over the frequencies. Practically, it is obvious that it is less easy for the lower frequencies to prove that the data follow the required statistical distribution than for higher frequencies. This will probably be the most important reason that it is advised to have longer time segments for lower frequencies.

Three frequency bands have frequently been used: a low (0.02 – 0.06 Hz), mid (0.07 – 0.14 Hz) and a high frequency band (0.15 – 0.40 Hz). The high frequency band mainly reflects respiratory related HRV (RSA), the mid frequency band reflects baroreflex related HRV, while the lower frequencies mainly are related slow task adaptation and temperature regulation (Mulder,1992). The procedure that will be described in the following will be applied to the mid and high frequency band, although there is no specific reason to restrict the method to these bands.

The described spectral profile method works as follows. The heart rate data to be analysed, which may last for several hours, are segmented in small highly overlapping time segments (e.g. window length: 60 seconds; step size: 5 seconds). For each of these time segments the spectral power in a number of specified frequency bands is computed, as well as the mean of the signal (heart rate) in exactly the same manner as is done for longer segments in normal HRV spectral analysis (Mulder, 1992). The time course of the spectral power in each of these specified frequency band is called a spectral profile. In the same manner also spectral profiles can be computed from the coherence, gain and phase functions between cardiovascular time series (e.g. systolic blood pressure-heart rate), again in each of the specified frequency bands (Mulder, 1992).

Theoretically it can be derived that it takes half of the window length before the optimal (theoretical) level of HRV is reached after a sudden change to a new level. In this sense the approach corresponds completely with the output pattern of a moving average filter. Extrapolating this idea it can be concluded that the time resolution of this technique is directly related to the window length; the step size is only relevant for the interdependency of consecutive spectral band values. The smaller the step size, the more smooth the time course of the profile will look. For practical research it is clear that when changes in task demands in consecutive segments have a duration of far less than the time window, the related HRV differences can not be detected. If the duration of such HRV-effects is longer than the time between consecutive task-events, overlap occurs. If there is little overlap, the HRV task-effects will be less than in cases without overlap, but probably differences can be detected. Additionally, the longer the time duration of the segments to be analysed, the higher the reliability of the computed spectral values will be. This reliability is here improved by taking the weighted average of a number of segments belonging to a specified class of task segments.

Study 1: SON intelligence test

The main goal of this study (Rusthoven, 2006) was to find out whether there is a direct relation between task performance in a verbal intelligence test and invested mental effort, as measured with HR and HRV profiles. An adapted version of the SON-R5.5-17 (Snijders-Oomen non-verbal intelligence test for ages between 5.5 and 17 years) was used (Tellegen, 2005). In particular it was studied whether there were indications that children were giving up in cases that the test items could not be solved adequately.

Methods

A specific task was constructed using four subtests of the SON-R5.5-17 (further indicated as the SON). Thirty-seven children in the age category between 9 and 11 years, with normal education and without known developmental problems, were tested. The four selected subtests were, respectively: Categories, Analogies, Mosaics and Patterns. The first two are abstract reasoning tests; the last two require mainly spatial insight (Snijders, Tellegen, & Laros, 1988). Each subtest consisted of two series of items, each with increasing level of difficulty. The number of items per subtest varied with the required solution time, with Categories and Analogies being the shortest (about 15 seconds) and Mosaics and Patterns being the longest (about 70 seconds). The short subtests had a maximum of 10 items per series, while the long series included 7 items as a maximum. A series of items was ended when 3 errors were made in the Patterns and Mosaics subtests and 5 errors in the Categories and Analogies subtests. Each new series started with easy items. In order to prevent effects of time-on-task, half of the subjects started with the short lasting items, while the other half started with the items of longer duration. Moreover, after the first and after the third subtest a resting period of 3.5 minutes was included that was used as baseline measurement.

HR and HRV measures were obtained from hardware triggered R-peak events in the ECG and were corrected for artefacts, using a combination of automatic detection/correction and visual inspection followed by manual correction where necessary in the Carspan spectral analysis programme (Mulder, 1992). Spectral profiles from HR and HRV (mid and high frequency band) were computed with the same programme. Data were analysed with a window length of 30 seconds and a time step of 1 second. With respect to the subtests, around each item a small time segment was selected that was aligned around the response of the participant. For Categories and Analogies this window started 20 seconds before and ended 6 seconds after the response. For the subtests with longer duration this segment was between 80 seconds before and 10 seconds after the response (for Patterns) or between 70 seconds before and 10 seconds after the response (for Mosaics). Two types of differences were studied: between the first and second half of each series and between items with correct and incorrect answers. In this way 4 averaging categories were obtained: CB: correct items in the first half (begin); CE: correct items in the second half (end); IB: incorrect, first half; IE: incorrect second half. It has to be realised that these categories are not completely independent: in the first half of each series more correct answers may be expected because the items are easier. Moreover, the defined time segments were further adapted by shortening these by the individual mean durations of the items in the CB, CE, IB and IE categories. Finally, HR and HRV profile-values were averaged over these newly defined segment values. For reasons of a having a more normal distribution, the natural logarithm of the HRV measures was taken (Van Roon, 1998).

It was expected that HR is higher and HRV lower in the more difficult (effortful) items; items in the first half (CB, IB) are estimated as easier than those in the second half (CE, IE), while correct answered items (CB, CE) are estimated as easier than incorrect items (IB, IE). No signs of giving up during difficult items were expected. HRV was expected to be higher in the baseline conditions, while HR would be lower in the two (averaged) baseline conditions. Data were statistically analysed using two-sided paired t-tests after Bonferoni-Holm correction (Van Peet, Wittenboer, den Hox, 2001). For all tests a significance level of 5% was applied.

Results and discussion

Only the results of the subtests Categories (figure 1) and Patterns (figure 2) will be described in detail. From other subtests only general effects will be mentioned.

In all subtests HRV (mid and high frequency bands) is lower during task than in the baseline conditions; HR is higher during task performance than in the baseline conditions, for the tests with the longer lasting items (Patterns, Mosaics), but not for the subtests Categories and Analogies. HRV-high distinguishes items from the first and the second half in all the subtests except Mosaics: HRV is higher in the first half; the same pattern is found when comparing correct with incorrect items, but is only significant in the Categories and Patterns subtests. HRV-mid shows similar patterns as HRV-high, but the level of significance is only reached in the Patterns subtest (both comparing first-second half and correct-incorrect items). The Mosaics subtest shows a different pattern: no differences are found on HRV (high and mid frequency band) between first and second half and correct versus incorrect items, although all task conditions are strongly different from the baseline condition in the expected direction. It is remarkable in this case that HR is different between first-second half and correct-incorrect items, but in the other direction than expected: HR is higher in the first half than the second and higher during the correct items. As a matter of fact this same pattern was found for HR in the other subtests, but not significantly.

In more detail: figure 1 shows the results for the Categories subtest. Although HRV-high and mid frequency bands show very similar patterns, the effects are only significant for the high frequency band. Note the small (non-significant) differences on HR between baseline and tasks and the task conditions mutual.

Figure 2 shows the results of the Patterns subtest. Now all HRV effects are clearly significant, both when comparing task with baseline values as well as the task conditions mutual. HR is higher during task performance than during baseline conditions, while the task conditions do not differ mutually.

The study shows that there are signs of increased effort in incorrect items, therefore, no arguments are found for the idea that children give up during the most difficult items. All together, the results are remarkable clear and consistent, while interesting details are found between the subtests and the used variables. In general, HRV-high seems to be the most sensitive variable; this holds in particular for the subtests with the shortest item-durations (Categories, Analogies). For the Pattern subtest high and mid frequency band have similar sensitivity. For Mosaics a quite different pattern occurs in both bands: no differences between the task conditions, but large differences with baseline values, probably related to the high difficulty level of all items.

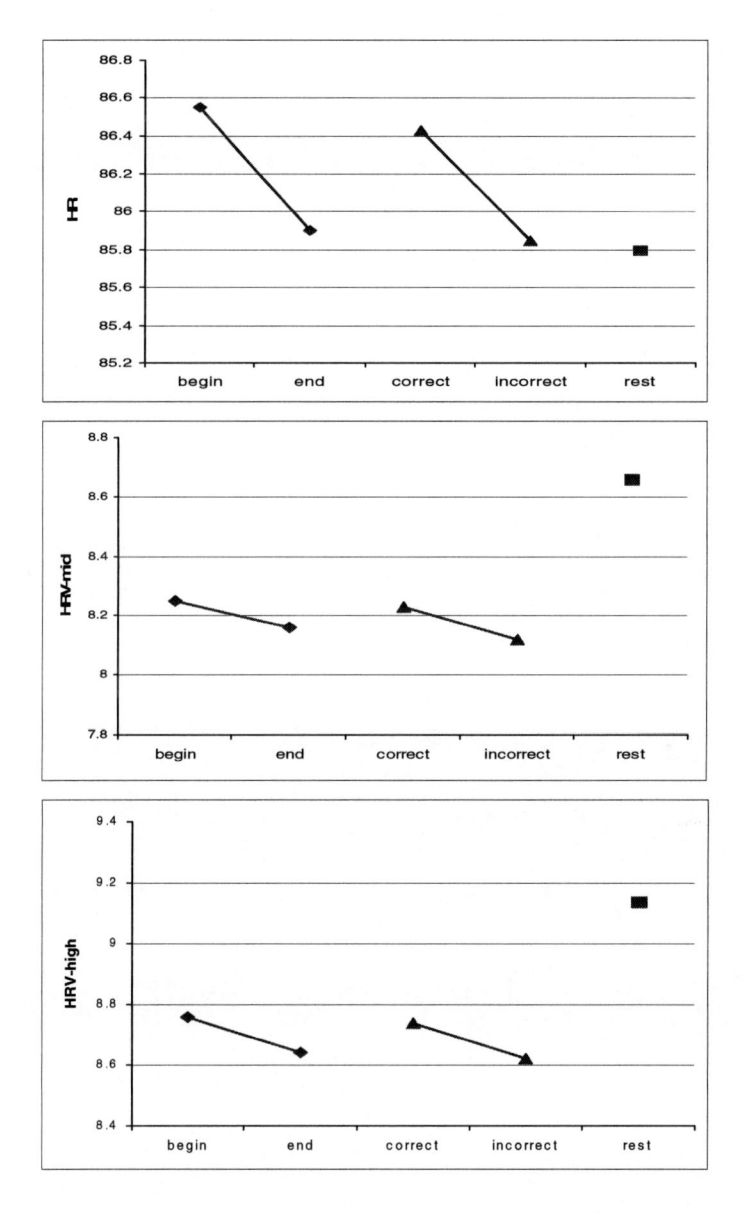

Figure 1. HR and HRV results of Categories sub-test. HR (upper panel), HRV in mid (middle panel) and high frequency band (lower panel) as a function of task conditions. Begin/end indicates first/second half of the items, correct/incorrect indicates correct vs. incorrect items, rest indicates baseline data. HRV measures are natural logarithms

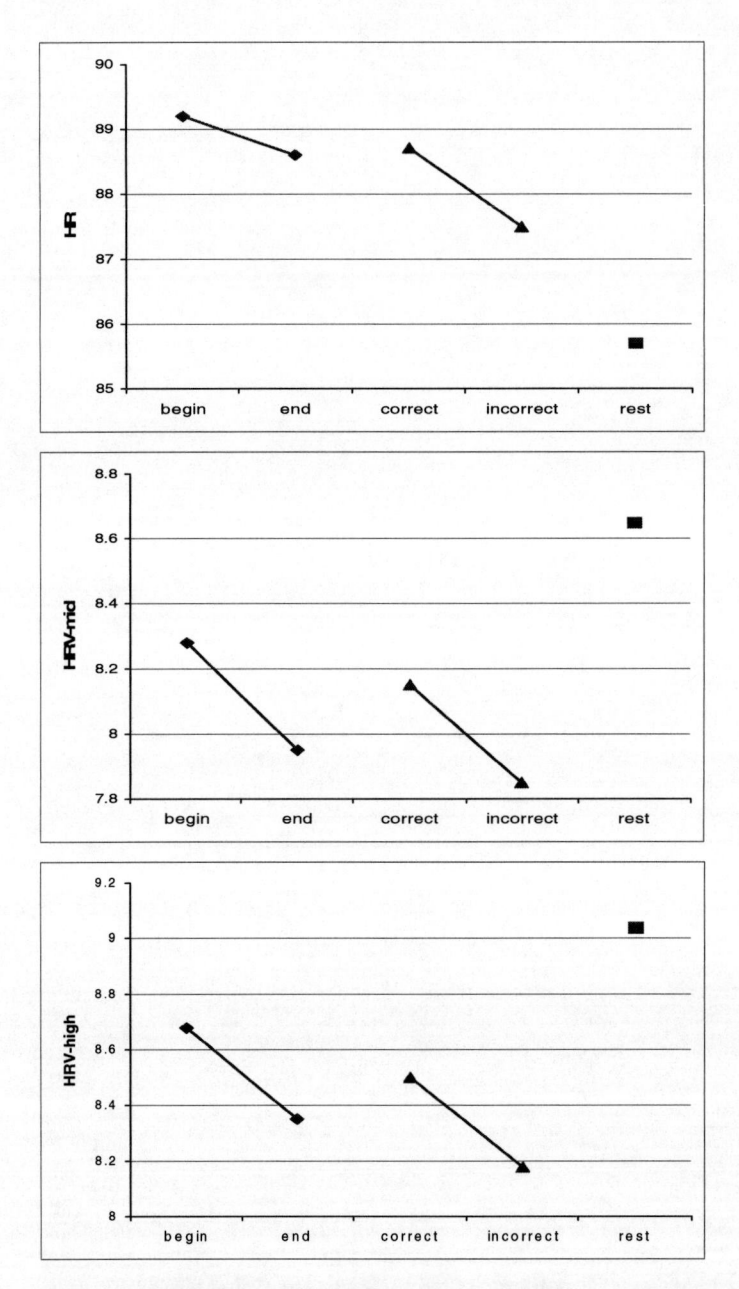

Figure 2. HR and HRV results of Patterns sub-test. HR (upper panel), HRV in mid (middle panel) and high frequency band (lower panel) as a function of task conditions. Begin/end indicates first/second half of the items, correct/incorrect indicates correct vs. incorrect items, rest indicates baseline data. HRV measures are natural logarithms

So, in contrast to many other laboratory studies, it seems that here the high frequency band is more sensitive to changes in mental effort than the mid frequency band in the described setup for the subtests with the short lasting items. This finding corresponds well with the position of the Committee Report in Psychophysiology (Berntson et al., 1997) that segments of longer duration are necessary for lower frequency bands. Whether this has to do with the statistical distributions of these variables or with the fact that there is more overlap in HRV profile-patterns between the segments is still unknown.

In many laboratory experiments with heavy mental loading tasks (memory search and counting, mental arithmetic, etc.) it is found that HRV in the mid frequency band is reduced with about a factor 2 (for natural logarithm this is a difference of 0.7), while differences have to be about 0.4 (on a ln scale) for getting significant results, assuming about 20 participants (Van Roon, 1998). In the present experiment with 37 participants, differences in the high frequency band lower than 0.2 were significant (Categories, Analogies). This means that the presented method is certainly not less sensitive than when having united task segments.

Conclusions

- There are signs of increased effort when dealing with the most difficult items of the test.
- Despite the short duration of the items stable HRV differences can be found.
- The high frequency band of HRV seems to be more sensitive in the tests with the shortest item durations than HRV the mid frequency band, probably related to the restricted time-resolution of the latter.
- Comparison of these results with other types of task can probably clarify whether these findings are task related or have to do with the item duration itself.

Study 2: mental effort in simulated flight

The main aim of this study (De Rivecourt & Kuperus, 2006) is to find out whether different task difficulty levels of a simulated flight are reflected in corresponding HR and HRV profiles. Knowing that in this task the pattern of task demands is changing very rapidly one has to find out whether it is still possible to work with HRV profiles that require relative long time durations. Moreover, it is has to be found out which variables are the most sensitive for this approach.

Method

Nineteen male participants from the Royal Netherlands Air Force selection and training programme, in the range of 17 to 27 years, performed an instrument flight task on an ALSIM AL 100 Flight Trainer. The participants had some experience in a flight simulator but had not yet started their military flight education. They all had less than 100 flight hours and can be considered as relatively inexperienced.

After a short instruction and familiarisation in a training flight (24 minutes) participants were expected to have sufficient control and track of the task to be performed. Before the experimental flight (that lasted 28-30 minutes) they were instructed about the flight profile, which was available during the whole flight in a written form attached to their knee. The participants had to perform an instrument flying task with increasing task complexity, starting with straight and level flight, followed by a horizontal turn, a climbing turn, a descending turn and combinations of these elements with at the end relatively fast transitions. Six flight segments could be distinguished, which lasted each between 1.5 and 2.5 minutes. More detailed task analysis led to a description of the task in 39 consecutive flight elements that could be assigned to four increasing levels of task complexity: 1. horizontal flight, 2. horizontal turn or climbing/descending, 3. turns in combination with climbing/descending, and 4. transitions. Transitions from one phase to another were considered to be more complex than category 3. The duration of each of these flight elements was variable and lasted between 5 and 100 seconds. In particular, most transitions were not longer than 20 to 25 seconds. Although the flight scenario was very detailed and precisely prescribed in time, individual variations could occur when participants started a new phase too early or too late.

HR and HRV profiles were obtained in the same way as described in study 1, while in this case, for reasons not relevant for the present chapter, the window length for HR was 4 seconds, while it was 30 seconds for the HRV profiles. The step size was 1 second for all variables. HRV power values for the 4 levels of complexity were obtained by computing weighted averages of the short segment HRV profile values. Baseline values for the heart rate data were computed by taking the average of a five-minute rest before the start of the flight and a same resting period after the flight. Next to heart rate also eye fixation patterns were measured, as well as subjective indications of task complexity in the 6 consecutive flight phases. These data will be described elsewhere.

To summarize, data are analysed in two ways: on the basis of the 6 consecutive flight segments and on the basis of the segments belonging to the 4 levels of complexity. It is expected that HR increases and HRV deceases with increasing task demands. This will be tested using multilevel analysis (MLWin) with a random effect model (Wright, 2004; De Rivecourt & Kuperus, 2006). A one-sided significance level of 5% was used for all tests.

Results and discussion

The HR and HRV results with respect to the 6 consecutive flight segments are illustrated in figure 3. In comparison to the baseline values HR is strongly increased in all flight segments, while there is a continuous ongoing increase of HR as a function of time (and task load, as task load increases as a function of flight time). Multilevel analysis shows that all segments differ from rest, while segments 1, 2, 3 and 4 can be distinguished from each other. No differences are found between segments 4, 5 and 6. The HRV patterns in both the mid and high frequency band show differences between the first segment and all others, while these other segments are mutually not different, except segment 6 for the high frequency band which is statistically different from the other segments. Segment 1 does differ from baseline in both frequency bands.

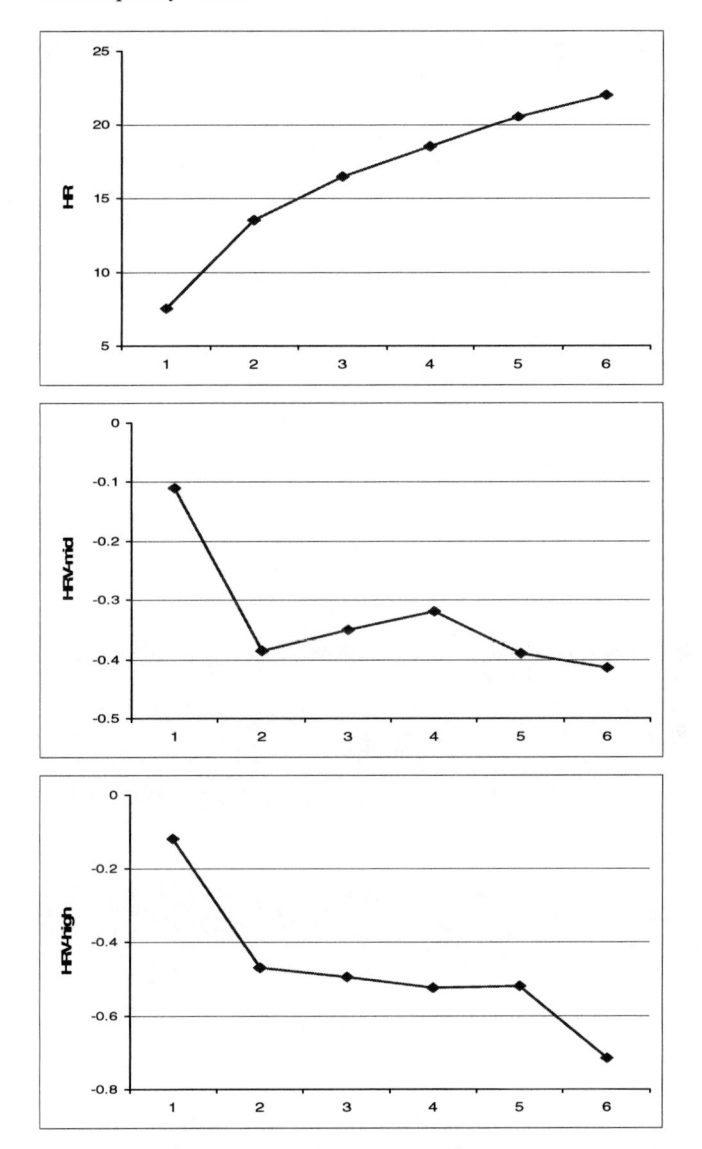

Figure 3. HR and HRV results as a function of flight segment. Changes in HR (upper panel), HRV in mid (middle panel) and high frequency band (lower panel) as a function of flight segment complexity; level 1 corresponds with the most simple task elements, level 6 with most complex ones. All values are related to baseline. HRV measures are natural logarithms

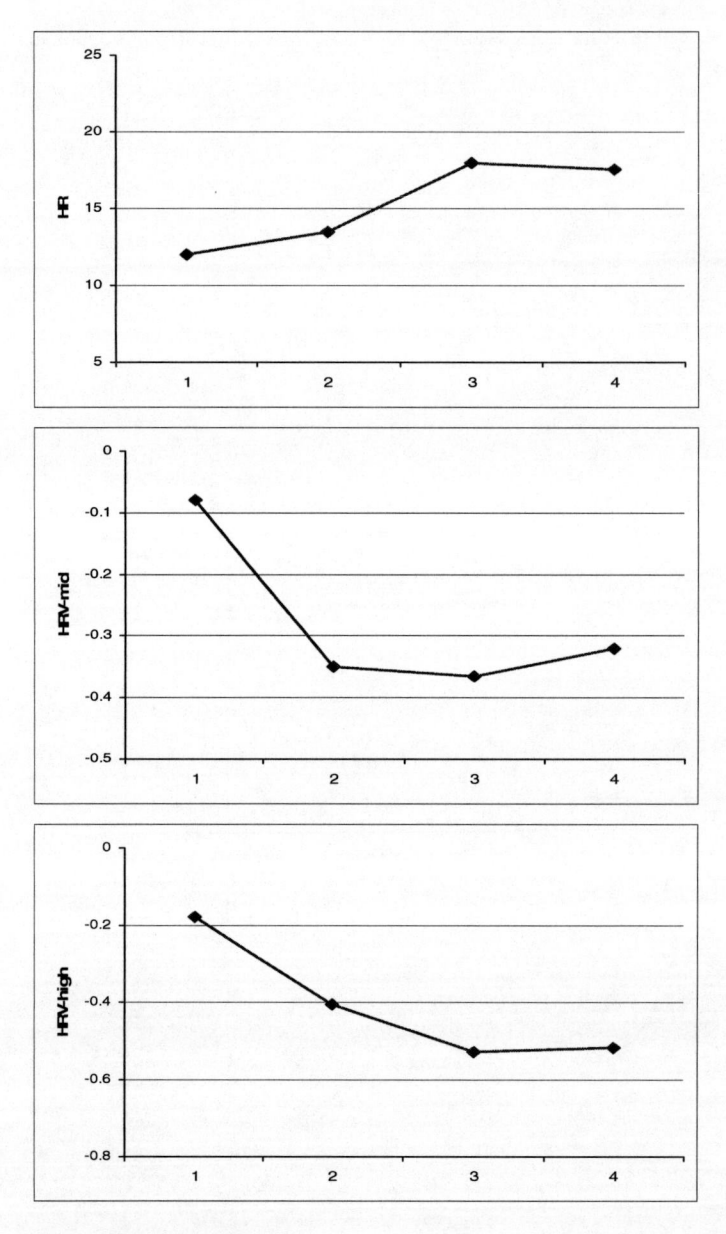

Figure 4. HR and HRV results as a function of task levelChanges in HR (upper panel), HRV in mid (middle panel) and high frequency band (lower panel) as a function of increasing task level complexity: 1. horizontal flight, 2. horizontal turn or climbing/descending, 3. turns in combination with climbing/descending, and 4. transitions.. All values are related to baseline. HRV measures are natural logarithms

The HR and HRV results on the basis of the four task demand levels are illustrated in figure 4. For HR, all task demand levels differ from the baseline, while HR increases with task demand level. Multilevel analysis shows that level-pairs 1,2 differ from level-pairs 3,4, while the levels are not mutually different within these pairs. HRV decreases strongly with increasing task demand level in both frequency bands. Multilevel analysis shows that in both frequency bands level 1 can not be distinguished from the baseline periods. In the mid frequency band levels 2, 3 and 4 differ from level 1, while these levels do not differ mutually. In the high frequency band level 1 differs from level 2, level 2 differs from the pair 3,4, while these latter levels can not be distinguished mutually.

The HR data in this study show much larger increases compared to baseline values than in Study 1. This finding corresponds with other studies in flight simulators and in driving simulators, which illustrates strong effects of manual control on the HR level in comparison to mental tasks that require more working memory operations (Veltman & Gaillard, 1996, Wilson, 1992, De Waard, 2002). HRV level changes in the present study are in the same range as those found in Study 1 and in many other mental loading studies (Van Roon, 1998). Although there seems to be a problem in this study that task load effects are confounded by time-on-task, it has to be mentioned that in general time of task effects are in the opposite direction than found in this study. Usually HR decreases, while HRV increases as a function of time on task (Mulder, et al. 2003).

The two approaches, one based on continuous task segments with lengths between 1.5 and 2.5 minutes and the other based on short segment analysis related to task demand level give, in great lines, similar results. For HR, the analysis based on consecutive segments seems to be the most informative, because more levels can be distinguished. For HRV-high the task demand level analysis seems to be at least even informative as the segment analysis, because in this case the levels 2 (curves or climbing/descending) and 3 (curves in combination with climbing/descending) can be distinguished. Furthermore, using this task demand level analysis the problem of untangling time on task effects from task load effects is less prominent. Moreover, in the present setup differences in the high frequency band of HRV of about 0.15 (ln scale) can be distinguished, both in the segment analysis (level 6 compared to 2, 3, 4 and 5) as in the task demand analysis (level 2 compared to 3), which is quite sensitive compared to other studies using data segments of longer duration.

Conclusions

- Both HR and HRV differences can be detected between the different task segments as well as between task demand levels.
- The differences in HR, compared to baseline are remarkably larger than in Study 1.
- Again, HRV in the high frequency band seems to be more sensitive in both types of analysis than HRV in the mid frequency band.
- Also in this study the short segment analysis based on the profiles approach is suitable, both for HR and HRV analysis.

- This study shows, once again, that the combination of HR and HRV measures gives more information than taking just one of these types of measures.

General discussion and conclusion

The proposed short segment analysis technique based on (spectral) profiles worked well in both experiments. Despite the short duration of some segments (certainly in Study 2, related to flight transitions) different task demand levels could be distinguished by averaging HRV band values and HR values for relevant short segments. It is certainly not denied that overlap will exist between the HRV effects in consecutive short task segments, but the results of these two short studies show that despite this overlap relevant task effects can be found at the level to be studied. In general, it may be expected that the less overlap exists between segments the better the statistical resolution will be. This is a hopeful conclusion for all those experimental situations at which partly overlap can not be avoided. Moreover, it is remarkable that the standard error of the spectral band values (not shown in the data presentation) is not larger for baseline data (relative long consecutive segments) than for short segments from, for instance, flight transitions.

In both studies the HRV effects in the mid and high frequency band showed about the same pattern, but in both cases the effects in the high frequency band were more sensitive to task load. Effortful laboratory tasks in the past (Van Roon, 1988) showed more consistent effects in the mid frequency band, based on longer lasting consecutive task durations (about 5 minutes of data). At least two explanations can be given for this difference. The first is related to possible statistical distributions of these spectral band data. The 10-second rhythm constituting the power in the mid frequency band shows in general, for instance during longer lasting baseline measurements, an on-off going burst pattern. If this occurs in the same way during the type of tasks as described in this paper, large random variations may be expected; these will then result in large standard errors and statistical distributions far from normal. The second possible reason has to do with control of the autonomic nervous system. It may be expected that HRV patterns in the high frequency band are directly related to vagal control, while changes in the mid frequency band are related to both vagal and sympathetic effects (van Roon, 1998). Knowing that in sympathetic control much longer time constants are involved, having effects over 10 or 20 seconds, while in comparison vagal effects are restricted to 2 or 3 seconds it is to be expected that much more overlap will exist in effects in the mid frequency band than in the high frequency band. This would then result in smaller differences between different types of task segments in the mid frequency band compared to the high frequency band.

It can be concluded that the described short segment spectral profile approach looks very promising for use in (semi-)realistic working situations. The important prerequisite is that on the basis of simple task analysis relevant segments have to be detected that do not overlap too much with respect of the HRV patterns. It is advised to use both HR and HRV measures (in both the high and mid frequency band); combination of these measures gives more information than taking just one type of measures.

Acknowledgments

The authors wish to thank the staff of the Centre for Human Factors in Aviation (Soesterberg, The Netherlands) for their support, the Air Force cadets, as well as Evelien Kums, Michiel de Leeuw, and Siemen Henk Sikkema for fruitful co-operation in Study 2. In Study 1 the help of parents and participating children and the intensive support of Peter Tellegen and Bas Kortmann are greatly acknowledged. For both studies we thank the technical staff of the department of Psychology of the University of Groningen for their support.

References

Bendat, J.S. & Piersol, A.G. (1986). *Random data: analysis and measurement procedures*. New York: John Wiley and Sons.

Berntson, G.G., Thomas Bigger JR, J., Eckberg, D.J., Grossman, P., Kaufmann, P.G., Malik, M., Nagaraja, H.N., Porges, J.P.S., Stone, P.H. and Van der Molen, M.W. (1997). Committee Report - Heart rate variability: Origins, methods and interpretive caveats. *Psychophysiology, 34*, 623-648.

Boucsein, W. & Backs, R.W. (2000). Engineering Psychophysiology as a Discipline: Historical and Theoretical Aspects. In R.W. Backs and W. Boucsein (Eds.). *Engineering Psychophysiology: Issues and applications* (pp. 3-30). Mahwah, NJ: Lawrence Erlbaum.

De Rivecourt, M., & Kuperus, M.N. (2006). *Heart rate and eye activity measures as indices for mental effort in aviation*. Master thesis. Groningen: University of Groningen.

De Waard, D. (2002). Mental Workload. In R. Fuller and J.A. Santos (Eds.) *Human Factors for Highway Engineers* (pp. 161-175). Oxford: Pergamon.

Mulder, G. (1980). *The heart of mental effort*. Ph.D. thesis. Groningen: University of Groningen

Mulder, G. (1986). The concept and measurement of mental effort. In G.R.J. Hockey, A.W.K. Gaillard, and M.G.H. Coles (Eds.), *Energetics and human information processing* (pp. 175-188). Dordrecht, The Netherlands: M. Nijhoff Publishers.

Mulder, L.J.M. (1992). Measurement and analysis methods of heart rate and respiration for use in applied environments. *Biological Psychology, 34*, 205-236.

Mulder, L.J.M., Van Roon, A., Veldman, J.B.P., Laumann, K., Burov, A., Quispel, L., & Hoogeboom, P. (2003). How to use cardiovascular state changes in adaptive automation. In G.R.J. Hockey, A.W.K. Gaillard, and O. Burov (Eds.), *Operator Functional State*. (pp. 260-269). Amsterdam: IOS Press

Nickel, P. & Nachreiner, F. (2003). Sensitivity and diagnosticity of the 0.1 Hz component of heart rate variability as an indicator of mental workload. *Human Factors, 45*, 575-590.

Rusthoven, H. (2006). *De hartritmevariabiliteit tijdens afname van de SON-test. Masters thesis*. Groningen: University of Groningen.

Snijders, J.Th., Tellegen, P.J. & Laros, J.A.(1988). SON-R 5.5-17 *Verantwoording en handleiding*. Groningen, The Netrherlands: Wolters-Noordhoff BV.

Van Steenis, H.G. (2002). *On Time Frequency Analysis of Heart rate Variability.* PhD thesis. Rotterdam, The Netherlands: Erasmus University.

Van Peet, A.A.J., Wittenboer, G.L.H., & Van de Hox, J.J. (2001). Toegepaste statistiek: Inductieve technieken. Groningen, The Netherlands: Wolters-Noordhoff BV.

Van Roon, A.M. (1998) *Short-term cardiovascular effects of mental tasks, physiology, experiments and computer simulations.* PhD thesis. Groningen, The Netherlands:University of Groningen.

Veltman, J.A. & Gaillard, A.W.K., 1996, Physiological indices of workload in a simulated flight task. *Biological Psychology, 42,* 323-342.

Wilson, G.F. (1992), Applied use of cardiac and respiration measures: practical considerations and precautions. *Biological Psychology,* 34, pp. 163-178.

Wright, D.B. (2004). Statistical software review. *British Journal of Mathematical & Statistical Psychology,* 57, 383-384.

Concurrent validity of an ocular measure of mental workload

Marco Camilli, Michela Terenzi, & Francesco Di Nocera
University of Rome "La Sapienza"
Italy

Abstract

In previous studies, eye fixations were recorded from participants playing a videogame and from professional pilots during a simulated flight. Ocular data were then analyzed using spatial statistics algorithms, and results showed sensitivity of fixations' dispersion to variations in mental workload. Particularly, a tendency towards spatial randomness of fixations was associated to the most demanding phases. Implementation of this procedure is still in its early stage, thus making it necessary to assess its validity. In the present study, the index has been used to assess mental workload during the execution of another visuo-motor task: the Tetris game. Task demand was manipulated by varying the degree of difficulty of the game. This was accomplished implementing three levels of difficulty of the game that were selected in a pilot study involving a sample of gamers. Additionally, the amplitude of the P300 component of ERPs was used as a concurrent measure of mental workload. Results showed that fixations dispersion is a valid index of mental workload.

Background

Ocular activity has been often related to mental workload and different attempts have been made to find ocular indices that showed variable diagnostic power (e.g., eye-blinks, pupil diameter, fixations frequency and duration). However, the relation between ocular activity and mental workload load is not straightforward, mostly because there is a lack of agreement about the nature of this construct. Indeed, while mental workload is a key topic in Human Factors / Ergonomics (HF/E) research, its definition and assessment are still a matter of debate (see Annett, 2002 and commentary for a recent discussion). For example, it is still unclear whether mental workload is associated with the activity of functionally separated resources, or if those modular resources are combined with a general-purpose resource that is invoked for all processing activities (Parasuraman & Caggiano, 2002). Nevertheless, most theories and models agree on a basic set of assumptions: "(a) people have a limited mental and attentional capacity with which to perform tasks, (b) different tasks will require different amounts (and perhaps different types) of processing resources from the same individual, and (c) two individuals might be able to perform a given task equally well, but it may be more difficult for one than the other" (Baldwin, 2003, pp. 132 f.).

In D. de Waard, G.R.J. Hockey, P. Nickel, and K.A. Brookhuis (Eds.) (2007), *Human Factors Issues in Complex System Performance* (pp. 117 - 129). Maastricht, the Netherlands: Shaker Publishing.

The multi-dimensional and modular nature of mental workload is also reflected by visual scanning behaviour. For example, individuals appear to trade the cost of sampling movements (needed to gather visual information) against the cognitive demands of maintaining information in working memory (McCarley & Kramer, 2007), and different types of task demands have been found to differently affect visual scanning (e.g., Recarte & Nunes, 2000, 2003). Seminal work in this field has been carried out to obtain a quantitative measure of visual scanning strategies, possibly linked to mental workload and thus varying with task demands. Some of these studies have been carried out to test whether the scanpath was based on random sampling or if statistical dependencies could be found. For example, using an information-seeking task performed by airline pilots, Ellis and Smith (1985) found that the pattern of scanning deviates systematically from random sampling and could be explained by more deterministic models. Ponsoda et al. (1995) also investigated the relationship between successive saccades finding statistical dependencies, but failed to show any effect of task complexity. More importantly, their finding might not hold when complex scanning patterns are taken into account as in their study stimuli were "arranged in such a way that the task could be completed with only horizontal and vertical saccades" (p. 173).

An explicit account on the relation between scanning strategies and mental workload can be found in those studies based on the concept of entropy (Harris et al., 1986; Hilburn et al., 1997; Tole et al., 1983). As in thermodynamics the concept of entropy is related to the quantity of disorder in a system, in those studies the "disorder" (or randomness) in visual exploration was taken into consideration. All these studies have reported that randomness in the visual scanning and workload were inversely correlated: the higher the workload, the more stereotyped was the scanpath (but see Kruizinga et al., 2006 for a different account). The common denominator of these contributions is that they were basically based on the analysis of transition matrices, which have been the key method for studying visual scanning strategies for years. In the entropy analysis reported above, for example, randomness was due to frequent transitions between areas of interest (as opposed to dwells, in which eyes remained within the same area of interest). Clearly, the spatial information that eye movements bring with them has been neglected by those methods, which have confined fixations location to *a priori* regions of interest. On the contrary, recent studies (Di Nocera et al., in press; Di Nocera et al., 2006) have considered fixations coordinates as a valuable source of information to establish how they were distributed.

The type of spatial distribution produced by a pattern of fixations can be assessed using spatial statistics algorithms that are frequently used to study other spatial patterns (e.g., plant, animals, and fossils) in other research domains (e.g., Ecology and Palaeontology). Particularly, Di Nocera and colleagues (see below) used the Nearest Neighbour Index (NNI). A comprehensive description and demonstrations can be found in Clark & Evans (1954). The index is the ratio between (1) the average of observed minimum distances between points and (2) the mean random distance that one would expect to find if the distribution were random. This ratio is equal to 1 when the distribution is random. Values lower than 1 suggest grouping, whereas values higher than 1 suggest regularity (i.e., the point pattern is dispersed in a non-random way). Theoretically, the NNI lies between 0 (maximum clustering) and 2.1491 (strictly regular hexagonal pattern) (Clark & Evans, 1954, p. 447). In a first study (Di Nocera et al., 2006), two versions of the arcade game "Asteroids" were used to impose different levels of task load. In a successive study (Di Nocera et al., in press), ten professional pilots were required to complete a simulated flight imposing variable task load across five segments. In both studies participants' ocular behaviour was recorded and later analysed to compute the NNI. The index always showed sensitivity to task load: more demanding conditions led to significantly higher NNI values (i.e., wider fixation distributions) than the easier conditions. Furthermore, the NNI can be computed over relatively small epochs (1-minute), making it possible to obtain "continuous" information about the functional state of an individual. This is particularly appealing in a measure of mental workload, as it opens to the opportunity of using it as a trigger for adaptive systems. However, in order to achieve this goal, a critical step will be to demonstrating the validity of the NNI computed over eye fixations, thus casting out any doubt that NNI variations might be due to factors other than changes in mental workload (e.g., changes in ocular strategy due to task constraints). The validation strategy employed in this study is that of contrasting the NNI with other measures that have been frequently used as indicators of mental workload, namely: the NASA - Task Load IndeX and the amplitude of the P300 component.

The NASA-Task Load indeX (NASA-TLX: Hart & Staveland, 1988), is a multi-dimensional rating procedure that derives an overall workload score based on a weighted average of ratings on six subscales (mental demand, physical demand, temporal demand, effort, performance, and frustration). Its main advantages are the ease of use and the short time needed to fill in the form and to compute the ratings, not to mention its low cost. Although there are known issues related to the subjective estimation of mental workload (e.g., vulnerability to context effects), many studies have shown the validity of the NASA-TLX, which has become a standard in HF/E research. However, the TLX is nothing more than a subjective assessment provided in discrete periods of time, making it impossible to obtain information on the ongoing state of an individual. The P300 (see Kramer, 1991 for a HF/E account) is a positive component of the Event Related Potentials (ERPs) occurring about 300 milliseconds from stimulus onset. This component has been shown to be inversely related to stimulus probability: in the so-called odd-ball paradigm, target (infrequent) tones occurring among a series of standard (frequent) tones elicit the largest P300 amplitudes. In HF/E studies the odd-ball is typically used as secondary task and the amplitude of the P300 has been shown to decrease as the demands imposed by the primary task increase (e.g., Israel et al., 1980). This makes the P300 a very useful psychophysiological index of mental workload (i.e., processing resources). However, the fact that the electrophysiology can be used to monitor the ongoing neural activity does not mean the P300 can be used to obtain a constant monitoring of an individual's mental workload. Theoretically, using "single trials" (the neural response to a single stimulus) it might be possible to monitor the ongoing amount of resources invested in a task. Practically, this is a rather complicated procedure that has been rarely applied, because several methodological manipulations are needed to overcome the signal-to-noise ratio issue (Di Nocera, 2003).

By contrasting NNI, P300, and NASA-TLX it is expected to find convergent evidence that the proposed index varies with workload. In consideration of its advantages as a continuous measure, if that were true it would provide further support to the use of the NNI for the assessment of mental workload in many real-world tasks. Even if the studies reported in this paper examined participants' performance while playing the Tetris game, results could be as well generalised to performance in complex systems. In fact, this task imposes the same type of visuo-spatial demands typically associated with the operators' procedures in a variety of complex domains (Nikolic et al., 2001) and its requirements are highly representative of the abilities needed in many real-world operative conditions that often involve numerous and dynamic displayed elements (e.g., Air Traffic Control and baggage screening).

Pilot study

The aim of this pilot study was to select three among ten levels of difficulty of a visuo-motor task (the Tetris game). These three levels should clearly generate "high", "intermediate" and "low" workload levels to be implemented as task load conditions (hereinafter reported as "Hard", "Medium", "Easy") in the successive experiment. This is a necessary step in order to assess the validity of the proposed index.

Method

Participants
Twenty undergraduate students (10 females and 10 males; mean age = 23 years, SD = 2.41) volunteered in this study. All participants reported to be right-handed, with normal hearing and normal or correct to normal vision.

Apparatus
The Tetris game used in this study was coded using Microsoft® C# and the .Net standard GDI+ Libraries. The game area consisted of 300 cells deployed on 15 rows. Each block was randomly extracted from a pool of 7 different block types and descended at a constant speed. In order to generate the ten levels of difficulty, the speed was varied from 600 ms per cell (level 1) to 60 ms per cell (level 10).

Procedure
Participants received training prior experimentation and were included in the sample only when they became able to play for 10 minutes without filling completely the game area. Participants sat in dark and sound-attenuated room and were asked to play the game gaining as many points as possible. Each level of difficulty lasted 3 minutes and the order of presentation was randomised across participants. After each level, participants compiled the NASA-TLX for the subjective assessment of mental workload.

Data analysis and results

NASA-TLX weighted scores and number of completed lines (an index of performance in the Tetris game) were analysed by ANOVA designs using the level of difficulty as independent variable. Results showed a main effect of the level of difficulty in both cases ($F_{(9,171)}$ = 56.56, $p<0.0001$ and $F_{(9,171)}$=37.01, $p<0.0001$, respectively). Selection of the conditions (falling speed levels) to be used in the successive experiment was based upon Duncan post-hoc testing. Particularly, levels 1 to 6 showed no significant differences in the amount of mental workload that was generated. Levels 7 to 10 were significantly different one from each other (and from the lower levels). Similar results were obtained for the number of completed lines. Accordingly, levels 6, 7, 8, 9, 10 could be used to generate significantly different levels of mental workload. However, levels 9 and 10 showed too poor performance (see Figure 2) in order to be used (less than 4 and 1 completed lines, respectively). Levels 6 (Easy), 7 (Medium), and 8 (Hard) were then considered the best compromise in order to grant equal "distance" between falling speeds and to avoid disproportionate overload that could affect results in unpredictable ways.

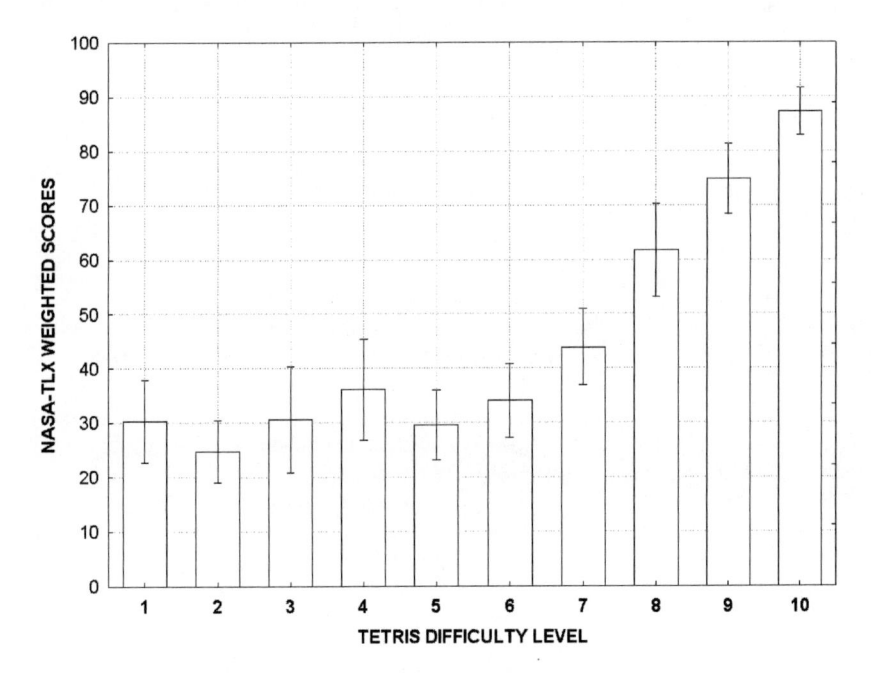

Figure 1. NASA-TLX values (weighted scores) separately for level of difficulty. Error bars denote 0.95 confidence intervals

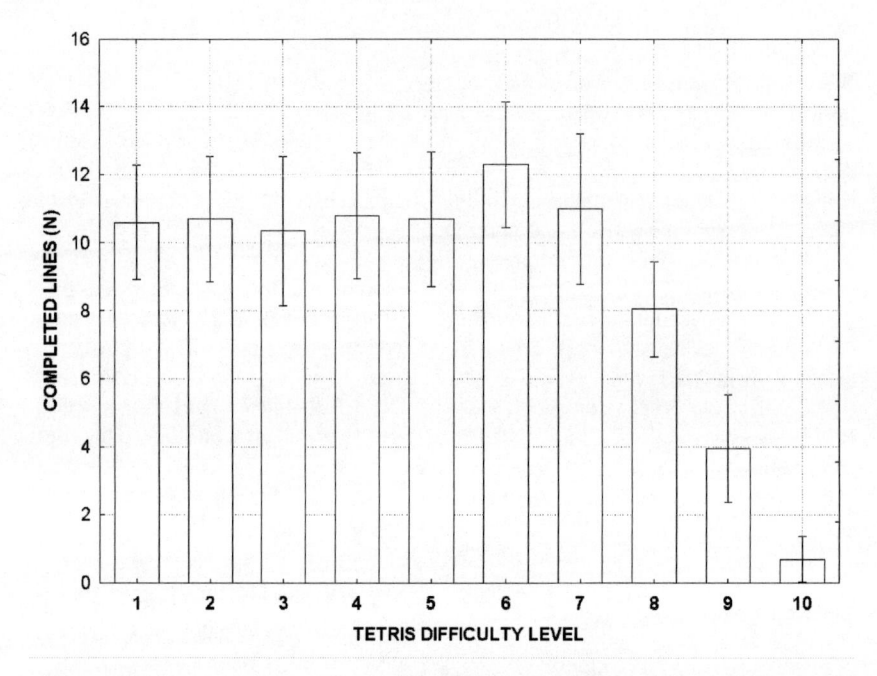

Figure 2. Number of completed lines separately for level of difficulty. Error bars denote 0.95 confidence intervals

Experiment

The Tetris game is a common visuo-motor task that has been successfully used for generating mental workload in the scientific literature (e.g., Trimmel & Huber, 1998). The game is also well-known so that little participant training is necessary, and – as reported above – its requirements are highly representative of the abilities needed in many real-world operative settings. Using this task, one of the primary concerns in the present research was to define task load conditions that could clearly generate different amount of mental workload. To this aim, ten levels of difficulty based on increasing speed were used in a pilot study, and twenty participants were requested to play those levels (randomly presented). Results allowed selecting three speed levels to be used as "Easy", "Medium", and "Hard" task load condition in the successive experiment.

Method

Participants
Ten undergraduate students (5 females and 5 males; mean age = 23.6 years, SD = 2.01) volunteered in this study. All participants reported to be right-handed, with normal hearing and normal or correct to normal vision.

Apparatus

Three levels of difficulty of the Tetris game defined by block falling speed (Easy = 360, Medium = 420, Hard = 480 milliseconds per cell) were used for generating different amounts of mental workload. An odd-ball task was used as secondary task. Three-hundred tones (65 dB SPL, 100 ms), were presented through headphones. Seventy-five percent of the tones were 850 Hz (standards) and the remaining 25 percent were 1100 Hz (targets). These tones were presented randomly intermixed at a variable rate (ISI ranging from 1000 to 1500 ms).

EEG recordings

The Mizar 33 System (EBNeuro, Italy) for physiological data acquisition and analysis was used for recording the EEG sampled at 128 Hz for 1 s starting 100 ms prior to each stimulus onset and averaged off-line for target and standard tones separately. Trials judged on a visual inspection as contaminated by artefacts (eye movements or muscular activity) were excluded from the averaging. P300 amplitudes were measured individually for each participant's data as the difference between N2 and P3 (peak-to-peak amplitude) in the Fz, Cz, and Pz electrode sites.

Ocular activity recordings

The ET17 eye-tracking system (Tobii, Sweden) was used for recording ocular activity. This system allows the researcher to collect ocular data without using invasive and/or uncomfortable head-mounted instruments. ET17 uses near infrared diodes to generate reflection patterns on the corneas of the eyes of the user. These reflection patterns, together with other visual information, are collected by a CCD camera. Image processing algorithms identify relevant features, including the eyes and the corneal reflection patterns. Three-dimensional position in space of each eyeball, and finally the gaze point on the screen are calculated. Sampling rate was approximately 33 Hz.

Procedure

After the electrode cap application, participants sat in a sound-attenuated room and were asked to remain relaxed during the recording session. Their task was to play the game completing as many lines as possible, to ignore the standard tones (225 out of 300) and to count target tones (75 out of 300). Each game level lasted 12 minutes and the order of presentation was randomised across participants. After completing each level, participants were requested to fill the electronic version of NASA-TLX (U.S. Naval Research Lab).

Data analysis and results

NASA-TLX weighted overall ratings were used as dependent variable in a repeated measures ANOVA design using Task load (Easy vs. Medium vs. Hard) as repeated factor. Results showed a significant difference between the levels of difficulty ($F_{(2,18)}$ = 4.83, $p<0.05$). Duncan post-hoc testing showed that the Hard condition was significantly different from the other two ($p<0.05$).

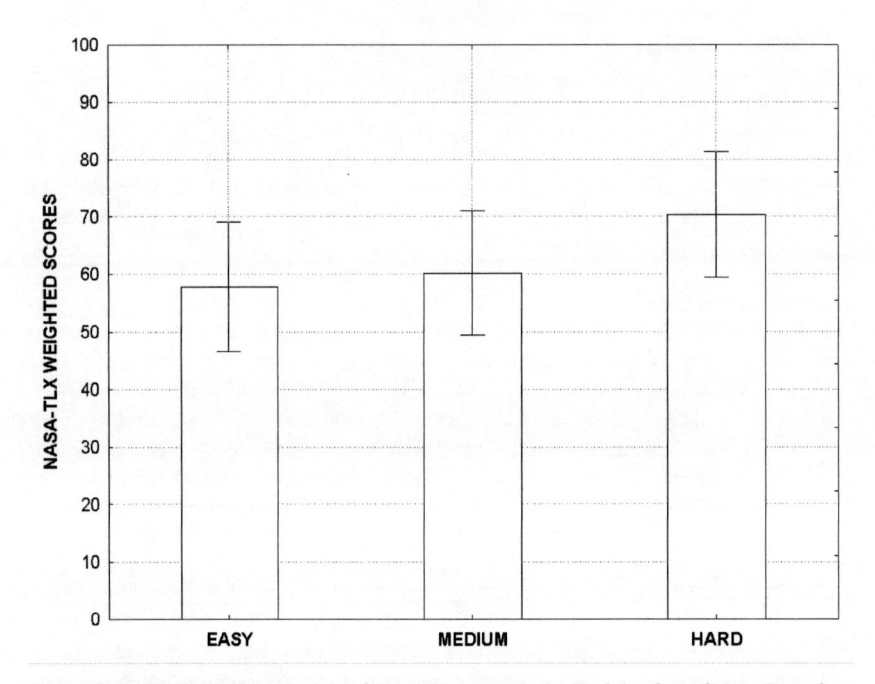

Figure 3. NASA-TLX values (weighted scores) separately for Task load condition. Error bars denote 0.95 confidence intervals

Secondary task performance
Counting errors (deviation from the actual number of target trials) were used as dependent variable in a repeated measure ANOVA using Task load (Easy vs. Medium vs. Hard) as repeated factor. Results showed no significant effect of Task load ($p>0.05$).

Nearest Neighbour Index
As suggested elsewhere (Di Nocera et al., in press), the NNI was computed on epochs of 1 minute for each participant. This strategy is necessary because the index evolves over time. NNI fluctuations over time are shown in Figure 4. Averaged NNI values were used as dependent variable in a repeated measures ANOVA design using Task load (Easy vs. Medium vs. Hard) as repeated factor. Results showed a main effect of Task load ($F_{(2,18)} = 4.22$, $p<0.05$). Duncan post-hoc testing showed that the hard condition was significantly different from the other two ($p<0.05$).

Event-Related Brain Potentials
The difference between N2-P3 amplitudes to standard and target stimuli were used as dependent variables in an ANOVA design Task load (Easy vs. Medium vs. Hard) x Site (Fz vs. Cz vs. Pz). Results showed a main effect of Task load ($F_{(2,18)}=4.40$, $p<0.05$). Post-hoc Duncan testing showed that only the difference between the "Hard" task load condition and the other two was significant ($p<0.05$).

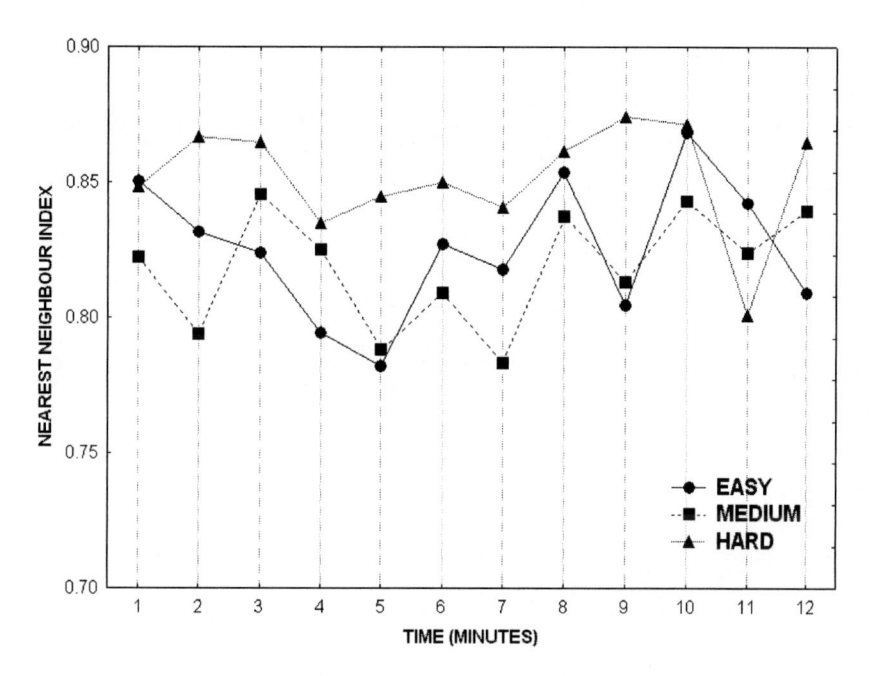

Figure 4. Variation in time (minutes) of the NNI separately for Task load condition.

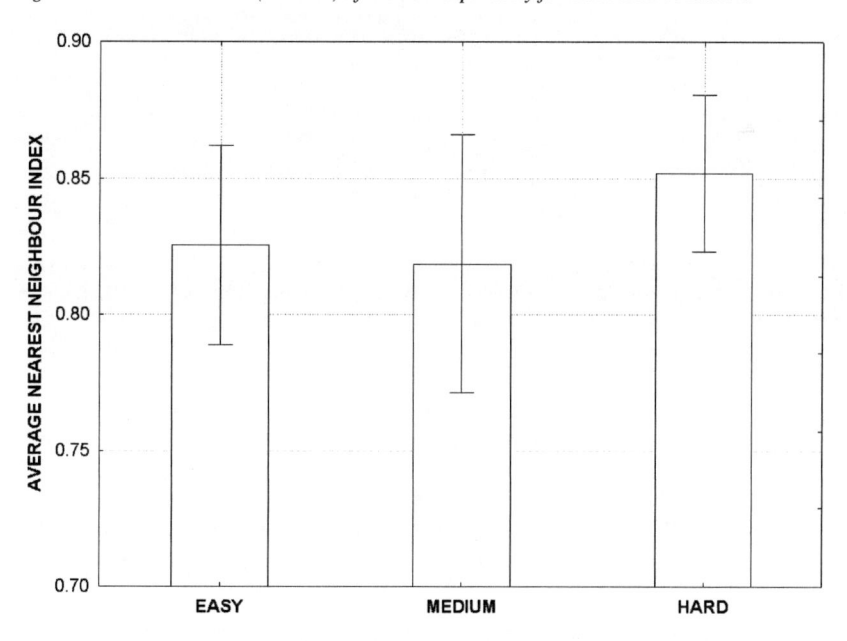

Figure 5. Average NNI separately for Task load condition. Error bars denote 0.95 confidence intervals

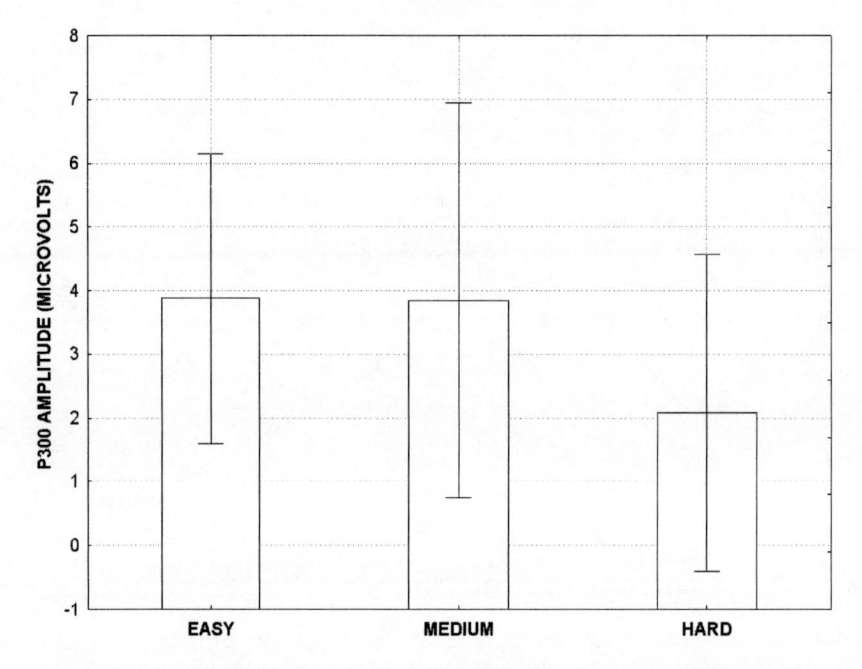

Figure 6. P300 amplitudes by Task load. Only the difference between the "Hard" task load con-dition and the other two was significant. Error bars denote 0.95 confidence intervals

Discussion and conclusions

This study represented a first attempt to assess the validity of the dispersion of eye fixations as an indicator of mental workload. Two studies (Di Nocera et al., 2006; Di Nocera et al., in press) had reported the usefulness of the NNI, but its validity was not specifically assessed. The strategy adopted here was that of using multiple measures in order to estimate the concurrent validity of the index. Of course this study cannot contribute to the definition of which aspect of mental workload these measures contribute to assess, though the task load manipulation was obtained by changing the temporal demand (block falling speed). Nevertheless, consistent results were found across the three measures. The most difficult condition was found to generate significantly different values in the NASA-TLX ratings, in the P300 amplitude, and in the NNI values. However, all measures failed to show differences between the easiest and the intermediate task load conditions. This might be due to two reasons. The first is the great variability affecting the data (mostly in the intermediate condition), which is probably due to the small sample size. Indeed, the three conditions were selected from a pilot study in which twenty participants had rated their subjective workload, whereas in this case only ten people participated in the experiment. The second reason might be a lack of perceivable difference between the easiest and the intermediate conditions. In fact, in the pilot study ten levels of difficulty were administered, and participants might have been able to experience the entire spectrum of the imposed workload, generating fine-grained assessments. Contrarily, in the experiment reported above, participants only experienced three levels of difficulty, making it hard to generate accurate estimates. This effect is known as "context effect" and has been studied experimentally by Colle & Reid (1998) who demonstrated that subjective estimates of mental workload are biased when participants cannot experience the full range of task difficulty. This explanation may be quite convincing for the subjective measure. However, also the ocular strategy and the brain activity showed the same pattern. Can context effect account for those measures too? This is difficult to demonstrate post-hoc, and one should expect to observe changes in perceived workload due to the differential allocation of mental resources. Nevertheless, one could also consider the possibility that perceived workload affects the amount of resources actively allocated by participants during the execution of a task. After all, the operator's perceptions are always reported to be an important factor in the definition of mental workload as a multidimensional construct.

However, the most noticeable result of this study was that all measures showed sensitivity in the same task load conditions. This supports the validity of the proposed index as a measure of mental workload. The main advantage of using the ocular measure (over ERPs and subjective measures) is that it allows to compute the index for epochs of one minute, making the NNI a good candidate measure for triggering some automated systems (see Di Nocera et al., 2003) adaptively.

Acknowledgments

This work was supported by the European Office of Aerospace Research and Development, United States Air Force Office of Scientific Research, grant #FA8655-05-1-3021.

References

Annett, J. (2002). Subjective rating scales: science or art? *Ergonomics, 45*, 966-987.

Baldwin, C.L. (2003). Neuroergonomics of mental workload: New insights from the convergence of brain and behaviour in ergonomics research. *Theoretical Issues in Ergonomics Science, 4*, 132-141.

Clark, P.J., & Evans F.C. (1954). Distance to nearest neighbor as a measure of spatial relationships in populations. *Ecology, 35*, 445-453.

Colle, H.A., & Reid, G.B. (1998). Context effects in subjective mental workload ratings. *Human Factors, 40*, 591-600.

Di Nocera, F. (2003). On Reliability and Stability of Psychophysiological Indicators for Assessing Operator Functional States. In G.R.J. Hockey, A.W.K. Gaillard, and O. Burov (Eds.), *Operator Functional State: The Assessment and Prediction of Human Performance Degradation in Complex Tasks* (pp. 162-173). Amsterdam, The Netherlands: IOS Press.

Di Nocera, F., Camilli, M., & Terenzi, M. (in press). A random glance to the flight deck: pilot's scanning strategies and the real-time assessment of mental workload. *Journal of Cognitive Engineering and Decision Making*.

Di Nocera, F., Terenzi, M., & Camilli, M. (2006). Another look at scanpath: distance to nearest neighbour as a measure of mental workload. In D. de Waard, K.A. Brookhuis, and A. Toffetti (Eds.), *Developments in Human Factors in Transportation, Design, and Evaluation* (pp. 295-303). Maastricht, The Netherlands: Shaker Publishing.

Di Nocera F., Lorenz, B., Tattersall, A., & Parasuraman, R. (2003). New Possibilities for Adaptive Automation and Work Design. In G.R.J. Hockey, A.W.K. Gaillard, and O. Burov (Eds.), Operator Functional State: The Assessment and Prediction of Human Performance Degradation in Complex Tasks (pp. 162-173). Amsterdam, The Netherlands: IOS Press.

Ellis, S.R. & Smith, J.D. (1985). Patterns of statistical dependency in visual scanning. In R. Groner, G.W. McConkie, and C. Menz (Eds.), *Eye movements and human information processing* (pp. 221-238). Amsterdam, The Netherlands: Elsevier.

Harris, R.L., Glover, B.L., & Spady, A.A. (1986). *Analytic techniques of pilot scanning behavior and their application* (NASA Technical Report 2525). Hampton, VA, USA: Langley Research Center.

Hart, S.G., & Staveland, L.E. (1988). Development of a multi-dimensional workload rating scale: Results of empirical and theoretical research. In P.A. Hancock & N. Meshkati (Eds.), *Human Mental Workload* (pp. 139-183). Amsterdam, The Netherlands: Elsevier.

Hilburn, B., Jorna, P.G., Byrne, E.A., & Parasuraman, R. (1997). The effect of adaptive air traffic control (ATC) decision aiding on controller mental workload. In M. Mouloua and J. Koonce (Eds.), *Human-Automation Interaction: Research and Practice* (pp. 84-91). Mahwah, NJ, USA: Erlbaum Associates.

Israel, J.B., Wickens, C.D., Chesney, G.L., & Donchin, E. (1980b). The event-related potential as an index of display monitoring workload. *Human Factors*, 22, 212-224.

Kramer, A.F. (1991). Physiological Metrics of Mental Workload: A Review of Recent Progress. In D.L. Damos (Ed.), *Multiple-Task Performance* (pp. 279-328). London, UK: Taylor and Francis.

Kruizinga, A., Mulder, B., & de Waard, D. (2006). Eye scan patterns in a simulated ambulance dispatcher's task. In D. de Waard, K.A. Brookhuis, and A. Toffetti (Eds.), *Developments in Human Factors in Transportation, Design, and Evaluation*. (pp. 305-317). Maastricht, the Netherlands: Shaker Publishing.

McCarley, J.S., & Kramer, A.F. (2007). Eye movements as a window on perception and cognition. In R. Parasuraman & M. Rizzo (Eds.), *Neuroergonomics. The Brain at Work* (pp. 95-112). New York, USA: Oxford University Press.

Nikolic, M.I., Orr, J., & Sarter, N.B. (2001). The effects of display context on the effectiveness of visual onsets for attention capture. In *Proceedings of the IEEE/AIAA 20th Digital Avionics Systems Conference (DASC)*, vol. 1, pp. 5A3/1-5A3/7. Madison, WI, USA: Omnipress

Parasuraman, R., & Caggiano, D. (2002). Mental workload. In V.S. Ramachandran (Ed.), *Encyclopedia of the Human Brain* (vol. 3, pp. 17-27). San Diego, USA: Academic Press.

Ponsoda, V., Scott, D., & Findlay, J.M. (1995). A probability vector and transition matrix analysis of eye movements during visual search. *Acta Psychologica, 88*, 167-185.

Recarte, M. A., & Nunes, L.M. (2000). Effects of verbal and spatial-imagery task on eye fixations while driving. *Journal of Experimental Psychology: Applied, 6*, 31–43.

Recarte, M.A., & Nunes, L.M. (2003). Mental Workload While Driving: Effects on Visual Search, Discrimination, and Decision Making. *Journal of Experimental Psychology: Applied, 9*, 119-137.

Tole, J.R., Stephens, A.T., Vivaudou, M., Eprath, A., & Young, L.R. (1983*). Visual scanning behavior and pilot workload* (NASA Contractor Report 3717). Hampton (VA), USA: NASA Langley Research Center.

Trimmel, M., & Huber R., (1998). After-effects of human-computer interaction indicated by P300 of the event-related brain potential. *Ergonomics, 41*, 649-655.

Enhanced decision support for train drivers: "Driving a train by the seat of your pants"

Anjum Naweed, Richard Bye, & Bob Hockey
The University of Sheffield
Sheffield, UK

Abstract

Train drivers in the UK travel at speeds of up to 125 mph (200 km/h). At such speeds it takes over a mile for the train to stop so drivers must initiate speed control actions long before the target comes into view. Safe and efficient performance is achieved via a reliance on the driver's memory of the infrastructure and terrain, known as route knowledge. Much work has been undertaken to provide more information to support route knowledge so that the driver can operate efficiently at levels well below the limits of human performance, even in degraded conditions. Examples include in-cab signalling systems and the European Rail Traffic Management System (ERTMS) interface, designed to facilitate interoperability throughout Europe. The standardisation of in-cab interfaces has clear advantages; but the resulting 'all-in-one' design may provide insufficient support to suite the natural environments and driver preferences in each country. This paper used cognitive task analysis and cognitive field research methods to understand the requirement of UK train driving tasks and explore the potential impact of ERTMS information on driver decision making. The results recognise several types of driving task in existence on the domestic network and consider the suitability of ERTMS integration into the country.

Scope and introduction

The Railway Gazette's recent Speed Survey tables (2005), record the British InterCity 225 High-Speed Train (HST) as the 8th fastest train in the world (see Table 1). The fastest entry time for this train highlights a start-to-stop journey covering a distance of 77.8 miles (125 km) from Stevenage to Grantham, travelling at an average speed of 112 mph (181 km/h). The train itself is easily capable of exceeding the stipulated track limits of 125 mph (200 km/h), and in practise, drivers regularly attain these sorts of speeds in an effort to optimise the journey, adhere to scheduled times and generally bring about greater efficiency to the task.

In trying to define a 'High-Speed Train,' the industry appears to encounter a number of obstacles. Whilst the ability to achieve/exceed a particular speed provides a clear basis for a set of criteria, a parallel school of thought considers the quality of the service of trains running at lower speeds but with specific features, e.g. tilting

In D. de Waard, G.R.J. Hockey, P. Nickel, and K.A. Brookhuis (Eds.) (2007), *Human Factors Issues in Complex System Performance* (pp. 131 - 144). Maastricht, the Netherlands: Shaker Publishing.

mechanisms, as important competitors for the coveted title. The definition for a HST provided by the International Union of Railways (UIC, 2006) therefore indicates no single definition of the term, but instead a combination of elements - most notably operating practices and new or upgraded track and rolling stock that define such high-speed rail operations. This denotes a degree of international variability to the top speeds a train must attain in order to qualify as 'high-speed', typically ranging from 100 mph (160 km/h) to over 185 mph (300 km/h). Train drivers apply the relevant throttle and braking controls in order to drive at these speeds, but to optimise the navigation of the train safely and efficiently, the task traditionally involves a reliance on their knowledge of the infrastructure, trackside signals, familiar landmarks and general geography around them. Train drivers have to rely on this very specific and expert *route knowledge* to adjust to movement authority, speed limits, temporary restrictions, and so on. However, as a human cognitive dynamic, route knowledge is a concept sensitive to outside influences.

Table 1. World Train Speed Survey Tables – 2005

	Country	Train	Speed - km/h Average	Top
1	France	Train à Grande Vitesse (TGV)	263	320
2	Japan	Shinkansen	262	300
3	International	Thalys Soleil	242	320
4	Germany	InterCityExpress (ICE)	234	300
5	Spain	Alta Velocidad Española (AVE)	205	300
6	Sweden	X2000	191	200
7	South Korea	Korea Train Express (KTX)	190	300
8	**United Kingdom**	**InterCity 225 HST**	**181**	**200**
9	Italy	Eurostar	167	250
10	USA	Acela Express	165	240

A general search of literature in the both rail industry and human factors discipline, reveals a large body of work exploring human susceptibility to performance degrading threat factors such as fatigue and mental workload. The Speed Survey table above highlights the need to investigate human performance against these kinds of human threat factors. The additional variable of driving at faster speeds is arguably of great concern as it not only lowers the reaction time required for implementing a throttle change, but also increases the processing demand per unit time on the driver (Einhorn, Sheridan, & Multer, 2005), including a degraded awareness of the train's position and colour aspect of trackside signals. Train manufacturers recognise this issue to some extent as most HSTs now also incorporate in-cab signalling instruments in the driver-cab interface, though the principal explanation for this is arguably more practical – the trains are simply much too fast for drivers to react to or indeed *see* upcoming trackside signals in time. The importance therefore of exploring the extent to which faster rail may affect driver workload and fatigue is self-evident.

The majority of the HSTs in the survey's top ten, including the Italian Eurostar ranked 9th in the table, possess in-cab signalling. It may therefore come as a surprise to learn that British HSTs, currently contain no in-cab signalling devices or indeed *any* in-cab equipment that would support decision-making beyond simple train state indicators (e.g. a speedometer). This perceived imbalance in the use of available technologies is of particular concern as the increased demand for performance in British rail service delivery has resulted in an increased speed of operations. Passenger trains now generally aim to operate at the maximum speed the rail infrastructure will allow within the boundaries of safety.

Whilst the introduction of automated train protection devices has helped shape British rail travel in into a safe and dynamic system, much can still be done to aid in train driving. The rail industry has indeed recognised the limitations posed by the current, and comparatively antiquated driver-cab interface, and plans to address them by piloting a European Initiative called the European Railway Traffic Managing System[*] (ERTMS) on the Cambrian Line in Wales in 2008 (Network Rail, 2006). ERTMS as a train control and management solution was first conceived in the early 1990's, and eventually translated into the end product of a specification written in 1996 in response to the EU Council Directive (96/48/EC, EU, 1996) on the interoperability of the trans-European high-speed rail system. The European Union confirms the existence of more than 20 heterogeneous signalling and speed control systems operating in Europe, with at least 14 incompatible safety systems. In short, the EU considers this as a barrier to trade and interoperability, and a hindrance to cost-efficiency, quality improvements and growths in the economy in general.

The driver-cab interface proponent of ERTMS, called the European Train Control System Driver-Machine-Interface (ETCS DMI), contains some enhanced display features, including accurate track information, infrastructure details and a level of in-cab signal preview that is unprecedented in UK rail travel. Should the system be successfully implemented nationwide, it has the potential to revolutionise the industry and support driver route knowledge, especially in degraded conditions. However, as an initiative designed to primarily establish uniformity in international signalling policies, there is a concern that an 'all-in-one' design philosophy may provide insufficient support to suit particular natural environments, driver preferences and potentially different driving tasks. The design intention behind the initiative seems to have narrowed its focus to interoperability alone, rather than appraise the original reasons behind the acculturated characteristics of each signalling standard. Rail research has moved forward tremendously in recent years, and with the developmental programme for ERTMS commencing over 15 years ago, there is also the concern that the features may be outdated in consideration of subsequent research. This issue is somewhat reinforced by the Strategic Rail Authority announcing a realistic target date for ERTMS stretching into the 2020s (SRA, 2005), at least 10 years after the deadline laid down following the Paddington rail crash.

The current deadline may however be reinterpreted as the ideal opportunity to develop a more informed model of the driver-cab interface, study the British train driving task from first principles, consider the surrounding environment and identify

---

[*] Information accessible at http://www.ertms.com/

what the information needs of the train driver *really* are at the sharp end. There is little doubt that ERTMS would be of tremendous benefit to the UK rail industry, but its suitability on an infrastructure very different to that in other European countries should be considered, along with the number of different driving tasks that may be currently in use. This paper sets out to explore these contentions, via Cognitive Task Analysis techniques such as the critical incident method (Klein, Calderwood, & MacGregor, 1989) and cognitive field research methods designed to elicit expert knowledge. Finally, it also considers whether driver information needs stretch beyond those which the ETCS DMI can cater for.

Data collection

Overview

It is difficult for researchers to unwrap the complexity of the UK rail system because decisions, plans and actions are layered within the tasks and subtasks deeply embedded within goal-directed work activities. To overcome such difficulties and investigate the fundamental needs of driver Subject Matter Experts (SMEs), a novel suite of cognitive field research methods was employed to capture the requisite detail of rail operations in which work is complex, dynamic, unpredictable and distributed in space and time.

Methods

Table 2 provides a brief overview of some core methods used in the investigations. The power of the approach lays in the application of the techniques coordinated as an iterative suite of methods where emergent findings informed subsequent analysis. The most fundamental objective driving this approach was to investigate what could be done – independent of the technical and organisational constraints imposed by existing systems.

Participants

A great number of interviews were conducted with driving SMEs including professional train drivers, Operations Managers and Train Crew Managers (see Table 3), and ranged in length from 30 minutes to 2 hours depending on the operational constraints of the particular Train Operating Company (TOC) and Freight Operating Company (FOC). Interviews were conducted in order to provide a supplementary commentary to the observations and to deepen understanding. The structured interviews were all recorded following signed consent and involved capturing individual career histories and demographic information before progressing further. A significant number of train driver interviews were conducted following live cab rides in the presence of a Driver Trainer Manager.

Table 2. Overview of research methods used

Method	Description	Notes
Documentation Analysis	Early phase Bootstrapping	Review of SOP and other documentation. Indispensable stage for domain familiarisation
Ethnographic Field Observations	Observational	Structured techniques to understand the work through direct observation
SME Work Shadowing	Unstructured Interview	Close observations and informal discussions with SMEs during operations
Task Diagram	Structured Interview	To capture and understand the core elements of work
Knowledge Audit	Structured Interview	Identification of domain expertise based on probes of experienced events
Simulation Interview	Structured Interview	Analysis of decision making processes for a fictional scenario
Recent Case Walkthrough	Structured Interview	Precursor to Critical Decision Method to inform more detailed analysis
Critical Decision Method	Structured Interview	Intensive interview technique to capture detailed information about past events
Verbal Protocol Analysis	Real time analysis	Analysis of event transcripts in which operators provide a live verbal commentary
Concept Mapping	Structured Interview/ workshop	Iterative technique where the analyst structures an SMEs account of the core concepts for particular domains or operations
Verification Workshop	Discussion forum	Presentation and revision of findings with SMEs

Table 3. Summary of site visits for familiarisation and data capture

Service Type	Locations	SMEs	Methods
TOC	York London Doncaster Leeds	Driver Driver Trainer Managers Train Crew Manager Train Dispatchers	Direct Observations Cab Ride x 3 (25 hours) Informal Interview (x5) Structured Interview (x5)
FOC	Sheffield Doncaster Livingstone (Scotland)	Operations Manager Driver Driver Trainer Managers Trainee Drivers Engineering Supervisor PICOP	Direct Observations Informal Interview (x6) Structured Interview (x7) Cab Ride
Rail Consultancy	York Livingstone	Human Factors Consultant	Informal Interview (x1) Structured Interview (x2)

Analysis of data

The analysis was structured through the development of an abstraction hierarchy, adapting constructs and techniques from Cognitive Work Analysis (CWA; Vicente, 1999; Rasmussen, Pejtersen, & Goodstein, 1994) to develop a veridical representation of the cognitive work required by driving. The model was sufficiently flexible to adjust the scale and focus in the evaluation of rail system interactions, and provided a granular picture at different levels of analysis. The structure of the domain decomposition enabled the coordination of individual research elements so that the analyses in the driving task could be assimilated. This was an important feature and reflected the influence of goals and constraints that shape work in rail operations, permeating both vertically and horizontally to affect decisions between and within levels of the hierarchy. Figure 1 illustrates how the domain was decomposed to facilitate analysis at different system levels.

Domain Decomposition

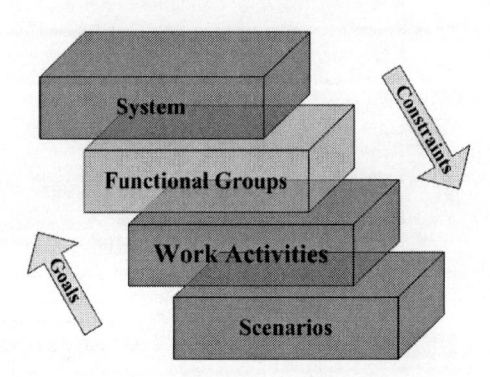

Figure 1. Decomposition of the rail domain and basis for subsequent distributed cognitive model

Results & discussion

The introduction set up a methodology which embarked on a programme to learn and recognise train driver information needs at both the blunt and sharp ends of the domain. The results help to clarify those issues most pertinent to the aims of the train driving task, the existence of different subtasks, and the prospective suitability of ERTMS deployment in the UK. The overall aim was to identify the key elements that may be incorporated into an enhanced display to aid driving. The following discussion is based on the results of the data collection efforts and is supported with the use of selected narratives, which have been extracted from the data to illustrate the core issues.

The analysis of the data took different forms and resulted in the production of diagrams, concept and process maps, interview transcripts and other artefacts that were used to both deepen and document understanding. The products of the analysis were time consuming to generate but yielded much information that was used to populate the representation of cognitive work in rail operations.

Track profile and route knowledge

The drivers considered an awareness of the track profile to be of the utmost importance when driving a train. As a key proponent of route knowledge, they consistently commented upon the track's curvature and gradient, reflecting on how instrumental it was to the role. Some drivers grouped the importance of this information in the same category as signal preview and asserted how, in an ideal world, it would be a given feature on an integrated train display;

> "You'd need to know well in advance your signals, your speeds and your stopping places, your gradients, things like that."

> "A driver should know things like gradients etc, but maybe something like knowing the gradient profile, where's he stood or travelling at that moment, that may assist him."

Awareness of the track profile features heavily in driver route knowledge acquisition programmes, mainly as a result of the innumerable variations to train handling characteristics that the curvature and gradient of the line can cause. The ability to utilise this information into the driving task effectively is also often attributed to high levels of skill as highlighted in the following quotation;

> "If you go on a rising gradient or a falling gradient, sometimes when you get to the top of a falling gradient you'll be shutting power off, and the driver will know this well before he gets to his place."

Incorporating this information into the driver-cab interface would obviously aid the driver enormously, particularly in situations requiring faster decision-making. The ETCS DMI contains many important track features in its interface, such as level crossings, stations and so on that would help the driver localise their train. It also contains information related to the track's gradient but seems to have omitted information related to the curvature. The drivers generally grouped these characteristics together, which implies both curvature and gradient play an executive role in the task. In some ways the location, radius, cant and length of rail or transition curves are easier to detect in the upcoming field of view, and therefore less important than the gradient. However, traversing the curved rails which characterise railways in the UK, whilst encountering dense foliage at high-speed could reduce efficiency in the task, particularly in degraded conditions;

> "Stations that are usually overrunning are usually on falling gradients, tucked around bends and suffer from low adhesion."

A display afforded with these features would be a tremendous aid from the perspective of interoperability, as continental drivers may potentially traverse differing natural environments daily. The human factors in the driving task clearly highlight the ease with which driving skill can be comprised, as shown in the following statements:

> "It's amazing a driver could be driving along a route for years and doesn't realise the gradient's falling - or rising, not until somebody tells him."

> "The railway can be deceiving."

> "When you're going into Dewsbury, it looks like it's going up but its dropping."

"Visually you think you're rising but you're actually falling, and it is an important part of driving because if you approach a station on a rising gradient you find that you don't need as much braking, you need less braking, whereas if you're doing it the other way around you need more braking."

The quote below shows what the driver's generally agree upon at most important aspects of route knowledge:

"Gradients, curvature of the line, signals, speeds, the weight of his train, speed of his train."

Different train driving tasks

The quote immediately preceding this section highlights another very important element to the train driving task, and one which appears to play a pivotal role distinguishing between different types of train driving – the train's weight. The interviews uncovered differences in the weight of passenger and freight operated trains and the associated handling characteristics as key players within this theme. When questioned about the main differences between freight and passenger train operation, the driving technique and the weight of the train was frequently mentioned:

"[In] freight trains you're supposed to run it in a 'goods mode' as opposed to a 'passenger mode' – so if you drop DSD or something like that the brake doesn't go straight on, it's a more gradual application and gradual release."

"Most passenger trains would drive roughly the same day in and day out because of the unit type and the formation that they're made of, but because with our [Freight trains] they are a little bit different."

"Varying trains. Varying lengths, weights. It all comes into it. Being able to drive a heavy train for one part of your shift and a light train for another."

"Every day is different. You can have different weight of train on, different length of train on."

These excerpts highlight the extent to which passenger and freight operations differ. Fluctuations in weight on most passenger trains are regulated by a device which redistributes air to the suspension and brake cylinders as the load increases. The resulting driving experience does not differ noticeably. Freight trains on the other hand vary enormously in load type, length and weight. It is a daily event for individual freight drivers to haul significantly varying loads on a round trip. The drivers used their own experiences to convey the importance of these distinctions:

"I'm not being biased because I've driven both, I've driven Electrics, Diesels, Passengers and Freight trains, and every train driver's skilled, but I would say Freight train driver's are more skilled than Passenger train drivers."

"Stress on the couplings yes, for different trains, but for us no, we don't need that. So it would have to be tailored for different types of trains. With heavy freight trains if you get an inexperienced driver there, and creates too much stress on the couplings that's when you get trains breaking loose which often happens, but you wouldn't want this on a passenger train like ours."

These quotes indicate the kind of enhanced information that could aid a freight train driver. Train separations or derailments resulting from excessive stress on the couplings are a danger to the driver and other rails users, as well as costly to the freight operator. Considering this, the potential benefits that provision of information such as the aerodynamics of train buffering or coupling stress could provide are very meritorious. This type of information is generally omitted from displays, and not featured within the ETCS display. The example below further illustrates the differences in the task:

"Freight trains stop more frequently, so they have a better use of the brake, the brakes are not as sharp as a passenger train, a passenger train's brakes will go on quicker and come off quicker, whereas a freight train go on a lot slower obviously because there's the weight of the train, and they'll come off a lot slower as well."

The third easily distinguishable component of the train driving task can be seen in yard work which includes marshalling and shunting of trains, and the operation of a train in engineering worksites as illustrated in the quotes below;

"When you're on an engineering worksite, you're always aware, that there are contractors working on or about the line."

"There is a lot more to be aware of with regard to engineering worksites. Mainly because we know that to some degree that some of the contractors, are hired hands who don't understand the dangers of working on or about the line. A 127 ton engine at ½ mph will kill you."

The train driver's duties in these tasks are generally a lot less predictable and coordinated through outside authorities. The safety issue here becomes not one of speed, but rather one of optimum communication and slow, intricate, precise movement.

In-cab signalling and interoperability

As is the expected and observed case, the drivers all supported the importance of signal preview information for safe and efficient train driving. The current British trackside signalling system facilitates preview of the next upcoming signal, but the drivers all thought that more is often much better on the grounds that it allows the driver the ability to plan the journey ahead:

> "In foggy conditions and things like that, it would be nice to have what his next signal's displaying in front of him, even the next one or two, just so that he's got some idea."

One Driver Train Manager maintained "Someone keeping time in foggy conditions is the sign of a good driver." This credits the in-cab signalling perspective enormously in providing drivers in the UK with information above and beyond what they are currently familiar with. The ETCS DMI excels in this respect, and as an initiative containing an excellent resolution of upcoming signals, it satisfies the most basic component of enhanced interface design. By displaying signal preview, in-cab signalling systems may also alleviate the train driver's mental workload when running at high-speed by increasing their awareness of the environment around them, and allowing greater foresight for time-keeping strategies. When asked about an important feature an in-cab display should contain to help with the task, the drivers again asserted the importance of signal preview:

> "Well you'd have to have some kind of system that told you the line speeds that you were travelling over, the line speeds coming up, it would have to tell you things like if there is signalling."

> "Driver's are always planning ahead, so you'd have to know at least three. Your mind's always got to think ahead, so you'd have to be thinking three miles ahead."

However, the drivers also brought up examples of potential issues when asked about continental interoperability:

> "One of the problems is we have a different kind of railway to where that does work efficiently."

> "Even though [the driver's] allowed to do 40 mph, they slow the speed of the train down to 30, so they can take into account that type of line, you know the curvature and the gradient and all that."

The latter quote is important in that it distinguishes track characteristics that vary internationally, as a result of both the existing infrastructure and constraints placed by the natural environments. Sweden and the UK for example are two European countries with railways characterised by curved rails. Both countries have addressed this property by utilising trains possessing tilt-type technology in order to compensate for the varying forces and to bring about a more comfortable journey at high speed. Whilst interoperability may be less of an issue for British rail travel, train drivers navigating across a multitude of adjoining countries cannot expect the ETCS DMI as an all inclusive solution to route knowledge acquisition.

> "A lot of people say you drive a train by the seat of your pants..."

Skilful train operation has traditionally evolved from the driver's ability to attune their senses to fluctuating train characteristics such as the weight of the train and track adhesion conditions - what some Driver Train Managers affectionately dubbed as 'Dining Room Drivers.' These driving parameters are generally agreed upon as an important distinction for driving skill, where the 'feel' of the train is most important.

Conclusions

Though the article set out to investigate information needs in the context of high-speed trains, it is apparent that enhanced interface features, such as that of signal preview, can benefit every type of train driving strategy, and is a particular necessity on curved railways. Consequently, the results on a whole imply that the number of different train tasks in existence on UK rail, vary enough to warrant different levels of information for aiding the driver. The question is therefore not whether the ETCS DMI proponent of the European management initiative can fulfil driver information needs in the UK, but rather whether an all-in-one integrated solution is the right way to go about it, without introducing any redundancies or unnecessary clutter.

This study also infers the importance of a number of display features absent from the ETCS DMI. Though this is more of a secondary issue, it necessitates some further clarification as to why British train drivers would deem these features useful. The curvature of the track for example is something that is generally expressed in the ETCS locally allowed speed display, and an integration of this data within ETCS has been selectively omitted at some stage of the conceptual or developmental process. Nevertheless, the drivers in this study insist upon a tangible display of this information, even when the influence of a curve is itself expressed through the permitted speed signage on the railway. It may be the case that this information need is simply a peculiarity to British train drivers, and would in reality be redundant on a display. Alternatively, it may be the case that the presentation of this information is a sort of visual proprioceptory indicator, and part of situation awareness, helping the drivers know where they are. Whatever the case may be, further research is required to clarify its uses.

The issues unveiled in this study are important enough to investigate further at research level, not with a view to create a new display prototype or replace the ETCS DMI, but perhaps design a comprehensive research tool that can consider the cost-benefit ratio of display features in UK rail for a future generation of trains.

Visualising new displays

In view of the results it seems appropriate to further differentiate train driving tasks, and explore the ways in which display variables can contribute to information needs. More importantly, it seems appropriate to discuss the alternative ways in which information can be presented in a specific enhanced display research *tool*. This section therefore represents a blank canvas of exploratory initiatives approaching the subject from a 'blue-skies' perspective as a playground housing ideas outside any practical or indeed, political constraints.

Signal preview & track profile

As previously stated, the issue of signal preview will benefit any train, but more so, those involved in high-speed operations. The pertinacious properties of Britain's Victorian railway network, coupled with the highly specific terrain, denote this feature of particular use. Drivers tend to require the gradient, curvature, speeds and signals as external sources of information. A display must therefore realise this information in an easily viewable and digestible form. Vertical displays like the ECTS DMI work very effectively by mapping the direction of movement with the direction in the display. However, research indicates that displaying this information horizontally need not compromise performance (Askey & Sheridan, 1996; Einhorn, Sheridan, & Multer, 2005) though mapping real-time corresponding information such as the gradient is more of an issue. The ETCS DMI has addressed this particular obstacle by weighting any incremental level increases or decreases in the form of a bar with a directional arrow and numerical value denoting any change. Figure 2 illustrates a simple mock-up of how the track structure, signalling and profile can be integrated horizontally in a way that compliments the different types of information. Representing any level differences in the form of a Z axis on a horizontal plane, may or may not be any more effective than the way it has been implemented in the ETCS DMI, but as a diagram on a blank canvas, it certainly is an alternative display variable that can be developed and explored further.

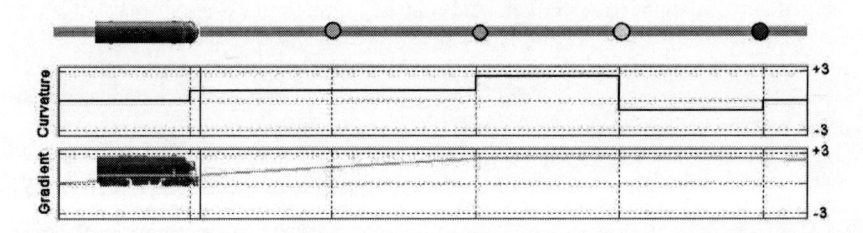

Figure 2. Horizontal display signal preview and track profile components. A colour image is available at http://extras.hfes-europe.org

Aerodynamics and train buffering

Figure 3 shows a mock-up detailing the train's aerodynamics, buffering and coupling stress information. This sort of information is readily available in some train simulators (Dorrian, Roach, Fletcher & Dawson, 2006) and imparts information that would be specifically useful to the operation of freight trains, or a train hauling weighty cargo distributed over a multitude of wagons.

Good freight driving skill usually appears to manifest itself in the executive ability to recognise when to implement the throttle and when to make advantageous use of track gradients. The latter is critical not only for fuel economy, but also for preventing undue stress on the couplings which must be stretched and compressed smoothly in order to prevent separation. The display of this information is supplementary to route knowledge and when used in simulators, invariably assists in transmitting the realism of the simulation. In practise, this information may be a useful aid not only for novices, but continental drivers where it would facilitate interoperability across neighbouring countries, varying terrains and different weather systems.

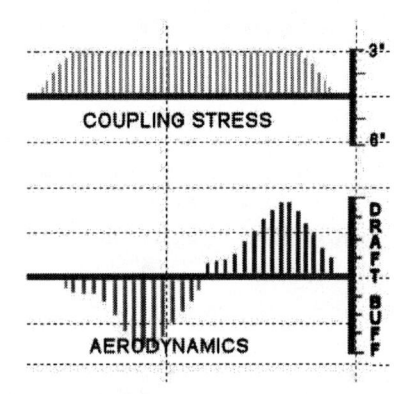

Figure 3. Train aerodynamics and buffering. A coulour image is available at http://extras.hfes-europe.org

Topographical structure and routing

The information shown in Figure 4 (modified from Einhorn, Sheridan, & Multer, 2005) depicts a display component with details of the top-down track topography including key wayside structures, immediate track layout and correct routing direction. Not dissimilar to navigation equipment in road vehicles, this type of information is more 'blue skies' than that which has already been suggested, and is rarely included in trains.

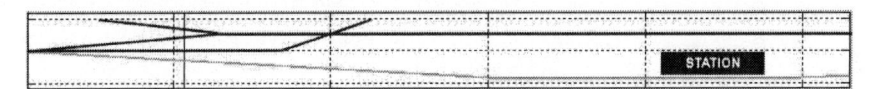

Figure 4. Track topography and routing components. A coulour image is available at http://extras.hfes-europe.org

In terms of information it would be of tremendous support to route knowledge and useful for virtually every driving task, especially if integrated with time-keeping information. Although there is no high-speed involved in the tasks, this display component would be very helpful to drivers engaged in operation on yards or engineering sites, imbuing them with a greater awareness of the environment around them due to high level of detail and intricacy the continually updating display would convey.

Of course these display variables and ideas are but skirting the surface of the potential features that could be investigated – in particular, the use of braking curves and optimal trajectories as enhanced features ubiquitous in the maritime sea navigation and aviation industries have already been implemented in rail research with promising results. The rail industry appears to be converging with next generation research initiatives at a time when there is a great deal to be excited about, but as a field involving a great deal of politics and sensitivities at both the sharp and blunt ends of the domain, psychological research in this area must aim to look at the advantages worth implementing, and consider the costs of doing so.

Acknowledgements

The work was funded by the EPSRC Rail Research UK and would not have been possible without the considerable support and assistance provided by colleagues and subject matter experts within a number of rail companies. We gratefully acknowledge the contribution of individuals from Atkins, ATOC, EWS Railways, First Engineering, GNER, Network Rail, Northern Rail, and RSSB.

References

Askey, S. & Sheridan, T. (1996). *Human Factors Phase II: Design and Evaluation of Decision Aids for Control of High-speed Trains: Experiments and Model Safety of High-speed Ground Transportation Systems.* (DOT/FRA/ORD-96-09). Cambridge, MA: John A. Volpe National Transportation Systems Center.

Dorrian, J., Roach, G., Fletcher, A., & Dawson, D. (2006). The effect of fatigue on train handling during speed restrictions. *Transportation Research Part F, 9*, 243-257.

European Union (1996). *The interoperability of the trans-European high-speed rail system* (96/48/EC of 23 July 1996 – 31996L0048). Retrieved November 1, 2006, from http://europa.eu/

Einhorn, J., Sheridan, T., & Multer, J. (2005). *Preview information in cab displays for high-speed locomotives: Human Factors in Railroad Operations.* (DOT/FRA/ORD-04/12). Cambridge, MA: John A. Volpe National Transportation Systems Center.

International Union of Railways (2006). *General definitions of high speed. Union Internationale des Chemins de fer.* Paris, France. Retrieved August 9, 2006, from http://www.uic.asso.fr/gv/article.php3?id_article=14

Klein G.A., Calderwood. R., & MacGregor D. (1989). Critical decision method for eliciting knowledge. *IEEE Transactions on Systems, Man and Cybernetics, 19*, 462-472

Network Rail (2006). European Rail Traffic Management System. London, UK Retrieved November 27, 2006, from http://www.networkrail.co.uk/aspx/3677.aspx#WhatDoingCambrian

Railway Gazette International (2005). World speed survey tables. Retrieved August 9, 2006, from http://www.railwaygazette.com/Articles/2005/11/01/1222/2005+World+Speed+Survey+tables.html

Rasmussen, J., Pejtersen, A.M., & Goodstein, L.P. (1994). *Cognitive systems engineering.* New York: Wiley.

Strategic Rail Authority (2005). *National ERTMS Programme Team* (2004/05 Progress Report). London, UK. Retrieved November 1, 2006, from http://www.dft.gov.uk

Vicente, K.J. (1999). Cognitive work analysis. Toward safe, productive, and healthy computer- based work. Mahwah, NJ, USA: Lawrence Erlbaum Associates.

Human reliability: analysis of procedure violations on traffic control of a light railway network

Pedro Ferreira
Network Rail, London
UK

Abstract

The purpose of this paper is to present a study that aimed to investigate the context in which violations of procedures took place, and to understand what resources were used by the traffic controllers to ensure the safety of the operation of a light railway network.

The methodology implemented consisted of two different phases. The first one was based on an ergonomic analysis of the traffic controller's job and their working context. Dispatchers were interviewed using a questionnaire for subjective assessment of working conditions, and video recordings were collected and scored to support debriefing interviews with subjects. The second phase consisted on the analysis of violations of operation and safety procedures, and the circumstances in which they occurred.

The methodology used, led to the identification of the major types of violations, as well as the unofficial strategies used by the dispatchers to cope with the unpredictability of controlling traffic. It was also established that the communication and cooperation between traffic controllers and their supervisors was a key element to ensure the reliability of this operation.

Introduction

The light railway sector in Portugal, has known a significant growth in recent years. On the one hand, this trend is motivated by an increasing quality demand on public transportation. On the other hand, when compared with heavy metro systems, tramway networks require a considerably lower infrastructural investment. However, the fast growth in the sector and its pursuit for higher safety and quality standards has brought profound job modifications for workers such as tramway drivers and traffic controllers (Wilson & Norris, 2005).

To ensure the necessary high standards of human resources reliability, working conditions must be improved and made suitable to a higher task complexity and increased cognitive job demands. Modern computer networks have made it possible to collect all the necessary information on a single system and control the majority of traffic control operations from a distance. In this environment, the dispatchers' tasks consist of information processing and decisions making that can have a critical impact on the safety of the whole operation. Like many other light rail networks in major European cities, the one in this study operates in close relation with motor vehicle traffic and pedestrians pathways such as road crossings or sidewalks. These characteristics do not only have an impact on the dispatchers' and drivers' job, but it also requires strict safety and operation procedures for traffic control activities.

With the purpose of providing health and safety guidelines, a project was developed by the Ergonomics Department of the Technical University of Lisbon, together with a company operating a tramway network in Portugal. This project was based on a thorough ergonomic job analysis and addressed more or less independently, tramway drivers and dispatchers of the traffic control centre. The traffic control study was followed by a study aiming to characterise human reliability through the assessment of the potential for the occurrence of violations to safety and operation procedures.

Aims

The study on tramway drivers will not be discussed here, although its outcome provided important insight over the dispatchers' job and working context.

The research on the occurrence of violations in traffic control was preceded by a first step that consisted of an ergonomic job analysis, which aimed in particular to assess mental workload and characterise stress and fatigue factors. This analysis was then followed by a second project phase that focused on the identification of procedure violations and the characterisation of the organisational and technical factors that contributed to those behaviours. The focus was to address behaviours outside the boundaries of safety and operation procedures, and to tease out the unofficial strategies used by dispatchers to overcome difficulties and insure the required safety standards. During the two different project phases, the following objectives were considered:

- Characterise the working context of traffic regulation;
- Identify risk factors as well as organisational and technical constraints contributing to an increase in mental workload and higher levels of stress and fatigue;
- Identify and characterise the occurrence of violations;
- Identify the environmental, organisational and technical factors that motivated deviant behaviours;
- Characterise the unofficial problem solving strategies used by dispatchers and assess their potential contribution for the improvement or degradation of the safety of the whole operation.

Methodology

Traffic control tasks are performed in dynamic and complex environments, under which workers must be able to perceive and understand multiple characteristics and anticipate events. This complexity is closely related to the significant unpredictability of events taking place on a rail network operating in an urban context. Thus, tasks are characterised by a constant need of information processing and decision making. Job analysis in a work context where activity consists almost exclusively of cognitive processes has proven often to be a difficult task, as very little can be observed that will allow a clear understanding of the work carried out and the constraints that it imposes on workers. Nevertheless, a methodological approach mainly based on behavioural observation was considered adequate, given the complexity of the tasks in question and the time frame available to carry out this analysis.

Questionnaire for subjective assessment of working conditions

The first analysis step was the development and application of a questionnaire to obtain an overall perception of working conditions. Although its main focus was the characterization of stress and fatigue symptoms, other issues like health and work time related matters were addressed as well. This questionnaire was applied as an interview (using the questionnaire as guide), so that particular remarks made by workers could be registered, as well as additional information on several work related issues.

Job analysis

After completing a consistent characterisation of all mental workload related aspects, a job analysis was carried out, with the aid of video recordings. A protocol for video sampling and analysis was defined based on the data previously collected. The following objectives were considered for this procedure:

- Register observable elements, such as the direction of the eyes, posture and other behavioural aspects;
- Register potential fatigue signs such as yawning or eye rubbing;
- Characterise all significantly different work periods and environments (day and night, the beginning and end of working shifts, normal and critical circulation conditions);
- Identify differences of work methods among dispatchers.

The considerable variability of the tasks performed, required the collection of continuous video records throughout a whole working shift. Four cameras were used that were connected to a multiplexer and a video recorder and provided images from the following elements:

- Workers' facial expressions;
- Workers' postures and movements;
- Working desk activities and manual activities (form filling and written records);
- General view of the control centre.

Due to the nature of the activities under observation, audio was also registered via a microphone placed over the main traffic control systems desk. The content of the communications between on duty dispatchers and drivers was considered fundamental to understand the decision making processes.

A chart was prepared to support debriefing interviews, based on relevant issues gathered during video observation. Basically, these interviews consisted on the interpretation of different observed behaviours, to understand the hidden aspects required by task performance. Subjects verbalized certain aspects of their behaviour and identified potential fatigue and stress causes, as well as factors contributing to a mental workload increase. These interviews also aimed to obtain an overview of the impact of fatigue and stress on dispatchers' performance.

Methodologies for the subjective assessment of mental workload

From all the known subjective methods for mental workload assessment, the NASA-TLX, developed by NASA (Hart & Staveland, 1988) is probably the one most used for the driving work context. Within the same scope, Pauzié and Pachiaudi (in Lenné *et al.*, 2004) developed the DALI (Driving Activity Load Index) method, adapting the NASA-TLX to the automotive driving context. This tool integrates a set of 6 factors for mental workload:

- Attention effort
- Visual demands
- Hearing demands
- Time pressure
- Interference
- Stressful situation

Each of these factors is assessed on a progressive scale of 1 to 6. Factors are then organized into 15 pairs, from which subjects are asked to select the more significant one. From the combination of these two step outcomes a corresponding level of mental workload.

Analysis of the occurrence of procedure violations

Violations consist of a deliberate deviation from the established rules, procedures or instructions (HSE, 1999). For traffic control, a failure to comply with procedures can jeopardise the safety of workers, clients or anyone who interacts with the network. The analysis carried out considered the following goals:

- Identify organisational factors that combined or isolated can increase the potential for the occurrence of violations within traffic control;
- Provide guidelines on priority issues and adequate course of action for improvement;
- Determine what processes are informally established among dispatchers and how these can impact safety.

The methodology used was developed by the Human Factors in Reliability Group (HFRG, 1995) and published by the Health & Safety Executive (HSE).

The first step should be the selection of procedures or rules to be submitted for analysis, after which, interviews are conducted with those who are responsible by the design of these procedures (management) and to those compelled to apply them (workers). Through this process, it is possible to characterise, not only, the companies' safety trends and main concerns, but also to compare different perspectives regarding safety culture. In a more objective manner, the selected procedures are then characterised through a set of 48 concise statements, which workers should score with 0 if they do not agree with the statement in question, and scores 1, 3 or 6 according to the degree in which they concur with it. The results of this classification are then imputed into a set of matrixes, which will output the final scores and the guidelines for intervention, according to 13 possible categories of measures as shown in Table 1.

Table 1. Categories of measures for intervention

A. Rules and procedures - objectives
B. Rules and procedures - application
C. Rules and procedures - training
D. Hazards and risks - training
E. Commitment to safety - workers
F. Commitment to safety - management
G. Supervising - control and detection
H. Supervising – supervising style
I. Modification in equipment design and productive area
J. Job design
K. Working conditions
L. Logistics support
M. Organisation

Results

To gain a better understanding of the analysis, it is necessary to briefly describe the working context of a Light Railway Traffic Controller.

The traffic control tasks and subtasks

In a dynamic and complex environment, the traffic control of a tramway network consists of performing multiple subtasks. These subtasks often require simultaneous attention while demanding considerable levels of awareness and vigilance. An efficient time management strategy becomes crucial for the performance of the following subtasks:

- Monitor the network's performance and if needed, carry out immediate corrective actions;
- Ensure the predicted transportation services to customers meets with the necessary quality standards ;
- Supervise the operation of all plant and equipment directly related to the network;

- Instruct drivers, and all other workers related to the network on the adequate course of action under all circumstances;
- Ensure that incident related information is recorded and can be made available to those whom might need it;
- In case of accident or incident, inform the proper emergency services.

During network operation, there are two controllers at the CCP (Central Command Post, the traffic control office). A third controller is on location at the network, who operates as an on site support for critical situations. This job organisation permits an efficient problem solving in traffic control.

Questionnaire for working conditions assessment

The total population of traffic controllers was interviewed, consisting at the time of 12 participants. All were male and their ages ranged between 24 and 43 years.

The noise levels at the CCP were one of the main reasons for complaints. Due to the large number of controlling tasks performed at the CCP, frequent audio alarms required the controllers' attention. In addition, there was a repeated coming and going of people from outside the CCP that significantly contributed noise distraction. Although these noise levels were found to be below the legal requirements, they clearly represented an important disturbance factor and an increase of mental workload, stress and fatigue.

Traffic control also depends upon effective communication. In fact, to oversee and manage the network operations, dispatchers must efficiently make decisions and promptly pass them on to those responsible for their implementation. This capability depends entirely on the telecommunication devices at the CCP. For this reason, controllers had severe criticism on these communication devices, especially with regard to the audio quality of the radio system on board each vehicle, which sometimes made it difficult to clearly pass through instructions to tramway drivers. Because of their impact on traffic control activities, communication difficulties and malfunctioning were considered one of the most stress inducing elements. Workers stated that whenever communications were down, they were powerless to pass instructions to on site co-operators.

The responsibilities of traffic controllers to the network operation, made it impossible for them to perform regular meal breaks and working schedules. It was established as normal and necessary to sometimes skip the lunch break in order to attend a critical event or emergency situation. In these instances, after recovering normal circulation conditions, they would have a light meal during a short break. Under these circumstances, it was noticed that workers were deprived of a fundamental resting period and that stress and fatigue indicators became more significant.

As previously mentioned, the constant need for attention and awareness were the main causes for high levels of stress and fatigue. The effects perceived by workers were a reduced ability of reasoning and, a delay in decision making.

Video analysis and debriefing interviews

This process included 22 hours of video records during two different working shifts. Eight dispatchers were filmed and three of them were debriefed, aiming to obtain a reasonable sample of different levels of experience.

This approach considered the following variations on operation mode:

- During the night when vehicles were retrieved from circulation and parking management was carried out, as well as vehicle maintenance and cleaning;
- Dawn when circulation began with the replacement of vehicles in circulation;
- A period before noon and before afternoon rush hour, when circulation assumed normal standards;

The debriefing interviews were based on a set of hypotheses and questions raised during video analysis. Thus, the interviews would either confirm or refute these hypotheses. They can be summed up as follows:

- Under more demanding circumstances, are there matters that are of less concern or have a lower priority that can be delayed or suppressed?
- What is the role of informal job strategies within the operation?
- How important is job experience?
- What is the importance of cooperation between both on duty controllers for the efficiency of the operation?

According to the respondents, traffic regulation relies on the definition and constant reassessment of priorities. Inevitably, when faced with more pressing matters the lower priority issues are postponed or might not even be perceived.

Regarding stress and fatigue effects, controllers associated them more with bad humour and aggravating moods during tense situations, rather than the usual yawning and stretching physical behaviours, which were singly associated with undemanding and monotonous situations.

Job experience was considered a fundamental component for an efficient traffic controlling. Experience outcomes from the application of procedures as they in return, profit from accumulated experience. Since it was based on experience that controllers were able to achieve an increased promptness and confidence when facing complex situations, they tend to value this component of their job. Nevertheless, training was considered as a fundamental basis from which one can then optimise performance through experience.

Teamwork was also characterised as a crucial element for traffic control. In fact, all participants stated that their performance was greatly dependent on how duty controllers co-operate.

Subjective assessment of mental workload

The DALI protocol was applied to six traffic controllers and the results found were consistent with high levels of mental workload. For all 6 controllers, one assessment was carried out, except for controller 4, for whom there were two different moments of evaluation, as shown in Table 2.

Table 2. Mental workload indexes obtained with DALI

	Workload index	
Assessment	1	2
Controller 1	100	
Controller 2	99	
Controller 3	93	
Controller 4	75	93
Controller 5	80	
Controller 6	77	

Analysis of procedures and violations

Although designed for industrial purposes, the HFRG method was useful for the identification of inadequacies of the procedural contents and organisation.

From an initial list of 40 operation and safety procedures, 20 were selected according to their significance. Three dispatchers were selected for the interviews based on their different degrees of experience, and the CCP supervision together with the safety management represented the decision makers in the companies' structure. For the second step of this procedure, 10 dispatchers filled out the 48 statements list, representing approximately, 75% of all controllers on active duty.

The information collected from all five interviews was used to establish comparisons on three different levels:

- Comparison between perspectives of different dispatchers;
- Comparison between perspectives of the two levels of management;
- Comparison between perspectives of dispatchers and management.

Traffic controllers, more or less shared the same perspective on safety issues. Management was considered a participative element and generally opened to debate, especially on issues concerning the CCP management. Nevertheless, controllers were unanimous in recognising a strict attitude of safety management in regard to errors, no matter how inconsequential they might seem. As for violations on safety or operation procedures, it was also unanimously assumed that they sometimes occurred, even if they were at all times acknowledged and overseen by the CCP supervisor.

The interviews of the two management levels stressed out different perspectives regarding the application and contents of procedures. Whilst management revealed total confidence on the efficiency of procedures, the CCP supervisor does not rely so much on them, as they are able to identify and follow up on everyday constraints that these procedures impose on traffic regulation. Given the high complexity of the operation, the development of documents and procedures becomes also very complex as it has to go through an extensive process of teamwork discussion, and it depends on the approval of many different entities.

When comparing dispatchers and management, it was first noticed that the CCP supervisors had a perspective rather closer to dispatchers than to safety management. In fact, the participative attitude is reflected mostly by this level of management, and not so much by top level. On the other hand, any reprehension or punitive action comes from the top, and CCP management usually adopts a sympathetic position in regard to controllers. It was promptly admitted by all those working within the CCP that procedure violation was necessary to maintain network operation and in particular, to efficiently recover from critical situations.

Based on the list of statements filled out by 10 dispatchers, different priorities for intervention were obtained. The issue that appeared as a first priority was the "Modification in equipment design and productive area" (I). This concerns the adequacy of systems, technical requirements and limitations to the individuals' aptitude, and safety and comfort conditions. The definition of procedures should aim for a better compromise between job demands and the workers' aptitude, thus reducing the potential for the occurrence of violations. In fact, another issue that out came as a priority refers to the reviewing of rules and procedures and establishing whether or not they effectively meet their purposes (A).

Throughout this study, it was made clear that the non compliance of procedures by traffic controllers was mostly due to the acquired notion that their violation simplifies the task to be performed. The reason for this attitude was found in the inadequacy of the following systems, which strongly contributed for the increase of the potential for violations:

- The radio communications that sometimes make it difficult to pass through the necessary information;
- The high frequency of audio alarms that constantly draw the controllers attention from other tasks, that could be proprietary;
- Computer software and devices, despite their reasonable reliability, are subject to flaws that are well known by controllers. In case of doubt, controllers often question the information that these systems provide and try to verify it by other means some times less reliable and more time consuming.

Discussion

By confronting all data collected throughout the whole project, the more frequent procedure violation scenarios were identified, as well as the dispatchers' course of action to avoid potential impacts over safety and normal circulation conditions. What follows does not correspond to a complete and thorough discussion of all cases but rather a comprehensive outlining.

The noise level at the CCP

During the questionnaire application, the job analysis and the procedure violations study, noise levels were identified as the major disturbance factor for dispatchers. Apart from communications within the room and telecommunications to and from the network, there is a high variability and frequency of other audio features such as alarms. On the one hand, this noise clearly demands an increased effort from dispatchers to maintain adequate awareness and concentration levels, thus representing an increase in mental workload and an important stress and fatigue factor. On the other hand, the disturbance it creates to vital information acquisition processes also increases the potential for the occurrence of several kinds of errors, such as communications misunderstanding.

To cope with these circumstances, dispatchers make use of many strategies that clearly violate safety and operation procedures. One of the most frequently observed behaviours was the blocking of the space bar on the computer keyboard, which would automatically deactivate the audio message whenever an alarm was received by the system. Naturally, by doing so, dispatchers would disregard potentially critical information for their decisions. When confronted with these facts during debriefing interviews, dispatchers promptly admitted and recognised this behaviour as a violation and argued that they would previously assess circulation conditions and monitor the network using alternative systems such as the Closed Circuit Television, thus aiming to ensure safety requirements.

Unofficial procedures

The interviews carried out during the procedure violation analysis revealed that dispatchers rely as much on their formal work procedures as their job accumulated experience. It was stated that procedures serve as guidance, whilst experience is the foundation of a more efficient decision making and troubleshooting strategy.

According to dispatchers some procedures can be contradicting due to the fact that they are some times produced or submitted to revision without carefully considering previously established rules. Also, the complex institutional relations between the network operating company and other parties such as metropolitan authorities require a very thorough procedural description and design which, as dispatchers avowed, can be conflicting with the imperativeness of, among others, re-establishing normal circulation conditions after critical occurrences. In case of malfunction or critical operating modes, it was frequently mentioned by dispatchers that acting within the boundaries of official procedures without any resource to informal and in many cases, rule violating strategies, would mean paralysing the train circulation for a minimum of several hours, regardless of the scenario under consideration.

Whenever acting in divergence from official procedures, dispatchers rely on their job experience that serves as a basis for cooperation between both on duty dispatchers, and the CCP management to ensure safety requirements.

The reduction of the potential for the occurrence of violations

When considering the priorities for intervention that outcome from the applied HSE methodology, one can consider that the behaviours previously described clearly demonstrate the need for an intervention focused on improved equipment such as the alarm system to high demanding working circumstances, as well as the development of procedures that are more robust with regard to the main goal of traffic control, i.e. to maintain train circulations according to schedule and when faced with undesired events, carryout all necessary actions to avoid circulation disturbance or re-establish it in the shortest period of time possible.

Concerning the main issues already discussed, it was recommended that information (alarms) should be provided to dispatchers according to several levels of priority, appropriate to their specific needs for decision making. For example, an audio signal that alerts routine maintenance operation might not be necessary when such interventions are scheduled and registered at a daily journal already provided to dispatchers.

Conclusions

Considering that the main purpose of this project was to study the occurrence of violations in traffic control, the method developed by the Human Factors in Reliability Group (HFRG, 1995), although intended for industrial context applications, provided valid and extensive data when applied in this particular field. Nevertheless, the knowledge regarding the specific causes and means by which violations take place was made possible through the development of a thorough job analysis. Not only were characterised the more significant violations and identified the specific processes by which dispatchers aimed to ensure safety and train circulation in these circumstances, but it also became clear that these behaviours did not necessarily compromise safety requirements. As Amalberti (2001) argued, the seriousness of the consequences resulting from a given event are not so much related to the human error or violation in its origin, but rather to the technical and organisational characteristics in which this event occurs.

Despite the inadequacies of technical and organisational elements in regard to the high job demands, dispatchers together with CCP management have been able to developed informal teamwork resources that reveal a constant concern in providing fast and efficient solutions whilst keeping safety as a top priority. This would lead us to conclude that a more flexible and comprehensive procedure organisation is necessary to cope with traffic control job demands. On the other hand, the high level of responsibility of this company towards its counterparts and to the public in general requires a clear and precise structure of procedures that unequivocally, sets the limits of safety and the accountability of all those who have a responsibility towards this operation.

Research developed in transportation systems (Dekker 2004) have many times revealed that serious accidents can have their origins in a complex chain of events that amount several years back. According to Starbuck and MilliKen (1988) *in*

Dekker (2004), the job experience such as one dispatcher has shown to develop, can compensate for many insufficiencies in systems and improve its performance. However, this improvement, which in the end is a normal evolution process of organisations, represents a slow but constant push to the limits of safety. Thus, one can say that more and more often, as systems become more and more complex, accidents tend to happen in the sequence of everyday and normal events that constitute a slow drift into failure.

Acknowledgements

The author wishes to acknowledge the team that worked with him on the full research project for their fundamental contribution to this particular study (Miguel Lourenco, Julia Correia, Jose Carvalhais and Anabela Simões – Technical University of Lisbon).

References

Amalberti, R. (2001). The paradoxes of almost totally safe transportation systems. *Safety Science*, 37, 109-126.

Dekker, S. (2004). *Ten questions about human error – A new view of human factors and system safety*. Aldershot, UK: Ashgate.

Hart, S.G. & Staveland, L.E. (1988). Development of NASA-TLX (Task Load Index): results of empirical and theoretical research. In P.A. Hancock and N. Meshkati (Eds.), *Human Mental Workload* (pp. 139-183). Amsterdam: North-Holland.

Health and Safety Executive - HSE (1999). *Reducing error and influencing behaviour. Individual job organization*. Suffolk, UK: HSE Books.

Human Factors in Reliability Group - HFRG (1995). *Improving compliance with safety procedures – Reducing industrial violations*. Suffolk, UK: HSE Books.

Lenné, M., Regan, M., Triggs, T., & Haworth, N. (2004). *Review of recent research in applied experimental psychology: Implications for counter measure development in road safety* (Report 223). Victoria, Australia: Monash University. Accident research Centre.

Wilson, J.R. & Norris, B. (2005). Rail human factors: Past, present and future. *Applied Ergonomics*, 36, 649-660.

Railway infrastructure engineering in the wild

Richard Bye[1] & Anjum Naweed[2]
[1]Network Rail
[2]University of Sheffield
UK

Abstract

Classical decision theory is supported by laboratory studies in which participants are charged with selecting between known alternatives with fixed aims, purposes and values. Such work supports the assumption that decision makers weigh up the relative merits of competing options to make an optimal choice. In the wild however the costs and benefits of competing options are ill defined, and real time, high stake decisions are based on experience, pattern matching and parsimonious analyses of rich data streams. The following case study highlights some of the patterns and complexities of real time railway track renewal work in the UK.

Background

The UK rail infrastructure dates back to the Victorian era and an extensive programme of track maintenance and renewal is necessary to preserve the integrity of the network. The decision to renew a section of track and associated assets is taken when routine maintenance becomes ineffective or when qualitative upgrades are required to support increases in line speed or in the intensity of use.

The work presented here is a case study of the renewal of a short section of track (approximately 1400 yards, or 1.2 kilometres) on a busy UK commuter route. The renewal was planned a year in advance with line blockages, isolations and possessions spread over 13 weeks and with approximately 93 track workers employed on the weekend of the observations. Track renewal work is therefore expensive and its complexity can be demonstrated by the scope of work for ergonomists, which ranges from information support for planners, on site manual handling and safety critical communication, to work organisation, supporting shared situation awareness and distributed team performance.

The work aimed to gain an insight into the patterns and complexities of track renewal work and produce a model of integrated rail operations (Bye et al, in press) to show how operators could be better supported in future to enhance safety, efficiency and productivity. This outline provides a snapshot of the work to give an indication of some features that contribute to the complexity of railway infrastructure renewals 'in the wild' (Hutchins, 1996).

In D. de Waard, G.R.J. Hockey, P. Nickel, and K.A. Brookhuis (Eds.) (2007), *Human Factors Issues in Complex System Performance* (pp. 157 - 160). Maastricht, the Netherlands: Shaker Publishing.

Methods

The work utilised a bootstrapping approach in which numerous cognitive systems engineering methods were combined to develop a picture of how track renewal work is conducted. Methods included analyses of documentation and standard operating procedures, workshops with subject matter experts (Figure 1, left), concept mapping, critical decision method interviews (Kelin et al, 1989) and live on-site observations. The live on-site observations (Figure 1, right) were perhaps the most interesting and useful stage in the research, although they did not necessarily produce the highest quantity (or quality) of data, and required the completion of early document-based methods in order to understand the nature and consequences of observed actions.

Figure 1. Left: Early workshop methods, right: live field observations

Results

A heavy snowfall, freezing temperatures and blizzard conditions provided a unique opportunity to observe the adaptive response of the track workers whose already tight schedule of work was severely disrupted. This was not the intention of the visit (as we had to adapt too) but the conditions enabled us to observe first hand the need for flexibility in response to severe environmental constraints and the resulting difficulties (Figure 2, right). The features of the work listed below were distilled from the observations to illustrate some of the issues faced and also serve to support the need for ethnographic field observations as a coherent approach to understand the railway as a complex sociotechnical system.

The need for high stake decision making under uncertain, dynamic conditions

Although snow had been forecasted, it had not arrived at the point when the decision to proceed or cancel the renewal work was required. The severity of the weather could not be predicted but the consequences of project failure, such as the cost of delays, were clearly understood. Many additional problems were ill defined, time pressured and had conflicting goals, meaning that it was extremely difficult to ascertain what, how, or when decisions were made. Although all other planned works in the area were cancelled the decision to go ahead did not result in adverse outcomes, but this was mainly due to the positive 'can do' attitude of the workers.

Figure 2. Left: extreme weather conditions, right: problems with automated systems

The delay or unavailability of workers and equipment

It was so difficult to get to and from the worksite that members of the nightshift simply never arrived. Team dynamics were therefore disrupted by relief staff arriving late and without the appropriate knowledge, certification or shared experiences required to establish common ground (e.g. Klein, 2001) and work under their own initiative. A second tamper failed to materialise and an engineering train was unable to fulfil the necessary requirements to depart the worksite due to the weather conditions, time pressure and staff shortages.

The conditions reducing the speed and effectiveness of work

Snow and ice prevented automated track clipping (Figure 2, right), delayed load examining and reduced the efficacy of tamping. Increased risk of slips, trips and falls, combined with poor visibility and low temperatures increased the physical effort required to complete routine tasks. It was very difficult for the Engineering Supervisor (ES) to move around the worksite and maintain awareness of overall progress.

The failure in communications, technology and power supply

The ES was forced to rely on communication by SMS text message due to a damaged cell phone and disrupted radio communications. The generator in the site cabin ran out of fuel resulting in heat and power failure so the site access manager was unable to act as a central hub of communication, which had been the emergent strategy to support the ES. Information from external sources was slow to arrive and incomplete, reducing the ability to implement revised work plans.

Conclusion

The site working conditions were extraordinarily difficult and despite highly detailed and thorough planning, nearly all tenets of ergonomic best practice were violated. Task difficulty scored highly on factors including control, criticality, complexity, ambiguity, anomaly and rule incongruity (Kirschenbaum, 1990), workload was high, decisions were time-pressured and physical conditions were challenging. And yet, in the face of these overwhelming odds, the work was completed on time and scored highly on objective quality measures.

Track renewal work relies on detailed plans and formal procedures which are necessary but not sufficient to get the job done, especially under abnormal, degraded or otherwise challenging conditions. There is an obvious need to employ experienced track workers who can work around emerging problems, but there is also scope to provide additional support to increase jobholder safety, effectiveness, productivity and satisfaction. Ongoing work is in progress to provide such support.

Acknowledgements

This work would not have been possible without the generous support of Tom Wilson (Atkins Rail), David Tomnay (First Engineering), John Robinson (Network Rail) and all on site personnel.

References

Bye, R., Farrington-Darby, T., Cox, G., Hockey, G.R.J., Wilson, J.R., & Clarke, T. (in Press) Grounding research: From work analysis to a macrocognitive representation of integrated rail operations. In Wilson, J.R., Norris, B.J., Clarke, T. and Mills, A. (Eds). *People and Rail Systems: Human Factors at the Heart of the Railway*. Ashgate Publishing: Abingdon, UK.

Hutchins, E. (1996) *Cognition in the wild*. Cambridge, MA: MIT Press.

Kirschenbaum, S.S., (1990) *Command Decision Making: Lessons Learned*. (NUSC TM No.902149). Newport, RI: Naval Underwater Systems Center.

Klein, G.A., Calderwood, R. & MacGregor, D. (1989). Critical Decision Method for Eliciting Knowledge. *IEEE Transactions on Systems*, Man and Cybernetics, 19(3), 462-472.

Klein, G. (2001). Features of team coordination. In M. McNeese, M. R. Endsley & E. Salas (Eds.), *New trends in cooperative activities* (pp. 68-95). Santa Monica, CA: HFES.

Biomechanics of securing vehicles for transport

Sandra Anstaett Metzler, Jeffrey Bookwalter, & Nick Eiselstein
SEA Ltd., Columbus, Ohio
USA

Abstract

Vehicles are transported from the assembly plant to the dealer using multi-vehicle tractor-trailer systems, and are secured by the drivers using chains or straps that are tightened by ratchet mechanisms. To our knowledge, no detailed biomechanical study has previously been conducted on the procedure of securing the vehicles to the transport system, a manual handling activity. This study presents the results of research conducted to study the biomechanics of this activity on a tractor-trailer system utilizing metal chains to secure the vehicles. Three different body positions were analyzed, which encompass the majority of the different ratchet configurations. To perform the analysis, a six-camera motion capture system was used to capture the body positions throughout the process. A standard ratchet bar was instrumented with a strain gauge to record the force exerted, and these data were captured and synchronized with the motion via the motion capture system. The body postures and external hand forces associated with the securing process were then input into the 3-D Static Strength Predictor Software program, and the individual joint strength requirements and low back compression forces analyzed. The external hand loads necessary to secure the vehicles to the transport system ranged from 165 to 485 N. The combination of postures and external hand forces required at the peak force were determined to be achievable by 75% or more of the female workforce population, and the low back compression forces did not exceed the NIOSH Back Compression Design Limit value of 3400 N.

Background

The transporting of automobiles from the factory to the dealer typically involves the use of a multi-vehicle tractor-trailer system. The vehicles are loaded by the truck driver onto the tractor-trailer individually, and must then be secured prior to transport. There are two types of systems used for securing the vehicles, one involving a system of chain, hook, and ratchet mechanisms that are secured to the vehicle undercarriage, and the second involving straps that mount over the wheels. Securing the vehicles using either system includes the use of a hand-held bar to tighten either the chains or straps, in either a pull or a pull that transitions to a push. This process therefore has much in common with other types of manual material handling processes found throughout industry. The force required to tighten and secure the vehicles varies throughout the tightening process, as does the specific

In D. de Waard, G.R.J. Hockey, P. Nickel, and K.A. Brookhuis (Eds.) (2007), *Human Factors Issues in Complex System Performance* (pp. 161 - 166). Maastricht, the Netherlands: Shaker Publishing.

body position of the operator. As a result, performing a biomechanical analysis of this process is more complicated than that involved in a task with a constant force load, such as many manual material-handling operations. It requires that the body position of the operator be recorded in a synchronized manner with forces being exerted on the hand-held bar (commonly referred to as a "ratchet bar"). This information can then be used to perform a biomechanical analysis on the tightening process to determine the joint strength necessary for the operation. The required joint strengths can then be compared to the strengths of the population to determine what section of the population is capable of performing this task, and whether the task is likely to result in musculoskeletal injury, when performed in the manner analyzed. This paper presents the results of such an analysis, performed on a tractor-trailer manufactured by Cottrell, Inc. a manufacturer who sells vehicles in Europe, Africa, Australia, and North and South America. The tractor-trailer analyzed utilized the hook, chain, and ratchet type of system to secure vehicles.

Methods

The analysis was performed on a multi-vehicle tractor-trailer system (Figure 1). The vehicles are secured by means of a system of chains that are connected to four specific points in the vehicle undercarriage. The chains are then tightened via a ratchet mechanism to compress the suspension of the vehicle no more than 5 cm vertically, thereby securing the vehicle to the trailer (Figure 2). To capture the force exerted on the end of the ratchet bar, a strain gage was mounted on a standard production model ratchet bar. The strain gage was calibrated by placing the ratchet bar in a horizontal position in a locked ratchet assembly on the truck, and then hanging calibrated weights on the handle end of the ratchet bar.

Figure 1. Auto hauling tractor-trailer assembly, fully loaded

The operator postural information was obtained via a Motion Analysis Corporation motion capture system. A standard Helen Hayes marker set, including medial markers, was used for the motion capture, with either medial or lateral markers omitted when necessary due to line of sight obstructions. Using both medial and lateral markers, rather than omitting the medial markers during active motion, allowed for greater flexibility and maintained better visibility.

The combined operator posture and force level exerted at the time of maximum force, as well as at one-half second intervals throughout the ratchet tightening process, were input into the University of Michigan 3-D Static Strength Predictor

(3DSSPP) software (University of Michigan, 2005) to perform the biomechanical analysis. In order to eliminate potential analyst bias, the operator posture was first input into the 3DSSPP and then the individual hand loads were entered. As a general rule, designing tasks so that at least 75% of the female work population has the necessary joint strength to perform the operation will offer the best protection against musculoskeletal injury (Snook, 1978, Snook & Cirello, 1991). Therefore, a female operator performed the tasks, and the 3DSSPP analysis was performed using female anthropometry and comparisons to the female population strengths. A male operator, however, also performed the tasks and the male operator obtained a similar range of force values when securing the vehicles.

Figure 2. Sample ratchet assembly

The testing and analysis was performed using a compact car, the Hyundai Sonata and a large truck, the Ford F-150 pickup, in order to test a range of suspension stiffness. The vehicles were secured in each of three positions: an overhead ratchet position, a mid-level ratchet position, and a low-level ratchet position. In addition, the process of extending and retracting the skids on the rear of the trailer was tested and analyzed. The skids are extended and retracted manually, using the ratchet bar as a handle. The ratchet bar is inserted into a hole in the end of the skid, designed for this purpose, and then the skid is extended by pulling it backward out of the trailer assembly, or retracted back into the trailer assembly by pushing it forward.

In addition to analyzing the biomechanics of the task of securing the vehicles, other ergonomic aspects were considered, including the frequency with which the task is performed, the task duration, the availability of rest and recovery periods, and the quality of the "coupling" or interaction between the system and the operator.

Results

The forces necessary to secure the Hyundai Sonata and the Ford F-150 pickup truck ranged from 165 to 489 Newton for the positions tested in this analysis. The ratchet tightening procedure was performed at each position both with the other 3 chain positions tightened and loose. The maximum force values obtained at each position are shown in Table 1. The results of the 3-D Static Strength Predictor software analysis for the process of securing the vehicles to the trailer show that more than

75% of the female work population is capable of performing all these tasks. Additionally, the lower back compression forces for all tasks were below the National Institute of Occupational Safety & Health (NIOSH) recommended Back Compression Design Limit (BCDL) value of 3400 Newton.

Table 1. Maximum forces obtained securing vehicles and manipulating skids.

Task	Max force (N)
Tighten rear of car	489
Tighten mid car	391
Tighten car overhead	236
Tighten rear of truck	360
Tighten mid truck	480
Tighten truck overhead	294
Skid extension	98
Skid retraction	133

The percentage of the female population capable of producing the required force and torque levels at each joint are shown in Figures 3 and 4 for the mid level position on the car, which (along with the front truck and rear car positions) had the lowest percentage capability at 77% for the shoulder, and for the rear of the car, which had the highest force value of 489 Newton.

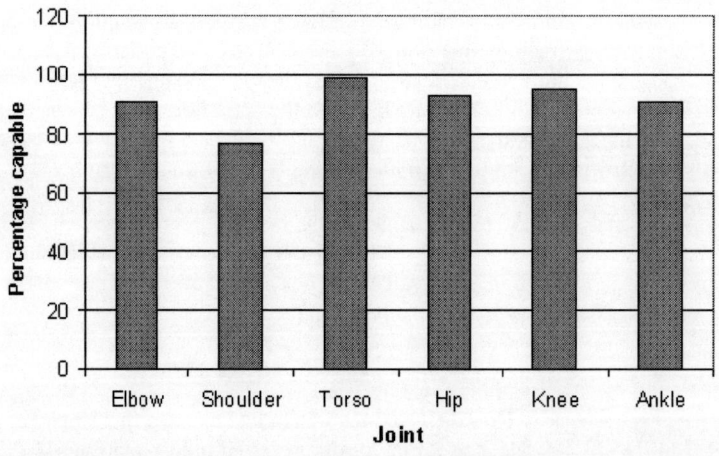

Figure 3. Percentage of female work population capable of producing mid car position required joint forces

Rear car, 489 Newton

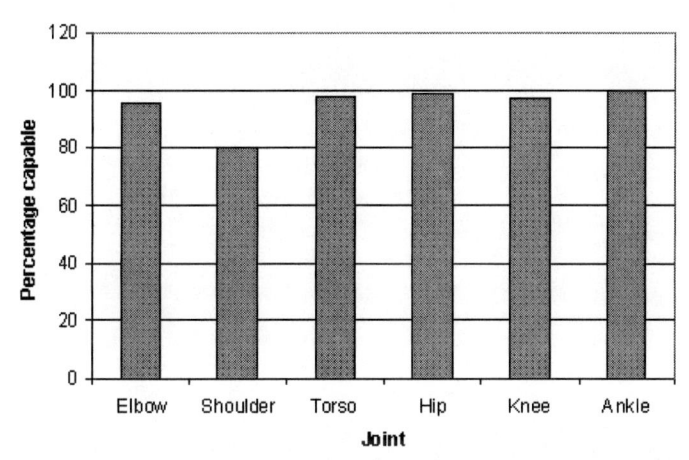

Figure 4. Percentage of female work population capable of producing rear car position required joint forces

Securing the vehicles to the trailer is a task that is performed intermittently and for short durations throughout the workday. The nature of the task automatically provides rest and recovery periods between exertions. The hand-ratchet bar interface provides the highest quality of coupling or interaction possible.

Discussion

More than 75% of the female work population is capable of producing the forces and torques at the joints analyzed in this research. This includes the elbow, shoulder, torso, hip, knee, and ankle. Previous research indicates that tasks that 75% or more of the female work population have the requisite joint strength to perform, represent a low risk of overexertion type injuries. Therefore, the process of securing vehicles to the trailer is associated with a low risk of overexertion injuries. This process is also relatively short in duration and performed only intermittently throughout the day, so it would not be considered repetitive in nature, and would not lead to repetitive stress type injuries. The vehicles are secured initially after loading onto the trailer, and then released via a quick release ratchet mechanism. Therefore, the highest force exertions will occur during the loading and securing phase of the operation.

The design of the ratchet and ratchet bar allow the operator to position the bar in an almost infinite range of positions, which is desirable in order to make the operation as flexible as possible. In addition to positioning the bar in a variety of radial positions, the bar can be rotated in the ratchet so that the operator can position him or herself slightly away from the truck, if that provides a more biomechanically advantageous position. This flexible design allows the operators to adaptively position themselves based on their own stature and strength ability, thereby providing an automatic adjustment for different anthropometries seen throughout the working population.

References

3D Static Strength Predictor Program (2005), version 5.05. University of Michigan, Michigan, USA: The Regents of the University of Michigan.

Snook, S.H. (1978). The design of manual handling tasks, *Ergonomics, 21*, 963-985.

Snook, S.H. & Cirello, V.M. (1991). The design of manual handling tasks: revised tables of maximum weights and forces. *Ergonomics, 34*, 1197-1213.

Transportation

vibrotactile collision warning

In D. de Waard, G.R.J. Hockey, P. Nickel, and K.A. Brookhuis (Eds.) (2007), *Human Factors Issues in Complex System Performance* (pp. 167). Maastricht, the Netherlands: Shaker Publishing.

'Intuitive' vibrotactile collision warnings for drivers

Cristy Ho[1], Nick Reed[2], & Charles Spence[1]
[1]University of Oxford, Oxford
[2]Transport Research Laboratory, Wokingham
United Kingdom

Abstract

A study was designed to investigate the possibility of improving driver responses to potential critical emergency situations by implementing vibrotactile warning signals that indicated the likely direction of potential collision events. Normally-sighted participants drove in a driving simulator in which a car following scenario was modelled. The participants were instructed to try and maintain a safe headway distance to the lead car, and they had to respond as quickly as possible to the sudden deceleration of the lead car which had its brake lights disabled. The participants performed the task either with or without the aid of vibrotactile warning signals (presented to their waist) that indicated the direction of potential collision events (front vs. rear). The results demonstrated significantly faster (> 400 ms faster) braking responses and larger (> 3 m) safety margins when the vibrotactile warning signal was presented than when it was absent. These findings therefore demonstrate the potential effectiveness of 'intuitive' vibrotactile cues in helping drivers to orient their spatial attention in the appropriate direction and respond appropriately, especially in situations where the effectiveness of visual or auditory driving aids may be impaired. Given the robust benefit attributable to the provision of vibrotactile cues even for drivers with normal vision, the benefits for low-vision drivers are likely to be even greater.

Background

The sense of touch provides a potentially effective, but at present underutilized, alternative to the traditional focus on vision and audition in automobile interface design. In particular, recent research has demonstrated the feasibility of using vibrotactile cues to communicate directional and distance information to drivers via vibrotactile displays embedded in the driver's seat (e.g., van Erp & van Veen, 2004), worn around their waist (e.g., Ho et al., 2005), or via a vibrotactile display worn on their torso (e.g., van Erp et al., 2004). The rapid growth of interest in the design of tactile applications (see Gallace et al., in press) is supported by robust neuropsychological evidence from studies on the multisensory integration of information available from various different sensory modalities (see Calvert et al., 2004; Spence & Driver, 2004). Given drivers' frequent complaints regarding visual overload (Sivak, 1996) and the potential benefits of using touch as an alternative or as a redundant channel for information presentation (see Jackson & Selcon, 1997; Spence & Driver, 1999; van Erp & van Veen, 2004), it seems possible that this currently underutilized sense will increasingly be used in a variety of settings in the years to come.

A review of the extant literature on tactile communication highlights several potential advantages of touch over vision and, in some cases, audition. These include: the rapid transmission of tactile information to the brain (Harrar & Harris, 2005; Mowbray & Gebhard, 1961); the attention-capturing nature of tactile stimuli (i.e., regardless of the current direction of a driver's gaze); their relatively automatic ability to alert (Geldard, 1960; von Haller Gilmer, 1961); their inherent directionality (i.e., the fact that tactile stimuli are naturally mapped to bodily coordinates; van Erp & van Veen, 2001; see also Ho & Spence, 2007); the fact that they are private to the driver; and hence will not be as annoying as auditory signals (e.g., Lee et al., 2004; McGehee & Raby, 2003); and unlike vision, the tactile system cannot be 'shut out' voluntarily (see von Haller Gilmer, 1960, 1961). Taken together, these advantages of tactile stimulation appear to coincide with the properties required of an effective warning signal that is capable of alerting drivers and redirecting their attention to potentially dangerous road events. Given the above, Ho et al. (2006) recently conducted a driving simulator study in which they attempted to examine whether vibrotactile cuing would provide a particularly effective and practical means of alerting drivers to potential front-to-rear-end collisions. The study examined whether there was any 'intuitive' mapping between particular driving actions and the positioning of vibrotactile cues.

Ho et al.'s (2006) study

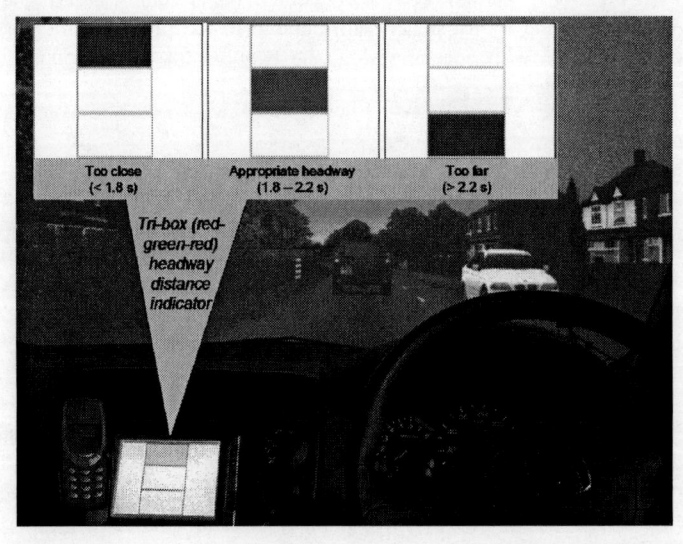

Figure 1. Sample shot of the driving scene in Ho et al.'s (2006) study taken from behind the driver's seat. The tri-box headway distance indicator is also shown (numbers in parentheses represent the actual time headway of the participant's car to the lead vehicle

Eleven participants (one extra participant was excluded due to their failure to follow the task instructions) drove in a high-fidelity driving simulator in which a car following scenario was modelled (see Ho et al., 2006, for a detailed description of the methodology). The participants were instructed to try and maintain a safe headway distance (2 s time headway) to the lead vehicle. An in-car navigation screen displaying a tri-box headway distance indicator was presented in the centre of the driving console to assist the driver in maintaining a safe headway distance (see Figure 1). In particular, the tri-box screen would display a green box in the middle when the participant's car was travelling at the correct headway distance. The tri-box screen changed to the upper red or lower red box when the participant was travelling either too close or too far, respectively, from the lead vehicle. This tri-box headway distance indicator acted as an analogue to the visually-demanding in-car technology that is increasingly proving to be a distraction to drivers' attention (e.g., Ashley, 2001).

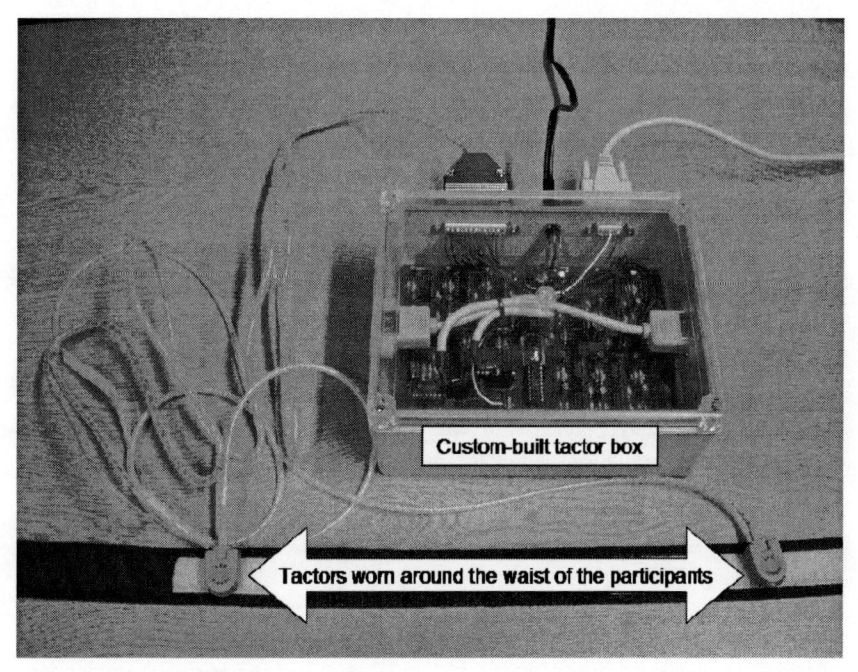

Figure 2. Photograph of the custom-built tactor box hardware used to present vibrotactile stimuli to the participants (via a belt worn around the participants' waist) in Ho et al.'s (2006) study

During the course of the experimental drive, the participants had to respond as quickly as possible to the sudden deceleration of the lead car, which had its brake lights disabled. The participants had to perform the task either with or without the aid of vibrotactile warning signals that were presented to their waist (which indicated the direction of potential collision events). Specifically, one of the tactors was positioned in the middle of the participant's stomach, the other in the middle of their back (see Figure 2). A vibrotactile warning signal, consisting of a 500 ms vibration, was presented from either one of the two tactors at the onset of a critical event (i.e., at the initiation of the sudden deceleration of the lead car) in the blocks with vibrotactile cuing. The vibrotactile cues used were spatially predictive, meaning that on 80% of the trials, the cues correctly indicated the direction of the potential collision event, while on the remaining 20% of the trials, the cues were presented from the direction opposite to the collision event.

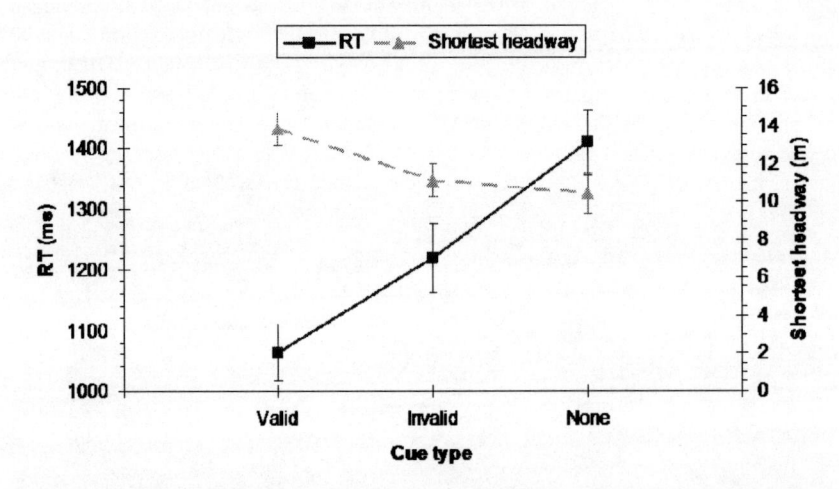

Figure 3. Summary graph of the mean RT (ms) and shortest headway (m) results from Ho et al.'s (2006) study as a function of cue type (valid, invalid, or no cue). Error bars indicate standard errors of the means

The results of Ho et al.'s (2006) study revealed significantly faster braking responses and larger safety margins when the vibrotactile warning signal was presented than when it was absent (see Figure 3). In particular, mean response times (RTs; the time after the onset of a critical frontal event to the participants depressing on the brake pedal) were 348 ms faster and the stopping distance to a potential collision increased by 3.5 m when a valid vibrotactile cue (that indicated the correct direction of the critical event) was presented than when no cue was present. These results reflect a 24.7% reduction in response latency and a 33.7% increase in safety margin to a potential collision. These results have important safety implications for the application of tactile warning signals in real driving environment (see Suetomi & Kido, 1997).

Discussion

The results of Ho et al.'s (2006) study demonstrated the efficacy of directional vibrotactile cues in eliciting a braking response from drivers. In particular, the results highlighted the potential benefits of using this seemingly 'intuitive' vibrotactile displays to present time-critical information to drivers. In fact, the term 'intuitive' has been used by many researchers when they described the presentation of information via the tactile channel (e.g., Eves and Novak, 1998; Rupert, 2000; van Erp, 2005; van Erp and van Veen, 2004). Specifically, Rupert defined 'intuition' as 'the power of attaining direct knowledge or cognition without rational thought and inference' (p. A96). This implies that an 'intuitive' tactile signal can presumably bypass the traditional routes in information-processing to elicit the most rapid response from an operator. The results of Ho et al.'s study provides clear evidence that the valid frontal vibrotactile cues (i.e., cues coming from the same direction as the potential event on the road) effectively elicited a braking response from the participants who had had no training using the vibrotactile display before the study. This also reflects the inherent direct mapping of bodily coordinates to external events (with the valid vibrotactile cues coming from the same direction as the sudden deceleration event in front being most effective).

The results of Ho et al.'s (2006) study suggested that the directional information conveyed by the vibrotactile cues presented on the front of the driver's torso might be particularly effective in getting the driver to depress the brake pedal. It might be argued that it is even more practical to vibrate the foot pedal(s) that the driver would need to release (or depress), as this will provide the driver with a straightforward signal concerning the appropriate action that they should take (e.g., Kume et al., 1998). Essentially, the question here refers to the distinction between the presentation of vibrotactile cues for their effectiveness in terms of stimulus-response compatibility versus spatial cuing effects (i.e., orienting a driver's gaze to the direction of interest; see Proctor et al., 2005, for a detailed discussion of spatial compatibility vs. spatial cuing effects). For example, while vibrating the pedals may be effective in signalling to the driver that they should perform an action with the pedals (i.e., the appropriate response modality), it may not be particularly effective in signalling to the driver whether he/she should depress or release the accelerator (i.e., the appropriate action), and given that drivers do not normally have their foot on the brake pedal, warning signals consisting of vibrating the brake pedal may even be left unnoticed. On the other hand, several researchers have shown that vibrotactile cues are particularly effective for signalling lane departure information (e.g., McGehee & Raby, 2003). McGehee and Raby (2003) provided the drivers of snowplows with lane departure information via tactile stimuli presented to the drivers' thighs through the driver's seat. Taken together, the inherent directionality and alerting properties of tactile sensations appear to be best for use in conveying directional information concerning events that a driver should pay attention to, as compared to visual and auditory forms of information presentation.

Ho et al.'s (2006) study examined the case of a front-to-rear-end collision in a normal car following condition in a rural area (i.e., low traffic flow). Given the robust benefit attributable to the provision of vibrotactile cues under normal conditions, it seems plausible that even bigger benefits of vibrotactile cuing will be evidenced in situations that are more visually attention-demanding or degraded, such as in low visibility or heavy traffic, when drivers are under high perceptual load (see Janssen et al., 1976; Lavie, 2005).

In addition, given the wide availability of tactile displays for blind people (see e.g., Bach-y-Rita, 2004; Jansson, 1983; Segond et al., 2005), it is possible that vibrotactile cuing may provide a particular effective means of assisting drivers with visual impairment (i.e., for those who are not classified as legally blind and are thus still allowed to drive). For instance, the technology is now sufficiently advanced for sophisticated radar systems to detect dangerous road situations ahead of time (even before the driver his/herself is aware of them). It is possible that these systems could be used to provide advanced warnings about the road situations to drivers to counteract any slowing in responses due to their impaired vision. With a growing population of elderly drivers, the communication of redundant information via touch also holds great promise as studies have demonstrated greater performance gain in the elder population than the younger population in multisensory integration (see Laurienti et al., 2006; Poliakoff et al., 2006).

References

Ashley, S. (2001). Driving the info highway. *Scientific American, 285(4)*, 44-50.
Bach-y-Rita, P. (2004). Tactile sensory substitution studies. *Annals of the New York Academy of Sciences, 1013*, 83-91.
Calvert, G.A., Spence, C., & Stein, B.E. (Eds.). (2004). *The handbook of multisensory processes.* Cambridge, MA: MIT Press.
Eves, D.A., & Novak, M.M. (1998). Extraction of vector information using a novel tactile display. *Displays, 18*, 169-181.
Gallace, A., Tan, H.Z., & Spence, C. (in press). The body surface as a communication system: The state of the art after 50 years. *Presence*.
Geldard, F.A. (1960). Some neglected possibilities of communication. *Science, 131*, 1583-1588.
Harrar, V. & Harris, L.R. (2005). Simultaneity constancy: Detecting events with touch and vision. *Experimental Brain Research, 166*, 465-473.
Ho, C., Reed, N., & Spence, C. (2006). Assessing the effectiveness of "intuitive" vibrotactile warning signals in preventing front-to-rear-end collisions in a driving simulator. *Accident Analysis & Prevention, 38*, 989-996.
Ho, C. & Spence, C. (2007). Head orientation biases tactile localization. *Brain Research, 1144C*, 136-141.
Ho, C., Tan, H.Z., & Spence, C. (2005). Using spatial vibrotactile cues to direct visual attention in driving scenes. *Transportation Research Part F: Traffic Psychology and Behaviour, 8*, 397-412.
Jackson, M. & Selcon, S.J. (1997). A parallel distributed processing model of redundant information integration. In D. Harris (Ed.), *Engineering psychology and cognitive ergonomics, Vol. 2: Job design and product design* (pp. 193-200). Aldershot, England: Ashgate.
Janssen, W.H., Michon, J.A., & Harvey, L.O., Jr. (1976). The perception of lead vehicle movement in darkness. *Accident Analysis & Prevention, 8*, 151-166.
Jansson, G. (1983). Tactile guidance of movement. *International Journal of Neuroscience, 19*, 37-46.
Kume, Y., Shirai, A., Tsuda, M., & Hatada, T. (1998). Information transmission through soles by vibro-tactile stimulation. *Transactions of the Virtual Reality Society of Japan, 3*, 83-88.

Laurienti, P.J., Burdette, J.H., Maldjian, J.A., & Wallace, M.T. (2006). Enhanced multisensory integration in older adults. *Neurobiology of Aging, 27*, 1155-1163.

Lavie, N. (2005). Distracted and confused?: Selective attention under load. *Trends in Cognitive Sciences, 9*, 75-82.

Lee, J.D., Hoffman, J.D., & Hayes, E. (2004). Collision warning design to mitigate driver distraction. *CHI 2004: Proceedings of the SIGCHI conference on human factors in computing systems, 6*, 65-72.

McGehee, D.V., & Raby, M. (2003). *The design and evaluation of snowplow lane awareness system* (Report No. HF-PPC 2003-1). Iowa City: University of Iowa Public Policy Center.

Mowbray, G.H. & Gebhard, J.W. (1961). Man's senses as informational channels. In H.W. Sinaiko (Ed.), *Selected papers on human factors in the design and use of control systems* (pp. 115-149). New York: Dover.

Poliakoff, E., Ashworth, S., Lowe, C., & Spence, C. (2006). Vision and touch in ageing: Crossmodal selective attention and visuotactile spatial interactions. *Neuropsychologia, 44*, 507-517.

Proctor, R.W., Tan, H.Z., Vu, K.-P.L., Gray, R., & Spence, C. (2005). Implications of compatibility and cuing effects for multimodal interfaces. *Proceedings of the 11th International Conference on Human-Computer Interaction, 11*, Paper No. 2733.

Rupert, A.H. (2000). Tactile situation awareness system: Proprioceptive prostheses for sensory deficiencies. *Aviation, Space, and Environmental Medicine, 71*, A92-A99.

Segond, H., Weiss, D., & Sampaio, E. (2005). Human spatial navigation via a visuo-tactile sensory substitution system. *Perception, 34*, 1231-1249.

Sivak, M. (1996). The information that drivers use: Is it indeed 90% visual? *Perception, 25*, 1081-1090.

Spence, C. & Driver, J. (1999). A new approach to the design of multimodal warning signals. In D. Harris (Ed.), *Engineering psychology and cognitive ergonomics, Vol. 4: Job design, product design and human-computer interaction* (pp. 455-461). Aldershot, England: Ashgate.

Spence, C. & Driver, J. (Eds.). (2004). *Crossmodal space and crossmodal attention*. Oxford: Oxford University Press.

Suetomi, T. & Kido, K. (1997). Driver behavior under a collision warning system - A driving simulator study. *SAE Special Publications, 1242*, 75-81.

van Erp, J.B.F. (2005). Presenting directions with a vibrotactile torso display. *Ergonomics, 48*, 302-313.

van Erp, J.B.F., Jansen, C., Dobbins, T., & van Veen, H.A.H.C. (2004). Vibrotactile waypoint navigation at sea and in the air: Two case studies. *Proceedings of EuroHaptics 2004*, 166-173.

van Erp, J.B.F., & van Veen, H.A.H.C. (2001). Vibro-tactile information processing in automobiles. *Proceedings of EuroHaptics 2001*, 99-104.

van Erp, J.B.F., & van Veen, H.A.H.C. (2004). Vibrotactile in-vehicle navigation system. *Transportation Research Part F: Traffic Psychology and Behaviour, 7*, 247-256.

von Haller Gilmer, B. (1960). Possibilities of cutaneous electro-pulse communication. In G.R. Hawkes (Ed.), *Symposium on cutaneous sensitivity* (pp. 76-84). Fort Knox, KY: U.S. Army Medical Research Laboratory.

von Haller Gilmer, B. (1961). Toward cutaneous electro-pulse communication. *Journal of Psychology, 52*, 211-222.

Driver behaviour analysed by image analysis

Gaetano Bosurgi, Antonino D'Andrea, & Orazio Pellegrino
University of Messina
Messina, Italy

Abstract

Driving behaviour is a direct consequence of the stimuli that the driver receives from the road infrastructure, from the surrounding environment and from the environment inside the vehicle. There is consensus that all these factors affect driving behaviour and it has been confirmed by the recent advances in road safety research. Driver perceptions of the road context are the result of analyses based on an unconscious selection of information received from the surroundings. To examine these issues, the present study focused on driver behaviour in relation to both road environment and interaction with other vehicles. This was achieved by calculating a series of characteristic variables such as distance, speed, and relative acceleration to a vehicle ahead from video recordings.

Introduction

The impact of visual behaviour on driving has been well examined and documented over the years (Land, 1992; 1998). Nevertheless, for the road engineer, whose ultimate objective would be the safety of road users, the relationship between driving activity and the physical characteristics of the road context such as geometry, traffic, speed, and visibility, remain insufficiently explored.

Methodology

To perform this study, some videotape recordings of road contexts and eye movements of 30 drivers were made, while sensors tracked variables such as distance covered, speed, longitudinal acceleration and use of the accelerator and brake pedals. A portable GPS was also used to track the driver's position on the road. The results were subsequently further filtered and analyzed in order to extrapolate key parameters and to correlate them appropriately. The aim of this study was to interpret driver visual behaviour to define a number of indicators that would add to the explanation of driving behaviour, and therefore also road safety.

The recordings permitted to recognize head-eye movements and certain postures of the driver associated with specific manoeuvres. The raw data for movements of the head-eye system were compared with road geometry, environmental context and traffic conditions to indicate information overload. The index that quantifies this activity is the Visual Load Index (VLI), which has been described previously

(Bosurgi et al., 2004a, b; 2005) as a sudden deviation from trajectory of the driver's gaze to sample visual information of interest both inside and outside the standard field of visual activity. In the subsequent phase, data relative to eye movement coordinates were filtered using regression analysis. This allowed the elimination of data relating to impulsive behaviour, which VLI determination allows for, and produced a function that represents only the "macro" movements of the head-eye system.

The function chosen for the approximation of experimental data, indicated as Context Information, was that of Fourier, i.e. a sum of sine and cosine equations up to the eighth order, of the type:

$$y = a_0 + \sum_{i=1}^{n} a_i \cdot \cos(n \cdot \omega \cdot x) + b_i \cdot \sin(n \cdot \omega \cdot x) \qquad (1)$$

Where a_0 models any DC offset in the signal and is associated with the $i = 0$ cosine term, the ω is the fundamental frequency of the signal, and n is the number of terms (harmonics) in the series.

Analysis of this function has permitted to derive other important parameters. For example, knowledge of first and second order derivatives has allowed identification of maximum, minimum and inflection points. With reference to the models of visual behaviour exposed by Land (1992; 1998), it was found that the inflection point in the Context Information function is that one at which the driver begins to analyse the geometric element situated within his field of visual activity. The strict relationship among the Context Information (CI) function and eye movements has been confirmed by the recorded video tape.

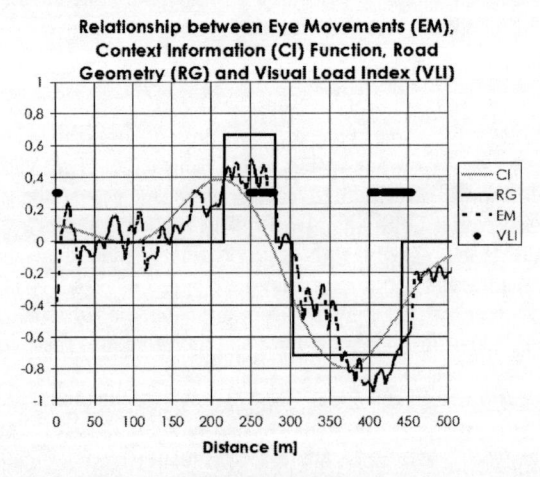

Figure 1. In the section of the road from 0.00 to 500.00 m with this representation it is possible to study the relationship of the visual behaviour (by means of the Context Information function, deduced by eye movements) and the road geometry (RG function). Sudden variation of movements are recorded by VLI index

Relationship between ΣE (Energy), Road Geometry (RG) and Visual Load Index (VLI)

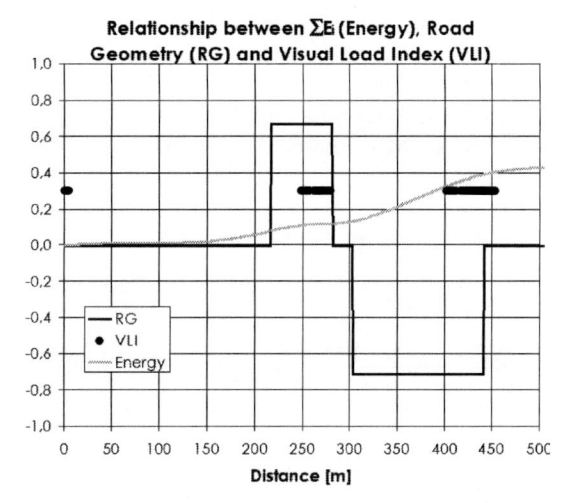

Figure 2. Relationship among Road geometry function, VLI index and Energy function spent in the visual activity. This last parameter rises during the distance and could be represent an index of driver's fatigue

If the element is a curve, attention is focused on the tangent point. As the driver entered the curve, observation of the inside road edge caused the Context Information function to identify a maximum or minimum point (depending on whether the curve is to the right or to the left). Beyond the maximum (or minimum) point, the driver has no further need for additional information and proceeds with examination of the next element.

As stated before, the maximum or the minimum point coincides with the point inside the curve beyond which the driver has no further need to acquire information about the geometric element negotiated and can direct his attentions to the next element. Therefore, the space and time spent (velocity function) are the space and time necessary to negotiate an element in total safety; these two points, together with the width of the maximum or minimum point (depending on whether the curve is to the left or to the right), therefore provide information on any difficulties encountered in the interpretation of the geometric element, the curve radius function, the deviation angle between the straight lines, traffic, visibility and other factors that may make driving activity more difficult.

Another interesting parameter is given by the quantification of the integral of the above function since it represents the energy expended by the driver in interpreting the road. This energy (E) can be measured for a single geometric element, such as a curve, or for a whole stretch of roadway in order to assign a specific or general level of difficulty.

This energy expended by the driver might be considered one of the components of the workload and, indeed, a measurement of the latter parameter using established techniques, such as the technique known as visual occlusion (Tsimhoni et al., 1999), would constitute a valid benchmark for the variable proposed in this study.

Method

Experimentation was performed in two main phases. The first was characterised by on-road trials, undertaken at the same time and under similar traffic conditions for all participants. The second phase concerned the post elaboration of telemetric data (speed, longitudinal and transversal acceleration, vehicle position and, therefore, trajectory) and, more importantly, examination of the relationship between these measurements and the driver's visual behaviour (Gonzales & Woods, 2001).

Eye movements were represented in a Cartesian diagram with units of measurement expressed in pixels. A number of flashing signals were superimposed on the graph thus obtained to highlight sudden variation in driver visual behaviour and therefore show the potential overload described as Visual Load Index. In the figures 1 and 2, VLI was shown using a segment of consistent height to represent the spatial coordinate at which the anomalous visual behaviour occurred.

Results

Results assuming identical contour conditions indicated good correlation between individual driving styles, as indicated by the figure 3 in the case of speed and for three different drivers. The quantification of the correlation has been omitted for the sake of brevity.

The differences between the drivers were mainly caused by local traffic conditions (junctions, passing, etc.) that had produced a different behaviour in term of speed, acceleration and eye movements.

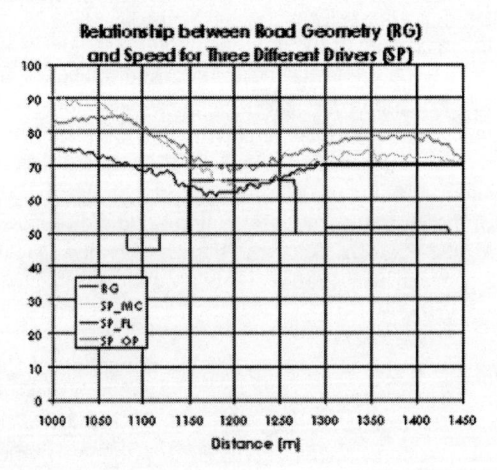

Figure 3. Speed behaviour of three different drivers in the section between 1000 and 1450 m

Some tables, as Table 1, summarise the performances for each driver. These indexes, some of which are totally original, are very useful to understand the driver behaviour. They are:

- Radius R [m].
- The speed maintained by the driver throughout negotiation of the entire section of road ΔV [km/h].
- Operating speed V_{85} [km/h], derived from the expression proposed by Lamm et al. (1999) and equal to $V_{85}= 105.31 + 2 \times 10^{-5} \times CCR_s^2 - 0.071 \times CCR_s$, where the Curvature Change Rate (CCR) is given by the following expression:

$$CCR_s = \frac{\left(\frac{Lc_{l1}}{2R} + \frac{Lc_r}{R} + \frac{Lc_{l2}}{2R}\right)}{L} \cdot \frac{200}{\pi} \cdot 10^3 \quad [gon/km] \qquad (2)$$

in which Lc indicates the length of any clothoids (not present in the stretch of road used in these tests) and Lc_r indicates the length of the circular curve.

- The deflection angle α [deg].
- The length of the circular curve Lc_r [m].
- The distance d_1 between the inflection point of the function representative of head-eye
- movement and the start of the circular curve [m] (Figure 4).
- The time t_1 required by the driver to reach the start of the curve following identification of the tangent [sec] (Figure 4).
- The distance d_2 between the curve bisector and the maximum (or minimum) point of the function illustrating head-eye movement [m] (Figure 4).
- The distance d_3 between two consecutive inflection points, indicative of the distance required to interpret the whole curve [m] (Figure 4).
- The ordinate of the maximum or minimum point, indicated by K here; the greater the 1/R curvature, the greater this ordinate should be (Figure 4).
- The energy E_i expended by the driver in negotiating the whole curve, equal to the integral determined between the abscissas of the inflection points [pixel^2].
- The energy ΣE_i progressively expended by the driver over the whole stretch of road negotiated up to the element under consideration [pixel^2].

Table 1. New Proposed Indexes. These new indexes help the analyst to understand the relationship among the single geometrical elements of the road and the visual behaviour of the drivers

	\multicolumn{8}{c}{Bend n°}
	1	2	3	4	5	6	7	8
R	75	70	180	160	160	400	130	1350
ΔV	65-73	66-68	72-74	74-80	85-88	84-76	67-70	72-74
V$_{85}$	66	62	97	94	94	109	89	116
α	80	113	32	26	22	5	52	6
Lc$_r$	64	137	99	70	60	35	116	133
d$_1$	55	12	83	39	44	-	156	-
t$_1$	0,80	0,18	1,14	0,51	0,51	-	2,28	-
d$_2$	37	2,5	48,5	18	-10	-	-49	-
d$_3$	50	78	84	56	84	-	156	-
K	0,3894	0,8024	0,0795	0,1257	0,3396	-	0,3946	-
1/R	0,0133	0,0143	0,0056	0,0063	0,0063	-	0,0077	-
E$_i$	34,02	91,17	22,24	8,82	57,05	-	65,23	-
ΣE$_i$	41,51	136,60	166,91	181,09	210,13	248,55	300,16	323,61

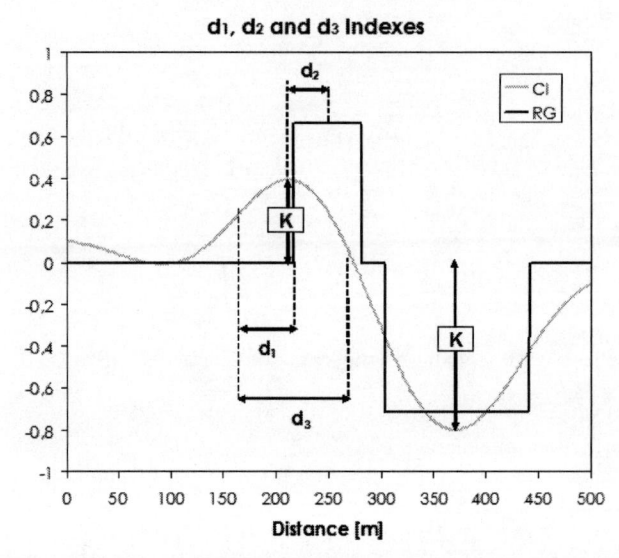

Figure 4. Meaning of d1, d2, d3 and K indexes: relationship among road geometry (RG function) and visual behaviour (CI function)

Discussion

V_{85} values, calculated according to Lamm's formulation for quite small radii (70-75m), reflect real driver behaviour, but differ considerably for larger radii. In the examined trials, the driver identified a comfortable driving speed and maintained it regardless of the fact that the curve radius would have allowed higher speeds. Presumably, other factors, such as traffic, the transversal section and conditions of visibility inhibited further acceleration.

The distance d_1 (and the time t_1 necessary to cover it) can have no generally valid relationship with road geometry, because the driver simply cannot look ahead the curve and is, therefore, forced to perform this activity over a shorter distance and space of time. In this case, the very limited length of the straight stretch of road preceding the curve under examination made a decisive difference.

It could be said that the magnitudes d_1 and t_1 are highly dependent on the geometry of the elements that precede them and that it is, therefore, important for curve radii not to be too dissimilar from each other because if the driver does not have sufficient time to interpret a new curve, he will deal with it in much the same way as he dealt with the previous one. This observation casts further doubt on the current trend to design roadways with continuous curves, i.e. with no straight sections between one curve and the next.

Distances d_2 and d_3 are also affected by the above constraints; the variable d_2 can assume negative values; this situation occurs when the driver continues to sample useful information despite having travelled beyond the bisector point in the curve.

The same observations can be made for Energy values (E), both in respect of an isolated geometric element and of the overall extension of roadway. Parameter E_i is, in some respects, more interesting than the previously calculated distances d_1, d_2 and d_3 in that it takes the value of the function into account. As stated in the paragraph on methodology, ΣE_i could be used in conjunction with existing methods to quantify the workload the driver is subject to.

In this sense, it would be interesting to hypothesise a threshold value for driver ability, even though this is a very subjective parameter. Working with a higher number of drivers than used in this study, it would be possible to define a value which would constitute the insuperable limit. It would be useful to establish two threshold values: the higher one representing driving ability, and the lower one being necessary to avoid a too much boredom at the steering wheel.

References

Bosurgi G., D'Andrea A., & Pellegrino O. (2004a). *Visual Load Index in Roads*. 82rd Transportation Research Board Annual Meeting 2004, Washington DC, USA.
Bosurgi G., D'Andrea A., & Pellegrino O. (2004b). Visual Complexity in traffic as indicated by image analysis. In D. de Waard, K.A. Brookhuis, and C.M. Weikert, *Human Factors in Design* (pp.321-326). Maastricht, The Netherlands: Shaker Publishing.
Bosurgi G., D'Andrea A., & Pellegrino O. (2005). *A methodology to study driving behaviour based on the visual activity*. 83rd Transportation Research Board Annual Meeting 2005, Washington D.C., USA
Gonzales, R.C., & Woods, R.E. (2001). *Digital Image Processing*. Second Edition, New York: Prentice Hall.
Lamm, R., Psarianos, B., Mailaender, T. (1999). *Highway Design and Traffic Safety Engineering Handbook*. New York: McGraw-Hill.
Land, M.F. (1992). Predictable eye-head coordination during driving. *Nature, 359*, 318-320.
Land, M.F. (1998). The visual control of steering. In L.R. Harris and K. Jenkin (Eds.) *Vision and Action* (pp. 163-180). Cambridge University Press
Tsimhoni, O., Yoo, E., & Green, P. (1999). *Effects of Visual Demand and In-Vehicle Task Complexity on Driving and Task Performance as Assessed by Visual Occlusion*. Technical Report UMTRI 99-37. Ann Arbor: The University of Michigan, Transportation Research Institute.

Evaluation of different ergonomic factors in the cabin of drivers in public transport

Iva Macku & Alexandr Pesak
CDV, Transport Research Centre
Brno, Czech Republic

Abstract

An exploratory questionnaire study was conducted on perception of ergonomically relevant factors of the design of driver cabins in public transport operations. The focus was on driver's satisfaction with using different vehicles with different designs of panel boards. Of the 1500 questionnaires distributed to drivers due to low rate of return and missing answers only 403 could be considered for analysis. One third of the drivers admitted that using different types of vehicles could lead to a higher probability of error, wrong manoeuvres or delayed reactions. According to the answers given switching between different interface layouts requires an adaptation to different driving characteristics of the vehicle, characteristics of braking and different display and control settings and arrangements. One third of the drivers conceded that shifting vehicles contributes to an increase in effort especially in demanding traffic situations. Nearly two thirds of the respondents said they would support technical standards or guidelines that would enforce consistent design of vehicle panel boards. Although results could be based on a small number of questionnaires only a more systematic evaluation of working conditions in public transport operations based on representative samples of driving situations and subjective as well as observational measures seems to be urgently necessary to improve safety and well being of the drivers as well as the passengers.

Introduction

Professional drivers, including drivers in public transport, present one of the most endangered professions (Hladký, 2005). Among other stressors that occur in the everyday work those of high impact for professional drivers are high demands on cognitive processes (perception, attention, memory, decision making), high responsibility, monotony of work, time pressure, social conflicts (dealing with passengers), physical stressors, such as noise and vibrations (Duffy & McGoldrick, 1990; Kompier, 1996; Kompier et al., 2000; Peters & Nilsson, 1997). For bus, trolleybus and tram drivers it is therefore necessary to successfully balance the competing demands of safety, customer-focused services and company regulations (Tse et al., 2006).

Responses on stress can be expressed in the area of emotions or in the area of vegetative functions, like increased blood pressure or body temperature, which may lead to different negative consequences for professional drivers' health. The intensity of potential impairments depends on the individual coping strategies, attitudes to work, resistance to stress, motivation and other factors. In other words, stressors can lead to certain physical (e.g., cardiovascular disease, gastrointestinal disorders, musculoskeletal problems, fatigue), mental (e.g., anxiety, depression) and behavioural (e.g., substance abuse) consequences (Tse et al., 2006). It is therefore to be assumed that driving a vehicle is a relatively demanding task. Reed and Cronin (2003) highlight the fact that professional drivers are daily exposed to multiple stressors. Long and irregular working hours of drivers contribute to high workload, fatigue and stress. The combination of these stressors can lead to risky or inappropriate behaviour and inappropriate conflict management, and thus has negative consequences on safety (Machin, 2001).

In the area of stress prevention, ergonomics and optimisation of working conditions are considered as very important factors. The aim is to improve the effectiveness of the operator-system interaction by optimising his or her workload. In this respect stressors for bus drivers include poor cabin ergonomics (Bakalář, 1985). Dashboard displays and controls should be visible and simple (Štikar et al., 2003). Moreover, the buttons should be placed close to the centre of the view or within the primary visual area, so that drivers do not have to take away their attention for longer periods of time. However, some of the recommendations for prevention of occupational stress may cause conflicting results; ergonomics and human factors analysis and design of driver cabins is therefore required. According to Štikar et al. (2003) appropriate arrangement and design of the driver dashboards have the potential to decrease the risk of operating errors, to improve driver reaction times and to reduce level of fatigue.

Recommendations for prevention of occupational stress of drivers refer e.g. to the following aspects (see e.g. also Grösbrink & Mahr, 1998):

- Ergonomics of driver's cabin (special attention should be devoted e.g. to the position and adjustment of the seat position, steering wheel and pedals, visibility of symbols and settlement of actuators and overall adjustment of the working area to the drivers)
- Working time schedules (including e.g. quality of rest breaks, reduced time constraints)
- Psychosocial environment (e.g. training of the social skills, programmes for coping with stress and fatigue, dealing with management, colleagues and customers, consultation of problems)

The aim of this exploratory study is to gain information on public transport drivers´ perception of the design quality of ergonomic factors in the cabin of their vehicle. The special focus will be on switching between the vehicles during public transport operations and drivers´ perception of these aspects and cabin design issues – and how they can influence their everyday job in terms of stress, comfort and safety.

Method

A questionnaire was specifically created for exploration of drivers' perception of ergonomic factors of panel board design, especially their perception of different arrangements of displays and controls with arrangement of displays and controls arrangement of displays and controls on the dashboard, and of drivers' satisfaction with usage of different types of vehicles within their everyday task. The development of the questionnaire was based on information gathered in a focus group previously carried out with 6 drivers of public transport vehicles in Brno and their supervisor. The questionnaire included 22 questions concerning drivers' satisfaction with usage of different types of vehicles, disposition of controls, number of accidents during their professional life, years of professional driving, and other questions regarding age, gender, education, marital status and health conditions. The questionnaire itself has not yet been standardised and published.

1500 questionnaires have been distributed to public transport drivers in two cities of the Czech Republic (Brno and Ostrava). In Brno, drivers filled in the questionnaires during at the beginning of their regular training sessions. All drivers in the classroom received the questionnaire. In Ostrava, questionnaires were distributed through the managers of the drivers. In total 403 questionnaires were filled in and returned (153 from Brno, 250 from Ostrava). Because of the low rate of return the samples of drivers were not representative. The average age of the respondents (86 % males and 14 % females) was 44.5 years. The average age of drivers' experience of drivers in public transport was 12 years. The biggest group of drivers was bus drivers.

Questions of the questionnaire referring to core issues of the study were as follows:

- Are drivers in public transport satisfied with the usage of different types of vehicles within their job?
- How drivers perceive shifting between different vehicles and usage of different dashboards?
- What drivers do like and do not like on the dashboard?
- What risks may arise from different inter-vehicle design of dashboards?
- Is there any link between satisfaction or dissatisfaction with dashboard design and the number of drivers' accidents, or possibly with other factors under investigation?

Results

The analysis of the questionnaires resulted in some interesting findings. Although the hypothesis that dissatisfaction with dashboard design and/or switching between vehicles correlates with higher numbers of accidents in drivers' history was not confirmed, approximately one half of the respondents admitted that using different types of vehicles *may lead to higher risk of a wrong manoeuvres*. Drivers also found that in the case of shifting between vehicles, they had to *devote more effort in demanding traffic situations*. Drivers also said that these risks could not be reduced by training, but by optimisation of their work and equipment in this respect.

According to the results presented in Figure 1 drivers admitted the possibility of wrong manoeuvre (i.e. choice of a driving behaviour that is not appropriate for the context in terms of safety), which may be caused by shifting between vehicles and different types of dashboards. On the one hand 30% of the drivers absolutely agreed with this statement and another 18% rather agreed. On the other hand, almost 16% of the drivers did not agree at all and another 15% rather disagreed.

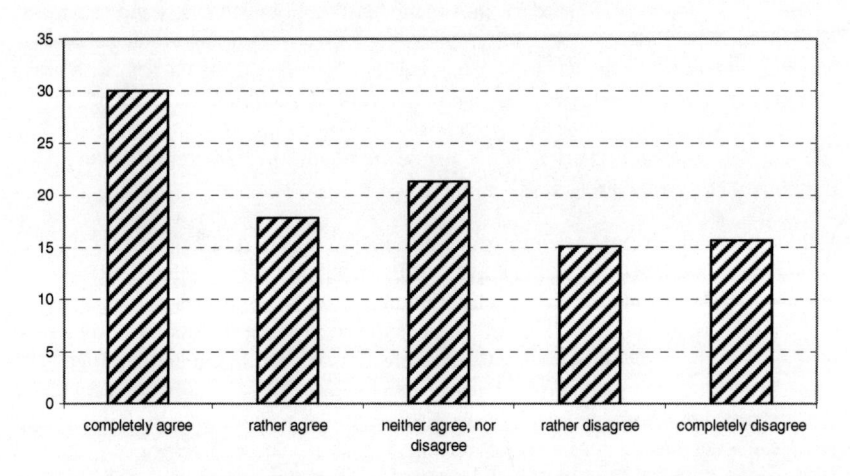

Figure 1 Switching between different types of vehicles may lead to higher probability of wrong manoeuvre (responses in %)

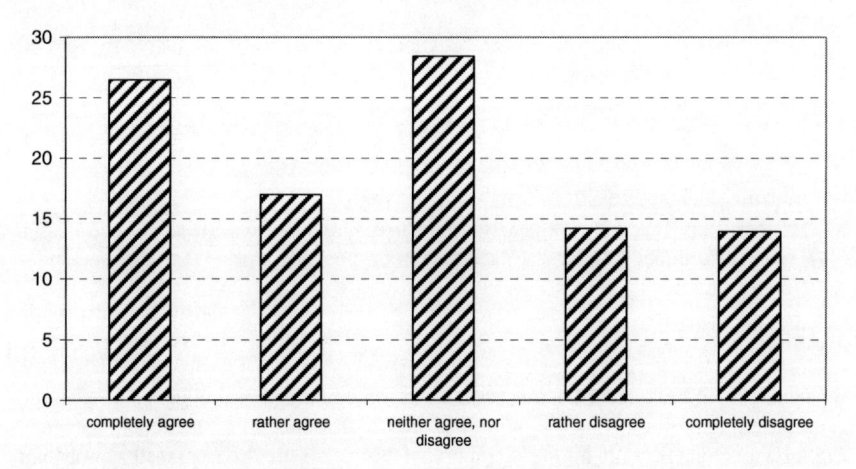

Figure 2. Switching between different types of vehicles contributes to higher mental effort during the driving task (responses in %)

Approximately one third of the drivers confirmed that shifting between different types of vehicles may have contributed to higher mental effort during driving (Figure 2). More than half of respondents thought that the possibility to change the vehicles led to an increase of concentration necessary for the driving task (Figure 3). Also approximately half of the drivers thought that the possibility to change the vehicles increases the variety of work (Figure 4).

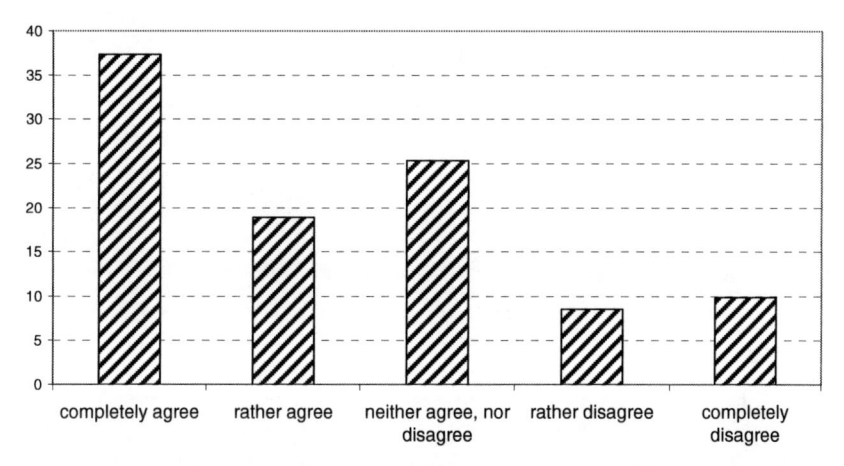

Figure 3. Switching between different types of vehicles contributes to better concentration on the driving task (responses in %)

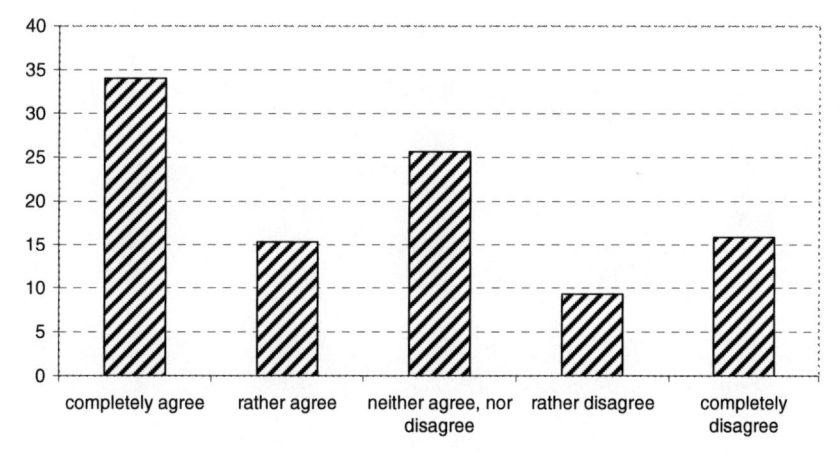

Figure 4. Switching between different types of vehicles contributes to a higher diversity of work (responses in %)

Although most of their working time drivers drove one type of the vehicle, 46% of the drivers used different types (mainly three different ones). As illustrated in Figure 5, drivers are mostly satisfied with these conditions, although almost 25% of drivers (both drivers that always drove the same type of vehicle and drivers who drove different types of vehicles) preferred to drive one type of vehicle only. As negative features, drivers mentioned that each vehicle has different qualities, different braking characteristics and in particular different arrangement of dashboards (displays and controls), e.g. the control for the emergency brake.

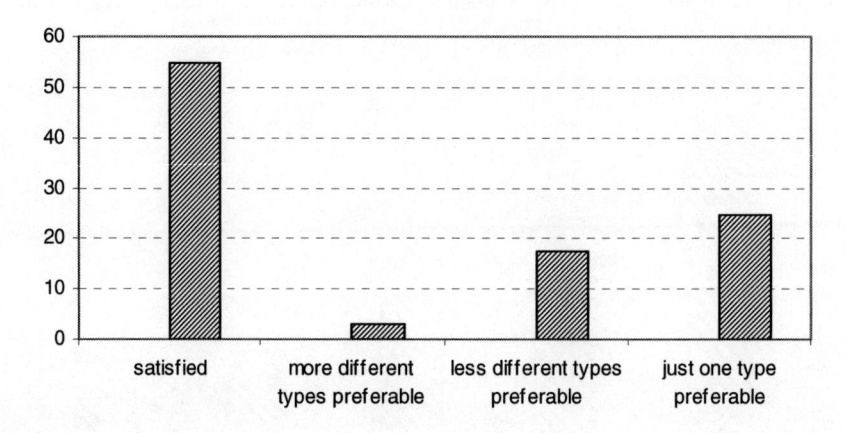

Figure 5. Drivers´ satisfaction with switching between different types of vehicles (responses in %)

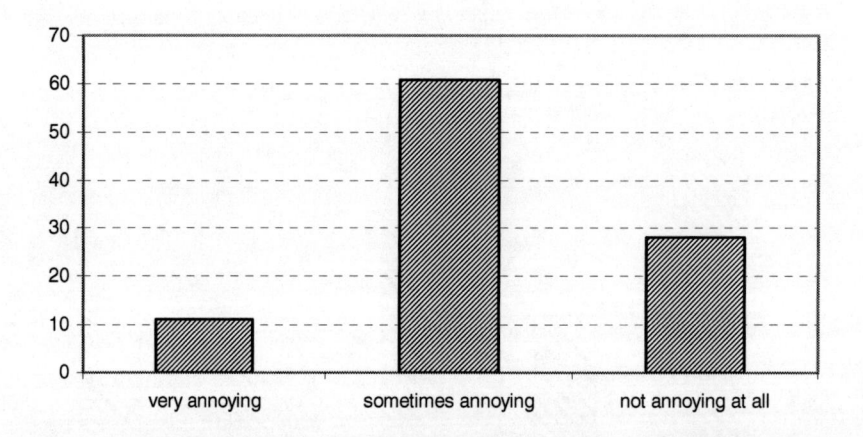

Figure 6. Perception of different disposition of operating buttons in different types of vehicles (responses in %)

Most of the drivers perceived using different types of vehicles as negative because there is a *risk of overlooking a signal, wrong manoeuvre and late or incorrect reaction*. In general, drivers thought that if they use different vehicles, they have to devote *more effort in demanding traffic situations*. Drivers also perceived that these risks cannot be minimised by the training, but by a *more consistent design of dashboards across vehicles*. Approximately 60% of respondents said that sometimes they mind the different disposition of actuators on the dashboard (Figure 6). The majority of drivers (62%) would support application of technical standards or guidelines, which would *guarantee a more uniform design of dashboards* (Figure 7). As crucial drivers considered colour coding of different buttons and they recommended that colours and coding should be consistently used for *operating doors, bells and hand brakes* across all vehicles in public transport.

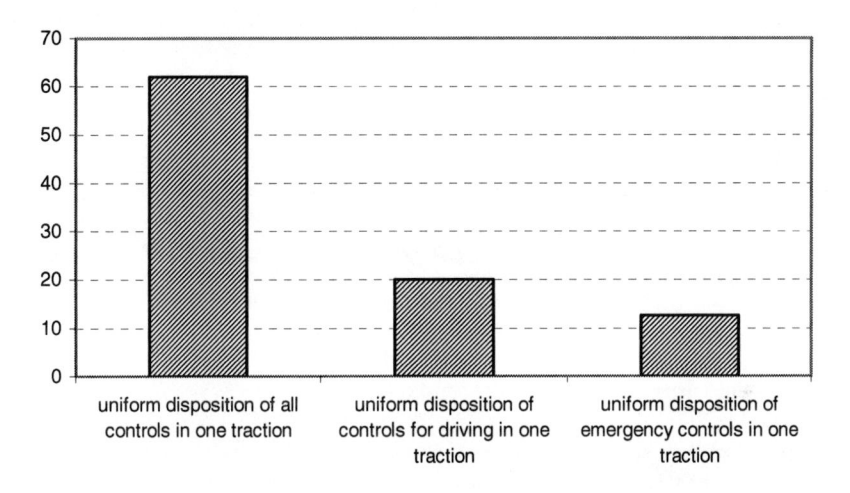

Figure 7. Support for technical standards and guidelines that would provide uniform presentation of displays and controls within a system for transportation (bus, tram, trolleybus) (responses in %)

Discussion and Conclusions

The results of the study are in accordance with findings of Kompier et al. (2000; Kompier, 1996) and Peters and Nilsson (1997), who highlight the importance of consistent design across different types of vehicles for the safety reasons and satisfaction of professional drivers. Based on the driver's feedback it can also be suggested that dashboard design may influence the level of mental and visual workload and that optimal ergonomic conditions would allow for eliminating or at least reducing the risk of wrong actions, errors or slowed down reaction especially in difficult driving situations. It seems to be necessary to devote more attention to public transport drivers and an ergonomic design of driver cabins. Often it is not possible to significantly change cabin design for vehicles already in use. However, it can be assumed that even slight adaptations and practical interventions can lead to improvements of driver wellbeing when taking into account a work systems approach and variations in demands imposed on drivers (as with switching between different types of vehicles) and when systematically implemented and evaluated. By improving ergonomically relevant factors within and across vehicles, it can be expected that the efficiency and safety of transport will be enhanced for drivers and passengers.

The authors of the study are aware of limitations of the results presented. Although questionnaires were addressed to all public transport drivers in two different cities rate of return was rather low and it therefore remains unclear whether results presented are representative. As the questionnaire study had exploratory character a follow up study should not only include efforts to increase rate of return and by that allow for a more sophisticated analysis of data but also include systematic task analyses and some observational measures to allow for deducing more specific interventions for cabin design especially with regard to the need to switch between different types of vehicles or generations of vehicle design.

References

Bakalář, P. (1985). *Bližší analýza psychických nároků na vybrané kategorie řidičů ČSAD a MHD*. Prague, Czech Republic: Ústav silniční a městské dopravy

Duffy, C.A., & McGoldrick, A.E. (1990). Stress and the bus driver in the UK transport. *Work and Stress, 4*, 17-27.

Grösbrink, A., & Mahr, A. (1998). Ergonomics of bus driving (in Chapter 102: Transport Industry and Warehousing. In J.M. Stellman (Ed.), *Encyclopaedia of Occupational Health and Safety* (vol. 3). Geneva, Switzerland: International Labour Office.

Hladký, A. (2005). Prevence stresu v práci: Strategie vládních orgánů v evropských zemích. *Psychologie v ekonomické praxi, 1-2*(ročník XL), 1-26.

Kompier M.A. (1996): *Bus drivers: Occupational stress and stress prevention* (CONDI/T/WP.2/1996). Geneva: International Labour Office.

Kompier, M.A., Aust, B., van den Berg, A.M., & Siegrist, J. (2000). Stress prevention in bus drivers: Evaluation of 13 natural experiments. *Journal of Occupational Health Psychology, 5*, 11-31.

Machin, M.A. (2001). *Evaluating a non-prescriptive fatigue management strategy for express coach drivers. A report prepared for the Australian Transport Safety Board.* Toowoomba, Australia: University of Southern Queensland. (Retrieved 05.04.2007 from http://www.usq.edu.au/users/machin/atsb.htm)

Peters, B., & Nilsson, L. (1997). Professional Drivers. In D. Brune, G. Gerhardsson, G.W. Crockford, & D. Norbäck (Eds), *The Workplace, Volume 2, part 3* (pp. 239-265). Oslo, Norway: Scandinavian Science Publisher.

Reed, D.B., & Cronin, J.S.: (2003). Health on the road: Issues faced by female truck drivers. *American Association of Occupational Health Nurses Journal, 51*, 120-125.

Štikar, J., Rymeš, M., Riegel, K., & Hoskovec, J. (2003). *Psychologie ve světě práce (Psychology in the world of work)*. Prague: Karolinum

Tse, J.L.M., Flin, R., & Mearns, K. (2006). Bus driver well-being review: 50 years of research. *Transportation Research Part F, 9*, 89-114.

Perceived styling and usability in integrated centre panel layouts as a function of interaction style and age

Robert Broström[1,2], Peter Bengtsson[1], & Jakob Axelsson[2]
[1]Luleå University of Technology, Luleå
[2]Volvo Car Corporation, Göteborg
Sweden

Abstract

In the past ten years information and entertainment functionality has become an increasingly important part of the car interior. Infotainment functions have been growing in number and diversity, concurrently with a trend towards utilization of fewer controls and graphical displays in integrated centre panel layouts. This evolution has solved many functional and styling issues. However, as a consequence, several usability and safety concerns have been raised. A number of these concerns are related to age, a factor that is especially important in the premium car segment where a majority of drivers are older than 50 years. This study investigated perceived styling and usability of premium car centre panel layouts among different age groups. The investigation was based on APEAL customer survey data from the North American market, associated with the sound system. Questions on the appearance (styling), understanding (usability) and ease of use while driving (usability/safety) of the stereo faceplate and controls were analysed. The results showed that all age groups perceived the appearance of integrated centre panel layouts similarly. However, with rising age, there is a decrease in perceived understanding and ease of use while driving in the case of a number of premium car models.

Introduction

The use of secondary task functions, such as information and entertainment devices, while driving is under debate owing to possibly increased driver distraction and traffic safety risks. From the 100-car Naturalistic Driving Study, conducted in the United States of America, Klauer et al. (2006) concluded that 78 percent of all crashes and 93 percent of rear end crashes were caused by the driver's visual inattention to the forward roadway. The study also indicated that inattention caused by secondary tasks accounted for 23 percent of all crashes and near crashes in the study. Today, in premium cars, hundreds of functions are incorporated in the context of the centre panel, known earlier as "the radio". In addition to the traditional AM/FM channels, modern radios also offer a variety of media such as CD, mp3, DVD and over 100 channels of satellite audio programs (Lind et al., 2004). The centre panel control and display layout in premium cars also integrate other systems, such as navigation, telephone, climate, vehicle settings, television etc.

According to Tan et al. (2004) there are three main centre panel layout configurations on the market today, conventional, hybrid and integrated centre panel layouts (Figure 1). These can be characterized as follows: *Conventional centre panel layouts* – Dedicated displays and controls for each sub-system (e.g., audio, climate control or navigation) grouped horizontally and stacked. *Hybrid centre panel layouts* – At least one common display shared by individual sub-systems. Layout retains some conventional aspects. *Integrated centre panel layouts* – A single, common display and a control configuration that breaks the visual and physical barriers of conventional and hybrid layouts. In this study the integrated layout group was divided into touch screen, close control and remote control interaction styles.

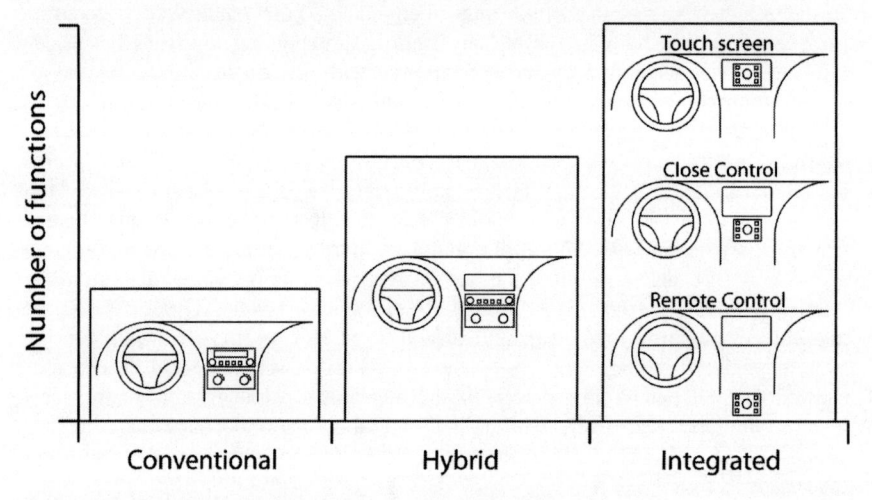

Figure 1. Conventional, hybrid and integrated centre panel layouts with the number of functions increasing

The premium segment for modern cars is dominated today by hybrid and integrated layouts. However, there seems to be an inevitable drive towards integrated centre panel layouts caused by the introduction of new technologies, evolving interior design trends and new methods for interaction processes, such as touch screen and multifunction rotary controls. This functional evolution can be compared with mobile phones. Because of large feature sets, contemporary mobile phones, state of the art 2002, had to change mapping for a majority of functions from control keys to menus, an indirect manipulation style (Kiljander, 2004). In an indirect manipulation the user first selects the object and then uses a pushbutton or the like to initiate the operation (Davies & Thomas, 2001). In the car domain indirect operations can be demanding for driver resources because of their interactive visual and manual demands (Wierwille, 1993). In a study done by Transport Canada, Burns et al. (2005) found when assessing two premium cars with integrated centre panel layouts that these could contribute to cognitive distraction by requiring drivers to remember what mode they were in. The layouts, which consisted of a centrally mounted LCD screen and a console mounted multifunction rotary control knob, were also criticised since information that was once a button press away was now hidden in hierarchical menu structures, hence an indirect manipulation style. Methods for the interaction processes and the position of controls and displays have also been studied. Zwahlen et al. (1988) suggested that operating touch screens while driving is visually demanding if not dangerous based on the lane position measures in the test. Moreover, in a comparison of a high and a low touch screen display position, no significant differences were found for number of glances. Manes and Green (1997) showed when assessing control and display position in a simulation study that locating the display high on the instrument panel and the control low was recommended, even if the differences between the locations were not significant. Pak et al. (2002) found, when comparing performance for a touch screen and a rotary control that precise operations and long distance moves were more effectively carried out with the rotary control. However, the touch screen performed better when the system required button pushing or other pointing tasks. Absolute positioning of a secondary task display may also have an effect on safety and usability. In a simulated driving task Wittman et al. (2006) concluded that the distance between the onboard display and the outside line of sight had an effect on both behavioural data and subjective scores on workload. Vertical eccentricities had a more destructive effect than horizontal distance. These results are in line with the principles of the Alliance of Automobile Manufacturers (AAM, 2002), where for example principle 1.4 states that a visual display should be placed high on the instrument panel towards the driver's side of the central console. The explicit recommendation is that a display should be mounted at a position where the downward viewing angle is less than 30 degrees at the geometric centre of the display.

When interaction becomes more complex in terms of locating and activating certain functions it is likely that increasing age has a negative influence on usability. Dukic et al. (2006) found when testing different button locations in a real driving task that older drivers had significantly longer visual time off the road and larger steering wheel deviation than younger drivers for all positions. However, in the subjective ratings on safety, the older group had a higher perceived safety on all button positions than the younger group. In a simulator study where visual information was presented and the participants were to respond by pressing a button, Liu (2001) found that older drivers performed worse regarding both response time and accuracy in the response. Manes and Green (1997) also found that the effect of age was significant for total task time and task accuracy, and Baldwin (2002) concluded that contrast sensitivity, dynamic visual acuity, peripheral vision skills, motion perception and visual search abilities were affected by advanced age. On the other hand, Pak et al. (2002) found that a larger training effect was present for old compared to young subjects using a rotary control.

The harmonization of strategic attributes in developing new centre panel layouts is a multifaceted process influenced by several stakeholders. Various assessment methodologies are utilized to evaluate the effects on attributes. Safety measures are regulated by different principles and guidelines agreed upon for example within the Alliance of Automobile Manufacturers and the International Standards Organization and by local requirements (e.g. Stevens et al., 2002), hence with a primary focus on injury prevention. Styling and usability measures are shaped both by internal car company studies (e.g. expert evaluations) and by customer satisfaction surveys. The results of customer satisfaction surveys, which are subjective evaluation methods, are particularly important from a sale and repurchase point of view and therefore a key factor in decisions on new design concepts. However, in subjective evaluations of usability, participants may be biased by their opinions of styling. For example, Tractinsky et al. (2000) and Kurosu and Kashimura (1995) found when studying computerized systems that perceived usability was affected more by the interfaces' aesthetics than by the actual usability of the systems examined. These results suggest that users are affected by their opinions of styling, even when interfaces are assessed in their usability aspects. These studies indicate that there may be a divergence between the results from customer surveys and human factors studies on usability.

The purpose of the present study was to analyse how different interaction styles in integrated centre panel layouts affected car owners' ratings of styling and usability based on APEAL customer survey data. The increasing number of new in-vehicle functions makes studies of systems integration important for the purpose of mobility and road safety. Moreover APEAL data has influence on design assessment within automotive industry.

Method

The APEAL USA market survey of 2005 (J.D. Power, 2005) assessed customer satisfaction issues based on over 115,000 new vehicle owners (model year 2005 and 2006) during their first 90 days of ownership. Nine categories of vehicle performance and design data such as cockpit/instrument panel, comfort/convenience, heating, ventilation/cooling and the sound system were collected.

In this study answers concerning the sound system from 2365 owners of premium cars with integrated centre panel layouts were extracted from the APEAL survey. The questions selected were:

- appearance of the stereo faceplate and controls
- ability to easily understand the controls
- ability to easily use the controls while driving

Answers were given on a scale of 1 to 10, where 1 denotes unacceptable, 5 average and 10 outstanding. The integrated centre panel layouts were further sorted on the basis of their interaction style (Figure 1): first, the "touch screen interaction style", implying a touch screen with mode buttons on or in close proximity to the display; second, the "close control interaction style", meaning a layout where a display, mode buttons and multifunctional controls are arranged in close proximity; finally, the "remote control interaction style", signifying mode buttons and multifunctional controls grouped in remote proximity to the display.

To study related differences, the answers were also divided into five groups based on the car owners' age, from up to 34 to over 65 years of age (Table 1).

Table 1. Distribution of age groups and interaction styles for integrated centre panel layouts.

Interaction style	–34	35-44	45-54	55-64	65+	All age groups
TS1	1	8	24	32	56	121
TS2	23	43	82	108	102	358
Touch screen	**24**	**51**	**106**	**140**	**158**	**479**
CC1	15	67	126	155	121	484
CC2	10	17	41	37	24	129
Close Control	**25**	**84**	**167**	**192**	**145**	**613**
RC1	39	84	129	153	79	484
RC2	88	178	233	199	91	789
Remote Control	**127**	**262**	**362**	**352**	**170**	**1273**
Total per age group	*176*	*397*	*635*	*684*	*473*	*2365*

The data were analysed with two factors ANOVAs with Age group as the within subject factor and Interaction style as the between subject factor. An alpha level of .05 was used in the analyses. The Tukey HSD procedure was used for post hoc pairwise comparisons of means.

Results

Appearance of the stereo faceplate and controls

For the question concerning the appearance of the stereo faceplate and controls the two-way ANOVA showed no significant effect for Interaction styles or Age group (Figure 2, Figure 3(a)).

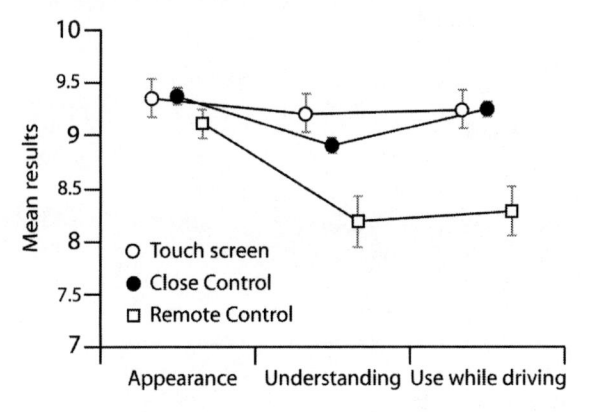

Figure 2. Mean values for answers on appearance, understanding and ease of use while driving for different interaction styles. Answers were given on a scale of 1 to 10, where 1 denotes unacceptable, 5 average and 10 outstanding

Ability to easily understand the controls

In the question on ability to easily understand the controls the analysis indicated significant main effects for both Interaction style, $F(2, 15) = 61.9, p < .001$, and age group, $F(4, 15) = 9.45$, $p < .001$. An Interaction style x Age interaction was also present, $F(8, 15) = 5.58$, $p < .01$. The post hoc test revealed a lower result for remote control compared with the other two interaction styles (Figure 2).

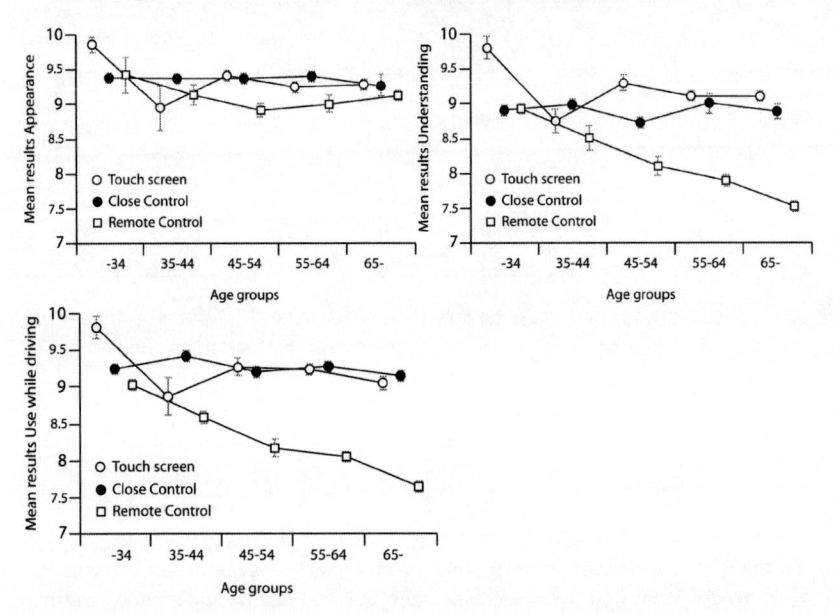

Figure 3 (a)-(c). (a) Mean values for the answers on appearance, (b) understanding and (c) ease of use while driving for integrated centre panel layouts with rising age. Answers were given on a scale of 1 to 10, where 1 denotes unacceptable, 5 average and 10 outstanding

For age groups, one-way ANOVAs and post hoc tests revealed differences between interaction styles for all age groups except the 35-44 group (Figure 3(b)). For the age group up to 34 the touch screen interaction style had a significantly higher result than the other two interaction styles, $F(2, 3) = 13.23$, $p < .05$. In the 45-54 age group the remote control interaction style had a significantly lower result than the touch screen interaction style, $F(2, 3) = 16.18$, $p < .05$. For the two oldest groups, 55-64 and 65+, there were significantly lower results for the remote control interaction style compared to the other two interaction styles, $F(2, 3) = 24.94$, $p < .05$ for 55-64 and $F(2, 3) = 71.56$, $p < .01$ for 65+. Furthermore, analysis of each interaction style over age groups using one way ANOVAs showed significant differences for the remote control interaction style, $F(4, 5) = 11.97$, $p < .01$ (Figure 3(b)). The post hoc test showed significantly higher results for the youngest (up to 34) compared with the two oldest age groups (55-64 and 65+). The oldest age group (65+) showed a significantly lower result than the two youngest (up to 34 and 35-44) for the remote control interaction style. There was no indication of significant differences over age within the other interaction styles.

Ability to easily use the controls while driving

In the question on ability to easily use the controls while driving the analysis also showed significant main effects for both interaction style, $F(2, 15) = 80.12, p < .001$, and age groups, $F(4, 15) = 11.48, p < .001$. An Interaction style x Age interaction, $F(8, 15) = 5.08, p < .01$, was also present. In the same manner as in the question on ability to easily understand the controls the post hoc test revealed a lower result for the remote control- than the other interaction styles (Figure 2). One-way ANOVAs and post hoc tests done on age groups revealed differences between interaction styles for all age groups except the 35-44 group (Figure 3(c)). For the up to 34 age group the touch screen interaction style showed a significantly higher result than the other two interaction styles, $F(2, 3) = 9.5, p < .05$. In all the other older groups (45-54, 55-64, 65+) there were significantly lower results for the remote control interaction style compared to the other interaction styles. $F(2, 3) = 20.49, p < .05$ for 45-54, $F(2, 3) = 76.6, p < .005$ for 55-64 and $F(2, 3) = 124.1, p < .005$ for 65+. In contrast to the question on understanding sound controls a difference between interaction styles was found in a younger age group for ease of use while driving. Furthermore, analysis of each interaction style over age groups with one-way ANOVAs showed significant differences for the remote control interaction style, $F(4, 5) = 24.7, p < .005$ (Figure 3(c)). The post hoc test showed a significantly higher result for the youngest (up to 34) as compared to all age groups except the 35-44 group; moreover, the oldest age group (65+) had a significantly lower result than the two youngest (up to 34 and 35-44) for the remote control interaction style. No significant differences were indicated over age within the other interaction styles.

In summary, the results for appearance of the stereo faceplate and controls were similar for all interaction styles. Results on the ability to easily understand the controls and the ability to easily use the controls while driving were reduced with rising age for remote control layouts. There were no significant differences between age groups for touch screen and close control layouts in terms of ability to easily understand the controls and ability to easily use the controls while driving.

Discussion

The purpose of the present study was to analyse how different interaction styles in integrated centre panel layouts affected car owners' ratings of styling and usability based on APEAL customer survey data.

Even though cars with integrated centre panel layouts incorporate a great many functions, they seem preferable to cars with conventional and hybrid layouts. Interior space, instead of being cluttered with buttons and controls, can be used for sophisticated styling elements and for other high priority functions in the interior of the car. The results show agreement with the industrial rationale for increased integration, i.e. integrating state of the art functionality and increasing styling possibilities despite the growth in functions. The result for appearance of the stereo faceplate and controls is similar for interaction styles in integrated centre panel layouts (Figure 2).

Although all of the interaction styles had a similar number of functions, the ratings on ability to easily understand the controls and easily use the controls while driving are significantly lower for remote control than for touch screen and close control interaction styles (Figure 2). Three major discrepancies within integrated layouts that may affect these results are control-display proximity, display position and the ability to operate functions in a direct manner (Figure 4). However, in the study by Pak et al. (2002) the nature of the tasks, e.g. pointing or moving, defined what control type, touch screen or rotary control, was more effective. This suggests that some tasks are easier with touch screen than with rotary control and may be the case for some of the sound functions. However that does not explain the difference between results for close control and remote control interaction styles.

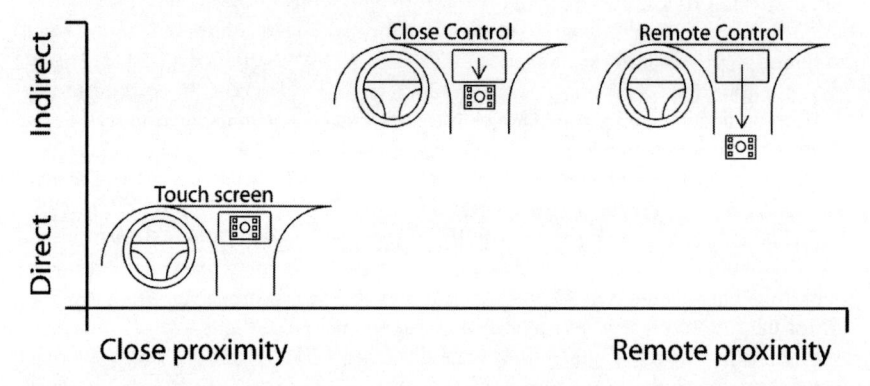

Figure 4. Interaction styles within integrated centre panel layouts. Three major factors may affect the variation: (1) control-display proximity, (2) display position and the ability to (3) operate functions in a direct manner

For all interaction styles, the results for appearance of the stereo faceplate and controls are constant over age (Figure 3 (a)). For remote control interaction style the ratings for the ability to easily understand the controls and to easily use the controls while driving significantly decrease with rising age. This is not the case for close control- and touch screen interaction style over age (Figure 3 (b)-(c)).

The remote control interaction style has due to its rotary control a higher degree of indirect manipulation compared to the touch screen interaction style (Pak et al., 2002). This may explain the decreasing ratings for understanding with age. The close control interaction style also comprises a high degree of indirect manipulation, however, although with no age effect on understanding. This result is not expected since the display position is the same as that of the close control interaction style. The only major difference between close control and remote control interaction styles is the lower control position in the remote control interaction style. It is reasonable to assume that the lower control position is not the only factor that contributes to the poorer understanding with age in the case of the remote control interaction style. Further studies are thus needed to gain an understanding of this relationship. The touch screen interaction style shows no significant decrease for the combination of understanding or ease of use while driving and rising age. The results observed over age seem to be due to the high degree of direct manipulation that is present in the touch screen interaction style. Direct manipulation supports novices, most probably among older age groups, in their learning of basic functionality quickly, but it also supports knowledgeable intermittent users in retaining the conceptual model (Hutchins et al., 1985).

In terms of the remote control interaction style the ratings on ease of use while driving decrease with rising age. For the close control- and touch screen interaction style, however, there is no effect with higher age. An increasing age-related demand on the primary task can affect the efficiency as concerns secondary tasks, especially in locating, identifying and selecting buttons and controls with regard to the roadway. For example, Baldwin (2002) explains that contrast sensitivity, dynamic visual acuity, peripheral vision skills, motion perception and visual search abilities are affected by advanced age. This may support the lower rating for ease of use while driving in the case of the remote control interaction style due to higher visual demands in locating controls. However, the low control position encourages blind location and operation, which should be the best control position according to Manes and Green (1997).

Even though the touch screen interaction style has the shortest distance between controls and display, the position of the display is further down in the centre panel owing to reach issues. In addition, interacting with a touch screen demands actual transfer of visual attention away from the road to the screen due to lack of tactile feedback (Stevens et al., 2002). The lower display position for the touch screen interaction style as compared to the other two styles is not beneficial for a user of any age. Wittmann et al. (2005) concluded that the best display position is the same as that of the close control- and the remote control interaction styles.

In premium cars of today it is becoming increasingly common to implement integrated centre panel layouts. The drives for change are functional growth and styling issues. All age groups appreciated the integrated centre panel layouts from a styling perspective. Nonetheless, it is noticeable that older people have difficulty understanding and using the remote control interaction style. It seems paradoxical that more than 70 percent of cars with integrated layouts are purchased by customers older than 45 years (Table 1). The subjective results for easily understanding the controls and ability to easily use the controls while driving seem to be dependent on age group. The next generation of older users of cars equipped with integrated layouts will most likely find it easier to understand the structure of a menu-based system because of their greater experience with computers and consumer electronics. However, it is not clear whether their experience will balance the physical and cognitive impairments that are inevitable with increasing age. Moreover the findings from the study by Dukic et al. (2006) indicate that the subjective ratings on safety were perceived higher for the older group, irregardless of the control position, even if their driving performance were worse. This may point towards additional differences between age groups regarding driving performance than the subjective ratings reveal in this study. In previously mentioned studies that have analysed effects in age differences, the comparisons have often been based on two groups where one is below 20 and the other above 65 years of age. The results for remote control interaction style in this study indicate that there are perceived differences between age groups within a narrower age span. Further research is needed here.

In the development of new cars, data from customer surveys are a key factor in decisions about new design concepts. This study shows that some aspects about perceived usability in the APEAL data are supported by the literature. In other cases, however, the results concerning users' perceptions fail completely in matching reports in the literature. As customer surveys have a central role in indicating customer opinions, there is a need to be able to interpret the data within a consistent framework. This must be further investigated.

In summary, the results reported in this paper indicate that subjective differences exist between interaction styles and age groups for two questions on the usability of sound controls. Age must be considered when designing usable centre panel layouts. However, other factors may be hidden within the age factor, and this is thus an interesting topic for further research. The proximity between controls and display has an effect on perceived usability. Display position has been thoroughly investigated in the literature, while the proximity between controls and the corresponding display is not clearly described. Further studies are welcome. The effects of directness in manipulation in different driving situations must also be investigated further, especially in terms of safety aspects. Interaction styles based on ecological control and display positions must be further investigated, particularly in regard to safety aspects.

Acknowledgement

This study is part of the OPTIVe project for studies of the integration of HMI systems and is financed by the Swedish IVSS (Intelligent Vehicle Safety Systems) Research Foundation.

References

AAM (Alliance of Automobile Manufacturers, Driver Focus-Telematics Working Group) (2002). *Statement of Principles, Criteria and Verification Procedures on Driver Interactions with Advanced In-Vehicle Information and Communication Systems*—Version 2.0. Retrieved 04.04.2007 from http://www.autoalliance.org/archives/driver_guidelines.pdf.

Baldwin, C.L. (2002). Designing in-vehicle technologies for older drivers: application of sensory-cognitive interaction theory. *Theoretic Issues in Ergonomic Science, 3*, 307-329.

Burns, P.C., Trbovich, P.L., Harbluk, J.L., & McCurdie, T. (2005). *Evaluating one screen/one control multifunction devices in vehicles* (Report 05-0339). Ottawa, Canada: Transport Canada.

Davies, M.L., & Thomas, B.H. (2001). An animated 3D manipulator for distributed window-based applications. In *Proceedings of the 2nd Australasian Conference on User Interface* (pp. 116–123). Washington, DC, USA: IEEE Computer Society.

Dukic, T., Hanson, L., & Falkmer, T. (2006). Effect of drivers' age and push button locations on visual time off road, steering wheel deviation and safety perception. *Ergonomics, 49*, 78-92.

Hutchins, E.L., Hollan, J.D., & Norman, D.A. (1985). Direct Manipulation Interfaces. *Human-Computer Interaction, 1*, 311-338.

J.D. Power (2005). *New-Vehicle Buyers Increasingly Attracted to Models with Innovative Features Highlighting Comfort and Convenience* (J.D. Power and Associates Reports). Retrieved 04.04.2007 from
http://www.jdpa.com/corporate/news/releases/pressrelease.asp?ID=2005174.

Kiljander, H. (2004). *Evolution and Usability of Mobile Phone Interaction Styles* (PhD thesis, Helsinki University of Technology). Helsinki, Finland: Telecommunications Software and Multimedia Laboratory.

Klauer, S.G., Dingus, T.A., Neale, V.L., Sudweeks, J.D., & Ramsey, D.J. (2006). *The Impact of Driver Inattention on Near-Crash/Crash Risk: An Analysis Using the 100-Car Naturalistic Driving Study Data* (Report DOT HS 810 594). Blacksburg, Virginia, USA: Virginia Tech Transportation Institute.

Kurosu, M., & Kashimura, K. (1995). Apparent Usability vs. Inherent Usability: Experimental analysis on the determinants of the apparent usability. *Conference companion on Human factors in computing systems* (Denver, USA) (pp. 292-293). New York, NY, USA: ACM Press.

Lin, B., & Jones, C.A. (1997). Some issues in conducting customer satisfaction surveys. Journal of Marketing Practice: *Applied Marketing Science, 3*, 4-13.

Lind, R.C., Yen, H.W., & Welk, D.L. (2004). *Evolution of the Car Radio: From Vacuum Tubes to Satellite and Beyond* (Report of the Convergence Transportation Electronics Association 2004-21-0001). Tokyo, Japan: Delphi Electronics.

Liu, Y.C. (2001). Comparative study of the effects of auditory, visual and multimodality displays on drivers' performance in advanced traveller information systems. *Ergonomics, 44*, 425-442.

Manes. D., & Green. P. (1997). *Evaluation of a Driver Interface: Effects of Control Type (Knob Versus Buttons) and Menu Structure (Depth Versus Breadth)* (Report UMTRI-97-42). Ann Arbor, MI, USA: Transportation Research Institute (UMTRI), University of Michigan.

Pak, R., McLaughlin, A.C., Lin, Ch-Ch., Rogers, W.A., & Fisk, A.D. (2002). An age-related comparison of a touchscreen and a novel input device. Proceedings of the Human Factors and Ergonomics Society 46th Annual Meeting (pp. 189-192). Santa Monica, CA: HFES.

Tan, A.K., Okamoto, M., & Irinatsu, T. (2004). *Strategy and Challenges for an Integrated HMI* (Report Convergence Transportation Electronics Association 2004-21-0091). Tokyo, Japan: Nissan Motor Co.

Tractinsky, N., Katz, A.S., & Ikar, D. (2000). What is beautiful is usable. *Interacting with Computers, 13*, 127-145.

Stevens, A., Quimby, A., Boards, A., Kersloot, T., & Burns, P. (2002). *Design Guidelines for Safety of In-vehicle Information Systems* (Report PA3721/01). Berkshire, UK: Transport Research Laboratory.

Wierwille, W.G. (2002). Visual and manual demands of in-car controls and displays. In B. Peacock and W. Karwowski (Eds.) *Automotive Ergonomics* (pp. 299-321). London, UK. Taylor and Francis.

Wittmann, M., Kiss, M., Gugg. P., Steffen. A., Fink. M., Pöppel, E., & Kamiya. H. (2006). Effects of display position of a visual in-vehicle task on simulated driving. *Applied Ergonomics, 37*, 187–199.

Zwahlen, H.T., Adams, C.C., & DeBald, D.P. (1988). Safety aspects of CRT touch panel controls in automobiles. In A.G. Gale, M.H. Freeman, C.M. Hasselgrave, P.A. Smith, and S.P. Taylor (Eds.), *Vision in Vehicles II* (pp. 335-344). Amsterdam, The Netherlands: Elsevier.

Driver attitudes towards advanced driver assistance systems – a cross-cultural study

Anders Lindgren[1], Robert Broström[2], Fang Chen[1], & Peter Bengtsson[2]
[1]Chalmers University of Technology, Gothenburg
[2]Luleå University of Technology, Luleå
Sweden

Abstract

Over the last years active safety has become an increasingly important factor within the automotive industry. Active safety systems, also known as Advanced Driver Assistance Systems (ADAS), have the function of actively assisting the driver in avoiding accidents by providing information about current and upcoming traffic situations and helping the driver take proper actions before a potential accident occurs. In this paper, differences and similarities in attitude towards three different ADAS were investigated. A set of three focus group discussions were conducted with Swedish, US American, and Chinese participants. The analysis of subjective data showed differences between the three groups regarding attitudes towards system feasibility, information presentation and need for system adjustability. Results also showed that factors such as driving conditions, infrastructure, and traffic regulations all seemed to influence the hypothesised usefulness of the different systems.

Introduction

Although our roads are more congested now than ever, the number of people killed or seriously injured in Western countries has decreased by 50 percent since 1980. Much of this progress is done thanks to improved crumple zones, airbags, seat belt tensioners and other passive safety technologies (Curtis, 2004). However, even with these improvements a large amount of fatal injuries still occur across the world every day. Therefore, Advanced Driver Assistance Systems (ADAS) have become a growingly important factor when further developing the area of traffic safety. Today there are only a few ADAS available on the market but new systems are continuously introduced by car manufacturers' world wide. One of the major challenges is to integrate these systems in order to make them work optimally together with the driver. Research concerning system sensitivity, alarm signals and alarm modalities is therefore of vital importance. Besides these factors, Trivedi et al. (2001) points out the importance of considering cultural differences in order to improve safety of upcoming generations of automobiles. This means developing systems optimally suited for different types of drivers in different situations. It is hypothesised in this paper that there, besides individual physical and cognitive differences, also are cross-cultural differences in attitude towards ADAS concerning usage, system sensitivity

In D. de Waard, G.R.J. Hockey, P. Nickel, and K.A. Brookhuis (Eds.) (2007), *Human Factors Issues in Complex System Performance* (pp. 205 - 215). Maastricht, the Netherlands: Shaker Publishing.

and interface modality. In this paper, the term *attitude* is defined as people's *opinions*, *thoughts* and *preferences* concerning ADAS.

ADAS are electronic systems designed to support the driver with the driving task. This support can range from simple information presentation through more advanced assisting, and in critical situations, even taking over the driver's task in order to prevent an accident. In this study, attitudes toward three different ADAS are being investigated:

Collision Warning & Brake Assist (CWBA)

The CWBA is a system developed to help the driver avoid a collision with an obstacle ahead of the vehicle. A system sensor is located at the vehicle's front and constantly scanning the road ahead. If an obstacle is detected, the CWBA decides whether or not the vehicle is in an imminent risk of crashing. If the system senses an imminent risk, the driver is provided with a warning to notify him/her of the potential danger (Flodas et al., 2005).

Blind Spot Information System (BLIS)

When driving in urban traffic, critical situations may arise if the driver overlooks vehicles in the so called blind spot. With the help of a sensor or camera based technique, the BLIS provides the driver with information about vehicles, pedestrians or cyclists in areas not visible to him/her. This information is often provided through a red lamp on the car's A pillar and generated depending on the speed difference between the driver's own vehicle and others (Flodas et al., 2005).

Lane Departure Warning (LDW)

One of the most common causes to fatal accidents is unintended lane departures (Headley, 2005). LDW is a camera based system that recognises lane markings and is activated when the driver is about to leave the lane he/she is travelling in without using the blinker signal. If the system recognizes the start of an unintended lane change, it notifies the driver with a visual warning. Some LDW systems combine this warning with a combination of steering wheel vibrations, rumble strip sounds, or/and a slight automatic correction in order to return the vehicle to its original lane (Siemens VDO, 2005).

Although the purpose of ADAS is to generate a positive effect on traffic safety, negative effects on e.g. driver behaviour have been found as well (Dragutinovic et al., 2005; Saad, 2004; Brookhuis et al., 2001; Kovordányi, 2005). Hence, a poorly designed and/or overly sensitive system may increase the driver's workload and thereby decrease his/her situation awareness, comfort and safety (Vahidi & Eskandarian 2003). Additionally, Zeidel (1992) mentions that social environment, including other road users, social norms, formal and informal traffic rules are factors that influence every individual driver. These differences in social environment vary from one region of the world to another. For example, in Turkey, the traffic flow's speed tend to be much higher than the speed limit, as the Turkish drivers do not see speeding as a serious offence compared to what Western Europeans might do (Özkan et al., 2006). As another example, highways in Sweden may be crowded only during rush our traffic while a whole day average speed on the expressways surrounding Beijing is around 35 km/h, due to congested traffic (Huang & Wu, 2006). Beside the infrastructural dissimilarities there are also cultural differences concerning attitudes on aspects like aggression and moral. Sounding one's horn is an obviously aggressive behaviour in Scandinavia while in Southern Europe the threshold for using the horn is much lower and does not essentially indicate aggression. Another attitude example by Social Attitudes to Road Traffic Risk in Europe (SARTRE, cited in Lajunen et al., 2004) shows that "71% of Swedish drivers report that they never drive their car 'after consuming even a small amount of alcohol' whereas the same result for Italians was 8%" (p. 237). Results like these shows that informative values of other road users' behaviour are very high, but only as long as all road users share a common driving culture (Zaidel, 1992). These examples all indicate that, in order to develop useful and safe ADAS, much work must be focused on studying cultural differences with drivers that are to use the systems in environments and contexts consistent with their natural driving habitat. These opinions are supported by Trivedi et al. (2001), who points out the importance of successfully accomplishing these research goals in order to improve safety of new generations of automobiles and telematic devices used in the vehicle industry. Moreover, when concentrating on existing ADAS, some systems that take control of the vehicle in an emergency situation may make an action that differs from the driver's interpretation of the situation. Chalmers (2001) mentions that this may be a reason for why driver attitudes are more favourable towards systems that assist the driver but less favourable towards more automated systems that take control of the vehicle. Chalmers also remarks that there may be variances in driver attitude towards the system depending on the external infrastructure. The purpose of this study is to investigate driver attitude towards ADAS and it is hypothesised that the differences in infrastructure and traffic culture between Sweden, USA, and China would also be reflected in the participants' attitudes towards the systems.

Method

To investigate people's attitudes towards different ADAS a set of three focus-groups were being held during May of 2006; a Chinese, a Swedish, and an US American group. The decision to use participants from these three particular cultures was based on both the distinct differences in road infrastructure and vehicle fleets that are apparent between the three countries. Before beginning the focus-group studies, a pilot study was conducted. This study was set up as the focus-group studies that were to follow and consisted of six persons. Information gathered from this pilot study was then evaluated and resulted in some minor changes in structure and questions used in the group discussions.

Material

The focus groups were carried out in a conference room with the participants seated around an oval table with a projector screen located at one short end of the table. A laptop connected to a projector was used to present videos of the ADAS. The videos were 2-3 minute introductions of the systems with some sample scenarios and did not contain any detailed demonstrations of technical functionalities. After each video the participants were asked to individually answer a questionnaire about the systems' *feasibility, reliability, willingness to pay for the systems, and need for personalisation*. These categories of questions were based on both earlier research on integration of driver support functions (van Driel & van Arem, 2004) and system reliability and feasibility research, originally performed within the area of intelligent speed adaptation systems (Piao et al., 2005).

The participants answered the questionnaire by selecting a number on a 1-7 scale were 1 was considered "not useful" and 7 "very useful". The question about system feasibility was a four level question (how feasible the participants hypothesised the system in *city traffic, suburbs, country road, and motorway*) while the remaining questions were single level. The following group discussions were partly based on questions from the questionnaire. Other questions brought up in the group discussion concerned preferred warning modalities and positive versus negative aspects of each ADAS. All three focus group sessions were moderated by one discussion leader making sure that all participants had a chance to express their opinions. All focus group sessions were recorded both using a video camera and a MP3 sound recorder with permission from the participants.

Participants

Each group consisted of six participants (two female and four male), all with higher educational background and at least two years experience from driving in urban and motorway traffic in their native country. The average age for the US American, the Chinese, and the Swedish group of participants was 26 years (SD 3), 33 years (SD 12) and 40 years (SD 14), respectively. The participants were selected through an independent recruitment company and informed that they would participate in a workshop concerning traffic safety and new vehicle technologies. They all received approximately € 30 in value checks for participating in the study.

Procedure

The focus group consisted of several sections. To start with, the participants were assured of anonymity and confidentiality. They were then asked to complete a form with general questions about age, profession, yearly driving mileage etc. When this was done, the moderators presented three videos/animations of the different ADAS and explained their believed traffic safety benefits. After each video the participants were asked to individually answer a questionnaire. The participants were also encouraged to write down personal comments on the system. After completing the questionnaires the participants were given a 15 minute coffee break. Then a general discussion was held where the moderator presented questions related to the questionnaires' topics. The moderator also encouraged the participants to discuss the different systems and the possible effects that each system might have in their native country. The questionnaires were written in English for the Chinese and the US American group and in Swedish for the Swedish group. The US American and Chinese group discussions were held in English. However, in the Chinese group discussion a translator was present to assist one participant with difficulties in understanding English. The other participants in the Chinese group all spoke and read English fluently. The Swedish group discussion was held in Swedish as this was both the moderator's and participants' mother tongue.

Data analysis

When analysing the question about each system's feasibility a two-way mixed ANOVA with one within-subjects factor was used: Driving environment feasibility (four levels: city traffic, suburbs, country road, and motorway). The question about the Lane Departure Warning's feasibility was only a two level question (country road and motorway) since the system is only active in speeds above 70 km/h. When analysing the remaining parts of the questionnaire, one-way between subjects ANOVAs were used. In all ANOVAs, the three different groups were used as a between-subjects factor. The focus-group discussions were transcribed at a level three exactitude (Wibeck, 2000), were only the information thought to be relevant for the purpose of the study was noted.

Results

The results showed differences in attitudes between the different groups concerning the discussed areas, i.e. warning and information modalities, feasibility, reliability, system personalisation and willingness to pay. During the discussions, the participants' attitudes sometimes differed within the groups. It was therefore decided to define a group attitude as an attitude agreed on by a majority (minimum four out of six) of the group's participants. Below, results from both the questionnaires and group discussions are presented for each system separately. Statistical analysis revealed an effect for LDW system feasibility only with no further significant effects.

Collision Warning & Brake Assist (CWBA)

System feasibility
The common opinion in all three groups was that the CWBA was best suited for highway driving, as the high travelling speed often leads to serious rear-end collision accidents with severe injuries. The Swedish and Chinese participants found the system feasible and could imagine using it while the US Americans had the opinion that the CWBA would not improve their driving.

Preferred warning modality
The US Americans asked for a vocal warning with the motivation that a warning sound would probably only confuse the driver. They also believed that this vocal warning would help them separate between different warnings if several systems start off simultaneously. The Chinese, on the other hand, preferred audible warnings from the CWBA with an increasing sound if the driver does not react to the warning immediately. This opinion was shared by the Swedish participants, who also preferred an audible warning in order to get the drivers attention. In addition, they believed that a complementary warning light would be useful to make sure the driver notices the situation instantly and takes a proper action.

Reliability
All three groups considered system reliability as the most important question concerning the CWBA. False alarms were considered a major issue since they would probably affect the driver's trust to the system in a negative way and most likely make the driver either ignore the warnings, or eventually shut the whole system off.

System personalisation
The wish to individually adjust the CWBA was something that differed between the US Americans and the other two groups. The US American group preferred a system that allows the driver to manually adjust settings like system sensitivity. They also made it clear that the system needs to be transparent in a way that the driver understands at what sensitivity level the system is currently set. These thoughts were not shared by the Swedish and Chinese participants, who believed that the system sensitivity level set by the manufacturer must be optimal and therefore trustworthy. However, these two groups wanted the possibility to manually switch the system on/off, in specific traffic situations.

Lane Departure Warning (LDW)

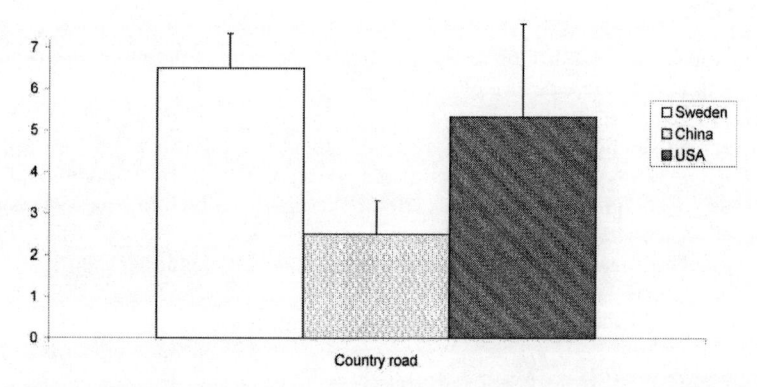

Figure 1. Average results for the focus groups on the question about hypothesised feasibility for the LDW system concerning the driving environment "country road" (with the y-axis ranging from 1 'not useful' to 7 'very useful')

System feasibility
The hypothesised usefulness of the LDW differed between the three groups. The Chinese group found the system superfluous (Figure 1) as few roads in China have lane markings (which are necessary for the system to work). This opinion was also evident in the questionnaires were there was a significant Country x Driving environment feasibility interaction effect, $F(2, 15) = 7.71$, $p < .01$. Further, there were main effects for Country, $F(2, 15) = 7.30$, $p < .01$, and Driving environment feasibility, $F(1, 15) = 20.50$, $p < .001$. To further explore the interaction effect, two one-way ANOVAs were conducted (one for each road type). No significant effects were found for the level *highway*. Significant differences were however found for the driving environment *country road*, $F(2, 15) = 10.48$, $p < .001$. Tukey HSD post-hoc tests showed significant differences between the Chinese and US American groups, $p < .017$, and Chinese and Swedish groups, $p < .001$. No significant differences were

found between the Swedish and US American groups. In detail, the Swedish group found two main uses for the system. The LDW could help the driver in case he or she falls asleep during long distance highway driving. Also, it could help notifying the driver in case he or she gets distracted and drifts out of the intended lane. The US American group shared the Swedish group's opinions on issues with driver distraction and did also find the system useful in case the driver falls asleep while driving. In addition, they believed that the system could work as an assistant, and allowing them to drive some extra miles when feeling tired. The Chinese participants, however, were extremely negative towards using the system as a help for driver drowsiness with the explanation that one should not drive if one is feeling tired.

Preferred warning modality
When discussing warning modalities, the Swedish group preferred an audio warning, but also discussed the eventual problems with differentiating between different audio warnings. Therefore, some of the participants presented the idea of complementing the audio warning with some kind of information presentation on the dashboard. This idea, however, was questioned by others in the group as they believed that the time it takes for the driver to notice that form of information is not enough, especially not in an emergency situation. The US American and Chinese participants appreciated an audible warning. The Chinese group, however, insisted that this warning must not be irritating and the US American group pointed out the importance of presenting the warning in a way that it does not scare the driver and makes him or her overreact.

Reliability
System reliability was an important question for both the Swedish and the US American participants. Both groups believed that the manufacturer has great responsibility in making this system reliable. Additionally, the Swedish group pointed out, that a system which warns the driver more than necessary, is preferable compared to a system that misses a warning. They also believed that driver acceptance to false warnings may be depending on how expensive the system is.

System personalisation
Both the Swedish and US American groups wanted the possibility to turn the LDW on and off. The Swedish participants felt that they trusted the manufacturer's sensitivity levels and did not want the opportunity to adjust system settings. The US American participants on the other hand would like the possibility to change the settings, but only if it was clear to the driver what effects a change would have on the system's reliability.

Blind Spot Information System (BLIS)

System feasibility
When discussing the BLIS's usefulness, all three groups had similar opinions. The participants believed that this system would help them spot motorcycles and bicycles when changing lanes, and when turning in an intersection. The Chinese group found this particularly important as the intense city traffic in China is a very complex driving environment. The three groups also agreed on possible issues that may arise

when using this system. They believed that the main problem would be if drivers put too much trust into the system without bothering about turning their heads and making sure that no object is within the blind-spot area. Especially the Swedish and US American participants feared that this system could make the driver lazier and less focused on the main task of driving.

Preferred warning modality
All three groups believed that visible warnings through an integrated lamp near the rear-view mirror would be a preferable way to get the driver's attention, as it is easily recognisable for the driver when looking in the rear-view mirror.

Reliability
The Swedish and US American groups had the opinion that BLIS is a system that they would not put too much trust in. The reason for this was the possible difficulties the driver might have interpreting the warning together with the current traffic situation. The Swedish groups believed that a small display showing the blind-spot area visually would be a better and more easily understandable way of presenting information. The Chinese group was more benevolent towards the BLIS. They were of the opinion that if the system fails to notice an object in the blind-spot area, the manufacturer would have to retrieve the car to improve the system. However, they also agreed on the driver responsibility to think about eventual consequences. If the system fails, an accident may occur. However, the driver still remains utmost responsible for his or her own actions.

Finally, there were differences in how much money the groups were willing to spend on the systems if buying a new car. Participants from all groups were willing to spend more than € 400 on buying the CWBA. When it came to the LDW and BLIS, the Swedish participants were the only group that clearly indicated their interest to spend more than € 400 on the systems.

Discussion

Qualitative results from this study show differences between the three groups in attitude concerning hypothesised daily usage and expected traffic safety benefits of today's ADAS. However, even with these differences between the groups, the sample sizes in this study were small and can not be said to represent the countries' populations. This also might have been one of the reasons for lack of significant effects in statistical analysis of the questionnaire data. Further, data gathered from the group discussion was subjective and it is possible that the participants may have influenced each other, making them change their opinions or keeping thoughts and opinions for themselves. One common factor referred to by the participants, was the traffic environment in their native countries. The differences in road congestions and types of other road users apparently play a considerable role when looking at the different systems' feasibility. Chalmers (2001) mentions possible variances in driver attitude towards ADAS depending on the external infrastructure. This theory is further supported in this study. As an example, the Chinese participants find the BLIS very usable, as the streets in China often tend to be crowded with people travelling on bicycles, scooters and motorcycles. Further, the US American participants (used to good quality motorways and long distance driving) find the LDW-system very useful. The Chinese participants were more negative to the system due to the limited amount of roads with lane markings in their native country. Results like these suggest that the participants' attitudes towards the ADAS were principally influenced by the infrastructure in their native countries. This could also imply that this may be more a question on infrastructure than on attitude, especially since the participants were asked to focus on the traffic environment in their native countries.

Beside the infrastructural considerations, moral dissimilarities between the Chinese participants and the group of US Americans emerged during the group discussions. While the US American participants found no problems using the system as a drowsiness warning, the Chinese group clearly dissociated themselves from this type of usage. This type of moral diversities complies with earlier work by SARTRE (cited in Lajunen et al., 2004) and Özkan et al. (2006) concerning driver attitudes towards drinking and driving, and speeding as a driving offence. However, one has to take into consideration factors like sample size and age differences between the two groups, as well as the willingness to discuss this possibly sensible subject.

Further, Chalmers (2001) mentions, that drivers favour systems that aid the driver over automated systems taking control of the vehicle. When comparing the groups' attitudes towards the highly automated CWBA and the more informal BLIS, it can be seen that the Chinese participants were positive both to the CWBA and the BLIS. They found the CWBA to be feasible in motorway traffic and the BLIS very useful in hectic traffic situations in their home country. These results indicate that factors like system feasibility and social environment (see Zadkiel, 1992) may be equally important when investigating driver attitudes as level of system automation and control. This also agrees with earlier work on traffic safety research by Trivedi et al. (2001) pointing out the importance of considering cultural differences in order to improve safety of upcoming generations of automobiles.

The questionnaires were written in English for the Chinese and US American groups while written in Swedish for the Swedish group. Although all Chinese participants but one were fluent in English there is always a risk that words and sentences have different meaning in different countries and that they may not always be directly translatable. The same issue may have occurred with the Chinese participant that did not speak English well. Even though a Chinese translator was present (both during the questionnaire and discussion session) information exchange between translator and participant may have been misunderstood and incorrectly translated. Also, there is a possibility that the Swedish words and expressions used were not fully synonymous with their English counterparts. Additionally, it has to be taken into consideration that some information may have been lost or transformed when translating information both from the moderators to the participants and vice versa. Finally, the participants' opinions may have been biased by the different ADAS' introduction videos and animations. However, it was thought that this way of presenting the systems was preferable compared using for example toy cars or photographs, as it was believed to give a more realistic view of the systems intended use.

Conclusion

In conclusion, the results presented provide preliminary evidence for the hypothesis that there are attitude differences between the three groups concerning the hypothesised usage, feasibility, system sensitivity and interface modality of the three ADAS; i.e. CWBA, BLIS and LDW. It is also concluded that a large amount of these differences seem to depend on infrastructural factors. This makes e.g. two options available for car manufacturers; either change the infrastructure in these countries to fit their ADAS design or take these cultural differences into consideration when developing and evaluating new systems, with the latter option being more realistic. However, it has to be taken into account that the number of participants in this study was small and that more extensive research within this area is needed before more general conclusions can be drawn.

Acknowledgement

This study is part of a series of studies on differences in driver attitude towards active safety systems carried out by the OPTIVe project, financed by the Swedish IVSS research foundation.

References

Brookhuis, K.A., de Waard, D., & Janssen, W.H. (2001). Behavioural impacts of Advanced Driver Assistance Systems—An overview. *European Journal of Transport and Infrastructure Research, 1*, 245-253.

Curtis, A. (2004). ADAS – What are the barriers to adoption and how can they be solved? *Traffic Engineering & Control, 45*, 88-89.

Chalmers, I.J. (2001). User Attitudes to Automated Highway System. *Proceedings of the International Conference on Advanced Driver Assistance Systems* (pp. 6-10). (September 18-19, 2001, Birmingham, UK). IEEE Conf. Publ. No. 483.

Dragutinovic, N., Brookhuis, K.A., Hagenzieker, M.P., & Marchau, V.A.W.J. (2005). Behavioural effects of Advanced Cruise Control Use – a meta-analytic approach. *European Journal of Transport and Infrastructure Research, 5*, 267-280.

Flodas, N., Admitis, A., Keinath, A., Bengler, K., & Engeln, A. (2005) *Review and Taxonomy of IVIS/ADAS applications (AIDE Deliverable D2.1.2)*. Brussels, Belgium: Information Society Technologies.

Headley, P. (2005). *ESC as a baseline for active safety* (Paper Number 05-0332). Culpeper, USA: Continental Teves. Retrieved 28.03.2007 from http://www-nrd.nhtsa.dot.gov/pdf/nrd-01/esv/esv19/05-0332-O.pdf.

Huang, L., & Wu, J. (2006). Evaluation of Performance of Beijing Expressway Based on Integrated GPS/GIS Data. *Proceedings of the IEEE Intelligent Transportation Systems Conference* (pp. 927-932) (Toronto, Canada). IEEE.

Kovordányi, R., Ohlsson, K., Alm, T. (2005) Dynamically Deployed Support as a Potential Solution to Negative Behavioral Adaptation. *Proceedings of the 2005 IEEE Intelligent Vehicle Symposium* (pp. 613-618). (Las Vegas, USA). IEEE.

Lajunen, T., Parker, D., & Summala, H. (2004). The Manchester Driver Behaviour Questionnaire: a cross-cultural study. *Accident Analysis and Prevention, 36*, 231-238.

Özkan, T., Lajunen, T., El Chliaoutakis, J., Parker, D., & Summala, H. (2006). Cross-cultural differences in driving behaviours: A comparison of six countries. *Transportation Research Part F, 9*, 227-242.

Piao, J., McDonald, M., Henry, A., Vaa, T., & Tveit, Ø. (2005). An Assessment of User Acceptance of Intelligent Speed Adaptation Systems, *Proceedings of the International IEEE Conference on Intelligent Transportation Systems* (pp. 1045-1049) (September 13-15, Austria). IEEE

Saad, F. (2004). Behavioural adaptations to new driver support systems - Some critical issues. *Proceedings of the IEEE International Conference on Systems, Man and Cybernetics, vol. 1* (pp. 288-293). IEEE

Siemens VDO Automotive AG (2005). *Increasing Comfort – Boosting Safety* (j71001-A-A669-X-7600 I 09.2005). Regensburg, Germany: Siemens VDO Automotive AG Corporate Communications.

Trivedi, M.M., Rao, B.D., Hollan, J.D., Pashler, H.E., & Boer, E.R. (2001). *Human Centered Intelligent Driver Support Systems: A Novel Multi-Modal "Driving Ecology" for Enhanced Safety (Research Proposal).* La Jolla, USA: UCSD Distributed Cognition and Human Computer Interaction Laboratory. Retrieved 28.03.2007 from http://hci.ucsd.edu/220/dimi-proposal.pdf.

Vahidi, A., & Eskandarian, A. (2003). Research Advances in Intelligent Collision Avoidance and Adaptive Cruise Control. *IEEE Transactions on Intelligent Transportation Systems, 4*(3), 143-153.

Van Driel, C.J.G., & van Arem, B. (2004). Integration of driver support functions: the driver's point of view. *Proceedings of the IEEE International Conference on Systems, Man and Cybernetics*, vol. 4 (pp. 3988- 3994). IEEE.

Wibeck, V. (2000). *Fokusgrupper: Om fokuserade gruppintervjuer som undersökningsmetod.* Lund, Sweden: Studentlitteratur.

Zeidel, D.M. (1992). A Modeling Perspective on the Culture of Driving, *Accident Analysis & Prevention, 24*, 585-597.

Solving communication problems in the transportation sector

Claire Huijnen[1] & Ilse Bakx[2]
[1]European Centre for Digital Communication, Hogeschool Zuyd
Heerlen, The Netherlands
[2]Centrum voor Usability Onderzoek, Katholieke Universiteit Leuven
Leuven, Belgium

Abstract

The methods and results are presented of a study within the "Virtual lab for ICT Experience Prototyping" (VIP-lab). This case study deals with communication problems and limited comprehension of safety instructions caused by language barriers in the industry sector. An interactive application is proposed as solution.

Introduction

When developing (ICT) applications the emphasis is increasingly put on the experience of the end-user. Related to this trend, User-Centred Design (UCD) techniques are emerging and applied more frequently in the development of ICT systems. Moreover UCD eventually found a place in an ISO standard 13407. Norman (1988) introduced and defined the term "User-Centred Design" as: "a philosophy based on the needs and interests of the user, with an emphasis on making products usable and understandable". The "Virtual lab for ICT Experience Prototyping" (VIP-lab) is a project and a virtual lab where different research groups have integrated their knowledge and know-how with respect to designing the user's experience (Coninx, Haesen, & Bierhoff, 2005). VIP-lab is a project that tries to make companies aware of the advantage of ICT Experience Prototyping by providing a multidisciplinary, profiled, and accessible service for enterprises by means of conducting User Centred research and design. The project consists of five pilots in different application domains: media, e-government, health-care, services, and industrial settings. Each pilot delivers one or more prototype(s). In this contribution the focus will be on the industrial sector.

Bridging language barriers

In industrial and transportation contexts, safety instructions often play a crucial role. With the disappearing (formal) borders between European countries, more and more diversity is encountered in the languages that are spoken by truck drivers that are visiting (Dutch and Belgian) industrial company grounds. This encounter often causes (severe) communication problems. A great potential risk arises when safety instructions and procedures have to be understood and adhered by truck drivers. The aim of this study is to find a user friendly (ICT) solution for these problems.

Methods

To better understand the current situation and possible solutions, extensive (user and task) analysis is carried out with employees and visiting truck drivers of industrial company grounds at three companies in Belgium and the Netherlands. Extensive observation and interviewing were done while conducting Contextual Inquiry (analysis in context) (Beyer & Holtzblatt, 1998). A prototype of a possible solution, with a touchscreen interface was created and then tested by means of a Heuristic Evaluation (Nielsen, 1994). Several UCD methods have been applied in different (iterative) steps in the project (see Figure 1).

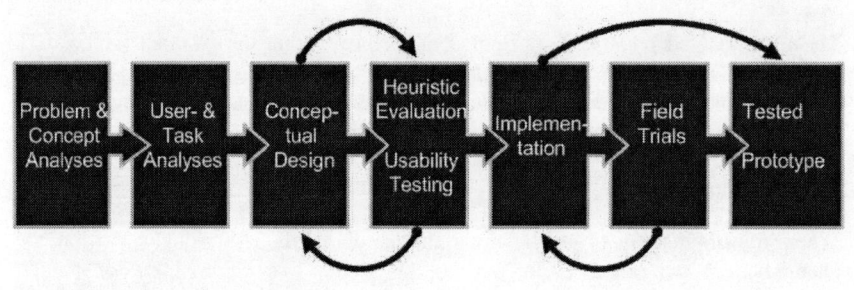

Figure 1. Steps in the VIP-Lab project

Results

It became evident from the contextual inquiry that many truck drivers who are crossing the European borders regularly experience communication problems in their daily work due to language barriers. This results in situations in which safety instructions can not be read nor understood by the drivers.

Most of the truck drivers in the study mentioned that understanding safety instructions is (very) important to them. A large number of them devoted much attention to these instructions. Nevertheless, it seems that for more than half of them it is common that they do not (fully) understand the safety instructions. Causes that respondents mentioned for this are:

- Not understanding the presented text because of language differences
- Text is presented or shown too fast
- Not understanding the receptionist or the text is too complicated
- The text is easily forgotten

With these and other results in mind, a possible solution was suggested.

Solution

The created prototype solution to this problem is a user friendly and interactive, touch screen based, application that utilizes a number of important characteristics:

1. Language personalisation
   - truck drivers are able to select their mother tongue or their preferred language in which the information will be presented
2. Clear and consistent instructions
3. Pace personalisation
   - Truck drivers can, themselves, determine the speed at which they receive the instructions
4. Audio and visual aids to enhance memory for the safety instructions and procedures
   - Besides textual information, pictograms and pictures will be used
   - Audio will be provided. It is expected that recall and memory will increase when auditory information is presented in a proper manner (Baddely, 1997).

This prototype has been evaluated by a number of truck drivers in the Netherlands and Belgium (13 in total). A majority (N=11) of these truck drivers indicated that this application would definitely solve a lot of the communication problems they currently experience in foreign countries.

Discussion

The VIP-lab project has adopted methods of User-Centred Design, which inherently means that a lot of attention is devoted to the end user. It is expected that this attention and expertise will result in more usable and more appropriate applications for the end user.

Specifically for this pilot, a number expected effects of the developed application can be distinguished:

- less communication/language problems,
- increased understanding and recall for safety instructions,
- improvement of work efficiency (for truck drivers and receptionists),
- positive effect on the safety.

Whether these expected effects will indeed occur will be the focus of the study of the field trials that will be conducted in February 2007. More information on VIP-lab is available at: www.vip-lab.org.

Acknowledgements

VIP-lab is financed by the "Interreg Benelux-Middengebied" authorities and is co-financed by Province of Limburg (B), Province of Limburg (NL), Ministry of Economic Affairs (NL) and Ministry of Flemish Government/Economic Affairs (B). We acknowledge the contribution of the VIP-lab consortium partners: European Centre for Digital Communication (EC/DC) (NL), Expertise Centre for Digital Media (B), Centre for Usability Research (B), Technical University of Eindhoven (NL) and De Vlijt (B).

References

Baddely, A. (1997). *Human Memory. Theory and Practice*. Bristol, UK: Psychology Press.
Beyer, H.; Holtzblatt, K. (1998). *Contextual Design: Defining Customer Centered Systems*. London, UK: Morgan Kaufmann.
Coninx, K., Haesen, M., & Bierhoff, J. (2005). VIP-lab: A virtual lab for ICT experience prototyping. *Proceedings of Measuring Behavior 2005*. Wageningen, The Netherlands: Noldus.
ISO *13407:1999 Human-centred design processes for interactive systems*, April 2004
Nielsen, J. & Mack, R.L. (Eds.) (1994). *Usability Inspection methods* New York: John Wiley & Sons.
Norman, D. (1988). *The Design of Everyday Things*. New York: Basic Books.

Correlates of simulator sickness in a truck driver training programme and the development of an effective screening process

Nick Reed & Andrew M. Parkes
TRL Limited, Wokingham
UK

Abstract

The incidence of simulator sickness impacts all simulators that purport to provide drivers with a realistic experience. It has symptoms similar to motion sickness but can occur in the absence of physical motion of the observer. TRL was commissioned by the Scottish Executive to train 700 professional commercial vehicle drivers on two full mission truck simulators. Monitoring the incidence and effects of simulator sickness were paramount to the success of the programme. The aim of the driver training was to improve driver safety and fuel efficiency. Drivers on the programme completed a short familiarisation drive before completing two sets of four exercises, spending about an hour in the simulator in total. The simulator recorded drivers' fuel efficiency, gear changes, speed, and time taken. Drivers also completed questionnaires as part of the training programme, one of which was the simulator sickness questionnaire (SSQ) proposed by Kennedy, Lane, Berbaum, and Lilienthal (1993), completed before and after driving the simulator. This enabled drivers' subjective feelings of sickness to be recorded. Drivers rated their experience in the simulator very highly and showed significant improvements in their driving performance. Driver age and previous experience of motion sickness were both correlated with reported sickness level. There was also a significant correlation between drivers' attitudes to technology and their susceptibility to simulator sickness. The implications of these results for the development of screening processes to reduce the incidence of simulator sickness and the consequences for the use of simulators for driver training are discussed.

Introduction

Simulator technology is well established in the aircraft industry for pilot training. It offers the trainee the opportunity to experience (potentially dangerous) training scenarios repeatedly in a safe environment where performance can be studied and reviewed with a high degree of accuracy. With the increased availability of low cost computer technology capable of displaying realistic virtual environments and managing complex vehicle dynamics calculations, simulators are now being used for training in other domains such as road vehicles. However, an important problem that

In D. de Waard, G.R.J. Hockey, P. Nickel, and K.A. Brookhuis (Eds.) (2007), *Human Factors Issues in Complex System Performance* (pp. 221 - 234). Maastricht, the Netherlands: Shaker Publishing.

to some degree afflicts all simulators based on virtual environments is simulator sickness.

Simulator sickness is a condition with symptoms similar to motion sickness but whereas vestibular stimulation can be sufficient to cause motion sickness (although visual stimulation can be contributing factor), simulator sickness can be caused by visual stimulation alone. To refine the definition, simulator sickness can be defined as discomfort resulting from performing a task in a simulator for which performance of the same task in the real-world does not produce similar sickness or discomfort. Symptoms can include eye strain, headache, pallor, sweating, dryness of mouth, fullness of stomach, disorientation, vertigo, ataxia, nausea, and vomiting (see Kennedy, Lane, Berbaum, & Lilienthal, 1993). The accumulation of these symptoms can be sufficient to cause participants to withdraw from exposure to the simulation. There may also be after-effects whereby the participant experiences disorientation, elevated nausea levels, and oculomotor disturbances following virtual environment exposure (Stanney & Kennedy, 1998).

In a research programme, the incidence of simulator sickness is at best, a nuisance requiring the recruitment of additional participants. At worst, it can compromise the research findings by causing participants to adopt unrealistic behaviours in order to ameliorate the sickness symptoms. The consequences when significant numbers of participants suffer from simulator sickness in a training programme are similarly damaging. Firstly, the trainee (or their employer) will have paid for the simulator training. If the trainee is unable to complete the training due to symptoms of simulator sickness, this money must be refunded. Secondly, the reputation of the simulator training programme will suffer if there are a number of participants who have had discomforting experiences on the simulator. This may lead to participants arriving anxious about how they will feel in the simulator or perhaps avoiding simulator training altogether. Drivers failing to complete their training or avoiding simulator training may result in a simulator facility failing to achieve the trainee throughput required to remain financially viable, thus jeopardising the operation. A third possible outcome when a driver is suffering from simulator sickness is that the driver will adopt behaviours to minimise the symptoms. There is a danger that it is behaviours adopted to reduce the sickness symptoms that will transfer to the real situation rather than the true training objectives for which the simulator exercises were created. These behaviours may in fact cause a driver to perform less safely when driving their real vehicle; a negative training effect. Furthermore, simulator sickness after-effects such as disorientation are of particular concern where a participant may drive on public roads soon after synthetic training.

In the SCOTSIM project, the requirement was to provide simulator training for 700 professional truck drivers based in Scotland using two full mission truck simulators. The training objective was to improve drivers' fuel efficiency and to encourage safe driving habits. As discussed, simulator sickness is an unavoidable side effect of apparent self motion through a virtual environment for a proportion of the population. It was therefore important to monitor its occurrence and where possible take steps to minimise the severity of symptoms.

Method

Equipment

Drivers experienced training on one of two simulators, both provided by Thales. The TRUST 3000 (T3000) was housed in an expandable trailer unit and was therefore mobile, providing training at various locations around the Scottish mainland. The TRUST 5000 (T5000) was installed at a fixed facility in Bellshill, near Glasgow, Scotland. Both simulators use a real truck cabin mounted on a Stewart platform (see Stewart (1965)). However, the one major technical difference between the simulators is that the screens of the T3000 visual system are mounted on the floor, independent from the motion platform whereas on the T5000, both the cabin and the visual system are installed on the motion platform. Figures 1 and 2 show the two simulators.

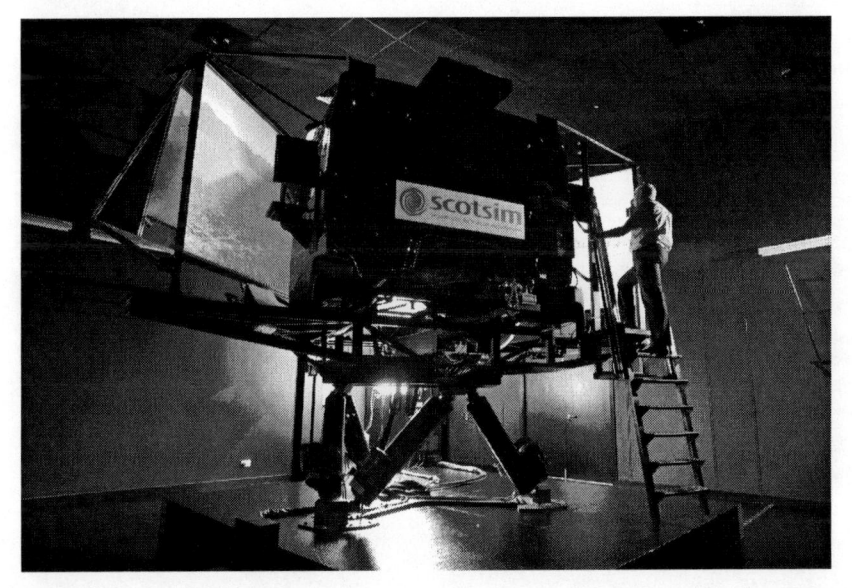

Figure 1. Fixed location T5000 simulator

The driver cabin on both simulators is the distribution version of Renault Premium truck cabin. It was converted for use in a simulator and all instruments and controls interface with the simulator's computer system. All the dashboard controls work in the same way as in a real truck with force feedback for the steering wheel, pedals and gear stick. Table 1 shows the technical characteristics of the motion system used in the simulators.

The visual system uses three video channels to generate a 180° horizontal forward field of view. Three further video channels provide the images for the rear view mirrors and the pavement mirror on LCD monitors. The images are displayed at a refresh rate of 60Hz, a resolution of 1280 × 1024 pixels per channel, and with up to 24 sub-pixels anti-aliasing. The three front channels are powered by three Evans &

Sutherland simFUSION imaging computers. Two Intel processor based PCs with high-end graphics boards control the other channels. The audio system simulates engine noise, aerodynamic/friction noises, braking noises, and the vehicle noise of other road users. The instructor station is the trainer's workplace and consists of displays of the front channel and the rear-view mirrors plus a control screen and a display showing the driver in the cab.

Figure 2. External view of mobile trailer housing the T3000 simulator in training mode

Table 1. Characteristics for the motion systems on the T5000 and T3000 simulators

	T5000		T3000	
DOF	Excursion	Acceleration	Excursion	Acceleration
Pitch	±16°	±250°s^{-2}	±16°	±500°s^{-2}
Roll	±16°	±250°s^{-2}	±16°	±500°s^{-2}
Yaw	±16°	±250°s^{-2}	±16°	±500°s^{-2}
Heave	±0.25m	±7ms^{-2}	±0.15m	±5ms^{-2}
Surge	±0.30m	±7ms^{-2}	±0.20m	±6ms^{-2}
Sway	±0.30m	±7ms^{-2}	±0.20m	±6ms^{-2}

Participants

All participants in the SCOTSIM training programme were working for companies based in Scotland and were professional commercial vehicle drivers. Participation guidelines were given in the letter sent to driver managers. These suggested that drivers should be under 50, in good health, have good eyesight (including corrected to normal), not prone to motion sickness, and not sensitive to flickering lights.

Exercises

The simulated vehicle that trainees were required to drive was a fully loaded rigid lorry (UK vehicle category C: large goods vehicle above 3.5t). Before completing the training exercises, all drivers were required to complete a short (5 minute) familiarisation drive to enable them to become accustomed to the controls of the simulator vehicle and the feel of driving in the virtual environment. Four training exercises were created.

(i) Industrial exercise (approximately 5 minutes)
In a depot; the trainee must reverse the vehicle into a loading bay taking care to avoid pedestrians, exit the depot, and make progress on a rural A-road for a short time. This is a single carriageway that has one lane in each direction. The speed limit is 64km/h (40mph) for trucks.

(ii) Village exercise (approximately 10 minutes)
Rural roads with sweeping bends, some shallow gradients, and some single track roads. Trainees were challenged by unexpected pedestrian events and vulnerable road users. The exercise was ended by a triggered vehicle malfunction that caused the simulated vehicle to overheat, thus requiring the driver to stop.

(iii) Highway exercise (approximately 7 minutes)
Dual carriageways (two lanes in each direction with central reserve; speed limit 80km/h (50mph) for trucks) and motorways (two lanes plus hard shoulder in each direction with central reserve; speed limit 96 km/h (60mph) for trucks) requiring the trainee to overtake a slow moving vehicle, manage motorway junctions, and negotiate a traffic jam.

(iv) City exercise (approximately 8 minutes)
A built up environment requiring the trainee to negotiate tight turns and busy junctions. It included unexpected events and vulnerable road users and ended with a reversing manoeuvre into a pedestrianised precinct.

The total distance driven across the four exercises was approximately 13.5 km (8.5 miles). After completing the four exercises, each participant was given feedback on their performance and training advice by the instructor. They were then required to complete the four exercises a second time to demonstrate the skills that they had been taught.

Questionnaires

Participants completed a range of questionnaires during their training session. Before driving the simulator, they completed a questionnaire that required them to give information about their background, their perceived driving abilities, their general health state, and their attitudes to computers. They were also required to complete the Simulator Sickness Questionnaire (SSQ) as presented in Kennedy, Lane, Berbaum, & Lilienthal (1993). This was to ascertain their health state before using the simulator. The SSQ requires participants to rate the severity of sixteen different symptoms of simulator sickness on a four point scale: 'None'; 'Slight'; 'Moderate'; 'Severe'; scoring 0, 1, 2, and 3 respectively. The scores for each symptom are aggregated into an overall SSQ score and can be separated into three components representing different aspects of simulator sickness: Nausea; Oculomotor Discomfort; and Disorientation. Participants completed the same SSQ after they had finished driving. By comparing scores before and after driving, it was possible to assess how much driving the simulator contributed to any feelings of discomfort.

Trial schedule

Each participant spent a half day at the simulator facility engaged in the training process, managed at all times by a trained driver instructor. On arrival at the simulator facility, participants would receive a short briefing about the purposes of the study and were informed of their right to withdraw from the study at any time. Next, they completed the pre-drive questionnaires before driving the familiarisation exercise. They would then begin the training exercises. Participants completed exercises in the order Industrial; Village; Highway; City.

Results

Participants

A total of 641 participants completed the SCOTSIM simulator training programme between August 2005 and April 2006. Their age, sex, and experience profiles are shown in table 2 below. Participants were not asked whether they had any experience of driving simulators before. To now, the limited number of driving simulators in the UK means that the number with past experience would be small. However, as simulation technology becomes more common, this factor should be considered.

Table 2. Age, sex, and experience profile of participants in the SCOTSIM training programme

		T5000	T3000	Total
	N	471	170	641
Age (years)	Mean	41.8	41.4	41.7
	Min	18	21	18
	Max	72	67	72
	SD	9.5	9.8	9.6
Sex	Male N	467 (99.2%)	168 (98.8%)	635 (99.1%)
	Female N	4 (0.8%)	2 (1.2%)	6 (0.9%)
Years as a professional truck driver	Mean	13.8	14.3	13.9
	Min	0	0	0
	Max	45	44	45
	SD	10.3	10.4	10.3

There were no significant differences in the age, sex, or experience of drivers attending the T5000 compared to those attending the T3000. Table 3 shows drivers' reported health state.

Table 3. Reported health state of participants in the SCOTSIM training programme (N (T5000) = 471, N(T3000) = 170)

	T5000 Number reporting condition (%)	T3000 Number reporting condition (%)
Inner ear problems	13 (2.77%)	6 (3.55%)
Diabetes	3 (0.64%)	1 (0.59%)
Respiratory disorder	16 (3.40%)	4 (2.35%)
Mood problems	3 (0.64%)	0 (0.00%)
Motion sickness	62 (13.2%)	30 (17.8%)
Migraine	18 (3.82%)	9 (5.33%)
Claustrophobia	2 (0.42%)	4 (2.35%)
Serious/terminal illness	1 (0.21%)	1 (0.59%)
Heart condition	9 (1.91%)	4 (2.35%)
Brain damage	6 (1.27%)	2 (1.18%)
Seizures/epilepsy	2 (0.42%)	0 (0.00%)

It is clear from the age distribution and health questionnaire results that the participant recruitment guidelines were largely ignored by the transport managers who selected the drivers to participate in the programme. It is likely that this was for pragmatic operational reasons: companies would send the drivers who were available for training, regardless of compliance with the recruitment criteria. No further details were asked about the type of brain damage, seizures, or epilepsy symptoms that participants suffered. Participants were given adequate warnings about what they would experience in driving the simulator and it was presumed that any reported health condition would not be worsened by their participation. Drivers who have suffered from epilepsy must satisfy strict criteria before returning to work in the UK as a professional driver of a commercial vehicle. The driver must:

- hold a full car licence and
- have been free of seizures for ten years and
- have not had to take anti-epileptic drugs during this ten year period and
- have been declared 'fit to drive' after a medical examination by a consultant nominated by the Driver and Vehicle Licensing Agency (DVLA).

SSQ and driver drop-out

A driver was considered to have dropped out of the programme if s/he were unable to complete all the required training exercises due to symptoms of simulator sickness. Drivers failing to complete the training programme due to other reasons (e.g. required back at work, simulator technical problem) were not counted as drop-outs due to simulator sickness. Table 4 shows the SSQ scores reported by drivers in the two simulators.

The negative minimum values shown in the 'Total due to simulator' row indicate that some participants felt notably *better* after driving the simulators than when they arrived at the facility, perhaps indicating that they were not in an optimum health state on arrival. The largest improvement scores were observed on the oculomotor discomfort and disorientation SSQ subscales. Independent samples t-tests show that there were no significant differences across the simulators in the SSQ scores reported. The variation in N values across the different SSQ score measures is caused by drivers who failed to complete part or all of the SSQ questionnaire such that SSQ score values could not be calculated.

Table 4. SSQ scores reported by participants in the SCOTSIM training programme

	T5000					T3000				
SSQ score	N	Mean	Min	Max	SD	N	Mean	Min	Max	SD
Nausea	451	27.2	0	190.8	37.9	156	33.2	0	162.2	41.5
Oculomotor discomfort	451	16.0	0	128.9	23.1	156	15.3	0	91.0	19.5
Disorientation	453	27.3	0	222.7	39.8	154	24.3	0	208.8	36.2
Total post drive SSQ score	446	25.6	0	179.5	33.7	152	26.3	0	123.4	31.5
Total SSQ due to simulator	443	22.5	-29.9	179.5	32.6	149	22.4	-41.1	112.2	31.3

Table 5 shows the number of participants that dropped out due to simulator sickness at each of the simulator facilities and the mean SSQ scores for drivers completing and drivers dropping out of the training programme.

Table 5. Drop-out status of participants in the SCOTSIM training programme

				Total SSQ score	
Simulator	Drop-out status	N	%	Mean	SD
T5000	Completed	364	78.4%	15.6	22.8
	Dropped out	100	21.6%	65.9	40.5
	Total	464	100.0%	25.8	33.9
T3000	Completed	114	67.1%	14.5	22.2
	Dropped out	56	32.9%	57.3	31.2
	Total	170	100.0%	26.3	31.5
Total	Completed	478	75.4%	15.3	22.6
	Dropped out	156	24.6%	63.1	37.9
	Total	634	100.0%	25.9	33.3

Table 5 shows that the drop-out rate was high for both simulators, particularly for the T3000 where practically one third of drivers were unable to complete the training programme due to symptoms of simulator sickness. An independent samples t-test comparing drop-out rate revealed that there was a highly significant difference across the two simulators ($t(632) = -2.97$; $p = 0.003$), suggesting that drivers were significantly less likely to drop-out using the T5000 rather than the T3000. SSQ scores were similar across the two simulators despite the difference in drop-out rates.

No motion on T5000

A technical fault caused the motion system to be inoperative on the T5000 for approximately six weeks between September and October 2005. The simulator exercises could still be driven therefore training continued but the driver did not experience the motion cues that the system should provide. This allowed comparison of sickness rates with and without an active motion system. Table 6 shows the post-drive SSQ scores and percentage drop-out rates for drives completed on the T5000 with and without the motion system.

Table 6. Comparison of post drive SSQ scores and percentage drop-out rate of participant experiencing an active or inactive motion system on the T5000

	Motion status	N	Mean	SD
Post drive SSQ score	Active	350	27.6	35.4
	Inactive	96	18.2	25.6
% Drop-out rate	Active	363	24.0%	42.7
	Inactive	101	12.9%	33.7

Table 6 shows that simulator sickness, in terms of both driver drop-out and reported SSQ, were reduced when the motion system was inoperative. An independent samples t-test on both the post drive SSQ scores (t(444) = −2.42; p = 0.016) and percentage drop-out rates (t(462) = −2.41; p = 0.016) shows that the differences were significant. The difference in drop-out rate between the T5000 and the T3000 remains significant if the participants that did not experience motion in the T5000 are removed from the comparison (Drop-out rate; T5000 = 23.4%; T3000 = 32.9%; t(536) = −2.35; p = 0.019). The difference in SSQ becomes insignificant.

Correlations with SSQ and driver drop-out

To understand the factors contributing to the observed sickness rates, a multi-factorial Pearson correlation procedure was performed to investigate which factors were strongly correlated with high SSQ scores and driver drop-out. The first result was that drivers' SSQ scores were unsurprisingly highly positively correlated with drop-out (N = 592; r = 0.60; p < 0.001). Furthermore, drivers' age also showed a weak but significant positive correlation with drop-out (N = 633; r = 0.12; p = 0.003). Four of the health characteristics showed positive correlations with drop-out. The strongest correlation was where the participant recorded suffering from motion sickness (N = 633; r = 0.32; p < 0.001). There were also weak but significant correlations between driver drop-out and drivers who reported suffering with (respectively) migraine (N = 633; r = 0.079; p = 0.047), claustrophobia (N = 634; r = 0.13; p = 0.001), and brain damage (N = 634; r = 0.080; p = 0.045).

Drivers also completed a questionnaire that asked them to rate their agreement with each of 18 statements relating to the use of technology. Agreement was measured on six point scale (1-6) where a score of 1 indicated that the driver completely disagreed with the statement and a score of 6 indicated that the driver completely agreed with the statement. Correlations were taken between participants' agreement with these statements and SSQ scores and with driver drop-out. Eight of the statements showed weak but significant correlations. These are shown in table 7. Note that correlations with statements that are generally positive towards technology are negative and correlations with statements that are generally negative towards technology are positive.

Table 7. Statements in the Attitudes to Technology questionnaire that show significant correlations with either SSQ or driver drop-out

Statement	Correlation with SSQ score			Correlation with driver drop-out		
	N	r	p	N	r	p
"I enjoy watching widescreen TV"	578	-0.083	0.045		NS	
"I am very unsure of my abilities to play computer games"	583	0.117	0.005	618	0.084	0.038
"I seem to have difficulties with most video players I have tried to program"		NS		619	0.080	0.046
"I am very confident in my abilities to use different technical equipment"		NS		622	-0.097	0.016
"I would rather that we did not have to learn how to use computers"		NS		620	0.114	0.005
"I always seem to have problems when trying to use computers"	587	0.094	0.023	622	0.113	0.005
"Playing computer games is something I rarely enjoy"	578	0.108	0.009		NS	
"I don't consider myself a competent player of computer games"	583	0.111	0.007		NS	

Table 7 shows that the significant correlations are all in the direction where a driver who has a negative attitude towards technology is more likely to report a high SSQ or drop-out of the simulator training programme. Although the correlations are significant, the small magnitude of the correlation coefficients suggests that the observed relationships are mere indications of a very weak relationship between attitude to technology and simulator sickness.

Screening criteria

The items that showed significant correlations with either SSQ or drop-out were used to generate screening criteria that could be applied to drivers wishing to participate in a simulator training programme. These were evaluated by applying them retrospectively to the 641 drivers participating in the training programme to investigate how many drivers would be excluded using such criteria and to examine sickness and drop-out rates for included and excluded drivers. For drivers' age, the threshold was set at 60 years, such that drivers aged 60 years and over would be excluded from participation. This excluded 16 drivers from the original dataset. For the health criteria, if a driver reported any of the conditions that were correlated with drop-out, then they were excluded. This meant that 92 drivers who reported suffering from motion sickness were excluded; 27 participants who reported suffering from migraine were excluded; 6 participants who reported suffering from claustrophobia were excluded; and 8 participants who reported suffering from brain damage were excluded[*]. Finally, scores from the eight questions that showed significant correlations with SSQ score and/or driver drop-out were aggregated such that if a drivers' total agreement scores with the statements (measured on the 1-6 scale) was below a threshold score of 20, the driver would be excluded from the analysis[°]. This resulted in the exclusion of 33 participants in the retrospective analysis.

Sufficient data were available to apply the exclusion criteria to 625 of the 641 participants in the training programme and resulted in the (retrospective) elimination of 149 participants (23.8%) from the training programme. Table 8 shows the drop-out rate for the included and excluded participants.

Table 8. Driver drop-out rate and mean post-drive SSQ score observed for participants included and those excluded using the exclusion criteria

Driver group	N	Completed	Drop-out	% drop-out	Mean SSQ
Included	476	397	79	16.6%	20.9
Excluded	149	74	75	50.3%	43.2
Included+Excluded	625	471	154	24.6%	25.9

Table 8 shows that for drivers who are considered eligible for simulator training based on these exclusion criteria, the drop-out rate has fallen from the original overall rate of 24.6% to 16.6%. However, for the excluded drivers the drop-out rate exceeds 50% with drivers reporting higher SSQ scores more than double those reported by the included group. An independent samples t-test across the included/excluded groups shows that the differences in drop-out rate ($t(623) = 8.83$; $p < 0.001$) and post-drive SSQ score ($t(588) = 7.06$; $p < 0.001$) are highly significant. Furthermore, independent samples t-test comparisons between the included group and the original driver group (included and excluded drivers) for drop-out rate ($t(1054) = 2.49$; $p = 0.013$) and post-drive SSQ score ($t(1108) = 3.25$; $p = 0.001$) are also highly significant, suggesting that filtering participants before training began would have improved throughput.

---

[*] Some of the participants may have met several of the criteria known to be correlated with simulator sickness. Consequently the total number of participants excluded is less than the sum of the number of participants that would have been excluded under each of the exclusion criteria.
[°] Scores relating to some questions were reversed such that all significant correlations became positive; high agreement score indicated highly positive attitude towards technology

Discussion

The training programme conducted as part of the SCOTSIM research study provided an opportunity to monitor the incidence of simulator sickness for a large number of drivers completing the same exercises on two similar simulator systems. Before discussing simulator sickness further it should be noted that drivers achieved significant improvements in their performance across the two drives. Drivers demonstrated an average reduction in fuel consumption of 11.2%, an average reduction in the number of gear changes of 16.0%, and a reduction in the time taken to complete the exercises of 10.3%. However, the focus of this paper is the incidence of simulator sickness and the driver drop-out rate as a result of its symptoms was considerably higher than was expected, particularly for the T3000. It is conceivable that the greater range of motion and flying screens available on the T5000 are a significant factor in the lower SSQ scores and drop-out rate observed on that system. Certainly the T5000 motion system would offer the potential to reduce the mismatch between visual and vestibular cues in a simulator, which has been suggested as the main cause of motion- and simulator sickness (see Claremont, 1931; Guedry, 1968). However, the large reduction in SSQ scores and drop-out rate during the period in which the T5000 motion system was inactive suggests that it is not the presence of the T5000 motion system that is responsible for the reduction in sickness rates. The observation of reduced sickness rates in the absence of a functional motion system suggests that there may even have been a problem with the motion cues delivered by the motion system such that they served to exacerbate the sickness symptoms.

The large reduction in both SSQ scores and driver drop-out rate following the technical fault with the motion system on the T5000 calls into question the need to use large scale motion systems for driving simulators or at least, suggests that care must be taken to ensure that motion cues provided by such systems are appropriate. If drivers can more readily complete exercises in a simulator that does not have a motion system, this has consequences for future purchasers of simulator technology since the motion system represents a significant proportion (as much as half) of the cost of a full mission simulator. Aviation literature suggests that because experienced pilots often rely on motion rather than instrument readings, motion becomes more important as experience level increases (Briggs & Wiener, 1959, cited in Williges, Roscoe, & Williges, 1973). It could be argued that the cues provided by a motion system to indicate vehicle behaviour become more important for experienced truck drivers than dashboard displays, particularly in emergency situations; circumstances for advanced training. Novice drivers on the other hand might derive substantial benefit from systems that focus on instrument display and may gain little tangible benefit from large scale simulated motion cues.

Reason and Brand (1975) suggested that motion sickness is almost non-existent for adults over the age of 50. However, in this study a positive correlation was observed between age and simulator sickness suggesting that, unlike motion sickness, older drivers suffered greater symptoms of simulator sickness. This may be related to the sensory conflict theory since older drivers have more experience of driving and may be more sensitive to any mismatch between visual and vestibular sensations experienced in a simulator (see Kennedy & Frank, 1985). Furthermore, younger drivers are more likely to be familiar with computer games and the suspension of disbelief required to become immersed in a virtual environment. Older drivers' difficulty in overcoming this hurdle may contribute to their experience of sickness symptoms. A related point is that Bertin, Collet, Espie, and Graf (2005) found that feelings of sickness were strongly correlated with anxiety. The results of this study support their findings since drivers' attitudes to computers were correlated with sickness where participants who were less confident/comfortable using technology were more likely to experience symptoms of simulator sickness. This has implications for the recruitment of drivers to participate in simulator research and training programmes, particularly since the population that are of interest for training and research are sometimes those who are inexperienced with technology.

Driver exclusion criteria were generated using factors that were correlated with high SSQ scores and driver drop-out. Applying these criteria retrospectively to the 641 drivers trained in the SCOTSIM programme revealed that drop-out would have been lowered from 24.6% to 16.6% and the drop-out rate for drivers who would have been excluded was 50.3%. However, this means that nearly 50% of drivers that would have been excluded did successfully complete the training programme despite meeting the post-hoc exclusion criteria. The decision as to whether this would be acceptable would be down to those responsible for training operations. If driver recruitment was a problem, the exclusion criteria could be relaxed in order to increase the number of drivers who are able to participate but at the risk of an increased drop-out rate. Alternatively, if drop-out rate was too high, the exclusion criteria could be tightened but at the risk of rejecting many drivers who would have successfully completed the simulator training.

The screening criteria proposed here are hypothetical and were generated simply through the correlation with drop-out rate and/or SSQ scores. However, it may be considered unethical to exclude drivers, particularly based on their age. Rather than strict exclusion criteria, the factors found to correlate drop-out rate and/or SSQ scores in this study could be considered as guidelines for companies wanting their drivers to participate and operators of research and training simulators may choose to adapt their procedures for drivers such that more care is taken with drivers who are considered susceptible to simulator sickness, as predicted by the exclusion criteria. This could entail the use of different, less challenging exercises or restricting the motion settings on the simulators to be used. An investigation is currently underway into the effect of improved familiarisation and the application of screening processes on sickness rates.

To conclude this study has demonstrated that drivers recruited to take part in the SCOTSIM training programme experienced relatively high levels of simulator sickness with around one in four participants unable to complete the programme due to discomfort caused by driving the simulator. A comparison of the incidence of sickness when the motion system on the T5000 was active to that when it was inactive revealed that the motion system may have played a significant role in the severity of the symptoms. An investigation into the factors correlated with sickness was used to create exclusion criteria and when applied retrospectively, these would have successfully excluded a majority of the drivers who dropped-out due to symptoms of sickness. Further research is required to validate these exclusion criteria and to investigate the cost/benefit analysis of different levels of motion system for different simulator research and training operations.

References

Bertin R.J.V., Collet C., Espié S, & Graf W. (2005) Objective measurement of simulator sickness and the role of visual-vestibular conflict situations. In *Driving Simulation Conference North-America (DSC-NA) proceedings*, Florida, USA, November 2005.

Claremont, C.A. (1931). The psychology of seasickness. *Psyche, 11*, 86-90.

Department for Transport, UK (2003) *The safe and fuel efficient driving (SAFED) standard.* Good practice guide 2100. London, UK: Department for Transport.

Guedry, F.E. (1968). *Conflicting sensory orientation cues as a factor in motion sickness. Fourth Symposium on The Role of the Vestibular Organs in Space Exploration.* Naval Aerospace Medical Institute, Pensacola, FL, 24-26 September, 1968, 45-51. Washington D.C: U.S. Government Printing Office.

Kennedy, R. S., & Frank, L. H. (1985). *A review of motion sickness with special reference to simulator sickness.* (Tech. Rep. NAVTRAEQUIPCEN 81-C-0105-16). Orlando, FL, USA: Naval Training Equip

Kennedy, R.S., Lane, N.E., Berbaum, K.S., & Lilienthal, M.G. (1993). Simulator Sickness Questionnaire: An Enhanced Method for Quantifying Simulator Sickness. *The International Journal of Aviation Psychology, 3*, 203-220.

Reason, J.T. & Brand, J.J. (1975). *Motion sickness.* London: Academic Press.

Stanney, K.M., & Kennedy, R.S. (1998). Aftereffects from virtual environment exposure: How long do they last? *Proceedings of the 42nd Annual Human Factors and Ergonomics Society Meeting* (pp.1476-1480). Santa Monica, CA, USA: HFES.

Stewart, D. (1965) *A Platform with six-degrees-of-freedom.* Proc. Inst. Of Mechanical Engineers, vol. 180, part 1, no. 5, 371-386

Triesman, M. (1977). Motion sickness: an evolutionary hypothesis. *Science, 197*, 493-495.

Williges, B.H., Roscoe, S.N., & Williges, R.C. (1973). Synthetic flight training revisited. *Human Factors, 15*, 543-560.

Enhanced information design for high speed trains

Anjum Naweed, Richard Bye, & Bob Hockey
The University of Sheffield
Sheffield, United Kingdom

Abstract

Train drivers have traditionally 'navigated' by processing information from trackside signals and familiar landmarks, though such direct sources may be difficult to use at high speeds. Drivers have to rely on expert knowledge about the route such as movement authority, speed limits etc in order to initiate speed control actions. However, effective use of route knowledge can be compromised by the faster decision-making required at high speeds, and by temporary increases in workload and fatigue, which may reduce drivers' situational awareness (SA). A general solution is to develop enhanced cab displays to support decision-making by providing preview and predictive information. Preliminary work has employed a range of cognitive engineering techniques to assess the driver operational demands. Data analysis will consider how drivers acquire and use route knowledge to influence their decision making, what information is effective for different driving tasks, and how it impacts on their SA. Early analysis indicates that drivers employ quasi-mathematical operations obtained from route knowledge, train state indicators and environmental conditions to maintain SA and evaluate safe and efficient journey trajectories. It is anticipated that this will lead to the development of prototype display interfaces to support the effective use of route knowledge and driver SA.

Background

Train drivers have traditionally 'navigated' by processing information from knowledge of track infrastructure, trackside signals, familiar landmarks and other such geographical markers. In practice, drivers have to rely on this expert knowledge about specific route information, to adjust to movement authority, speed limits, temporary restrictions, and so on, and thus implement appropriate throttle or braking control. In the UK, the increased demand for performance in rail service delivery has resulted in an increased speed of operations. Passenger trains now operate at the maximum speed the rail infrastructure will allow within the boundaries of safety. However, as with all safety critical industries (road traffic, maritime navigation, process industries) safety and performance are often in conflict as competing goals, and the severity of rail incidents in the UK in recent years (e.g., Watford Junction, Southall, Ladbroke Grove, Hatfield, Potter's Bar), have raised public questions of rail safety. Whilst most serious accidents are attributable to poorly maintained infrastructure or a chain of events involving several people, those which occur as a

In D. de Waard, G.R.J. Hockey, P. Nickel, and K.A. Brookhuis (Eds.) (2007), *Human Factors Issues in Complex System Performance* (pp. 235 - 240). Maastricht, the Netherlands: Shaker Publishing.

result of serious omissions or errors in driving are potentially the most costly. In 1999, the Ladbroke Grove incident cost 31 lives with over 400 people suffering serious injuries. Investigations following the incident revealed a signal passed at danger (SPAD) as the principle cause (Uff & Cullen, 2001).

However, a thorough analysis of rail safety statistics since 1945 has concluded that safety is no longer a compelling enough a reason for restructuring the railway (Evans, 2004). The recent introduction of automated train protection technology - such as the Automatic Warning System, which generates in-cab alarms associated with upcoming signals, and the Train Protection Warning System, which applies an automated full service brake application in the event of excessive speed or a SPAD - has played an instrumental role in minimising train accidents. Whilst the implementation of these systems into cabs has proven to be a lengthy, often technical and invariably costly campaign, the successful results have established rail travel as a safe, dynamic system. Nevertheless, any growing concerns over the safety of rail travel are not completely unfounded, as SPADs continue to occur. Authorities have reported 94 individual SPADs for the 3rd quarter of 2006 alone, 4 of which were potentially severe, and 11 cases which resulted in trains running past the signals by 200 yards (approximately 180 metres) or more (HM Railway Inspectorate, 2006). As is the case, the majority were invariably due to an omission or unintentional error on the part of the driver.

Whilst SPADs may not be indicative of failing safety levels in rail, their insistence to occur may evidence a failing reliability and effective use of route knowledge associated with the faster decision-making required at higher speeds. When a driver initially misreads a signal displaying a stop indication, or has misread a signal displaying a warning indication, they are very unlikely to have sufficient time or distance to stop at the signal, in spite of ultimately realising the error and attempting to stop. This may be because the faster decision making required at high speeds temporarily increases driver workload and fatigue, whilst at the same time reducing their situational awareness (SA). SA is a constantly evolving picture of the state of the environment, formally defined as a person's 'perception of the elements in the environment within a volume of time and space, the comprehension of their meaning, and the projection of their status in the near future' (Endsley, 1988). The higher levels of SA incorporating the operational goals and ability to project future states of the system are particularly critical for effective functioning in the complex train driving environment. The reduction in driver SA and effective use of route knowledge at high speeds highlights the need to interrogate the driver-cab interface for possible enhancements to address the problem. Locomotives in the UK, currently contain no equipment beyond train state indicators such as analogue dials (e.g., speedometer; brake pipe pressure) that would support decision-making.

A general solution would be to reduce the reliance on trackside infrastructure by integrating and displaying all the information deemed necessary to aid the driver. This would provide drivers with preview information for optimal trajectories and predictive displays illustrating the effects of 'what-if' control actions. Dynamic systems analogous to rail where collision avoidance plays a pivotal role, such as in aviation and maritime sea navigation incorporate these features within their standard operator control panels, whilst the technology within locomotives is comparatively antiquated. By providing drivers with more readily accessible information, and decreasing their chances for perceptual memory errors, omissions and inaccuracies in route knowledge, it would increase efficiency and punctuality and generally optimise the progress of the train for example by aiding in the pursuit of fuel economy and out of course events (e.g., diversions; wrong-routing; adverse weather conditions).

A European initiative called ERTMS* (European Railway Traffic Management System), contains some enhanced display features and is currently under negotiations for integration into the UK Rail industry. Research in Sweden (Stjernström, 2001) has also looked at decision-support in the cab-interface and a prototype set of displays developed at the Volpe/MIT centre (Askey & Sheridan, 1996; Einhorn, Sheridan & Multer, 2005) has attracted limited testing within the USA. However, the research base for such applications is not well developed, and a more informed model of the driver-cab interface is required as a basis for future information design initiatives. This should consider: how drivers acquire and use route knowledge to influence their decision making; what information is effective for different kinds of driving; how SA is affected by driving conditions and alternative display configurations.

This work aims to gain insight into the information needs for drivers in the UK, understand the task at both the blunt and sharp ends of the scale, and in doing so, use this information to develop a number of candidate auxiliary displays and alternative prototype display interfaces to support the effective use of route knowledge and driver SA.

Method and analysis

Unwrapping the complexity of the UK rail system is generally a very difficult task, mainly because decisions, plans and actions are layered within the tasks and subtasks deeply embedded within goal-directed work activities. During early familiarisation of the task, train driver skill and expertise was found to be very much an intuitive, tacit form of knowledge resistant to conventional interviewing techniques, therefore a novel, hybrid approach of several cognitive analysis techniques was used to effectively elicit the most detailed information. Amongst these were Cognitive Work Analysis (CWA; Vicente, 1999; Rasmussen, Pejtersen & Goodstein, 1994), used to decompose the domain into functions, work activities, tasks and scenarios, and a range of Cognitive Task Analysis (CTA) interview techniques such as the critical decision method (Klein, Calderwood & MacGregor, 1989), to incorporate a series of information-gathering sweeps in order to guide the interviewee into salient knowledge recall.

---

* Further information accessible at http://www.ertms.com/

A significant amount of time was invested becoming familiar with the train driving task and associated rail functions. This information was obtained at both the sharp and blunt ends of the domain through informal interviews with rail subject matter experts. This invariably helped shape the structure of the subsequent interviews which were arranged on an opportunity sampling basis, and coordinated within the offices and live cab rides of the relevant rail companies. Driving subject matter experts included professional train drivers, Operations Managers and Train Crew Managers. The interviews were all recorded following signed consent and involved capturing individual career histories and demographical details before progressing further. The power of this approach lay in the application of the techniques coordinated as an iterative suite of methods where emergent findings informed subsequent analysis. The most fundamental objective driving this approach was to investigate what could be done – independent of the technical and organisational constraints imposed by existing systems.

The analysis was structured through the development of a veridical representation of cognitive work in the task (for more details of development and analysis see Naweed, Bye, & Hockey, 2007). The model was sufficiently flexible to adjust the scale of research and focus on individual research elements to build a complete representation of the driving task. This was an important feature and reflected the influence of goals and constraints that shape work in rail operations, permeating both vertically and horizontally to affect decisions between and within levels of the hierarchy. The analysis of the data was qualitative and took many different forms, resulting in the production of diagrams, concept and process maps, interview transcripts and other artefacts that were used to both deepen and document our understanding for subsequent display design. As with all cognitive systems engineering methods, the products of the analysis were very time consuming to generate but yielded much information and emergent themes that were used to populate the representation of cognitive work in rail operations.

Results and discussion

Though analysis is still in its early stages, it has revealed the most important components of driver information needs, as far as train drivers familiar with UK signalling standards recognise. The coding of the data uncovered some interesting themes, broadly grouped into three categories as shown in Table 1.

Table 1. Important components of driver information needs

Environmental Conditions	Train State Indicators	Route Knowledge
Visibility	Speed	Gradients
Feedback	Weight	Curvature
Forces	Passenger/Freight	Signals
Drag	Freight Type	Speed Restrictions
Weather/Seasons/Adhesion	Fuel Usage	Geographical Markers

The following excerpt from the data indicates the importance of route knowledge is to the task, "Most drivers would say that route knowledge is the key to driving a train." Subject matter experts generally agreed upon the following criteria as the most important and salient aspects of route knowledge; "Gradients, curvature of the line, signals, speeds, the weight of his train, speed of his train." The data implicates that quasi-mathematical operations obtained from train state indications, trackside signage and extensive route learning are employed in order to maintain SA. This information is seemingly combined with recognition of environmental conditions in order to evaluate time-keeping, and practice safe and efficient journey trajectories. As issues central to the problem, this information will be used to drive the prototype interface, and if incorporated effectively, may help the driver plan the task more efficiently. The ability to recognise and subsequently adapt to environmental changes in particular is considered an important proponent of train driving expertise as shown in the following; "If you're going to work in a foot of snow, you're expected to work that train in a foot of snow from A to B in the same time you would on a normal dry day, clear day."

Though information pertaining to environmental conditions and fuel is generally omitted from train displays, the data also indicates that including this type of real-time information may help the driver optimise the task further. At this stage, the data also reveals the existence of several train driving tasks which differ in the amount and type of information required. For example, the subject matter experts frequently commented on the clear distinctions between passenger and freight train driving; "Freight trains stop more frequently, so they have a better use of the brake, the brakes are not as sharp as a passenger train." This brought about another important issue; "We need to compensate for the weight difference." These findings highlight the importance of train weight, and posit the existence of innumerable variations in train handling physics. They also raise important questions concerning the suitability of the ERTMS initiative (Naweed et al., 2007) scheduled for integration into the rail network in the next decade or so. In short, this implies that the provision of in-cab support must not end with high-speed operations - Freight trains driving at slower speeds with an array of comparatively antiquated technology will also reap significant benefits from more information available at their fingertips.

Future work

Future work will revolve around the development of the interface and subsequent testing and evaluation of alternative configurations, using both performance criteria (time-keeping, trajectory tracking, fuel use etc) and assessment of processing demands. Preliminary work will be carried out using a PC simulation, with software enhancements and possibly the use of train control hardware. Students will be used for early testing, but experts (both simulation users & drivers) will be used for advanced development and evaluation.

References

Askey, S. & Sheridan, T. (1996*). Human Factors Phase II: Design and Evaluation of Decision Aids for Control of High-speed Trains: Experiments and Model Safety of High-speed Ground Transportation Systems.* (DOT/FRA/ORD-96-09). Cambridge, MA: John A. Volpe National Transportation Systems Center.

Einhorn, J., Sheridan, T., & Multer, J. (2005). *Preview information in cab displays for high-speed locomotives: Human Factors in Railroad Operations.* (DOT/FRA/ORD-04/12). Cambridge, MA: John A. Volpe National Transportation Systems Center.

Endsley, M.R. (1988). Design and evaluation for situation awareness enhancement. In *Proceedings of the Human Factors Society 32nd Annual Meeting* (pp. 97-101). Santa Monica, CA: Human Factors Society.

European Union (1996). *The interoperability of the trans-European high-speed rail system* (96/48/EC of 23 July 1996 – 31996L0048). Accessible at http://europa.eu/

Evans, A.W. (2004). *Rail safety and rail privatisation in Britain.* Centre for Transport Studies, Imperial College London, June.

HM Railway Inspectorate (2006). *SPADS (Signals passed at danger) report for Q3 2006* (October, 2006, 253330.01). London, UK: Office of Rail Regulation. Accessible at http://www.rail-reg.gov.uk/

Klein G.A., Calderwood. R., & MacGregor D. (1989). Critical decision method for eliciting knowledge. *IEEE Transactions on Systems, Man, and Cybernetics, 19*, 462-472.

Naweed, A., Bye, Richard., & Hockey, G.R.J. (2007). Enhanced decision support for train drivers: Driving a train by the seat of your pants. In D. de Waard, G.R.J. Hockey, P. Nickel, and K.A. Brookhuis (Eds.), *Human Factors Issues in Complex System Performance* (pp. 131-144). Maastricht, the Netherlands: Shaker Publishing.

Rasmussen, J., Pejtersen, A.M., & Goodstein, L.P. (1994). *Cognitive systems engineering.* New York: Wiley.

Stjernström, R. (2001). *User-centred Design of a Train Driver Display.* (Technical Report 2001-016). Department of Information Technology. Uppsala University

Uff, J. & Cullen, W.D. (2001). *The southall and ladbroke grove joint inquiry into train protection systems.* London: HSE Books.

Vicente, K.J. (1999). *Cognitive work analysis. Toward safe, productive, and healthy computer- based work.* Mahwah, NJ: Lawrence Erlbaum Associates.

Effects of a new railway information system on train driver efficiency and subjective performance

Karel Brookhuis[1], Irene Taroni[2]
[1]Delft University of Technology
[2]University of Groningen
The Netherlands

Abstract

The purpose of the present study was to investigate effects of providing accurate and dynamic in-vehicle information to train drivers by means of a kind of digital map on a PDA (personal digital assistant). It may be that enhancing the content of the task of the train driver by providing extra information affects efficiency, job satisfaction and subjective performance. It may also be that providing information distracts driver attention in such a way that it has negative effects on performance and acceptance, specifically with respect to safety. The objective of the underlying project was to determine whether the railway system would be safer and more efficient if train drivers are provided with an overview of the traffic situation in front of them by displaying accurate and dynamic context information.

To assess the effects of the new information system a group of professional train drivers was tested in a train driving simulator study on their objective and subjective responses to the provided information. The performance results indicate that provision of forward information on a PDA may potentially enhance the train drivers' awareness, improving decision making, and might lead to a decrease in energy consumption. The results from the questionnaires show that the train drivers indicate that decision-making, safety and personal satisfaction were enhanced with the use of the additional information given by the PDA.

Introduction

All sorts of traffic are rapidly increasing in volume and complexity, with concomitant increase in accident risk. Graham and Pollock's (1997) research on railway accidents shows that an alarming increase of "signals passed at danger" (SPADs) by train drivers (150 in 1995; 281 in 2003) has established, similar to red light running in road traffic. While SPAD cases rarely result in fatalities or injuries, they do create situations where the potential for increased risk is high. Missing relevant information in the operator environment is a well-known problem in a vigilance task when attention deteriorates (Brookhuis et al., 2004). In agreement with previous (rail) research, sustained attention is one of the most salient contributing (human) factors across all incident types in rail traffic (Graham & Pollock, 1997). Enhancing sustained attention may lead to a better performance of the train driver, for instance, by using a new generation of displays providing relevant information with respect to the situation ahead. Livingstone et al. (2005) developed the train driver situation awareness model, combining and integrating internal and external information factors to improve decision-making, by focussing on information processing.

The requirements of sustained attention, or vigilance, in operator performance constitute a well known problem in the transport industry (Smiley, 1990; Haga, 1984; Michaut & McGaughey, 1974). The railway operating environment requires that the driver remains constantly alert, often under monotonous conditions, and responds immediately to irregular and, therefore, largely unpredictable critical signals. Although trains are controlled by the train drivers, they mostly do not make their decisions based upon any general overview of the traffic situation. Their decisions are based upon orders given by the signalling system, the time schedules and central command centres. The railway system lacks the flexibility that is found in other modes of transportation and this may have a negative effect on safety and efficiency (Schotanus & Zigterman, 2004).

Background

A few things are important for railways in this respect. Firstly, it seems that driving a train is seen as a very simple task, i.e. just following simple orders. Secondly, the culture of the railways has always been based on rationality, hierarchy and safety. Thirdly, the amount of information that train drivers, being human beings, can process is considered to be limited, therefore they should do only simple tasks and technology is used to dominate the railway process.

In the rail industry, applied organizational research in the area of vigilance has resulted from concerns about rail safety for quite a long time. Hildebrandt et al. (1975) found that the monotonous task of the train driver can result in alertness decline, particularly when drivers are fatigued. Haga (1984) studied signal vigilance errors among train drivers and found that sustained attention was particularly influenced by distraction. Other studies have documented the unfavourable nature of the train drivers' working environment in terms of temperature, humidity and noise levels, and their detrimental effects on alertness (Michaut & McGaughey, 1974).

Originally, studies on sustained attention have typically been constrained to the laboratory environment, where research has consistently found that decrement occurs over the first 20-35 minutes of vigilance conditions depending on the task being performed (Parasuraman, 1986; Levine & Craig, 1988). While laboratory studies have been helpful in guiding vigilance research, laboratory conditions and real life piloting or driving tasks have little in common, at least according to some experts (Nachreiner, 1977), and investigation reports have questioned the generalization of experimental results to real life performance (Adams, 1987; Nachreiner, 1977; Farber, 1999, but see also De Waard et al., 1999). As a result, simulator studies of car, truck and train driving have been initiated, focusing on examining manipulable criteria, such as psycho-physiological processes like activation, arousal or alertness in a quasi realistic environment (De Waard et al., 1999).

Train drivers' support

The Dutch railway system includes a careful interplay between traffic management and train driving, organised in a top-down fashion. The traffic manager plans the routes (time schedules) to avoid conflicts, and train drivers integrate various information orders (signage, signals, and temporary orders) to drive their trains (NS, "Dutch Railways", 1999). The current situation on the railways in the Netherlands suffers from capacity and punctuality problems. To improve this situation, a bottom-up approach is applied to enhance decision-making and empowerment of train drivers by providing more and accurate context information (Biemans et al., 2004). A simple input-output research model was applied, of context information and driving decisions, leading to the *Het Spoor Meester* (HSM, "mastering the rail") project, started in April 2003. The main objective of HSM was to realize an optimal combination of human being and technology (Van Luipen, 2005). A new electronic information display, called RouteLint, might help the train driver by providing a better overview of the traffic situation.

The starting point of the HSM project is that the railway system may become more efficient and safer if the train drivers are given the space to express their abilities. They are talented problem solvers after all that can handle complex and sometimes unpredictable tasks. The main hypothesis of this project is that extra information improves railway performance through enhanced self-empowerment (Biemans et al., 2004). Railway performance consists of safety, punctuality, energy-costs, personnel satisfaction and passenger satisfaction. Additional information affects decision making directly through better projection ahead, and indirectly through motivating and empowering train drivers (Biemans et al., 2004). The explorative part of the project, i.e. this study, is about how the train driver perceives the extra information in a working situation, in a simulator environment.

The first goal of the present study, as part of the HSM project, is to investigate whether simulated railway performance improves in terms of efficiency after providing more dynamic and accurate information to the train driver with the use of a personal digital assistant (PDA) equiped with the digital map RouteLint. It may be that enhancing the content of the task of the train drivers by providing information helps to improve their performance. The second objective is to identify the impact of the RouteLint information on the driver, using a questionnaire on usability and subjective aspects of the information system (Taroni, 2006).

Method

The present paper is mainly focussing on subjective measures using the RouteLint information system in a simulation study, carried out in a special train driving simulator. In Figure 1 a schematic representation of the situation of the train driver is depicted, including the PDA with route information that was used during the experiment.

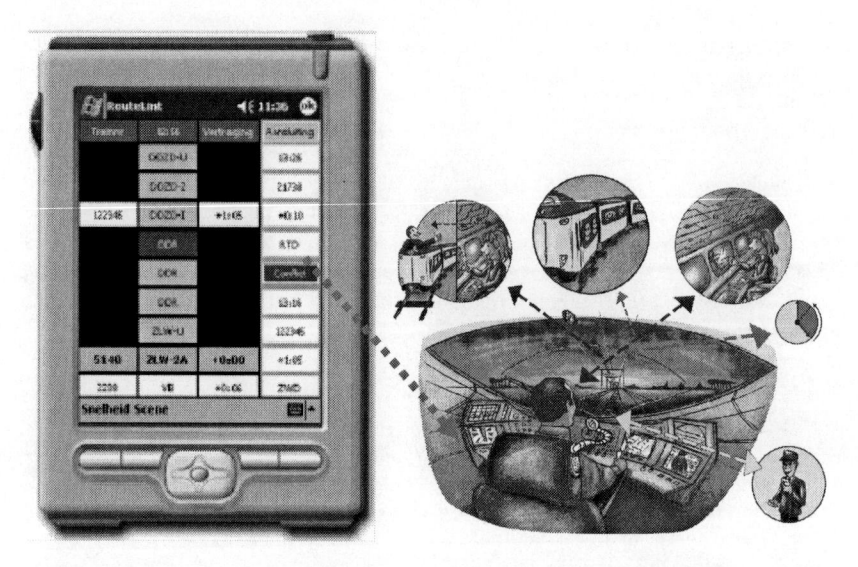

Figure 1. The train driver has advanced information about the traffic situation [images available in colour at http://extras.hfes-europe.org].

The picture of the PDA shows an image of the new display, the RouteLint information system. A detailed ergonomic analysis of the image is not included in this study (Taroni, 2006). Briefly it can be stated that the image shown on the display helps the train drivers decide how to optimize speed regulation. They can anticipate what happens in front, slowing down in a gradual way in advance of a regular red light signal or stop immediately in case of emergency. From the display it is clear where and when they will encounter a yellow or a red light and this knowledge helps to regulate speed and indirectly energy consumption. This new PDA image has interesting consequences on the communication between train drivers and traffic controllers as well.

The study sets out to investigate whether train drivers with a traffic image are more efficient in terms of speed control, i.e. energy use, than without it. The most important objective is to see what kind of information is relevant during the traffic situation and if RouteLint is capable of transferring that kind of information in an easily perceivable and comprehensible way. This is done in a within-subjects, cross-over design, including a training session, a treatment and a control condition. A train driving simulator, measuring a few relevant train driving aspects, and questionnaires, measuring acceptance (Van der Laan et al. 1997), subjective driving quality (Brookhuis et al., 1985) and perceived mental effort (Zijlstra, 1993) are used to assess the objectives. Furthermore, (virtual) energy use is estimated during the simulations, to measure efficiency performance.

In the simulator experiment 40 licensed and experienced train drivers participated, in the control condition without PDA and in the experimental condition with PDA, counterbalanced in a cross-over design. Train drivers came in groups of four, firstly trained to operate the relatively simple simulation device, using a laptop and a joystick. The total session lasted 4 hours, the first (training) session supposedly giving a sufficient virtual-reality feeling of "really" driving a train to start with. After the training session, firstly a questionnaire was completed with respect to personal information, subjective safety aspects of train driving and initial ideas about the RouteLint facility that was explained to the participants before the actual start of the experimental runs. After the two experimental runs, the participants were again asked about their feelings with respect to RouteLint.

Results

Energy consumption

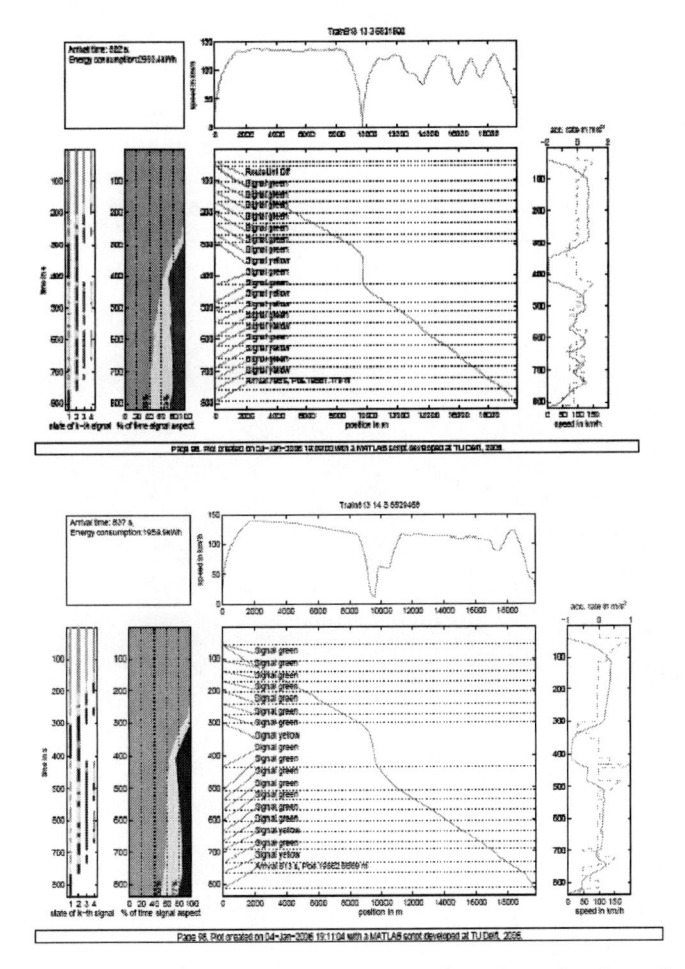

Figure 2. Performance of the train in terms of speed, acceleration and energy consumption, without and with the RouteLint information system (from top to bottom, left to right: energy consumption and speed, signage, position development, speed & acceleration) situation [images available in colour at http://extras.hfes-europe.org].

With respect to energy use during the rides, information provision using RouteLint was expected to help decrease energy consumption. The use of the PDA may stimulate the train drivers to monitor the route with respect to throughput and thus save energy consumption of the trains. In Figure 2 examples of train performance are depicted of one single train driver, without and with the information system. The pictures display speed development over the rides, signage, position development, and speed and acceleration.

From the numbers in the example in Figure 2, it is clear that the train driver adapted acceleration and speeds in this specific ride (lower panel, compared to upper panel), based on the information from the system. In the baseline condition (upper) 2950 kWh was used, while only 1960 kWh was used in the condition (lower) with the RouteLint information system. Not all drivers were able to use RouteLint that efficiently during the experiment, however.

Subjective impressions

The train drivers were asked if they thought that the new information system would be safe, useful and pleasant, before the experimental sessions from a description, and after each session by experience with the RouteLint information system.

Figure 3 shows that on average the population of train drivers perceived the extra information provision as safe while they were driving with the information displayed on the PDA, as compared to the feeling from the description beforehand.

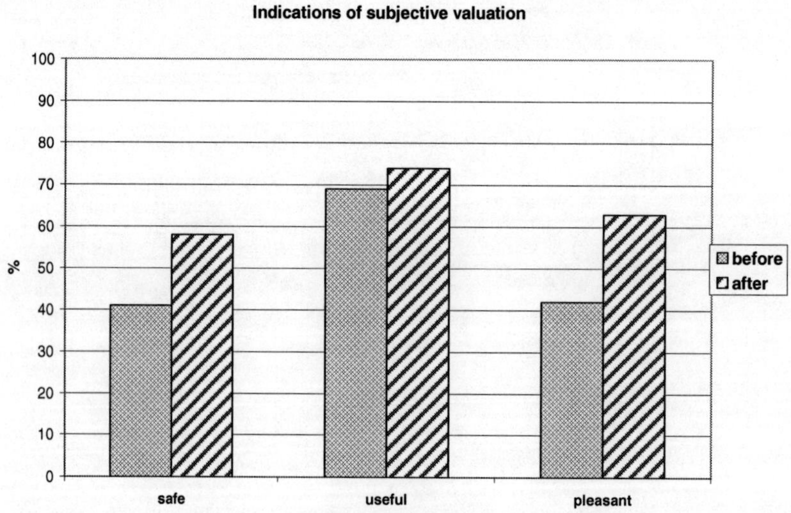

Figure 3. Percentage of answers that agree with safety, usefulness and pleasantness, before and after experiencing Routelint

Train drivers feelings with respect to the use of the device were measured by asking the train drivers if they experienced the information system as useful and pleasant.

Figure 3 shows that the majority of the train driver population perceived the extra information as useful while they were driving with the display, while Figure 4 shows the same for pleasantness. However, the difference between before and after experience with the system was not the same for useful and pleasant.

Figure 4 shows that the participants needed time and experience to get used to the train simulator; they indicated a decrease in mental effort as they gained more experience with the simulator during the three sessions.

Indications of subjective valuation

Percentage answers

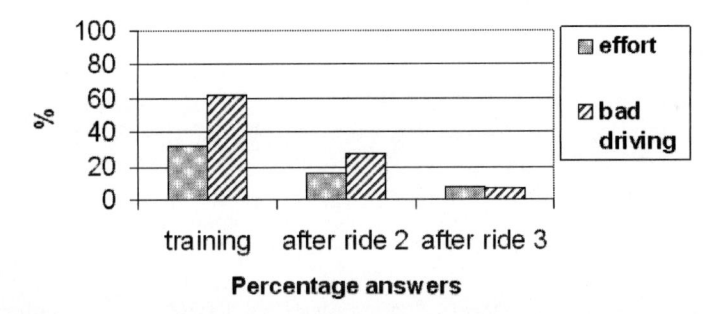

Figure 4. Indications on the rating scale of mental effort and driving quality in the course of the three rides.

Certainly in the beginning, when the train driver were still familiarizing with the train simulator and the PDA, the number of SPADs (signals passed at danger) were quite numerous, much more than in normal circumstances. The train drivers were well aware of their poor performance, as witnessed by their indications on the scale for self-judgement of driving quality (Figure 4).

The subjective qualifications were age- and education-dependent, as demonstrated by a regression analysis of the results of invested mental effort. Mental effort was related to both age and education, especially in ride 2 when RouteLint information was added, as the concomitant correlation coefficients in Table 1 show.

Table 1. Correlation coefficients of mental effort for age and education (* $p < 0.05$, ** $p <0.01$)

Mental Effort	Training	Ride 2	Ride 3
Age	.319	.559*	.342
Education	.406	.428**	.304

Discussion and conclusions

The present study adds to the literature concerning the effects of adding context information on the performance of train drivers (Biemans et al., 2004). In particular, in this study explicitly the relationship concerning the RouteLint information effect with train drivers' performance of speed management as reflected in energy costs and subjective assessment of personal performance in a simulated work setting is elaborated. Results from the questionnaires indicate that decision-making and feelings of personal satisfaction are enhanced with the use of the additional information given by the RouteLint system. Most of the train drivers perceived the extra information as useful and pleasant while they were driving with the information display. The train drivers reported that the extra information can make them more efficient through better anticipation and decision-making. Moreover, after the test the train drivers showed enthusiasm and they reported to expect enjoy working with it in practice. Thus, performance and work satisfaction in general may be improved by introducing context information in the everyday work setting of train drivers.

However, the value of the study is limited for a couple of reasons. First of all, the train drivers had no experience with the train simulator beforehand. It took a while to familiarize, clearly reflected in the subjective reports on mental effort and self-reported performance. Some did not get used to it completely at all; they kept on having difficulties while operating the simulation. Secondly, at the same time they had to familiarize with the RouteLint information system, on a PDA not equipped with a very obvious and user-friendly interface (see Figure 1). The measurements and observations revealed that some train drivers had trouble and needed time to get used to the extra information. The ease to understand quickly what they could do with the context information turned out to be age- and education dependent. Some train drivers may have problems in integrating new information in their daily driving routine. Skill-acquisition takes time, in particular the development of routine (Biemans et al., 2004). The train drivers in the experiment had only 2 hours to practice driving with the RouteLint information system on a PDA. In this short amount of time they had to learn how to operate a train simulator and incorporate new information from an unfamiliar system into their supposedly normal train driving routine.

The results show that providing extra information potentially improves railway performance, but not without problems with regard to specific information processing. Therefore, training is needed to learn how to interpret and process the information while driving with the display. Additionally, since the actual scenarios are outside, it is important that the train drivers learn to keep on looking outside sufficiently while they use the PDA to get a better perspective of the whole situation. Some train drivers were concerned that their attention might be too much directed towards the new display which might have a negative effect on safety. The ability to divide and allocate attention may be a good predictor of job success (Johnson & Proctor, 2004), while candidate train drivers are engaged in the training process in train simulators.

With the development of the RouteLint information system it is hoped that there will be an opportunity in the Netherlands to extend this initiative in order to provide more accurate, timely and understandable information to train drivers, to support them in their jobs, enhancing safety and performance in the rail services (see also Bye & Hockey, 2005).

Acknowledgement

We are grateful to Jelle van Luipen (ProRail) and 40 professional train drivers that enabled us to carry out this study.

References

Adams, J.A. (1987). Criticisms of vigilance research: a discussion. *Human Factors, 29*, 135-141.

Biemans, M. Swaak, J., Van Velde, S., & Huppertz, M. (2004). *Empowering Train Drivers: Designing and testing context information.* Enschede, the Netherlands: Telematica Instituut, University of Twente.

Brookhuis, K.A., De Vries, G., Prins van Wijngaarden, P., Veenstra, G., Hommes, M., Louwerens, J.W., & O'Hanlon, J.F. (1985). *The effects of increasing doses of Meptazinol (100, 200, 400 mg) and Glafenine (200 mg) on driving performance* (Report VK 85-16). Haren, the Netherlands: Traffic Research Centre, University of Groningen.

Brookhuis, K.A., De Waard, D., Marberger, C., & Bekiaris, A. (2004). Design and implication of Driver Drowsiness Warning Systems. In D. de Waard, K.A. Brookhuis and C.M. Weikert (Eds.), *Human factors in design* (pp. 63-70). Maastricht, The Netherlands: Shaker Publishing.

Bye, R., Hockey, R. (2005). *A Cognitive Analysis of Train driver Information Requirements* (Report S10 2TP). Sheffield, UK: Department of Psychology, University of Sheffield.

De Waard, D., Van der Hulst, M., Hoedemaeker, M., & Brookhuis, K.A. (1999). Reply to comments on "Driver behavior in an emergency situation in the Automated Highway System". *Transportation Human Factors, 1*, 87-89.

Farber, E.I. (1999). Comments on "Driver behaviour in an Emergency Situation in the Automated Highway System". *Transportation Human Factors, 1*, 83-85.

Graham, D., & Pollck C. (1997). The Influence of Sustained Attention On Railway Accidents. In: *Elsevier Science.* Vol. 29. No 4.

Haga, S. (1984). An experimental study of signal vigilance errors in train driving. *Ergonomics 27*, 755-765.

Hildebrandt et al. (1975). 12 and 24 hour rhythms in error frequency of locomotive drivers and the influence of tiredness. *International Journal of Chronobiology, 2*, 175-180.

Levine, B., & Craig, A (1988). Self-control over performance in situations that demand vigilance. In J.P. Leonard (Ed.), *Vigilance: Methods, Models and Regulation*, Frankfurt: Lang.

Livingstone, H., Gipson, T., & Luther, R. (2005). Development of a risk-based approach to training and assessment in safety critical roles. In *Training Education and Simulation International,* (pp. 22-24), The Netherlands.

Michaut, G.M.E., & McGaughey, T.P. (1974). *Work Conditions and Equipment Design in Diesel Locomotives: Feasibility Study and Recommendations.* Canadian Institute of Guided Transport. Kingston, Canada: Queens University.

Nachreiner, F. (1977). Experiments on the validity of vigilance experiments. In R.R Mackie (Ed.), *Vigilance, Theory, Operational Performance and Physiological Correlates,* New York: Plenum Press.

NS (Nederlandse Spoorwegen) (1999). Voorschriften voor de bediening van wissel- en seininrichtingen. Automatische Trein –Beinvloeding (Nieuwe Generatie) C5504/II (NG).

Parasuraman, R. (1986). Vigilance, monitoring and search. In K. Boff, K. Kauffman and J. Thomas (Eds.), *Handbook of Perception and Human Performance.* Volume 2: Cognitive processes and performance, New York, USA: Wiley.

Schotanus, B., & Zigterman, L. (2004). *De orde van het seinhuis en kan de mens het spoor veiliger en efficienter maken.* Internal Report ProRail (Dutch Rail).

Smiley, A.M. (1990). The Hinton train disaster. *Accident Analyses and Prevention,* 22, 443-445.

Taroni, I. (2006). *PDA to avoid SPAD.* Master thesis, University of Groningen.

Van der Laan, J.D., Heino, A., & De Waard, D. (1997). A simple procedure for the assessment of acceptance of advanced transport telematics. *Transportation Research C,* 5, 1-10.

Van Luipen, J. (2005). *HSM: Op zoek naar optimale combinatie van mens en technologie.* Internal Report ProRail (Dutch Rail).

Zijlstra, F.R.H. (1993). *Efficiency in work behaviour. A design approach for modern tools.* PhD thesis. Delft, The Netherlands: Delft University Press.

Situation Awareness

three dimensional animations

In D. de Waard, G.R.J. Hockey, P. Nickel, and K.A. Brookhuis (Eds.) (2007), *Human Factors Issues in Complex System Performance* (pp. 251). Maastricht, the Netherlands: Shaker Publishing.

The use of three-dimensional animations in aircraft maintenance documentation

Joël Tapie, Yvonne Barnard, Patrick Mazoyer, Jonathan Devun, & Marie Moal
EURISCO International
Toulouse, France

Abstract

Technical documentation for aircraft maintenance includes black and white two-dimensional graphics. They are a support for the written text of the maintenance procedures. In current practice text is still a main source of information on how to perform a maintenance procedure. It is printed out in the form of a job-card and taken to the aircraft to be maintained. This study on the use of maintenance documentation for the future addresses the use of three-dimensional animations. Interviews were conducted with both experienced maintenance operators and students about their ideas, wishes and mental models concerning three-dimensional animations. The general procedure was to give participants a task (such as the removal of an aircraft system), to show them the (written) procedure in the existing electronic manual, complemented with three-dimensional animations. Questions were asked about how they would use these during task-performance, necessary improvements, and the relation with the text. Outcomes show that although there was a positive attitude to three-dimensional animations, critical questions were also asked. Assessments differed as to the way in which different technicians use the technical manuals. Differences also relate to experience and to tasks. The outcome of the study is discussed and related to the literature on both maintenance practices and the use of three-dimensional animations.

Introduction

In technical documentation for aircraft maintenance, pictures of systems are provided in black and white graphics. They are a support for the written text of the maintenance procedures. In the new generation of electronic documentation it is possible to include interactive three-dimensional animations (3D). However, providing what is technically possible is not necessarily supporting the users. In current practice, text remains the major source of information on how to perform a maintenance procedure. It is printed out in the form of a job-card and brought to the aircraft to be maintained.

Text and 2D images are sources of information that have been used for centuries. In education, children learn to use these from an early age on. In technical education, future technicians learn how to work with texts, images of systems and schematics.

In D. de Waard, G.R.J. Hockey, P. Nickel, and K.A. Brookhuis (Eds.) (2007), *Human Factors Issues in Complex System Performance* (pp. 253 - 265). Maastricht, the Netherlands: Shaker Publishing.

There are teaching programs for learning how to interpret these data and how to use them to perform technical tasks. The youngest generation of technicians also grew up playing computer games, with (fast) moving 3D animations. However, in school, they are rarely (yet) confronted with technical 3D animations for educational purposes.

As 3D animations are becoming more widespread, and as their creation will become easier and cheaper, new questions emerge:

- How do users of technical manuals perceive the use of 3D animations for maintenance purposes?
- How will the use of these animations relate to the tasks they have to perform?
- What are the advantages and the disadvantages of 3D animations in technical manuals?

This paper starts with an introduction on the perception of 3D used in interfaces. Next a description is given of a study in which maintenance operators, both experts and novices, were presented with 3D animations about which they were asked to give their opinions and thoughts.

3D animations

Human beings live in a 3D environment. It is therefore tempting to infer that 3D representation is a natural way to present volumetric information. Things may, however, be more complicated since 3D images have an ambiguous relationship with the represented element. A 3D representation provides a direct image, easy to perceive. Nevertheless, the information management in a 3D display needs to take into account 3D space specific rules. Objects in the background are hidden by those in the foreground. Distant objects are no longer noticeable. Scale problems may occur when small elements are placed next to larger ones. Beyond these basic aspects, Wickens & Alexander (Wickens, 2002; Alexander & Wickens, 2005) in their work on interface design and space awareness in aviation, identified a set of cognitive biases related to the use of 3D displays. These biases lead operators to make errors estimating distances and inclination angles.

Most computer interfaces are 2D WIMP (Window Icon Mouse Pointer) interfaces. They are made up of many windows enclosing elements (scrollbars, buttons, etc.), and managed by rules. The design recommendations of the WIMP interfaces are now stabilized, which leads one to suppose that they all react in the same way. Users' competences can easily be transferred from a 2D interface to another one. This is not yet the case with 3D display interfaces. Since these interfaces are not widespread, users do not possess sufficient experience with 3D interfaces to consolidate 3D behaviour rules (Tapie et al., 2005). This may evolve in the future when 3D becomes more common in computer applications. The younger generation, familiar with 3D computer games, already shows fewer problems in using 3D and deriving information from it.

3D presentation of information does not automatically lead to a better performance of the task than a 2D presentation, especially when performance is evaluated by speed and accuracy measurement (Van Orden & Broyles, 2000; Mejdal, McCauley & Beringer, 2001). 3D does not make searching faster but induces the building of another kind of mental representation of information than 2D. 3D supports a spatial representation of information. That is why using 3D is best suited for some tasks but not for others. 3D display is best suited to visualize and understand space layouts. On the other hand, 2D provides better results estimating precise sizes and distances (St John & Cowen, 1999).

3D animations are also known as 4D. 4D represents the features of 3D in a time sequence. Concerning information presentation, 3D animations are useful to illustrate data that vary in time like sequences, procedures and movements (trajectories). Using 3D animations, the user usually does not act on the 3D representation itself, but rather on the time sequence (pause, rewind, slow motion).

The use of multi-media documents

With the introduction of 3D animations into maintenance manuals, the documentation becomes a multi-media document. Obtaining information from multi-media documents requires a different mental process from reading a text document. Tricot (2003) constructed a model of the various levels on which multimedia documents can be used and understood, and the processes involved (see Figure 1).

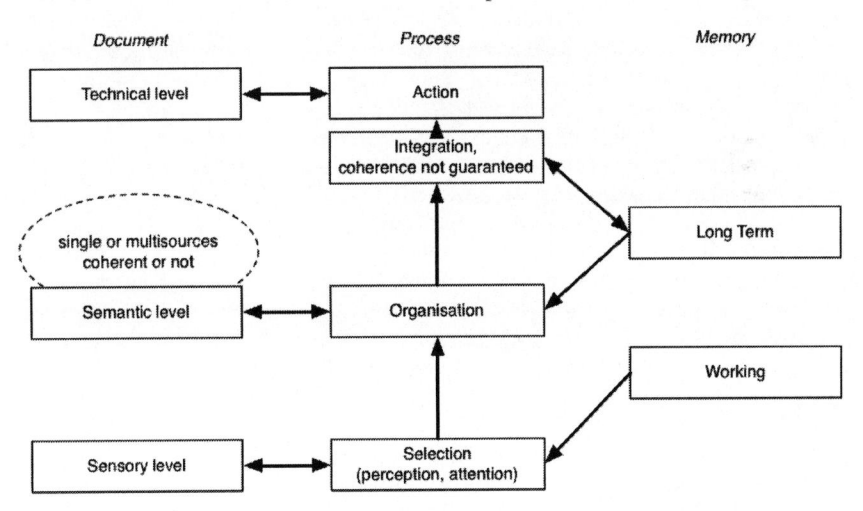

Figure 1. Levels of document, types of handling and memory involved in the understanding of multimedia. Taken and translated from Tricot (2003)

This model is of interest for the use of 3D animations because it puts an emphasis on the distinction between the selection and perception of information (the sensory level), the organisation of the information, that is to say the understanding of what the documentation is presenting (the semantic level) and the integration into what the user already knows, and finally, the action resulting from reading the multimedia documentation (technical level). Although this is also true for text reading, 3D animations put a heavier load on the sensory level, especially when the animation is not self-paced, as in reading or studying a 2D drawing. From the model it becomes clear that improving documentation is not just a question of improving it at a sensory level, for example having an interface that is easier to use or to provide more multimedia. All the levels are closely linked, and in order to improve the actions (such as doing more efficient maintenance work, by understanding and using the correct information) all levels need to be paid attention to. Especially for the use of multimedia, the organisation of information from different media or from different parts of the documentation is an aspect that should be taken into account. In other words, does providing multi-media information support the technician in organising and understanding the information (building a correct mental model) or does it lead to more confusion and incorrect mental models?

The use of maintenance manuals

Maintenance manuals are used for a variety of purposes (Barnard & Reiss, 2006). A distinction may be made according to the job of the persons working in maintenance, such as maintenance planners, line maintenance operators who work at an airfield preparing aircraft for take-off, maintenance operators working in scheduled maintenance, working on regular maintenance and installing and modifying systems, inspectors, people working in design offices, teachers and students in maintenance education etc. Maintenance operators may be specialised in avionics or in mechanics. Another way of looking at the use of maintenance documentation is looking at the tasks people have to fulfil and for which the documentation provides guidance and support. Examples of these maintenance tasks are: following a maintenance procedure, preparing and planning a maintenance procedure, ordering parts, testing and troubleshooting, etc. Maintenance tasks have different characteristics, they may be familiar or novel, complex or simple, taking much time or not, potentially dangerous or not, etc.

Yet another way is to look at the activities involved in using the documentation itself. In interviews with maintenance operators conducted throughout the study (Barnard, Reiss, & Mazoyer, 2006) different uses were mentioned. Maintenance operators search for general and for specific information, they use documentation to make sure that they perform their work correctly and they want to learn from it. The different uses mentioned are listed below.

Searching information to have a general idea about the work to perform:
Scanning to get an overview of the procedure; Scanning to refresh the memory about a procedure and to check whether there is something important; Getting an overview of how to perform a task; Being able to see related information; Going from one information to another, within the same procedure.

Searching for precise information:
Being aware of warnings; Localising components and access; Knowing how to work in areas that are not easily accessible; Making sure to have the right information for a specific aircraft; Knowing how to perform a specific subtask or to find a specific

component; Being able to order or to identify parts; Making sure no information is missed.

Using documentation to be sure the work is performed correctly:
Following a procedure step by step, for tests or for new or unknown procedures; Knowing the sequence of performing a task/procedure, not forgetting a step; Going from one task to another, embedded tasks; Interpreting test results; Connecting information in text and images; Having information near the aircraft.

Using documentation to gain knowledge:
Knowing more about how a system functions; Understanding the behaviour of a system; Knowing all the details of a system/task; Learning how to do a new/unknown task; Knowing what faulty systems look like; Using documentation for training purposes; Ongoing and unconscious training growing into the maintenance culture.

When 3D animations are introduced into maintenance documentation, all or a subset of these different activities have to be supported.

At the moment, electronic maintenance documentation is most often used on an ordinary workstation. The documentation is consulted in planning, preparation, and when unexpected problems arise. The maintenance procedures, and related information, are printed out in the form of job-cards and taken to the aircraft. Although it is possible to take the manuals on a laptop, or other hand-held devices, the use of paper job-cards is widespread and it is often a convenient way of dealing efficiently with information in a dynamic environment, with dirty hands, gloves, outdoors etc. Research is going on at several places to mount the manuals on dedicated hardware, such as head-mounted displays. This kind of use was not addressed in this study.

Studies with people working in aircraft maintenance

Two studies were performed in which maintenance operators were interviewed and presented with an electronic maintenance manual extended with several innovative features. One of them related to a 3D animation demonstrating a maintenance procedure. This study was not limited to 3D animations but other innovations tested will not be discussed in this paper (for more detailed information, see Barnard, Reiss, & Mazoyer, 2006).

Study 1

In the first study, five maintenance operators with 10 to 20 years experience were interviewed while being presented with and using the electronic documentation. They were experienced in various types of maintenance work, line maintenance and scheduled maintenance. All but one had extensive experience in working with electronic documentation. They were all used to working with paper documentation, and some of them with older versions of electronic documentation. Most of them had experience with leading teams of technicians, and with preparing and supervising work. Students involved in aircraft maintenance education (second year of the

Master course) were also included in the panel of participants. Four of them, with no experience in working with electronic documentation, were interviewed during a single session, while three more experienced students were interviewed in individual sessions. In addition, a demonstration was given to a classroom of 41 students, followed by a discussion and a questionnaire in which students were asked to list positive and negative aspects of the innovative features.

Differences in the assessments between the experienced, older interviewees and the students were clearly revealed. Experienced operators have very strong and mixed judgements about the animations. Positive statements about animations relate to being able to locate systems, to see how a task is performed step-by-step, and to less well-known tasks. Negative statements especially concern the primary role text should play. The maintenance operators suggested improvements, such as providing relations between text and animations (and prints), and improving details and the interface. Free exploration of 3D images was seen as even more negative. 3D seemed too complex to use to them. One operator also signalled a danger in the freedom of exploration that 3D brings; it might induce operators to not follow the procedure strictly. Another interesting objection made was that 3D may provide a false impression of the physical reality, for example a very heavy component seeming small and transparent. And it seemed, quite surprisingly, that improving the quality of the part of the aircraft modelled, might magnify this problem.

The vast majority of the students really appreciated the 3D, especially for complex tasks or tasks the operator is not familiar with. Their main positive comments were related to animations supporting a better understanding of the task by facilitating its mental representation. According to them, a task becomes far more understandable by watching the animation than by just reading the document. It is also important in helping to judge the complexity and difficulty of the task. And they saw it as a good tool for conveying knowledge, for explaining how to do things.

Study 2

In the second study, a more in-depth study on the perception and use of 3D animations was performed. For this, two animations presenting the (de)installation of aircraft systems were used. The first 3D animation showed all the manipulations described in the written procedure of the maintenance manual, which is long and repetitive. The other one related to only a part of another procedure. For the study, the 3D animations were displayed in a new window superimposed on the text in the background.

Twenty persons were interviewed, and filled out the questionnaire. They all studied, or had a professional activity related to aircraft maintenance. Five of them were students in a maintenance course. Three others were teachers at a maintenance school, but not experienced maintenance operators. The twelve remaining subjects were engineers working on planning and work preparation. Before their actual job, four of the engineers were maintenance technicians on aircraft, and three of them regularly performed inspections on aircraft. The diversity of interviewees ensured that inexperienced persons of different ages (the younger ones were students aged

20-21, and the older ones were teachers aged 41-59), were represented. The younger ones all had experience with 3D, mostly gained by playing computer games. The experienced persons, working in maintenance jobs, were aged between 26 and 44.

The aim of this study was to gain more insight into the possibilities and problems of the future use of 3D animations and to formulate recommendations for further development. It was not imperative for the study to be fully representative of the whole maintenance population. Its main purpose was to gather a variety of viewpoints. One of the problems with this kind of study is that it is not so much the opinion of the current generation of operators and the use of 3D for their current work that is at stake, but rather a projection for the future. Experienced maintenance operators have, given their age, usually not much experience with 3D, so will have more problems getting information out of it. On the other hand they do not need much information because they can rely on their knowledge and experience. Inexperienced operators need much more information and for them it may be easier to use 3D. The study should not be seen as a usability test of a product (3D animations) but as an empirical study on the usefulness of 3D in maintenance documentation.

The use of 3D animations requires spatial mental processes. People vary in their abilities to perform these mental processes, especially mental rotations (Vandenberg & Kuse, 1978), where an object has to be imagined in a position different from how it is perceived. It was expected that people with good skills in mental rotation feel more comfortable with 3D animations than others. This may have an impact on their evaluation of 3D animations. It was therefore decided to assess the mental rotation skill of the participants. In order to do this, a mental rotation test, presented as a little game, was added. For practical reasons, only five figures (plus one example) from the original Vandenberg & Kuse (1978) test were used.

All 20 participants were interviewed individually, using the following protocol: (1) Presentation of the aim of the study by the experimenter; (2) Asking information about the participant and taking the Mental Rotation test; (3) Viewing one shot of the two 3D animations; (4) Presentation of the existing electronic documentation augmented with the 3D animations, to let the persons explore it in order to answer the questionnaire; (5) Answering the questions of the questionnaire, concerning the 3D animations; (6) Open discussion and review of the answers (audio recorded). The average time needed for a session was about one hour and half.

The questionnaire addressed 11 themes, concerning viewpoints & visibility, orientation & localisation on aircraft, temporal aspects, warning/cautions/notes, complex steps, relation between text and animation, information to add to 3D animations, showing tools and equipment, showing maintenance operator, using prints and general questions on using 3D.

Results

Four themes turned up as especially interesting for the research. The first one concerns the use of 3D animations. The second one is about features of the 3D animation (viewpoints & visibility, orientation & temporal aspects). The third one relates to additional information (information to add, operator & tools). The fourth one concerns relation between text and 3D animations.

Use of 3D animations

First of all, it is noteworthy that the general assessment of 3D animations was positive; all participants found them useful in giving a global view and an overall understanding of the task that text alone is unable to provide. An important problem with the animations, which emerged from the interviews, relates to their role as compared to text (see below). 3D animations were not seen as an active support of information during the performance of the task, but rather as an upstream support in the preparation of the task, for becoming familiar with the task, recalling it easily, briefing support for team work, and helping to visualise the system and its environment. This is partly due to the problem of taking a laptop to the aircraft. The benefits and drawbacks of the 3D animations indicated by the participants are given in the Table 1.

Table 1. Benefits and drawbacks of 3D animations

Benefits	Drawbacks
Present information clearly	Are less precise than text
Make spatial orientation east	May have some missing information
Give a good visualization of the task	Do not rigorously follow the procedure
Enable a good comprehension of the task	May involve omissions (of steps)
Provide a global point of view	Need attention resources from the user
Make the procedure explicit	Are different from the real situation
Allow to recognize systems and components	Lose benefits when too much displayed
Have educational value	May divert from textual procedure and
Allow to identify localisation of screws	2D figures
Give direct information	
Are convivial	
Are playful	

All but one of the participants stated they would have used 3D animations to do the maintenance tasks. They gave different reasons for this (see Figure 2). Most of them wanted to use the 3D animations to get acquainted with the task, to quickly remember the job to do, to help them during briefing when several operators are needed and to visualize the system and/or its environment that is consistent with the benefits expressed in Table 1. Less than one third of the participants mentioned they could use the animations for support during the performance of the task. Verifying that steps are done seemed not to be relevant to 3D animations. Finally, one participant proposed the idea of using them during training sessions. Participants were asked when they would use 3D animations. All of them said they would watch an animation just before actually performing the task, and also during the task if they should need more information or if the text were not sufficiently clear.

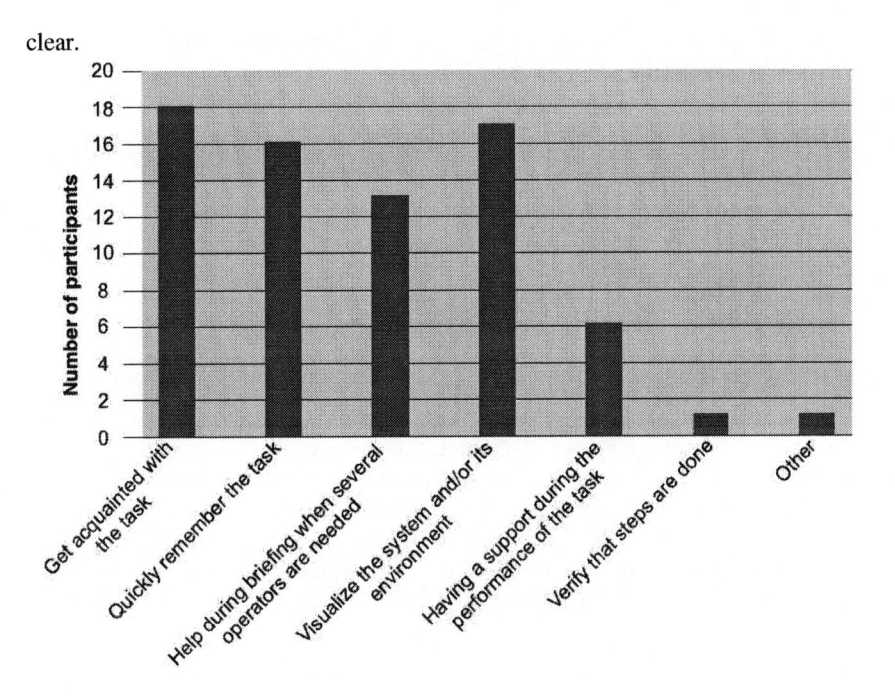

Figure 2. Assessment of participants concerning the utility of 3D animations

Features of 3D

The general layout and visibility of the animations was rated to be positive (see Table 1). All users with maintenance operator experience wanted a global view of the system at the beginning of the animation in order to show what systems should be removed to achieve the task. It would also be advisable to distinguish between base maintenance, where surrounding systems may have been removed, and line maintenance where they are still in place. Only one situation is taken into account in the animations. This may result in a difference in the perception of the difficulty of the task between animation and reality. When proposed to add location information (zone and access panels visualization) in the animations, only half of the participants were interested. On the other hand, controlling the angle of view was desired by all participants for working on the preparation of maintenance tasks, or for training purposes. With regard to the default speed of the animations, in general the participants were satisfied, although showing texts in the animations is often too quick for full comprehension. However, 50 percent of the participants thought that showing repetitive steps may be accelerated. The option to see the complete animation at an accelerated speed did not seem useful, and even considered risky. However, the option "be able to regulate the speed" by the user is desired by most of the participants. All participants who have experience with working on aircraft did not want interruptions (with the ability to continue when desired) in the video. The others liked to have stops for Warnings, torque values and all textual instructions. Finally, half of the participants thought that the possibility to access a step of the animation directly by clicking on a step in the text greatly augments the usability of the electronic manual.

Additional information

Although 3D representation in general causes problems in estimating size and distances (in contrast with 2D where no problems of perspective occur), nobody expressed the wish to have a scale in the animation. The reason is that the systems shown during the interviews were well-known by the users, they already had an idea of their scale. The movements in the animation may give the impression that parts are of light weight, which may give the false impression that the task is easy to perform (see Table 1). The majority of the participants thought that heavy parts ("more than 10-15 kg" is the value most mentioned) should have a weight indication. Moreover, participants were very interested in the possibility to show the tools during manipulations. This would be efficient when using special equipment or when the system is so placed that it is difficult to use a tool. However, they did not think it would be useful to see the arms of a technician. Opinions were divided on the visualization of a manikin showing the position the technician should take during task performance. Some thought it useless or not realistic, others thought this might be interesting for critical or dangerous situations.

Relation with other information

Most participants in the study were explicit (and especially those who already worked on aircraft) that 3D animations should not replace text. Their role is to help the user to get a clear and global view of the task. To attain these objectives, 3D animations need to be as bare and text-free as possible. All written information needed by the user is to be found in the text of the manual, not in the animations where they might be forgotten. Text in the animations might also distract attention from the images. However, keeping animations as basic as possible may become an impediment if users rely exclusively on them to achieve their task and consider that what does not appear in the animation is not relevant (torque values for instance). Specifying that reading the manual is compulsory will not ensure one hundred percent that such a scenario will never occur. A fundamental aspect of the animations relates to their consistency with the text. In particular, it is crucial that the chronology is identical in both. If not, the user may rely spontaneously on the animation and thereby make errors. An interesting result was that most of the users admitted needing to follow the text while watching the 3D animation. However, only half of them would welcome a multi-windows screen with the step of the procedure highlighted in text while being played in the animation.

Differences between types of user

Some of the results differ between user groups. Most participants experienced in maintenance did not want stops during the animation except when solicited. Less experienced participants generally wanted to add stops for torque and warning messages. Moreover, experienced users were against the superimposition of any text onto the animation, whereas less experienced users were for it. Regarding the Mental

Rotation Test, the participant who was fastest to complete it, and with only one error, thought the scroll speed of the 3D animations was too slow. The participants who had the lowest scores thought that the scroll speed was too quick. Moreover, there seems to be a link between the scores on the Mental Rotation Test and the feeling of being lost in the aircraft. The great majority of participants who complained about orientation on the aircraft were in the lowest part of the Mental Rotation Test scores. This result is only an indication, but it may be interesting to investigate further whether this is a valid correlation.

Conclusions and discussion

In general, most participants in the two studies were positive about the use of 3D animations in maintenance documentation. This is in line with the findings of the study of Chaparro et al. (2004) who performed evaluations of technical manuals using different evaluation strategies and different types of users. Most of the remarks made by the users are related to visualization: there are many requests for illustrations, pictures, figures, and videos. There may be several reasons for this need. As maintenance work has a very strong motor-perception component, visual information relates easier to understanding a task than texts. Also, people with a technical education are usually comfortable with the use of images of different natures. Another problem is the fact that texts are not always clear. In the study of Chaparro et al., unclear descriptions are mentioned, especially the use of too many and ambiguous words.

The interviewees differed in their preferences about the features of 3D animations, such as speed, added information, controls etc. A solution for this would be a customisation feature according to individual preferences. An objection to having individualised documentation is that documentation also has other functions than just supporting the performance of a maintenance task. It also has an organisational and cultural role to play. Technicians work together in teams and collaborate with other actors such as pilots and people from technical offices. One of the experienced maintenance operators in the first study emphasised the binding role of documentation within the organisation.

The interviewees were also aware of problems related to the use of 3D animations. Some problems are related to the features of the 3D used in the studies. Conceptual and technical solutions are feasible. However, some of the problems are related to the use of 3D as such. Most of the interviewees saw the principle use of 3D in relation to preparing a task or getting a better understanding of the task, rather than in following the animation step by step while working on the aircraft. According to Tricot's model (see Figure 1), there are several areas that need attention. The first is memory: as the animation develops at its own pace, it is easy to forget a step or a warning. Reading is self-paced and paper may always be used as a memory aid. Second is the sensory level: for the same reason, one might not notice a step in an animation, because it passes too quickly or not enough attention is paid. At the semantic level, there are also issues to be investigated. As 3D animations are relatively new, the body of knowledge about how people interpret this kind of data is not extensive enough to fully understand the mental processes involved. Especially in the 3D animations investigated, the difference between animation and reality is relatively large. Surrounding systems are not shown, neither are tools nor the technician, and the environment is transparent and clean. However, this is regarded by many as a strong point, abstracting from the reality and therefore providing a better understanding. Most of the interviewees preferred this kind of abstraction to realistic films and videos. The integration of data is another issue. As text and animations will be provided at the same time, the user has to make an effort for their integration. Also for legal reasons, text will remain the primary source of information that technicians are obliged to use. Text can also describe things that cannot be shown. The opposite may also be true. Although in general, presenting information by using different modalities provides an advantage, the integration of text and 3D will remain a topic for further investigation: both from the users' and the authors' point of view. Finally, more work needs to be done on the action level if 3D animations are also to be used during task performance on the aircraft.

References

Alexander, A.L. & Wickens, C.D. (2005). *3D Navigation and Integrated Hazard Display in Advanced Avionics: Performance, Situation Awareness and Workload*. Technical Report AHFD-05-10/NASA-05-2. Urbana, IL: University of Illinois.

Barnard, Y. & Reiss, M. (2006). User-centered innovation of electronic documentation for maintenance. In D. de Waard, K.A. Brookhuis, and A. Toffetti (Eds.), *Developments in Human Factors in Transportation, Design and Evaluation* (pp. 129-142). Maastricht, the Netherlands: Shaker Publishing.

Barnard, Y., Reiss, M., & Mazoyer, P. (2006). Mental Models of Users of Aircraft Maintenance Documentation. In F. Reuzeau, K. Corker, and G. Boy. *Proceedings of the International Conference on Human-Computer Interaction in Aeronautics* (pp. 232-239). Toulouse, France: Cépaduès-Editions.

Chaparro, A., Rogers, B., Hamblin, C., & Chaparro, B. (2004). *A Comparison of Three Evaluative Techniques for Validating Maintenance Documentation*. Washington, D.C.: Federal Aviation Administration.

Mejdal, S., McCauley, M.E., & Beringer, D.B. (2001*). Human Factors Design Guidelines for Multifunction Displays.* Report FAA/AM-01/17, Washington D.C.: Office of Aerospace Medicine.

St John, M. & Cowen, M.B. (1999). *Use of Perspective View Displays for Operational Tasks*. Technical Report 1975, San Diego, CA: SPAWAR System Center.

Tapie, J. Terrier, P., Perron L., & Cellier J.-M. (2005). Should remote collaborators be represented by avatars? A matter of common ground for collective medical decision-making. *AI & Society, 20*, 331-350.

Tory, M. (2004). *Combining 2D and 3D Views for Visualization of Spatial Data*. Phd Thesis, School of Computing Science. Vancouver, B.C., Canada: University of British Columbia.

Tory, M., Möller, T., Atkins, M.S., & Kirkpatrick, A.E. (2004). Combining 2D and 3D Views for Orientation and Relative Position Tasks. *Proceedings of the SIGCHI 2004 Conference on Human Factors in computing systems* (pp. 73-80). ACM Press.

Tricot, A. (2003). *Apprentissage et recherche d'information avec des documents électroniques. Mémoire en vue de l'habilitation à diriger des recherches.* IUFM de Midi-Pyrénées ERT «hypermédias et apprentissages» & Laboratoire Travail et Cognition UMR CNRS et Université de Toulouse le Mirail.

Vandenberg, S.G. & Kuse, A.R. (1978) Mental rotations, a group test of three dimensional spatial visualization. *Perceptual and Motor Skills, 47*, 599-604.

Van Orden, K.F. & Broyles, J.W. (2000). Visuospatial task performance as a function of two- and three-dimensional display presentation techniques. *Displays, 12*, 17-24.

Wickens, C. (2002). *Spatial Awareness Biases*. Technical Report AHFD-02-6/NASA-02-4.Urbana, IL: University of Illinois.

Shared situational awareness as a systems-level phenomenon: applying propositional networks to shared awareness in teams

Chris Baber[1], Robert J. Houghton[1], Richard McMaster[1], & Neville A. Stanton[2]
[1]The University of Birmingham, Birmingham
[2]Brunel University, Uxbridge
UK

Abstract

Previously, work has sought to demonstrate how shared or overlapping individual mental models could be used to describe 'shared situational awareness' amongst a team of individuals. It is argued that such an approach is difficult to apply and potentially misleading. For example, gaining access to the individual mental models and then developing a means by which they could be shown to overlap requires a level of data collection and analysis that could be extremely challenging. In the present paper a more parsimonious approach is offered that assumes a 'systems level' view of the situation that can be ascertained through the observation of the utterances and behaviour of team members together with input from subject matter experts and represented as a propositional network model. Upon this network model one can then represent incidences when 'knowledge objects' are shared and used over different phases of a scenario. The approach is illustrated with examples taken from an example of a Fire Service training exercise.

Introduction

The advent of modern electronic networking technology, such as the internet, and the related development of military concepts such as Network Enabled Capability (NEC, see MoD 2004) has given rise to interest in 'Shared Situational Awareness' (SSA). The general notion appears to be that through the use of networked systems the members of geographically or functionally distributed teams will be able to have a common view of the situation (e.g., through a Common Operational Picture) and so arrive at a shared understanding of the situation that will enable improvements in the quality and speed of decision making (e.g., see MoD 2004 for a description of a "benefit chain" relating technology to decision making via SSA. In terms of cognitive psychology and philosophy of mind, there are a number of highly problematic assumptions underlying this notion of 'shared situation awareness'. While this paper is not the place to debate all of these problems, it is worth asking whether there can be a 'common view' of a situation for distributed participants. Normally, this is dealt with simply through the provision of a map of the terrain with markings to indicate locations and movements of entities. At this level, it could be safe to assume that the same map conveys the same information to all who see it. However, by way of a simple example, not everyone who looks at a map can instantly recognise and interpret contour lines as indicating variation in height above sea level. This could mean that an 'obvious' route from A to B for one viewer can mistakenly assume a straight line and not consider the impact of climbing hills. In order to avoid this sort of error (and in order to ensure a truly *common* view) it is necessary to train users of the displayed information to read it in the same manner and to the same degree of accuracy, but even here there may be problems of ensuring that all features are attended to with equal focus by all viewers.

One reason for the use of Standard Operating Procedures (SOPs) could be seen from this perspective, i.e., to support mutual monitoring through shared (trained) understanding of roles and responsibilities (Shu & Furtura, 2005). It is often argued that in order for the effective communication of SA information to occur, the team need to have a common frame of reference. However, it is the case that people will not always be dealing with the same aspects of a situation, and so 'sharing' awareness could even be detrimental to performance. Alternatively, a 'system' frame of reference has been considered as a mental model, which is shared amongst the team. However, low levels of overlap in SSA do not necessarily hamper group performance. Groups of people engaged in complex activities are able to perform them effectively despite having different viewpoints, backgrounds and goals (Artman and Garbis, 1998), e.g. a multi-service response to an emergency, where the police, fire and ambulance have differing views of the situation as a result of different training and experience and therefore have different priorities in terms of activities to carry out or even conflicting goals.

There appear to be two major difficulties for the analyst; first, if Situational Awareness itself has long-standing difficulties in terms of its definition and scope, this problem is made worse by considering how it might be 'shared' (see Nofi, 2000 for a review) and second; the problem that standard approaches to empirical investigation of situation awareness such as lab studies or probes of individual activity, such as SAGAT, may not practically scale-up to large groups carrying out diverse activities over a long period of time. The present paper describes a tractable and pragmatic approach to producing an analysis of the spread and sharing of knowledge and information in teams based on a combination of a Systems-level view of teamwork inspired by notions of Distributed Cognition and the use of network analysis techniques. We begin by discussing what Shared Situational Awareness might be considered to be, describe the Distributed Cognition concept and how it might contribute to a useful re-conceptualisation of SSA, consider how networks might represent these distributed processes and conclude with an example of the approach as applied to a Fire Service exercise.

In this paper, it is suggested that the practical questions we might ask about SSA in a team concern what information the System as a whole needs to know so that various sub-tasks may be adequately performed and what information will need to be shared amongst members of the team as the situation unfolds. From this it follows that in System redesign terms we might be less interested in how specific individuals utilise information about the situation (so long as they can, and are not for example overloaded), and more interested in evaluating and, perhaps, adjusting the System as a whole to improve overall performance. This assumes that it is the System as a whole that can take in and be 'aware' of the required information is the ideal outcome, i.e., we follow a Distributed Cognition perspective in viewing cognitive processes as occuring at a 'systems level' (Artman & Garbis, 1998; Flors and Hutchins, 1991; Hutchins, 1995; Perry, 2003; Poirier & Chicoisne, 2006). This is potentially an interesting line of enquiry for three reasons: First, if one can distinguish relevant knowledge objects, then it might be possible to indicate changes in the focal activities of the distributed system; Second, if one can show how different agents make use of the various knowledge objects, then one can indicate how and when 'sharing' (of awareness or understanding) might occur; and Third, if one can define relevant elements, then one can evaluate self-reports from people against an objective (or at least external) frame of reference.

Networks of knowledge

The notion that knowledge (however it is described) can be represented in the form a network has long been important in many areas of psychology including animal learning, psycholinguistics and cognitive science. This approach appears variously as connectionism and neural networks (see Rummelhart & McClelland, 1996). Some of the earliest uses of networks to represent knowledge can be seen in the work of Quillian (1969) who proposed a model of semantic memory that was based on a network. This semantic network has units, i.e., 'objects', which are the nodes of the network and can be thought of as nouns, such as 'hydrogen chloride', 'hydrochloric acid', or 'moisture'. The nodes of the network have 'properties', which can be thought of as adjectives or verbs, such as 'toxic' or 'corrosive'. Usually, the elements are represented in the form of a 'network diagram' in which the words are linked together by arrows to show associations between them.

In a modification to the Semantic Net idea, Anderson (1980) suggested the use of Propositional Networks, which are like semantic networks in that they contain nodes (with words) and links between nodes, but differ in two ways. First, the words are not necessarily randomly added to the network but involve the definition of propositions. A proposition is a basic statement, i.e., "...the smallest unit about which it makes sense to make the judgment true or false" (Anderson, 1980, p.102). Second, the links between words are labeled to define the relationship between propositions. On the basis of such descriptions, it is possible to claim that one can produce dictionary-like definitions of concepts through the application of basic propositions and operators (Ogden, 1987). These relations might be in terms of subject and object (in grammatical terms), with a corresponding relation term, e.g., the sentence 'Hydrogen chloride is toxic' has a subject (Hydrogen chloride), an object (toxic) and a relation (is).

Data to populate the propositional network can be gathered in two ways. The first approach is to use the Critical Decision Method (Klein et al., 1989) in which Subject Matter Experts (SMEs) are interviewed post-hoc. First, SMEs are asked to decide upon the critical incidents at which key decisions were made; Second, SMEs are asked to list the information required to make these decisions. An alternative, but complimentary technique is to subject records of communications between individuals to automated analysis. The present authors have had success using a very simple statistical approach to sentence processing generating propositions from co-occurring nouns (which constitute knowledge objects) and verbs (which can be used as linking propositions) in sentences.

It is possible to represent networks as matrices of 1s and 0s (see Wasserman & Faust, 1994 for a review) and the propositional network is no exception to this, albeit it is necessary to lose the propositions themselves and simply regard nodes (knowledge objects) as linked or not linked. This is a slightly counter-intuitive view because it implies that we are attempting semantic analysis with no access to the semantics of the words themselves. However, it may be claimed that that the 'semantics' arise as much from the combination and co-occurrence of words and phrases in a given domain as in the specific meaning associated with the words. Because the network can be rendered mathematically it is possible to use a wide range of statistical techniques to identify patterns amongst nodes based on their linkage. It is suggested that these techniques can be used to identify patterns in System knowledge. Two particularly useful metrics that we employ are Status and Centrality. Status is an indication of the relative 'connectedness' of a node; it is calculated in terms of the sum of inputs and outputs to a node. In this case a node is a knowledge object, and its status is calculated relative to the overall size of the network itself (that is, the number of other knowledge objects). Bavelas-Leavitt centrality calculates a similar index of the standing of a knowledge object within a network, but this time it is in terms of geodesic paths (the shortest path between any two given nodes). Centrality therefore gives an indication of how close (and thus how central) a node is on average to all the other nodes in the network. A highly central node is one that can communicate with (and thus influence) many other nodes. A lower scoring and thus more peripheral node is one that can exert influence on relatively few nodes and is at a great geodesic distance from the majority of other nodes in the network. Calculating the sum of all geodesic distances in the network and dividing it by the geodesic distances to and from that node under examination produces the reported index. Whilst it is outside the scope of the present paper to describe the derivation of the necessary formulae, the interested reader can find full accounts in Wasserman and Faust (1994).

Fire Service incident example

The scenario is based on an exercise at the Fire Service Training College, addressing the management of a (simulated) road traffic accident involving a chemical tanker and a car. In this incident, the car was traveling along a country road and collided with the chemical tanker, carrying twenty-thousand liters of Methyltrichlorosilane, at a junction. The tanker was ruptured and a chemical leak occurred. A member of the public dials '999' to report an emergency and the Fire Service response is mobilized. The response involves two pumps from a local Fire Station, together with units from other Stations, including a Rescue Unit, a Support Pump and an Environmental Pump. The accident has blocked a main road and is causing severe congestion, which slows down the arrival of the units. The Station Officer who is first on scene reports that there is a definite leak of liquid from the tanker, that casualties are reporting eye and skin irritation (implying some vaporization leading to the chemical becoming airborne), and this is leading to people abandoning the vehicles to seek safety away from the tanker.

Data collection and propositional network production

Through observation of the exercise and two subsequent debriefs, we were able to build a detailed collection of knowledge objects that were relevant to the situation. The relationship between knowledge objects was defined through collaboration with SMEs, and a propositional network produced. Figure 1 shows detail from the network as the full network would be difficult to reproduce legibly here. This network was then reviewed with SMEs from both Fire and Police operations in order to produce a version that was felt to be a fair reflection of how the incident could have been managed. The key requirement here is to ensure that as many relevant knowledge objects as possible are collected and that their relationships are valid.

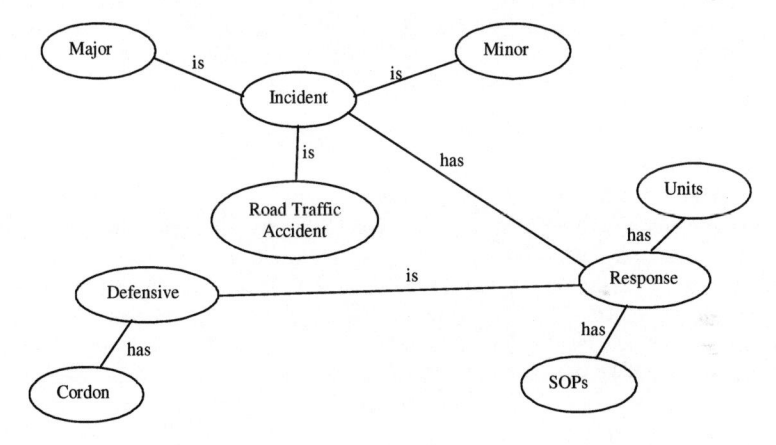

Figure 1. Extract of Fire Incident propositional network

In Figure 1 each node represents a specific knowledge object and that each link represents a specific relationship between knowledge objects. For example, <Road Traffic Accident> is <incident>; <incident> is <major, minor> and has <incident response>; <incident response> has <units, SOPs1> and is <Defensive, Offensive> etc.

Analysis of the Propositional Network

Having built a propositional network, the next step is to relate this to concept of distributed cognition. As mentioned above, we view the incident in terms of specific phases and in terms of specific agents. From this, it is a simple matter to use the overall network as a means of indicating which knowledge objects are activated for a given phase and a given agent. Initially, we use a color-coding scheme to indicate agents in a given phase. The incident itself consisted of five phases; 1. Handling of the initial call; 2. Travel to the scene; 3. Investigation of the scene; 4. Treatment of casualties and 5. Standing down. Notice that the activation of knowledge objects changes over the course of the incident, and that use of knowledge objects changes across agents. The fire-fighters do not know the nature of the chemical until phase 3 (Investigation of the scene). With this knowledge, the definition of response is made easier, the question of which Personal Protective Equipment to wear can be solved and the search strategy simplified. From the perspective of a distributed cognition analysis then, the challenge in incident management becomes one of ensuring that the appropriate agents have access to appropriate knowledge objects at the right time. This provides an indication of the manner in which situation awareness changes over time, that is, the dynamic nature of SA, and also provides a cue to where sharing might be required in terms of identifying those knowledge objects used by more than one agent. Whilst color-coding the network is a simple process, it has proved useful. For example, the Fire Service Training College has responded favorably to the concept and is using large versions of the networks to support their training and debriefing of the exercise. The presentation of the entire network and the activating of specific knowledge objects provide a useful means of focusing discussion of related concepts and on who knows what and when they know this.

Quantitative Analysis of Propositional Networks

The propositional networks, coded by Agent and Phase, can be interpreted in terms of the number of active (i.e., coloured) nodes in any given network and the number of shared (i.e., striped) nodes. Thus, in phase 1, out of 73 nodes in the propositional knowledge network, 16 are active, and of these 4 are used by only one agent. Thus, there are 12 shared nodes. We can represent these numbers in a variety of ways to show, for example, that at the initial stage of the incident, the active knowledge is relatively low, i.e., 16 / 73 = c.22%, or that the amount of shared knowledge is quite high, i.e., 12 / 16 = 75%. In phase 5, there are 62 active nodes and 15 nodes used by one agent, giving 47 shared nodes. Thus, at the close of the incident, the relative active knowledge is much higher, i.e., 62 / 73 = c.85%, but the amount of shared knowledge is similar, i.e., 47 / 62 = c.76%. The implication, for this incident at least, is that the amount of active knowledge increases during the course of the incident, e.g., as the fire-crews and associated services discover more information about the incident, but the rate of sharing remains constant, e.g., because much of the decision-making is performed through collaboration over the course of the incident. While these numbers provide points of comparison over the course of an incident, and between incidents, they are only simple reflections on the content of the networks.

Quantitative analysis of the networks was also undertaken using metrics of status (Table 1) and centrality (Table 2). In order to decide which nodes to consider as most important from the perspective of status, it was decided to report only those nodes with a status score in excess of one standard deviation of the mean, i.e., where Status = 0.078 + 0.045 = 0.123. This gives 9 knowledge objects out of the total set of 77, i.e., 11.7%, which are shown in Table 1. Centrality was calculated and knowledge objects with a score in excess of one standard deviation of the mean, i.e.,

Centrality = 37 +6.25 = 43.25, were returned. This gives 11 knowledge objects out of the total set of 77, i.e., 14.3%, as shown in Table 2.

Table 1. Calculated status of knowledge objects across the entire incident

Node	Status
Condition	0.24324325
Other Agencies	0.22972973
Chemicals	0.1891892
Incident Response	0.16216215
Road	0.13513513
Police	0.13513513
Casualties	0.13513513
Incident	0.13513513
Offensive	0.13513513

Table 2. Calculated centrality of knowledge objects across the entire incident

Node	B-L Centrality
Chemicals	49.71239
Hazardous Materials	47.305264
Hazard	45.120483
Fire Control	44.94
Casualties	44.583332
Incident Response	44.49505
Other Agencies	44.407116
Condition	43.972603
Type	43.88672
Information	43.462284
Incident	43.462284

Validation

In order to determine whether the propositional network bore any resemblance to reality, we performed two validation activities. In the first activity, we presented the final network to SMEs for their opinion. It was felt that the network provided a fair and accurate reflection of the issues that needed to be addressed for an incident of this type. However, we wished to get a clear sense of the correctness of the network and decided to compare the output against SOPs. Taking the two sets of results yields a combined set of six knowledge objects which have both high status and high centrality, i.e., {Casualties, Condition (of casualties), Chemicals, Incident, Incident Response, Other Agencies}. The implication is that these knowledge objects represent the main aspects of tactical response for this incident. In other words, at the level of tactical situation awareness within the system, it is important for agents to consider the condition of casualties, the fact that the incident involves chemicals, the type of incident response and the liaison with other agencies. HM Fire Inspectorate (2002) states that, when an Officer assumes command of an incident, then it is essential to attend to the following elements: 1. Confirm tactics and mode of response; 2. Ensure resources as appropriate; 3. Ensure communications; 4. Review operations; 5. Ensure welfare of Civilians, Crew, and Other Personnel. Table 3 shows that the knowledge objects extracted through the analysis of proposition networks compare favorably with the topics covered in the Fire Service Manual. This suggests that the objective analysis of the propositional network provides an output with reasonable content validity, in that it concurs with the theory of command espoused by the training manual. Given that the scenario observed was in training it seems reasonable to assume that it would be likely performed "by the book". It is to be noted that agreement between SOPs and the propositional network metrics has come about as a result of a "blind" analysis performed by the researcher; whilst the input of SMEs is essential; these outputs were automatically produced without the researcher having to have a detailed understanding of Fire Service procedure.

Table 3. Comparison of extracted knowledge objects with advice from fire service manual

Fire Service Manual Advice	Extracted Knowledge Objects
Confirm Tactics and Mode	Incident Response
Ensure Resources Appropriate	Chemicals
Ensure Communications	Other Agencies
Review Operations	Incident
Ensure Welfare	Casualties, Condition

Core knowledge objects as critical success factors

It is interesting to consider the role of the knowledge objects that are rated highly on the measures of centrality and status. In the case of the example of this paper these objects were identified as the casualties, the condition of the casualties, the chemicals, the incident, the response to the incident, and other agencies. We suspect that analysis of the quality of information held in each of these core objects could be used to predict system success or failure. For example, in the specific case of the incident that we have presented there are a number of questions that can be addressed to each of the core knowledge objects. Do we know how many casualties there are and their location? Do we know the nature of the injuries of the casualties and any complications that they may have? Do we know what chemicals were involved, their identification code, their location and their strength? Do we know the cause of the incident, who was involved and who has been informed? Do we know which agencies have been informed of the incident and what response plan is being put into action? Has the response plan been checked to ensure that it is working? Do we know that all the relevant agencies have been informed and do we know that each agency has the appropriate information to make sure that their response is effective? The answer to each of these questions, if negative, could mean failure of part or the whole of the response to the incident. We feel that, in general terms, identification of core knowledge objects is essential in these multi-faceted, distributed, systems. The core knowledge objects can be thought of as factors that will be critical to the success of the system. When the quality of information held in each of these core objects is close to the actual situation (and the appropriate response is known and can be brought into effect) then the system is likely to succeed. Thus, we argue, knowledge objects as critical success factors can be used to predict both success and failure of the system.

System redesign

This paper has addressed the major issues with SSA facing human factors practitioners engaged in systems redesign activity that were identified earlier in this paper. Namely, it has been demonstrated that the problem of establishing what situation awareness is and how individuals share it can be side-stepped through focussing our attention on systems-level processes. Furthermore, the practical problems associated with applying existing analytical techniques to large systems have been addressed through the development of a methodology for analysing systems-level situation awareness. Finally, it has been shown that the DC/propositional network approach answers the key questions with regard to Shared Situation Awareness, i.e. regarding the information that the team as a system needs to know in order to achieve its goals and establishing the requirements for information sharing between agents at various stages during a situation. In terms of System Design, our approach to the analysis of team performance is useful, in that it identifies the key processes that Systems Designers should ensure they preserve during any subsequent redesign activity. In order to ensure that new technological systems meet the requirements of their users, it is necessary to have an accurate understanding of how the work environment currently operates and the impact that new technologies will have on the performance of work. The design of appropriate C2 environments and technologies requires not only an understanding of the tasks that the (work) system must complete, but also the wider social, organisational and cultural elements of coordinated activity (Vincente, 1999). The adoption of a more sociotechnical systems based approach to the design of work systems is known as macroergonomics and is increasingly acknowledged as necessary for the development of successful innovations within complex work systems (Hendrick, 1997).

References

Anderson, J.R. (1980). *Cognitive Psychology and its Implications*. San Francisco, CA: Freeman.
Artman, H. & Garbis, C. (1998). Situation Awareness as Distributed Cognition. In T.R.G. Green, L. Bannon, C.P. Warren and J. Buckley (Eds) *ECCE 9: Proceedings of theNinth European Conference on Cognitive Ergonomics*, (pp. 151-156). Le Chesnay, France: European Association of Cognitive Ergonomics (EACE).
Flor, N.V. & Hutchins, E.L. (1991). Analyzing Distributed Cognition in Software Teams: A Case Study of Team Programming during Perfective Software Maintenance. In J. Koenemann-Belliveau, T. G. Moher and S. P. Robertson (Eds.) *Empirical Studies of Programmers: Fourth Workshop*. 36-64. Norwood, New Jersey: Ablex.
Hendrick, H.W. (1997). Organizational design and macroergonomics In G. Salvendy (Ed.), *Handbook of Human Factors and Ergonomics*. London: Wiley.

HM Fire Inspectorate (2001). *Fire Service Manual volume 2 - Fire Service Operations: Incident Command*. London: Her Majesty's Fire Inspectorate Publications Roger Section.

Hutchins, E. (1995), How a Cockpit Remembers Its Speed. *Cognitive Science, 19*, 265-288.

Klein, G.A., Calderwood, R., & MacGregor, D. (1989). Critical decision method for eliciting knowledge. *IEEE Transactions On Systems, Man, And Cybernetics, 19*, 462-472.

Ministry of Defence (2004). *Network enabled capability*. HM Stationary Office.

Nofi, A. (2000). *Defining and measuring shared situational awareness*. Alexandria, VA: Center for Naval Analysis, Thoughtlink Inc.

Poirier, P. & Chicoisne, G. (2006). A framework for thinking about distributed cognition. *Pragmatics and Cognition, 14*, 215-234.

Perry, M. (2003). Distributed cognition, In J.M. Carroll (Ed.) *HCI Models, Theories and Frameworks* (pp. 193-224). San Francisco, CA: Morgan-Kaufmann.

Quillian, R. (1969). The teachable language comprehender: a simulation program and theory of language. *Communications of the ACM, 12*, 459-476.

Rummelhart, D.E. & McClelland, J.L. (1996). *Parallel distributed processing: Explorations in the microstructure of cognition, Vol. 1: Foundations*. Cambridge, MA: MIT Press.

Shu, Y. & Furuta, K. (2005). An inference method of team situation awareness based on mutual awareness. *Cognition, Technology and Work, 7*, 272-297.

Vicente, K. (1999). *Cognitive work analysis: Toward safe, productive, and healthy computer-based work*. Mahwah, New Jersey: Lawrence Erlbaum Associates.

Wasserman, S. & Faust, K. (1994). *Social Network Analysis: Methods and Applications*. Cambridge: Cambridge University Press.

Representing Distributed Situation Awareness: a case study in Multi-National operations

Paul M. Salmon[1], Neville A. Stanton[1], Chris Baber[2], Guy H. Walker[1],
Rob Houghton[2], Daniel P. Jenkins[1], & Richard McMaster[2]
[1] Human Factors Integration Defence Technology Centre
Brunel University, Uxbridge
[2] University of Birmingham, Birmingham
UK

Abstract

The concept of Distributed Situation Awareness (DSA) is currently receiving increasing attention from the human factors community. Despite this, some researchers argue that theory and methods for representing SA in collaborative systems are lacking. This article describes a DSA approach to viewing SA in collaborative systems and outlines the propositional network method, a new methodology for evaluating and representing DSA. To demonstrate, examples taken from a recent case study on DSA in multinational warfare operations are presented. The findings are discussed in relation to their implications for DSA during the multinational operations observed, including the structure of DSA in terms of the usage of knowledge by the different agents involved, the distribution and sharing of knowledge between agents, and the salience of the different knowledge items identified.

Introduction

Interest in Situation Awareness (SA) continues to expand. Ostensibly, SA refers to the awareness that an individual has of a situation, an operator's dynamic understanding of 'what is going on' (Endsley, 1995). Of the SA theories presented in the literature, Endsley's information processing based three-level model is the most popular. The three-level model, depicts SA is a *product* comprising three hierarchical levels: *level 1*, the perception of task relevant elements in the environment; *level 2*, the comprehension of their meaning in relation to task goals; and *level 3*, the projection of their future states. Interest in the concept of *team SA* has increased markedly over the past decade. Endsley's model has subsequently been applied to team SA in a wide variety of domains, including the military (e.g. Endsley, Holder, Leibricht, Garland, Wampler & Matthews, 2000). Much, however, has been written on the need for a greater understanding of team SA during collaborative activity and for the development of more sophisticated SA measures for collaborative systems (e.g. Artman and Garbis, 1998; Salmon, Stanton, Walker and Green, 2006; Siemieniuch & Sinclair, 2006). In this article we describe an

---

In D. de Waard, G.R.J. Hockey, P. Nickel, and K.A. Brookhuis (Eds.) (2007), *Human Factors Issues in Complex System Performance* (pp. 277 - 289). Maastricht, the Netherlands: Shaker Publishing.

alternative approach to viewing SA in collaborative environments, the Distributed Situation Awareness (DSA) approach, which attempts to describe team SA from a systems level perspective. Further, we present the propositional network (prop net) method, a methodology for evaluating and representing DSA in collaborative environments and use examples from a recent case study on multinational warfare operations to demonstrate DSA and the prop net method.

Distributed Situation Awareness

DSA approaches take their theoretical underpinning from Hutchins (1995) seminal work on distributed cognition. Distributed cognition theory focuses on cognition at the systems level, suggesting that the people and artefacts comprising a system conjugate together to form a so-called 'joint cognitive system' and that cognitive processes emerge from, and are distributed across, the system itself. Cognition is therefore achieved through co-ordination between system units (Artman & Garbis, 1998). Mirroring this approach, DSA theories argue that SA too exists at a systems level. Team SA is therefore viewed not as a shared understanding of the situation, rather as an entity that is separate from team members and is in fact a characteristic of the system in which the team is working (Artman & Garbis, 1998). Whilst recognising that individuals within a team possess their own SA and that team members may share their understanding of the situation (Artman & Garbis, 1998), DSA approaches assume that SA is an *emergent property* (i.e. relationship between system elements) of the system that is independent from individual cognition. The authors recently described an approach to DSA in complex sociotechnical systems (See Stanton, Stewart, Harris, Houghton, Baber, McMaster, Salmon, Hoyle, Walker, Young, Linsell, Dymott & Green; 2006). According to Stanton et al SA-related information is distributed across the agents and artefacts (human and non-human) comprising the system. These knowledge 'themes' or 'topics', labelled *knowledge elements*, represent what agents 'need to know' in order to achieve success during task performance. In this case, the term knowledge represents the relationship between concepts (Shadbolt & Burton, 1995) and refers to task-level knowledge, which relates to the goals and sub-goals of the task being performed. The ownership, usage and sharing of knowledge is dynamic and is dependent upon the task and its associated goals. Agents therefore have 'different' SA for the same situation, but their SA is typically overlapping and complementary, and deficiencies in one agents SA can be compensated by another agent.

SA is therefore defined as 'activated knowledge for a specific task, at a specific time within a system' (Stanton et al, 2006), echoing Bell and Lyon's (2000) assumption that, "SA could be defined as knowledge (in working memory) about elements of the environment" (Bell & Lyon, 2000). Stanton et al propose then, that a situation requires the use of appropriate knowledge (held by individuals, captured by devices etc.) that relates to the state of the environment and those changes as the situation develops. The 'ownership' of this knowledge is initially at the system, rather than individual level. This notion could be further extend to include 'meta-SA', where its knowledge of other agents' knowledge is contained in the system, such that each agent could potentially know where to go when they need to find something out.

Measuring and representing Distributed Situation Awareness

A review of SA measurement approaches suggested that existing SA methods, in isolation, may be flawed when used to assess team SA in real-world collaborative environments (Salmon et al 2006). Subsequently, a new approach to evaluating and describing DSA, the *prop net* (propositional network) methodology, was developed. Taken from the Event Analysis of Systemic Teamwork (EAST; Stanton, Salmon, Walker, Baber & Jenkins, 2005) methodology, prop nets are used to evaluate and represent DSA in complex sociotechnical systems. Prop nets are typically constructed from Critical Decision Method (CDM; Klein & Armstrong, 2005) and Hierarchical Task Analysis (HTA; Annett, 2005) outputs using a simple content analysis and depict the *knowledge elements* that are used by the different agents during task performance. Essentially prop nets display the information that comprises a particular systems DSA. These knowledge elements represent what the agents 'needed to know' in order to achieve their goals during task performance and are linked based on causal links that emerged during the task under analysis (e.g. enemy '*has*' location, commander '*knows*' plan etc). Knowledge element usage is also represented via shading based on their usage by different agents during task performance. To demonstrate, in constructing the prop nets, the hypothetical verbal transcript: "We need to identify the source and location of the enemy's radio transmitters within the Internally Displaced Persons (IDPs) Camps" would be subjected to a simple content analysis which produces the key words: source, location, enemy, radio transmitters, IDPs, IDP camps. The resultant prop net for this portion of the transcript is presented in Figure 1.

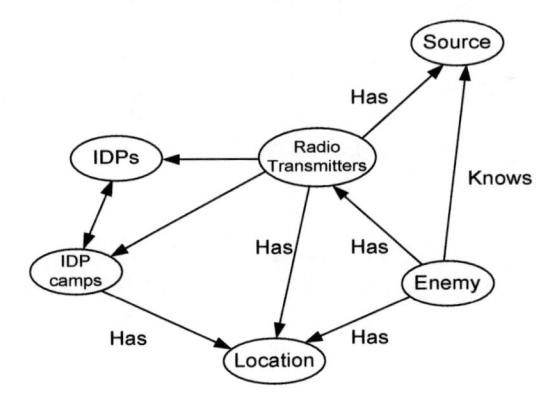

Figure 1. Propositional Network Example

Case Study: Distributed Situation Awareness in Multi-National Operations

HFI-DTC researchers were invited to undertake an analysis of the recent Multi-National Experiment 4 (MNE4). One component of this analysis involved the use of prop nets to evaluate DSA throughout the experiment. Additional analyses included HTA, CDM interviews, and social network analyses, however these results are not presented here (see Verral, 2006 for the full analysis). MNE4 was undertaken in order to examine the robustness (i.e. reliability of process) of an Effects-Based

Operations (EBOs) approach to modern day warfare and involved the conduct of a simulated multinational warfare scenario using a virtual, distributed, ad hoc, multinational Coalition Task Force (CTF) headquarters (HQ). EBOs are a new approach designed to support warfare operations within network-centric warfare environments and have been defined as "co-ordinated sets of actions directed at shaping the behaviour of friends, foes, and neutrals in peace, crisis and war" (Smith, 2002). Effects-based approaches use a combination of military and other activities (e.g. Diplomatic, Information and Economic) in order to direct behaviour in the warfare environment, with the focus being on *effects* (desired end states) rather than *actions*. Thus planning, execution and assessment efforts focus primarily on effects and the actions required to achieve these effects.

Apparatus

A total of 132 military and civilian participants from eight countries (United States, United Kingdom, Australia, Sweden, Germany, Canada, France and Finland) took part. Each of the countries involved undertook the experiment within secure laboratories and all information was shared over a secure network. Participants interacted with one another and undertook daily activities (e.g. planning, meetings, after action reviews etc) on the Information Work Space (IWS) collaborative system, which is a collaborative environment comprising chat rooms, email, information databases and Microsoft office tools (e.g. PowerPoint, word etc). Participants also had access to the internet, printing facilities and telephones.

Stimuli

The participants were presented with a hypothetical modern day Afghanistan coalition warfare scenario. Players were instructed to use a new EBO Concept of Operations (CONOPS) to support achievement of the desired end state of establishing a secure environment (free from internal and external threats) within the Afghanistan area of operations.

Methodology

HFI-DTC analyst's were located at the UK headquarters during the three weeks of MNE4 and observed activity taking place on the IWS collaborative planning system. This gave the analyst's access to voice communications and text chat taking place between all players. At least two analysts were on duty at any time during the experiment (often three people and occasionally four). Each analyst concentrated on meetings and planning sessions and recorded information on what was happening during a meeting, including the *communications* between players, the *content* of the communications, the *topics* being discussed and any *documents* referred to. The primary sources of information used by the HFI-DTC team were the Concept of Operations (CONOPS), the Commander's briefs, observation of meetings and any documents referred to during the meetings and briefs. The analysis focused specifically on the following five functional groups involved in the scenario:

1. Knowledge Based Development (KBD). The KBD group were responsible for building and maintaining a knowledge base that players could use for developing SA and understanding, including SA on the operating environment, the adversary, friendly, and neutral forces.
2. Effects Based Planning (EBP). The EBP group were responsible for developing and refining operational plans designed to enable the achievement of the desired effects and end state.
3. Effects Based Execution (EBE). The EBE group were responsible for co-ordinating, directing and monitoring task force operations.
4. Effects Based Assessment (EBA). The EBA group were responsible for assessing the actions and effects in order to identify operational deficiencies and recommend methods to improve force effectiveness.
5. Multi National Interagency Group (MNIG). The MNIG were responsible for the civilian component of the response.

Due to article size restrictions, only extracts of selected prop nets taken from the commander's briefings and the evolving humanitarian aid scenario are presented.

Results

Commanders brief Prop nets

Prop nets were constructed from the commander's briefs that were given at the start of each day. The commander's brief described all activities from the previous day, forthcoming activities and included situation reports from each of the different groups (e.g. KBD, EBP, EBE, EBP, EBA and MNIG). Extracts from the prop nets constructed from the commander's briefs on the 3rd and the 9th March are presented in Figure 2. The prop nets presented in Figure 2 demonstrate firstly how the information required for SA acquisition and maintenance increased as the scenario unfolded and secondly how more groups began to use the information provided by the KBD group as the experiment progressed.

Following the ideas presented by Stanton et al (2006), it is possible to identify the key knowledge elements that have salience for each scenario phase, salience being defined as those knowledge elements that act as hubs to other knowledge objects (i.e. the heuristic of five or more links). This can also be calculated more formally using SNA statistics such as degree centrality. In this case the key knowledge elements were extracted from the prop nets based on the causal links between them. The key knowledge elements from each prop net are presented in Table 1 and the total use of knowledge elements by each group is presented in Table 2.

The prop net extracts presented in Figure 2 represent some of the knowledge themes that the different groups were using at that point in the warfare scenario. They demonstrate that, as the scenario unfolded, there was increasing usage and sharing of information by the different parties involved. In the initial commander brief propositional network (3rd March), the KBD group held the majority of the information related to the scenario, and this information is yet to be used by the other groups. Over the course of the experiment, however, the information used by other groups increased, as demonstrated by the 9th March prop net which shows that more groups are using more of the information that was initially held by KBD.

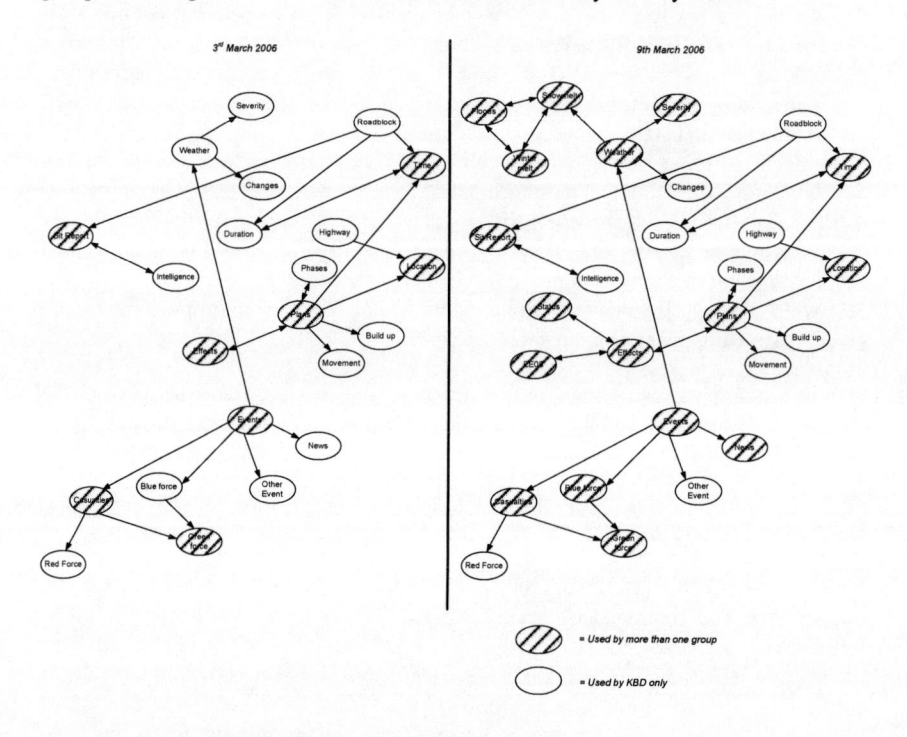

Figure 2. Commanders Brief Propositional Networks

Table 1. Key Knowledge Elements

Key Knowledge Elements 3rd March	Key Knowledge Elements 9th March
Roadblocks	Weather
Locations	Effects
Plans	Coalition Task Force
Effects	Capability
Coalition Task Force	Humanitarian Aid
NGO	IDP Camps
Weapons	Refugees
Taliban	Transportation
Afghanistan	Shortages
Expectations	Taliban
Security Risk	

This is indicated by the increase in striped nodes in the 9th March prop net. This is taken to show greater consensus on the scenario and activities required and a commonality on themes between groups. The initial lack of usage of the information held by the KBD has interesting ramifications for technologically supported and distributed multinational warfare operations. The usage (or provision) of this information by the KBD group indicates that the information was available (and to some extent required) to other groups. The non usage of the information by other groups suggests that either they could not access this information as they could not locate it on the IWS or did not know who to speak to within the organisation to find the information, or that they were not aware of the existence of the knowledge. Further, it might also demonstrate that the KBD were waiting for information requests (rather than proactively contacting the groups). Certainly our observations indicate that there was some confusion over the KBD groups role, with some players seeing them as *'sign posters'* (i.e. pointing players to information) and other seeing them as *'gatekeepers'* (i.e. supplying information on demand). The CONOPS suggested that the KBD group's role was as *gatekeepers*, supplying information to other players as and when requested. The commander's brief prop nets also suggest that common themes emerged as the experiment progressed. Initially groups were clustered (as can be seen by the grouping of specific colours), which indicated that they were performing separate activities. However, as the experiment developed and the process evolved, commonality in themes began to emerge. This resulted in the increase in information required by groups and also some sharing of knowledge between groups.

Table 2. Knowledge Element Usage

Group	March 3rd	March 9th
KBD	62	46
EBP	14	33
EBE	8	13
EBA	4	9
MNIG	8	12

The total number of knowledge elements used by the different groups involved was also derived from the prop nets. A general increase in usage by the different groups demonstrates how knowledge requirements increased as the experiment unfolded. For example, knowledge elements used by the KBD group decreased from 62 items on the 3rd March to 46 items on the 9th March. The knowledge used by the EBP and EBE groups increased from 14 items and 8 items respectively on the 3rd March to 33 and 13 on the 9th March respectively, and the knowledge used by the EBA and MNIG groups increased from 4 items and 8 items on the 3rd March to 9 items and 12 items 9th March respectively. Perhaps of more significance is the finding that, on the 3rd March, a total of 40 knowledge elements being held by the KBD group remained unused, whereas on the 9th March, this figure had decreased to 21 knowledge elements. This demonstrates that the other groups (e.g. EBP, EBA. EBE & MNIG) were able to access and use more information as the experiment progressed.

Humanitarian Aid Propositional Networks

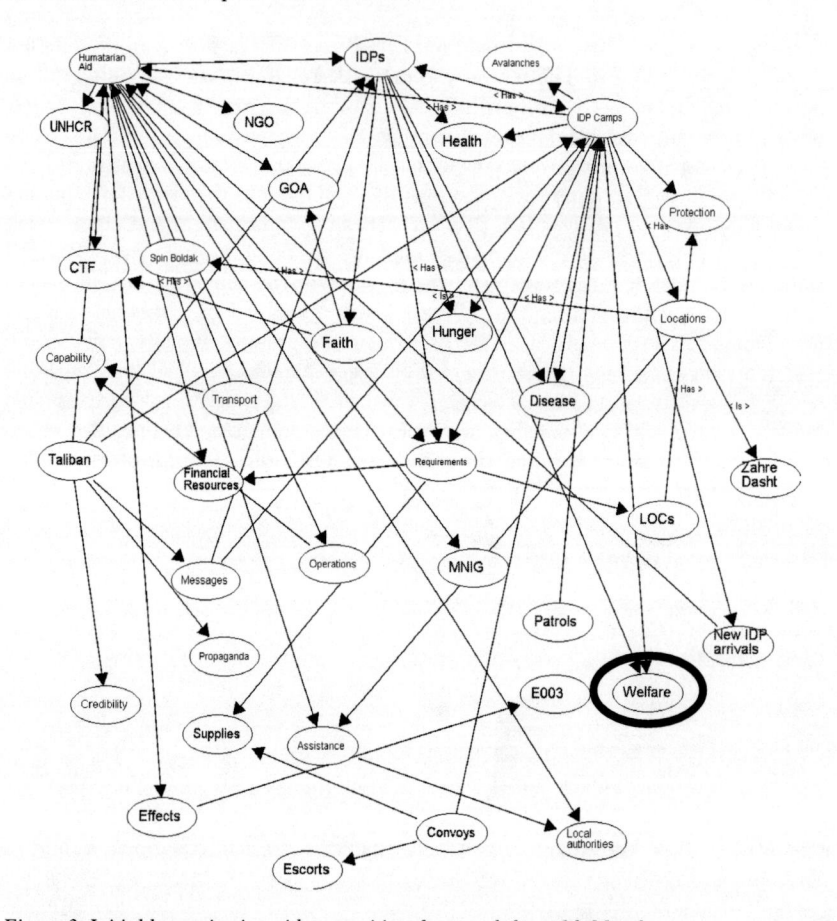

Figure 3. Initial humanitarian aid propositional network from 6th March

A humanitarian aid situation unfolded over the course of MNE4. Prop nets related to the humanitarian aid situation were constructed from the daily updates and Situation Reports (SitReps). The prop nets demonstrate the increase in knowledge related to the humanitarian aid situation over the course of the experiment. As the situation unfolded, there was a requirement for awareness of more knowledge topics and information. As more events occurred and the humanitarian aid situation deteriorated, the different players and groups needed to know more about the situation in order to deal with it. Further, the increased knowledge depicted in the prop nets demonstrates how more information related to the humanitarian aid situation was made available and shared by different groups within the organisation. This demonstrates that, as the experiment progressed, groups began to find out more about the situation and make this information or knowledge available to other groups. For example, the initial prop net from the 6th March (Figure 3) presents a very high-level overview of the humanitarian aid situation at that time. This indicates that the different groups had only a limited, very high level SA of the humanitarian aid situation at that time, including a very basic knowledge of the humanitarian aid requirements and of the different locations of the internationally displaced persons (IDP) camps. In short, they had some SA, but did not have a detailed knowledge of the situation, its implications and requirements. Significantly, some of the information required to enhance their knowledge of the situation was available on the IWS collaborative system, but was not accessed. This again indicates that the players either did not know that the information was available or that they could not find or access the information on the IWS system.

Over time, as more information related to the situation is discovered and made available by the KBD group, and as more events begin to occur in the camps, the different groups begin to develop a very detailed, specific awareness of the situation. As a result of this the prop nets expanded considerably over the course of the experiment. To give an example, further information related to the knowledge element 'Welfare' (circled in Figure 3) was made available and used by the actors involved, including 'Water', which referred to the water shortages in the IDP camps. Similarly, further knowledge elements related to 'water' appeared in the following prop net (14th March), such as *supply, streams* and *local suppliers, distribution* and *transport, treatment* and *storage*. An extract taken from the final the prop net constructed on the 15th March, showing the additional knowledge elements related to 'Water', is presented in Figure 4.

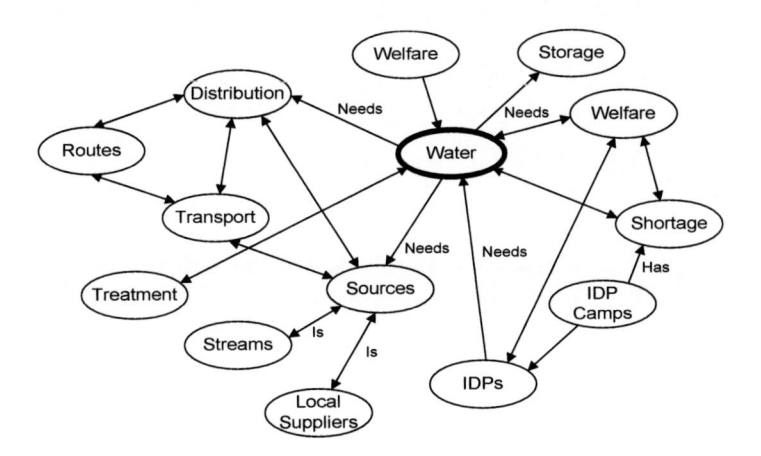

Figure 4. Water-related knowledge elements

Figure 4 demonstrates that, rather than simply knowing that the IDPs need water (as depicted by the 6th March prop net in presented in Figure 3), the groups were now considering where the water will come from, how the water could be treated and distributed, and how it could be stored. The final prop net developed on the 15th March was considerably larger than the initial prop net developed on the 6th March. This demonstrates how the different groups had developed a richer and more detailed SA of the humanitarian aid situation and the subsequent requirements in each of the Internally Displaced Persons (IDPs) camps. This increase in information related to different themes presented in the initial prop net was a feature of the additional prop nets developed. This was taken to show that, as events unfolded, the different groups were able to access more detailed information about the humanitarian aid situation. As a result of this, the systems DSA became far more detailed and richer as this additional information was assimilated and understood and so task performance (i.e. responses to the humanitarian aid situation) was supported more effectively. To reinforce this conclusion, the total number of knowledge elements related to the humanitarian aid situation increased from 37 in the initial prop net (Figure 3) to 111 in the final humanitarian aid prop net constructed on the 15th March. The key knowledge elements related to the humanitarian aid scenario were extracted form the prop nets. The key knowledge elements identified are presented in Figure 5.

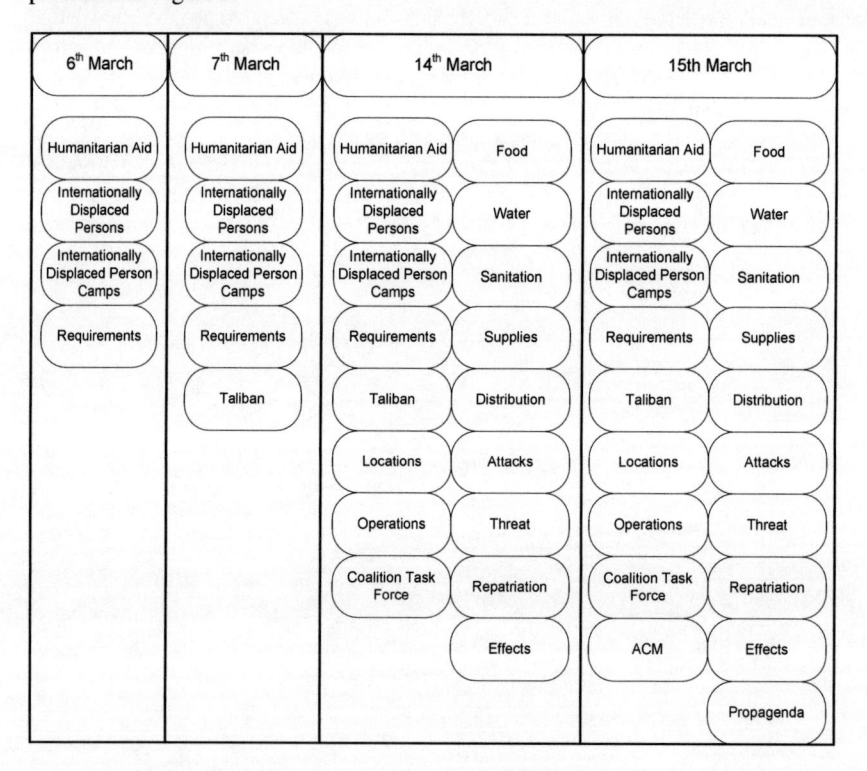

6th March	7th March	14th March		15th March	
Humanitarian Aid	Humanitarian Aid	Humanitarian Aid	Food	Humanitarian Aid	Food
Internationally Displaced Persons	Internationally Displaced Persons	Internationally Displaced Persons	Water	Internationally Displaced Persons	Water
Internationally Displaced Person Camps	Internationally Displaced Person Camps	Internationally Displaced Person Camps	Sanitation	Internationally Displaced Person Camps	Sanitation
Requirements	Requirements	Requirements	Supplies	Requirements	Supplies
	Taliban	Taliban	Distribution	Taliban	Distribution
		Locations	Attacks	Locations	Attacks
		Operations	Threat	Operations	Threat
		Coalition Task Force	Repatriation	Coalition Task Force	Repatriation
			Effects	ACM	Effects
					Propaganda

Figure 5. Humanitarian Aid Scenario Key Knowledge Elements

As demonstrated by Figure 5, the key knowledge elements at the beginning of the scenario (6h and 7th March) as the humanitarian aid situation began to unfold were the overall humanitarian aid situation, the IDPs and IDP camps and the humanitarian aid requirements. As the situation began to deteriorate, the key knowledge elements began to increase. Factors such as food, water, sanitation, supplies and supply distribution began to become of primary concern, along with the Taliban, who were beginning to infiltrate IDP camps, attacks on IDP camps and United Nations (UN) workers within the IDP camp, the effects being planned, the coalition task force and repatriation efforts and the ACM and Taliban propaganda.

In summary, the prop net analysis highlights how events occurring 'in theatre' can quickly lead to increased SA requirements and also suggests that system and procedural design should consider communications links and access to, and dissemination of, SA related information in multinational systems. As the scenario progressed, increasing amounts of information were required by agents in order to keep up with the situation and develop and maintain an appropriate level of SA. The communication, availability and presentation of knowledge to agents in collaborative and distributed systems thus become key system design requirements. In this case it was apparent that much of the information required for detailed SA of the humanitarian aid situation was available to players on the IWS collaborative system. However, the prop nets demonstrate that this information was not accessed initially and that it took time for the agents to access the knowledge that they required. This can be attributed to two factors: firstly, that the different groups found it difficult to use the IWS system and to locate the required information within the system; and secondly that the groups waited for the information to be given to them rather than pro-actively seeking the information themselves.

Conclusions

The aim of this article was to outline a new approach to describing SA in complex collaborative environments and to demonstrate a new approach of evaluating and representing SA in these systems. We contend that viewing SA as a systems level emergent property is fruitful for a number of reasons, including that it permits a systemic description of the knowledge comprising SA (which can be extrapolated to an individual SA level) and it allows judgements to be made on potential barriers to SA acquisition and maintenance. Further, considering SA in this way ensures that team SA within complex collaborative systems is viewed in its entirety, rather than as its component parts (i.e. individual team member SA). In such systems, tasks are rarely performed entirely independently of others, especially in complex situations and when critical decision-making is required (Artman & Garbis, 1998) – these activities tend to require coordinated activity between several individuals (Cannon-Bowers and Salas, 1990; cited in Salas, Prince, Baker and Shrestha, 1995). It is important therefore that team SA assessments consider this co-ordination. The prop nets presented demonstrate that, as the experiment unfolded, more information was used by, and shared between, the different groups involved. It was concluded that this was due to a number of factors, including that the different groups were becoming more efficient with the IWS system and so were able to locate the information that they required as the experiment progressed, and also that more and more information was created and became available as the scenario progressed (as the KBD group was able to find and present more information as the scenario progressed). The humanitarian aid prop nets also demonstrate how information requirements increase as warfare scenarios unfold, and also how the key knowledge elements required for the humanitarian aid scenario increased as the situation 'on-the-ground' deteriorated.

The DSA approach, along with the prop net methodology, permits a comprehensive analysis of SA in collaborative systems. In addition to judgements on the content and quality of individual, team and system SA, it is possible to identify instances in systems where the information required for SA is either not available (i.e. not presented by interfaces) or its dissemination is not supported (i.e. the information cannot be communicated to the people who require it). Secondly, it is also possible to identify the key knowledge elements within a particular network. This information can be used to strengthen or increase the communication channels that disseminate this information within a particular system, or to develop and introduce new interfaces that present this information more explicitly.

In closing, both the theory and the case study evidence suggest that communication, communication links and the availability of information are the key elements involved in the acquisition and maintenance of DSA. This follows on from Stanton et als (2006) notion that the links between agents in a network are more crucial than the nodes themselves in maintaining DSA. It follows then, that the network links (between agents) in a system are critical. According to Stanton et al (2006) knowing which links to use (and where to offer information when needed) will determine the quality of DSA. Further study investigation into the concept of DSA is required, including case studies of DSA in other domains and research to support theoretical and methodological validation. One particularly interesting aspect relates to the effects that the communications between agents have on each individual agent's propositional network (i.e. SA). Although individual agent prop nets were not constructed in this case, this is one avenue of research that the authors are currently pursuing.

References

Annett, J. (2005). Hierarchical task analysis. In N. A. Stanton, A. Hedge, E. Salas, H. Hendrick, and K. Brookhuis, (Eds.), *Handbook of Human Factors and Ergonomics Methods* (pp. 33.1-33.7). Boca Raton, Florida: CRC Press.

Artman, H., & Garbis, C. (1998). Situation awareness as distributed cognition. In T. Green, L. Bannon, C. Warren, and J. Buckley (Eds.) Cognition and cooperation. Proceedings of 9th Conference of Cognitive Ergonomics. (pp. 151-156). Limerick, Ireland.

Bell, H.H, & Lyon, D.R. (2000). Using observer ratings to assess situation awareness, In M.R. Endsley (Ed.) *Situation awareness analysis and measurement* (pp 129-146). Mahwah, NJ: Laurence Earlbaum Associates.

Endsley, M.R. (1995). Towards a theory of Situation Awareness in Dynamic Systems, *Human Factors*, 37, 32-64.

Endsley, M.R., Holder, C.D., Leibricht, B.C., Garland, D.C., Wampler, R.L. & Matthews, M.D. (2000). *Modelling and measuring situation awareness in the infantry operational environment* (pp. 1753). Alexandria, VA: Army Research Institute.

Hutchins, E. (1995). *Cognition in the wild*. Cambridge Massachusetts: MIT Press.

Klein, G. & Armstrong, A. A. (2005). Critical decision method. In N. A. Stanton, A. Hedge, E. Salas, H. Hendrick, and K. Brookhuis, (Eds.), *Handbook of Human Factors and Ergonomics Methods* (pp. 35.1-35.8). Boca Raton, Florida: CRC Press.

Salas, E., Prince, C., Baker, P.D., & Shrestha, L. (1995). Situation awareness in team performance. *Human Factors, 37*, 123-126.

Salmon, P. M., Stanton, N., Walker, G., & Green, D. (2006). Situation awareness measurement: A review of applicability for C4i environments. *Applied Ergonomics, 37*, 225-238.

Shadbolt, N. R., & Burton, M. (1995). Knowledge elicitation: A systemic approach. In J.R. Wilson and E.N. Corlett (Eds.) *Evaluation of Human Work: A Practical Ergonomics Methodology* (pp. 406-440). London: Taylor & Francis.

Siemieniuch, C.E., & Sinclair, M.A. (2006). Systems Integration. *Applied Ergonomics, 37*, 91-110.

Smith, E.A. (2002). Effects based operations: Applying network centric warfare in peace, crisis, and war. DoD Command and Control Research Program (CCRP) Report, retrieved 05.04.2007 from http://www.dodccrp.org/html3/pubs_download.html

Stanton, N.A., Salmon, P., Walker, G.H, Baber, C. & Jenkins, D. (2005). *Human Factors Methods: A Practical Guide for Engineering and Design.* Aldershot, UK: Ashgate.

Stanton N.A., Stewart, R., Harris, D., Houghton, R.J., Baber, C., McMaster, R., Salmon, P., Hoyle, G., Walker, G.H., Young, M.S., Linsell, M., Dymott, R., & Green, D.A., (2006). Distributed situation awareness in dynamic systems: theoretical development and application of an ergonomics methodology. *Ergonomics, 49*, 1288 – 1311.

Verrall, N.G. (2006). *Multinational experiment 4: UK analysis of the operational-level headquarters organisation.* Salisbury, UK: Defence Science & Technology Laboratory/TL18781 V0.1

Users' mental models of infotainment systems

Tanja Schilling
Humboldt Universität zu Berlin
Germany

Abstract

This article presents the results of two studies concerning the nature of users' mental models of infotainment systems in passenger cars. The content of a mental model formed by a user in a certain situation during the operation of an infotainment system is defined here as the user's expectancies towards the system in that situation. In both studies verbal protocol analysis and *process tracing* were used to obtain the data. The first study found differences between the users' mental models and the conceptual model of an existing infotainment system with regard to menu structure, system reactions, and labelling. Aggregating the obtained data, the users' expectancies towards the course of operation were extracted for several operational tasks and graphic representations of the mental models were derived. Hypotheses were formed referring to those aspects of the mental models which exist independently of the specific interaction concept of the first system. Since these aspects are thought to be independent of a specific interaction concept, they were expected to manifest in the interaction with a second system that is operated using a different interaction concept. The second study verified the mental models and allowed general recommendations for the design of future systems. Those recommendations are planned to be evaluated in a following prototype study.

Introduction

Modern cars offer more and more infotainment features to the driver and passengers. So-called in-car infotainment systems include the functionality from different domains, such as audio/video entertainment, navigation, and telecommunication. Because several formerly separate devices (e.g. radio, navigation system, mobile phone) have been integrated under one sophisticated user interface, the outer appearance and the interaction concept of the system have changed. Instead of separate devices with several buttons each representing a fixed function, the user encounters a single menu-controlled system. Users will not only expect to find the functionality that they are familiar with in the menu, but also to be able to operate the desired functions in the same way as they are used to. The challenge for the designer during the development process of the infotainment system is to map the operation from a formerly separate device onto a system with a new interaction concept. Since technical devices differ in their interaction concepts and since users have different experiences with various technical devices, the expectancies toward the use of an infotainment system will vary among different users. But despite all inter-individual variation, some aspects in the expectations may be the same for most or even all users, because some basic interaction principles are common to different devices.

The aims of the two studies described in this paper are the following: to identify the common aspects of different users' expectancies toward the use of an infotainment system and to verify which of these expectancies exist independently of a certain system's specific interaction concept. Furthermore, the methodology developed to achieve these aims will be presented and explained in detail. This methodology will be applicable during the design of any kind of user interface, especially for the kind of devices which integrate the functionality from several different domains.

Theoretical assumptions

The present research work seeks to identify users' mental models which can be used as a basis for designing any infotainment system's operational paths. Four questions will be addressed to illuminate the major theoretical principles related to this research aim.

Why are users' mental models important for interaction design?
Interacting with different technical devices in the past (infotainment systems and others), users have acquired schematic knowledge of how these devices function and how to use them. According to theory (Dutke, 1994; Johnson-Laird, 1983), users construct mental models about how a specific system should be used from their background knowledge and from cues given by this system's properties. With the help of these mental models of a system, a person will be able to predict and interpret the system's status and reactions and derive the actions necessary to complete a certain task (Kluwe & Haider, 1990).

Knowledge about the users' mental models will enable researchers and system designers to create the paths of operation in a system according to these mental models. Systems that are designed with respect to the users' expectations should permit a more effective task performance and lead to a greater user satisfaction than other systems.

Which part of the users' mental models' content is relevant?
Because of the individual differences in the experience of users one cannot speak of the one mental model for any task. Mental model analysis should therefore aim at determining those expectancies that are shared by a majority of users. Here those parts will be called *interindividually congruent mental models*. Unlike research in the field of shared cognition (Cannon-Bowers & Salas, 2001; Langan-Fox, Code & Langfield-Smith, 2000; Mohammed & Dumville, 2001), the work conducted in this project does not evaluate the congruence of mental models with regard to its role in team work, but rather with the interest of using it for the design of user interfaces.

Even if an expectation is shared by a majority of users it will only be relevant for the design of in-car infotainment systems if this expectation can be applied to infotainment systems in general. Aspects of mental models which can be applied to any in-car infotainment system concern the menu structure and the labelling of menu options. In contrast to these aspects, the mapping between controls and menu will depend largely on a system's specific properties. In the literature (Landauer & Nachbar, 1985; Larson & Czerwinski, 1998; Miller & Remington, 2002; Norman, 1999; Pirolli & Card, 1998; Rauch, Totzke & Krüger, 2004; Resnick & Sanchez, 2004; Totzke, Rauch & Krüger, 2003) an inappropriate menu structure, labelling, and/or mapping seem to be potential sources for users' errors during the operations of a system, when a system's user interface does not match with a user's expectations. Therefore, examining the mismatches between mental model and system using the categories menu structure, labelling, and mapping should help in separating the content of the mental model which is relevant to system design from the irrelevant system-specific aspects.

Which level of abstraction seems adequate?
To analyse mismatches between the users' expectations and the system's user interface, an adequate level of abstraction has to be defined. Every task has to be divided into meaningful units, allowing the researcher to identify those parts of the user's mental representations, which cause him or her to execute a certain action.

In the present research work, the definition of appropriate units roughly follows Norman's definition of menu functions (Norman, 1991). Any sequence that effectuates one of these menu functions counts as a step of operation. This way, the task of dialling a telephone number, for example will be divided into the steps "enter digits", "activate call", and "hang up". This definition fits very well with the claims of action regulation theory (Hacker, 1986; Hacker, 1994). According to this theory, any goal-directed behaviour can be hierarchically structured into subunits. The smallest independent unit of an activity is called an *action*. Each *action* is separated from the next one by its own small subgoal within the task. When all actions have been completed, the main goal of the task is achieved. Further subdividing an action leads to units of operation that are regulated on the skill-based level (Rasmussen, 1983) and are not planned deliberately.

Unitising operational activities into actions permits the analysis of mental models with regard to their relevance to meaningful units of operational behaviour and to identify which parts of the mental model cause the user to execute a certain step of operation.

How can mental models be measured adequately?
An adequate methodology has to be used to gain information about mental models and describe them in a way suitable for user interface design. The above mentioned theoretical concepts imply several conditions a suitable methodology will have to meet. The methodology should:

1. measure mental models in an authentic setting,
2. capture the mental models in adequate units,
3. exclude those aspects which are irrelevant for selecting an action, i.e. filter the skill-based/"unconscious" errors/mismatches,
4. detect any mismatches between the mental model and the user interface,

5. analyse the nature/content of any mismatches,
6. identify congruent expectations, and represent them graphically, and
7. extract the system-independent aspects.

Method

Two studies were conducted. The first one identified users' interindividually congruent mental models for one specific system and extracted the system-independent aspects. The second one verified the system-independent aspects for a system with a different interaction concept. For this purpose the mental models were elicited in both studies and compared to the conceptual model of each of the two systems. A *process tracing* methodology was developed to extract mental models and to identify the congruent and system-independent aspects.

Instantiating the conceptual model

For the two studies, two real infotainment systems from serial production were selected. The two systems had very similar functions but a different user interface. A conceptual model was derived for both systems through system and document analysis. For each investigated task the conceptual model outlined the path of operation, and subdivided it into the actions that are required to solve the task as described above. For each task, the path of operation was depicted graphically in a state-action-diagram.

Design and procedure

Study 1

Thirty-four employees of a German car manufacturer, averaging 42.2 years of age (sd=8.47), participated in the first study. All participants had a technical profession. None of them had ever used the infotainment system under investigation before and nobody had any experience with the design of user interfaces.

The infotainment system used in Study 1 is operated by a set of hardkeys, softkeys and a central control (eight-way-arrow-button with confirmation-button) for operating the menu. All controls and the display are integrated in one device located in the centre console of the car.

The aim of the study was to identify as many deviations between the users' mental models and the system's conceptual model as possible. Therefore, data were collected for a total of 39 typical tasks from the applications navigation, audio and telephone. To limit the time for each participant's session, the tasks were divided into three sets, each set including about the same total amount of actions required to solve the tasks. Some tasks were common to two or to all three sets of tasks. Every participant worked on one set, thus 15 to 17 tasks. Interindividually congruent and system-independent aspects of the users' expectations were extracted using the coding scheme described in the next subchapter ("obtaining the data using process tracing").

Study 2
Twenty participants took part in Study 2. As in the proceeding study, all participants were employees of the same German car manufacturer. None of them had participated in Study 1, but all of them had a very similar professional background, average age (m=42.2; sd=6.24), and experience with infotainment systems as the participants of the first study. As in Study 1, none of the participants had ever used the infotainment system under investigation before and nobody had experience in user interface design.

The infotainment system used in Study 2 is operated by a central control for menu operation and a few hardkeys. Unlike the first system, display and controls of the second system were not integrated in one device. The display was located in the centre console, but at a higher position than the first system's display. The most important controls were located in the centre armrest.

On the basis of the results in Study 1, 20 tasks were selected to verify the users' assumedly system-independent expectations. For these 20 tasks, some of the required steps of operation had emerged from Study 1 as potentially deviating from the users' system-independent expectations. Others were expected to fulfil the users' system-independent expectations better than system 1. Detailed predictions were formed for all required steps of operation within the 20 tasks used in Study 2.

111 predictions were made because the path of operation in system 1 was in line with the users' expectations and was implemented in the same way in system 2. No deviation was predicted in these cases for system 2.

Two predictions were made because the steps of operation were implemented in system 2 in the same way as in system 1 and had shown to deviate from the majority's mental model in Study 1. Therefore, it was assumed that, as the same interindividually congruent expectations as in system 1 would be true also for these required actions, the same mismatches as in system 1 would also occur in system 2.

Fourteen predictions were made because the corresponding steps of operation are implemented in system 2 somewhat differently from the way they are implemented in system 1. The second system's conceptual model also deviated from the users' expectancies. It was predicted, that mismatches would occur but that these mismatches would be different from the ones in system 1.

Eleven predictions referred to steps of operation that are implemented according to the users' expectations in system 2, but not in system 1. Therefore, no mismatches were predicted to occur for these steps of operation.

Finally, eight predictions referred to steps of operation which were implemented differently in system 2 than in system 1. They did not cause any mistakes in system 1, but were expected to cause mistakes in system 2, because the second system's conceptual model deviated from the majority's mental model.

Obtaining the data using process tracing

This section describes the developed methodology with respect to the conditions set out earlier in this article. To measure the mental models in a most realistic setting (condition no. 1), participants were observed while operating real infotainment systems, positioned in a set-up which imitated a real car's interior. The study focused on typical tasks from the most important applications: navigation, audio functionality and telecommunication. A natural order of tasks was chosen.

Condition no. 2: in both studies the participants were asked to think aloud while solving tasks. Verbal protocols and logfiles of all operations were recorded. Verbalisations were transcribed and integrated with the actions into one complete chronological report of all events during the operation. This method of *process tracing* has been used before to analyse operators' behaviour in interaction with complex systems (Bainbridge, Lenior, & van der Schaaf, 1993; Ericsson & Simon, 1993; Patrick, Gregov, Halliday, & O'Reilly, 1999). The experimental arrangement used in studies 1 and 2 is illustrated in figure 1.

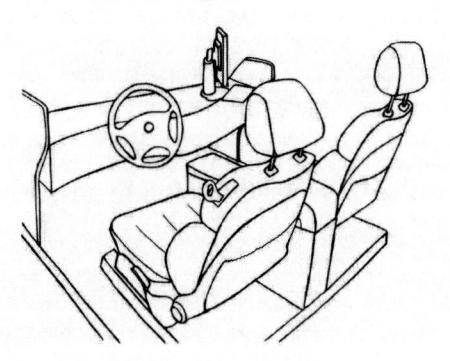

Figure 1. Experimental arrangement used in studies 1 and 2

In each participant's report, seven steps of quantitative and qualitative analysis were conducted to capture the relevant content of the mental models in adequate units.

Step 1: for each task every action executed by the person was marked in the protocol. All verbalisations were associated with the corresponding action. All required actions were marked and any unneeded additional actions were ascribed to the corresponding required action.

Step 2: on the basis of the corresponding verbalisations, every action was categorised as either having been executed intentionally or not (condition no. 3). Unneeded actions which resulted from deficits in attention, perception, or manual dexterity were regarded as irrelevant for the qualitative analysis of the mental models and were therefore filtered. This kind of error has been called *slips* and *lapses* (Reason, 1990). An intentional action could be classified a) as a correct action matching the one required by the system's interface, resulting from a mental model matching the system's conceptual model or b) as a false action resulting from a mental model deviating from the system's conceptual model or c) as trial and error behaviour resulting from the lack of a specific mental model.

Step 3: the number of actions executed intentionally in order to complete the required action was summed up for every required action. All required actions where the participants' incorrect expectations lead to an average of three or more actions being executed before the required action was completed were identified. They mark the instances where on the average users executed a first inappropriate action, then a second inappropriate action to correct the first one and finally a third and correct action fulfilling the next required step. These instances will be referred to as *critical actions* in the following because they hint at major deviations between mental and conceptual models (condition no. 4).

Step 4: for every critical action, each participant's first intentional action and the corresponding part of the verbal protocol were analysed with regard to the underlying mental model. The content of each deviating mental model was identified by assessing from the participant's comments which action this user had expected instead of the one required by the system (condition no. 5).

Step 5: for every critical action, frequencies for the identified mental models were counted. Deviating mental models shared by more than 50% of the users were identified as *deviating mental models of high interindividual congruence*. Mental models shared by 25% to 50% of the users were identified as *deviating mental models of medium interindividual congruence*. Mental models shared by less than 25% of the users were identified as *deviating mental models of low or no interindividual congruence*.

Step 6: all deviations from the conceptual model were represented graphically in the state-action-diagrams which up to this point represented only the conceptual model. This way the deviations could be illustrated visually (condition no. 6).

Step 7: all mental models of high and medium interindividual congruence were analysed with regard to the system properties that they referred to. They either referred to the menu structure, the labelling of menu options, or the mapping between controls and menu. Mental models referring to the menu structure, or the labelling of menu options were classified as system-independent expectations, whereas mental models referring to the mapping between controls and menu were classified as either system-specific or system-independent, depending on their content (condition no. 7).

Results

This section will report the major results of both studies and detailed results for two tasks exemplarily for both studies.

Study 1

In total, all 39 tasks consisted of 159 required actions. For the 39 tasks all actions carried out by the participants totalled a sum of 6,498.

Step 2 of the analysis lead to the classification of all actions according to whether they had been executed intentionally or not. They were classified as shown in table 1.

Table 1. Classification of all executed actions, studies 1 and 2

Classified as	Study 1 sum	perc.	Study 2 sum	perc.
Correct actions (appropriate mental model)	2162	33.3%	2479	33.6%
Intentionally executed, incorrect actions (specific, deviating mental model)	777	12%	1693	22.3%
Trial and error behaviour (lack of a specific mental model)	2275	35%	1356	17.8%
Attention, perception and dexterity deficits	543	8.4%	404	5.3%
Actions executed intentionally outside of the required tasks, and non-classifiable	741	11.4%	1693	22.3%

Step 3 of the analysis identified major deviations between the users' expectations and the implemented path of operation. Out of the 39 tasks, only 19 included required actions, not matching with the users' expectations. Out of the total of 159 required actions, 30 actions evolved as critical, requiring each an average of at least 3 intentional actions to be completed.

Steps 4 and 5 of the analysis output the frequencies for the users' expectations deviating from the implemented critical required actions. It thus permitted to identify which contents of the expectation are shared by a majority of the users. For 9 of the critical actions, more than 50% of the users shared the same mental model (high interindividual congruence) deviating from the conceptual model. For 12 of the critical actions, 25% to 50% of the users shared the same mental model (medium interindividual congruence). For the remaining nine of the critical actions, only low interindividual congruence existed. Here, either less than 25% of the users shared the same expectation, or most of the users had no specific expectation at all (trial and error behaviour).

Step 6 of the analysis lead to the graphical representation of the mental models as state-action-diagrams. Figures 2 and 3 show each an example of these depictions for a deviating majority model.

The first example (figure 2) shows the deviation between the users' mental models and the system's conceptual model for the task of setting the current radio station to a desired preset position. In order to do so, the user had to first open the preset menu, then manoeuvre the cursor to the desired preset position, and finally confirm the desired preset position via a long press on the confirmation button of the central control (labelled "ok"). Alternatively, the user could execute a long press on the hardkey corresponding to the desired preset position.

Of the eleven users working on this task, five users used the preset menu, four users used the preset hardkey, and two users tried both paths, one after the other. Counting all actions that were executed for this required action, all participants executed an average of 10.8 actions before either successfully terminating the task or giving up.

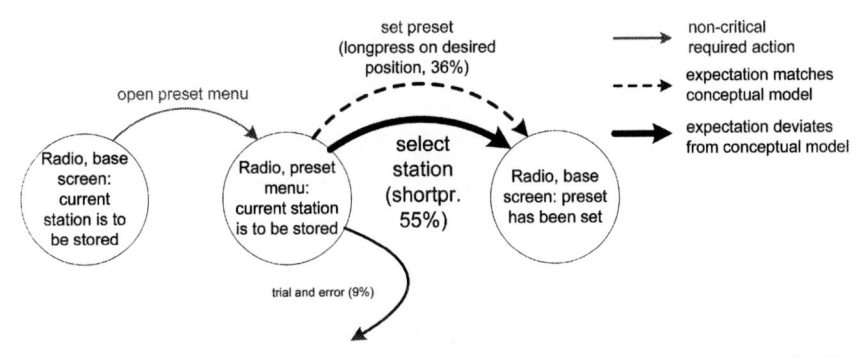

Figure 2. System 1: mental and conceptual models for the task of setting a designated radio station as a preset

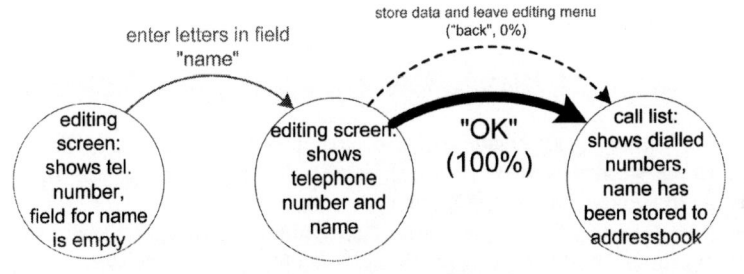

Figure 3. System 1: mental and conceptual models for the last two required actions of the task of permanently storing a phone number to the address book

As shown in the state-action-diagram in figure 2, only 36.4% of the users managed to confirm the desired preset position via long press in either of the two possible ways. Another 9.1% of the users, not having a specific mental model of how to confirm the desired preset position, showed trial and error behaviour. 54.5% of the users expected to confirm the preset position via a short press on either the confirmation button while the desired position was marked in the preset menu or by a short press on the hardkey corresponding to the desired preset position. Since more than 50% of the users expected to perform the same action, this expectation was identified as a mental model of high interindividual congruence.

The second example (figure 3) shows the way in which the users' mental models deviated from the system's conceptual model for the task of permanently storing a phone number contained in a call list to the system's address book. In order to do so, the user had to first open the call list, then position the cursor on the number to be stored, continue by starting the storing process, then enter the name in the editing screen, and finally terminate the storing process and leave the editing screen by pressing the softkey "back". Only the last two actions are depicted in figure 3. To complete the last required action of terminating the storing process users performed an average of 7.27 actions.

As shown in figure 3, 100% (n=11) of the users expected to be able to terminate the storing process by pressing the confirmation button ("ok"). None of the users chose the correct softkey labelled "back". Since all of the users expected an action different from the one required by the system and since they all expected the same action, this deviation was also identified as a mental model of high interindividual congruence.

Finally, step 7 analysed the system-independent aspects of the previously identified expectations. Both highly congruent mental models mentioned in the two examples were caused by misleading menu labels. In the first example, the desired function was available but hidden to the users because no label existed indicating the function of the key when pressed for a longer time interval. In the second example, the desired function was also available, but hidden under an inadequate label ("back"). In both cases the function was looked for but could not be found by the user. Also, the majority's mental model referred to the label of the function which could be used in any infotainment system regardless of its interface's specific properties. Both deviations between mental and conceptual model were thus identified as system-independent and therefore an attempt was made to verify them in Study 2.

Study 2

For the task of setting a radio station to a desired preset position, the paths of operation were the same in systems 1 and 2. It was thus predicted that the same deviation between mental and conceptual model as had become evident in system 1 would also occur in system 2. This means that the action of confirming the desired preset position (via a long press) was predicted to evolve as a critical action after step 3 of the analysis. Instead of storing the current station as a preset to the designated position, users were expected to commit the error of activating the station on which they had positioned the cursor within the preset menu by a short press on the central control element. Moreover, since the percentage was estimated to be at least 50%, this deviating expectation was prognosticated to turn out as a mental model of high interindividual congruence after step 5.

For the task of storing a telephone number permanently from a call list to the address book, system 2 used a different path of operation than system 1. In system 2, the menu option "OK" is available after entering the name and should be used to terminate the storing process. Since in system 1 all users had expected this function to be labelled "OK", it was assumed that users in system 2 would have no problems terminating the storing process. No deviation between mental model and conceptual model was predicted for system 2. This means that the action of terminating the storing process by confirming "OK" in the menu was predicted not to turn out as a critical action in Study 2.

In total, all 20 tasks used in Study 2 included 146 required actions. For these 20 tasks all actions carried out by the participants totalled a sum of 7605. In step two of the analysis, these actions were classified as shown in table 1.

In step 3, major deviations between mental and conceptual models were found for 13 of the 20 tasks. Of the 146 required actions, 28 evolved as critical, again with regard to the three-action threshold. For the first example of confirming the designated preset position, users performed an average of 5.1 actions to complete the required action. Thus this required action did evolve as critical as had been predicted on the basis of the results in Study 1. The conceptual model for this task's path of operation deviates from the users' expectations. For the second example of terminating the storing process, users performed an average of 1.2 actions to complete the required action. Thus this action did not turn out as critical, as had been predicted. The conceptual model of system 2 is in line with the users' expectations.

Step 5 identified deviating mental models of high interindividual congruence for six required actions, mental models of medium interindividual congruence for 11 required actions, and mental models of low or no interindividual congruence for another 11 of the 28 critical actions.

Figures 4 and 5 show the graphical depiction of mental and conceptual models for the tasks of setting a radio station as preset and storing a telephone number for system 2.

As shown in figure 4, 76.5% of the users expected to be able to confirm the designated preset position in the preset menu via a short confirmation of the central control. Instead, this is how the highlighted radio station is activated. 5.9% of the participants had no specific mental model (trial and error behaviour) and 17.6% had an expectation in line with the conceptual model. The expectation of a short confirmation was identified as an interindividually highly congruent mental model, as had been predicted on the basis of the results in Study 1. It was thus verified as a system-independent expectation.

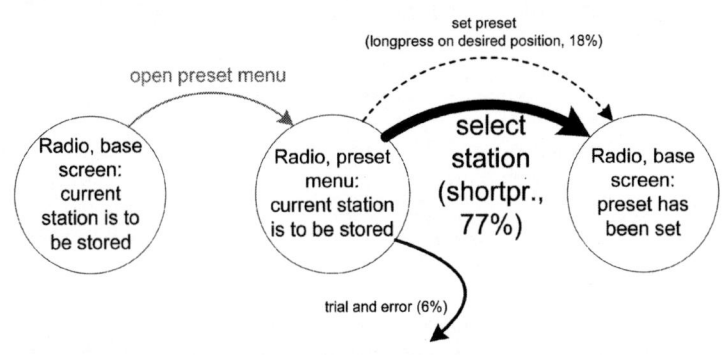

Figure 4. System 2: Mental and conceptual models for the task of setting a designated radio station as a preset

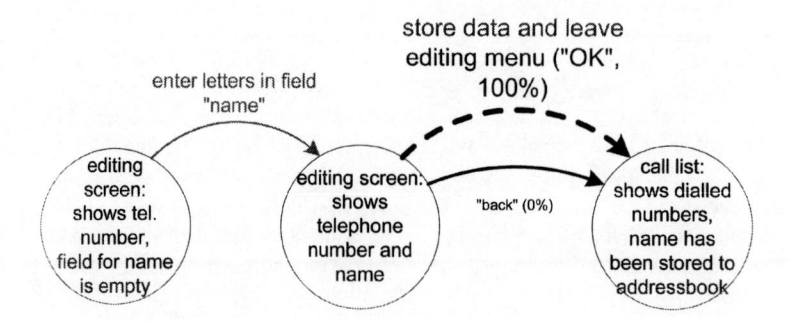

Figure 5. System 2: Mental and conceptual models for the last two required actions of the task of permanently storing a phone number to the address book

Figure 5 shows that no deviation between the users' expectations and the system's conceptual model occurred for the storing task. Again, only the last two required actions are shown. The expectation that OK will terminate the storing process was thus confirmed as system-independent..

Summary of results

For 126 of the 146 required actions in system 2 the users' expectations were predicted correctly. For eight required actions the predictions of a specific deviating mental model were only partly fulfilled. For twelve required actions the predictions about the nature of the users' mental models were incorrect: Three times the majority's mental model was predicted to deviate from the conceptual model, but turned out to be in line with it. Nine times, te opposite was the case. These predictions about user behaviour which turned out as not being supported by the data of Study 2, however permitted conclusions about the mental models. All assumed mental models which turned out to be in deed system-independent as confirmed by the results of Study 2, lead to a set of rules that should be respected as guidelines when designing the user interface of an infotainment system.

Discussion and future prospects

The two presented studies intended to extract and verify users' mental models of how to operate an infotainment system. It is shown by the results of these studies that users' behaviour and mistakes during the operation of such a system can be predicted on the basis of the content of users' expectations in a certain situation and the nature of the conceptual model of this system. The results also show on the one hand that the two systems, as they are, contain many paths of operation that are very much in line with the users' expectations. On the other hand they show that even in existing fully developed infotainment systems, systematic deviations from users' mental models can be found.

The methodology used in these studies, even though time consuming and cumbersome, provides a useful and appropriate way to extract the relevant content of the users' expectations from the data. Unlike other usability methods, it permitted identifying the specific aspects of the nature of users' expectations as emerging in a realistic setting during the operation of an infotainment system.

Since paths of operation which are in line with the users' mental models will lead to a better user performance than paths of operation that deviate from the mental model, predicting the user behaviour for any kind of infotainment system on the basis of the mental models found in these studies will be helpful for the design of the system's user interface. Unnecessary actions executed by the user because of a mental model which differs from the system's path of operation can be avoided.

To find more evidence for this presumption, a third study is planned in which a prototype will be used to evaluate paths of operation which eliminate the deviations between mental model and conceptual model as they were found in the reported two studies. The third study will compare performance measures, perceived task difficulty and user satisfaction for two versions of this prototype, one version containing deviations and one without deviations.

References

Bainbridge, L., Lenior, T.M.J., & Van der Schaaf, T.W. (1993). Cognitive processes in complex tasks: Introduction and discussion. *Ergonomics, 36,* 1273-1279.
Cannon-Bowers, J.A. & Salas, E. (2001). Reflections on shared cognition. *Journal of Organizational Behavior, 22,* 195-202.
Dutke, S. (1994). *Mentale Modelle: Konstrukte des Wissens und Verstehens.* Stuttgart: Verlag für Angewandte Psychologie.
Ericsson, H. A. & Simon, H. A. (1993). *Protocol analysis: Verbal protocols as data.* Cambridge, MA: MIT Press.
Hacker, W. (1986). *Arbeitspsychologie.* Berlin: VEB Deutscher Verlag der Wissenschaften.
Hacker, W. (1994). Arbeits- und organisationspsychologische Grundlagen der Software-Ergonomie. In E. Eberleh, H. Oberquelle, and R. Oppermann (Eds.), *Einführung in die Software-Ergonomie* (pp. 53-93). Berlin: De Gryuter.
Johnson-Laird, P.N. (1983). *Mental Models.* Cambridge: University Press.
Kluwe, R.H. & Haider, H. (1990). Modelle zur internen Repräsentation komplexer technischer Systeme. *Sprache & Kognition, 9,* 173-192.
Landauer, T.K. & Nachbar, D.W. (1985). Selection from alphabetic and numeric menu trees using a touch screen: Breadth, depth, and width. In *Proceedings of CHI '85 Human Factors in Computing Systems* (pp. 73-78).
Langan-Fox, J., Code, S., & Langfield-Smith, K. (2000). Team mental models: Techniques, methods, and analytical processes. *Human Factors, 42,* 242-271.
Larson, K. & Czerwinski, M. (1998). Web page design: Implications of memory, structure and scent for informations retrieval. In *Proceedings of CHI 98* (pp. 25-32). New York, NY: ACM.
Miller, C.S. & Remington, R.W. (2002). Effects of structure and label ambiguity on information navigation. *Proceedings of CHI 2002: Human Factors in Computing Systems* Retrieved 01.05.2007 from http://facweb.cs.depaul.edu/cmiller/eval/chi2002.pdf

Mohammed, S. & Dumville, B.C. (2001). Team mental models in a knowledge framework: Expanding theory and measurement across disciplinary boundaries. *Journal of Organizational Behavior, 22,* 89-106.

Norman, D.A. (1999). *The psychology of everyday things.* New York: Basic Books.

Norman, K.L. (1991). *The psychology of menu selection: Designing cognitive control at the human/computer interface.* Norwod, NJ: Ablex Publishing Corporation.

Patrick, J., Gregov, A.D., Halliday, J., & O'Reilly, S. (1999). Analysing operator's diagnostic reasoning during multiple events. *Ergonomics, 42,* 493-515.

Pirolli, P. & Card, S.K. (1998). Information foraging models of browsers for very large document spaces. In *Proceedings of the Advanced Visual Interfaces Workshop, AVI '98* (pp. 83-93).

Rasmussen, J. (1983). Skills, rules, and knowledge: Signals, signs, and symbols and other distinctions in human performance models. *IEEE Transactions on Man, System, and Cybernetics, SMC-13,* 257-266.

Rauch, N., Totzke, I., & Krüger, H.-P. (2004). Kompetenzerwerb für Fahrerinformationssysteme: Bedeutung von Bedienkontext und Menüstruktur. In *Integrierte Sicherheit und Fahrerassistenzsysteme* (pp. 303-322). Düsseldorf, Germany: VDI-Verlag.

Reason, J. (1990). *Human Error.* Cambridge: Cambridge University Press.

Resnick, M.L. & Sanchez, J. (2004). Effects of organizational scheme and labelling on task-performance in product-centered and user-centered retail web sites. *Human Factors, 46,* 104-117.

Totzke, I., Rauch, N., & Krüger, H.-P. (2003). Kompetenzerwerb und Struktur von Menüsystemen im Fahrzeug: "Breiter ist besser?". In C. Steffens, M. Thüring, and L. Urbas (Eds.), *Entwerfen und Gestalten: 5. Berliner Werkstatt Mensch-Maschine-Systeme* (pp. 226-249). Düsseldorf, Germany: VDI-Verlag.

Automation

hospital pharmacy automation

In D. de Waard, G.R.J. Hockey, P. Nickel, and K.A. Brookhuis (Eds.) (2007), *Human Factors Issues in Complex System Performance* (pp. 305). Maastricht, the Netherlands: Shaker Publishing.

A comparison of HEART and FMEA risk assessment results in evaluating an automated dispensing system in hospital pharmacy

Tabassum Jafri[1], Melinda Lyons[1], Shelly Jeffcott[2], James Ward[1], & John Clarkson[1]
[1]Cambridge University, Cambridge, UK
[2]Monash University, Melbourne, Australia

Abstract

Automation has been advocated by the Audit Commission (2001) in being instrumental in improving patient safety because it minimises human practitioner error, specifically within the pharmacy. Several automated dispensing systems have been or are in the process of being installed across the National Health Service (NHS). However, there seems to be a lack of literature published evaluating the vulnerabilities, problems and risks of introducing such systems into the complex, and often unpredictable, domain of healthcare. This paper presents an exploratory case study examining the impact of a new automated dispensing robot on the delivery of medicines to patients within a district general hospital. Two established risk assessment methods were used to analyse and compare the pre and post automated situations for one task: the Failure Mode and Effects Analysis (FMEA) and the Human Error Assessment and Reduction Technique (HEART). Low levels of risk were observed using the methods in both pre- and post-automated situations. However, a four-fold reduction was observed in risk with FMEA after automation had been implemented. HEART revealed a slight increase in risk after implementation, reflecting user-interface issues. Further research including all tasks of the dispensing process is required to assess the risk of automation in this domain of healthcare.

Introduction

Automation reduces the human contribution to certain stages of the dispensing process, namely the picking of medicines from shelves (Fitzpatrick, 2005). Hospital pharmacies are introducing automated dispensing systems because of perceived advantages of reduction in dispensing errors, distribution incidents, faster turn-around times for prescriptions, stock control and convenient and safer out of hours supply (Whittlesea, 2004; see Figures 1 and 2).

Automated dispensing has been associated with a 16% reduction in dispensing errors at the final checking stage by a pharmacist before medicines are given to patients (Fitzpatrick, 2005). Similarly Dean and Barber (2006) reported a drop in error at the final checking stage from 2.7% before automation to 0.9% after automation. There is a lack of literature exploring potential risks introduced by automation using engineering or human reliability risk assessment methods. This study uses two techniques to explore risk with hospital pharmacy dispensing systems.

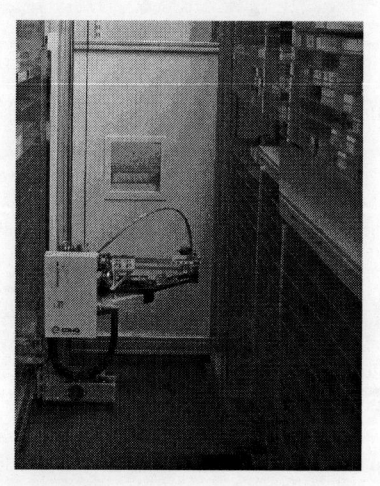

Figure 1. Automated dispensing robot

Figure 2. Hospital pharmacy dispensary showing dispensing terminal with delivery chutes of the automated system

Method

Risk assessment began with a detailed task analysis of the dispensing process. This was primarily developed from observations of how dispensing was done and literature descriptions of the dispensing process (Dean and Barber 2006). The research pharmacist (TJ) spent three one-hour sessions shadowing pharmacy staff and keeping a log of the tasks involved. The method was in-keeping with Kirwan and Ainsworth (1992) observational method. The completed task analysis was then confirmed with the dispensary manager for validation purposes. The task analysis served to focus attention on the hospital dispensing activities that changed the most due to automation i.e. tasks that were made redundant or replaced with a completely new task. A number of different tasks were identified in the dispensing process, however in this exploratory study for comparison the task of picking medicines done by staff in the pre-automated situations and done by the robot in the post-automated situation was risk assessed, using Failure Mode Effects Analysis (FMEA) as described by McDermott et al. (1996) and Human Error Assessment and Reduction Technique (HEART) as reported by Williams (1992). A brief description of these tools as applied in the present study follows below:

FMEA

FMEA considers the likelihood, impact and detectability of failure to give a risk priority number for each task.

- Failure causes and consequences were first considered for the one task.
- Likelihood, impact and detectability of failure were ascribed a rating ranging from 1 to 10
- These were then multiplied to give a risk priority number for the task

HEART

HEART provides an indication of the likelihood of task failure as a result of human reliability issues.

- The first stage of HEART was to select a task description from a list of available generic task descriptions by Williams (1992) that suited picking of medicines the most. Task G was chosen:
   Completely familiar, well-designed, highly practised, routine task occurring several times per hour, performed to highest possible standards by highly motivated, trained and experienced persons, totally aware of implications of failure, with time to correct potential error, but without the benefit of significant job aids. This task is mission orientated and could involve a great many discrete elements or actions, but would normally only involve one basic activity.
- From a list of Error Producing Conditions (EPCs), three likely EPCs for the task were selected and the proportion of the effect on the task was assigned by the researcher from a range of 0 to 1

- Mathematical manipulation was used to derive the assessed effect of each condition and then finally the combined effect of the EPCs and task generic characteristics on the likelihood of task failure

Results

Table 1 shows the results of the FMEA carried out for both the automated and non-automated picking of medicine in dispensing. A reduction in the risk priority number is observed after automation of this task. The risk assessment results of HEART are presented in Table 2. A slight increase in risk is observed as a result of automation but this is not significant.

Table 1. FMEA assessment for non-automated and automated dispensing

Task	Failure Mode	Potential causes	Potential consequences	Likelihood (1-10)	Impact (1-10)	Detectability (10-1)	Risk Priority Number (1-1000)
Non-automated: Pick medicine	Incorrect medicine picked	Error made in selection	Wrong medicine selected	4	8	2	64
Automated: Robot picks medicine	Incorrect medicine picked	Error made in selection	Wrong medicine selected	1	8	2	16

Table 2. HEART assessment for non-automated and automated dispensing

Factor	Total HEART effect	Proportion of effect (0-1)	Assessed effect	Likelihood of failure
Non-automated dispensing:				0.075
Unfamiliarity with a situation which is potentially important but which only occurs infrequently or which is novel	X17	0.4	(17-1)x0.4+1 = 7.4	
Shortage of time available for error detection and correction	X11	0.8	(11-1)x0.8+1 = 9	
Poor, ambiguous or ill-matched system feedback	X4	0.6	(4-1)x0.6+1 = 2.8	
Automated dispensing:				0.1
Unfamiliarity with a situation which is potentially important but which only occurs infrequently or which is novel	X17	0.4	(17-1)x0.4+1 = 7.4	
Shortage of time available for error detection and correction	X11	0.8	(11-1)x0.8+1 = 9	
A mismatch between an operator's model of the world and that imagined by the designer	X8	0.4	(8-1)x0.4+1 = 3.8	

Discussion

The aim of this study was to explore risk in automated hospital dispensing systems using two different risk assessment techniques. Low levels of risk are observed in the results for both FMEA and HEART in both the automated and non-automated situations. This may be due to differing approaches to risk taken by the tools, with HEART being more human-based in comparison to FMEA. It is important to note that as a method HEART is typically used to complement other technical risk assessment methods as it focuses on identification of human error in tasks. Therefore its findings tend to form part of a wider risk assessment process.

A four-fold reduction in the risk of picking the wrong medicine was observed with automation in the FMEA analysis. This is mainly due to barcode identification and pack size recognition, which removes confusion based on look-alike packaging and sound-alike medicines in non-automated picking. In contrast, a small difference is observed between the pre and post automated situations with HEART analysis of task failure, with picking medicines without automation being slightly more favourable. This may be attributable to HEART's consideration of design errors in the automated system and their effect on the working practice of staff. For example, the introduction of trolleys under ward boxes for ward box picking to catch medicines as they come down the delivery chute or keeping dispensing trays close to the chute to prevent medicines bouncing off the bench and falling on the floor. This is particularly important for large bulky medicines such as a box of glass ampoules for injection.

Dispensing errors according to Cina et al. (2006) arise from a dispensing process that relies exclusively on repetitive human inspection, which is subject to human fatigue. It is difficult for pharmacists to maintain vigilance and detect all errors that occur in a high workload environment with staff shortages. Automation may offer a reduction in picking the wrong medicine by barcode recognition and pack size. However, this does not necessarily mean that the entire dispensing process is safer, as it relies on the correct selection of medicine at the terminal by the operator in the first place.

Each dispensing task should be risk assessed to determine whether the risk observed in tasks in isolation are mitigated when they are considered as part of the process. This will be undertaken in the future with stakeholder engagement to allow for a careful evaluation of the system as "automated dispensing is not error free" (Coleman, 2004, p. 250) and improve the validity of the results.

Conclusion

It has been observed that calculating risk exemplarily for one task in the dispensing process depends upon the method employed. It is therefore important to select a risk assessment tool that captures the key features of the task or process being risk assessed. Using more than one tool can offer a greater understanding of risk, especially when different outcomes are observed. Human reliability methods are particularly relevant in identifying error producing conditions in an organisation and observe 'drift' towards a less safety conscience organisation. Further risk assessment of the dispensing process will help develop a thorough understanding of risk arising in pharmacy, with or without automation, to improve medication safety that will undoubtedly have knock on effects on increasing patient safety.

References

Audit Commission (2001). *A Spoonful of Sugar*. London, UK: Audit Commission Publications. Retrieved 29.03.2007 from http://www.audit-commission.gov.uk/Products/NATIONAL-REPORT/E83C8921-6CEA-4b2c-83E7-F80954A80F85/nrspoonfulsugar.pdf.

Cina, J., Gandhi, T.K., Churchill, W., Fanikos, J., McCrea, M., Rothschild, J.M., Featherstone, E., Keohane, C., Bates, D.W., & Poon, E.G. (2006). How many hospital pharmacy medication dispensing errors go undetected? *Joint Commission Journal on Quality and Patient Safety, 32*, 73-79.

Coleman, B. (2004). Hospital Pharmacy Staff Attitudes Towards Automated Dispensing Before and After Implementation. *Hospital Pharmacist, 11*, 248-251.

Dean, B. & Barber, N. (2006). *Evaluation of the Pack Picker Automated Dispensing Machine at Charing Cross Hospital*. London, UK: The School of Pharmacy Publication.

Fitzpatrick, R. (2005). Evaluation of an Automated Dispensing System in a Hospital Pharmacy Dispensary. *Pharmaceutical Journal, 274*, 763-765.

Kirwan, B., & Ainsworth, L.K. (1992). *A Guide to Task Analysis*. London, UK: Taylor and Francis.

McDermott, R.E., Raymond, J.M, & Beauregard, M.R. (1996). *The Basics of FMEA*. New York, USA: Productivity Press.

Whittlesea, C. (2004). Automated Dispensing. *Hospital Pharmacist, 11*, 283-285.

Williams, J. (1992). *A User Manual for the HEART – Human Reliability Assessment Method* (Report Number C2547-1.001). Cheshire, UK: DNV Technica Ltd.

Making it quantitative: early phases of development of a new taxonomy for levels of automation

Michela Terenzi, Marco Camilli, & Francesco Di Nocera
University of Rome "La Sapienza"
Italy

Abstract

The classic approach to the concept of "Level Of Automation" (LOA) is qualitative in nature: it simply describes the trading of system control between humans and computers. Since Sheridan's seminal work many taxonomies have been proposed, but they are all domain- and task-dependent. This makes it difficult to compare results from different studies. A different approach (that will eventually allow defining LOA quantitatively) has been introduced here. The basic idea was to characterise LOA in terms of number of processes traded by humans and machines. For example, at the information-acquisition level, LOA may be defined in terms of number of features of an object that has to be identified. Automation providing reliable information on 1 out of 4 possible features was set at LOA=.25, whereas for a system providing aid on 2 out of 4 features LOA=.50. In order to start a research program aimed at devising a general model, two experiments were run on 36 participants who were requested to perform a visual search task. Three LOA were tested: 0 (manual), .25 (intermediate), and .50 (high). These first studies were a necessary step in order to study the mathematical relation between LOA and human performance.

Introduction

In general, implementing automation support in a complex system implies the introduction an additional element that needs to be managed: humans and automation working together pose several problems in terms of authority for decision and action. As reported by Miller and Parasuraman (2007), in order to discuss alternative forms of automation, it is helpful to have a scheme for characterising roles and responsibilities. Such characterisations have been often made in terms of levels of automation (LOA) that define a spectrum of possible relationships ranging from full human to full automation control.

However, the classic approach to the concept of LOA is qualitative in nature: it simply describes the trading of system control between humans and computers. For example, the 10-point scale proposed in Sheridan's seminal work (Sheridan & Verplank, 1978) only describes the degree of human (or machine) involvement in system control. Consequently, it expresses the level of computer aiding to the human

In D. de Waard, G.R.J. Hockey, P. Nickel, and K.A. Brookhuis (Eds.) (2007), *Human Factors Issues in Complex System Performance* (pp. 313 - 323). Maastricht, the Netherlands: Shaker Publishing.

(e.g. showing all alternatives vs. narrowing alternatives). Parasuraman, Sheridan, and Wickens (2000) extended this approach including it within a four stage information-processing model, thus providing a framework to better designing automated systems. Albeit this qualitative approach is useful for function allocation in the design phase, a more formal model would be necessary for experimentation. Indeed, it is currently impossible to compare results from different studies, because each author characterises LOA in different ways.

To our knowledge, the only attempt to develop a universal LOA measure was made by Wei, Macwan, and Wieringa (1998), who proposed a model to quantify what they called "degree of automation" (DofA). Using this model, they showed that, when DofA increases above a certain threshold, performance improvements become very small. The most important aspect of this approach is its focus on the quantification of LOA, and the attempt to provide *descriptive model* (a representation of how humans and automation *actually* work) as opposed to a *normative model* (a representation of how humans and automation *should* work, see Sheridan, 2002).

The concept of DofA is very appealing, but two aspects of the model significantly limit its use. First, it is based on a detailed task definition, meaning that a lot of work has to be done to compute parameters and weightings. Second, it needs to include a workload parameter that is difficult to estimate prior experimentation, so that a task load measure is used instead. Both reasons might be the cause that -to date- the DofA approach has not gained much support in the field.

With that in mind, in the present paper, LOA has been defined in terms of the *amount* of information traded by humans and machines. For example, at the information-acquisition level, LOA may be defined in terms of number of features of an object that has to be identified. Consequently, automation providing reliable information about 1 out of 4 possible features has LOA equal to .25, whereas for a system providing specific aid about 2 out of 4 features, LOA is equal to .50. This might seem a very simple-minded model. Indeed, the point is that more complicated models might be not as useful as a simple one. Only accounting for the number of features (or alternatives, in case of a decision-making process) has its advantages: 1) it can be easily applied to any type of task, 2) it can be applied to design experiments as well as to compare results of experiments that have already been carried out, and 3) does not require complex calculations.

Of course, the scheme introduced here is not a normative model of human-automation interaction. This is rather a (basis for a) descriptive model aimed at explaining the effects of automation on human performance.

Study 1

Method

Subjects
Twenty students (mean age = 25.3, SD = 3.0, 10 females) volunteered in this study. All participants were right-handed, with normal or corrected to normal sight. No cases of Daltonism were reported.

Stimuli
Sixty-four digital rectangular shapes were used as stimuli. Shapes were created by manipulating three features: colour, texture and orientation. Each feature was implemented in four different alternatives. Particularly, colour was implemented as red / blue / black / green; texture was implemented as horizontal / vertical / right-tilted / left-tilted stripes; orientation was implemented as vertical / horizontal / right-tilted / left-tilted shapes. This manipulation allowed obtaining a set of stimuli that presented all combination of the given characteristics.

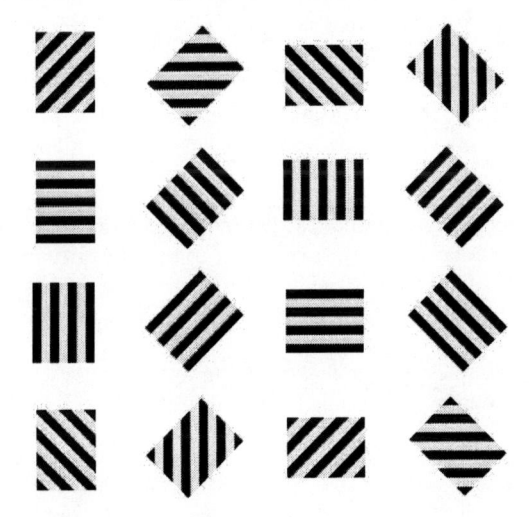

Figure 1. Examples of stimuli (black only)

Ocular activity recordings
The Tobii ET17 eye-tracking system was used for recording ocular activity. This system uses near infrared diodes to generate reflection patterns on the corneas of the eyes of the subject. The eye fixations data were used to compute an index of spatial dispersion known as Nearest Neighbour Index (NNI: Clark & Evans, 1954) that has been found to be correlated to mental workload (Di Nocera, Camilli, & Terenzi, in press; Di Nocera, Terenzi, & Camilli, 2006). The index provides information about the distribution of points (in this case eye fixations) in a 2D space. The index is equal to 1 when the distribution is random. Values lower than 1 suggest grouping, whereas values higher than 1 suggest regularity. Higher NNI values have been reported to indicate higher mental workload.

Procedure

Participants sat in a dark and sound-attenuated room, underwent a calibration procedure for the eye-tracker, and received instructions for the execution of the task. The target was always presented at the screen centre, followed by a screenshot containing 63 distractors and the target (set size = 64 stimuli). Across trials, targets were evenly scattered among 16 positions within a 4x4 ideal grid dividing the screen space in 16 quadrants (not visible to participants). Stimuli were presented on a 17" computer screen (screen resolution = 1024 x 768) with uniform grey background. Participants were required 1) to inspect the target as long as they wanted to 2) to press a key to perform a visual search task, and 3) clicking over the target shape as soon as they found it. Target inspection times, number of correct responses and search times were collected for successive analyses. Participants were instructed to prefer accuracy over speed, and performed the same task in three different blocks:

a. Manual control: a visual search task, with targets presented at each trial;
b. Moderate automation support: same task, but subjects received automation support consisting of the highlighting of those shapes sharing at least one out of four characteristics with the target (e.g., all red-coloured shapes were highlighted if the target were red);
c. High automation support: same tasks, but subjects received automation support consisting of the highlight of those shapes sharing two out of four characteristics with the target (e.g., all red horizontal shapes were highlighted if the target were red and horizontally oriented).

The highlighted stimuli were positioned approximately at the same distance from the centre of the screen. Participants were requested to perform six experimental blocks. Each block consisted of a sequence of 15 search trials, and no feeedback was provided for the correct response. The LOA sequence (manual-moderate-high vs. manual-high-moderate) was balanced across blocks. Automation was 100% reliable, but subjects were instructed to pay attention anyway, because (they were told) the system could occasionally provide unreliable information.

Data analysis and results

Performance and ocular data were analysed by repeated measures ANOVA designs using LOA (manual *vs.* moderate *vs.* high) as repeated factor. Number of correct responses, target inspection time, and target detection time were used as dependent variables. Results showed a main effect of LOA on target detection time ($F_{2,38}=12.86$, p<.0001). Duncan post-hoc testing showed that all conditions were significantly different one from each other (p<.05).

Number of correct responses in the visual search task showed a main effect of LOA ($F_{2,38}=6.12$, p<.01). Particularly, the high LOA led to a higher number of correct detections than the other two LOA (p<.01). No significant differences were found between manual control and the moderate LOA (p>.05).

A significant effect of LOA on target inspection time ($F_{2,38}=12.36$, p<0001) was found. Post-hoc testing showed that time dedicated to target inspection was significantly longer during manual control than the other two automation conditions (p<.001).

Nearest Neighbour Index values computed for each LOA were analysed by a repeated measures ANOVA design using LOA (manual *vs.* moderate *vs.* high) as repeated factor. One participant, whose ocular data contained artifacts (no valid eyes position in over 30% of the trials), was excluded from the analysis.

Results showed a significant effect of LOA ($F_{2, 36}$=4.8, p=.01). Post-hoc testing showed that NNI values computed from manual control condition were significant lower than those computed from the other two automation conditions (p<.05).

Table 1. Means and standard errors by LOA and measures (Study 1)

	Correct Responses	Detection time (milliseconds)	Inspection time (milliseconds)	Nearest Neighbour Index
Manual	13.25 (0.33)	5184.76 (285.05)	4089.87 (310.86)	0.86 (0.01)
Moderate	13.45 (0.32)	4515.62 (229.52)	3209.13 (336.32)	0.93 (0.01)
High	14.40 (0.12)	3621.76 (400.56)	3383.50 (313.13)	0.91 (0.02)

Discussion

Results showed that automation aids effectively supported performance. Of course, this is not surprising as the automatic aid made the task progressively easier. Participants were progressively faster in detecting targets as the LOA increased. Moreover, the number of correctly identified targets was significantly higher at the LOA=.50 than in the other two. However, no significant differences were found between manual control and the moderate LOA for successful target detection rate. In order to assess the effect of automation support on mental workload, the distribution of eye fixations was analysed. Result showed a more grouped distribution pattern during manual control, suggesting a lower level of mental workload when the task was performed without the use of automation aids. On the contrary, when automation aids were provided, the fixation distribution pattern approached spatial randomness (values near 1), suggesting an increase in mental workload.

One would expect automation support to reduce the amount of workload experienced by the individuals. However, that is not necessarily true, and it is strongly dependent on the type of task or strategy carried out by the operators. In the present study, for example, one key factor modulating mental workload might have been the time spent on the target shape memorisation prior searching. The decision of starting the search task was left to the participants, who examined the target until they were confident to remember it. This choice was made in order to avoid memory effects that might have been difficult to isolate post-hoc. Inspection times were thus collected in order to include them in the analyses. Interestingly, in the manual control condition, subjects inspected the target shape for a significantly longer time than in the other two conditions. For this reason, it may be hypothesised that this longer time was used for better "memorising the target" and led subjects to be more confident with the task when they had to carry it out manually. Nevertheless, as reported above, performance was better when automation support was provided both in terms of correctly identified targets and in target detection times.

In order to verify this interpretation, a further study has been run. Moreover, in order to gather additional information, this second study featured a concurrent measure of mental workload.

Study 2

The scope of this second study was to further investigate the effect on mental workload arose in study 1. To this aim, the same experimental task was used, but target inspection time was kept constant between trials (5 seconds, which was the average inspection time employed by participants in study 1). This change in the procedure should allow disentangling the effects of memorisation and LOA on mental workload. Moreover, in order to not rely on the ocular measure only, a concurrent measure of mental workload (subjective estimates) was implemented.

Method

Subjects
Sixteen students (mean age = 22.4, SD = 1.5, 12 females) volunteered in this study. All participants were right-handed, with normal or corrected to normal sight. Participants have not reported Daltonism.

Stimuli and ocular activity recording
The same set of stimuli and the same eye-tracking systems of study 1 were used.

Procedure
Participants sat in a dark and sound-attenuated room, underwent a calibration procedure for the eye-tracker, and received instructions for the execution of the task. As in study 1, target shapes were presented on each trial, followed by a screenshot containing 63 distractors and the target. Participants were requested to inspect the target (presented at the centre of the screen) for 5 seconds, then automatically switched to the search screen and were required to click over the target shape as soon as they found it. During the experimental session 6 blocks of trials were presented. Each block consisted of 3 sub-blocks supported by three different LOA (manual, moderate, and high) whose order was randomised across blocks. Each sub-block consisted of 15 search trials. At the end of each sub-block, participants were requested to fill the NASA – Task Load index (NASA-TLX; Hart & Staveland, 1986). Search times, number of corrects responses and NASA-TLX scores were collected for the successive analyses. The NNI was computed as in study 1. Also in this case subjects were told that the system could occasionally provide unreliable information (nevertheless, the system was 100% reliable).

Data analysis and results

Performance and ocular data were analysed by repeated measures ANOVA designs using LOA (manual *vs.* moderate *vs.* high) as repeated factor. Number of correct responses and target detection time were used as dependent variables. Results showed a main effect of LOA on target detection time ($F_{2,30}$=28.17, p<.0001). Particularly, high-LOA detection times were shorter then those recorded from moderate-LOA and manual control (p<.001). Number of correct responses in the visual search task showed a main effect of LOA ($F_{2,30}$=7.65, p<.01). Particularly, the high LOA led to the highest number of correct detections (p<.05). No significant difference was found between manual control and the moderate LOA (p>.05).

NASA-TLX scores were analysed by repeated measures ANOVA designs using LOA (manual *vs.* moderate *vs.* high) as repeated factor. Results showed only a tendency towards statistical significance ($F_{2,30}$=3.16, p=.06). Post-hoc testing showed that high-LOA led to significantly lower mental workload that manual control (p<.05).

Nearest Neighbour Index values computed for each LOA were analysed by repeated measures ANOVA design using LOA (manual vs. moderate vs. high) as repeated factor. Results showed no significant differences between the three LOA ($F_{2,30}$=1.36, p>.05).

Finally, in order to compare the fixation distributions arose from the two studies, an ANOVA design was run on NNI values, using LOA (manual *vs.* moderate *vs.* high) as repeated factor and Target Inspection (self-paced *vs.* 5-second) as fixed factor. Results showed a main effect of LOA ($F_{2,66}$=5.2735, p<.01). An interaction between LOA and Target inspection showed only a tendency toward a significance ($F_{2,66}$=1.83, p=.16). Duncan post-hoc testing showed a tendency toward significance comparing the manual control condition from the two studies (p=.08).

Table 2. Means and standard errors by LOA and measures (study 2)

	Number of hits	Detection time (milliseconds)	NASA Task Load indeX	Nearest Neighbour Index
Manual	13.69 (0.27)	4010.87 (134.72)	39.01 (4.27)	0.92 (0.02)
Moderate	13.98 (0.23)	3866.55 (227.92)	37.92 (4.45)	0.94 (0.01)
High	14.37 (0.17)	2904.44 (222.92)	36.91 (4.36)	0.94 (0.01)

Discussion

This experiment was primarily aimed at clarifying the effect of target memorisation on mental workload. Moreover, study 2 served also as replication experiment for testing the stability of the effects found. Results are fairly in agreement with those of study 1, always showing a beneficial effect of automation on performance. Participants were significantly faster in detecting targets in the "high" automation support condition. Moreover, the number of correctly identified targets was significantly higher at the high-LOA than in the other two LOA conditions.

Nevertheless, no significant differences were found between manual control and the moderate LOA. Also in this second study, the distribution of eye fixations was analysed to assess the effects of automation support on mental workload. The interpretation suggested for results of study 1 (namely, that low workload in the manual condition was due to longer target inspection time), was supported by results of this study. Implementing a fixed target inspection time resulted in no significant differences in the level of mental workload across the three LOA. This result was also confirmed by NASA-TLX scores, which were unavailable in study 1.

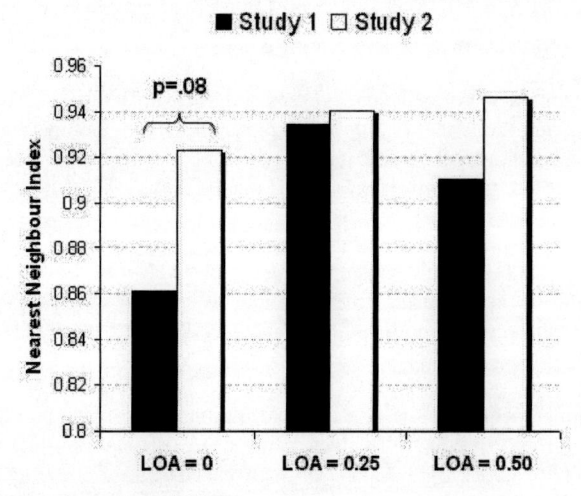

Figure 2. NNI values by study and LOA

General discussion and conclusions

The great variety of LOA taxonomies discussed in literature (e.g., Billings, 1991; Sheridan and Verkplant, 1978; Parasuraman et al, 2000; Endsley and Kaber 1997, Endsley and Kaber, 1999) suggest the need to develop a common theoretical platform in order to compare human performance across different LOA in different tasks and environments. One possible step in this direction is to migrate the LOA definition (and meaning) from qualitative to quantitative.

The general idea underlying the present paper was that automation could be defined in terms of the *amount* of information traded by humans and machines, thus allowing simple coding for identifying one particular LOA. Of course, this simplicity should be shown useful for discriminating between levels of performance and workload. The studies reported here only represent the initial phases of development and, although the research agenda includes the generalization to different stages of processing, only the "acquisition" level (see Parasuraman, Sheridan, & Wickens, 2000) was taken into consideration. Particularly, acquisition automation has been implemented in a visual search task. The use of this type of task has two main advantages. First, visual search is a very common task in experimental psychology and much is known about the changes in performance one should expect varying the degree of the difficulty of the task. Second, visual search is a typical human ability that is challenged in several complex tasks (e.g. baggage screening). Therefore, knowledge about the behavioural effects of the different levels of automation may have important implications for designing future systems. However, it should be pointed out that the type of task used here is quite different from baggage screening or other operative activities in which targets may be either absent or present. In this study a single target was always presented. This choice was made to avoid frequency related issues. Indeed, Wolfe, Horowitz, and Kenner (2005) showed that target prevalence has important effects on visual search performance. Observers abandon search in less than the average time required to find a target when targets are rare. Of course, given the methodological aim of this study, trials homogeneity was needed.

In both the present studies participants showed a higher rate of correct identifications and, as expected, they were faster in detecting targets at the highest LOA (the one making the task easier). Nevertheless, no significant differences were found between manual control and the moderate LOA, particularly for correct response rate. The lack of differences between these two conditions could suggest that the proportion employed here might not have been sufficient to affect performance. It will be critical for future studies to further investigate this issue.

Moreover, both studies have failed showing a clear effect of the three LOA on mental workload. Both the NASA-TLX and the NNI have showed that the three LOA generated about the same level of workload, and TLX scores indicate that the general workload level is very low (ranging from 37 to 39). Quite interestingly, the NNI showed values approaching spatial randomness (near 1), which has been reported to indicate high workload (Camilli et al., this volume; Di Nocera et al., 2006; in press). Albeit this was not the primary aim of this paper, this result is particularly interesting for clarifying the relationship between spatial distribution of fixations and mental workload. Indeed, the fact that a visual search task generated NNI values approaching randomness, whereas the workload was clearly too low (as demonstrated by the low TLX scores), might be considered as evidence that the spatial distribution needs to be related to the type of task from witch the ocular data are recorded. Visual search tasks are naturally aimed at maximizing the dispersion of ocular movements in order to detect the "hidden" target. This strategy can affect the spatial index. As a corollary, one should expect that high mental workload would generate more regular patterns of fixations representing the outcome of a strategy aimed at finding the target while optimizing the invested resources. Future studies should be devised to test this hypothesis as well as to investigate changes in the index by varying the number of targets and the degree of system reliability. This latter issue is particularly important as system reliability is expected to affect both performance and workload, and a descriptive model for types and levels of automation should be able to predict its effects.

Concluding, these studies represented a first step in developing a quantitative and general taxonomy for levels of automation. Such taxonomy would rely on a descriptive model of human performance at varying degrees of automation support, an aspect that has been neglected by all the available taxonomies.

This objective is quite ambitious and it is clear that the development of a general model may take years. Nevertheless, even at this early stage, the benefits in terms of comparability of results from different studies are large.

References

Bainbridge, L. (1983). Ironies of automation. *Automatica, 19*, 775–779.
Billings, C.E. (1991). Human-*centred aircraft automation: A concept and guidelines* (NASA Tech. Memo. No. 103885). Moffet Field, CA, USA: NASA-Ames Research Center.
Clark, P.J., & Evans F.C. (1954). Distance to nearest neighbor as a measure of spatial relationships in populations. *Ecology, 35,* 445-453.
Di Nocera, F., Camilli, M., & Terenzi, M. (in press). A random glance at the flight deck: pilot's scanning strategies and the real-time assessment of mental workload. *Journal of Cognitive Engineering and Decision Making.*
Di Nocera, F., Terenzi, M., & Camilli, M. (2006). Another look at scanpath: distance to nearest neighbour as a measure of mental workload. In D. de Waard, K.A. Brookhuis, A. Toffetti (Eds.), *Developments in Human Factors in Transportation, Design, and Evaluation* (pp. 295-303). Maastricht, the Netherlands: Shaker Publishing.
Endsley, M. R. & Kaber, D. B. (1997). The use of level of automation as a means of alleviating out-of-the-loop performance problems: a taxonomy and empirical analysis. In P. Seppala, T. Luopajarvi, C. H. Nygard, and M. Mattila (Eds), *13th Triennial Congress of the International Ergonomics Association*, Vol. 1 (pp. 168–170). Helsinki: Finish Institute of Occupational Health.
Endsley, M.R. & Kaber, D.B. (1999). Level of automation effects on performance, situation awareness and workload in a dynamic control task, *Ergonomics, 42,* 462–492.
Lorenz, B., Nocera, F., Rottger, S., & Parasuraman, R. (2002). Automated fault management in a simulated space flight micro-world. *Aviation, Space, and Environmental Medicine, 73,* 886–897.
Milewski, A., & Lewis, S. (1999). *When people delegate* (Tech. Memorandum). Murray Hill, NJ: AT&T Laboratories.
Miller, C. & Parasuraman, R. (2007). Designing For Flexible Interaction Between Humans and Automation: Delegation Interfaces for Supervisory Control. *Human Factors, 49*, 1, 57-75.
Parasuraman, R., Mouloua, M., & Hilburn, B. (1999). Adaptive aiding and adaptive task allocation enhance human-machine interaction. In M. W. Scerbo & M. Mouloua (Eds.), *Automation technology and human performance: Current research and trends* (pp. 119–123). Mahwah, NJ: Erlbaum.
Parasuraman, R., Sheridan, T.B., & Wickens, C.D. (2000). A model for types and levels of human interaction with automation. *IEEE Transactions on Systems, Man, and Cybernetics. Part A: Systems and Humans, 30,* 286-297.
Sheridan, T.B. (2002). *Humans and Automation: System Design and Research Issues.* New York, NY: Wiley & Sons.

Sheridan, T.B., & Verplank, W. (1978). *Human and Computer Control of Undersea Teleoperators*. Cambridge, MA: Man-Machine Systems Laboratory, Department of Mechanical Engineering, MIT.

Wei, Z., Macwan, A.P., & Wieringa, P.A. (1998). A quantitative measure for degree of automation and its relation to system performance and mental load. *Human Factors, 40*, 277-295.

Wolfe, J.M., Horowitz, T.S., & Kenner, N.M. (2005). Rare items often missed in visual searches. *Nature, 435*, 439-440.

Development of a cyclic loading method for the study of patterns of breakdown in complex performance under high load

Peter Nickel, Adam C. Roberts, Michael H. Roberts, & G. Robert J. Hockey
Department of Psychology
The University of Sheffield
United Kingdom

Abstract

Prediction of operator breakdown in complex systems depends on detecting states of extreme strain resulting from sustained compensatory activity, associated with fatigue and loss of control. This research is aimed at identifying the underlying state(s) that correspond to this limit in terms of key psychophysiological markers. To address these issues the study used a new 'cyclic loading' method, based on strain testing methods in mechanical engineering. Manual control load on a process control task is increased until compensatory control limits are breached and primary performance begins to fail; then reduced until performance recovers to within normal limits. The cyclic loading method is shown to be a valuable tool for exploring the dynamics of operator/task interactions under high demand. Principal component analysis of correlations between hysteresis functions for relevant markers of strain (differences between loading and unloading response) showed evidence of two distinctive psychophysiological patterns, corresponding to fatigue/control and effort management processes. These findings suggest that prediction of operator risk will need to consider both early onset of fatigue effects, leading to loss of task control, and differences in effort management strategies employed by operators to maintain performance goals.

Introduction

Operator performance in complex, highly automated tasks typically appears to be reliable, despite the constant threat of disruption from demanding workload, environmental stressors and increasing fatigue (Hancock & Desmond, 2001; Hockey, 1997). Particularly in situations where the operator is highly motivated to avoid error (for example, safety critical systems), top-level task goals appear to be protected by an increase of effort. However, the use of such compensatory strategies also attracts costs or 'latent decrements': the adoption of less demanding (riskier) strategies, secondary task decrements, and increases in both subjective strain and physiological activation (Hockey, 1997).

Effects such as these will to lead to manifest breakdown under extreme conditions. However, for a period before primary task failure becomes evident, the operator is likely to be in a vulnerable state, able to manage predictable demands but not unexpected or difficult problems. If this state could be detected and measured it might be possible to predict periods of increased operational risk and prevent serious breakdown. Such information could be used, for example, as an input to an adaptive interface that would transfer control to the computer system whenever a high risk state was detected. The approach taken here is developed within the operator functional state (OFS) framework (Hockey, 2005), in which performance is viewed as part of a broader human-task system, served by a complex psychophysiological state, including not only cognitive, but also energetical and subjective regulatory processes. Because of this, the dynamics of primary task breakdown can be understood only by reference to changes in other state variables. This paper reports a preliminary attempt to measure strain in operators responding to increasing levels of task demand. It asks whether there are distinctive patterns of changes in relevant OFS markers that signal periods of high risk and vulnerability to performance breakdown.

To study the development of strain leading to breakdown we adopt a new 'cyclic loading' method, based on strain testing methods used in mechanical engineering. In this, task load is increased (the loading phase) until compensatory control limits are reached and primary performance begins to fail, then task load is reduced progressively (unloading phase) until performance recovers to within normal limits. Measurement of the (maximum) strain state that precedes breakdown is the main aim, although it was anticipated that the method would also allow measurement of the characteristics of the recovery of the engaged state during unloading. This makes use of the standard hysteresis function (the difference in the load-strain relationship between loading and unloading phases attributed to a lag or inertia in system response). While such methods are common in engineering and electronics testing, there have been very few studies of hysteresis effects in human performance (Farrell, 1999). Conway (2005, 2006, Conway & Hockey, 2007) found that, although primary task performance was not impaired markedly with high load, there were marked increases in both fatigue and effort during unloading, supporting the interpretation of compensatory control under fatigue. To our knowledge, this is a new approach to the problem of measuring risk of breakdown in operational tasks. It recognises the adaptive nature of task management, and the need to titrate task load against adaptive costs as the operator attempts to maintain performance. A focus on individual adjustment is also required, since a generally applicable strain state may be unlikely. Use of the cyclic loading method allows the detection of person-distinctive patterns of both breakdown and recovery from overload.

Because of their high bandwidth and fast and reliable response, physiological measures of both autonomic (ANS) and central nervous system (CNS) activity are particularly strong candidates for OFS strain indicators. When combined with changes in primary task strategy, secondary task measures, and subjective ratings, they can provide a distinctive strain index (Hockey et al., 2006, Nickel et al., 2006). Cardiovascular (CV) indices, notably heart rate variability (HRV), as defined by power in the mid frequency (0.1 Hz) band, have been found to respond reliably to changes in workload and mental effort (Mulder et al., 2000), particularly in operational settings where executive problem solving is involved (Tattersall & Hockey, 1995). As with HRV, power spectrum analysis is usually necessary to reveal changes of mental states in EEG data. The NASA/Langley group (Pope et al., 1995) have developed an 'engagement index' (EI), based on the ratio of high (beta, 14-30 Hz) vs. low (alpha, 8-13 Hz, and theta, 4-8 Hz) frequency activity (beta/[alpha + theta]). Changes in EI have been used to switch successfully between manual and computer-aided modes of tracking and vigilance tasks, and offer considerable promise as a measure of changing levels of mental activity, though it may be limited as an index of strain per se. In emphasising generalised cortical activation, the engagement index may be better considered as a measure of generalised alertness, rather than engagement in the sense of focused task orientation, as assumed in the strain model of performance protection. However, it is retained in the analysis for comparison purposes.

Focussed attention has been more clearly related to the presence of the theta rhythm localised at frontal and anterior sites (Schacter, 1977), receiving projections from prefrontal and anterior cingulate cortical mechanisms associated with executive control function (Miller & Cohen, 2001). In the present study the level of executive control is inferred from Gevins' 'task load index' (TLI) (Gevins & Smith, 2003), defined as the ratio of theta band power localised at frontal midline sites to alpha derived from parietal/occipital areas (theta/alpha). As an index of the effectiveness of task control, increases in TLI would be expected as operators successfully protect primary task performance under increasing load, while reduced TLI values may be more likely if performance breakdown occurs (either because of control limitations, or through an adaptive reduction in task engagement under extreme load; Hockey, 1997; 2005). It may also be expected that it reflects the carry-over effects of fatigue by being less responsive during unloading (a reduction in executive control capacity). However, such a change can only be interpreted if the status of other markers of the strain state is known: whether there is evidence of secondary task decrements, whether effort is increased or not under high load, and/or whether general alertness is high or low. In addition, it is valuable to include the HRV (0.1 Hz band) index, because of its demonstrated sensitivity to workload increases. To provide for these possibilities the study adopts a hybrid approach, in which EEG indices are derived for both generalised alertness (EI) and executive control (TLI), as well as cardiovascular-related effort (HRV 0.1 Hz), both primary and secondary task measures, and indices of subjective strain (anxiety, fatigue and effort).

Method

Participants

Based on extensive training on the process control simulation autoCAMS (10-14 hrs) and appropriate results in training progress assessments (introduced at beginning, middle and end of the training programme; Roberts et al., this volume) 11 postgraduate students from engineering and science departments of The University of Sheffield were selected to work as operators with the process control simulation in the present study. Participants were financially compensated for taking part in the study.

Testing environment and apparatus

For each participant, two experimental sessions were scheduled in an air-conditioned room without windows, illuminated with two pairs of high-frequency fluorescent lamps and furnished with desks for the participant and the experimenter and movable walls for separation. The process control software and subjective ratings were presented on a 19" TFT monitor at about 50 cm from the participant who used a PC keyboard and a mouse as hardware controls. Subjective ratings and system performance parameters were recorded on the process control computer while psychophysiological data were recorded on a separate experimenter PC. The Active Two Base System (Biosemi, The Netherlands) was used for continuously acquiring psychophysiological data from 45 channels, for ECG (electrocardiogram; Nehb's triangle), respiration (nasal/oral thermistor for 3 point measurement), EMG (electromyographic muscle activity from the musculus trapezius; Hanson et al., 1993), EOG (vertical, horizontal electrooculogram), reference (left and right mastoids), and EEG referenced to linked matoids (32 sites on a headcap arranged in the 10-20 system with FC5, T7, T8, FC6 replaced by FPz, AFz, CPz, POz, respectively; American Electroencephalographic Society, 1994). All signals, except for respiration, were collected with Ag/AgCl active electrodes. Data acquisition for all signals sampled at 2048 Hz was controlled by an interface (ActiView 5.37, BioSemi, the Netherlands). The ActiView interaction interface provided for the experimenter on a monitor served for monitoring and control of signal pre-processing, for marking of specific events (environmental disturbances or other artefact indications), and for storing all psychophysiological and marker signals in BioSemi-data-files on the experimenter's computer.

Experimental tasks

An automation-enhanced modification (autoCAMS; Lorenz et al., 2002) of the Cabin Air Management System (CAMS; Hockey et al, 1998; Sauer et al., 2000) served as the process control environment. The task requires operators to manage a semi-automatic system that controls the atmospheric environment (air quality, temperature, pressure etc.) of a closed system such as a space capsule or submersible. Operators interact with a dynamic visual display that provides data on system variables and functions via a range of controls and automation tools. Figure 1 shows the simplified autoCAMS interaction interface as it was presented on the participants' monitors in the present study. Operators were required to monitor and control the system so that variables did not stray outside the strict limits imposed by the white and grey areas of the display meters. They were encouraged to try to remain within the ideal white zone, but told that deviations into the grey zone were allowable. System control errors were scored at two levels of magnitude: absolute control failures (% time variables were in the prohibited black zone) and the more strict measure of control deviations (% time variables were in either the grey or the black zone).

For the present study the primary task was simplified so that no fault detection, diagnosis or maintenance was required. The level of load imposed on the operator was defined in terms of the number of automation failures for the five sub-systems shown in Figure 1. These took the form of switch point failures for the controllers of the carbon-dioxide scrubber, nitrogen flow, oxygen flow, dehumidifier, and temperature cooler, respectively. The number of control panels that needed to be controlled manually was manipulated through a cyclic loading schedule of nine 15-min conditions, increasing stepwise from one to five (loading phase) then decreasing from five back down to 1 (unloading). For brevity, the nine conditions are referred to as combinations of phase (loading/unloading; L/U) and load level (1-5): 1L, 2L, 3L, 4L, 5L, 4U, 3U, 2U, 1U. The aim was to force instability and a breakdown in task performance, usually protected by compensatory control processes, allowing the detection of breakdown and pre-breakdown phases of strain states, and analysis of recovery from strain during unloading.

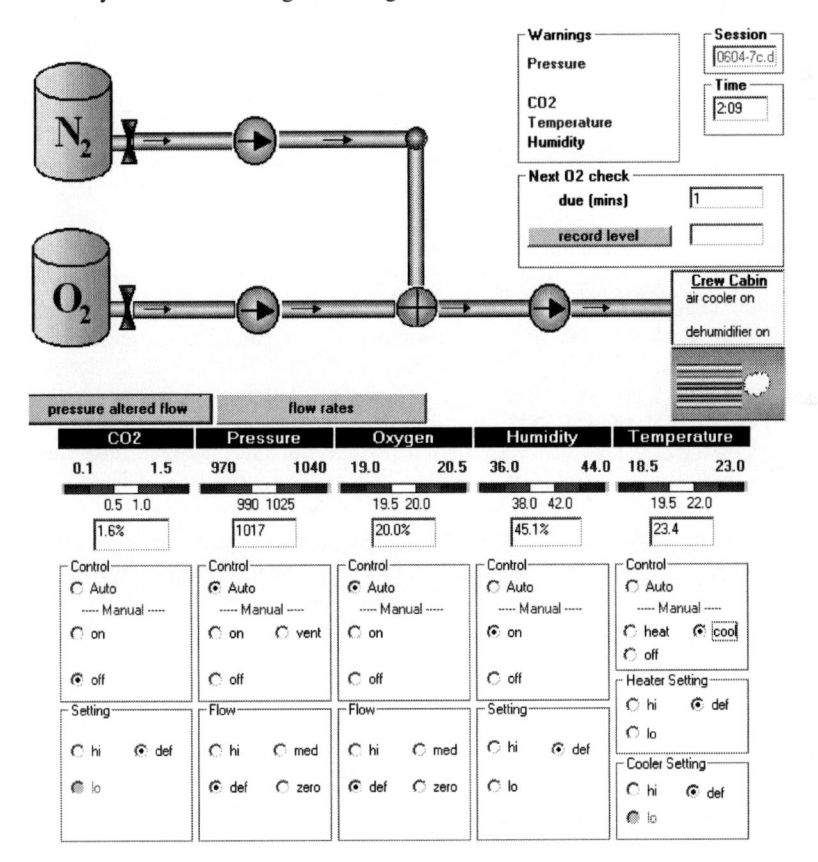

Figure 1. AutoCAMS interaction interface (originally coloured): see text for explanation

Since the focus of interest was manual control load, operators did not need to determine which faults were present in each condition: they were told which automatic control components would fail during successive conditions of the loading and unloading phases. Operators were required to maintain the system parameters within their target ranges (primary task) using the manual control mode. Two secondary tasks, alarm acknowledgement and tank level recording, were also incorporated into the structure of autoCAMS. The alarm acknowledgment task required operators to respond to alarms as soon as possible by clicking on the alarm message with the mouse cursor, providing a measure of alarm reaction time (ART). Tank level recording (TLR) was a prospective memory task (Brandimonte et al., 1996), requiring operators to maintain a precise electronic record of the current oxygen tank level at 1-min intervals. In addition, subjective state was measured at the beginning of the session and at the end of each load condition. Participants were required to indicate their current ratings of anxiety, fatigue and mental effort by moving a slider with the mouse along each of three visual analogue scales presented on the participant's monitor, with end points labelled 'calm - tense', 'alert - tired', and 'low - high', respectively (Sauer et al., 2003).

Psychophysiological measures

With Brain Vision Analyzer (Brain Products, Germany) the EEG electrodes were re-referenced to linked mastoids. For the EEG and EOG activity the high and low pass filters were set at 1.6 Hz and 55 Hz, respectively. Based on segmented data (epochs of 2s), first, ocular correction (Gratton et al., 1983), next, baseline correction (epoch length), and finally, semi-automatic artefact detection on the remaining amplitude (range 100 µV) was applied. The epoched EEG signals were further analysed via Fast Fourier Transform (FFT; 10% Hanning window) and normalised to obtain power spectra (0.5 Hz – 50 Hz) in 0.5 Hz resolution comparable across segments.

To calculate the so-called engagement-index (EI) (beta/[alpha + theta]) EEG sites (Cz, P3, Pz, P4) were pooled and three different bands (theta: 4-8 Hz, alpha: 8-13 Hz, beta: 13-22 Hz) were extracted as mean per spectral line. Different task load index (TLI) measures were derived, relating to alternative definitions of EEG sites and frequency bands: TLI/afz (AFz theta: 5-7 Hz / CPz and POz alpha: 8-13.5 Hz) and TLI/fz (Fz theta: 6-7 Hz / Pz alpha: 10-12 Hz), extracted as mean per spectral line for the appropriate site. The extracted data for each frequency band was exported to separate files and the indices were calculated using Office Excel (Microsoft, USA).

The ECG signal was composed of signals recorded from Nehb's triangle and afterwards 5 Hz high cut-off filtered using Brain Vision Analyzer (Brain Products, Germany). Application of the Vision Analyzer built-in solution "EKG Markers" allowed R-peak event detection and time-stamp by a marker. Artefact correction was done by visual inspection of the ECG signal and marked R-peaks and then corrected with functions provided by the Vision Analyzer interface, if necessary. Time stamps of the R-peak marker were exported to separate files. Instantaneous heart rate and the 0.1 Hz component of heart rate variability (HRV/0.1) were calculated using the LabVIEW (National Instruments, USA) virtual instruments and the procedure described in Nickel & Nachreiner (2003).

Procedure

Two experimental sessions of around 2.5 h each were run, to allow the assessment of reliability of OFS measures. These were carried out on subsequent days at the same time of day, to control for circadian effects. After fixing electrodes and acquiring psychophysiological data participants were asked, to move their eyes, then close their eyes and relax while sitting calmly and quietly for about 5 min, in order to collect data with low EOG activity. Next, they were asked to elevate both shoulders, to provide data on maximal voluntary contraction of the trapezius muscle. For about 60 min participants performed different component tasks in order to set up comparable pre-loading states for the simulated process control operations with autoCAMS. Prior to the simulated process control operations participants filled in the subjective ratings. Each of the nine conditions for simulated process control operation lasted 15 min (in total about 135 min) and the subjective ratings completed during the last 20 s in parallel with ongoing process control operations. Psychophysiological and performance data were continuously recorded on different computers during process control operations. Neither breaks nor system resets interrupted the sense of continuity from condition to condition.

Data analysis

The primary goal of the analysis was to assess the impact of strain in terms of its fatigue after-effect. The cyclic loading method imposes load on operators during the loading phase, and then removes it, leaving fatigue effects during unloading, as indicated by hysteresis. Analysis was based on data integrated over each of the nine 15 min conditions (L1, L2, L3, L4, L5, U4, U3, U2, U1) of simulated process control operations within experimental sessions. Operator functional state indicators (dependent variables relating to system performance, psychophysiology and subjective ratings) were analysed separately in relation to phase and load, and used to derive estimates of hysteresis for each. To do this averaged indicator values over the middle range of the loading and unloading phases ([L2 + L3 + L4] vs. [U4 + U3 + U2]) were compared, ignoring the common L5 condition and the lowest loads (L1 and U1), where differences would be expected to be attenuated. The presence of a typical hysteresis effect would be reflected by higher strain values during unloading than loading. To standardise the hysteresis values for the different indicators, unloading/loading means were computed from ratios of strain indicators for corresponding loading and unloading phases (rather than from differences between indicators). In order to reduce skewness (since positive hysteresis effects have ratios of 1-∞, and negative effects values in the restricted range 0-1) a further $\log_{10}$ transformation was applied to these ratios. The final $\log_{10}$ ratios are symmetrical for positive (>0) and negative hysteresis values (<0).

Principle Component Analysis (PCA) was used to examine the correlation matrix of these hysteresis values for evidence of underlying structure. As the main aim of the study was a detailed analysis of intra-individual strain patterns it did not provide a large enough sample for this to produce a reliable factor solution. For this a minimum observations/variables ratio of 5:1 is normally recommended (Gorsuch, 1983). However, the analysis is an exploratory one, and we improved the reliability by using sessions rather than individuals as the units of observation, and by adopting a restricted set of indicator variables. This also had the effect of removing interpretive problems associated with multicollinearity, since some of the EEG and subjective measures have high inter-correlations.

Results

Because the main purpose of this paper is to analyse patterns of hysteresis effects, only a brief summary of primary data is presented here, except for performance, which provides the focus for the analysis of breakdown patterns.

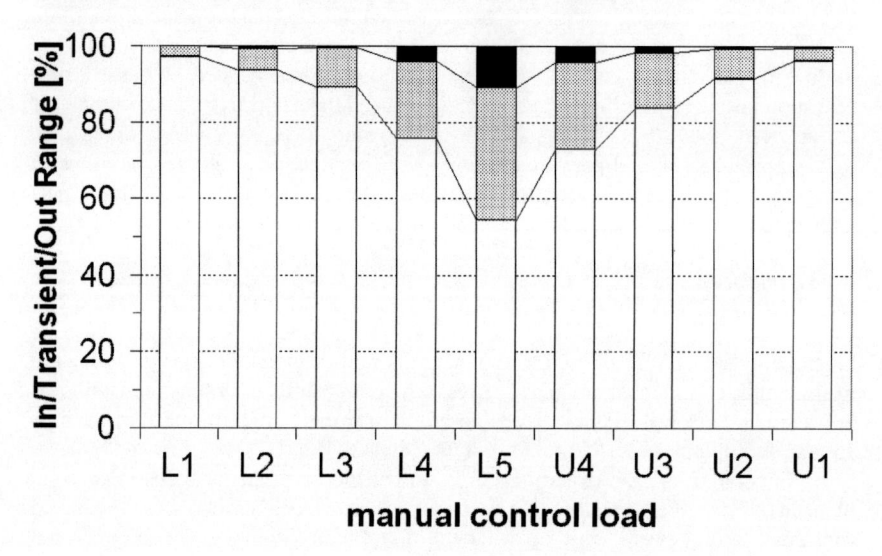

Figure 2. Primary task performance: percentage time total system is in range (white bars), transi-tional (grey bars), and out of range (black bars) for each condition of the load cycle (aggregated over all sessions and participants, N=22)

Task performance

Figure 2 shows the mean primary task performance over the loading and unloading cycle, based on all 22 sessions. Most operators performed very well despite increasing load, on average maintaining the system within the acceptable (white and grey) range for over 95 % of the time. Nevertheless, the data showed evidence of the beginning of performance breakdown (black bars) under the most demanding condition (L5), where all five control panels had to be controlled manually, as well as small disturbances in L4, U4 and U3. A more sensitive indicator of primary task strain is provided by the more strictly defined criterion of control deviations (grey and black bars). Deviations increased monotonically during the loading phase (L1 to L5), and decreased during unloading (L5 to U1). Additionally the comparison between phases appears to indicate the typical hysteresis carry-over effect, with performance impaired for longer during unloading. The data for secondary task performance measures also showed consistent increases and decreases with load changes, confirming the interpretation that the system was in a vulnerable state during the more demanding load conditions.

Subjective measures

All subjective state measures increased markedly during loading. There was also strong evidence of hysteresis, levels during unloading being much higher for fatigue and anxiety, with less marked increases for effort.

Psychophysiological measures

All psychophysiological measures responded to an increase in task load. Both TLI measures and EI increased monotonically with load, while HRV decreased (the expected effect of increased effort). Hysteresis effects were less marked than in performance and subjective indicators. Levels during unloading were slightly reduced for TLI, suggesting a tendency for reduction in executive control, and increased for EI and HRV.

Evidence for strain factors

Table 1. Rotated 2-component PCA solution for the analysis of hysteresis measure, showing factor loadings of >0.4

Hysteresis Indicators	Principal Components	
	C1	C2
Fatigue	.72	
Effort		-.53
Control deviations	.72	
TLR timing errors	.60	.62
ART		.56
EI		.55
TLI/fz	-.72	
HRV/0.1		.55
variance accounted for	28%	19%

The main purpose of this paper is to consider evidence for underlying psychophysiological strain patterns in relation to fatigue, effort and performance. The approach taken here is to look for evidence of general factors by exploring the structure of the relationships between the hysteresis estimates for the different indicator variables, through use of a PCA extraction with varimax rotation. Following preliminary screening of variables for multicollinearity and distributional properties, the analysis was carried out for the total 22 test sessions on eight key indicator variables: subjective measures (fatigue, effort), primary task performance (control deviations), secondary task performance (TLR, ART), and psychophysiological measures (HRV/0.1, TLI/fz, EI). To improve stability of factors a minimum value of 0.4 was imposed on including variables in a factor. A summary of the analysis is shown in Table 1.

Two factors were extracted, with all but one of the variables loading on one of the two factors in the rotated solution (the exception being TLR, which loaded equally on both). The first component (C1) shows positive loadings on fatigue and control deviations, with a negative loading on TLI. The second (C2) is characterised by a negative loading on effort, and positive loadings on ART, EI and HRV/0.1. TLR timing error loads equally on both factors.

Given the low resolution power of the analysis we need to exercise caution in interpreting these factors, though they fit well with current theories of the nature of executive function and strain. The two factors may be labelled, tentatively, as (1) fatigue and (2) effort, using the subjective state measures as marker variables. Fatigue is thus identified with a reduction in the effectiveness of control of primary task goals, represented by the increase in deviation errors and, interestingly, a reduction in TLI, thought to reflect activity of frontal executive control mechanisms (Gevins & Smith, 2003). The second factor, effort, is associated more with performance on secondary tasks, and inversely related to HRV/0.1 (as shown in previous work). The ambiguous loading pattern of TLR may genuinely reflect the demands of this task, requiring both control (maintenance of the goal to make checks at regular intervals in the absence of reminders), and its secondary task status (requiring allocation of effort).

Discussion

The PCA results suggest the presence of two interpretable and theoretically coherent factors in the hysteresis data. It suggests that fatigue and effort may be considered as two (quasi-) independent processes that, taken together, can be used to predict the pattern of breakdown observed in performance of the primary task. Clearly, any conclusions must be considered tentative, given the limitations of the data, but they offer considerable encouragement to further analysis, with much larger samples.

The two patterns emerging from the analysis map well onto existing theories of task performance and executive control. At one level it is consistent with current models of the role of cortical mechanisms in executive function, in particular the interdependent roles of Pre-Frontal Cortex (PFC) and Anterior Cingulate Cortex (ACC). A widely held view is that PFC is responsible primarily for control and maintenance of task goals, represented in this study by the close link between changes in primary task behaviour and power in frontal theta activity. A complementary role is thought to be served by ACC, monitoring and responding to goal disturbances and threats to effective control (Miller & Cohen, 2001; MacDonald et al., 2000), and signalling the need for additional effort when conflicts are detected (Botvinick et al., 1999). Other work (Critchley et al., 2003; Luu & Posner, 2003) indicates strong connections between ACC and activation of cardiovascular arousal, implicating HRV suppression under effortful behaviour as part of the ACC regulatory process.

The findings also resonate with expectations from Hockey's (1997; 2005) compensatory control model, where control of goal-related actions is separated from an effort-related response to goal disturbances. As in the patterns observed here, goal maintenance is associated with primary task performance and high levels of executive activity, while effort is associated with secondary task failure and autonomic activation. Hockey's model also accounts for operators responding with either of two different strategies under fatigue: (1) where they are highly motivated to protect performance goals, with a consequent increase in effort, and (2) where goal maintenance is allowed to slip, with no increase in effort. Some supporting evidence for this distinction is provided by this study. Control failures (the criterion of successful goal maintenance) varied considerably across individual sessions (from 0-53 % in L5), though there was a clear separation around a level of 10 %. Of the 22 sessions, 15 succeeded in protecting control performance from breakdown under increasing load, but the remaining 7 showed clear evidence of breakdown, with failure rates of 15-30 % at L4 and L5. When the PCA analysis is carried out separately on these two groups of sessions the patterns of loading are similar to that shown in Table 1, except for one striking difference. For good performance sessions, the tendency for TLI to be lower during unloading (as a consequence of fatigue) is associated with a compensatory increase in effort – an attempt by operators to overcome the loss of control experienced. However, for poor sessions, the pattern of increased fatigue and primary task errors and reduced TLI is negatively correlated with magnitude of effort response. The greater the increase in fatigue and task errors during unloading, the smaller is the effort response. In the first case, increased effort is clearly aimed at maintaining task goals under failing control; the second appears to be an example of the typically observed fatigue after-effect (Hockey, 1997; Hockey & Earle, 2006; Meijman, 1997; Van der Linden et al., 2003), aimed at avoiding further strain through a relaxation in effort expenditure and acceptance of a reduction in task performance levels.

Although these differences are based on very small samples of data, such findings offer rich insights into the dynamics of strain regulation in complex task management. Effort regulation appears to be critical in distinguishing successful from unsuccessful goal management. Taken together with the main findings, they support the interpretation of two different modes of interaction between fatigue/control and effort mechanisms, based on operator decision making relating to the relationship between task goals and personal state goals (since maintenance of high levels of effort may be aversive; Hockey, 2005). When control slippage is detected under fatigue (ACC function), some corrective action is required. Effort can be increased in an attempt to overcome the disturbance, leading to minimal risk of breakdown. Alternatively, an operator may decide not to increase effort, resulting in major breakdown.

In conclusion, notwithstanding the limitations of the study, the results of the analyses suggest the presence of two coherent underlying factors or patterns of strain response during demanding complex work, and two contrasting types of adaptive response. Any developments of adaptive automation that seek to make use of strain markers as inputs to the human-computer control interface will need to consider the implications of the adaptive complexity hinted at by such results. Minimally, they suggest the need for a two-module monitoring process, in which the adaptive controller needs to know not only whether the operator is fatigued/control-impaired, but whether they are in a high or low effort response mode.

Acknowledgements

This study is part of the project funded by the UK EPSRC grant GR\S66985\01. We thank Stefan Röttger and Dick de Waard for helpful comments on an earlier version of the manuscript.

References

American Electroencephalographic Society (AES) (1994). Guideline thirteen: Guidelines for standard electrode position nomenclature (AES). *Journal of Clinical Neurophysiology, 11*, 111-113.

Botvinick, M., Nystrom, L.E., Fissell, K., Carter, C.S., & Cohen, J.D. (1999). Conflict monitoring versus selection-for-action in anterior cingulate cortex. *Nature, 402*, 179-181.

Brandimonte, M., Einstein, G.O., & McDaniel, M.A. (1996). *Prospective memory: Theory and Applications.* Mahwah, USA: Erlbaum.

Conway, G. (2005). *Effects of workload, effort and fatigue on complex performance: Application and tests of compensatory control theory* (unpublished PhD Thesis). Leeds, UK: University of Leeds.

Conway, G. (2006). Noise and cyclic loading effects on performance and operator functional state. *Proceedings of the HFES conference 2006.* San Francisco, USA: HFES.

Conway, G. & Hockey, G.R.J. (2007). Effects of cyclic loading on complex performance and operator functional state. In D. de Waard, G.R.J. Hockey, P. Nickel, and K.A. Brookhuis (Eds.) (2007), *Human Factors Issues in Complex System Performance* (pp. 339 - 344). Maastricht, the Netherlands: Shaker Publishing.

Critchley, H.D., Mathias, C.J., Josephs, O., O'Doherty, J., Zanini, S., Dewar, B.-K., Cipolotti, L., Shallice, T., & Dolan, R.J. (2003). Human cingulate cortex and autonomic control: converging neuroimaging and clinical evidence. *Brain, 126*, 2139-2152.

Farrell, P.S.E. (1999). The hysteresis effect. *Human Factors, 41*, 226-240.

Gevins, A. & Smith, M.E. (2003). Neurophysiological measures of cognitive workload during human-computer interaction. *Theoretical Issues in Ergonomics Science, 4*, 113-131.

Gratton, G., Coles, M.G.H., & Donchin, E. (1983). A new method for off-line removal of ocular artifact. *Electroencephalography and Clinical Neurophysiology, 55*, 468-484.

Gorsuch, R.L. (1983). *Factor analysis.* Hillsdale, NJ, USA: Erlbaum.

Hancock, P.A. & Desmond, P.A. (Eds.) (2001). *Stress, Workload, and Fatigue.* Mahwah, USA: Erlbaum.

Hanson, E.K.S., Schellekens, J.M.H., Veldman, J.B.P., & Mulder, L.J.M. (1993). Psychomotor and cardiovascular consequences of mental effort and noise. *Human Movement Science, 12*, 607-626.

Hockey, G.R.J. (1997). Compensatory control in the regulation of human performance under stress and high workload: A cognitive energetical framework. *Biological Psychology, 45*, 73-93.
Hockey, G.R.J. (2005). Operator functional state: The prediction of breakdown in human performance. In J. Duncan, L. Phillips, and P. McLeod (Eds.), *Measuring the Mind: Speed, Control, and Age* (pp. 373-394). Oxford, UK: Oxford University Press.
Hockey, G.R.J. & Earle, F. (2006). Control over the scheduling of simulated office work reduces the impact of workload on mental fatigue and task performance. *Journal of Experimental Psychology: Applied, 12*, 50-65.
Hockey, G.R.J., Wastell, D.G., & Sauer, J. (1998). Effects of sleep deprivation and user-interface on complex performance: A multilevel analysis of compensatory control. *Human Factors, 40*, 233-253.
Hockey, G.R.J., Nickel, P., Roberts, A.C., Mahfouf, M., & Linkens, D.A. (2006). Implementing adaptive automation using on-line detection of high risk operator functional state. In ISSA Chemistry and Machine and System Safety Sections (Ed.), *Design Process and Human Factors Integration: Optimising Company Performance* (pp. 1/004:1-13). Paris, France: INRS.
Lorenz, B., Di Nocera, F., Röttger, S., & Parasuraman, R. (2002). Automated fault-management in a simulated spaceflight micro-world. *Aviation, Space, and Environmental Medicine, 73*, 886-897.
Luu, P. & Posner, M.I. (2003). Anterior cingulate cortex regulation of sympathetic activity. *Brain, 126*, 2119-2120.
MacDonald, A.W., Cohen, J.D., Stenger, V.A., & Carter, C.S. (2000). Dissociating the role of the dorsolateral prefrontal and anterior cingulate cortex in cognitive control. *Science, 288*, 1835-1838.
Meijman, T.F. (1997). Mental fatigue and the efficiency of information processing in relation to work times. *International Journal of Industrial Ergonomics, 20*, 31-38.
Miller, E.K. & Cohen, J.D. (2001). An integrative theory of prefrontal cortex function. *Annual Review of Neuroscience, 24*, 167-202.
Mulder, G., Mulder, L.J.M., Meijman, T.F., Veldman, J.B.P., & van Roon, A.M. (2000). Psychophysiological approach to working conditions. In R.W. Backs & W. Boucsein (Eds.), *Engineering psychophysiology: Issues and applications* (pp. 139-159). Mahwah, USA: Erlbaum.
Nickel, P. & Nachreiner, F. (2003). Sensitivity and diagnosticity of the 0.1 Hz component of heart rate variability as an indicator of mental workload. *Human Factors, 45*, 575-590.
Nickel, P., Hockey, G.R.J., Roberts, A.C., & Roberts, M.H. (2006). Markers of high risk operator functional state in adaptive control of process automation. In R.N. Pikaar, E.A.P. Koningsveld, & P.J.M. Settles (Eds.), *Meeting diversity in ergonomics* (pp. 0244:1-6). Amsterdam, The Netherlands: Elsevier.
Pope, A.T., Bogart, E.H., & Bartolome, D.S. (1995). Biocybernetic system evaluates indices of operator engagement in automated task. *Biological Psychology, 40*, 187-195.

Roberts, M.H., Roberts, A.C., Nickel, P., & Hockey, G.R.J. (2007). Training in micro-world simulation. In D. de Waard, G.R.J. Hockey, P. Nickel, and K.A. Brookhuis (Eds.) (2007), *Human Factors Issues in Complex System Performance* (pp. X - Y). Maastricht, the Netherlands: Shaker Publishing.

Sauer, J., Wastell, D.G., & Hockey, G.R.J. (2000). A conceptual framework for designing micro-worlds for complex work domains: A case study on the Cabin Air Management System. *Computers in Human Behavior, 16*, 45-58.

Sauer, J., Wastell, D.G., Hockey, G.R.J., & Earle, F. (2003). Performance in a complex multiple-task environment during a lab-based simulation of occasional night work. *Human Factors, 45*, 657-669.

Schacter, D.L. (1977). EEG theta waves and psychological phenomena: A review and analysis. *Biological Psychology, 5*, 47–82.

Tattersall, A.J. & Hockey, G.R.J. (1995). Level of operator control and changes in heart rate variability during simulated flight maintenance. *Human Factors, 37*, 682-698.

Van der Linden, D., Frese, M., & Sonnentag, S. (2003). The impact of mental fatigue on exploration in a complex computer task: Rigidity and loss of systematic strategies. *Human Factors, 45*, 483-494.

Effects of cyclic loading on complex performance and operator functional state

G.E. (Gareth) Conway[1] & G.R.J. (Bob) Hockey[2]
[1]University of Leeds
[2]University of Sheffield
UK

Abstract

Performance failures in complex work environments have widespread and profound consequences. Advances in the understanding of stress effects have been hindered by equivocal results and methodological and theoretical problems. Hockey's Compensatory Control Model (CCM) addresses these issues by emphasising the adaptive abilities of the responsible performer to protect important task goals, but at a cost of latent decrements on less salient tasks and compromised operator functional state. The present study tested CCM predictions under conditions of sustained task demand. Changing task load was manipulated using a cyclic loading method, with objective task demand increasing then decreasing over a 105 min session. Performance was assessed on a primary task and two embedded secondary tasks, using the Cabin Air Management System as an experimental test-bed. Sub-sessions and hysteresis measures were employed to assess fatigue accumulation and dissipation during performance, and allow the collection of self-report subjective ratings of effort, fatigue and anxiety. Primary task performance remained stable over changes in workload, with evidence of decrement only for secondary tasks. As predicted by CCM, effort was selectively increased towards the primary task under higher loads. Performance protection incurred fatigue costs, which failed to dissipate during the unloading phase. The present results offered broad support for CCM predictions of the pattern of breakdown under high demand.

Introduction

Though performance failures in complex work environments are uncommon, the costs associated with these rare events are high, as witnessed in large scale industrial and mass transportation accidents (e.g., Bhopal, Chernobyl, and Ladbroke Grove). Accordingly, efforts should be made to minimise the likelihood of accidents such as these taking place. Research examining the dynamic relationship between the human operators and their task environments plays a key role in this process. However, the safety-critical nature of operational work environments such as these all makes it impossible (or at least unlikely) to employ experimental manipulations of factors that may influence operator performance. Hence, any attempts to assess threat through empirical examinations must be conducted using analogue environments or laboratory-based simulations. One problem associated with this strategy is that laboratory examinations of load and stress effects on performance have historically often yielded equivocal findings (Hockey & Hamilton, 1983), with rapid performance breakdown observed in some studies but others showing undisturbed performance under stress. It is thought that this confusing picture might be a result of the fact that the experiments were based on flawed theoretical and/or experimental frameworks.

Laboratory examinations of performance under stress have typically employed tasks that only assess performance on a single level and participants that would not be as motivated as the trained staff in operational environments that the studies aim to generalise to. Hence, though performance decrements may be found when untrained or unmotivated participants are used, it is also important to recognise that responsible operators will attempt to adapt their performance under demanding conditions (see Kahneman, 1973; Teichner, 1968), and so observable performance levels may appear unaffected. The present study aimed to find evidence of potential threat to system safety under conditions of sustained and varied task demand. In order to capture the threat-related effects of exposure to sub-optimal conditions, a wider range of metrics was used, in accordance with the recommendations of Hockey's Compensatory Control Model (CCM; Hockey, 1997). As CCM proposes that performance can be maintained under demanding conditions but at a cost to performance levels in less salient tasks and decrements in subjective state, the framework proposes the use of measuring these hidden (or 'latent') decrements in addition to assessment of overt performance levels. This extended definition of performance moves beyond the typical definition of performance *effectiveness* in order to recognise *performance efficiency,* which contextualises the performance against the costs of maintaining it. The CCM proposes that latent decrement can be recognised through performance degradation to less salient tasks (as performance protection under stress is biased towards the primary task) and performance costs in the form of increased levels of effort investment to protect primary task goals, in addition to increased levels of subjective strain (e.g., fatigue, anxiety).

Method

The CAMS task

The Cabin Air Management System (CAMS; Sauer et al., 2000), a microworld simulation of the atmospheric control systems for a hyperbaric spacecraft living chamber, was used as an experimental framework as it provides opportunities for measuring the range of overt and latent effects identified by Hockey's CCM. These included primary and embedded secondary tasks, embedded self-report metrics, in addition to offering methods for effectively manipulating task load. Supervisory control of the system was designated to be the primary task, and required the operators to maintain the environmental parameters within designated 'safe' zones. Two embedded tasks were deemed to be subsidiary; the Alarm Reaction Task (ART; a simple reaction time task) required operators to acknowledge visual annunciators as when they appeared on display, whilst the System Status Check (SSC; a pulse-based prospective memory task) required the logging of system parameter information at set intervals.

Participants, design and procedure

Fifteen participants were recruited (8 male and 7 female, median age 26) from a sample of Post-Graduate students at the University of Leeds. Ten participants had taken part in a previous experiment using CAMS. They were trained for two hours, and were also required to pass a 30 min inclusion assessment under test conditions prior to data collection. The experiment was designed with cyclic loading as a central feature as it reflected variable task demands common across work environments. Load was manipulated through the primary task, with a 2 (phase) x 4 (task load) within-groups design used. Phase was defined by the direction in which the load levels were changing, either loading or unloading. Task load was defined by the three levels of task difficulty, in which the number of faults in the system varied from 2 to 5 faults. A 3 (task) x 2 (phase) x 4 (task load) within-groups design was used to analyse absolute effort changes to the three CAMS tasks. The experimental session took place in a quiet laboratory equipped with artificial lighting. The operators took part in a single 105 min experimental session, which consisted of 7 x 15 min sub-sessions. Task load levels were increased and decreased monotonically over the course of the session, with the load increasing gradually over the first three sub-sessions (the 'loading phase') and decreasing over the final three sub-sessions (the 'unloading phase'). The maximum load consisted of faults in the system controllers of all five parameters, which was found in the fourth sub-session only. The first and last sub-sessions contained the minimum loads of faults in the control systems of only two parameters. A 30 s pause between sub-sessions was used to collect self-report data.

Measures

Primary task performance was defined as the percentage of time that the parameters were in the unsafe 'red' zone. The results were computed across the five parameters to yield a mean percentage of the total time that the system is in a fault state. ART was assessed through the mean response time to the visual warnings. A measure of average response latency was used for the SSC. In addition to the performance assessments, subjective state measures were also used. Embedded (on screen) visual analogue scales were presented at the beginning and end of every sub-session for *perceived mental workload, overall effort intensity* and *fatigue*. The uni-dimensional measures allowed for quick and easy assessment of the variables, with the low level of intrusiveness minimizing the disruption to the experimental procedure and reducing the likelihood of strain dissipation (e.g., Tattersall & Foord, 1996). A pencil and paper measure of *effort direction* was also completed following each sub-session. This required participants to estimate the relative percentage of effort allocated to each of the three (primary and two secondary) tasks, by assigning a number to each (therefore, the total of the three ratings was required to be 100). The cyclic loading method enabled the use of hysteresis methods for the assessment of fatigue carry-over effects. This was defined as the difference between unloading and loading phases for the middle of the load range for each measure; [(the mean of the 3 + 4 fault sub-sessions from the unloading phase) – (the mean of the 3 + 4 fault sub-sessions from the unloading phase)]. A measure of 'absolute effort' for the primary task was computed as the product of effort intensity and direction (transformed to a proportional weighting (0-1).

Results

Performance

Fig 1a shows that primary task performance remained very high and stable with load changes. While the effect of load was significant [$F(1.41, 19.68) = 6.18, p = .014, f = .44$], the increase in error from load 2 to load 5 was very small (1-2%), supporting the prediction of performance protection. ART performance also showed a high level of stability across the session, though a non-significant but large effect of task load was found [$F(1.44, 20.11) = 2.08, p = .16, f = .38$]. SSC performance deteriorated as a function of increasing *task load* [$F(1.81, 25.29) = 5.37, p = .038, f = .062$] and *phase*, with larger decrements found in the unloading phase [$F(1, 14) = 5.24, p = .015, f = .61$].

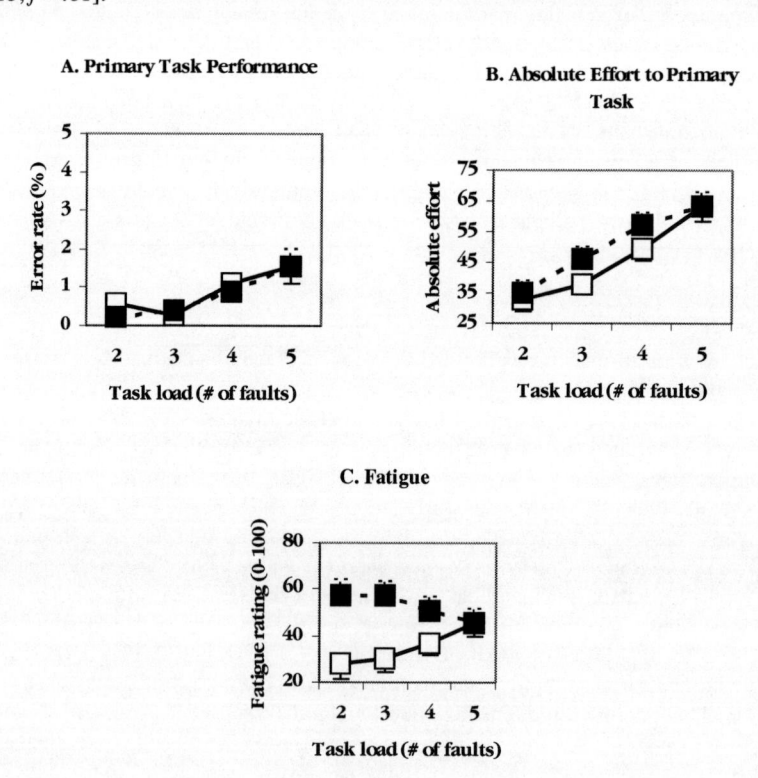

Figure 1. Changes in (a) Primary task performance, (b) Absolute effort to primary task, and (c) Fatigue, as a function of load and phase (loading = open symbols; unloading = filled symbols). For clarity standard error bars are shown as one-sided

Effort and fatigue

As a confirmation of the effectiveness of the load manipulation, subjective mental workload ratings increased dramatically as a function of *task load* [$F(1.50, 20.70) = 36.68$, $p < .001$, $f = 1.66$], and were also higher under the unloading phase (hysteresis estimate = 11.67) [$F(1, 14) = 6.95$, $p = .018$, $f = .52$].

Absolute effort (Fig 1b) showed differential effects of task load on the amount of effort allocated to the primary and secondary tasks, with increased effort on the primary task under unloading supporting the interpretation of protection of primary task performance [$F(1.05,14.67) = 230.05$, $p < .001$, $f = 4.07$]. The significant *task x task load* interaction [$F(1.47,20.63) = 29.80$, $p < .001$, $f = 1.46$] supported the interpretation of a strategic shift in resource allocation, with task load increases being met with slight decreases to the amount of effort allocated to secondary tasks, and large increases to the primary task. The absence of hysteresis effects for the two secondary tasks demonstrated similar effort allocations over the two phases, whilst an estimate of 7.87 indicated that the primary task received more effort in the unloading phase.

Fig 1(c) shows that fatigue ratings, as expected, also increased with load. However, they showed no sign of dissipation during the unloading phase. This strong carryover effect was confirmed by a significant effects of *phase* [$F(1,14) = 29.10$, $p < .001$, $f = 1.44$, and *phase x task load* interaction [$F(1.57,22.00) = 17.07$, $p < .001$, $f = 1.10$].

Discussion

Primary task performance was found to be actively protected under high demand, though at a cost to subsidiary task goals and compensatory costs. SSC performance showed a pattern of degradation with increases in task load and also during the unloading phase. Subjective mental workload ratings also increased with task load and during the unloading phase, a pattern that was reflected in the results for absolute effort to the primary task, suggesting that operators adaptively increased the effort levels to the most important goals in order to protect them under conditions of high load and during the unloading phase. Compensatory costs were also found in the form of large fatigue increases over the course of the session. Fatigue levels accumulated in response to load increases, but did not dissipate with load reductions, as they continued to increase before stabilising in the final (low load) sub-session. The present findings therefore support Hockey's (1997) assertion that even when overt performance may appear undisturbed under high levels of load, latent effects can be valuable indicators of strained performance and decreased operator functional state.

The present results have several implications for operational work environments. The assessment of latent decrements showed that the increased compensatory costs were found during the unloading phase, hence reflecting increased risk *after* rather than *during* periods of high load. As fatigue is as an adaptive response to the maintenance of task goals in focal attention, this 'stop emotion' increases the resistance to the investment of further effort, which could be problematic should load increase again. The lack of recovery during the unloading phase therefore represents a serious threat to system safety, with obvious implications for work scheduling interventions (rest breaks, shift transition, etc). It is therefore recommended that performance assessment in complex work domains should be able to identify these hidden threats.

Acknowledgements

A Ph.D. bursary from the Institute of Psychological Sciences, University of Leeds, supported this research.

References

Hockey, G.R.J. (1997). Compensatory control in the regulation of human performance under stress and high workload: A cognitive-energetical framework. *Biological Psychology, 45*, 73-93.

Hockey, G.R.J., & Hamilton, P. (1983). The cognitive patterning of stress states. In G. R. J. Hockey (Ed.), *Stress and human performance*. Chichester.: John Wiley & Sons Ltd.

Kahneman, D.E. (1973). *Attention and effort*. Englewood Cliffs, N.J.: Prentice Hall.

Sauer, J., Wastell, D., & Hockey, G.R.J. (2000). Using Microworlds to simulate highly-automated work environments: The case of the Cabin Air Management System. *Computers in Human Behaviour, 16*, 45-58.

Tattersall, A.J., & Foord, P.S. (1996). An experimental evaluation of instantaneous self-assessment as a measure of workload. *Ergonomics, 39*, 740-748.

Teichner, W.H. (1968). Interaction of behavioural and physiological stress reactions. *Psychological Review, 75*, 51-81.

How to develop and use assistance systems efficiently –Using the microworld to acquire knowledge for developers and operators

Barbara Gross[1] & Jens Nachtwei[2]
[1]Technische Universitaet Berlin
[2]Humboldt-Universität zu Berlin
Berlin, Germany

Abstract

This research considers how a human-machine system which is sufficiently complex to mimic real world conditions can be derived in an experiment. A Socially Augmented Microworld (SAM) is described in which the complexity of the microworld is augmented by a social component – so called microworld inhabitants. Humans, as an important factor for complexity in a system, are not simulated then but are used in determined roles as part of the experimental environment. It could be shown that a direct variation of the microworld's complexity can be achieved by choosing the microworld inhabitants on the basis of specific personal features as well as by task modification. The scope for further developments is discussed.

Introduction

The fit between humans and machines is an important aspect of the capability of a complex human-machine system. This applies especially to technical assistance and automated systems against the background of function allocation in supervisory control of industrial systems such as process control or telerobotics (Sheridan, 1978). Safe, reliable and cost-effective systems can only be designed if the human qualities and needs of the operators of such complex systems are considered. It also seems necessary to consider the system developers in this connection, because the quality of systems is determined by their abilities. Important basis for using abilities is knowledge about the matter of interest. The adaptation of technical systems to their users is only possible if the resources of the users are known to the developer. In addition, both the system's context of use and the goals and tasks of the developer must be known so that reasonable support can be offered.

If the resources of both the systems operators and developers are acquired in parallel, this can be used to optimise the function allocation in human-machine systems (e.g. Fitts, 1951; Sheridan, 2000; Fuld, 2000; Wright et al., 2000). An experimental setting is needed which offers challenging tasks to both operators and developers of complex man-machine systems and allows a comparison of their performance. A supportive task has been chosen in a specially developed Socially

Augmented Microworld (SAM) in the form of a road environment (Gross, 2006). The special feature of SAM consists of real human beings as inhabitants of a microworld. This paper aims at exploring the influence of personal features of microworld inhabitants on features of SAM.

Methods

Approach

Microworlds make it possible to examine behaviour under controlled laboratory conditions (DiFonzo et al., 1998). However, there are limitations. Either functions are deterministic and events can be foreseen in principle (even if these events are extremely complex and interdependent) or functions contain stochastic parts which makes prediction of behaviour of the microworld nearly impossible. Neither form is sufficiently suitable to observe human behaviour in complex systems. A promising approach is to augment the microworld with a social component – two so called microworld inhabitants (MI). Humans, an important factor for complexity in a system, are not simulated but are used in determined roles as part of the experimental environment.

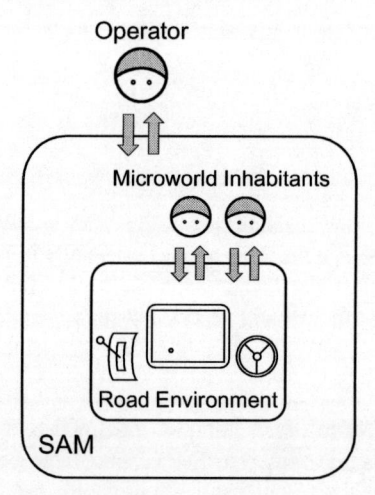

Figure 1. Supervising role of operator in the SAM environment

The experimental paradigm is supervised cooperative tracking. That means two persons have to work together to cope with the tracking task. An external operator (see Figure 1) supervises the process of cooperative tracking. S/he is able to block, to limit or to amplify certain actions of the microworld inhabitants and to give warnings, hints and feedback in real-time to enhance their performance, just like a technical assistance system would do.

Materials and equipment

Preliminary studies showed that the primary task "tracking in the microworld" is suitable to induce the desired support requirement (Gross & Nachtwei, 2006). The microworld inhabitants can cope with the task, but could proceed faster and make fewer mistakes. According to these findings the support requirement can be manipulated in the sense of experimental variation. Initially, three domains are used for the evolution of the microworld: Features of the route used in the tracking, selection and deployment of the microworld inhabitants, and the pairings with respect to certain personal features, as well as additional task features. The present study focusses on the influence of personal feature strategy (in the sense of driving style) on characteristics of the microworld. The preliminary studies showed that this offers considerable potential for adjusting the microworld. The research question was to what extent a fit of the two microworld inhabitants is suitable for influencing the complexity with respect to these personal features as a means for the manipulation. This study does not yet include a supervising operator.

The specially developed "Cooperation Conflict Complexity Model" describes a corresponding working mechanism (Gross & Nachtwei, 2006). Put simply, there is a correlation between certain personal features and performance variables which can objectively be captured during tracking (Elander et al., 1993). If cooperating microworld inhabitants differ in these features, which should lead to a higher conflict potential, mediated over subjectively observed differences in performance (Sell et al., 2004). Conflicts lead to a worse prediction of the course of events in the experimental environment. This in turn leads to a more challenging supportive task for the supervising operator. In the case of strategy the conflict consists in a divergence of goals. It was expected that the variance in personal features is reflected by performance differences: Speed-oriented microworld inhabitants go faster; the accuracy oriented ones make fewer mistakes on average. According to the assumption, the divergence of goals leads to a drop in performance, it was expected that the average cooperative performance of the microworld inhabitants is worse than the average single tracking control ride.

Design

For a sample of 50 participants in 25 teams, the personal feature strategy (in the sense of driving style) was examined as the independent variable. A number of researchers have shown that there is a relationship between speed and accuracy for movement tasks (e.g. Fitts, 1954). According to this, strategy is differentiated in speed orientation and accuracy orientation. This bipolar variable is considered in an unspecific and a specific form. Unspecific strategy describes a trait manifested in the individual, the personal inclination either for accuracy or speed orientation. Individuals' preferred strategy was determined prior to the investigation by an especially developed questionnaire, and used to assign the participants to the teams for the cooperative tracking. Therefore in a first step, participants with opposite features according to the results of the questionnaire were paired, so each team consisted of one speed-oriented and another accuracy-oriented microworld inhabitant.

The specific strategy was manipulated in the experiment by the individually given instruction to complete the tracking task either accurately or quickly. The instruction was assigned according to the individual's inclination for accuracy or speed. Dependent variables were the performance measures speed, number of incidents, i.e. when the driver fails to keep within the lane markings (Number_Incidents), and the duration of these violations (Time_Incidents). A session consisted of warming up for both participants followed by eight trips of a certain distance. To compare the microworld inhabitants performance in cooperative and single mode, cooperative rides and single tracking control rides have been alternated (cooperative – single MI1 – cooperative – single MI2 – etc.). A cooperative ride took about five minutes, a single ride about one minute. The first part of every cooperative ride is identical with the single ride; to compare both only this first part was taken into consideration. A log file was written continually, the system performance of the PC used to run the tracking task enabled to make a record every 40 milliseconds.

Results

As can been seen in Figure 2, the differences in personal features are reflected in performance differences.

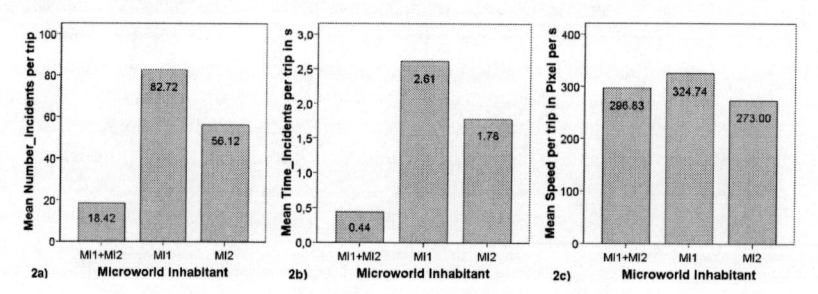

Figure 2. Average performance for the dependent variables: Number_Incidents, Time_Incidents, and Speed

Accuracy-oriented microworld inhabitants make fewer mistakes on average (see Figure 2a). The difference between the speed-oriented (MI1) and the accuracy-oriented (MI2) microworld inhabitants proved to be significant (independent samples t-test results: t = 2.47; df = 98; SE 10.77; p < .016). Speed-oriented microworld inhabitants go significantly more quickly (see Figure 2c). The difference between the speed-oriented (MI1) and the accuracy-oriented (MI2) microworld-inhabitants proved to be significant (t = 2.34; df = 98; SE 22.08; p < .016). The average performance of the microworld inhabitants is higher in the cooperative mode than in the single tracking mode for the Number_Incidents (see Figure 2a) and Time_Incidents (see Figure 2b), but not for Speed (see Figure 2c). The differences proved significant in independent sample t-tests for the smallest difference (MI1+MI2 vs. MI2) for Number_Incidents (t = –7.15; df = 148; SE 5.27; p < .016) and Time_Incidents (t = –8.26; df = 148; SE –1.34; p < .016), but not for Speed (t = 1.39; df = 148; SE 17.08; p < .016).

Discussion

The personal feature strategy was an effective way to influence the tracking performance. It is shown that a direct variation of the microworld complexity can be achieved by choosing the microworld inhabitants on the basis of specific personal features. This represents a step towards the development of the intended supportive task. The results for the performance variation in the cooperative tracking mode do not correspond to the expectations. Nevertheless this can be seen in the literature concerning compensatory strategies. Future research will investigate how the fit of personal features of microworld inhabitants impacts microworld complexity. If the combination of the manipulation of primary task sections, and selection and interaction of microworld inhabitants does not provide sufficient complexity for the operator's support task, then further task levels could be integrated. Supplementary perceptive and cognitive elements or decisions by the microworld inhabitants are conceivable.

References

DiFonzo, N., Hantula, D., & Bordia, P. (1998). Microworlds for experimental research: Having your (control and collection) cake, and realism too. *Behavior Research Methods, Instruments, & Computers, 30*, 278-286.

Elander, J., West, R., & French, D. (1993). Behavioral correlates of individual differences in roadtraffic crash risk: An examination of methods and findings. *Psychological Bulletin, 113*, 279-294.

Fitts, P.M. (1954). The information capacity of the human motor system in controlling the amplitude of movement. *Journal of Experimental Psychology, 47*, 381-391.

Fitts, P.M. (1951). *Human engineering for an effective air navigation and traffic control system* (Tech. Rep.). Columbus, OH, USA: Ohio State University Research Foundation.

Fuld, R.B. (2000). The fiction of function allocation, revisited. *International Journal of Human-Computer Studies, 52*, 217-233.

Gross, B. (2006). Mikrowelten in Squeak. In A.M. Heinecke and H. Paul (Eds.), *Mensch und Computer 2006. Workshop-Beiträge zur sechsten fachübergreifenden Konferenz* (pp. 59-64). München, Germany: Oldenbourg.

Gross, B. & Nachtwei, J. (2006). Assistenzsysteme effizient entwickeln und nutzen – Die Mikrowelt als Methode zur Wissensakquisition für Entwickler und Operateure. In M. Grandt & A. Bauch (Eds.), *Cognitive Systems Engineering in der Fahrzeug- und Prozessführung* (DGLR-Bericht 2006-02/07) (pp. 75-88). Bonn, Germany: Deutsche Gesellschaft für Luft- und Raumfahrt e.V.

Sell, J., Lovaglia, M., Mannix, E., Samuelson, C., & Wilson, R. (2004). Investigating Conflict, Power, and Status within and among Groups. *Small Group Research, 35*, 44-72.

Sheridan, T.B. (2000). Function allocation: algorithm, alchemy or apostasy? *International Journal of Human-Computer Studies, 52*, 203-216.

Sheridan, T.B., & Verplank, W.L. (1978). *Human and computer control of undersea teleoperators* (Man-Machine Systems Laboratory Report). Cambridge, MA, USA: Massachusetts Institute of Technology.

Wright, P., Dearden, A., & Fields, B. (2000). Allocation of function: scenarios, context and the economics of effort. *International Journal of Human-Computer Studies, 52,* 289-318.

Do cognitive assistance systems reduce operator workload?

Stefan Röttger[1], Krisztina Bali[2], & Dietrich Manzey[1]
[1]Berlin University of Technology
Berlin, Germany
[2]Budapest University of Technology and Economics
Budapest, Hungary

Abstract

As the operators' tasks in complex human-machine systems are often difficult and cognitively demanding, today more and more cognitive functions are aided or completely carried out by automated assistance systems (e.g. decision or diagnostic support systems in process control). One major purpose of providing such automated assistance is to reduce operator workload. Adding a system, however, also means adding tasks and complexity to a work environment. Thus, workload reduction is not granted when cognitive tasks are automated.

The present study addresses the impact of the introduction of automated assistance systems on operator workload in process control. Twelve participants were asked to detect, diagnose and repair any malfunctions occurring in a process control simulation (AutoCAMS). This had to be performed manually or was supported by automated assistance systems differing in their degree of automation. Workload effects were assessed with subjective (NASA-TLX), physiological (heart rate variability, HRV), and performance indicators (secondary task reaction time, RT).

Automation support significantly increased overall performance. Furthermore, subjective workload ratings were significantly lower in the assisted conditions as compared to the manual condition. This latter effect was not reflected in the HRV and RT measures, although these measures were sensitive to workload changes due to the presence or absence of faults. Possible explanations for the observed dissociation of workload measures are discussed.

Introduction

Many areas of human work are characterized by an increasing degree of automation, e.g. ground-, sea- and air transportation, chemical and power plants, and even health care (Sheridan, 2002). As the operators' tasks in such systems are often difficult and cognitively demanding, today more and more cognitive functions are automated, i.e. aided or completely carried out by assistance systems. Besides increasing performance, safety, and reliability of the overall system, one purpose of introducing such assistance systems often is to reduce operator workload. Adding a new (assistance) system, however, also means adding new tasks and complexity to a work environment. Thus, workload reduction may not be granted when cognitive tasks are automated. Some prominent examples for this are provided by approaches to cockpit automation in aviation. They have been criticized to often just shift workload of pilots from one area to another (e.g. decreasing manual but increasing cognitive workload), instead of achieving an overall workload reduction (Billings, 1997). Similarly, also the results of laboratory research provide some evidence for the ambiguous relationship between automated assistance and operator workload. Although an increased workload due to automation has not been reported, so far, the currently available evidence for workload reductions achieved by the introduction of assistance systems is at least equivocal.

On the one hand, there are a number of studies which indeed report workload benefits of assistance systems. For example, McFadden, Vimalachandran, and Blackmore (2004) studied performance and workload in a naval radar tracking simulation. Participants of their studies were asked to keep track of up to 20 vessels on a radar display. Even though the demands of controlling such a high number of vessels are high, comparatively low workload ratings were obtained when a reliable automated tracking aid was available. A similar result has also been described by Goteman and Dekker (2003) with respect to pilots flying approaches with support of an area navigation system (RNAV). Although the use of RNAV was linked with additional monitoring requirements, perceived mental workload of both pilot flying and pilot not-flying remained low. In addition, there are studies which suggest a more or less direct link between operator workload and different levels of automation (LOA). For example, Kaber, Onal, and Endsley (2000) investigated such a relationship in a telemanipulation taks and found higher LOA associated with lower workload ratings. Kaber and Riley (1999) showed that mandatory adaptive automation in an air traffic control-like laboratory task can lower workload as indicated by secondary task performance.

However, other studies have reported contradictory results. Using the same task as Kaber and Riley (1999), Kaber and Endsley (2004) failed to find any significant effect of LOA on secondary task performance and workload ratings. Endsley and Kiris (1995) investigated effects of different automated decision support systems on user performance and workload in a simulated planning task. Even though the assistance systems were found to affect performance, no clear relationships emerged with respect to the subjectively perceived workload in the different conditions. Similar results were obtained by Lorenz, Di Nocera, Röttger, and Parasuraman (2002) who studied the effects of different automated assistance systems which were introduced to support operators' fault identification and management in a simulated process control task. No effects of LOA of the assistance system on subjective workload ratings were found in this study either.

One shortcoming of the above-mentioned studies is that workload effects rarely have been the main focus of investigation. Instead, these studies mainly have focussed on performance-related effects of automation and workload rather was addressed as some kind of control variable. As a consequence, most of the studies relied on one single indicator of operator workload, only. This might have hindered to completely catch the pattern of workload-related effects associated with automated assistance systems, given the fact that workload appears to represent a multidimensional concept with differing workload assessment techniques differing in sensitivity and diagnosticity (O'Donnel & Eggemeier, 1986). Only recently, Metzger and Parasuraman (2005) examined workload effects of an assistance system for air traffic management using indicators from all three major categories of workload assessment techniques identified by O'Donnell and Eggemeier (1986): Subjective ratings, performance-based measures and physiological measures. While the participants of this study subjectively did not report a significant workload reduction when working with the automated assistance, secondary task performance was better indicating a higher amount of spare capacity in the automation condition. This latter result suggests that the introduction of the automated assistance system, on the one hand, successfully reduced the cognitive resources demanded by the primary tasks. However, because these "free" resources obviously were invested in order to enhance performance in the secondary task, the experienced overall workload remained constant. Although the results of the physiological data have been reported only partially, the results of the study of Metzger and Parasuraman (2005) can be taken as an example for the possible advantages of analysing several workload measures at the same time in order to provide a more complete pattern of workload related effects achieved by the introduction of automated assistance systems.

The present study shall contribute to further elaborate the relationship between operator workload and automated assistance systems. In order to catch possible dissociations and to obtain a more comprehensive picture of automation consequences with respect to operator workload, effects of *different* types of automation (Parasuraman, Sheridan, & Wickens, 2000) were studied using *different* workload measures. For this purpose, participants in the present study where required to perform what has been referred to as a supervisory control task. More specifically, they had to monitor a process control system and to perform effective fault management in case of malfunctions. Fault management included the detection, identification and correction of any faults occurring in different sub-systems of the overall process control. This latter task had to be performed manually or could be supported by one of two automated assistance systems varying in degree of automation. Workload effects were assessed by using subjective, behavioural (secondary-task performance), and physiological (heart rate variability) data. Three hypotheses were investigated: First, it was expected to find higher workload during periods where participants had to work on system malfunctions as compared to fault free phases. Second, it was expected that fault management performance would be increased and workload decreased by the provision of automated assistance. Third, the effect of workload reduction was expected to be dependent on the degree of automation of the assistance system, with higher degree of automation related to higher reduction in workload.

Method

Participants

Twelve engineering students (five male, between 20 and 27 years old with a mean age of 24 years) were recruited for the experiment and were paid for participation. All of them were familiar with the experimental paradigm from a previous study (Manzey, Bahner & Hüper, 2006). This allowed for a marked reduction of the pre-experimental training time, and the task was considered to be difficult enough to observe automation-induced workload reductions even in participants with prior task experience. As heart rate variability (HRV) measures were used in this study, only participants reporting to be without cardiac disorders and without diabetes mellitus, which can cause chronically decreased HRV (Kudat et al., 2006), took part in the experiment.

Tasks

The experiment was conducted using a modified version of AutoCAMS (Hockey, Wastell, & Sauer, 1998; Lorenz et al., 2002), a PC-based simulation of a process control task. This simulation is based on the Cabin Air Management System (CAMS) task originally developed by Hockey et al. in order to investigate stress effects on complex human performance. AutoCAMS simulates an autonomously running life support system of a spacecraft consisting of five subsystems that are critical to maintain atmospheric conditions in the space cabin with respect to different parameters (oxygen, nitrogen, carbon dioxide, temperature and pressure). By default, all of these subsystems are automatically maintained within their target range. However, different faults may occur occasionally, due to a malfunction in any subsystem (e.g. leaks or blocks of a valve or defective sensors). The primary task of the operator involves supervisory control of the subsystems. In case of a malfunction, fault diagnosis and management are to be performed, and an appropriate repair order has to be selected and sent to the spacecraft. Malfunctions always were indicated by an unspecific master alarm represented by a light turning from green to red. Fault diagnosis and management can be carried out manually or with support of an Automated Fault Identification and Recovery Agent (AFIRA). These systems can vary in their degree of automation. For the present study two types of AFIRA were used. The first one (AFIRA_1) represents a system which, in case of a fault, displays both, a fault-diagnosis as well as a supposed sequence of actions for effective fault management, which then has to be implemented manually by the operator. Using the model of Parasuraman et al. (2000), AFIRA_1 can thus be described as high level automation in the areas of information analysis and action selection. The second type, AFIRA_2, additionally offers a fully automated implementation of suggested interventions including and sending of the appropriate repair order, which constitutes a high-level automation of action implementation.

In order to obtain a behavioural workload measure, participants are given an additional *secondary task* which has to be performed in addition to the process control task. This secondary-task consists of a simple reaction time measure. Participants have to respond as fast as possible by a mouse-click to the appearance of a "connection-check icon", which is presented pseudo-randomly every 15 to 35 seconds. This task is introduced as a means of acknowledging seamless communication between control centre and remote life support system.

Measures

Data collection included four measures: Primary task performance, secondary task performance, subjective workload, and heart rate variability as a physiological workload indicator. *Primary task performance* was analysed separately for fault diagnosis and fault management during system malfunctions. Diagnose time, defined as mean time between master alarm and selection of correct repair order, was used as fault diagnosis performance indicator. Fault management performance was measured in terms of percent of time all relevant parameters remained within target limits.

Workload measures were based on self-reports performance, and physiological reactions. *Subjective workload* was assessed using the NASA Task Load Index (Hart & Staveland, 1988). Instead of using the original 100-point scaling, participants indicated perceived workload on a more common seven-point scale. *Secondary task performance* was defined by the median of connection-check reaction times. The mid-frequency (70 to 150 mHz) power spectrum component of *heart rate variability* was used in the present study. An all-pole autoregressive model was fitted to RR-interval time series, yielding the central frequency and bandwidth of the mid-frequency spectral peak. Spectral computations were carried out on a moving time window of 30 seconds, which was shifted along the data series by steps of one second. Thus, HRV values for each second of the experiment were obtained.

Procedure

The day before the experimental session, participants received a two-hour task training with AutoCAMS. Because all participants already had participated in a previous experiment using this task, training was limited to refresh their knowledge about the functionality of AutoCAMS components, and on procedures for fault diagnosis and fault management. They were briefed on the experimental procedures of the following day and signed informed consent. During the experimental session, electrocardiogram data were collected with precordial bipolar leads and three electrodes (positive, negative and ground) placed on the participants' chest. AutoCAMS was operated in three 30 minutes blocks, containing six malfunctions each. After every block, self-reports on workload were collected and extend of support for fault diagnosis and management changed. Thus, every participant operated AutoCAMS manually, and with support of AFIRA 1 and AFIRA 2. Order of automation conditions was balanced across subjects. Participants were instructed to verify AFIRA diagnosis before sending repair orders when working with AFIRA_1 or before starting automated action implementation of AFIRA_2, respectively.

Analysis

As the purpose of the assistance systems under study was to support operators during system malfunctions, workload effects of automation should be most pronounced during fault phases. However, awareness of availability of an assistance system may influence operator workload during fault free phases as well. For example, participants may not spend as much effort as in the manual condition on system monitoring to detect malfunctions and symptom patterns as early as possible. Moreover, higher workload levels were expected during fault phases as compared to fault free phase, which should be reflected by workload indicators as well. Therefore, a 2 × 3 repeated measures analysis of variance (ANOVA) with factors Fault (present vs. absent) and Automation (manual, AFIRA_1, AFIRA_2) was calculated for heart period variability and secondary task performance. As self-reports were collected only once after each block and performance measures are defined for fault-present phases only, these data were not available separately for fault-present and fault-absent phases and analysis was limited to a repeated measures ANOVA with Automation being the only factor. Greenhouse-Geisser correction was applied to degrees of freedom whenever sphericity assumption was violated.

Results

Mean values and standard deviations of all dependent variables are given in Table 1 for each level of factors Automation and Fault. ANOVA results are summarized in Table 2.

Table 1: Means and standard deviations of performance measures, subjective workload ratings and heart rate variability (HRV) in all experimental conditions

	Manual		AFIRA_1		AFIRA_2		Normal		Fault	
	Mean	SD	Mean	SD	Mean	SD	Mean	SD	Mean	SD
Diagnose Time (sec.)	107	57	45	13	56	16	--	--	--	--
Time Within Limits (%)	99.16	0.83	99.76	0.14	99.50	0.21	--	--	--	--
NASA-TLX	46.9	20.4	33.7	12.9	21.8	11.0	--	--	--	--
Secondary Task Performance (ms)	1395	282	1471	302	1616	558	1316	325	1673	423
HRV (ms^2)	201	177	189	163	182	114	210	152	171	142

Performance

Automation significantly influenced both diagnose time and time within limits with higher performance in assisted conditions. Post hoc t-test comparisons of diagnose times showed significant differences between Manual and AFIRA_1 (p=.002) as well as between Manual and AFIRA_2 (p=.01). Fault management performance, as indicated by the relative amount of time all parameters were kept within their predefined limits, was significantly higher with support of AFIRA 1 as compared to fault management carried out manually (p=.035) and with support of AFIRA_2 (p=.009). Secondary task performance, in contrast, did not differ significantly between Automation conditions. However, factor Fault had a significant main effect on prompted reaction times, which were slower during fault phases than during normal operation phases. There was no Automation x Fault interaction effect on secondary task performance.

Table 2: ANOVA results

	Diagnose Time		Time Within Limits		NASA-TLX		Sec. Task Performance		Heart Rate Variability	
Source	df	F	df	F	df	F	df	F	df	F
Automation	1.3	11.8**	1.2	4.6*	1.15	11.9**	1.1	2.0	1.1	0.2
Fault	--	--	--	--	--	--	1	11.9*	1	17.6**
Aut. x Flt.	--	--	--	--	--	--	1.3	1.4	1.7	1.0
Error	13.8	*1763*	12.7	*0.41*	12.7	*274*	13.9	*313826*	18.9	*3254*

Notes: Greenhouse-Geisser correction was applied to degrees of freedom (df) whenever sphericity assumption was violated. Uncorrected degrees of freedom are df = 2 for factor Automation, df = 1 for factor Fault, df = 2 for interaction, and df = 22 for error. Mean square error values are given in italics. *p < .05. **p < .01.

Subjective workload

There was a significant main effect of Automation on subjective workload ratings. Post hoc t-test comparisons showed that workload was rated significantly lower in the AFIRA_1 condition as compared to the manual condition (p=.023). AFIRA_2 led to a further significant reduction of experienced workload (p=.001).

Heart rate variability

A significant main effect of factor Fault on heart rate variability was observed, with lower HRV indicating higher workload during fault periods as compared to fault free periods of the experiment. There was no effect of Automation on HRV, and no Automation x Fault interaction was observed.

Discussion

Introducing an automated fault identification and recovery agent to support operators during system malfunctions in process control is beneficial for fault diagnosis and fault management. Diagnose times in both conditions with AFIRA-support were reduced considerably as compared to unsupported performance. Fault management performance in terms of the relative amount of time all parameters being within target range was above 99 percent in all conditions. From this very high performance level, only AFIRA_1 significantly enhanced the time all parameters being within target range. At the first glance, this is counterintuitive as AFIRA_2, not AFIRA_1, offers fault management support by automatically implementing all necessary interventions. However, these automatic implementations are realised on a step-by-step bases allowing operators to monitor and understand AFIRA_2 actions. Doing so, AFIRA_2 is somewhat slower than operators who manually implement the interventions suggested by AFIRA_1. Thus, the observed advantage of AFIRA_1 over AFIRA_2 is a matter of specific system design, not of general function allocation. On these grounds, it can be concluded that with respect to performance, assistance systems supporting information analyses and action selection with and without automated action implementation are both beneficial, and that there is no general performance advantage of leaving implementation to operators.

With respect to workload it was assumed that fault-management in general is more demanding than just monitoring the system in fault-free periods. Yet, the specific level of workload should be affected by the kind of automated support available. The first assumption got clear support from both measures used to assess differences in workload between fault-present and fault-absent periods. That is, during fault-present periods, heart-rate variability was lower and secondary-task reaction times were slower than during fault-absent periods. However, the additional assumption about the effects of automated assistance on workload only got support from the subjective workload assessment. Participants' workload-ratings in the most difficult manual condition were rather moderate, most probably because of their prior experience with the task from a previous study. Nevertheless, as expected, offloading participants from large parts of information acquisition, information analysis, and action selection tasks during fault phases by AFIRA_1 led to a significant decrease of experienced workload. Additionally automating action implementation (AFIRA_2) resulted in a further significant workload reduction on the subjective level. Thus, one could conclude that automating fault identification and recovery in process control indeed can lead to a reduction of the workload perceived by operators, and that this reduction is the stronger the higher the level of automation.

However, this kind of effect was not reflected in the more objective workload measures: Neither heart rate variability as an indicator of the physiological effort, nor secondary-task performance as indicator of spare capacity showed any systematic relationship to the extend of assistance available to operators during fault management. In fact, no differences emerged in these measures between the manual and both supported conditions. There are at least two possible explanations for this interesting dissociation between workload measures:

First, it could be supposed that both objective workload indicators were less sensitive and, thus, not capable of reflecting the workload differences induced by the different experimental conditions in the present experiment. However, the fact that both workload measures indicated workload differences between fault-present and fault-absent periods shows that they actually were sensitive to workload changes due to altered task demands. This would at least suggest that the workload-differences induced by the different assistance systems are only small, i.e. much smaller than those between fault-absent and fault-present periods. In this case they might have been strong enough to get recognized on a subjective level but too small to affect cardiac activity and secondary task performance. Inspection of participants' fault management behaviour supports this explanation: Operators carried out less information sampling and less interventions in the assisted conditions. This suggests that assistance systems did unload participants to some extend from activities necessary for fault management. This could have led to an experienced workload reduction which is correctly reflected in subjective workload reports.

However, findings regarding a similar dissociation of subjective, performance and physiological indicators of workload (e.g. Derrick, 1988) rather point to a second explanation of the observed effect. It might be that secondary task performance and heart rate variability correctly indicate that both assistance systems do not lead to any gains with respect to workload. In this case, the fact that participants did report workload alleviation might only reflect an evaluation they have inferred from the functionality of the assistance system at hand, i.e. the assumption that there must be a workload benefit if they get supported by such a system.

In any case, what seems to be a safe conclusion from the current study is that at least no increments of workload were introduced by the provision of the automated assistance systems. This result seems to be particularly important because both of the systems were found to yield significant benefits in performance. Obviously it is possible by means of these systems to gain an increment in performance while keeping operator workload at least constant. Furthermore, it seems that the differences in level of automation of the systems studied do not provide any considerable benefits or costs with respect to workload. Therefore, neither overall performance nor workload considerations may be sufficient to finally decide about the relative advantages of these systems with respect to implementation in real-world process control. As a consequence, other possible aspects of human-automation interaction have to be taken into account, in order to make and justify such a decision. These aspects might include all kinds of issues related to what has been labelled "out-of-the-loop-unfamiliarity" (Endsley & Kiris, 1995; Parasuraman et al., 2000), i.e. effects related to maintenance of situation awareness or avoidance of loss of skills after prolonged use of the automated systems. However, the currently available research does not provide clear guidelines in this respect (cf. Kaber & Endsley, 1999; Lorenz et al., 2002). More research clearly is needed in order to arrive at a more complete picture of automation consequences of cognitive assistance systems for fault management in process control.

Acknowledgements

We wish to thank Sabine Jatzev for her help during data acquisition and data analysis. We further highly appreciate the technical support from Marcus Bleil in configuring the experimental paradigm and setting up the equipment.

References

Billings, C.E. (1997). *Aviation automation. The search for a human-centred approach*. Mahwah, NJ: Lawrance Erlbaum Associates.
Derrick, W.L. (1988). Dimensions of operator workload. *Human Factors, 30*, 95-110.
Endsley, M.R., & Kiris, E.O. (1995). The out-of-the-loop performance problem and level of control in automation. *Human Factors, 37*, 381-394.

Goteman, Ö., & Dekker, S. (2003). Flight crew and aircraft performance during RNAV approaches: Studying the effects of throwing new technology at an old problem. *Human Factors and Aerospace Safety, 3*, 147-164.

Hart, S.G., & Staveland, L.E. (1988). Development of NASA-TLX (Task Load Index): Results of empirical and theoretical research. In P.A. Hancock and N. Meshkati (Eds.), *Human mental workload* (pp. 139-183). Amsterdam: North-Holland.

Hockey, G.R.J., Wastell, D.G., & Sauer, J. (1998). Effects of sleep deprivation and user interface on complex performance: A multilevel analysis of compensatory control. *Human Factors, 40*, 233-253.

Kaber, D.B., & Endsley, M.R. (2004). The effects of level of automation and adaptive automation on human performance, situation awareness and workload in a dynamic control task. *Theoretical Issues in Ergonomics Science, 5*, 113-153.

Kaber, D.B., Onal, E., & Endsley, M.R. (2000). Design of automation for telerobots and the effect on performance, operator situation awareness, and subjective workload. *Human Factors and Ergonomics in Manufacturing, 10*, 409-430.

Kaber, D.B., & Riley, J.M. (1999). Adaptive automation of a dynamic control task based on secondary task workload measurement. *International Journal of Cognitive Ergonomics, 3*, 169-187.

Kudat, H., Akkaya, V., Sozen, A.B., Salman, S., Demirel, S., Ozcan, M., et al. (2006). Heart rate variability in diabetes patients. *The Journal of International Medical Research, 34*, 291-296.

Lorenz, B., Di Nocera, F., Röttger, S., & Parasuraman, R. (2002). Automated fault-management in a simulated spaceflight micro-world. *Aviation, Space, and Environmental Medicine, 73*, 886-897.

Manzey, D., Bahner, E.J., & Hüper, A.-D. (2006). Misuse of automated aids in process control: Complacency, automation bias, and possible training interventions. In HFES *Proceedings of the Human Factors and Ergonomics Society 50th Annual Meeting* (pp. 220-224). Santa Monica,CA: HFES.

McFadden, S.M., Vimalachandran, A., & Blackmore, E. (2004). Factors affecting performance on a target monitoring task employing an automatic tracker. *Ergonomics, 47*, 257-280.

Metzger, U., & Parasuraman, R. (2005). Automation in future air traffic management: Effects of decision aid reliability on controller performance and mental workload. *Human Factors, 47*, 35-49.

O'Donnell, R.D., & Eggemeier, F.T. (1986). Workload assessment methodology. In K.R. Boff, L. Kaufman & J.P. Thomas (Eds.), *Handbook of perception and human performance* (Vol. II, Cognitive Processes and Performance, pp. 42-41 - 42-49). New York: Wiley

Parasuraman, R., & Riley, V. (1997). Humans and automation: Use, misuse, disuse, abuse. *Human Factors, 39*, 230-253.

Parasuraman, R., Sheridan, T.B., & Wickens, C.D. (2000). A model for types and levels of human interaction with automation. *IEEE Transactions on systems, man and cybernetics - Part A: Systems and humans, 30*, 286-297.

Sheridan, T.B. (2002). *Humans and Automation: System Design and Research Issues*. New York: Wiley-Interscience.

Supporting human-centred function allocation through animated formal models

Hendrik Oberheid, Bernd Lorenz, & Bernd Werther
German Aerospace Center (DLR)
Braunschweig, Germany

Abstract

Function allocation (FA) refers to the distribution of work across human and machine elements of sociotechnical systems. FA has an important impact on the human operators' roles within the final system and consequently on the systems' safety. It is therefore indispensable that human factors and domain experts' knowledge is integrated in the FA process. There is a need for a suitable design-artefact that facilitates a meaningful communication between engineers, human factors specialists and domain experts for use early in the design cycle. The paper proposes formal process models in combination with graphical animation to support a structured, scenario-based FA process.

Introduction

Function allocation (FA) is a central design step in the development of complex human-machine systems, it's principal aim being to determine which functions of the overall system should be carried out by the human operators and which by machine agents. Besides their criticality for the system's performance and system's safety function allocation decisions are often not made explicit because valid criteria for FA supported by a dedicated FA-method have not been established (Hancock & Scallen, 1996; Sheridan, 2000; Lim & Long, 1994). Instead it is assumed by many system engineering methods that designers will simply know which task are best performed by human operators and which ones should be automated. Extensive empirical evidence reported in human-factors literature and experience with human performance in complex interactive systems prove that this assumption is not a valid one (Parasuraman & Mouloua, 1996; Sheridan, 2002).

Development of FA methodologies

Since the early contributions to the field of function allocation (often also referred to as task allocation) by Fitts (1951) and Jordan (1963) the field has seen a number of notable developments (see Older, Waterson, & Clegg (1997) for a comprehensive survey on function allocation methods). Many of these developments have been reactions to technological advances on the side of automation such as the increasing introduction of higher-level automation, the consequent shifting of operator work to supervisory roles, and the technical potential for increasingly sophisticated dynamic and adaptive automation solutions (Rouse, 1981). Extensions to, and criticisms of existing methods therefore often reflected the need to adapt a method to cater for new trends in automation and e.g. develop a means to express differentiated characteristics of partial automation instead of solely distinguishing between the binary options of declaring a function as fully manual or fully automated.

A more recent trend in FA consists in the attempt to make function-allocation decisions more sensitive to the envisaged working-context in which the system will be used (Wright, Dearden, & Fields, 2000). This approach is motivated by a criticism that considering the allocation of individual functions in isolation as assumed by many former methods (Fitts, 1951; Pulliam & Price, 1984) fails to respect the complex interdependencies between those functions in actual working situations. Ignoring these interdependencies between functions can cause a high number of costly iterations in the FA process in which allocations have to be modified and corrected until a satisfactory global solution is found. Too many iterations are a problem of FA-methods frequently criticized by practitioners in system design. The consideration of each function in isolation also obscures important global trade-offs a development organization might have to make between potentially competing human-factors concerns (e.g. operator workload vs. situation awareness) (Dearden, Harrison, & Wright, 2000).

Scenario-driven FA methods have been proposed to better address the complex interdependencies between functions and to better account for the working context (Dearden et al., 2000; Harrison, Johnson, & Wright, 2002a,b; Sutcliffe, Shin, & Gregoriades, 2002). These approaches rely on scenarios as their basic unit of analysis. The scenarios convey during the function allocation process a rich picture of the actual working context under which the system will be used. The scenario-based approach is in line with more general developments in the field of software engineering where scenario-based system design becomes more widely used (Carroll & Go, 2004)

Objectives and structure of the paper

This paper strongly supports the case for a scenario-driven approach to FA. However, it argues that a procedure as described by Dearden et al. (2000) can be further enhanced through the use of appropriate formal process-models in the generation and selection of an optimal set of relevant and critical scenarios rather than authoring the scenarios manually as originally assumed by the method. It also claims, that by directly coupling the model with an appropriate graphical representation (animation) of the scenario, reasoning and communication about FA between the main stakeholders in the design process (System Designers, Human Factors specialists, Domain Experts) can be facilitated, and gives guidance to both the application points and the characteristics of the animated model. The remainder of the paper gives a brief overview over the scenario-based FA-method proposed by Dearden et al. (2000), referred to as the York Method, and identifies suitable application points for modelling and model animation to support the FA process. It then discusses characteristics of the proposed modelling support and the purpose and appropriate use of the model visualisation in the FA rating process.

Scenario-based function allocation

York method overview

The York method (Dearden et al., 2000) is a procedure for mapping system functions to high-level roles of human and machine agents. A flow chart of the basic steps of the method is shown in Figure 1, left box.

At the beginning of the procedure a list of system level functions is established from the user requirements (step 1). After identifying and sorting out the functions for which allocation to a certain agent is mandatory for reasons external to the design process (e.g. legal constraints, step 2) high-level role statements for the different agents are developed which describe the responsibility and authority of the agent at an abstract level (step 3). In the important next step of the method a number of scenarios are then constructed which describe the context for which the allocation of the remaining functions shall be optimized (step 4).

The actual core of the function allocation process consists of a rating process carried out by a team of system designers, human factors specialists and domain experts (steps 5-10). For the context of each individual scenario the functions are rated in two dimensions: (a) with respect to their centrality to each of the agents' roles and (b) with respect to the technical feasibility and cost of automation. The rating process itself consists of two main phases. In the first phase those functions are filtered out which are entirely separable from any of the human agents' roles and for which an automated solution is readily available (step 6). These functions are candidates for total automation. In the second phase for the remaining functions options for partial automation are created (step 7) and rated (step 8) with respect to selected human factors criteria such as workload, situation awareness and performance.

After running through the complete set of scenarios the different ratings are analysed and the most favourable automation options are selected. If results for different scenarios conflict, the concerned functions present potential candidates for dynamic allocation solutions (step 11). In the end all decisions are reviewed for global trade-offs between different human factors concerns (step 12). Additionally a number of further scenarios can be developed to test the output of the process (step 13).

Besides the theoretical advantage of the presented scenario-based method over approaches which consider each function in isolation, the practical application of the procedure is not without complications.

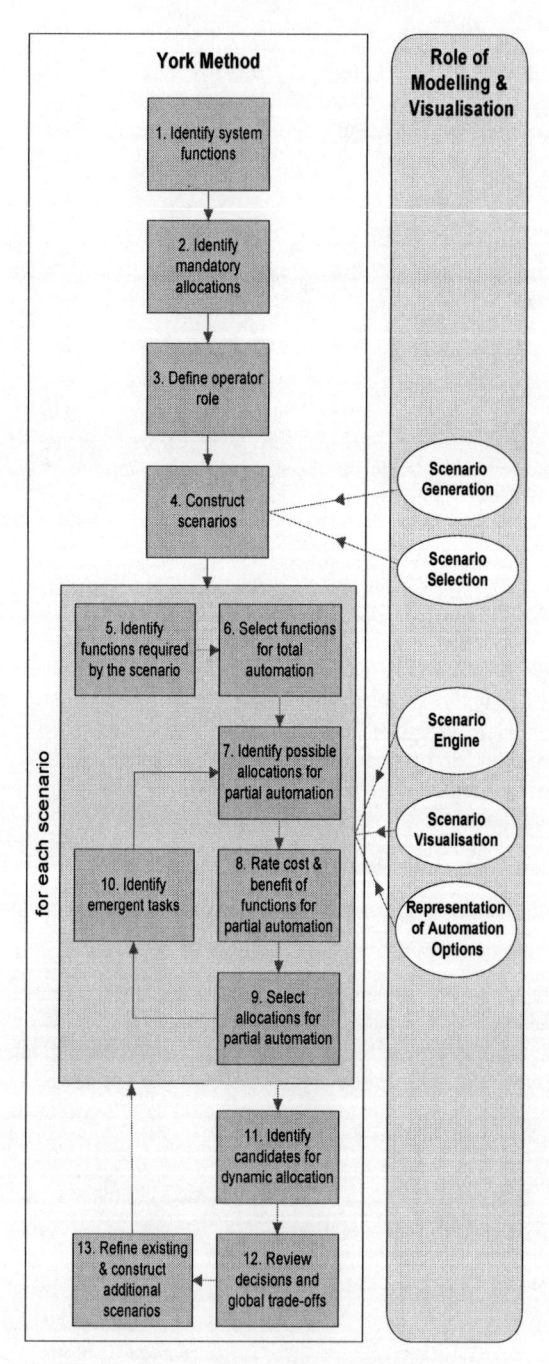

Figure 1. York method for function allocation, adapted from (Dearden et al., 2000)

As pointed out above a crucial step of the method consists in the generation and selection of an optimal set of scenarios. The authors of the method state that scenarios should focus on situations where workload is likely to be high, where complex cognitive work is likely to be required and where performance or safety might be compromised. Dearden et al. (2000) recommended that the selection should therefore be based on the experience of practitioners and accident and incident reports on previous systems. However the experience of practitioners and the information value of accident databases might be limited where the development of large and complex first-of-a kind systems is concerned as is currently for example the case in Air Traffic Management with the investigation of Airborne Separation Assurance Systems and 4D-Flight Management systems. The paper therefore proposes the usage of formal models to conduct preliminary analysis on possible scenario developments, the involvement of different agents in those scenarios and their associated (cognitive) resource usage.

A second critical point in the practical application of the method consists in choosing a suitable medium for the representation of both the scenario context and the potential automation solutions for step 6-8 of the rating process which can be used within the design meetings. A number of text-based templates have been developed by the authors of the method to fulfil this function, among others a scenario template and high-level human-automation interface template which the authors refer to as the IDA-S template standing for Information, Decision, Action and Supervision (Dearden, 2001; Harrison et al., 2002a).

The scenario template generally resembles a textual use case description as commonly used in software engineering or business process design (see Cockburn, 2001). An important difference however lies in the fact, that with view to the FA-process the scenario description must not pre-empt which agent performs a certain function, as this is a main output of the FA-method. On the contrary use case writing in software engineering practice explicitly demands to clearly state the actions of all actors.

The IDA-S template qualifies a given automation solution from a cognitive viewpoint and is supposed to encourage the function allocation team to explore systematically a range of alternative ways of using automation to support the performance of a function. For that purpose three major cognitive performance components of *information, decision,* and *action* are used along the perceive-decide-act stages of information processing. Superordinate to these three components is a fourth component *supervision,* hence the name of the framework IDA-S. Each component is further decomposed into a number of sub-elements (e.g. the component *information* contains the subcategories collection, integration and configuration for problem solving). This taxonomy provides a means to provide a representation of each suggested partial automation proposal that can be used in the allocation process to evaluate the consequences of the proposal against human performance criteria as well as against criteria of e.g. technical feasibility. This framework has some similarity with earlier level-of-automation taxonomies (Endsley & Kaber, 1999; Parasuraman, Sheridan, & Wickens, 2000). Specifying a human-machine system interface using such an abstract framework can indeed help the human factors engineer to compare and evaluate alternative automation options. However, for a non-human-factors specialist without prior training this representation is not always intuitive. In that line, Harrison, Johnson, and Wright (2003) report that during a workshop conducted with a mixed design team consisting of system engineers, human factors experts and domain experts the usage of the template was felt as being too complicated. This paper therefore proposes the use of model animation to combine an abstract notation such as IDA-S with a more intuitive graphical description of the automation solution. At the same time the scenario context can be visualized through the use of domain-specific symbols.

Modelling support for function allocation

At least three different roles can be identified which a formal executable model can fulfil during the application of a scenario-based function allocation method similar to the one described in the last section. Those roles are:

1) Scenario Generation: For the purpose of this paper a scenario can be defined as a description that contains (i) the system actors (ii) background information on the actors and assumptions about the environment (iii) sequences of actions events and possibly (iv) actor's goals and objectives (see Carroll & Go, 2004). The generation of scenarios consists in the calculation of a wide variety of possible actions and events sequences which the system might encounter during lifetime combined with information on the associated state of the system environment. Goals and objectives of actors may be treated explicitly through an appropriate cognitive task analysis and modelling approach or implicitly within a more limited process model.

2) Scenario Selection: Selection of a limited subset of scenarios generated in step 1, which on the one hand reflect the working context of the system under nominal conditions and on the other hand contain the off-nominal action and event sequences which will present a maximal challenge to the operators in terms of automation use and human factors criteria such as workload and situation awareness.

3) Scenario Engine: Real-time execution of the above subset of scenarios with the aim of driving a visualisation of the relevant processes and interactions as a design-artefact for communication purposes among stakeholders.

The three roles correspond to different steps in the York method as described above. While both scenario generation and scenario selection fit into step 4 of the method (construct scenarios) the role of the model as a scenario engine closely relates to step 8 (rate costs and benefits of possible allocations, see Figure 1, right box).

In order to fulfil these roles an appropriate modelling architecture has to be selected and a suitable modelling technique has to be chosen. Obviously, given the variety of potential target domains for the application of the FA-method and the vast number of different modelling paradigms and tools available, general guidance on this matter is hard to give. However a number of issues shall be raised in the following which reflect the background of this work in the field of air traffic management and flight guidance. A characteristic trait of many applications in this domain is the close connection and heavy interdependency of a large number of distributed agents. While expectations on the behaviour of individual agents can often be built from the knowledge of respective domain experts, the resulting properties of the complete system are generally hard to overview.

Scenario Generation: A key function of the model lies in the depiction of concurrency in the system under investigation. While purely sequential causal chains are comparatively easy to envisage for the human mind (and model based-scenario generation might therefore do little better than manual scenario authoring) human beings find temporal interdependencies of parallel processes hard to grasp. It was therefore found to be particularly helpful to use a modelling technique which provides an intuitive approach to concurrency. Therefore Petri Nets and Coloured Petri Nets were good candidates to model interactions between multiple airborne and ground actors.

Scenario Selection: Both performance analysis methods (quantitative methods) and formal analysis methods can be used to select the most relevant subset of scenarios. Formal analysis is particularly helpful for identifying system deadlocks, or searching the reachability graph for situations where a high number of human or machine resources is bound. However, only a limited number of modelling tools support such formal analysis.

Scenario Engine: For the use of the model as a scenario engine a suitable interface has to exist to connect the simulator with the animation module. Some tools offer dedicated interfaces for that purpose (e.g. CPN Tools with the SClub animation environment[*] and DESIGN/CPN with MIMIC/CPN). Other general simulation environments (such as Simulink/Stateflow) offer low-level generic interfaces which could be used to establish the communication. Generally it can be distinguished between tools which allow information to be sent only from the model to the visualisation front end and tools which allow for a two-way communication between the model and the visualisation, and are therefore able to incorporate user-feedback through the visualisation front end into the further progress of the simulation.

Visualisation support for function allocation

In their comprehensive survey on function allocation methods Older et al. (1997) identify the ability of a method to encourage participation of practitioners and end-users as one of the main requirements for a function allocation method in general (see also Grote, 1994). This requirement becomes increasingly important the more complex the target domain of the system is and the more difficult it gets for the system designers themselves to build up a comprehensive picture of the working context under which the system will be used. In the field of air traffic control and air

---

[*] Within a project at the German Aerospace Center CPN Tools (developed at the university of Aarhus, DK) is currently used in conjunction with the SClub visualisation tool (Westergaard & Lassen, 2005) to model trajectory negotiation processes between different airborne and ground actors.

traffic management the adequate involvement of domain experts (like e.g. controllers, pilots and airline personnel) and also human factors specialists through all phases of the system engineering process has become a major issue.

The demand for the participation of at least three different disciplines (system engineers, human factors specialists and domain experts) in the development of an initially only coarsely defined human-machine system raises the question for the most suitable design-artefact which the design team should build and discuss. Apart from the use of informal natural language for the description of the future system, a number of formal, abstract notations are commonly used in system engineering (such as UML, OMT). However as Parry et al. (1995) point out those abstract notations offer benefits mainly for developers as costumers often do not understand them. A similar difficulty can be observed in system engineers with the use of formal classification schemes for different levels of automation as have been proposed by the human-factors community (Endsley & Kaber, 1999; Parasuraman et al. 2000).

Within the system development process common in the air traffic management domain the use of animated formal models in the early phases of system design could contribute to filling the gap between the informal user requirements (derived from high-level strategic operational concept documents) and the later development of prototypes and full mission simulators. In a first step a formal model of an air traffic management application is built from the informal description found in the strategic concept documents (Eurocontrol, 2004, 2005; C-ATM, 2004). Animation is then used to validate through different stakeholders if the formalisation has been performed correctly and the model performs as expected. As this process will likely run through a number of iterations, it is highly desirable that the animation be tightly coupled to the model, so as to guarantee that the state of the model and the behaviour of the animation are always consistent. Once increasing confidence in the model has been built, it is then used to generate the scenarios for the actual function allocation process a described above. The most promising function allocation solutions discovered during the FA process and the most critical scenarios can present an important input to the planning of the time and cost intensive human in the loop simulations.

Within a project at the German Aerospace Center a so called ASAS application (Airborne Separation Assurance System) is currently investigated as an example case for the use of animated formal methods in function allocation. ASAS is a future air traffic management concept for delegating certain traffic separation and avoidance tasks from the groundside to the aircraft. It therefore has a potential to bring about major changes to current controller and pilot roles and self-conceptions. From a function allocation point of view ASAS is a particularly interesting example case, since the functions delegated to the aircraft will have to be distributed in a sound way across the flight crew and cockpit automation. Great care has to be taken that these tasks integrate seamlessly with current flightcrew (and controller) working practices.

So far within the project a cognitive task analysis of the ASAS application has been conducted and a number of potential automation options have been created and documented. Additionally a nominal scenario for the course of the application has been written. This scenario is currently being modelled with Coloured Petri Nets with the aim of subsequently extending the model to generate a number of alternative off-nominal scenarios. Also an animation for the ASAS application is currently being constructed which will serve to discuss the scenario and automation solutions with different stakeholders.

However, the concrete attempt to apply the proposed visualisation approach in practice reveals one important problem, which is what kind of visualisation exactly one should choose (see also Parry, Ozcan, & Siddiqi, 1995). Unfortunately no guidance was found in literature for the specific field of function allocation and very little seems to be available for the broader area of requirements engineering. This would leave the conception of the animation entirely to the judgement of the visualiser, a fact which could make animation difficult to apply in practice since the design team will not necessarily include people trained in creating technical animation or illustration. In the worst case the animation might then be misleading or simply miss out important aspects of the underlying model.

To tackle that problem of what exactly is to be visualized it might be helpful to have a look at the area of software and algorithm visualisation. Price, Baecker, and Small (1990) have presented a well-founded taxonomy for software visualisation which covers aspects such as visualisation content, form, method, interaction, and effectiveness. They therein discuss a wide number of issues such as the mapping between program time and visualisation time, the representation of control flows and data flows in the visualisation and the user interaction with the visualisation. Although narrower in scope and (as the name suggests) focused on software engineering instead of system engineering this taxonomy could present an stimulating framework and starting point for thinking about the animation of human-machine interaction. Further research should be conducted on in how this or a similar taxonomy could be applied or adapted to the area of system animation for function allocation.

Conclusions

Function allocation decisions (FA) for complex human-machine systems are typically taken during the early stages of the design process. Nevertheless they have a far reaching impact on the shaping of the human operators' roles within the final system and consequently on the resulting human-machine system's performance and safety. It is thus important to seek for ways to efficiently incorporate the knowledge of human factors specialists and domain experts into the FA process.

A recent development in the field of function allocation methods consists in the attempt to make FA decisions for human-machine systems more sensitive to the actual working context under which the system will be employed. In order to do so it is tried to consider function allocation decisions in the context of a wide range of future system scenarios and working situations.

The paper discusses the potential use of formal process models coupled with graphical visualisations of the model, to support a scenario-based function allocation process as proposed by Dearden et al. (2000). The role of the process model covers aspects such as the generation of a wide range of potential scenarios and the systematic selection of the most critical ones as an input to the FA-process and the stakeholder workshops. The main purpose of the visualisation consists in facilitating an efficient communication and shared understanding of both the scenarios and the potential automation options among the different stakeholders in the design process. Characteristics and application points for the different functions of the model and visualisations within the FA-process are pointed out throughout the article.

References

Carroll, J.M., & Go, K. (2004). The Blind Men and the Elephant: Views of Scenario-Based System Design. *Interactions, 11 (6)*, 44-53

C-ATM Consortium (2004). *C-ATM High-Level Operational Concept, Version 1.2*. Retrieved 03.04.2007 from :
http://www.eurocontrol.fr/Newsletter/2005/March/CATM/CATM_HLOC.doc.

Cockburn, A. (2001). *Writing Effective Use Cases*. Boston: Addison-Wesley.

Dearden, A., Harrison, M., & Wright, P. (2000). Allocation of function: scenarios, context and the economics of effort. *International Journal of Human-Computer Studies, 52*, 289-318.

Dearden, A. (2001). IDA-S: A conceptual framework for partial automation. In A. Blandford, J. Vanderdonckt, and P. Gray (Eds.), *People and Computers XV - Interaction without Frontiers Proceedings of IHM-HCI 2001* (pp. 213-228). Berlin: Springer.

Endsley, M.R. & Kaber, D.B. (1999). Level of automation effects on performance, situation awareness and workload in a dynamic control task. *Ergonomics, 42*, 462-492.

Eurocontrol (2004). Operational Concept Document (OCD), *Volume 1 (the vision)*. Document identifier FCO.ET1.ST07.DEL01. Retrieved 03.04.2007 from:
http://www.eurocontrol.int/oca/gallery/content/public/docs/OCD/OCD_2_1_Re leased.pdf.

Eurocontrol (2005). Eurocontrol ATM operational concept, *Volume 2, concept of operations*, year 2011. Retrieved 03.04.2007 from:
http://www.eurocontrol.int/oca/gallery/content/public/docs/op_concept/ConOps _2011_Edition%201_0_03-05-2005.pdf.

Fitts, P. (1951). *Human engineering for an effective air navigation and traffic control system*. Washington, DC: National Research Council.

Grote, G. (1994). A participatory approach to the complementary design of highly automated work systems. In G. Bradley and H. Hendrick (Eds.), *Human Factors in Organizational Design and Management* (Vol. IV, pp. 115-120). Amsterdam: Elesevier Science, North-Holland.

Hancock, P.A. & Scallen, S.F. (1996). The future of function allocation. *Ergonomics in Design, October, 4*, 24-29.

Harrison, M.D., Johnson, P.D., & Wright P.C. (2002a). Automating functions in multi-agent control systems: supporting the decision process. In F. Redmill and T. Anderson (Eds.), *Tenth safety-critical systems symposium*. Southampton, UK: Springer.

Harrison, M.D., Johnson, P.D., & Wright P.C., (2002b). *Automating functions in multi-agent control systems: supporting the decision process.* York, UK: Heslington.

Harrison, M.D., Johnson, P.D., & Wright, P.C. (2003). Relating the Automation of Functions in a Multi-Agent Control System to a System Engineering Representation. In E. Hollnagel(Ed.), *Handbook of Cognitive Task Design* (pp. 503-524). Mahwah, NY: Lawrence Erlbaum,.

Jordan, N. (1963). Allocation of functions between men and machines in automated systems. *Journal of Applied Psychology, 47*, 161-165.

Lim, Y.L. & Long, J.B. (1994). *The muse method for usability engineering.* Cambridge, UK: Cambridge University Press.

Older, M.T., Waterson, P.E., & Clegg, C.W. (1997). A Critical Assessment of Task Allocation Methods and their Applicability. *Ergonomics, 40*, 151-171.

Parasuraman, R. & Mouloua, M. (Eds.) (1996). *Automation and Human Performance.* Mahwah, NY: Lawrence Erlbaum,.

Parasuraman, R., Sheridan, T.B., & Wickens, C.D. (2000). A model of types and levels of human interaction with automation. *IEEE Transactions on Systems, Man, and Cybernetics – Part A: Systems and Humans, 30*, 286-297.

Parry, P.W., Ozcan, M.B., & Siddiqi, J. (1995). The Application of Visualisation to Requirements Engineering. Proceedings of the 8th International Conference on Software Engineering and Its Applications, Paris, France, (pp. 699-710).

Price, B.A., Baecker, R.M., & Small, I.S. (1990). A principled taxonomy of software visualization. *Journal of Visual Languages and Computing, 4*, 211-266.

Pulliam, R. and Price, H.E. (1984). Allocating functions to man or machine in Nuclear Power Plant Control. *The Nuclear Engineer, 25*, 79-85.

Rouse, W.B. (1981). Human-computer interaction in the control of dynamic systems. *ACM Computing Surveys, 13*, 71-99.

Sheridan, T.B. (2000). Function Allocation: Algorithm, alchemy or apostasy? *International Journal of Human-Computer Studies, 52*, 203-216.

Sheridan, T.B. (2002). *Humans and Automation: System Design and Research Issues.* Santa Monica: Wiley Interscience.

Sutcliffe, A.G., Shin, J.E., & Gregoriades, A. (2002). Tool support for scenario-based function allocation. In C.W. Johnson (Ed.), *Proceedings of the 21st European Conference on Human Decision Making and Control* (pp. 81-88). Glasgow, UK: University of Glasgow.

Westergaard, M. & Lassen, K.B. (2005). Building and Deploying Visualizations of Coloured Petri Net Models Using BRITNeY Animation and CPN Tools. *Sixth Workshop and Tutorial on Practical Use of Coloured Petri Nets and the CPN Tools*, Aarhus, Denmark: University of Aarhus.

Wright, P., Dearden, A., & Fields, B. (2000). Function Allocation: A perspective from studies of work practice. *International Journal of Human-Computer Studies, 52*, 335-355.

Design of alarm systems in different complex control settings

Anna Thunberg & Anna-Lisa Osvalder
Chalmers University of Technology
Gothenburg, Sweden

Abstract

Alarm systems play an important role in the maintaining of safe and efficient operation of complex process control settings. If the relationship between the operator's behaviour and the design of the human-system interface is clarified and more understandable, it will be possible to develop more efficient, effective and safe alarm systems. The results from five theoretical and empirical studies performed in different application areas (nuclear power, pulp and paper, oil refining, medical technology, and aviation) have been summarised to identify important design guidelines for alarm systems that take the operator's perspective into account.

The results show that adaptable alarm systems are needed since the operators have different roles and needs in different working situations. The alarm system should provide guidance for the operator to perceive the relevant information. Further, the operator's monitoring is greatly affected by information from colleagues. A main shared overview display should be provided to facilitate communication between team members. In addition, the operator and the team should have the ability to regulate their workload. Finally, increased transfer of knowledge between industry sectors can facilitate development of safe and efficient alarm systems.

Introduction

Alarm systems are important for the safe operation of many complex industrial settings, e.g., nuclear power, medical care, aviation, offshore, and process industries. Well-designed alarm systems help the operators to monitor and control the status of the process while alarm system design flaws can contribute to or worsen hazardous situations.

Alarm system research has mainly taking its starting point from existing alarm problems with the aim of reducing the problem. But to identify alarm system problems and act on them is not the most efficient way to develop systems. Prevention of alarms is better than cure (Hatch, 2005). And to prevent alarms, there is a need to understand how operators monitor the plant process as well as to predict the working performance of the operator.

This paper summarises the results from five theoretical and empirical studies performed within a research project with the objective of improving alarm system design in complex process control. The aim of the research project is to prioritise and complement existing guidelines about alarm system design with better relationships to existing knowledge about the operator's cognitive and physical abilities. The expected effects of deriving alarm system design guidelines that take the operator's perspective into account are that they should lead to safer, more user-friendly and efficient alarm systems in control rooms.

The main goal of an alarm system is to help the operator in different deviating working situations. Every alarm presented to the operator should be useful and relevant (EEMUA, 1999). The aim of an alarm system is to:

1. Alert the operator about a deviation
2. Inform the operator about the nature of the deviation
3. Guide the operator's initial response
4. Confirm, in a timely manner, whether the response corrected the deviation.
   (Hollnagel & Øwre, 1984; O'Hara et al., 1994; Karlsson et al., 2002)

The purpose of the research studies was to investigate how operators in various industry settings work with their alarm systems, to map the operator's monitoring process and to investigate how the characteristics of the operators influence the monitoring process and the decision making. The aim was to identify factors that influence the operator's performance and to identify alarm design guidelines.

Methodology

The research consisted of five studies (Table 1). The studies were performed in chronological order. The first two studies were performed across five industry sectors (nuclear power, pulp and paper, oil refining, aviation and medical care) whereas the final three studies were focused on the nuclear power operator's conditions and working situation.

Table 1. Study designs

	Study 1	Study 2	Study 3	Study 4	Study 5
Aim of study:	Investigate the design of alarm systems in different industries	Understand how operators handle deviations	Compile knowledge for nuclear power operator monitoring	Identify expertise and assess mental workload	Understand the influence of team members
Methods					
Interviews	X	X			
Observations	X	X			X
ACTA				X	
NASA-TLX				X	
Literature studies	X	X	X		

The first study (Jönsson & Osvalder, 2004; Thunberg, 2006) included 22 participants, 15 operators (including airline pilot and anaesthesia nurses) and 7 design engineers from the different industry sectors. Semi-structured interviews were performed with all participants. Observations of the operators, the nurses and the pilot were also conducted. The studies took place on-site in the control rooms during normal operation or in full-scope simulators.

In the second study (Jönsson & Osvalder, 2004; Thunberg, 2006), interviews with operators from the different industry sectors were performed. Further, a nuclear power plant shift team was observed for one day during training in a simulator. Several incidents were studied during these observations. In addition, two nuclear shift teams from two different units were observed during the yearly outage (a service and maintenance period). Both shifts were observed for six working days. Work shifts during daytime as well as evening- and nightshift were included.

Study three (Jönsson & Osvalder, 2005) consisted of a literature review aimed at compiling theories about operator monitoring.

In the fourth study (Thunberg & Osvalder, 2006a), six experienced turbine operators from two nuclear power units participated. Two working tasks with different characteristics were used in the study. The first task is characterised by task planning, process intervention and assessment of the effects of the actions taken whereas the second involves the use of checklists to assess and ensure a safe plant status. Applied cognitive task analysis (ACTA) (Militello & Hutton, 1998) was used to identify the operators' expertise. The NASA-Task load index (Hart & Staveland, 1988) was used to assess the overall mental workload of the investigated tasks.

The fifth study (Thunberg & Osvalder, 2006b) included observations of a nuclear power plant shift team during their yearly training sessions. The observations took place in a full-scope simulator. The shift team was observed during a session when they were trained on tasks and incidents related to the systems investigated in study four. The observations were performed from the instructor's room.

Results and analysis

A range of different questions have been used in order to drive the progress of the research project. The results are presented for each of the questions to be answered.

Question 1: How do operators in various industry sectors handle deviations and how do they work and interact with their alarm systems? What can explain interaction differences across the industries?

The operators' interaction with the alarm system showed many similarities across the settings (Jönsson & Osvalder, 2004; Thunberg, 2006). All operators from the case studies tried to optimise the process in normal operating conditions. Thus, they were interested in detecting small deviations and correcting these quickly. The observations showed that the operators responded to the alarms rapidly. The amount of alarms generated in normal operation ranged from 1-10 per hour depending on control setting which contributed to a relatively low workload which in turn facilitated fast response.

The alarm systems in the case studies in nuclear power, pulp and paper, and oil refining show deficiencies in large disturbances (Jönsson & Osvalder, 2004; Thunberg, 2006). A huge number of alarms (many of low value to the operator), with none or insufficient prioritisation, are generated and makes the alarm list or the annunciator tiles almost impossible to work with. Automatic safety functions are implemented to a great extent to ensure that the probability of severe consequences is low. The operators' main goal is to ensure safe shut-down for which they use emergency operating procedures. Further, operators monitor and control key parameters to keep the plant in a safe state. When the disturbance has subsided and the process is stabilised in a safe state, the operators deal with the cause of the deviation and the resulting effects in order to get the plant back into normal operation.

The operators in the case studies in aviation and anaesthesia did not consider large disturbances as a huge problem (Jönsson & Osvalder, 2004; Thunberg, 2006). The prioritisation and suppression of alarms in different flight modes in aviation made the situation easily manageable for the pilot. The ability to rapidly stop errors from propagating and to mitigate consequences was very important. The nurses experienced many alarms in deviations, but the disturbance situations could be managed since the alarms were prioritised and the nurse could use the patient as a secondary source of information. The nurses need to act very quickly to keep the patient alive without causing long-term injuries.

The way of interaction was dependent on the operating aim and the type of control system. Furthermore, the "size" of the system and the number of control and alarm signals affect how the alarm systems can be designed. The amount of alarm signals was estimated to be very high in the case studies in nuclear power, pulp and paper and oil refining. Several operators mentioned that *"We must have thousands of alarm signals in our system"*. The nurses and the pilot estimated that 100-300 alarm signals were representative for their systems.

Question 2: What is the current best practice regarding alarm systems, and how can the industries benefit from knowledge exchange with each other?

Of the alarm systems included in the study; the alarm system in the aviation case study of Airbus 320 best met the theoretical aim (Thunberg, 2006). The Airbus 320 alarm system alerts the operator with a sound and a lit lamp, it informs the operator about the deviation with a short informative message, it guides the response by presenting an action list with measures, and, finally, it confirms that the actions have been carried out by changing the colour of the text presenting the actions. In the other case studies, the alarm system alerts and informs the operator as well. However, it only does so on an individual alarm level. The guidance given by the action list in aviation is a possible improvement for alarm systems in other industries e.g., oil refineries (Mattiasson, 1999). The main drawback of the alarm system in aviation was the limited screen area used for alarm presentation. Further, the Airbus

320 alarm system proved very useful, since only relevant alarms were displayed. Alarms were suppressed in different operating modes. Thus, problems with alarm flooding were avoided.

The use of an always visible, spatially dedicated area for safety-critical alarms with tile-like representation was much appreciated by the operators in nuclear power. Alarms with spatial location were noticed easily and quickly. The spatial location ensured fast detection and pattern recognition which in turn simplified the interpretation of the alarm. As one operator said *"Since I know the location of the important alarms, I can see directly what has happened with only a quick look at the alarm annunciator panel"*.

Consistent use of alarm message text and colour coding were regarded as very important and are a recurrent guideline in standards and textbooks (e.g, O'Hara *et al.*, 2002; EEMUA, 1999). Intensive care nurses with equipment from many different suppliers complained about inconsistencies between the devices. According to the operators in nuclear power, pulp and paper, and oil refining, the problem with equipment from several suppliers and inconsistencies was also accentuated when add-on systems were introduced in the control rooms in these industries.

To meet operator demands in future alarm system designs, using experience from other companies and industries can be beneficial. The studies showed that there were resemblances between several of the settings in the case studies, both in working situation and the role of the operator which indicate that knowledge exchange of design solutions and lessons learnt can easily be made. For example, the suppression of alarms in different operating modes in the Airbus alarm system and the action list would be beneficial to implement in other industries as well to be able to reduce alarm flooding and to better guide the operator's response. An advantage in nuclear power was the use of always visible, spatially dedicated annunciator tiles for safety critical alarms. The spatial location facilitates process overview and makes it possible to act quickly and mitigate the consequences of an upset.

Stanton (1996) has found that even though operators believe their alarm system shows some deficiencies, many operators cannot think of a better alarm system. But when alarm systems in different settings are compared theoretically with the purpose and aim of an alarm system (Jönsson & Osvalder, 2004; Thunberg, 2006), many shortcomings and areas for improvements can be found. This is partly due to the operators' inexperience with other alarm systems than their own and partly because operators do not have human factors knowledge. Integration of human factors experts in development projects and an extension of the knowledge transfer between companies and industry sectors can open both the operators' and the system designers' minds.

Question 3: How does expertise influence the operator's performance when handling alarms and deviations?

The results from the applied cognitive task analysis method showed that the main advantage of being an experienced operator was to know reference values by heart

(Thunberg & Osvalder, 2006a). This made it easy to evaluate information and parameter values. This assessment information could however be implemented in the interface by e.g., adding colour coding to the scale indicating the set alarm limits. By superimposing the scale, it is possible to represent the parameter in different forms of representations, thereby increasing the flexibility of the interface (May & Petersen, 2006).

Another advantage of being experienced was that multiple information sources were accessible (Thunberg & Osvalder, 2006a). Multiple information sources were used both to confirm whether signals were valid and as back-ups if the primary information source was unavailable. A novice operator was strongly dependent on the primary source of information. Further, experienced operators were aware of typical problems that could arise in various situations, i.e., they were able to predict possible future incidents. Therefore, they monitored several important parameters to be able to quickly identify whether a fault had occurred and to avoid potentially hazardous situations.

During disturbances, the experienced operator perceived alarm patterns rather than individual alarms. In possession of many years of training and experience, the operator could use pattern recognition to identify the problem situation. Understanding process characteristics is another area in which the experienced operator has thorough knowledge. When an action is performed, the feedback in complex processes is usually slow. Therefore, it is important for the operator to know the process' time lags.

The level of expertise was most prominent in tasks requiring actions or assessment by the operator. The use of checklists is almost as easy for the non-expert operator as for the expert. Therefore, the use of checklists is necessary for hazardous or stressful situations.

Question 4: How do operators in nuclear power plants monitor the station's process, during both normal operation and deviations?

The studies emphasise that the operator's information processing is to a large extent based on the operator's own initiative (i.e. based on internal factors) rather than data-driven (i.e. based on external factors). Results from the interviews showed that the operators do not consider that the alarm systems are developed to match pro-active, knowledge-driven information processing. Instead, the operators believe that the existing systems support passive or reactive operators waiting for something to occur.

A model of the nuclear power plant operator's information process has been developed (Figure 1). The model is influenced by classic stage approaches of human information processing (e.g. Wickens, 1999), the cognitive model presented by Vicente *et al.* (2004) and the results from our empirical studies. The results show that early stages in the information-processing model are very important (Jönsson & Osvalder, 2005: Thunberg & Osvalder, 2006a, b). This indicates that the decision-making is mainly influenced by the information perceived rather than dependent on the operator's level of expertise. It is therefore crucial that the alarm system guides the operator's attention. The reason no large differences in the level of expertise in the operator's problem solving have been detected is probably due to the support of alarm handling procedures and the influence of shift team members.

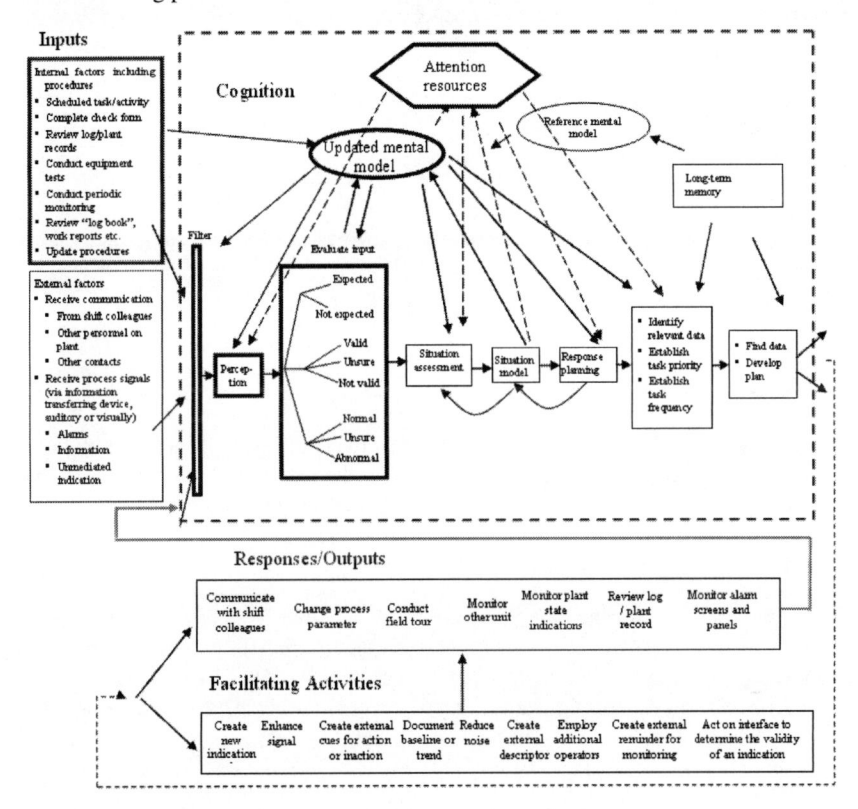

Figure 1. Model of the nuclear power plant operator's monitoring process

Since the operator's attention resources are very limited, they need to distribute and regulate their workload. Expert operators use external cues to reduce the workload and keep it at a manageable level. The mental model can also affect the mental workload. Process information can be more easily perceived, comprehended and integrated if the operator utilises a correct mental model (Johnson-Laird & Byrne, 2000). Mental model differences can be identified between novice users and experts. Expert operators have more detailed mental models where structural, functional and behavioural elements are integrated. Novice operators focus on static perceptually available components.

The monitoring of the plant is closely related to the working situation and the specific operative aim in that situation. Depending on the operative aim, the operator has different monitoring strategies. In normal operation, the operator follows a management-by-awareness principle. In deviations, the use of emergency operating procedures, the checking of key parameters, and the management-by-exception principle characterise the working procedure.

Question 5: What is the relationship between the work task characteristics and the behaviour of the operator, and which information needs do the operators have in various working situations?

Two types of work tasks were used in the study. The first task required operator intervention and the planning of task performance. The second task was characterised by automatic system processes and checking tasks for the operator under high time pressure.

The level of workload between the two investigated tasks was not easy to distinguish (Thunberg & Osvalder, 2006a). However, it could be seen that mental demands, temporal demands and performance were rated as the most important aspects when evaluating overall workload. None of the tasks were regarded as too difficult to handle, which indicates that the tasks are performed within the cognitive capabilities of the operator.

The results (Thunberg & Osvalder, 2006a) indicated that the operator used functional information about the system to assess the situation when performing the first task. The operator integrated information from several process objects to obtain an overall understanding of the task performance. The operator had to plan actions, execute them and confirm whether they worked out.

During the second task, the operator focused on specific parameters and controlled their discrete statuses (open/closed, on/off). The discrete information applies to unanticipated or stressful situations, whereas routine tasks rely on functional thinking (trends, increasing/decreasing value). Since the operator's mental representations and thinking can take different forms, the information presented by the alarm system needs to be adapted to the operator's different representation forms. Checklists should support high time pressure tasks in order to reduce the mental workload.

Question 6: How is an individual operator influenced by the work of the other shift team members, and how should this be attended to in the design of human-system interfaces?

The collaboration between the shift team members was very important (Thunberg & Osvalder, 2006b). The information given by other team members affected the performance of the other operators in the control room. The operators helped each other to maintain good process overview and to choose and use a correct mental model for the specific situation that had arisen.

Important parameters and trends were communicated in the team. The exchange of information made it easier for the operators to maintain an overall picture of the plant process and ensured that they did not get fixated on specific problems. The shift supervisor had a very important role, both to monitor the overall status of the plant and to ensure an overall manageable workload level for each operator.

The collaboration was very prominent in the nuclear control room. For example, all shift members are involved in the problem solving of various upsets. Thus, it is important that the information given by the system is easy to perceive and interpret by all operators on the shift, independent of level of expertise, years in profession, knowledge, training, etc. Therefore, an overview human-system interface must be designed with regard to the various needs of the different operators.

In a nuclear power plant control room, a combination of functional and structural mental representation is found. The physical layout of the plant is already well known, since the operators have worked as plant technicians before they started their education and training to become operators. The main function is also well known. However, since the system is very complex, it is impossible to have a completely updated functional mental representation of the whole process. Therefore, the overview displays should be based on structural representations (e.g., physical components and objects in the plant).

The simulator study and the tasks included in the training sessions originate from problems occurring in normal operation. Then, the dependency between the reactor operator and the turbine operator is strong. In the studies performed during the yearly outage, the collaboration between the operators was low. During the outage, the process dependency between the operators does not exist, since the plant is shut down for maintenance. But these two different working situations emphasise the importance of a flexible alarm system adapted to the different roles of the operator. However, since the process mostly is running in steady-state operation and the potential consequences of an incident are more severe if the plant is running, teamwork factors need consideration in control room operation.

information and overview for all of the team members. A shared overview interface is therefore necessary. Besides, performance can decrease if non-shared displays are used when a team handles faults (Banks & McKeran, 2006). Further, the Banks and McKeran study indicates that shared displays can reduce the need for complex situation awareness.

The shared display in the control room should use the main process and its main systems as a base for design. Almost all communication and problem solving relates to the main process in some way (Thunberg & Osvalder, 2006b). More detailed information, specific for the different operators in the control room, is better displayed on workstations.

Further, safety-critical alarms should be spatially located. This enhances the overview and is also very efficient in large disturbances. Less important alarms are preferably displayed on VDU screens. Then the amount of always-visible information is reduced, which will ease the situation for the operator (especially new ones) in large disturbances.

Every alarm that is triggered should require a response. This corresponds to the aim of the alarm system. It can also help to reduce the number of alarms in the system. Finally, it will minimise the risk of important alarms drowning in the flood of 'informative' alarms generated during a deviation. Alarms need to be consistent with other control and alarm systems in the control room. Therefore, the plant should have a documented philosophy on alarm system design. The alarm systems in the nuclear power plants today need to better support the operator to take corrective actions when anomalies occur. Today, the operators use paper-based procedures and instructions.

Conclusions

The following conclusions have been found about operator performance:

- The operator's differing roles in the different operational modes are very important for the processing of information.
    - Internal motivators drive the monitoring of the plant status. The operator aims to optimise the process and thus needs detailed information about the process.
    - In upsets, the operator manages the situation by following handling procedures to keep the plant safe. The alarm system is used only in a very limited fashion.
- Workload regulation is very important to maintain high overall performance. The operators regulate their workload by prioritising tasks according to available time and resources. They use external cues to decrease the workload. The supervisor has an important role in maintaining a manageable workload level for all operators.
- The operator's decision-making is very much influenced by the perceived information.
- The level of expertise affects the information processing and the experienced workload. The expert operators were able to chunk information, evaluate values immediately, and could more easily plan their work and foresee possible outcomes of their actions than the novices could.

Finally, the following conclusions have been drawn regarding guidelines for alarm systems:

- Future alarm systems should be adaptive. They should take the modes of operation, the role of the operator, and the aim of the operator into consideration.
- The operator needs guidance to perceive relevant information.
    - Use checklists in deviations.
    - Implement alarm prioritisation.
    - Implement alarm suppression techniques.
- Reduce distracting stimuli - Make it possible to silence alarms for a short period of time.
- Workload regulation is important - Allow operators to create and use external cues.
- A main shared overview display should be provided in the control room.
- Safety-critical alarms should be spatially located.
- Every alarm should require a response.

References

Banks, A.P., McKeran, W.J. (2006) The Influence of Sharing Displays on Team Situation Awareness and Performance. In P.D. Bust (Ed.) *The Ergonomics Society Annual Conference* (pp. 73-75) Cambridge, UK: Taylor and Francis.

EEMUA, the Engineering Equipment and Materials Users Association (1999) *Alarm Systems - A Guide to Design, Management and Procurement*, London, UK: EEMUA publication.

Hart, S.G., Staveland, L.E. (1988) Development of NASA-TLX (Task Load Index): Results of empirical and theoretical research. In P. A. Hancock, N. Meshkati (Eds), *Human Mental Workload* (pp. 239-250). Amsterdam: Elsevier.

Hatch, D. (2005) Alarms: prevention is better than cure. *Chemical engineer.* (Institution of Chemical Engineers), *769* (July), 40-42

Hollnagel, E., Øwre, F., (1984) *HWR-90 OECD Halden reactor project, The NORS/HALO system: background and methodology for experiment I.* Halden, Norway: Institutt For Energiteknikk.

Johnson-Laird, P. & Byrne, R. (2000) *Mental Models Website*. Retrieved 06.11.2006 from http://www.tcd.ie/Psychology/Ruth_Byrne/mental_models

Jönsson, A., Osvalder, A-L., Holmström, C., & Dahlman, S. (2004) *Alarm Systems in the Nuclear Industry.* Proceedings of the Man-Technology-Organisation Sessions, HPR-363, Vol. 1, EHPG Meeting. Halden, Norway: Institute for Energy Technology.

Jönsson, A. & Osvalder, A-L. (2005) *Development of a Theoretical Cognitive Model of the Nuclear Power Plant Operator's Information Process.* Proceedings of the Man-Technology-Organisation Sessions, HPR-365, Vol. 2, EHPG Meeting. Halden, Norway: Institute for Energy Technology.

Karlsson, T., Meyer, B.D., Jokstad, H., Farbrot, J.E., & Hulsund, J.E. (2002) *The alarm system for the HAMBO BWR simulator.* HWR-702 OECD Halden Reactor Project. Halden, Norway: Institutt for Energiteknikk,

Mattiasson, C. (1999) The alarm system from the operator's perspective. *International Conference on People in Control* (pp. 217-221). Human Systems Engineering Group. London: IEEE.

May, M. & Petersen, J. (2006) Media, Signs and Scales for the Design Space of Instrument Panels. In P.D. Bust(Ed.) *The Ergonomics Society Annual Conference* (pp. 93-97). Cambridge, UK: Taylor & Francis.

Militello, L.G., Hutton, R.J.B., (1998) Applied cognitive task analysis (ACTA): a practitioner's toolkit for understanding cognitive task demands. *Ergonomics, 41*, 1618-1641.

O'Hara, J.M., Brown, W.S., Higgins, J.C. & Stubler, W.F., (1994) *Human factors engineering guidance for the review of advanced alarm systems.* NUREG/CR-6105, BNL-NUREG-52391 Upton, NY: Energy Sciences & Technology Department, Brookhaven National Laboratory.

O'Hara, J.M., Brown, W.S., Lewis, P.M., & Persensky, J.J., (2002) *Human-System Interface Design Review Guidelines - NUREG 0700.* Upton, NY: Energy Sciences & Technology Department, Brookhaven National Laboratory.

Stanton, N. (1996) Operator reactions to alarms: fundamental similarities and situational differences. In N. Stanton (Ed.) *Human Factors in Nuclear Safety* (pp. 79-98). London, Taylor and Francis.

Thunberg, A. (2006) *A Cognitive Approach to the Design of Alarm Systems for Nuclear Power Plant Control Rooms.* Licentiate thesis. Göthenburg, Sweden: Chalmers University of Technology.

Thunberg, A. & Osvalder, A-L. (2006a) *Monitoring Complex Processes: Cognitive Model of the Control Room Operator's Information Process.* In R.N. Pikaar, E.A.P. Koningsveld, & P.J.M. Settles (Eds.), *Meeting diversity in ergonomics*. Amsterdam, The Netherlands: Elsevier.

Thunberg, A. & Osvalder, A-L. (2006b) *Human System Interface Design for Team Work in Complex Process Control.* In K.L. Saarela, C.-H. Nygård, and S. Lusa (Eds.) *Promotion of Well-being in Modern Society* (pp. 281-284). Tampere, Finland: Pk-paino.

Vicente, K.J., Mumaw, R.J., & Roth, E.M. (2004) Operator monitoring in a complex dynamic work environment: a qualitative cognitive model based on field observations. *Theoretical Issues in Ergonomics Science, 5*, 359-384.

Wickens, C.D. & Hollands, J.G. (1999) *Engineering Psychology and Human Performance.* New Jersey: Prentice Hall.

Woods, D.D., Patterson, E.S., & Roth, E.M. (2002) Can We Ever Escape from Data Overload? A Cognitive Systems Diagnosis. *Cognition, Technology & Work, 1*, 22-36.

Interface Issues

relevancy markers

In D. de Waard, G.R.J. Hockey, P. Nickel, and K.A. Brookhuis (Eds.) (2007), *Human Factors Issues in Complex System Performance* (pp. 385). Maastricht, the Netherlands: Shaker Publishing.

Locating task-objective relevant information in text

Martin Groen & Jan Noyes
University of Bristol
Bristol, UK

Abstract

Human task performance in dynamic and complex systems is considerably impaired by the reduced ability of operators to locate and act on task-relevant information. It is suggested that the highlighting of task-relevant information would facilitate expedient establishment of task objectives. This suggestion has been tested experimentally by investigating whether this task-relevant information can be located with *relevancy markers*. In telephone and email conversations it was found that across task (i.e. finance and logistics) and language (i.e. Dutch, English and Mandarin-Chinese) domains, humans seem to benefit from the presence of these markers when localising relevant information. It is suggested that this work has the potential to be used to inform the design of tasks and user interfaces of complex and other systems where user interaction is needed.

Background

Complex systems embody complex tasks, which are characterised by (a) the number of different information cues that must be processed; (b) the number of distinct processes that must be executed; and (c) the relationship between the cues and the processes (Speier, 2006). Dynamic complex systems add the continuous provision of new or changed information. The inherent challenges of complex tasks further aggravate the predicament of the human operator interacting with complex and dynamic automated systems. Over time, the situation awareness (SA) of the operator might diminish leading to the out-of-the-loop situation which might prohibit operators taking appropriate action if needed (Endsley & Kiris, 1995).

The problem of reduced SA is defined as an impaired "perception of the elements of the environment within a volume of time and space, the comprehension of their meaning, and the projection of their status in the near future" (Endsley, 1995, p. 36). The components of this definition which provide the current focus are those 'elements of the environment'. What are they? Are they all the elements in the environment or merely the task-related ones? How does the operator discriminate between task-relevant and irrelevant information? A review of research into SA is presented, with a focus on whether they address these questions. Following this, an alternative view is presented and the opportunities this promises to bring to the current practice are discussed.

Situation Awareness

An influential definition of SA, as given here, is from Endsley (1995). In this paper Endsley makes a laudable effort to define the SA concept and then relate it to human behaviour properties underlying and influencing SA. Note that the term SA is reserved for the result of the processes involved in establishing SA; the processes are called *situation assessment* (Endsley, 1995). Endsley concluded with a number of hypotheses about the underlying information processing mechanisms of SA. One of the open questions she identified is the way in which elements of the environment are acquired by individuals and teams to cope with dynamic, complex systems. What are useful critical cues vital to achieve good SA? This issue is taken up in this paper.

A review of 61 papers, which referred to the original Endsley (1995), was conducted. The criteria for the selection of papers as successful contenders for indicating the critical cues for the acquisition of good SA were based on the following considerations. First, the attractiveness of the SA concept is that it is a general description of task performance. In other words, SA is intended to be applicable "across a wide variety of domains" (Endsley, 2000, p. 6). So, an important selection criterion from an information processing perspective is that the cues considered are not limited to specific tasks. That is, they are used in a specific task, but are general enough to be useful in the execution of other tasks too. Second, the reported cues should be explicit. That is, cues should be manifest or readily available in the stimulus, for example a red flashing light. This criterion is adopted to ensure that there is a falsifiable relationship between the cue and SA. Thirdly, the choice of SA cues should be based on empirical tests, not analytical considerations.

Taking these three considerations into account, 19 papers reported research into acquiring SA. These were as follows:

Research into SA in simulated car driving tasks demonstrated:

- drivers, but not passengers, monitor changing spatial location of other cars as measured by recall tests (Gugerty, 1997);
- eye fixations on traffic scenes change as a function of increasing experience with driving a car (Underwood et al., 2003);
- feedback aids SA, especially auditory feedback. However, when particular types of feedback were removed, drivers were not aware of the resultant decrease in SA (Walker et al., 2006).

These findings inform which aspects of the car driving task appear to contribute to SA. However, the results appear to be limited to the car driving task, and therefore do not describe general task performance. Additionally, Gugerty's research used an indirect measure of SA.

Research into SA cues in air traffic control tasks showed:

- successful task completion by air traffic controllers seems to be related to accurate recall of aircraft altitude and direction of flight (Mogford, 1997);

- aircraft importance (i.e., potential traffic) affected memory for flight data (i.e., aircraft altitude and ground speed) in air traffic controllers (Gronlund et al., 1998).

The cues identified in these experiments appear to contribute to air traffic controller SA. However, it is hard to see how these results could be generalised to general task performance. Additionally, Mogford's research uses an indirect measure. Therefore, these cues do not meet the selection criteria.

In interface design, the following cues were identified to be associated with good SA:

- single, spatially contiguous configuration of letters on a display could be monitored better than separate areas (Brand & Orenstein, 1998);
- polychrome displays facilitate faster target detections than monochrome ones (Derefeldt et al., 1999);
- unique verbal labels support tracking of changed information (Hess et al., 1999);
- integrated spatial and temporal displays facilitate shorter fault detection times (Burns, 2000);
- more naturalistic depictions of terrain information lead to the best collision avoidance, compared to three other less naturalistic depictions (Billingsley et al., 2001);
- the effect of disruption of SA by extraneous background noise can be channelled by manipulating spatial and temporal characteristics of the auditory stream (Banbury et al., 2003);
- the interface should explicate the mental model used in the design of the system (Itoh & Inagaki, 2004).

This work provides some valuable advice for the design of interfaces. Distinctions in colour, unique verbal labels, and explicit mental models of the interface design are cues that appear to assist in realising good SA. However, four other studies do not provide information as to which cues contribute to good SA. They provide information on optimal information presentation on displays (Brand & Orenstein, 1998; Burns, 2000), but not what the SA cues were, or the SA cues were predefined, based on word length and jargon (Banbury et al., 2003). In another study, the results seem to be hard to generalise to other tasks (Billingsley et al., 2001).

Research in combat mission tasks reported SA to be aided by the following:

- a non-hierarchical (parallel, not serial) organisation of cooperation in commander teams working on a military task facilitates good SA (Artman, 1999);
- decisions about a course of action are made faster as command-post experience increases. This is not influenced by the level of confidence in the information gathered (Kobus et al., 2001).

These studies seem to be general enough, as they are potentially applicable to team work in other settings, to warrant studies in other task settings. However, no mention is made of the cues that are used to acquire SA.

In conjunction with acquisition, studies have often considered the establishment of SA. For example:

- information about current availability and workload of colleagues improved efficiency in establishing the task and collaborator SA (Xie & Salvendy, 2003);
- providing information about the current status of the task, such as task progress, time passed and mutual dependability of subtasks also improved SA (Xie & Salvendy, 2003);
- having a shared visual workspace increases the collaborators' understanding of the task and its current status, which is associated with faster and better task performance (Gergle et al., 2004).

These results are general enough to be studied in other task settings. The identified cues demonstrate that supplying this information results in good SA. However, in Gergle et al. (2004) the results imply that all available information could potentially be SA cues. Here, the aim is to identify a, hopefully, limited number of cues that could lead to good SA. So, therefore these SA cues do not meet the criteria.

Additional SA cues that have been identified are:

- emphasising information to which an operator is naturally less inclined, as in the situation when the information does not correspond with the currently held mental model (Jones & Endsley, 2000);
- providing cognitive support in the form of feedback or attentional resources, which may degrade performance on a real-time dynamic task (Lerch & Harter, 2001);
- paying specific attention to particular cues in a emergency medical dispatch task environment, such as job status, ambulances leaving the hospital, duration or frequency of emergency 'phone calls, all contribute to SA (Blandford & Wong, 2004).

It is difficult to generalise the last three findings. In order to be able to determine what characterises the mental model (Jones & Endsley, 2000), the experimenter needs to be aware of many aspects of the task. Also, the cues reported in Blandford and Wong (2004) are task restricted, although an effort is made to relate the findings to other types of tasks. In Lerch and Harter (2001) the SA cues used for feedback were predetermined, and as such cannot be regarded as generally applicable SA cues.

A concern that emerges from the literature is that analysing the mechanisms involved in the establishment of good SA seems to be similar to analysing the mechanisms involved in successful task objective realisation. However, they are not necessarily the same; one can have a good SA without being able to accomplish the task, or one can have poor SA and still be able to successfully realise the task objectives. How to discern between the two? This seems to be an additional pressing reason to investigate the basic environmental cues and cognitive and social mechanisms that contribute to achieving good SA. Or to question the validity of the SA construct, that is, do humans need good SA to establish task objectives?

Nevertheless, what emerges from the research literature is that the following cues appear to be related to the acquisition of good SA. They are colour of relevant cues (Derefeldt et al., 1999), unique verbal labels of relevant cues (Hess et al., 1999), information about current availability and workload of collaborating colleagues and task status information (Xie & Salvendy, 2003) and explicit mental models of the system and declaration of the control mode (Itoh & Inagaki, 2004). Note that these cues are considered as placeholders or variables allowing instantiation or an assigned value to be specified in particular contexts in which they are applied in order to acquire SA, or rather, establish task objectives. However, these cues might be informative as to what information people take into account while assessing a situation to come to awareness, it does not reveal *how* people discern between relevant information that might contribute to SA and task completion and irrelevant information. In the following section, a proposal is made that aims to address this 'how' question.

An alternative perspective

To distinguish between relevant and irrelevant information in dynamic complex systems, it is suggested that the information which deserves the operator's attention when attaining SA is the task-objective related information. The operator's SA could therefore benefit when this task-relevant information is highlighted in some way by the originator of the information, supplied either directly or via a medium, for example, a user manual, one-to-one instruction or via a user interface of a computer. The research question then becomes whether humans use particular information elements to highlight task-relevant information, and what these elements are. The aim of the present research is to identify these elements, called *relevancy markers*, and to investigate whether these are used by humans to localise task-relevant information when they attempt to establish task objectives.

To ensure that the indicators used to highlight task-relevant information are recognised as such, it is prudent to utilise conventional markers that are used to indicate relevant information in other dynamic and complex information exchange situations frequently encountered by humans. The most prevalent, encountered on a daily basis, are face-to-face dialogues (Clark, 1996; Fillmore, 1981; Pickering & Garrod, 2004). Knowing how humans highlight relevant information in face-to-face dialogues will allow the same mechanisms to be applied in other information exchange settings in order to increase the opportunities to maintain SA and achieve task objectives. The perspective on human dialogue as an instance of collaborative task execution has attracted considerable attention in the past two decades (e.g., Bangerter & Clark, 2003; Barr & Keysar, 2002; Boyle, Anderson, & Newlands, 1994; Brennan, 1991; Byron & Heeman, 1997; Clark & Krych, 2004; Clark & Wilkes-Gibbs, 1986; Garrod & Anderson, 1987; Garrod & Doherty, 1994; Pickering & Garrod, 2004). The dialogue partners that benefit from this highlighting of relevant information are the addressees, but also the bystanders. The addressees are the people that the originator or speaker sees as his or her audience. The bystanders are people who happen to be in hearing distance of the two (or more) dialogue partners.

The rest of this paper outlines the preliminary experimental work that has been conducted to examine the mechanisms humans employ to locate task-relevant information in dialogues. Note, that in this paper the focus is on the search behaviour of bystanders locating task-relevant information. Additionally, it needs to be emphasised that the aim of this work is to identify relevancy markers highlighting task-relevant information. These relevancy markers are not, by their very nature, task-specific. A number of suggestions are made about how the identified markers can assist acquiring and maintaining SA by addressing user interface design issues.

Locating relevant information

To develop an operational definition of relevancy markers the theory of *discourse markers* (Fraser, 1996; Levinson, 1983; Mey, 2001; Redeker, 1991, 2000; Schiffrin, 1987; Schourup, 1999) was consulted. Discourse markers signal to the dialogue partners that the stretch of discourse that follows the marker is a diversion from the normal flow of the discourse, for example, the term 'by the way' marks the start of a diversion and 'anyway' the return from it. The opportunity to introduce a diversion is dependent on the collaboration of the dialogue partners. Therefore, discourse markers are often uttered at the beginning of a contribution to a dialogue or, in other words, at a turn, so when the current speaker finishes talking and indicates that the addressee can initiate talking (Byron & Heeman, 1997; Sacks, 1995; Schourup, 1999).

In the context of this research, this property of discourse markers is very useful. The 'occurring at the beginning of a contribution'-property offers the possibility to distinguish the use of words such as discourse markers, from other uses of that same word. For example, the discourse marker 'so' can be used as a discourse marker *but also* as an adverb, a pronoun and an adjective. To distinguish between all these, it is useful to have a conventional location of these words. The property turn-initial or, similarly, at the beginning of a contribution provides this location. So, when a word occurs at a turn-initial position, then it is considered to be a discourse marker. When it is used in different locations than turn-initial it is considered to be uttered for one of the other uses, such as adverbial, as a pronoun or adjective. Note the circularity here.

No reference could be found as to how many words constitute 'beginning of a contribution' or *turn-initial*. For the current experiments, turn-initial is operationalised as the arbitrary number of *four words*. So, every discourse marker that occurs in the first four words of every contribution to a dialogue is considered a relevancy marker. In brief, relevancy markers are words from the set of discourse markers that are used at the beginning of a contribution of a speaker to a dialogue. In this preliminary work, beginning of a contribution, or turn-initiality, was defined as occurring in the first four words.

An inventory needed to be made of the markers of task-relevant information or *relevancy markers* that people use in dialogues. The candidate set is large, so the choice was made to examine conversations where the choice of signals is constrained. In telephone conversations, speakers can only use verbal markers to highlight relevant information and a subset of non-verbal markers, for example, intonation and pitch. It was decided to examine relevancy marker use in telephone conversations with particular reference to verbal relevancy markers.

A data set of 15000 email messages and 20 transcribed telephone conversations in Dutch was used to search for these words. Note that the set of emails was only used to assess the usage frequency of relevancy markers. The turn-initial ones were determined using the telephone conversation transcripts. The words 'well', 'so' and 'but' had the highest frequency in a turn-initial position (see Table 1 for details). Even though 'and', 'or' and 'then' had higher frequencies, they were not considered since they were not turn-initial in any of the contributions in the random sample from transcripts of telephone conversations.

Table 1. Usage frequency of discourse markers in the corpus used in the preliminary study

Rank	Discourse marker	Frequency
1	And	4214
2	Then	1872
3	Or	1456
4	But	653
5	So	409
6	Well	362
7	Y'know	73
8	Because	61
9	Now	12
10	Oh	2
11	I mean	2

The preliminary study identified the three potential relevancy markers. However, this was based on counting and theoretical considerations. So, empirical tests were needed to check this result against what humans actually do and to generalise the findings to other telephone conversations. Hence, three experiments were conducted to corroborate empirically the actual use of the candidate relevancy markers by humans.

Experimental findings

The experiments were conducted first with Dutch language speakers ($n = 31$), and later, with English ($n = 66$) and Mandarin-Chinese ($n = 37$), which have a more widespread use. Participants received a booklet with transcripts of three actual telephone conversations. Two dialogues had a topic from the financial-services domain and one was about a logistics problem. After reading each transcript the participants answered four questions relating to the transcripts. The first three questions requested the participants to assess the extent into which the dialogue partners, from each of the transcripts they had just read, succeeded in establishing their own or mutual goals. The fourth question requested to indicate on the transcript which stretches of dialogue were used to answer the first three questions. The distance in words (or characters in Mandarin-Chinese) was calculated between the participants' indicators and the candidate relevancy markers. All experiments demonstrated that in Dutch, English and Mandarin-Chinese the participants consistently oriented on, or were oriented by, the presence of the relevancy marker ('so', 'well' or 'but') to locate the relevant information. This outcome was not influenced by the participants being members of a particular language community (i.e., Dutch, English and Mandarin-Chinese), topic of the dialogue or domain of work. Details of these studies can be found in Groen and Noyes (2007).

The important finding for current purposes of this study is the demonstration that in English, Dutch and Mandarin-Chinese the words 'so', 'well' and 'but' (and their respective equivalences in Dutch and Mandarin-Chinese), appear to aid the information searcher to locate relevant information. Further, this effect occurs across disparate language communities. Thus, the results indicate that the relevancy markers appear to be structural elements, that is not domain-specific, that people use in dialogues to highlight the presence of relevant information.

Implications for situation awareness, task design and user interfaces

This work identified three potential relevancy markers. Within the context of SA, this result provides input to opportunities to maintain or improve SA and rapid task completion by including relevancy markers in the design of user interfaces. When establishing SA it is important that the task-relevant information receives priority in processing. The relevancy markers could assist in highlighting the relevant information in a visual array, thereby limiting the time and effort needed to find the needed information. The observed tendency to orient on relevancy markers lends support to the suggestion that addressees assume that the utterances of a speaker convey the person's intended message (Allen, 1983; Grice, 1989; Sperber & Wilson, 1995). In other words, addressees expect that the utterances of the speaker carry information that is relevant towards establishing the current goal. It is the task of the addressee to localise the information that is relevant to realise the goals of the speaker. However, since establishing his or her goals is important to the speaker, he or she will assist their addressees in recognising the stretches of dialogue that carry the goal-related information. To achieve this, it is suggested, speakers use relevancy markers. These results are based on reading transcripts of dialogues. Whether a similar mechanism is benefited from to localise task-objective relevant information in other formats is addressed in future research (there is some evidence for a similar mechanism in static images, e.g. Grant & Spivey, 2003). Addressees, in turn, can benefit from these relevancy markers in the swift localisation of task-relevant information.

The design of user interfaces of dynamic, complex systems could benefit from these findings. Information presented via a user interface can be regarded as a communicative act by the designers of the system. By presenting certain information via the interface they want to communicate that, for example, an important parameter has changed in value which is important to know. For example, the designers of the petrol level indicator in cars designed it in such a way that the car driver would recognise that he or she needs to fill up right away when not only the needle of the indicator is in the red area, but also a light emitting diode flashes. The addressee, in this case a human operator, needs to recognise this information as relevant, so that a decision can be made whether action is needed. The recognition of relevancy can be facilitated by highlighting this information with a relevancy marker. Note that relevancy markers can come in many different forms. This preliminary research found evidence for one format that humans seem to use to aid localisation of task-objective relevant information. In the case of images or machine control panels relevancy markers in other formats are potentially used to assist in highlighting task-relevant information (for example, animating as in Grant & Spivey, 2003). As the results of the study show, humans seem to expect the relevancy markers to be there, assisting them to localise task-relevant information. Translated to user interfaces, the mechanism of relevancy markers, that is first localising the relevancy markers and then assessing the relevancy of the localised information, can be benefited from to improve the SA of operators of dynamic, complex systems. As humans seem to expect to find relevancy markers in order to orient on task-relevant information, SA can be improved by aiding the operator to discriminate the relevant from the irrelevant by utilising relevancy markers. By doing so the operator is pulled 'back into the loop'. This should lead to a reduction of information overload which will allow SA to be acquired or maintained, and task objectives to be established faster.

An advantage of this approach is that studying human interaction with complex dynamic systems from this perspective expands accepted theories (Allen, 1983; Clark, 1996; Sperber & Wilson, 1995) which are supported by empirical evidence. Rather than studying humans performing tasks and ending up with results that demonstrate how participants attain SA in a particular task, an approach is taken which starts with a theory of basic human mechanisms of interaction and builds on that to study how humans interact with complex, dynamic systems. This should lead to results which are more straightforward to generalise and thus, beneficial to task and interface design, more effective in acquiring and maintaining SA and, ultimately, instrumental in improving the efficient and effective accomplishment of task goals.

References

Allen, J. (1983). Recognizing intentions from natural language utterances. In M. Brady, R.C. Berwick and J. Allen (Eds.), *Computational models of discourse* (pp. 107-166). Cambridge, MA, USA: MIT Press.

Artman, H. (1999). Situation awareness and co-operation within and between hierarchical units in dynamic decision making. *Ergonomics, 42*, 1404-1417.

Banbury, S., Fricker, L., Tremblay, S., & Emery, L. (2003). Using auditory streaming to reduce disruption to serial memory by extraneous auditory warnings. *Journal of Experimental Psychology-Applied, 9*, 12-22.

Bangerter, A. & Clark, H.H. (2003). Navigating joint projects with dialogue. *Cognitive Science, 27*, 195-225.

Barr, D.J., & Keysar, B. (2002). Anchoring Comprehension in Linguistic Precedents. *Journal of Memory and Language, 46*, 391-418.

Billingsley, G.O., Kuchar, J.K., & Jacobson, S.W. (2001). Head-up display symbology for ground collision avoidance. *International Journal of Aviation Psychology, 11*, 33-51.

Blandford, A., & Wong, B.L.W. (2004). Situation awareness in emergency medical dispatch. *International Journal of Human-Computer Studies, 61*, 421-452.

Boyle, E.A., Anderson, A.H., & Newlands, A. (1994). The Effects of Visibility on Dialog and Performance in a Cooperative Problem-Solving Task. *Language and Speech, 37*, 1-20.

Brand, J.L., & Orenstein, H.B. (1998). Does display configuration affect information sampling performance? *Ergonomics, 41*, 286-301.

Brennan, S.E. (1991). Conversation with and through computers. *User Modeling and User-Adapted Interaction, 1*, 67-86.

Burns, C.M. (2000). Putting it all together: Improving display integration in ecological displays. *Human Factors, 42*, 226-241.

Byron, D.K., & Heeman, P.A. (1997). Discourse marker use in task oriented spoken dialogue. In *Proceedings of the 5th Biennial European Conference on Speech Communication and Technology (Eurospeech '97)* (pp. 2223-2226). University of Rhodes, Greece.

Clark, H.H. (1996). *Using Language*. New York, USA: Cambridge University Press.

Clark, H.H., & Krych, M.A. (2004). Speaking while monitoring addressees for understanding. *Journal of Memory and Language, 50*, 62-81.

Clark, H.H., & Wilkes-Gibbs, D. (1986). Referring as a collaborative process. *Cognition, 22*, 1-39.

Derefeldt, G., Skinnars, O., Alfredson, J., Eriksson, L., Andersson, P., Westlund, J., et al. (1999). Improvement of tactical situation awareness with colour-coded horizontal-situation displays in combat aircraft. *Displays, 20*, 171-184.

Endsley, M.R. (1995). Toward a theory of situation awareness in dynamic systems. *Human Factors, 37*, 32-64.

Endsley, M.R. (2000). Theoretical underpinnings of situation awareness: a critical review. In M.R. Endsley and D.J. Garland (Eds.), *Situation Awareness Analysis and Measurement* (pp. 3-32). Mahwah, NJ, USA: Lawrence Erlbaum.

Endsley, M.R., & Kiris, E.O. (1995). The out-of-the-loop performance problem and level of control in automation. *Human Factors, 37*, 381-394.

Fillmore, C. J. (1981). Pragmatics and the description of discourse. In P. Cole (Ed.), *Radical pragmatics,* (pp. 143-166). New York, NY, USA: Academic Press.

Fraser, B. (1996). Pragmatic Markers. *Pragmatics, 6*, 167-190.

Garrod, S., & Anderson, A. (1987). Saying what you mean in dialogue: A study in conceptual and semantic co-ordination. *Cognition, 27*, 181-218.

Garrod, S., & Doherty, G. (1994). Conversation, co-ordination and convention: an empirical investigation of how groups establish linguistic conventions. *Cognition, 53*, 181-215.

Gergle, D., Kraut, R., & Fussell, S.R. (2004). Language efficiency and visual technology - Minimizing collaborative effort with information. *Journal of Language and Social Psychology, 23*, 491-517.

Grant, E.R., & Spivey, M.J. (2003). Eye movements and problem solving: guiding attention guides thought. *Psychological Science, 14*, 462-466.

Grice, H.P. (1989). *Studies in the way of words*. Cambridge, USA: Harvard University Press.
Groen, M., & Noyes, J. (2007). *Searching Task-Relevant Information in Unstructured Data Sets*. Manuscript submitted for publication.
Gronlund, S.D., Ohrt, D.D., Dougherty, M.R.P., Perry, J.L., & Manning, C.A. (1998). Role of memory in air traffic control. *Journal of Experimental Psychology-Applied, 4*, 263-280.
Gugerty, L.J. (1997). Situation awareness during driving: Explicit and implicit knowledge in dynamic spatial memory. *Journal of Experimental Psychology-Applied, 3*, 42-66.
Hess, S.M., Detweiler, M.C., & Ellis, R.D. (1999). The utility of display space in keeping track of rapidly changing information. *Human Factors, 41*, 257-281.
Itoh, M., & Inagaki, T. (2004). A microworld approach to identifying issues of human-automation systems design for supporting operator's situation awareness. *International Journal of Human-Computer Interaction, 17*, 3-24.
Jones, D.G., & Endsley, M.R. (2000). Overcoming representational errors in complex environments. *Human Factors, 42*, 367-378.
Kobus, D.A., Proctor, S., & Holste, S. (2001). Effects of experience and uncertainty during dynamic decision making. *International Journal of Industrial Ergonomics, 28*, 275-290.
Lerch, F.J., & Harter, D.E. (2001). Cognitive support for real-time dynamic decision making. *Information Systems Research, 12*, 63-82.
Levinson, S.C. (1983). *Pragmatics*. Cambridge, USA: Cambridge University Press.
Mey, J.L. (2001). *Pragmatics: An introduction*. Oxford, UK: Blackwell.
Mogford, R.H. (1997). Mental models and situation awareness in air traffic control. *International Journal of Aviation Psychology, 7*, 331-341.
Pickering, M.J., & Garrod, S. (2004). Towards a mechanistic psychology of dialogue. *Behavioral and Brain Sciences, 27*, 169-225.
Redeker, G. (1991). Linguistic markers of discourse structure. *Linguistics, 29*, 1139-1172.
Redeker, G. (2000). Coherence and structure in text and discourse. In H. Bunt and W. Black (Eds.), *Abduction, belief and context in dialogue. Studies in computational pragmatics* (pp. 233-264). Amsterdam, The Netherlands: John Benjamins.
Sacks, H. (1995). *Lectures on Conversation*. Malden, NJ, USA: Blackwell.
Schiffrin, D. (1987). *Discourse Markers*. New York, USA: Cambridge University Press.
Schourup, L. (1999). Discourse markers. *Lingua, 107*, 227-265.
Speier, C. (2006). The influence of information presentation formats on complex task decision-making performance. *International Journal of Human-Computer Studies, 64*, 1115-1131.
Sperber, D., & Wilson, D. (1995). *Relevance. Communication and cognition* (2nd. ed.). Oxford, UK: Blackwell.
Underwood, G., Chapman, P., Brocklehurst, N., Underwood, J., & Crundall, D. (2003). Visual attention while driving: sequences of eye fixations made by experienced and novice drivers. *Ergonomics, 46*, 629-646.

Walker, G.H., Stanton, N.A., & Young, M.S. (2006). The ironies of vehicle feedback in car design. *Ergonomics, 49*, 161-179.

Xie, Y.L., & Salvendy, G. (2003). Awareness support for asynchronous engineering collaboration. *Human Factors and Ergonomics in Manufacturing, 13*, 97-113.

Haptic, visual and cross-modal perception of interface information

Annie Rydström & Peter Bengtsson
Luleå University of Technology, Luleå
Sweden

Abstract

A cross-modal interface uses different modalities to present the same information. The objective of the present experiment was to investigate to what extent information provided in an interface can be shared across the haptic and visual modalities. The experiment had three feedback conditions, haptic, visual and haptic plus visual. The feedback was displayed haptically through a rotary device and visually on a computer monitor. The experimental task was to repeatedly locate and select textures in a menu of four rendered textures. The participants practiced the textures in one feedback condition and completed a test with 36 trials in the same or in a different feedback condition. There was a cross-modal transfer, although not effortless, and the transfer from haptics to vision seemed to be easier than from vision to haptics. The participants performed better in cases with the same feedback in both the training and test and in cases with visual feedback in the test. The asymmetry of the cross-modal transfer and the enhanced visual performance might be a result of the visual information being more useful for the task at hand.

Introduction

Humans are adapted to be able to simultaneously use information from several sensory modalities, and information can also be shared across modalities (Stein & Meredith, 1993). Hence, a lack of information from one modality can be compensated for by sensory information from another modality. For example, in the dark, haptic cues can substitute for vision. Since input from one modality can substitute for another, reliable information from multiple sensory systems provide flexibility when interacting with complex systems. In human-machine interaction (HMI) activities where visual information is not sufficient or is not optimal for conveying interface information, haptic cues can prevent an overload of vision (Hale & Stanney, 2004). Burnett and Porter (2001) recommended the use of haptic cues in the interaction with in-car equipment, to allow drivers keep their eyes on the road.

Although the visual, auditory and haptic senses can be utilized in HMI, most interfaces predominantly appeal to the visual sense. Unlike vision and audition, haptic interaction involves both sensing and manipulation (Hayward et al., 2004). Accordingly a haptic HMI device allows a user both to feel and interact with an interface. Computer devices such as the mouse and keyboard are not true haptic devices since the feedback is primarily visual through a visual display. Previous HMI research has shown that interfaces that appeal to both the visual and haptic sense have behavioural benefits over unimodal visual interfaces. For example, Grane and Bengtsson (2005) carried out an experiment in which participants were asked to identify and choose among five haptically and visually rendered textures. The textures were haptically displayed through a rotary type interaction device and visually displayed on a monitor. It was shown that haptic and visual feedback was preferable to visual feedback regarding accuracy and workload. Oakley et al. (2000) reported that the number of errors made in targeting, searching and scrolling tasks on a computer was reduced when redundant haptic feedback, such as gravity, friction and texture, was provided through the interaction device (a PHANToM force feedback device). Campbell et al. (1999) carried out an analogous experiment with a task equivalent to menu interaction with a pointing stick. In various visual and tactile feedback conditions with consistent, inconsistent and no tactile bumps the participants had to steer a pointer through a tunnel. There was a decrease in error rate and task time when consistent haptic and visual feedback was provided.

Information can either be modality specific or can be perceived through different senses. The perception of temperature is unique to the haptic system, and the perception of colour is unique to the visual system. Properties such as size, shape and texture can be perceived both visually and haptically, and the information can consequently be shared across the two modalities (Woods & Newell, 2004). Hoggan and Brewster (2006) defined HMI as multimodal when each modality is used to transmit a different type of information, and cross-modal when different modalities are used to present the same information.

Although information is shared across the haptic and visual modalities, the modalities experience the world in different ways. A sequence of impressions must often be gathered to identify an entity haptically (Lederman & Klatzky, 1987), while impressions through vision are gathered more in parallel (Hatwell, 2003). For geometric properties, such as size and shape, cross-modal transfer seems to be easier from haptics to vision than from vision to haptics (Hatwell, 2003). Switching from haptics to vision does not seem to increase cognitive load, while switching from vision to haptics seems to negatively affect cognitive processing (Hale & Stanney, 2004). Visual perception frequently dominates the visual-haptic percept when judging geometric properties but haptics have been shown to be as efficient as vision for texture information (Lederman et al., 1986). Ernst and Banks (2002) proposed a model that statistically determines the degree to which vision or haptic dominates. The modality that perceives the highest precision (the lowest variance) of the property to be estimated dominates a perception. The perception of natural textures includes attributes such as roughness, elasticy and viscosity (Loomis & Lederman, 1986). With haptic devices the touch sensation is remote, received through a tool, rather than directly by the skin, and it is a challenge to render reliable and useful sensations. However, it is shown that rendered textures provided through a haptic device can lead to a reliable sensation of roughness (Klatzky & Lederman, 2006).

The objective of the present experiment was to investigate to what extent information provided in an interface can be shared within and across the haptic and visual modalities. For the experiment a menu with different textures were rendered haptically, visually and haptically plus visually.

Method

Participants

A total of 54 engineering students, 18 females and 36 males, participated in the experiment. Their ages ranged from 18 to 35 years (M = 22.4, SD =3.7), and all but six were right-handed.

Equipment

The experiment ran on a laptop computer, and a programmable haptic rotary device (ALPS Haptic Commander, ALPS Automotive Products Division, Japan) with a knob diameter of 3.5 cm was used as an interaction device (Figure 1). The rotary device was mounted such that the participants' right arm was supported and the device could be grasped and operated comfortably. The experimental program was implemented in Macromedia Director 8.5 (Adobe Systems Inc., USA). The program managed the haptic feedback in the rotary device and the graphical scenes on the laptop computer. The presentation of the tasks was done orally in headphones and written in a 6.4" display. The program also recorded performance data for each participant. An audio stream of pink noise was played at a comfortable level through the headphones to block out sounds created when turning the rotary device. A similar experimental set-up was used by Grane and Bengtsson (2005).

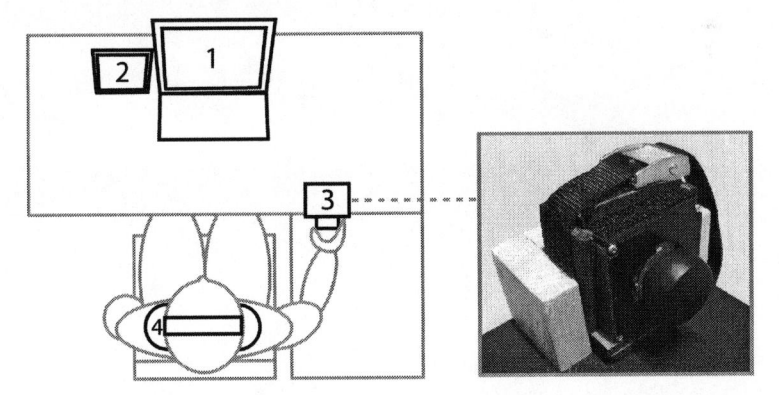

Figure 1. The experimental set-up, comprising a laptop computer (1), a 6.4" display (2), a haptic rotary device (3) and headphones (4)

Experimental conditions

With the intention that the participants would be able to comfortably rotate the device through a menu of four textures without changing their grasp, the total travel for a texture was limited to 30°. The haptic texture feedback was rendered as repeated and evenly distributed clicks, i.e. alternated high and low torque. To limit the number of possible textures, the peak torque was constrained to 10 mN·m. It was possible with these restrictions on angle and torque to design nine textures (with 0, 1, 2, 3, 5, 6, 10, 15 and 30 click repetitions). Eight participants were asked in a test to compare the textures in pairs in order to determine whether the textures felt the same or different. Textures with 0, 3, 6 and 30 repetitions were assessed to be the easiest to discriminate. Salient click effects were incorporated between every texture in the menu to indicate borders. The click angle was 10° and the amplitude of the elastic torque was 50 mN·m. The total angle of operation with the rotary device was consequently 150°. Restricting walls outside the scale limits on each end of the menu were also incorporated, and a damper torque made the forces increase and decrease with control speed. In a second test participants were asked to sketch visual representations of the haptic textures. Different graphical texture profiles were created from these sketches (three different profiles for each texture), and in a third test six participants were asked to match the haptic sensation with a representative visual image of the sensation. The outcome of these tests resulted in the haptic and visual feedback used in the cross-modal experiment.

The three feedback conditions, haptic (H), visual (V) and haptic plus visual (HV), are presented in Figure 2, where the textures are termed A, B, C and D. In the H feedback condition the rotary device provided the textures as haptic sensations, and no visual information was provided. In the V feedback condition the textures were visually displayed on the laptop monitor, but no textures or clicks in between could be felt through the rotary device. The participants thus had to rotate the device to move a transparent blue cursor in the texture menu. The textures were horizontally arranged, and each had a height and width of 25 mm. In the HV condition feedback was given both haptically through the rotary device and graphically on the laptop monitor.

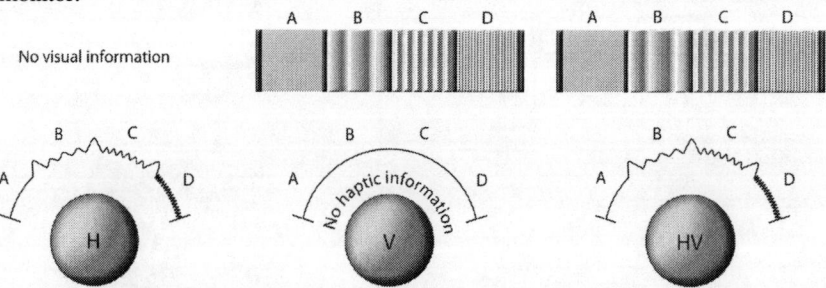

Figure 2. A representation of the haptic feedback provided through the rotary device and the visual feedback provided on the laptop display in the H, V and HV conditions. The textures are presented in alphabetical order from A to D. In the V and HV conditions the active texture was marked with a transparent blue cursor

Design and procedure

The experiment used a 3 x 3 between-subjects design and the independent variables were Training Condition (H, V and HV) and Test Condition (H, V and HV). The participants were randomly assigned to the resulting nine cases, so that each group of six participants was comprised two females and four males. Participants were informed that they would repeatedly locate textures among four textures. It was stated whether the discrimination would be by touch only, vision only or by touch and vision together, although it was not said that the test part for most of the participants was to be conducted in another feedback condition. After listening to instructions for the experiment, the participants were allowed to practice the four textures in two training series. In the first series the participants were free to explore a menu in which the textures were provided in alphabetical order. The name of the active texture (A, B, C or D) was displayed on the laptop display as the device was turned. The participants told the experimenter when they had learned the textures and were ready to continue. In the second training series the participants practiced the experimental task. The task was to repeatedly locate and select textures in the menu by turning and pushing the rotary device. The tasks, e.g. "Locate C", were automatically presented to the participants orally in the headphones and written in the 6.4" monitor. The target texture and the positions of the textures changed for every trial. However, if the wrong texture was selected, the textures stayed in the same order until the right texture was selected. After a successfully completed task a jingle was given as feedback. The device was programmed to start at the leftmost texture for every new trial, and the participants were to initially turn the device clockwise. The reset was not felt, and thus it was not necessary for the participants to let go of the device. The participants had to successfully complete 12 tasks in a row to pass the training series.

After the training series the participants were informed about whether they would do the test in the same or another condition in 36 trials. The participants were instructed to perform the tasks to the best of their ability, but were not informed about the recorded performance measures. To the greatest extent possible, the placement of the textures in the menu and the order in which the textures were displayed as targets were balanced so that each texture occurred in each position equally often and was equally often displayed as a target. A new task started every 13th second. If the participants did not finish a task during that time, the task time was logged as a missing value. When the wrong item was selected, the action was recorded as a push error: hence the participants had to select the right texture for the task to be completed. When the participants passed the right texture without selecting it, the action was recorded as a turn error. After the test the participants were asked to fill in a form with demographic information. To investigate whether the participants' perceived mental workload showed a similar pattern as the performance measures, the participants were asked to respond to NASA-TLX (Task Load Index) forms. NASA-TLX is a multidimensional workload scale in which the magnitudes of six workload-related factors (Mental Demand, Physical Demand, Temporal Demand, Performance, Effort and Frustration Level) are combined to derive an estimation of workload (Hart and Staveland, 1988).

Data analysis

Floor effects were present for most of the cases for the variables missing value and push error, and the data were therefore examined only on a percentage basis by calculating the total number of missing values and push errors for each case and divide it by the total number of tasks (36 x 6). Reiteration of a task may cause learning effects or fatigue-like effects. To check for these effects the time on task and turn error data were divided into two blocks with 18 tasks in each. The data were then analysed with mixed three-factor ANOVAs, with Block (1 and 2) as a within-subject factor, and Training Condition (H, V and HV) and Test Condition (H, V and HV) as between-subjects factors. The subjective workload (NASA-TLX) scores were analysed with a two-way between-subjects ANOVA, with Training Condition (H, V and HV) and Test Condition (H, V and HV) as factors. An alpha level of .05 was used in the analyses. The Tukey HSD procedure was used for post hoc pairwise comparisons of means.

Results

Missing values

There were few missing values in the experiment for most of the cases (fewer than 2% of the tasks were not completed in time). In the V-H (visual training and haptic test) and HV-H (haptic plus visual training and haptic test) cases, 13% and 10% of the tasks were not completed in time. Of the few missing values, 73% were made during the first block. Missing values were replaced by the maximum allowed task time, 13 s, in the task time data.

Task completion time

For task completion time the mixed three-factor ANOVA indicated a significant Block x Training Condition x Test Condition interaction, $F(4, 45) = 4.38$, $p<.01$, and a significant Training Condition x Test Condition interaction, $F(4, 45) = 3.62$, $p<.05$. The analysis also indicated significant main effects for Block, $F(1, 45) = 47.86$, $p<.001$, and Test Condition, $F(2, 45) = 36.52$, $p<.001$. In Figure 3 and Figure 4 mean task completion time is plotted as a function of Training Condition (H, V and HV) and Test Condition (H, V and HV) for Block 1 and Block 2. The figures reveal improvements for most of the cases over the two blocks. Within-groups t-tests made for each case over the blocks revealed that the improvements were significant for the cases H-HV, V-H, HV-V ($p<.01$), and H-V, V-V, HV-H ($p<.05$), but not for the cases H-H, V-HV and HV-HV. The interactions were further explored by conducting two separate two-way ANOVAs, one for each block.

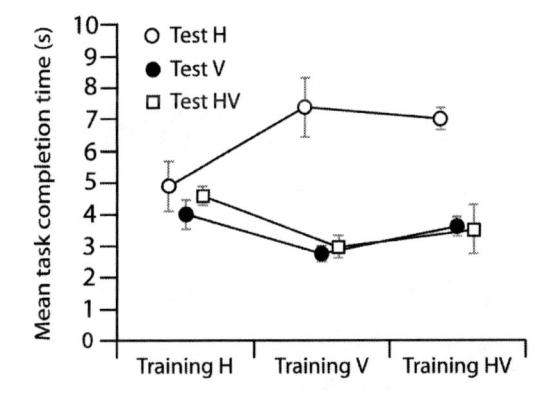

haptic, visual and cross-modal perception of interface information   405

Figure 3. A plot showing mean task completion time for the first 18 tasks in seconds (and associated standard errors) as a function of Training Condition (H, V and HV) and Test Condition (H, V and HV)

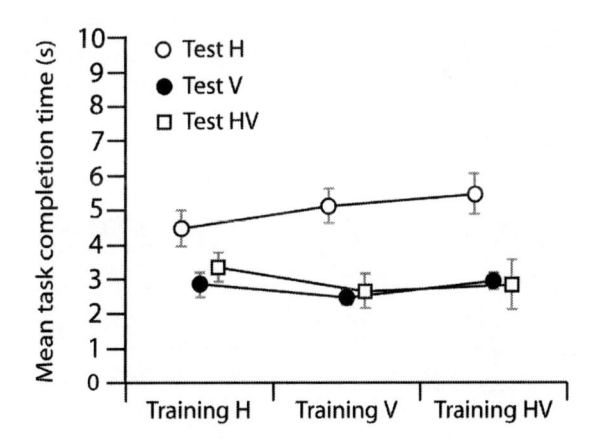

Figure 4. A plot showing mean task completion time for the last 18 tasks in seconds (and associated standard errors) as a function of Training Condition (H, V and HV) and Test Condition (H, V and HV)

The analysis for the first block (Figure 3) indicated a Training Condition x Test Condition interaction, $F(4, 45) = 4.88$, $p<.01$, and a main effect was found for Test Condition $F(2, 45) = 27.56$, $p<.001$. The main effect was interpreted in light of the significant interaction effect, and one-way ANOVAs were conducted for each training condition. There were no significant differences in the test when participants had gone through H training, but significant differences were found in the test when participants had gone through V training, $F(2, 15) = 15.49$, $p<.001$, and HV training $F(2, 15) = 15.88$, $p<.001$. Pairwise comparisons revealed that the H test condition was performed significantly slower than the V and HV test conditions, for both V and HV training. No significant differences were found among the V and HV test conditions.

For the second block (Figure 4) a main effect was found for Test Condition, $F(2, 45)$ = 36.12, $p<.001$. Pairwise comparisons of the three test conditions showed that the H test condition was performed significantly slower than the V and HV test conditions. These results indicate that interaction was faster in the test when visual information was provided, except at the beginning of the test (Block 1) when participants had gone through H training. H-H, H-V and H-HV were then conducted equally rapidly.

Push error

In the V-H case 7% of the tasks included a push error, and in the HV-H case 13% of the tasks included a push error. Few push errors were made in the other cases (fewer than 3%), and case HV-HV included no push errors at all. Of the few push errors, 56% were made during the first block.

Turn error

For turn error the mixed three-factor ANOVA indicated a significant main effect of Test Condition, $F(2, 45) = 5.99$, $p<.01$. Pairwise comparisons of the three test conditions showed that the H test condition generated significantly more turn errors than the V and HV test conditions.

NASA-TLX

No significant effects were found in the analysis of the NASA-TLX scores. However, Figure 5 gives an indication of a difference between cross-modal cases H-V and V-H. The workload seems to be lower going from the H training to the V test than when going from the V training to the H test.

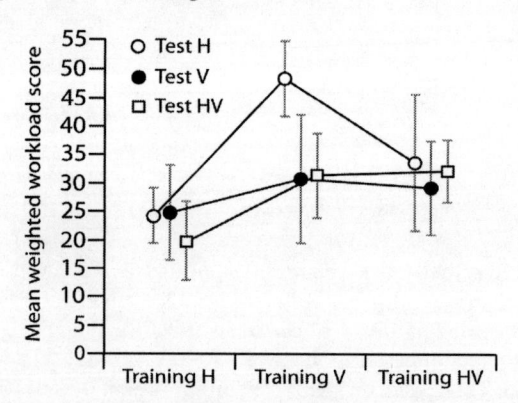

Figure 5. A plot showing the mean weighted workload score (and associated standard errors) as a function of Training Condition (H, V and HV) and Test Condition (H, V and HV). A high score indicates high workload

Discussion

This experiment investigated the extent to which information provided in an interface can be shared between the haptic and visual modalities. In the experiment menu information was coded in terms of textures. In the within-modal cases and the cases including visual feedback in both training and the test (H-H, V-V, V-HV, HV-V and HV-HV), there were no or small improvements in terms of time over the blocks, while there were clear improvements for the cross-modal cases (H-V and in particular V-H) (Figure 3 and Figure 4). These improvements indicate that the cross-modal transfer was not effortless and included learning. If the visual and haptic textures had been perfectly equivalent, the transfer would probably have been effortless. The task times for the H-V case would have been the same as for the V-V case, and the task times for the V-H case would have been the same as for the H-H case. The task times differed for Block 1 (H-V $\neq$ V-V and V-H $\neq$ H-H) but were almost equal for Block 2 (H-V = V-V and V-H = H-H). Hence, although the initial transfer was somewhat poor, the interaction became more rapid during the test. The HV-H case is not cross-modal but, even though bimodal information was provided during training, the participants performed no better initially on the test than when unimodal visual information had been provided during training (V-H). Since humans optimise the perception of haptic and visual information (Ernst & Banks, 2002), the visual information might have been perceived as being more useful for the task at hand, and the participants did not actively utilize the haptic information in the training. For the H-HV case there was also an improvement over the blocks, most likely for the reason that the participants initially utilized the somewhat more slow haptic interaction and after a while started to utilize the visual information also, with the result that the interaction became faster. That visual interaction is faster than haptic interaction was also observed by Grane and Bengtsson (2005).

In terms of missing values and push errors made, going from a training condition including visual cues to a unimodal haptic test condition (V-H, HV-H) seems to have been more troublesome than when the test condition included visual information. Hatwell (2003) and Hale and Stanney (2004) proposed that, for geometric properties, switching from haptics to vision is easier than switching from vision to haptics. This seems also to be the case for the textures used in this experiment. The workload scores point towards a lower workload going from the H training to the V test than going from the V training to the H test.

Both when interacting with the real world and in HMI haptic information is generally gathered in sequence and visual information is gathered to a greater extent in parallel. Hence, to perceive the textures haptically in this experiment, the participants went through the menu texture-by-texture, while the textures could be visually perceived simultaneously. The sequential versus simultaneous processing can be viewed in terms of turn errors. A comparison between textures could be made visually without turning the device, while the device had to be turned in order to perceive the textures in a haptic discrimination, and consequently more turn errors were made. The type of processing made may also explain that tasks including visual feedback were carried out faster. An issue that may have negatively affected the haptic processing was some unwanted buzzing in the device, and, when the device was moved over a texture, it was easy to accidentally slip over to the next.

Grane and Bengtsson (2005), Oakley et al. (2000) and Campbell et al. (1999) suggested redundant haptic to visual information in an interface. No significant difference between the V-V and HV-HV cases was found in this experiment. However, haptic or visual information can be more or less useful depending on the task at hand. In this experiment the participants could focus on the task. Perhaps haptic feedback could be used in a redundant fashion to facilitate interaction in visually demanding environments. Benefits of cross-modal and multimodal interfaces should be further investigated with realistic interaction tasks in different situations. When studying the interaction with in-vehicle systems, eye movements and distraction-related measures are probably more important to consider than task time and the number of errors made.

References

Burnett, G.E., & Porter J.M. (2001). Ubiquitous computing within cars: designing controls for non-visual use. *International Journal of Human-Computer Studies, 55*, 521-531.

Campbell, S.C., Shumin, Z., May, K.W., & Maglio, P.P. (1999). What You Feel Must Be What You See: Adding Tactile Feedback to the Trackpoint. In M. Angela Sasse, and Chris Johnson (Eds.), *Human-Computer Interaction – Proceedings of INTERACT'99*. (pp.383-390). Edinburgh, UK: IOS Press.

Ernst M.O., & Banks, M.S. (2002). Humans integrate visual and haptic information in a statistically optimal fashion. *Nature, 415*, 429-433.

Grane, C., & Bengtsson, P. (2005). Menu Selection Based on Haptic and/or Graphic Information. In G. Salvendy (Ed.), Human Computer International 2005 (CD-ROM). Las Vegas, USA: Erlbaum.

Hale, K.S., & Stanney, K.M. (2004). Deriving Haptic Design Guidelines from Human Physiological, Psychophysical, and Neurological Foundations. *IEEE Computer Graphics and Applications, 2*, 33-39.

Hart, S.G., & Staveland, L.E. (1988). Development of NASA-TLX (Task Load Index): Results of Empirical and Theoretical Research. In P.A. Hancock and N. Meshkati (Eds.), *Human Mental Workload.* (pp. 139-182). Amsterdam, The Netherlands: Elsevier.

Hatwell, Y. (2003). Intermodal coordinations in children and adults. In Y. Hatwell, A. Streri, and E. Gentaz (Eds), *Touching for Knowing: Cognitive psychology of haptic manual perception.* (pp. 207-219). Amsterdam, The Netherlands: J. Benjamins.

Hayward, V., Astley, O.R., Cruz-Hernandez, M., Grant, D., & Robles-De-La-Torre, G. (2004). Haptic interfaces and devices. *Sensor Review, 24*, 16-29.

Hoggan, E., & Brewster, S.A. (2006). Mobile Crossmodal Auditory and Tactile Displays. In *Proceedings of First International Workshop on Haptic and Audio Interaction Design.* (pp. 9-12). Glasgow, UK.
[http://www.dcs.gla.ac.uk/~mcgookdk/multivis/vol2.pdf]

Klatzky, R.L., & Lederman, S.J. (2006). The Perceived Roughness of Resistive Virtual Textures: I. Rendering by a Force-Feedback Mouse. *ACM Transactions on Applied Perception, 3*, 1-14.

Loomis, J.M., & Lederman S.J. (1986). Tactual perception. In K.R. Boff, L. Kaufman, and J.P. Thomas (Eds.), *Handbook of Perception and Human Performance. Vol 2, Cognitive Processes and Performance.* (pp. 1-41). New York, USA: Wiley.

Lederman, S.J., & Klatzky, R.L. (1987). Hand movements: A window into haptic object recognition. *Cognitive Psychology, 19,* 342-368.

Lederman, S.J., Thorne, G., & Jones, B. (1986). Perception of Texture by Vision and Touch: Multidimensionality and Intersensory Integration. *Journal of Experimental Psychology: Human Perception and Performance, 12,* 169-180.

Oakley, I., McGee, M.R., Brewster, S., & Gray, P. (2000). Putting the Feel in 'Look and Feel'. In *Proceedings of CHI'00.* (pp. 415-422). The Hague, The Netherlands: ACM Press.

Stein, E.S., & Meredith M.A., (1993). *The Merging of the Senses.* Cambridge, USA: MIT Press.

Woods A.T., & Newell, F. (2004). Visual, haptic and cross-modal recognition of objects and scenes. *Journal of Physiology – Paris, 98,* 147-159.

Control of information flooding and mode confusions: lessons from major engineering projects

W. Ian Hamilton[1], Joanne Stokes[1], & Graham Kenyon[2]
[1]Human Engineering Limited, Bristol
[2]Ultra Electronics Airport Systems, Manchester
United Kingdom

Abstract

The application of human factors practices to any systems development project should eliminate, or at least significantly reduce the risk of information overload or control mode confusion errors. Although human factors can enhance requirements capture and the anticipation and control of errors, the final quality of the system interface may be fixed by system design limitations unless these match user needs. Even where human factors techniques are applied to systems engineering, the translation of functional and task goals into design requirements may be of insufficient resolution to define necessary display performance characteristics. The resulting incompatibility of display performance and user needs may be realised only at the verification stage: too late to alter the design and leading to the delivery of an inadequate solution. This paper presents a technique for the specification of interface requirements, including detailed display performance characteristics based on task analysis data. The technique can be implemented as a simple database for display graphics rationalisation, and includes a comprehensive set of prompt fields for the capture of information and input requirements. The database, known as the Interaction Requirements matrix, can also support a basic assessment of the feasibility of the proposed interaction task. This is achieved using a GOMS style of analysis of unit task execution times, that are summed for a given interaction session or operational scenario to provide a time occupancy estimate of workload.

Introduction

Display and control systems are now widely used in supervisory control and monitoring situations. This is true not only in traditional process control applications but now too in large-scale facilities management applications. For instance in Heathrow's Terminal 5 the main control room houses a systems integration suite of displays that support operational and security monitoring activities, as well as facilities management, trouble-shooting and incident management tasks.

Figure 1. Depicting Heathrow Terminal 5 (picture from Cement Industry web site http://www.cementindustry.co.uk/main)

The effectiveness of these systems will rely on the quality of the human interface and its appropriateness for the human tasks to be performed. In particular, inappropriately designed information displays can make task performance inefficient or even lead to task performance failure. For example, a recent control system development for an oil and gas refinery included the addition of a set of displays for a new process train. Because the new process train was an exact replica of an existing train, the control and instrumentation engineers decided to make the new control displays a copy of the existing displays. This seemingly had advantages such as promoting consistency in operation and building on familiarity with established working practices. The two sets of displays where to be discriminated using different on-screen labels. Unfortunately the labels where identical except for a single 3.5 mm tall numerical character on each. When it was first put into operational use the control room operators quickly discovered that they found it hard to discriminate the process trains, and where often in the wrong mode. That is, when an outside operator radioed-in a request to start, stop or throttle some piece of equipment the panel operator sometimes chose the wrong one.

Fortunately no serious consequences arose as the operators reported the problem at once. A Human Factors specialist was called-in and advised on a simple re-design strategy to eliminate the risk of mode confusion. This simple example illustrates one consequence of not adopting a task centred approach to interface design. Any even limited human factors analysis of the operators' tasks would have revealed the potential for this confusion and the need for a solution. The design would then have been specified differently and the need for re-design work avoided. The only consequence here was financial in that additional work was required. But it could have been different.

This paper is concerned with the specification of display design requirements during early systems development. It is argued that a suitable and sufficient specification of the requirements for the display designs should take account of the operators' task goals and of the detailed requirements for information design and formatting to avoid clutter and confusion leading to information overload. This is closely related to the topic of alarm handling (EEMUA, 1999) but with the important difference that this concerns the whole user-system interface under normal as well as unusual working conditions.

The perspective presented here is strictly cognitive in that it is concerned with optimising the display design for the limited bandwidth and characteristics of human information processing. There are other valid perspectives but these are not addressed here. They include social, organisational, psychophysiological (e.g. stress), or communications perspectives, all of which are also relevant and are covered in more detail elsewhere such as in Christie et al. (2002).

User requirements

Factors affecting information overload

Displays will be seen to vary in complexity and clutter depending on a number of factors, including the competence and experience of the operator, the relevance of the information to the task to be performed, the way that the information is designed and presented on screen, and the time it takes to complete interaction tasks. The first of these factors is not within the control of the designer but should be considered during the implementation strategy. The issues of information relevance and the quality of presentation are directly relevant here.

Reducing clutter is not simply a matter of having less information on the screen. Artificially restricting the information content of a screen format can actually increase workload and complexity by demanding more time consuming navigation and option selection for the accomplishment of tasks. What is required is, therefore, a more systematic analysis of the user's interaction needs with respect to their task goals.

User centred design

Much has been written about user centred design and the high-level principles are expressed in numerous standards, for example BS EN ISO (1999), DD ISO/PAS (2003), and BS EN ISO (2004). However, it is often uncertain as to how best to translate these general principles into a design process. Task analysis is of course fundamental to achieving this but there are no established rules that guide the interpretation of task elements into display features, albeit that Wilson and Rajan (2002) provide some generic solutions based on Rajan's work in designing a control system application. In addition there are some published sources and standards that offer good generic advice on screen and dialogue design, for example the BS EN ISO 9241 series, in particular Parts 2, 3, 8, 10, and 11, and MacKendrick (1998).

The key to the success of the process is to capture the user's task goals at sufficient detail to be able to specify the display requirements at the correct resolution. For example, knowing that a user has to view information on flow rates, pressures or temperatures may be helpful, but it is essential to be able to define the required resolution of the information. For instance what is the smallest change in flow, pressure or temperature that is important to the operator, and what display update speed is required to best support the operator's scrutiny of these parameters.

The ability to display information in a standard, readily-recognisable, format is essential. In defining these requirements, and selecting suitable products, however, the system designer may need to take into account the capabilities of the graphical display technology to present the information in that format. As an example, functionality of a commercial off-the-shelf (COTS) product may not allow the presentation of Système Internationale (SI) units in the correct format under some circumstances. This can lead to the display feeling clumsy and perhaps alien or contrived.

Figure 2 compares an example of "ideal" display of units for quantitative information, along with an example displayed on a COTS product constrained by the inability to handle superscript text in mimics. The displayed units would be even less intuitive, if the constrained package did not allow the "slash" character.

No Constraint in COTS Package	Constraint in COTS Package	Comments
Airflow 20.0 ls^{-1}	Airflow 20.0 l/s	Example 1 – Units still easily assimilated with constraint
Acceleration 9.0 ms^{-2}	Acceleration 9.0 m/s/s	Example 2 – Units ambiguous with constraint

Figure 2. Presentation of Units Constrained by COTS Package Limitations

The context of use of information also has an important bearing on the identification of information needs. For example, Network Rail's signallers may often have to coordinate emergency service responses to road traffic accident locations where road vehicles have struck a railway bridge. The bridges have signs with phone numbers that will connect callers with a signaller who is perhaps at a relatively remote control centre. The caller can provide information that will help the signaller to identify the location of the bridge relative to the railway infrastructure under his supervision. However, the signaller's graphical displays provide relative position information and not absolute geographic position. The signaller then has to translate the information into a suitable coordinate system to direct emergency services to the location. The problem is compounded by the fact that the emergency services in some parts of the UK use different reference systems and not necessarily the Ordnance Survey reference system. Understanding these problems can have major implications for the detail and variety of information annotations that need to be available for a single bridge.

Capturing user interaction requirements

From the authors' recent project experience it is clear that the analysis of user requirements should consider the users' needs in terms of the following taxonomy of generic interaction behaviours:

- Identification – e.g. of display elements and their related system components.
- Discrimination – e.g. of similar systems such as parallel, redundant or back-up equipment, or camera views.
- Monitoring – e.g. of process or performance parameters or CCTV views.
- Interpretation – e.g. of data or messages, or the required resolution for camera search.
- Fault detection/diagnosis – e.g. of performance conditions, equipment status, or faults.
- Prediction – e.g. of future states, including the likely time frame required.
- Problem solving – e.g. taking account of the requirements to resolve uncertainty for both routine and unusual situations.
- Decision making – e.g. to deal with equipment failures or to determine an alternative configuration or working method, such as re-routing people to avoid a failed escalator or blocked passage or stairwell.
- Input – e.g. of date values or of menu choices or other types of selection.
- Communications – e.g. especially understanding the differences that may exist between each party's frame of reference.

These parameters are equally important whether the operator is involved in a continuous work stream, or performing a supervisory control task, which may be characterised by extended periods of relatively low monitoring workload, punctuated by short periods of time pressured activity. The supervisory control case is particularly important as the operator must be able quickly to gain an accurate appreciation of the situation.

The display design parameters that are available to the designer represent a small palette of choices. Typically the designer will be able to utilise:

- Labelling and annotation, including font parameters
- Menu structures and hierarchies of choices
- Symbology and pictorial representations, including icons
- Colour coding, including the use of background and foreground colours
- Spatial arrangement of display elements, windows, etc.

There will also typically be facilities for:

- Interaction with the individual display elements to accomplish necessary functions
- Navigation strategies, based on the relative frequency of links between items, and
- Information declutter, typically based on functional groupings and the levels of importance of information elements.

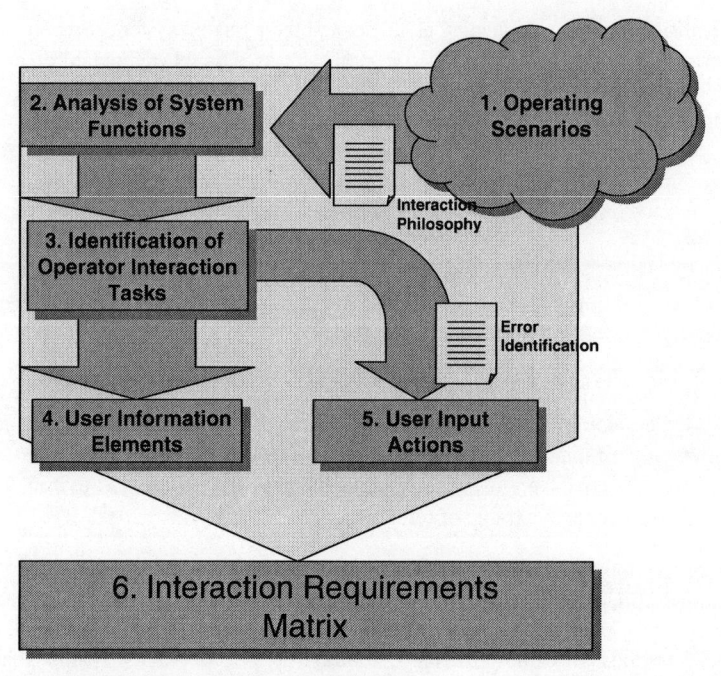

Figure 3. Capturing user interaction requirements

Figure 3 represents a flow chart process for the capture of user interaction requirements. The elements of the flow chart are explained below using the numbers to reference the elements of the chart.

1. *Operating Scenarios* – The system operating scenarios should be a complete list of all foreseeable operating modes, including normal and abnormal or unusual conditions.
2. *Analysis of System Functions* – This should identify all of the system functional goals with which the operator is concerned. This will likely be based on the system allocation of functions analysis that should have been done to determine the user's role in the system. There will probably be an interaction philosophy document to describe the planned interaction between operators and the system.
3. *Identification of Operator Interaction Tasks* – This will be a complete list of all of the users' interaction tasks with each task corresponding to the accomplishment of some goal. This will probably be developed through a hierarchical task analysis.
4. *User Information Elements* – Operator actions should be separated into inputs and outputs. This will be a list of the elements of information that should be provided to the user.
5. *User Input Actions* – This will be a list of the input functions that should be available to the operator.
6. *Interaction Requirements Matrix* – The outputs from stages 1 to 5 of this process are fed into a table of interaction requirements. This is intended to

support the translation of the task actions into specifications for the design of the system interface.

Interaction Requirements Matrix

This process of information needs analysis is designed to reinforce the link between the human factors analysis of operator tasks and the specification of the display graphic elements required to support the interaction philosophy. The analysis should take place early in the design process when there is time to properly influence the functionality and capability of the system interface to match the users' needs.

The Interaction Requirements Matrix is a simple technique to capture the functions and goals of the user interaction and to facilitate their translation into design specifications. The database contains no automation or algorithm for this translation as the analyst writing the requirements does it all. However the benefit to the design process is that it captures explicitly the requirements along with the rationale for the design. In this way an interface design emerges that addresses interaction requirements more completely, with greater consistency, and at an appropriate level of definition.

The Interaction Requirements Matrix is a simple table describing the hierarchical relationship between scenarios, functions, tasks and the interactive elements of the interface. The database's features are described in Table 1.

Application to design

The Interaction Requirements Matrix can be implemented as a simple table or relational database in Microsoft Excel or Access. It can be completed as a result of a workshop type exercise with the analysis of operator interaction tasks forming the primary input (i.e. step 3 in Figure 3). Once complete the matrix can act as support to the formal specification document and to promote the user centred objectives of the project. As the design develops the matrix can be extended to include images of the interaction elements. It can also be revised to ensure it remains complete.

The key advantage of this technique is that it explicitly and directly addresses the key principles of usability design. The interface features and functionality are driven by the requirements of accomplishing the tasks and functions necessary to complete operational scenarios. The information elements and interaction actions can be defined to achieve simplicity and consistency. User behaviour can be supported by positive feedback and guided to avoid errors in operation. The result should be a more intuitive interface design that matches the user's model of the system and expectations for its function.

Table 1. Interaction Requirements Matrix

Feature	Detail
Operating scenario	A title identifying the operating scenario
Scenario Description	A brief description of the scenario including any special terms
Scenario type	Normal/Abnormal/Degraded
Function	A title identifying the function
Function Description	A description of the purpose of the function and its goal within the system
Task	A title for the task to be accomplished
Task Description	A description of the task goal and its purpose for the function
Information Element	A description of the information element required. Typically a single entity of display information. This description will include its required purpose in support of the interaction task.
Item name	Label for the display information element, including any standard abbreviations to be used.
Frequency of use	An estimate of the number of occasions that this element is likely to be used in a session. A session may be any appropriate period of time.
Nature of use	This will define the behaviour associated with the use of the information element. The description will be compatible with the taxonomy of generic interaction tasks as outlined above.
Trigger	This is a description of the event or conditions that cause the element to be displayed. The initiating conditions may be a user selection, in which case the appropriate *input action* will be cross-referenced. If it is shown continuously this is stated here.
Resolution	This is an estimate of the frequency with which the information parameter is updated or changes, Typically frequency would be expressed on the same basis of the frequency of use.
Unit of Change	This is a statement of the required minimum unit of change to be displayed.
Display format	The element can be defined as a Label, Icon, or Symbol. This field contains the requirements for font, formatting, size, range of change in display characteristics, and position on the screen or within a window.
Colour property	This describes the colour to be used for the display parameter. If there are any colour changes these are described here too.
Action feature	This is a description of any interaction property associated with the display element; the relevant *input action* description would be cross-referenced.
Alerting feature	If the information item has an associated alerting feature
Input Action	This is a description of the interaction component and its purpose. This is typically a single screen element such as a symbol, icon, or graphic. Or may be a menu or menu item.
Action name	This is a name for the action
Frequency of use	This is an estimate of the number of occasions that this element is likely to be used in a session. A session may be any appropriate period of time, typically this would be the same as the time period used to define the frequency of use of *information elements*.
Details of action	This is a description of the interaction behaviour associated with the input action expressed in terms of the task step to be accomplished.
Action option	This is a description of the interaction behaviour associated with the input action. Typically this would describe keying actions, pointing device actions, or touch screen interaction behaviour as appropriate.
Timing	This field is to capture any timing parameters associated with the action, if it is time critical or an estimate of how long it may take to complete.
Feedback	This field contains a definition of the feedback that will be displayed to the operator following the input action.
Action constraint	This is a description of the safe guards required to ensure that the user cannot inadvertently perform the wrong action. Features might include two stage verification or conditions for 'greying out' options. Typically this will be informed by a suitable error identification study.

Interaction feasibility

The Interaction Requirements Matrix includes estimates of the frequency and duration of tasks concerned with information processing and interaction inputs. As a consequence a by-product of the technique is that it is possible to derive an estimate of interaction time for various functions, interaction sessions or scenarios.

The assessment is derived by using the GOMS (Card et al., 1983) human information processing model to calculate estimates of the execution time for the interaction tasks. The GOMS technique allows the analyst to construct a unit task expression for a short sequence of behaviour representing interaction tasks. For example, pointing to an icon with a mouse cursor, clicking to present a menu, and selecting an item from that menu might involve the following actions:

- Move mouse to icon
- Right click on icon
- Move cursor to target menu item
- Select menu item with left click.

It is possible to estimate the execution times for these actions from a range of timings for elementary behaviours supplied by the GOMS human information processing model. The data for these timings are provided as a range from 'fast', to 'median', and through to 'slow' and are detailed in Table 2 (extracted from data first published by Hamilton & Clarke, 2005).

Table 2. Timings for elementary behaviours

Element	Symbol	Timings (s) Fast	Median	Slow
Perceptual Processing	T_P	0.050	0.10	0.20
Cognitive Processing	T_C	0.025	0.07	0.17
Motor Processing	T_M	0.030	0.07	0.10
Cognitive Iteration Time	I_C	0.092	0.15	0.16
Eye Movement Time	E_M	0.070	0.23	0.70
Movement Iteration Time	I_M	0.070	0.10	0.12
Typing, Keystroke Time	T_{PTi}	0.158	0.33	1.15
Keying, Keystroke Time	T_{PKi}	0.300	0.58	1.09

The following is an example of how these elemental parameters can be used to construct performance time algorithms for the action of moving the mouse to a screen icon.

Unit task expression: $TPa = TP+TC+TM+ IM \log2 (D/S + 0.5)$

Where: $IM \log2 (D/S + 0.5)$ = an expression for the time accuracy trade-off for cursor movement given by Fitt's Law, which expresses movement time as a function of distance D and target size S, and *TPa = Time to Perform Action*

Other work by Hamilton et al. (2004) has provided evidence for the validity of the action execution times estimated from these data. As every interaction behaviour can be expressed as a unit task algorithm like the one above, predicted execution times can be generated for each interaction task. These can then be summed to provide an overall estimate of interaction task time for a given function, session or scenario.

The feasibility of the time taken to perform the interaction task may therefore be evaluated as:

$$T_p = \frac{\sum_{i=1}^{n}(A_i * D_i)}{H} * 100\%$$

where:
T_p is total time pressure, expressed as a percentage of time available,
A_i is the frequency with which each activity type i is required to be performed,
D_i is the duration of each activity type i,
H is the total time available for the interaction session or scenario.

This can be used to assess the feasibility of interaction tasks and provides a useful measure of the quality of the design. Recent work has applied this method to the assessment of the feasibility of control room tasks and to help to specify the necessary design features of the control system (Fisher & Hamilton, 2006).

Conclusion

The Interaction Requirements Matrix has been developed on the back of project work in support of a range of process and supervisory control systems. It can be applied from an early stage in the design process and greatly helps to manage the development of user requirements for the interactive systems. It is recommended to the reader as a useful device for the translation of user task requirements into system interaction requirements and, in conjunction with the GOMS technique as a means of assessing interaction task feasibility in terms of time pressure. The precise set of fields used can be modified to suit the particular application of the work, but it is hoped that the matrix presented here will offer a good starting point and a valuable aid to interface design specification work.

References

BS EN ISO (2004). *Ergonomic Principles in the Design of Work Systems* (BS EN ISO 6385:2004). London, UK: British Standards Institute.
BS EN ISO (1992). *Ergonomic Requirements for office work with visual display terminals (VDTs) - Part 2: Guidance on Task Requirements* (BS EN ISO 9241-2:1992). London, UK: British Standards Institute.
BS EN ISO (1993). Ergonomic *Requirements for office work with visual display terminals (VDTs) - Part 3: Visual Display Requirements* (BS EN ISO 9241-3:1993). London, UK: British Standards Institute.

BS EN ISO (1997). *Ergonomic Requirements for office work with visual display terminals (VDTs) - Part 8: Requirements for displayed colours* (BS EN ISO 9241-8:1997). London, UK: British Standards Institute.

BS EN ISO (1996). *Ergonomic Requirements for office work with visual display terminals (VDTs) - Part 10: Dialogue principles* (BS EN ISO 9241-10:1996). London, UK: British Standards Institute.

BS EN ISO (1998). *Ergonomic Requirements for office work with visual display terminals (VDTs) - Part 11: Guidance on usability* (BS EN ISO 9241-11:1998). London, UK: British Standards Institute.

BS EN ISO (1999). *Human Centered Design for Interactive Systems* (BS EN ISO 13407:1999). London, UK: British Standards Institute.

Card S.K., Moran T.P., & Newell A. (1983). *The Psychology of Human-Computer Interaction*. London, UK: Lawrence Erlbaum Associates.

Christie, B., Scane, R., & Collyer, J. (2002). Evaluation of human-computer interaction at the user interface to advanced IT systems. In J.R. Wilson and E.N. Corlett (Eds.), *Evaluation of Human Work: A Practical Ergonomics Methodology* (pp. 310-356). London, UK: Taylor & Francis.

DD ISO/PAS (2003). *Ergonomics of Human-System Interaction – Specification for the Process Assessment of Human-System Issues* (DD ISO/PAS 18152:2003). London, UK: British Standards Institute.

EEMUA (1999). *Alarms Systems: A Guide to Design, Management and Procurement* (EEMUA 191). London, UK: The Engineering Equipment and Materials Users Association.

Fisher, J., & Hamilton, W.I. (2006). Early Human Factors Interventions in the Development of an FPSO. In P.D. Bust (Ed.), *The Ergonomics Society: Contemporary Ergonomics 2006* (pp. 560-564). London, UK: Taylor & Francis.

Hamilton W.I., Lowe C.l, & Blanchard H. (2004). Cognitive Task Analysis And Performance Modelling For Early Human Systems Integration. In *Proceedings of The Human Factors and Ergonomics Society Annual Conference*, Santa Monica, CA, USA: HFES.

Hamilton W.I., & Clarke T. (2005). Driver performance modelling and its practical application to railway safety. *Applied Ergonomics, 36*, 661-670.

MacKendrick, H. (1998). *Development of a Human Machine Interface (HMI) Guidelines Database for Air Traffic Control Centres*. London, UK: National Air Traffic Services.

Wilson, J.R., & Rajan, J.A. (2002). Human-machine interfaces for system control. In J.R. Wilson and E.N. Corlett (Eds.), *Evaluation of Human Work: A Practical Ergonomics Methodology* (pp. 357-405). London, UK: Taylor & Francis.

Videoconferencing in a collaborative environment: Do partial gaze awareness and shared workspace make a difference?

Marc Arial & Brigitta Danuser
Institute for Work and Health, Lausanne University
Switzerland

Abstract

The goal of this study was to better understand the effects of partial gaze awareness and shared virtual workspace on dyads' performance and feeling of social presence. 80 participants took part in a 2 x 2 factorial experiment. The following factors were considered: (1) partial gaze awareness - tested with one or two computer screens to display the videoconferencing application and the cooperative application, and (2) shared virtual workspaces. Participants had 35 minutes to solve an optimisation problem. They were located in different rooms and communicated by means of videoconferencing systems and distributed – CSCW application. No significant main or interaction effect of partial gaze awareness was observed on social presence or performance. Similarly, there was no significant main or interaction effect of shared workspace on social presence or performance. However, average social presence was higher for group with two screens and partially shared workspaces than for group with two screens and fully shared workspaces.

Introduction

Systems for videoconferencing can be considered as cooperative technology supporting distributed and synchronous interactions among people (Baecker et al. 1995). As argued by O'Conaill et al. (1993), the idea behind the development of systems for audiovisual communication is to allow geographically remote users to gaze, use gesture, and improve the ability to monitor people's reactions. Videoconferencing technologies have the potential to facilitate frequent high-quality interaction between distant sites, and thus improve the quality of collaboration. For Isaacs and Tang (1994), visual contact is important in cooperative activities. It is used to express understanding, forecast responses, enhance verbal descriptions with gestures, convey purely non-verbal information, express attitudes in posture and facial expression, and manage pauses in speech. In this sense, it has the potential to enhance the degree of salience of another person in an interaction and the resulting salience of interpersonal relationship. This corresponds to the definition of social presence adopted by most researchers (Tu, 2002).

Whether it is possible to replace face-to-face meetings by video mediated ones still needs to be investigated. For Vertegaal (1999), video mediated communication has the potential to fully replicate face-to-face conditions, although current systems are far from producing a comparable context. Considerable research confirms many differences in conversational process and outputs between face-to-face and video mediated meetings. For example, video-mediated conversation is characterised by longer utterances, more frequent explicit handovers (O'Conaill et al. 1993), and less turn to talk (Isaacs & Tang 1994). Compared to face-to-face communication, usual systems for videoconferencing are characterised by the following flaws: they have a limited and fixed field of view, there is a discrepancy between the position of the camera and the position where the eyes are displayed on the screen, hearing and visual cues do poorly support precise spatial location. These flaws prevent to: convey natural eye contact and gaze related cues, easily access and track the point of interest, perform side conversation, and perceive peripheral cues and small movements (Sellen, 1992; Isaacs & Tang, 1994; Grayson & Monk, 2003; Arial, 2004). The potential of audiovisual communication for cooperation remain significant, but these limitations highlight the need for optimisation. Both gaze awareness capability and sharable workspace have the potential to improve video-mediated communication in CSCW applications; both might contribute to social presence and people's performance. These aspects are briefly explained in the following sections.

Gaze awareness

Gaze awareness refers to the knowledge of where someone is looking at, and has been identified as an important conversational resource (Grayson & Monk, 2003). For Gale and Monk (2000), there are three forms of gaze awareness. The first form is the partial gaze awareness, which refers to knowing the general direction where someone is looking. The second form, which is the full gaze awareness, refers to the knowledge of what object someone is looking at. The third form is the mutual gaze and refers to "eye-contact".

One goal of this paper is to verify whether partial gaze awareness improves social presence by emulating the affordances of physical workspaces. Partial gaze awareness is important in cooperative work. For example, it gives information on the point of attention of people involved in a cooperative task. As a consequence, partial gaze awareness contributes to improve the collaborators' degree of salience for each other. Although no such study was identified in the scientific literature, using two displays for videoconferencing (person view) and the cooperative application (task view) seems promising in enabling partial gaze awareness. For example, one could guess whether other collaborators are looking at the person or at the application. This is possible because a shift in the attention between the task view and the person view will be associated with a postural change (head movement) or a salient eye movement. The non-conflicting use of two screens also enables constant presence: the view of the remote collaborator is not hidden behind the application view. Therefore, facial expressions and other visual social cues are accessible for the whole cooperative session. In this view, using two screens to display the person and the task view should influence social presence in two ways: by enabling partial gaze awareness; and by allowing constant presence. No study was found investigating the effects of using two screens for distributed computer supported cooperative work on social presence. Such studies appear pertinent and important for designing distributed CSCW systems involving video-mediated communication.

Shared workspace

The way collaborators can access the workspace (virtual or physical) is an important determinant of communication process occurring in cooperative activities. For example, having a workspace that is shared among collaborators tends to improve cooperation performance (Tang & Minneman, 1990; Dourish & Bly, 1992; Fish et al., 1992). As stated by Decortis and Pavard (1994), knowing the actions performed, as well as the intentions behind these actions, are crucial mechanisms in cooperative activities. In remote environment, such mechanisms can be enabled by an unconstrained access to the virtual workspace where the collaborative actions are performed. Shared workspaces could also influence social presence. Not only the actions performed or the intentions behind them are relevant. The way they are performed could also possibly convey social relevant information e.g. emotive states like angriness (roughness) or doubt (hesitation). Therefore, teams using systems where the application has a fully shared workspace should perform better and report higher social presence than teams using systems with partially shared workspaces. However, no evidence supporting this was found in the scientific literature and further investigation is necessary.

The following questions appear relevant. Does using two screens (independent) to enable partial gaze awareness make a difference in terms of performance (dependent) and social presence (dependent) experienced by collaborators? Does fully shared virtual workspaces are an advantage compared to partially shared ones (independent) in terms of users' performance (dependent) and social presence (dependent)?

The following hypotheses were tested:

H1: Partial gaze awareness results in higher feeling of social presence
H2: Partial gaze awareness results in better cooperative performance
H3: Shared workspace results in better feeling of social presence
H4: Shared workspace results in better cooperative performance

Method

Participants

Participants were recruited by means of a classified advertisements website. An ad explained the research and offered 50 Swiss Francs compensation to each team of two participants selected. The ad mentioned the general topic of the research (cooperation and multimedia communication). It also mentioned that team members had to know each other before the experiment without having previous work experience together. Information about duration and location were also provided. Participants contacted the researchers and volunteered for the experiment. Teams were randomly selected and assigned to an experimental group. 80 participants (40 teams of 2 people) took part to the experiment. The sample included 44 men and 36 women. Their mean age was 26.6 (SD=4.67) years. Participants came from diverse occupations (i.e. engineer, physiotherapist, pharmacist etc.) and a majority were students (61/80, 76.2%). Participants reported to have either no experience or a very limited one in using systems for videoconferencing or CSCW groupware. 19 teams of participants reported having knowledge or previous experience with optimisation problems (engineers, students in engineering). In order to avoid a possible bias due to previous knowledge and experience, only these 19 teams were included for comparing groups' performance.

Design

The design used was a 2 x 2 factorial post-test only using between groups comparisons. A between groups design was used in order to avoid better participants' evaluation for a "nicer" and more sophisticated solution. Factors are partial gaze awareness (number of screens - one or two) and workspace (fully or partially shared). Four groups were created based on the factorial design:

Group A: One screen, fully shared workspace
Group B: Two screens, fully shared workspace
Group C: One screen, partially shared workspace
Group D: Two screens, partially shared workspace

Based on the hypotheses, the following results were expected:

Group B: more social presence and better performance than A, C, and D
Group A and D: more social presence and more performance than C

Items from Short et al. (1976) definition (unsociable-sociable; insensitive-sensitive, cold-warm; impersonal-personal) were used to measure social presence. As stated by Tu (2002), these items are too general to measure social presence in computer mediated communication. Five items were added to the multi-item scale for social presence. Additional items included for example: "How strong was your impression of being able to perceive when the other participant was smiling?", "How strong was your impression of establishing eye-contact?", "How strong was your impression of being able to perceive the other participant's facial expressions?". Items measuring the impression of reciprocity (i.e. "how strong is your impression that the other participant could perceive it when you smiled") were included as well. A score of 1.00 is the highest possible score for social presence. The indicator for social presence consisted in the average value for all items included. Possible values ranged from 0 to 1 with a resolution of 0.01. Items used to calculate the score for social presence were measured by means of visual analogue scales displayed as slider buttons on the videoconferencing monitors after of the cooperative session. The score for performance corresponds to the results obtained by the participants at the end of the cooperative session. As explained later in this text, the participants had to find a solution to an optimising problem. Performance was measured in terms of cost efficiency of the proposed solution. The score is presented in proportion of the highest score possible. Possible values ranged from 0 to 1 with a resolution of 0.01.

The participants were first invited to enter a meeting room. The researchers presented the experiment and its goals and procedure. A short introduction to videoconferencing was also given. The cooperative session lasted 35 minutes before the videoconferencing equipment and cooperative application were turned off. This duration was sufficient to allow people developing and trying out strategies for solving the problem, but was short enough to foster a certain pressure to perform efficiently. At the end of the session, the participants answered an electronic questionnaire measuring their satisfaction and the feeling of social presence they experienced during the cooperation.

Equipment and material

The goal of the experimental task was to create a context in which the participants would cooperate. The task had to be simple enough to allow a quick start. On the other hand, it had to be close to real cooperative context, as well as complex and difficult enough to foster cooperation and interactivity.

The experimental task consisted in an optimisation problem. The participants had to perform the production planning for seven weeks of production in the simulated context of a plastic moulding industry. Essentially, they had to consider different parameters in order to optimally choose when and which product they would produce. They were responsible for producing three different products using four different machines. Parameters they had to consider were, for example, the costs for storage, the amount of units in storage, the number of units ordered, the production capacity, the forecasted demand etc.

A synchronous cooperative application was developed in order to support teams performing the experimental task. The goals for this application were to support the people in cooperation, to allow a certain degree of flexibility in the problem definition (modify easily some parameters), as well as to non-invasively record all actions performed by participants. Participants were allowed to make some changes to previous choices, allowing an iterative task solving process. They were not limited for the number of trials. The task and the application are described in Arial et al. (2006).

Data analysis

The Cronbach α value was used in order to test the internal consistency of the social presence multi-item scale. The sample was first divided into two groups of equal size (n=40) in which all cases were randomly assigned. The α value was calculated for these two groups. An alpha value higher than 0.70 was observed for both groups for social presence (α_1=0.886; α_2=0.918). ANOVA (analysis of variance) was used in order to compare group characteristics. The Tukey's honestly significant difference post hoc test (HSD) was used to perform multiple comparison statements while assuring the overall confidence coefficient. Statistical significance was considered present when the p value was <.05.

Results

Only one participant rated the experimental task as "too difficult" and a large proportion of participants (56/80, 70.0%) rated it as "difficult" or "very difficult". No participant rated it "very easy". In general, participants reported positive attitudes towards the solution used to support them while cooperating. For 71/80 (88.8%) participants, the application was good or very good. The application reaction time was good or very good for 72/80 (90.0%) participants. Results for social presence and performance are presented at Table 1.

Table 1. Mean scores for social presence and performance by experimental group

Group					
	A	**B**	**C**	**D**	**F-Fisher**
Performance	(n=4) M=.631 (SD=.375)	(n=5) M=.783 (SD=.192)	(n=5) M=.847 (SD=.142)	(n=5) M=.642 (SD=.156)	1.075 (p=.39)
Social presence	(n=20) M=.575 (SD=.217)	(n=20) M=.515 (SD=.248)	(n=20) M=.627 (SD=.198)	(n=20) M=.686 (SD=.134)	2.566 (p=.06)

No significant difference for performance was observed between groups (at p<.05). A significant difference was observed between Group B and Group D (HSD, p=.046) for social presence. The group D reported the highest average score for social presence (M=.686, SD=.134). The group B was characterized by the lowest average score for social presence (M=.515, SD=.248). None of the 4 hypotheses were confirmed by the experimental results.

Discussion

No difference was observed between the experimental groups in terms of performance. This can be due to small sample size (among 40 teams who participated to the study, 19 were included in comparing score for performance).

The results of this study tend to indicate that partial gaze awareness alone is not sufficient to increase users' feeling of social presence. However, comparing average values for social presence between Group B and Group D showed interesting and unexpected result. A significant difference (HSD, p=.046) between average values was observed. Partial gaze awareness resulted in higher social presence only when associated with partially shared workspaces. It appears that due to the nature of the task to perform, the attention of participants was often oriented towards the application view. As a consequence, participants from Group B and Group D adopted a head-down posture. Because of the respective position of the camera (over the screen showing the view of the person) and the screen displaying the application view, the face of the subject was often only partially visible, and the impression of eye contact, as well as the access to facial expression was impeded. In one-screen conditions (Group A and C), the point of attention had only a limited impact on the position of the head because all the information (the application view and the person view) was displayed on the same screen. Therefore, a head-up position appeared natural in this condition. In addition, it is probable that the participants from group C and D had to compensate the lack of certain information with an increase in verbal interactions. In other words, team members had to talk more to each other in order to compensate for the lack of relevant information, ensuing in a more conversational session resulting in higher feeling of social presence. Because they probably addressed each other more often, they were also more likely to adopt frequent head-up posture allowing some social cues to be visible on the camera. This could also partially explain a rather high and unexpected feeling of social presence.

Using two screens to display the person view and the application does not ensure a better feeling of social presence. It seems crucial to consider the task to perform, as well as users' preferences, for better adapting CSCW solutions. Although it sounds obvious, new systems for distributed CSCW do not always offer the possibility to adjust the position or size of the person and application views (e.g. Ganser et al., 2005).

The reason for using a between group design was to avoid positive evaluation of the two screens system due to its more sophisticated appearance. A direct comparison of both systems by each participant would have probably resulted in a higher systems' differentiation. Alternative solutions (e.g. within-design with sequence as an additional factor) for comparing systems, while avoiding bias resulting from system's appearance, are relevant. The experimental task was difficult but feasible. All the teams used an iterative process in order to reach and improve a valid solution to the experimental problem. The simple computer application was helpful and necessary considering the task's complexity. Only one type of collaborative assignment was tested because the general goal was more to focus on partial gaze awareness than on task requirements. One might argue that using an experimental task such as the one used in the present study might have led to its mitigated results in terms of social presence. However, the average level of social presence was rather high for each experimental group. In addition, using a more conversational task (debating, negotiating, etc.) might have led to decrease the importance of the application view, which had to be preserved in order to emulate current distributed CSCW situations.

The cooperative session had a rather short duration (35 minutes). Different phases characterize a collaborative experience. Further experiment should address in a qualitative manner the evolution of social presence during cooperative sessions or projects. Such experiment should also last longer than 35 minutes or include repeated sessions. A crucial question would be how the work evolves from a mutual problem to a collective process of resolution, and how this evolution influences (or is influenced by) social presence.

Dyads were used for practical and methodological reasons. First, the type of experimental task was well adapted for dyads. Second, a bias due to inactive participants in the cooperative process had to be prevented. Although using dyads does not force participants to be active, small size teams could possibly encourage the involvement of team-mates. Third, this decision was made in order to keep the experiment as simple as possible and avoid testing additional variables, such as the number of points to connect or the number of persons per point to include. However, using teams of two people has drawbacks. Videoconferencing is particularly relevant for small group cooperation because it allows people to monitor the behaviours (e.g. non verbal expression, attention) of other participants than the one who speaks. Although dyads were suitable for this study, further research about social presence and video-mediated communication should involve small group distributed cooperation. Using early prototypes like the Hydra described by Buxton (1992) or one of its numerous successors (i.e. Quante & Mühlbach, 1999; Ganser et al., 2005) could enable such experiments.

Conclusion

Using two screens to enable partial gaze awareness does not necessarily lead to higher feeling of social presence for people involved in distributed computer supported collaborative work. The same conclusion applies to fully shared workspaces. In addition, such system characteristics appear to have no effect on performance. Optimisation of systems for cooperative work involving video-mediated communication should take advantage of other aspects (e.g. usability, mobility, sound quality, delay, etc.) than the ones investigated in this study. Implementing two screens or fully shared workspaces in a solution for distributed cooperation should be performed only when justified by specific task requirements.

Acknowledgments

This study was funded in part by the Swiss KTI (Kommission für Technologie und Innovation) Grant 4569.3 IMS, by the Swiss Federal Institute of Technology in Zurich (ETHZ) and the Institut de Santé au Travail (IST) in Switzerland. The authors also thank S. Mueller and A. Kunz (ETH Zurich) for programming the cooperative application.

References

Arial, M. (2004). *Integration of videoconferencing in distributed collaborative technologies* (PhD Thesis, Swiss Federal Institute of Technology in Zurich (ETH), Institute for Hygiene and Applied Physiology (IHA)). Zürich, Switzerland: ETH.

Arial, M. & Danuser, B. (2006). Communicate-IT; an experimental task/server-based application for testing communication conditions in D-CSCW. In R.N. Pikaar, E.A.P. Koningsveld, and P.J.M. Settels (Eds.), *Meeting diversity in ergonomics: proceedings IEA 2006 Congress* (pp.5485-5488). Amsterdam, The Netherlands: Elsevier.

Baecker, R.M., Grudin, J., Buxton, W.A.S., & Greenberg, S. (1995). *Readings in computer interactions: toward year 2000.* San Francisco, USA: Morgan Kaufmann Publishers.

Buxton, W.A.S. (1992). Telepresence : Integrating Shared Task and Person Spaces. In *Proceedings of the conference on Graphics Interface '92* (pp. 123-129). San Francisco, USA: Morgan Kaufmann Publishers Inc.

Colston, H.L., & Schiano, D.J. (1995). Looking and lingering as a conversational cues in video-mediated communication. In *Proceedings of the Conference on Human Factors in Computing Systems CHI'95 'Mosaic of creativity'* (pp. 278-279). New York, USA: ACM Press.

Decortis F., & Pavard, B. (1994). Communication et cooperation: de la théorie des actes de langage à l'approche ethnométhodogique. In B. Pavard (Ed.), *Systèmes coopératifs: de la modélisation à la conception* (pp. 21-50). Toulouse, France: Octarès.

Dourish, P., & Bly, S. (1992). Portholes: supporting awareness in distributed group work. In *Proceedings of the SIGCHI conference on Human Factors in computing systems* (pp. 541-547). New York, USA: ACM Press.

Egido, C. (1988). Videoconferencing as a Technology to Support Group Work: A Review of its Failure. *Proceedings of the 1988 ACM conference on Computer-supported cooperative work* (pp. 13-24). New York, USA: ACM Press.

Fish, R., Kraut, R.E., Root, R., & Rice, R.(1992). Evaluating video as a technology for informal communication. *Communications of the ACM, 36*(1), 48-61.

Ganser, C., Kennel, T., Birkeland, N., & Kunz, A. (2005). Computer-supported environment for creativity processes in globally distributed teams. In A. Samuel, and W. Lewis (Eds.), *Proceedings of the 15th International conference on engineering design* (ICED 05, August 15-18, 2005, Melbourne, Australia) (pp. 15-18). Barton: Institution of Engineers.

Gale, C., & Monk, A.F. (2000). "Where am I looking?" The accuracy of video mediated gaze awareness. *Perception and Psychophysics, 62*, 586-595.

Grayson, D., & Monk, A.F. (2003). "Are you looking at me? Eye contact and desktop video conferencing." *ACM Transactions on Computer-Human Interaction, 10*, 221-243.

Isaacs E.A., & Tang, J. C. (1994). What Video Can and Can't Do for Collaboration: A Case Study. *Multimedia Systems, 2*, 63-73.

O'Conaill, B., Whittaker, S., & Wilbur S. (1993). Conversations Over Videoconference: an Evaluation of the Spoken Aspects of Video-Mediated Communications. *Human-Computer Interaction, 8,* 389-428.

Quante, B., & Mühlbach, L. (1999). Eye-Contact in Multipoint Videoconferencing. *Proceedings of the 17th International Symposium on Human Factors in Telecommunication* (CD rom). Norway: Information Gatekeepers.

Sellen, A.J. (1992). Speech Patterns in Video-Mediated Conversations. In *Proceedings of the SIGCHI conference on Human Factors in computing systems* (pp. 49-59) New York, USA: ACM Press.

Short, J., Williams E., & Christie, B. (1976). *The social psychology of telecommunication.* London, UK: John Wiley & Sons.

Tang, J.C., & Minneman, S.L. (1990). Videodraw: A Video Interface for Collaborative Drawing. In *Proceedings of the SIGCHI conference on Human factors in computing systems: Empowering people* (pp. 313-320). New York, USA: ACM Press.

Tu, C.H. (2002). The measurement of social presence in an online learning environment. *International journal on E-learning, 1*, 34-45.

Vertegaal, R. (1999). The GAZE groupeware system: Mediating joint attention in multiparty communication and collaboration. In *Proceedings of the SIGCHI conference on Human factors in computing systems: the CHI is the limit* (pp. 294-301). New York, USA: ACM Press.

Inspection & Monitoring

time pressure X-ray

In D. de Waard, G.R.J. Hockey, P. Nickel, and K.A. Brookhuis (Eds.) (2007), *Human Factors Issues in Complex System Performance* (pp. 433). Maastricht, the Netherlands: Shaker Publishing.

Effects of time pressure on searching for terrorist threats in X-ray air passenger luggage images

Xi Liu & Alastair Gale
Loughborough University
UK

Abstract

In order to understand the development of skill in the domain of airport security an experiment was performed to examine how naïve observers searched a range of X-ray images of air passenger luggage for potential terrorist threat items. For each image their eye movements were recorded remotely and participants had to rate their confidence in whether or not a potential threat item was present. Half of all observers had a restricted search time of 10 seconds and the others had an unlimited search time. Observer performance in identifying targets correctly was measured as the areas under their receiver operating characteristic (ROC) curves. Results showed that observers with an unlimited viewing time exhibited significantly better detection performance than those under the time pressure condition. The eye movement data revealed that naïve observers could fixate on a potential target early in their visual search of each image. Observers were particularly inclined to fixate on targets earlier and process visual information faster (i.e. with a shorter visual dwell time on the area of interest in the X-ray luggage image) in the time pressured condition. One possible interpretation between performance and the eye movement data is a speed-accuracy relationship. The naïve observers lacked knowledge of possible threats which degraded their performance. Implications for training of security screeners are discussed.

Introduction

Aviation security greatly depends on the performance of security screeners in detecting items which pose potential threat to air travel when they visually examine X-ray images of passenger luggage. The work environment of screeners is time-pressurised and difficult as passenger flow must be maintained whilst the X-ray images are difficult as these have low signal-to-noise ratio with widely varying backgrounds. Generally the search time for experienced security screeners is between six to ten seconds per luggage item (Gale et al., 2000). In such a short period the screener must not only select the appropriately potential target area of the luggage item (which contains a possible threat item) but also correctly recognize the target object - even when it is in a camouflaged situation or in a cluttered background.

In D. de Waard, G.R.J. Hockey, P. Nickel, and K.A. Brookhuis (Eds.) (2007), *Human Factors Issues in Complex System Performance* (pp. 435 - 442). Maastricht, the Netherlands: Shaker Publishing.

A series of research studies are underway as part of the UK EPAULETS research project to investigate just how such expertise develops. In the present work the interest is in how naïve observers visually examine X-ray images of luggage items either with an unlimited time to do so or in a time equivalent to that taken by experienced airport security screeners. Just how does limiting the search time affect the performance of such observers and also in what way is their performance affected?

Previous research has shown that under time pressure, individuals trade-off time for accuracy, such that their performance is decreased and information is processed more rapidly (Payne et al., 1988). Also under time pressure humans are more risky at higher risk levels and more conservative at lower risk levels (Dror et al., 1999). Several possible strategies can be adopted under time pressure: *acceleration* - processing is accelerated under a deadline; *filtering* - some information is skipped due to the time constraint; *strategy shift* – the strategy is changed from a compensatory one to a simpler, non-compensatory strategy by which information acquisition is faster and easier to complement (Ben-Zur & Breznitz, 1981; Zakay, 1985).

The purpose of the present study is to explore how time pressure affects performance, and the acquisition of visual information, in the task of examining airport passengers' X-ray luggage images. The visual search behaviour of participants was recorded when they examined X-ray luggage images for threat items: namely guns, knives and improvised explosive devices (IEDs). It was hypothesised that when time was limited naïve observers would search the images faster for target threat items but they would make more errors. The nature of the errors made would be important and have implications for the design of training for airport security screeners.

Method

Participants

Twenty-one participants (12 male, 9 female) took part in the study. All of them had no experience on this kind of task. All participants had normal or corrected-to-normal visual acuity apart from one person who had nystagmus, consequently whilst the eye position data were not used the decisions on each image were employed.

Stimuli and apparatus

Stimuli were 50 X-ray luggage images. Half of all images were normal bag images containing no threat items. The remaining images contained threat items: five images had multiple threat items and twenty images had a single threat item. Participants' eye movements were recorded by a Tobii eye-tracker (X50) with a temporal resolution of 50 Hz and spatial resolution of 0.35°. They viewed images on a 53cm monitor at a distance of 70cm.

Procedure

Participants were instructed that their task was to search for potential threat items (guns, knives and IEDs) in X-ray images of passengers' luggage items - as if they were security screeners at an airport check-in point. The compositions of IEDs were explained to participants in an introductory section before the experiment began. To familiarise participants with the experimental procedure they first viewed five X-ray luggage images and identified whether a target was present or not; feedback was provided for each image. Then participants examined fifty X-ray luggage images. For each image, they had to rate their decision confidence concerning a potential threat target being present using a five-point rating scale (1 – definitely absent, 2 – probably absent, 3 – possibly present, 4 – probably present and 5 – definitely present). Other than for decisions of 1 or 2, participants were then asked to indicate the locations of potential threat items.

Ten participants inspected the images in an unlimited viewing time condition and the remaining participants inspected images with a 10 seconds time limit. In the time pressure condition, participants rated their decision confidence and located any threat item on a simulated image which was immediately displayed after 10 seconds of stimuli presentation and which had the same overall profile as the previous X-ray luggage image they had just viewed. In the unlimited viewing time participants first indicated they made a decision and then rated the image and located any threat item. Each participant was shown the images in a randomized order.

Results

Participants' confidence ratings of 3, 4 or 5 were scored as positive threat target responses and responses of 1 and 2 were scored as negative responses. For target-present images, the location of a threat item was also considered so that a positive target response but with a false location was treated as a 'miss' decision, in the same way as the responses of 1 and 2 for target-present images. A 'hit' decision was recorded only if both a positive response and the correct target location were identified. For the target-absent images only false alarm and correct rejection responses were possible.

Data were analysed using Receiver Operating Characteristics (ROC) methodology and participants' accuracy was expressed by the area under the ROC curve (A_z). Only confidence rating data of single-threat images were used in this performance analysis. Figure 1 shows the mean overall performance of these naïve participants as pooled ROC curves with an accuracy measure (A_z) value of 0.74 for the unlimited viewing time and 0.61 for the 10s condition. A one-way analysis of variance (ANOVA) showed a significant effect of viewing time on sensitivity ($F(1, 19) = 17.044$, $p \leq .001$) reflecting a better overall hit rate in the unlimited time (0.69) than that of time pressure (0.45). There was no difference in false alarm rates between two viewing conditions; 0.41 for the unlimited time and 0.42 for the 10s situation.

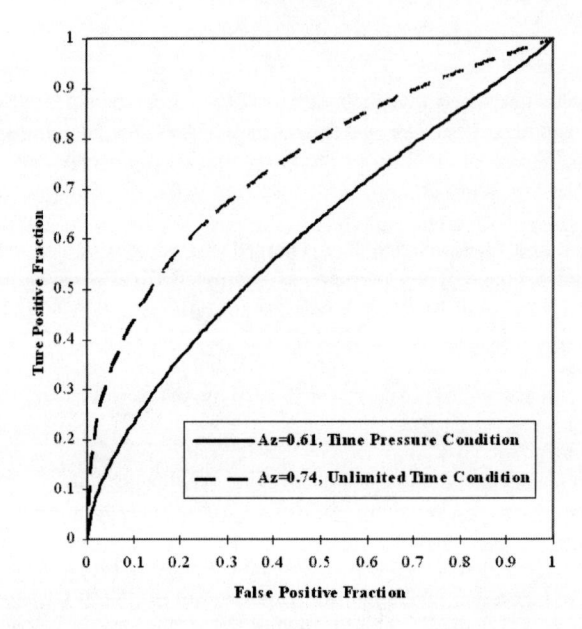

Figure 1. Mean overall performance of the naïve participants in pooled ROC curves under unlimited time and time pressure conditions.

An Area of Interest (AOI) was defined around each target in order to analyze how important visual information is both acquired and processed for decision making. In consideration of the irregular form of threat items the dimensions of the AOI were determined by: the form of the individual threat item in a bag; the visual angle subtended by the foveola (circa 1.2°, Schwartz, 1994), and the accuracy of the eye-tracker (0.5~0.7°). Consequently each AOI was empirically determined as an area which had a similar shape to the threat item profile but was slightly larger so as to subtend an additional 1° visual angle on each side.

Table 1 Hit rate, mean time to first enter AOI and dwell time on AOI for the two viewing conditions in the single-threat images.

Group	Response or Threat Item Category	Time to first enter AOI (msec)	Dwell time on AOI (msec)	Hit rate
Unlimited time	Hit	1053	5621	0.69
	Miss	1376	6692	–
	Gun	2431	2662	0.68
	Knife	1099	5129	0.8
	IED	794	7140	0.62
Time pressure	Hit	794	7140	0.62
	Miss	690	2187	–
	Gun	2151	1350	0.65
	Knife	474	2746	0.65
	IED	522	2960	0.33

The mean time it took for participants to first gaze within the AOIs of threat items and the overall dwell time on the AOIs under the two experimental conditions for the single-threat images are shown in Table 1. For the hit responses, the time to first enter the AOIs under unlimited viewing time was longer than that of the time pressure condition, but the difference was not significant. The dwell time within the AOIs of unlimited viewing time was significantly longer than that of the 10s condition, $F(1, 18) = 11.455$, $p \leq .003$. For the miss responses the time to first enter the AOIs and the dwell time on the AOIs of unlimited viewing time were both reliably longer than these measures in the time pressure condition ($F(1, 18) = 12.670$, $p \leq .002$ and $F(1, 18) = 14.431$, $p \leq .001$ respectively). An ANOVA indicated that the dwell time on the AOIs for hit responses was significantly longer than that of the miss responses in the time pressure condition, $F(1, 18) = 5.373$, $p < .05$. However, in the unlimited time condition the dwell time in the AOIs for hit responses was shorter than that of the miss responses, although the difference was not significant.

The time to first enter the AOIs of guns was longer than that of IEDs - both in the unlimited viewing condition, $F(1, 18) = 14.936$, $p \leq .001$, and in the time pressure condition, $F(1, 18) = 18.323$, $p < .001$. Furthermore, the dwell time on AOIs of guns was shorter than that of IEDs, both in the unlimited viewing condition, $F(1, 18) = 16.263$, $p \leq .001$, and in the time pressure condition, $F(1, 18) = 20.306$, $p < .001$. There was a similar relationship between knives and IED target items for both conditions but the differences were not significant.

Multiple-threat images

For the unlimited viewing time, the mean total search time was 17.5 seconds for single-threat images, 19.8 seconds for multiple-threats and 19.8 seconds for threat-free images. The difference in search time between single-threat and multiple-threat images was 2.3 seconds (not significant).

Overall, the miss rate for multiple-threat images was 8% (4/50) in the unlimited viewing time and 22% (11/50) in the 10s situation, this difference was significant, $\chi^2 = 3.843$, $p \leq .05$. For multiple-threat images, the time to first enter AOIs was 1,872 ms in the unlimited time condition and 1,339 ms in the 10s condition, this difference was significant, $F(1, 18) = 5.031$, $p < .05$. The dwell time on AOIs of unlimited viewing time was significantly longer than that of the 10s condition (4039 ms vs. 2100ms), $F(1, 18) = 11.167$, $p \leq .004$.

Previous studies indicated that missed errors in tasks involving the visual search of images have been divided into three categories: search, recognition and interpretation errors (Kundel et al., 1978). If the target AOI area is not encompassed by any eye fixation points then the miss responses were scored as search errors. If fixations, or cumulative clusters, hit on threat AOIs, and the gaze duration was less than 1,000 ms, then the miss responses were taken as recognition errors. If fixations, or cumulative clusters, hit on threat AOIs areas and the gaze duration was longer than 1000 ms, then the miss responses were scored as interpretation errors. The mean cumulative gaze duration on threat areas and percentage of missed responses according to image category in both conditions are listed in table 2. Interpretation errors were the main error type in all situations. The cumulative gaze duration of interpretation errors in the unlimited viewing condition was longer than that of the 10s condition for both single-threat and multiple-threat images.

Table 2. Mean gaze duration and % of the three types of missed errors according to image category in both viewing conditions

Image Category		Total No. of Missed Threat Items	Search Errors Gaze Duration (msec)	Search Errors Missed Responses (%)	Recognition Errors Gaze Duration (msec)	Recognition Errors Missed Responses (%)	Interpretation Errors Gaze Duration (msec)	Interpretation Errors Missed Responses (%)
Unlimited Time Condition	Single-threat	67	0	10.5	655	13.4	7659	76.1
	Multiple-threat	55	0	29	456	16.4	6602	54.6
Time Pressure Condition	Single-threat	107	0	8.4	519	15.9	2960	75.7
	Multiple-threat	70	0	10	545	28.6	2963	61.4

Discussion

In this study, visual scanning and information acquisition were examined under an unlimited viewing time and a time pressured condition in a simulated airport security examination task. As expected, participants were inclined to accelerate their visual search in the time pressure condition where they fixated on target areas more quickly and were faster to detect and recognize targets than they were in the unlimited time situation. The hit rate under time pressure was clearly worse than that of unlimited viewing time. A high number of threat items were used here as we were not trying to directly simulate the full airport screening situation itself (where a threat item occurrence is a relatively rare event) but rather our interest is in the training of individuals to detect and identify threat items correctly.

Previous research shows that limiting time on a task might increase incentive and psychological stress so that individuals reduce the threshold of their decision criteria or accelerate information processing (Ben-Zur & Breznitz, 1981). In the present study when time was limited then participants searched faster and made more errors. Generally, performance on a task is measured by accuracy and speed, which tend to be positively related. Participants under time pressure in this study had to trade-off speed and accuracy as their decision confidence had to be rated and potential areas of threat items indicated after 10 seconds viewing.

More than seventy percent of the miss errors of the single-threat images under both viewing conditions were due to interpretation errors. Clearly, one of the possible interpretations is that naïve participants lack the knowledge of what a potential threat item is and also what the X-ray image of a threat item looks like so that they could not recognize these threat items easily, even when they fixated on them.

For multiple-threat images, the phenomenon of satisfaction of search (SOS, is where an observer stops searching an image when a target is found and in doing so can then miss other additional targets present in the image display), which is common in medical imaging studies, occurred in both viewing conditions. Most of the targets were missed due to interpretation errors. Whilst observers fixated on the proper image areas with long eye fixation durations, they still missed them. Again, one possible reason is lack of knowledge of the appearance of threat items. Moreover, the low performance criteria of these naïve participants caused an early halt of their visual search of the display, this was reflected by there being no difference in decision times between the single-threat images and multiple-threat images in the unlimited viewing time condition. The results of SOS are not as severe as in the medical domain because participants detected one or two threat items in most of the multiple-threat images. Hand-check in airport security examination could prevent miss errors.

Decision making is a complex cognitive activity, sensitive to situational and environmental conditions (Payne, 1982). Airport screeners would be expected to adopt a conservative strategy which would search available information completely as their decisions are significant and they are responsible for these decisions. However, screeners have to accelerate their visual search of luggage images in order to cope with maintaining passenger throughput. The effect of time pressure is strong such that performance has been shown to improve after training under an unlimited time condition but that this does not transfer to a time pressured condition (Zakay & Wooler, 1984). If training with limited search time is employed then screeners are given a chance to study how to allocate attention, organize information and make decisions under time pressured conditions so that they should easily adapt to the real airport security situation. Some of our results provide useful guidance about training schemes for naïve observers who wish to become security screeners: firstly threat items should be updated constantly and a certain number of X-ray luggage images should be read in order to develop skills and expertise. This is based upon finding that although naïve observers fixated threat items they failed to recognise them. Secondly, training under time pressured conditions is recommended for ensuring adequate high detection ability in real life situations. Observers under the time pressure condition were faster to process visual information then made a decision so that accuracy rate was affected by their limited resource arrangement. Experience of this demanding situation would then we argue be a potential aid for ensuring good detection performance.

Acknowledgement

This research is supported by the EPSRC.

References

Ben-Zur, H. & Breznitz, S.I. (1981). The effect of time pressure on risky choice behaviour. *Acta Psychologica, 47*, 89-104.

Dror, I.E., Busemeyer, J.R., & Basola, B. (1999). Decision making under time pressure: An independent test of sequential sampling models. *Memory & Cognition, 27*, 713-725.

Gale, A.G., Mugglestone, M., Purdy, K.J., & McClumpha, A.. (2000). Is airport baggage inspection just another medical image? In E.A. Krupinski (Ed.), *Medical Imaging: Image Perception and Performance. Progress in Biomedical Optics and Imaging*, 1(26) (pp. 184-192). Bellingham, UK: SPIE.

Mackworth, N.H. (1974), Stimulus density limits the useful field of view. In R.A. Monty and J.W. Senders (Eds.), *Eye movement and psychological processes*, (pp. 307-321). New Jersey: Lawrence Erlbaum

Payne, J.W. (1982). Contingent decision behavior. *Psychological Bulletin, 92*, 382-402.

Payne, J.W., Bettman, J.R., & Johnson, E.J. (1988). Adaptive strategy selection in decision making. *Journal of experimental psychology: learning, memory, and cognition, 14*, 534-552.

Schwartz, S.H. (1994). *Visual Perception: A Clinical Orientation*. East Norwalk, Connecticut: Appleton and Lange.

Zakay, D, & Wooler, S. (1984). Time pressure, training and decision effectiveness. *Ergonomics, 27*, 273-284.

Zakay, D. (1985). Post-decisional confidence and conflict experienced in a choice process. *Acta Psychologica, 58*, 75-80.

Methodological approach to advancing airport screener X-ray threat detection skills

Gerald D. Gibb, Bill C. Fischer, & Brett R. Cabeca
SRA-Galaxy International
New Jersey, USA

Abstract

The U.S. Transportation Security Administration seeks improving screener proficiency in X-ray technology; the principle method to screen passenger belongings at airport security checkpoints. Previous approaches have relied on classroom instruction, simulation, TIP (threat image projection) and on-the-job training. A review revealed repetition, trial-and-error learning, and exposure to threat images are the fundamental tenets of such approaches. These traditional approaches emphasize drill and practice vice learning targeted techniques and strategies.

Currently the TIP system is partly employed to assess performance (an electronic means to project threat images on actual baggage in operational environments). Analysis of national data indicated there are exceptional performing screeners who consistently exhibit expert threat detection capabilities well above norms with low false alarm rates.

This paper presents a methodology to identify critical cues, strategies, techniques, decision points produced by difficult threat detection scenarios, subtle perceptual features of suspect items, and application of unique knowledge used by exceptional performing screeners (EPs) that contribute to successful threat detection for later dissemination via training. The premise employed an empirical framework by quantitatively identifying the target population, item analysis to select difficult threats which discriminate performance between EPs and the workforce, tailoring scenarios on a simulator, and adapting applied cognitive task analysis and critical decision making protocols to elicit and capture techniques. Such data forms the content for an empirically-based training regime. The study is ongoing and findings will be published at a later time.

Introduction

On November 19th, 2001 U.S. President Bush signed the Aviation and Transportation Security Act that established the Transportation Security Administration and mandated the restructuring of the entire U.S. aviation security program. This legislation established provisions for the federalization of airport security screeners; effectively transferring all responsibilities for the recruitment, training, evaluation, certification and retention from the air carriers and airport authorities to the federal government (with the exception of five test site airports manned by privately employed workforces). Under the new structure major milestones were established, goals set, and challenges to improve airport security put forth.

A number of research and development questions were raised as how improvements could be made to aviation security, specifically airport security checkpoints. Much attention was placed on the threat detection performance of the workforce for the X-ray screening process, because this is widely understood as the most difficult task for airport screeners. Improving the detection of improvised explosive devices is among the leading goals as a result of dramatic advances in the security of the flight deck. While conventional weapons still pose a threat, increased use of air marshals, training of flight crew members and modified cockpit entry security protocols has greatly diminished the potential of these threats in comparison to explosive devices.

Few would debate a key element of improving human performance first requires the capability to assess such performance in objective, quantifiable and practical terms. The deployment of TRX systems (Threat Image Projection Ready X-ray) enabled the capability to objectively, quantitatively, and fairly evaluate the relative threat detection performance of the screener workforce. While there are nuances and differences among systems that can impact performance, TRX remains one of the most advanced and effective deployed systems for measuring human performance. Screener threat detection performance is well defined and significant differences are observed among individuals. Each TRX system produces performance data that easily establishes a screener's performance relative to all others operating on the same system under similar operating conditions (e.g. TIP settings, number of bags per month screened, number of TIPs seen, TIP: Bag ratio, etc.).

TRX systems are essentially X-ray machines that are equipped to implement TIP. The TIP programme was designed by aviation security human factors engineers and at a conceptual level is quite simple to express. Loosely based on Signal Detection Theory (Green & Swets, 1988), airport screeners are presented with threats (signals) that are seamlessly integrated into the images of actual passenger bags (noise). They indicate that a potential threat is perceived by a single input button. The frequency of presentation, projection distribution among different threat categories, decision time limits and a number of other parameters is easily programmed. Performance is assessed using many of the classic Signal Detection Theory metrics including Pd, probability of false alarm, d', and so forth.

The process of detecting threats against a background of noise is a rather daunting task. Unlike related tasks (e.g. radiologists, sonar operators, industrial inspectors) where the aberration or peculiarity appears against a background of known and relatively consistent 'noise', each image is completely unique; varying across many dimensions (size, composition, clutter, level of organics and electronics, density, orientation), and contains any number of possible configurations of threats. The signal and the noise vary across an almost infinite range.

Early task analysis and personnel selection studies demonstrated cognitive processing (e.g. decision making, perceptual, higher order analysis, memory, hypothesis testing, mental rotation, etc.) takes place for screeners as they interpret each X-ray image while scanning passenger baggage. Screeners also have a limited range of image interpretation tools available to support the X-ray interpretation process. During this process each image is interpreted and assessed within a few seconds to determine whether the item is clear, contains a threat, or requires secondary screening. Screeners differ substantially in their individual capabilities to detect threats using X-ray technology as is evident when examining available TIP performance metrics.

In numerous analytical studies and investigations of screener performance it has been shown that there is substantial variability in performance. Although there is some relationship to historically demonstrated factors (e.g. job longevity, signal-to-noise ratio, threat saliency), much variability is unexplained. Regardless, many studies have demonstrated that there are individuals that consistently excel above their peers relative to TIP performance measures. The term EP Screener (exceptional performer) has been coined to describe such individuals.

The purpose of this paper is to demonstrate that EPs can be empirically identified. That there are TIP images – as with many performance assessment tools – that are highly effective discriminators of performance. And that these images can be designed into a high fidelity scenario where a number of human factors techniques can be utilized to capture the strategies, techniques, approaches, decision-making processes, cues, image characteristics, of EPs. This elicited knowledge thereby forming the foundation of an innovative training programme.

We make no claims that the deployment of an empirically-based training programme such as this will increase the efficiency of all personnel to the level of our experts, the EPs. To the contrary, as experts perform at high levels because their problem solving skills are advanced, having a deeper breadth and application of knowledge, and have more experience than novices (McGraw & Harbison-Briggs, 1989). The goal of this work is to isolate those elements of knowledge that are acquired through experience and disseminate the information across the workforce, consequently accelerating the knowledge acquisition processes typically gained over time. Indeed, it is anticipated that this work will increase the underlying knowledge of the majority of the workforce, with the greatest commensurate gains in performance occurring with novice workers and those with insufficient time on the job to have developed mastery level skills.

Analysis

Whilst it is neither permissible nor prudent to communicate threat detection performance of airport security screeners in absolute values, it is reasonable to describe the process and outcomes in relative terms. For it is the basis of this study that EP screeners can be demonstrated to exhibit an extraordinary level of performance comparative to their peers, and that the TIP library contains images that effectively discriminate their performance from that of the workforce. The former analytical process identifies the participants for the study whilst the latter component determines the images that are used to elicit the cues, techniques, principles, strategies, and approaches they use. This section describes the analytical processes that were used.

Selection of study participants

The first stage entailed forming an equal basis of comparison. That is to say that in order to compare individual performance, the workforce had to be examined under similar conditions. The TIP database is robust with operational data as it is with performance data. Therefore a number of conditions were used to establish the initial pool of individuals such as: 1) verifying that the performance was indeed that of the individual, 2) current TIP library used, 3) projection distributions were equivalent (e.g. the proportion of TIPs that are IEDs were the same) and 4) projection frequencies were set to standards (e.g. the ratio of TIP projections to passenger bags, variance around the ratio, and the percentage of TIP projections that were entirely random).

Screeners have unique login names and pass codes used to track their performance and it is possible, using filtering algorithms to verify the performance is theirs. For example, logon and logoff patterns should demonstrate within an expected range the number of shifts/day worked, not indicate simultaneous logons, and the number of bags screened should fall within expected ranges. The remainder of filtering tools are used to confirm the operating conditions – such that each individual is subject to the same TIP images under the same projection parameters.

The second stage of the analytical process follows straightforward techniques of establishing performance distributions. Essentially the mean and range of performance, variability within and between individuals, and the skewness and kurtosis of the distributions are examined. However, complexities arise as the operational environment introduces uncontrollable intervening factors that influence performance. Such factors include passenger/baggage volume differences (related to the size of the airport), type of TRX unit operated (four currently in use), number of different TRX units operated by the individual, job tenure, and varied TIP projection frequencies (smaller airports generally operate on smaller ratios than larger airports in an attempt to provide standardisation in the number of TIPs per month). Consequently "peer groups" are created such that an individual is compared amongst other co-workers operating under similar conditions.

Once peer groups (and the associated distributions) are established, the third stage examined individual performance within the respective distribution. Although a considerable number of dimensions are considered; the primary elements are Pd (Probability of detection), Pfa (probability of false alarm), number of TIPs seen monthly, and durability of exceptional performance. The Signal Detection Theory classic metric of d' is not used because the probability of false is highly skewed and weights equally with Pd in the computations. It offers little information since false alarms: 1) exhibit rates well below laboratory studies, and 2) are not necessarily true false alarms in the sense that the screener may be responding to an actual or perceived threat in the bag image – and the TIP system treats the event as a false alarm if no TIP was projected.

Consequently screeners were designated EP when a minimum threshold number of TIPs have been viewed each month and when their Pd and Pfa were above or below, respectively, thresholds based on their peer group distribution. These criteria had to be met consistently over a several month period. The absolute threshold values vary from one distribution to another somewhat, but the final result is that an EP falls within the upper first percentile of their respective peer group.

Selection of test stimuli

The fourth stage of the process necessitated identifying TIP images that effectively discriminated EPs from the remainder of the workforce. Conventional item analyses were conducted whereby TIP images were treated as items on a traditional written examination (for a full treatment of Item Analysis see Anastasi, 1976). Unlike conventional techniques applied to standard test instruments, the processes took into account that the "items" were visual images (the response is essentially binary – hit or missed) and the 'test' had considerably more 'items' than typical (more than 2000 images are in the TIP library).

Since the response set for any TIP image is limited (hit or miss), it was possible to compute a Pd metric for all images. Therefore an item difficulty level is derived as the number of hits to aggregate number of projections for each TIP image. These analyses were conducted for each TRX machine separately. The difficulty level is range bound between 0 and 1.00, independent and offers a relative ranking of detection difficulty. Since these data are ratio in nature, a mean Pd and standard deviation was computed for the TIP library for each TRX machine. A cut-off for further consideration was set as a threshold where the individual TIP image Pd could not exceed one standard deviation below the mean Pd.

TIP image Pds are a remarkably stable metric. Linear correlations between both absolute TIP Pd values and rank orderings month-over-month consistently generated correlation co-efficients above + .90. This is not unexpected given that the number of times an image is projected each month numbers in the hundreds nationwide, and that the each image never appears twice in the same passenger bag. Each image therefore always appears in background noise that varies on each trial. The result of these processes was a pool of difficult TIPs with low Pd values.

The final analytical process involved linking the performance of difficult TIPs to the EP group. In short, the empirical question can be phrased as "how do EPs perform on each of the difficult TIPs?" Consequently the performance to all difficult TIPs for the EP groups (independently for each TRX machine) was tracked over a six-month period. It would be rare for any EP to see such TIPs more than once over the six months. Therefore a Pd was computed for each of these difficult TIPs for each EP group. Comparisons in Pd, for each of the difficult TIPs, were made between the EP populations and the workforce at-large. It was found there was a sub-sample of difficult TIPs that discriminated performance exceptionally well (e.g. EPs generated

Pds that represented high detection rates that were significantly higher than those of the general workforce) and could be used as the target threats for later phases of this work. It is not surprising that the majority of the discriminator TIPs were improvised explosive devices.

In summary, the performance analysis studies demonstrated it was possible to classify airport screeners quantitatively with regards to their threat detection capability, and that a sub-group existed that consistently performed at very high levels with low false alarm rates. This phenomenon was independent of TRX machine type. Further, it was found, adapting classical item analysis techniques, there were TIP images that discriminated performance between EPs and the workforce in general. The remainder of this paper describes the methodology that will be used to elicit the cognitive processes and information used by EPs in successfully identifying difficult threats.

Methodology

The analytical work was designed to identify participants for the study and in selecting the appropriate stimuli. Success, however, in gaining the information needed to develop a training programme that is based on capturing the expertise of highly skilled workers is dependent on two major elements: 1) providing a realistic setting with the necessary tools that evokes the desired skills and cognitive processes, and 2) adapting cognitive task analysis techniques to thoroughly capture and define those capabilities (Klein, 1996; Hoffman et al., 1995; Cooke, 1994).

This study will elicit the best practices of EPs while engaged in X-ray image interpretation in a simulation environment. The simulation environment provides complex scenarios that challenge the participants in order to effectively tap into the skills, knowledge, and abilities used on the job. The simulation exercises have been carefully selected using those TIPs that have previously been demonstrated to discriminate performance and pose challenges in detection. The knowledge elicitation methods chosen for this study were selected on the basis of the task requirements, nature of the information sought, and their adaptability to the simulation environment. All test trials shall be conducted at selected U.S. airports.

Testing platform

A key study factor is the availability of an appropriate simulator platform. The TRX Simulator developed by the TSA as an X-ray training and testing tool faithfully emulates each of the TRX systems under evaluation in this study. The simulator has full image analysis features functionality and displays the resultant X-ray images on a standard computer monitor. All bag movement control functions (e.g. Stop, Forward, etc.) are also incorporated.

The simulator includes an expandable clear bag and threat library (clear bags are bags containing varied amounts of typical travel item clutter but no threats or hazardous materials). "Bag Builder" and "Session Builder" features allow administrator selection of clear bags, threats, the rotation and placement of threats in the image, and the creation of complete scenarios. The threat library however shall be created using the discriminator TIPs and not the one resident on the device. The test threat images will be captured and installed in a special use library on the simulator. Each test threat image is captured from the original physical threat that was used to create the TIP for the library in the same original view angle and orientation.

The test bag images are drawn from the TRX Simulator library, reflecting a wide range of bag types (e.g. Rollabag, duffle bag, suitcase, etc.), but always selected from among the most complex clear bag images available. As an illustration, complex clear bag images typically were highly cluttered, high density images which contained metals, electronics, or a considerable number of dense organics. In general, discrimination of individual objects is considerably difficult to the untrained observer. The TRX Simulator library classifies the complexity of each clear bag image and assigns a numerical rating along a simple scale. The TRX Simulator development team classified bag complexity from a value of 1 – 9, however, these ratings are not interval in nature and are based solely on the judgements of subject matter experts.

The simulation exercise consists of 23 – 26 bag images (dependent upon TRX machine) that participants interpret. Participants only interpret image sets for one TRX machine. Each bag image provides a highly complex scenario and contains one threat image. There is no time limit for any bag image or the exercise as it is dependent on the pace of each participant.

Test protocol and paradigm

A key facet of the work focuses on eliciting and capturing the information in real time as the task of image interpretation occurs. Since the task is primarily cognitive and few behavioural components are observable, the data collection techniques selected are derived from the field of cognitive engineering, applied cognitive task analysis and naturalistic decision-making (Salas & Klein, 2001; Klein et al., 1989; Olson & Reuter, 1987; Diaper, 1989; National Institute for Aviation Research, 2004; Klein, 1998; Cooke, 1994; Seamster et al., 1997; Hoffman et al., 1995; Militello & Hutton, 1998; Militello, 2001; Militello et al; 1997). These data are primarily qualitative and therefore is not specified in scales and units more commonly associated with human factors engineering approaches. This however is common in applied cognitive task analyses methods (Ericsson & Simon, 1996; Ericsson & Simon, 1980).

There are four methods selected to implement the knowledge elicitation protocols: 1) Critical Decision Method, 2) Think-Aloud Protocol Analysis Method, 3) Teachback Technique, and 4) Coaching Method. These methods were used in similar tasks and have proven technical merit (Hoffman et al., 1998; Thordsen, 1991; Miller et al., 1999). They are especially useful in environments where the cues used by experts are subtle and the decision processes not readily discernible (Dubois, 2002). An abbreviated summary of each is provided:

Critical Decision Method
Historically this technique evolved from critical incident methodologies of the 1950's. The method involves multiple-pass events guided by probe questions (e.g. How did you immediately decide this bag was not 'safe'? What is it that immediately "jumped out" at you?) to isolate the specific decisions and the critical information those decisions are based upon (Klein, 1996; 1997; Gordon & Gill, 1997). The technique is particularly powerful with highly skilled experts in eliciting knowledge about perceptual cues that are not observed using behaviour-based task analysis procedures (Hoffman et al., 1998). It is applied here during the image interpretation process to identify the visual cues (including identification of 'mismatches' [e.g. only one piece of footwear in the image]) and how these data are used, leading to the search for other information, or how decisions are reached to use image analysis features.

Think-Aloud Protocol Analysis
A technique developed from naturalistic decision-making research and oft used in the past decade in the development of expert systems. Although this technique has a broad scope of applications it is particularly suited to identifying the types of information attended to, thinking processes, and decision sequences of experts performing complex non-procedural tasks. This technique is adapted here such that the EP "steps through" the discrete elements of the image analysis process (Someren et al., 1994). The data produced would resemble in many respects those obtained in more traditional task analytic approaches.

Teachback Technique
This methodology has roots in a number of disciplines. The primary use for TB is clarification of the data obtained through other methods, and to "backfill" gaps in the information. The techniques are used as a corollary to other cognitive task analysis methods. In its most rudimentary form the investigator paraphrases the information back to the subject matter experts in a re-iterative format until comprehensiveness and accuracy are achieved (Johnson & Johnson, 1987; Someren et al.; 1994). The technique is highly effective in capturing the nuances of cues and less salient information that is used from the images.

Coaching Method
This technique essentially involves a role reversal where the subject matter expert assumes the role of mentor or trainer as the investigator becomes the protégé. The cues and information that are used to perform the task are transmitted during the process. The technique has limited value outside of an actual live task performance environment. This paradigm is modified such that the EPs are placed in the role of instructor whilst the researchers serve as "trainees" as they are guided through the cognitive processes involved in examining X-ray images.

The applied cognitive task analysis methods described were selected for their relevance to the type of information sought, application to the X-ray task, and the participant population under study. These methods are easily integrated and can be migrated fluidly from one to the next. The methods are deployed to varying degrees with each EP Screener. That is to say the communication skills of the EP participant determine movement from one method to another. To illustrate, a simulator session may begin with the use of the Think Aloud Protocol Analysis method, and then intermittently use either Teachback or Coaching approaches to obtain clarity or fill in knowledge gaps. Likewise, Critical Decision method can be used alongside of the Think Aloud Protocol Analysis method to identify what cues and characteristics are used to base image analysis feature use decisions upon.

The research study is a unique and unfamiliar environment for most screeners and therefore requires some degree of participant preparation. As such, considerable indoctrination is needed to: 1) address concerns about the study and why they were selected for participation, 2) discuss confidentiality and use of the information, 3) prepare them for their role as participants, 4) convey the role of the research team, 5) communicate the parameters of the simulation exercise, and 6) train them in the protocols. Since the TRX Simulator is widely deployed as a training tool EPs are familiar with its operational characteristics.

After appropriate training in knowledge elicitation techniques and study protocols, EPs are presented approximately 25 combined threat images, bags containing threats, on the TRX. The sets of discriminator TIPs used are specific to each machine and EPs only view image sets on the TRX machine that they were qualified as EP screeners. Although threat images have been selected on the basis of treating each TRX machine as statistically independent, there is some convergence regarding threat images used, and the image sets all have high proportions of improvised explosive devices.

Data capture forms were tailored specifically for capturing and categorizing best practices of EPs during the simulation exercise. General categories of cognitive processes have been structured on the data capture forms (e.g. Procedures, methods and approaches; techniques and strategies; critical cues; potential errors [i.e. why other screeners would miss the cue]; situational awareness; knowledge and decision making) to facilitate the data capture. Because of the high volume of data generated from using applied cognitive task analysis techniques, only one data capture form is used for each presented threat image. This facilitates examining the strategies, techniques, cues, etc. to specific images in the simulation exercise.

Although no single standardized procedure exists for coding and synthesizing data derived from cognitive task analysis methods, the general consensus is such methods produce large volumes of data. Several methods and practices have been suggested from the literature for effective protocol analysis procedures (e.g. Ericsson & Simon, 1980; 1996; Sanderson & Fisher, 1994; Woods, 1993) to develop a taxonomy of the best practices across all TRX machine types, and to isolate those strategies that are TRX machine specific.

The resultant taxonomy (Fleishman, 1967; 1975) will contain a highly detailed categorization of techniques and processes that lead to effective threat detection. It is understood that although there may be some commonalities across the different TRX platforms, this study is machine independent (as a result of differences between machines not related to TIP); and the cues, information used, techniques, approaches, application of image analysis features, strategies, and cognitive processes involved in analyzing images are different. Consequently the taxonomies may be different and machine-independent, but having convergence where the machine displays, features, and controls share similarities. Potentially the greatest domain for divergence will exist in the visual cues and the application of image analysis features.

Many such proposals involve a careful integration of the data collection and analysis processes to produce encoding schemes that are matched to how verbalizations are classified during the data acquisition phase. Accordingly, we have developed a system to target and classify the type of information during the simulation exercise that readily can be analysed using accepted techniques and will generate a taxonomy suitable for training requirements.

References

Anastasi, A. (1976). *Psychological Testing*. New York: Macmillan Publishing.
Cooke, N. (1994). Varieties of knowledge elicitation techniques. *International Journal Human-Computer Studies, 41*, 801-849.
Diaper, D. (1989). *Knowledge Elicitation: Principles, Techniques, and Applications*. New York: John Wiley & Sons.
Dubois, D. (2002). Leveraging hidden expertise: Why, when and how to use cognitive task analysis. In D. Dubois (Ed.), *Creating, implementing, and managing effective training and development*. San Francisco, CA: Jossey-Bass Publishing of Wiley Company.
Ericsson, K. & Simon, H. (1980). Verbal reports as data. *Psychological Review, 87*, 215-251.
Ericsson, K. & Simon, H. (1996). *Protocol analysis: Verbal reports as data*. Cambridge, MA: Massachusetts Institute of Technology Press.
Fleishman, E. (1967). Performance assessment based on an empirically derived task taxonomy. *Human Factors, 9*, 349 – 366.
Fleishman, E. (1975). Toward a taxonomy of human performance. *American Psychologist, 30*, 1127-1149.
Gordon, S. & Gill, R. (1997). Cognitive task analysis. In C. Zsambok and G. Klein (Eds.), *Naturalistic Decision Making* (pp. 131-140). Mahwah, NJ: Lawerence Erlbaum Associates.
Green, D. & Swets, J. (1988). *Signal detection theory and psychophysics* (2nd edition.). Los Altos, CA: Peninsula Publishing.
Hoffman, R. Shadbolt, N, Burton, A., & Klein, G. (1995). Eliciting knowledge from experts: A methodological analysis. *Organizational Behaviour and Human Decision Processes, 62,* 129-158.
Hoffman, R. Crandall, B., & Shadbolt, N. (1998). Use of the Critical Decision Method to elicit expert knowledge: A case study in the methodology of Cognitive Task Analysis. *Human Factors, 40*, 254-276.
Johnson, L & Johnson, N. (1987). Knowledge elicitation involving Teachback interviewing. In A. Kidd (Ed.), *Knowledge Elicitation for Expert Systems: A Practical Handbook* (pp. 91-108). New York: Plenum Press.

Klein, G. (1996). The development of knowledge elicitation methods for capturing military expertise (Report ARI Research Note 96-14). Alexandria, VA.: United States Army Research Institute for the Behavioral and Social Sciences.

Klein, G. (1997). An overview of naturalistic decision making applications. In C. Zsambok and G. Klein (Eds.), *Naturalistic Decision Making* (pp. 49-59). Mahwah, NJ: Lawerence Erlbaum Associates.

Klein, G. (1998). The current status of the naturalistic decision making framework. In R. Flin, E. Salas, M. Strub, and L. Martin, (Eds.) *Decision Making under Stress: Emerging Themes and Applications,* (pp.11-28). Brookfield, Vermont: Ashgate Publishing.

Klein, G., Calderwood, R., & MacGregor, D. (1989). Critical decision method for eliciting knowledge. *IEEE Transactions on Systems, Man, and Cybernetics, 19*, 462-472.

McGraw, K. & Harbison-Briggs (1989). Knowledge acquisition, principles and guidelines, London: Prentice-Hall International.

Militello, L. (2001). Representing expertise. In E. Salas and G. Klein (Eds.), *Linking Expertise and Naturalistic Decision Making,* (pp. 245-262). Mahwah, NJ.: Lawerence Erlbaum Associates.

Militello, L. Hutton, R., Pliske, R, Knight, B., & Klein, G. (1997). Applied Cognitive Task Analysis (ACTA) Methodology (Report NRRDCTN-98-4). San Diego, CA.: Naval Personnel Research and Development Centre.

Militello, L. & Hutton, R. (1998). Applied cognitive task analysis (ATCA): A practitioner's toolkit for understanding cognitive task demands. *Ergonomics, 41*, 1618-1641.

Miller, T, Copeland, R., Phillips, J., & McClosky, M. (1999). A cognitive approach to developing planning tools to support air campaign planners (Report AFRL-IF-RS-TR-1999-146). Rome, NY: Air Force Research Laboratory.

National Institute for Aviation Research (2004). Evaluation Toolbox. Human Factors Laboratory, Wichita, Kansas: NAIR, Wichita State University and the Federal Aviation Administration.

Olson, J. & Reuter, H. (1987). Extracting expertise from experts: Methods for knowledge acquisition. *Expert Systems, 4*, 152-168.

Salas, E. & Klein, G. (2001). Expertise and naturalistic decision making: An overview, In E. Salas and G. Klein, (Eds.), *Linking Expertise and Naturalistic Decision Making,* (pp. 3-10). Mahwah, NJ.: Lawerence Erlbaum Associates.

Sanderson, P. & Fisher, C. (1994). Exploratory sequential data analysis: Foundations. *Human-Computer Interaction, 9*, 251-317.

Seamster, T., Redding, R., & Kaempf, G. (1997). *Applied Cognitive Task Analysis in Aviation.* Brookfield, Vermont: Avebury Aviation Publishers.

Someren, W., Barnard, Y, & Sandberg, J. (1994). *The Think-Aloud Method: A Practical Guide to Modelling Cognitive Processes.* London: Academic Press.

Thordsen, M. (1991). A comparison of two tools for Cognitive Task Analysis: Concept Mapping and the Critical Decision Method. *Proceedings of the Human Factors Society 35th Annual Meeting.* Santa Monica, CA: HFES.

Woods, D. (1993). Process-tracing methods for the study of cognition outside of the experimental laboratory. In G. Klein, J, Orasanu, R. Calderwood, and C. Zsambok, (Eds.), *Decision Making in Action: Models and Methods,* (pp. 228 - 251). New Jersey: Ablex Publishing Company.

Using SWOT and risk analysis in prevention of coal dust emission during its transportation in Tallinn ports

Piia Tint[1], Henn Tosso[1], Karin Reinhold[1], & Kai Aava[2]
[1]Tallinn University of Technology
[2]Energo Management Ltd
Tallinn, Estonia

Abstract

The Muuga Coal Terminal in Tallinn together with the transportation of coal accounts for a substantial part of Estonia's income. The port is situated very near to the garden-town and represents a big pollution problem for people living there in summer or all year around. SWOT and risk analysis were used in the present study to establish a Multi-Dimensional Risk Assessment Model RAM-MD(3). The RAM-MD model enables the analysis the following aspects in global systems: the consequences of hazards on human life and health; on the environment (sea, nature pollution) and on the property.

Introduction

On the 1st of May 2004 The Baltic Sea became an inner sea of Europe. Estonia is the eastern border of The European Union since then, and it plays a role of a bridge between Russia and the united Europe. Estonian legislation supports the development of business and active innovative politics.

The construction of the Muuga Coal Terminal (Muuga CT) enhances the economics of the country, improving the collaboration between Estonia and Russia that makes it mutually beneficial both for European Union and Russia. The Muuga CT in Tallinn including the transportation of coal accounts for a substantial part of Estonia's income. The Muuga CT equipment has a high productivity profile. The coal unloading speed at the Terminal is approximately 20 wagons of 60 tons each per hour while the loading speed is 1800 tons per hour. The hole storage area provides a capacity of simultaneously keeping up to 750 000 m^3 of coal and three moorages with sum length of 770 metres and depth of 11 to 17 metres. The last number, a depth of up to 17 metres, is one of the advantages of Muuga CT over other portal terminals situated on the Baltic Sea. That assures serving practically all vessels passing through the Denmark Strait.

In D. de Waard, G.R.J. Hockey, P. Nickel, and K.A. Brookhuis (Eds.) (2007), *Human Factors Issues in Complex System Performance* (pp. 455 - 460). Maastricht, the Netherlands: Shaker Publishing.

A disadvantage is that the port is situated very close to the city's garden-town and represents a big source of pollution for people living there during summer or all year around.

The coal is coming to Estonia by railway transport from Kuzbas, which is located over 4000 km away and other Russian coal mines. In the Muuga CT the coal is loaded on the ships in order to transport it further by the sea to the Eastern Europe.

The dust is originating from coal particles (the coal particle size from 1 mm - 50 mm) released during this loading process. One possible way for solving the dust emission problems is based on integrated SWOT and risk analysis worked out in the current study.

The aim of the study

The aim of the study was to work out a scientifically based model for assessment and prevention of Tallinn inhabitant's health risks who are living near-by the Muuga CT caused by the coal dust emission during the loading from the wagons to the ships.

Materials and methods

One of the methods for solving the problem politically and socially is SWOT analyses method, as well as risk analysis. A SWOT (strengths, weaknesses, opportunities and threats) analysis is a technique for understanding the Strengths and Weaknesses and for looking at the Opportunities and Threats in the systems. A SWOT analysis is usually applied in business context, but it is also possible to use it for the investigation of complex systems such as pollution processes. Strengths and Weaknesses are internal factors, Opportunities and Threats relate to external factors of the system. A SWOT analysis may be related to risk analysis as well as to other problem solving techniques.

The method of risk assessment for preventing the major accidents, including environmental (Harms-Ringdahl, 2001) is more complicated and consists of more risk levels as it is used in the assessments of hazards in the work environment (Reinhold, Tint & Kiivet, 2006). The widely used risk assessment method in the work environment is based on BS 8800 and one of many versions for risk assessment in the chemicals industry, worked out by Rantanen (1999). The application of the latter method in the course of the Estonian legislation with respect to risk assessment is presented in the Table 1 (Reinhold, Tint & Kiivet, 2006).

Table 1 contains risk phrases (R20, R21, R65 etc.). Those risk phrases (like R20: harmful in contact with skin) characterize the hazardous effect of chemicals on a worker's health in EU and Estonian legislation. The above mentioned methods do not take into consideration the exposure time of hazards influencing on people. To get rid of this disadvantage, the Multi-Dimensional Risk Assessment Model RAM-MD(3) (Table 2A & 2B) was worked out in the present study.

Table 1. Determination of risk level for hazardous chemicals in workplace air

Consequences → Probability ↓	**Slightly harmful** uncomfortable, irritable feeling, overcoming illnesses R20, 21, 36, 37, 38[1]	**Harmful** burning, skin diseases, long-lasting severe damage, permanent slight disorders R23, 24, 25, 33, 34, 40, 43, 48, 62, 63, 64	**Extremely harmful** poisoning, occupational cancer, asthma, permanent severe damage, illnesses dangerous to health R26, 27, 35, 39, 41, 42, 45, 49, 60, 61, 65
Highly unlikely severe damage from <10% of the exposure limits, other 10–50% of the exposure limits[2]	trivial risk no risk reduction measures needed	tolerable risk follow-up of risks	moderate risk risk reduction measures needed
Unlikely severe damage from 10–50% of the exposure limits, other 50–100% of the exposure limits	tolerable risk follow-up of risks	moderate risk risk reduction measures needed	substantial risk risk reduction measures inevitable
Likely severe damage from 50-100% of the exposure limits, other over exposure limits	moderate risk risk reduction measures needed	substantial risk risk reduction measures inevitable	intolerable risk risk reduction measures to be implemented at once

[1] R-phrases (short for Risk Phrases) are defined in Annex III of EU Directive 67/548/EEC: *Nature of special risks attributed to dangerous substances and preparations.*
[2] concentrations of chemicals defined by Rantanen (1999). Exposure limits for chemicals given in the legislation (Resolution, 2001).

Table 2. Multi-Dimensional Risk Assessment Model RAM-MD(3) for analysis of global systems 2A – Definitions[3]

Exposure E		Likelihood L		Consequence C	
Continuously	8.1 – 10	Almost Certain	0.81 – 1.0	Critical	8.1 – 10
Frequently	6.1 – 8.0	Likely	0.61 – 0.8	Major	6.1 – 8.0
Occasionally	4.1 – 6.0	Possible	0.41 – 0.6	Moderate	4.1 – 6.0
Infrequently	2.1 – 4.0	Unlikely	0.21 – 0.4	Minor	2.1 – 4.0
Rarely	0.1 – 2.0	Rare	0.01 – 0.2	Insignificant	0.1 – 2.0

[3] The likelihood ranges from 0.01 to 1.0 (zero- risk is impossible). Exposure and consequences are given in 10 point scale in the Risk Assessment 3 D Model (2004).

2B - Risk Score & Legend[4]

Risk Score	Risk Level; Legend
RS> 40	**Ext**: extreme/significant risk; immediate action needed; must be managed by senior management with a detailed plan.
RS= 25-40	**High**: high risk; senior management attention needed, detailed research and management planning at senior levels.
RS= 10-24	**Mod**: moderate risk; management responsibility must be specified; manage by specific monitoring or response procedures.
RS< 10	**Low**: low risk; manage by routine procedures; unlikely to need specific allocation of resources.

[4] There are 4 risk levels: low, moderate, high and extreme. Risk score is obtained with the formula RS= E x L x C (exposure x likelihood x consequence).

Description of the present situation

The Muuga CT is situated 17 km from Tallinn and 20 km-s from Airport of Tallinn. Terminal is situated in direct vicinity to the Muuga railway station, which allows a notable reduction in carriage delivery time. The area of the Muuga CT is 45 hectares.

The processes which are taking place in Muuga CT:

- transferring – unloading of carriages, warehousing on the platform and loading on ship either from warehouse, or via basic variant from railway carriages;
- crushing – served coal can be crushed to size 0-50 mm;
- magnetic purification – coal is refined from iron scrap while receiving carriages and loading on ship;
- warehousing and storing – this service is rendered on basis of internal regulations and tariffs.

The station for tracking concentration of dust in the air is located close to the coal terminal. The management and personnel of the terminal perform constant monitoring of the station's indicators (for instance, the concentration of dust in the environmental air was from 20 mg/m^3 – 100 mg/m^3 in summer 2006) and try to keep the concentration of the dust low, according to modern ecological requirements - under 50 mg/m^3. The health and environmental risks caused by coal dust are as follows: health hazards, explosion and fire hazards, possible break-down of equipment and apparatus, decrease of visibility in the environment, worsening of the air quality, problems with local authorities and environmental board.

Results

In order to assess the present situation at the Muuga CT in the initial stage two models were combined: PEST (political, economical, social & technical aspects) and SWOT (strengths, weaknesses, opportunities and threats) analysis. The results are given in Table 3.

Table 3. Integrated PEST & SWOT method for solving the health and environmental problems related to coal dust emission at Muuga CT.

Political aspects	
Strengths P1	Geopolitically advantageous location for coal transportation & storage; Russian ambitious politics on export of natural resources, including coal.
Weaknesses P2	Muuga Port as a risk for Estonian security as indirectly connected to the Russian capital.
Opportunities P3	The usage of Muuga Port is an effective transit corridor between Russia and Western Europe.
Threats P4	The aggravation of the political situation between Estonia and Russia.
Economical aspects	
Strengths E1	Good economic potential enables to develop as technical-technological as social-political programmes, involving high scientific potential.
Weaknesses E2	Additional costs connected with technical and technological problems (breaks of the technological line; unloading and uploading are not synchronized).
Opportunities E3	The activities of Muuga CT enable to reinforce the economy of the Estonian Republic, gives force to economic collaboration between Estonia and Russia and

Threats E4	for Estonia with other European countries. The permission for activities is given to Muuga CT for one year, until July 2007. If the permission is not renewed, the closing threatens Muuga CT.
Social aspects	
Strengths S1	The firm has highly qualified and motivated personnel.
Weaknesses S2	The complaints are coming from the citizens because of the nearness that spoil the reputation of the firm and cause complications.
Opportunities S3	The economical potential of the Muuga CT and the social-political vision help the close-surrounding area municipally organs to realize different social-political programmes originating from the healthful living environment.
Threats S4	Jõelehtme county in the nearness of Muuga CT wishes the closing of the terminal originating from the environmental aspects.
Technical aspects	
Strengths T1	Professional knowledge in coal overloading and storage. The use of the latest technological achievements in coal transit. Minimal use of manual work. The process management is computerized.
Weaknesses T2	In winter the coal is freezing in the wagons into big chunks, therefore the discharge of the wagons demands notable big additional expense of energy, time, and workload. The emission of fine fraction coal takes place in the technological joints, storage territory, and in the neighbourhood.
Opportunities T3	The high productivity of the used equipment. The velocity of unloading is 20 wagons per hour; 1800 tons coal per hour. It is possible to store 750 000 m^3 of coal at the same time. The length of 3 mooring lines in 770 metres and depth 11-17 metres.
Threats T4	The mechanical and electronical parts of the technological joints come out from the bridging with dust, followed by the stop of all unloading process.

Table 4. Risk Assessment in Muuga CT

Identified hazards	Risk Assessment			Risk Score	Risk Level Ext; High; Mod; Low
	Exposure E	Likelihood L	Consequence C	E x L x C	
Political					
P1	8.0	1.0	0.1	0.8	Low
P2	8.0	0.6	6.0	28.8	High
P3	10.0	0.8	0.1	0.8	Low
P4	6.0	0.6	6.0	21.6	Mod
Economical					
E1	6.0	0.6	2.1	7.56	Low
E2	8.0	0.6	4.1	19.68	Mod
E3	8.0	0.6	0.1	0.48	Low
E4	10.0	1.0	10.0	100.0	Ext
Social					
S1	6.0	0.4	4.1	9.84	Low
S2	8.0	0.6	4.1	19.68	Mod
S3	4.0	0.6	6.0	14.4	Mod
S4	10.0	1.0	8.0	80.0	Ext
Technical					
T1	6.0	1.0	0.1	0.6	Low
T2	8.0	0.6	4.1	19.68	Mod
T3	10.0	1.0	0.1	1.0	Low
T4	6.0	0.4	6.0	14.4	Mod

The connections between SWOT-analysis and risk assessment on the basis of Model RAM-MD(3) are given in the Table 4. The risk is assessed on four levels; extreme (Ext), high (High), moderate (Mod) and low (Low). The greatest risk (Ext) is connected with the economical threat E4: the permission for activities is given to Muuga CT only for one year, until the July, 2007. If the permission is not renewed, closing threatens the terminal. The other extreme risk (S4) is connected with the pollution of the nearness to Muuga CT living area; all the efforts have to be used for improving the situation. As a high risk level, P-2 (Muuga CT is indirectly connected to the Russian capital) is considered. The other risks are assessed as moderate or low.

Conclusions

A major challenge in using SWOT analysis lies in identifying the position the business is actually in. SWOT analysis helps to resolve one fundamental concern in selecting a strategy. The Muuga Coal Terminal main strengths are the geopolitically advantageous location, the good economic potential, highly qualified and the motivated personnel and the professional knowledge on coal overloading and storage. There are also some weaknesses such as dust emission during coal overloading in a place that borders near-by inhabitants.

The problems have been analysed with the help of integrated PEST-SWOT and risk analysis methods. The RAM–MD(3) – Multi-Dimensional Risk Assessment Model – enables the analysis of the following aspects in global systems: the consequences on human life; on human's health; on environment (sea, nature pollution) and on the property.

References

British Standard 8800. (1996). *Guide to Occupational Health and Safety Management Systems*. London: British Standards Institute.

Council Directive 67/548/EEC of June 27 (1967) on the approximation of laws, regulations and administrative provisions relating to the classification, packaging and labelling of dangerous substances. *Official Journal of the European Communities, 196*, August 16, 1967.

Harms-Ringdahl, L. (2001). Safety Analysis. *Principles and Practice in Occupational Safety*. London: Taylor & Francis.

Rantanen, S. & Pääkkönen, R. (1999). *Työympäristön kemiallisten ja fysikaalisten riskien arviointi ja hallinta. [Assessment and management of occupational chemical and physical risks]*. Helsinki: Finnish Institute of Occupational Health.

Reinhold, K., Tint, P. & Kiivet, G. (2006). Risk Assessment in Textile and Wood Processing Industry. *Reliability, Quality and Safety Engineering, 13*, 115-125.

Resolution of the Estonian Government No.293 of September 18, 2001 on the occupational exposure limits of chemicals (2001). State Gazette in Estonia RTI 2001, 77, 460.

Risk Assessment 3D Model (2004). *EHS Manual*. The University of Melbourne. Melboure, Australia: Risk Management Office. Retrieved 15.05.2007 from www.unimelb.edu.au/ehsm

Training and Organisational Issues

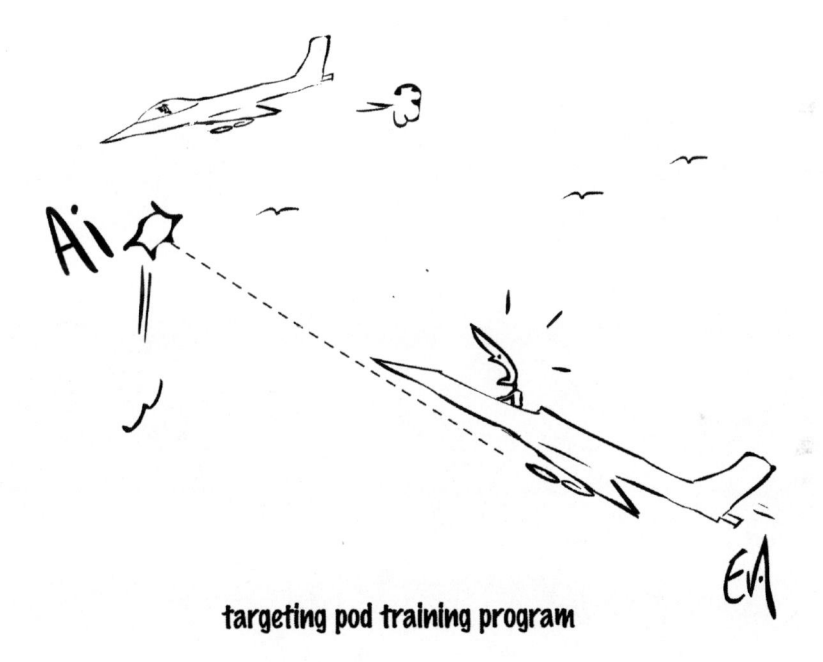

targeting pod training program

In D. de Waard, G.R.J. Hockey, P. Nickel, and K.A. Brookhuis (Eds.) (2007), *Human Factors Issues in Complex System Performance* (pp. 461). Maastricht, the Netherlands: Shaker Publishing.

Adaptive training methodology: skills analysis for the design of a Targeting Pod training programme

Jelke van der Pal & Machteld van der Vlugt
National Aerospace Laboratory NLR
Amsterdam, The Netherlands

Abstract

Finding and tracking a target, and delivery of a weapon onto the target, using a targeting pod (TGP) requires a highly complex set of skills of a fighter pilot. Considerable amounts of training time and effort are required to master these complex skills. However, available training time is limited. Training effectiveness can be improved by using adaptive training, meaning that the difficulty of the task being trained is varied as a function of actual trainee performance. This paper describes a skills analysis method that facilitates the design of an adaptive training programme for mastering TGP skills based on the 4C/ID method, which assumes that complex skills should be mastered by practicing whole tasks like e.g. typical TGP missions. A systematic analysis of the complex skills that are required for operating the TGP is carried out in consultation with experts. Based on an operational conditions analysis, the difficulty of the task (and hence the level of required skills) is determined. Results of this analysis can be used to adjust the actual training level related to trainee performance.

Introduction

A typical task for a fighter pilot is to eliminate an indicated enemy target. To facilitate this task modern fighter aircrafts are equipped with a targeting pod (TGP). The camera of the TGPs allows the fighter pilots to see the environment farther, sharper and more detailed, and therefore improve their ability to precisely pin-point an enemy target. The TGP is controlled via multifunctional user interfaces (Multi-Function Displays or MFDs). Given the high velocity of the aircraft to minimise amongst others exposure time to threats, it follows that the operation of the TGP requires complex skills. Training of those complex skills takes considerable time. However, available training time is limited. Therefore the training has to be efficient, i.e. it has to produce the desired effect in a minimum amount of time. A training programme is considered to be effective when the necessary skills mastered in training situations are transferred successfully to real-life situations. A training programme is efficient when it realises the same effect for less (e.g. time, effort, or money). Efficient training takes place when training is at an appropriate level of difficulty. The essence of adaptive training is that the difficulty of the training programme is adjusted based on how well the trainee is performing during the

In D. de Waard, G.R.J. Hockey, P. Nickel, and K.A. Brookhuis (Eds.) (2007), *Human Factors Issues in Complex System Performance* (pp. 463 - 473). Maastricht, the Netherlands: Shaker Publishing.

training such that it realises the same effect in less time than a fixed training programme. The next section will briefly outline training design principles that ensure effective training and provide a basis for adaptive training.

No efficiency without efficacy: the 4C/ID method

If a training programme has poor transfer to real-life situations, making this programme adaptive will not likely result in a high transfer. Van Merriënboer's (1997) 4C/ID (Four Component Instructional Design) model meets the requirements for designing an effective training programme for the following reasons. First, 4C/ID intents to design the training programme so as to maximize the transfer of skills from the training environment to real situations. The focus on the integration and coordinated performance of task-specific skills is a central design aspect of 4C/ID. Second, the 4C/ID model recommends a mixture where part-task practice supports the complex whole task learning. Finally, the 4C/ID method uses standard performance requirements as the criterion when assessing the trainee's actual performance.

4C/ID based training contains a sequence of whole tasks, a set of part tasks, and two types of knowledge presentation. The sequence of whole tasks is formed by main learning tasks which aim to integrate sub-skills by emphasising authentic, whole-task situations from the very beginning. "Authentic" means that the exercises are derived from real practice. "Whole task" implies that sub-skills should be practised in an integrated way. Learning should be practice-based, and training should focus on integration of the complex skill as a whole, instead of isolated sub-skills. To prevent that trainees get overloaded, training should start with simple situations, which gradually become more complex. Furthermore, learning tasks of similar difficulty, but varying in operational conditions and particular problems, should be grouped together. Learner support is provided to a high extent in the first learning tasks, which is decreased gradually such that finally the trainee is able to perform the task without support. The set of varying learning tasks with similar difficulty and gradually decreasing amount of learner support is called a task class. The sequence of task classes makes the backbone of training and will be designed first. The part tasks are designed for those actions that require a high automatism and need to be trained extra to gain these automatisms. Only after having sequenced whole and part tasks, knowledge presentations are being added to the design in order to support either insight (supportive information presentation) or task execution (just in time information presentation).

The 4C/ID model forms the basis for the adaptive training principles that are currently being developed at the National Aerospace Laboratory for the purpose of TGP Training. A previous attempt to use 4C/ID principles for adaptive training was a project using fuzzy logic principles (Van Merriënboer, Luursema, Kingma, Houweling, & de Vries, 1995). A 6th Framework EU project (ADAPT^{IT}, Van der Pal, 2003) was dedicated to develop a pragmatic version of 4C/ID and to ease the construction of adaptive algorithms. The resulting ADAPT Method (De Croock, Van Merriënboer, Van der Pal, Abma, Paas & Eseryel, 2002) has identified more specific ingredients for adaptive training and made it easier for training designers to use them. A recent project focused on a particular algorithm in which trainee performance and mental workload were used to select the next exercise in a part task sequence (Salden, 2005). While these efforts were successful or promising, they were providing adaptive training only in a limited way and did not provide a systematic adaptive principle for the full training design method.

The next sections attempt to relieve the design gap for adaptive training programmes. The starting point for a well-developed adaptive training programme is a systematic and sufficient differentiation of difficulty levels, combined with an easy application of these difficulty levels. Only then, the task difficulty can be optimized to the individual trainee's needs. This paper discusses a method that systematically differentiates between difficulty levels of the task. The method will be illustrated with the target targeting task.

Efficient adaptive training programme: the adaptive variable

Efficient training takes place when training is at an appropriate level of difficulty. Each adaptive training programme consists of three elements: an element that can be adjusted (the adaptive variable), an element that measures how well the trainee is doing (the performance measurement), and an element that changes the adaptive variable based on the performance measurement (Kelley 1969). In Figure 1 these elements and their relationship are illustrated. The appropriate level of difficulty is realised through the adaptive variable. Therefore, the critical element of an adaptive programme is the design of the adaptive variable.

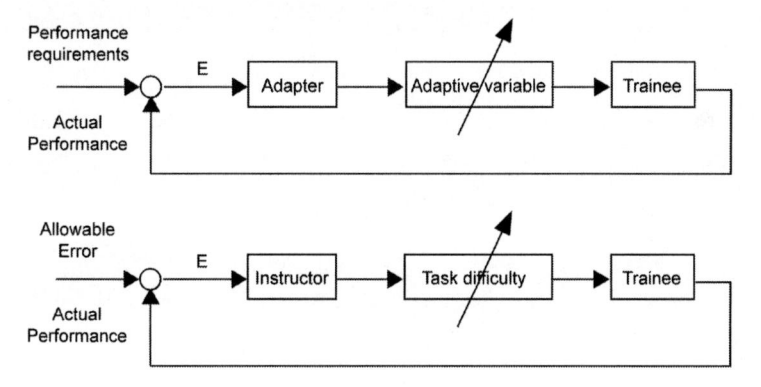

Figure 1. Elements of adaptive training environment. The adapter is played by the instructor, the adaptive variable can be any adaptable component of the training environment, the variable that is chosen is the task difficulty because it comes close to the variations that occur in real life situations

Defining the adaptive variable: task difficulty

The adaptive variable can be any component of the training environment that can be adjusted, for example the performance requirements, the amount of learner support or the difficulty of the task. It is impractical to vary all the possible components together. Therefore some decisions have to be made with regard to the choice of the adaptive variable.

In contrast to most training principles, the 4C/ID ideal is to keep the performance requirements at the required (real life) level already from the start of training. In practice, standard performance requirements define a maximum allowable deviation from pre-set targets. For instance, a beginning pilot must land the aircraft safely on the runway as well as the expert pilot. However, the expert pilot may be allowed to land under more severe conditions like having more side-wind or using a short runway. Due to its resemblance with real life it is not illogical to use the allowable performance error as the standard at which the performance of the trainee is measured. Naturally, such standards are difficult to reach for trainees without introducing certain instructional arrangements and/or environmental conditions.

The primary instructional instrument to accommodate to trainees is the task difficulty. This is a variable that can be considered as the global tuning knob on old radios. The radio channel searched for may be reached, but it is not easy to set it sharp. For fine tuning, another control is required. A similar principle is suggested by 4C/ID. Once a rough indication of task difficulty has been set (for a range of training tasks), further fine tuning can be achieved by varying the learner support to ensure the trainee can deal with the given task.

In this paper we focus on the primary variable: task difficulty. How the standard for the allowable performance error and the function between the actual error and the task difficulty should be designed is not discussed in this paper.

Analysing the task difficulty

A task requires a set of actions, and is person independent. The way an individual person carries out the required set of actions are the skills. Skills are person dependent. Some skills take more time to master than other skills. The task difficulty depends on the number and type of actions that have to be combined concurrently and on the precision this combination has to be carried out. A task becomes more difficult when more actions have to be executed simultaneously. The type of action also determines task difficulty (compare 'making decisions with incomplete information' with 'executing a standard procedure').

To determine the task difficulty, the task has to be analysed based on the required actions that have to be carried out concurrently including the precision of their (concurrent) execution. Actions that are interrelated such that they cannot be trained separately are combined into action sets. An example of a set of actions that cannot be separated is, for instance, engaging the clutch and pressing down the gas pedal when driving off in a vehicle. The analysis is illustrated in Figure 2.

The number of actions that has to be carried out concurrently and the required precision (i.e. the task difficulty) can be manipulated by system and by operational conditions. An example of system conditions that influence the difficulty of the task driving-off is the kind of car that is used. Driving-off is classified as more difficult for a petrol car than for a diesel car, because for a (low-power) petrol car it requires a concurrent combination of engaging the clutch and pressing down the gas pedal whereas for a diesel car it may require only engaging the clutch. Operational conditions can be the weather, day time, traffic, the target, or the slope of the road.

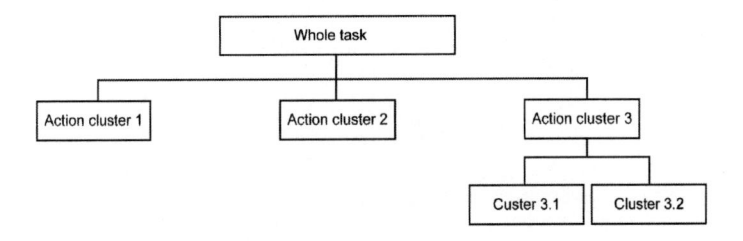

Figure 2. Action (skills) analysis and combined actions based on a whole task

During normal basic training, system conditions do not change during the task, e.g., there is no unexpected malfunctioning of the system. Therefore, the operational conditions remain for manipulating the task difficulty.

Structuring the differentiation of task difficulty

The differentiation of the task difficulty from easy to difficult should be logical and should lead the trainee through a sequence of task difficulties that are highly relevant to the skills he is expected to master (Kelley, 1969). For structuring, two basic methods of differentiation can be distinguished, the part-task and the whole-task methods. Part-task methods differentiate between task difficulties by isolating part tasks from the whole task. The trainees are lead through the part tasks one by one. Once they have reached the required performance level for a part task they are offered another part-task until they are able to carry out the whole task at the required performance level. The progression method from the part tasks to whole task can be pure part-task training, progressive part-task training, or repetitive part-task training. Whole-task methods offer a whole task directly at the outset of the training. The whole task ideally incorporates all the interrelated skills the trainee has to master. The training starts with the easiest whole task that can be encountered in real life and progresses to the most difficult whole task. The difference between part-task and whole-task progression methods is illustrated in Figure 3.

The part-task method guarantees that all tasks and related skills are covered in the training programme. A drawback with regard to effectiveness is that it may neglect the interrelation between skills across the part tasks, which may result in a hampered transfer of the skills to real-life tasks (Farmer, 1999; Van Merriënboer, 1997). A drawback with regard to efficiency is that the part-task methods can result in a roundabout progression taking more time than strictly necessary. Another drawback with regard to efficiency of adaptation is that part-task methods offer a less flexible differentiation of task difficulty. Nevertheless, part-task methods remain necessary for those part tasks that require precise execution of tightly interrelated actions that have to be practiced often before it is mastered at the required level.

	Whole task		
Cluster 1	Cluster 2	Cluster 3	
		Cluster 3.1	Cluster 3.2
Level 1	Level 0	Level 0	Level 0
Level 2	Level 0	Level 0	Level 0
Level 3	Level 0	Level 0	Level 0
Level 3	Level 1	Level 0	Level 0
Level 3	Level 2	Level 0	Level 0
Level 3	Level 3	Level 0	Level 0
Level 3	Level 3	Level 1	Level 0
Level 3	Level 3	Level 3	Level 3

Figure 3. Illustration of the progressive part-task method. Four levels of difficulty are distinguished in this example. The (part)-task difficulty is classified from 0 to 3, level 0 means no actions required, level 1 minimum action is required and level 3 maximum action is required. The most difficult whole-task level implies that the trainee must have mastered all the required actions at level 3

Whole-task methods partly solve the drawbacks of the part-task methods. For whole-task methods there are theoretically a vast number of possibilities for structuring the difficulty progression, as is illustrated in Figure 3. The training designer needs to define in consultation with subject matter experts, a criterion which reduces the vast number of possibilities to a manageable set of possibilities. Criteria that can be used are, for example, the frequency of certain task situations, importance of certain task situations, or the time available for training. Whole-task training is unavoidable for those tasks which require closely interrelated skills (Salden, 2005). The drawback of the whole-task method is that the easiest task can still be too demanding for the trainee. In this case the trainee must be given extra support.

Trainee support takes the care of those actions (skills) which the trainee cannot handle concurrently: at first the trainee gets much support, which will be decreased gradually as the trainee gains more proficiency. The trainee support may be provided by an instructor, by simulation or by an intelligent tutor system. Using trainee support, a simple part-task event (cf., the first row in figure 3: a level 1 practise of cluster 1 action) may change into a simple whole task event. And yet, no action is required from the trainee on the other action clusters, but the trainee does achieve some understanding, awareness of the actions in the whole task context, even though it is merely performed by the instructor or the system. This differs from a purely part-task training sequence, in which the whole task context is not given at all. Note, that for the TGP example presented below, no trainee support is considered and therefore, the first whole task is defined such that all actions are performed at least on the easiest level.

Designing the adaptive variable for training the TGP

Each real life task poses different questions for which decisions have to be made, requiring each adaptive programme to be developed specifically. A typical task for a fighter mission is to eliminate a specific target at a given location in a short time period.

The TGP is a system that is designed for precision pin-pointing of targets. The high quality cameras (visible and infra-red spectrum) with extreme zoom capabilities allow pilots to attack the enemy targets with precision-guided weapons. The latter may use a laser designator for precise delivery of laser guided weapons. The TGP is mounted externally to the fighter aircraft, and is operated through the man-machine interfaces in the cockpit: the multifunctional display (MFD), the side stick controller (SSC) and the throttle. These interfaces are also used to control the aircraft itself and other systems such as the radar and navigation system.

Skills analysis for the task difficulty: the targeting task

According to a pure whole-task method, a fighter pilot should be trained how to concurrently fly, navigate, communicate and target the enemy from the outset of the training. In practice this is not the case because carrying out the whole task is much too difficult. Therefore, for the whole "eliminate enemy" task, the required actions are identified and combined in part-tasks based on the required actions and their extent of interrelationship. A criterion for prioritizing the part-tasks that is used in practice is the interrelationship of the required actions across the part-tasks. First, the part task is trained for which skills has to be mastered that are a prerequisite for carrying out the other part tasks. For training for fighter tasks, this implies that the pilot first is trained to fly, navigate and communicate because these skills are general and conditionally for carrying out more specific tasks such as targeting. Nevertheless, these actions can be trained such that they prepare the pilot for specific tasks in the future. For example skilful manoeuvring of the fighter aircraft may make striking the enemy target easier. Flying and targeting are not entirely independent from each other. When the trainee has mastered the required general skills, the skills specific for carrying out the targeting task are trained.

For the present, the design of the adaptive variable is limited to the part-task "targeting". This has two main practical reasons. First, the preferred means for training are desktop trainers since they can be taken to mission locations to practice on site specific situations. Second, usually the use of the TGP is trained only after the pilots obtained their flight license. TGP training is an additional qualification-training. To preserve the idea of whole-task training, the flying, navigation and communication tasks are offered but kept at a difficulty level that the pilot is able to handle himself. In Figure 4 this analysis is illustrated. The tree shows which actions may have to be carried out concurrently and repeatedly

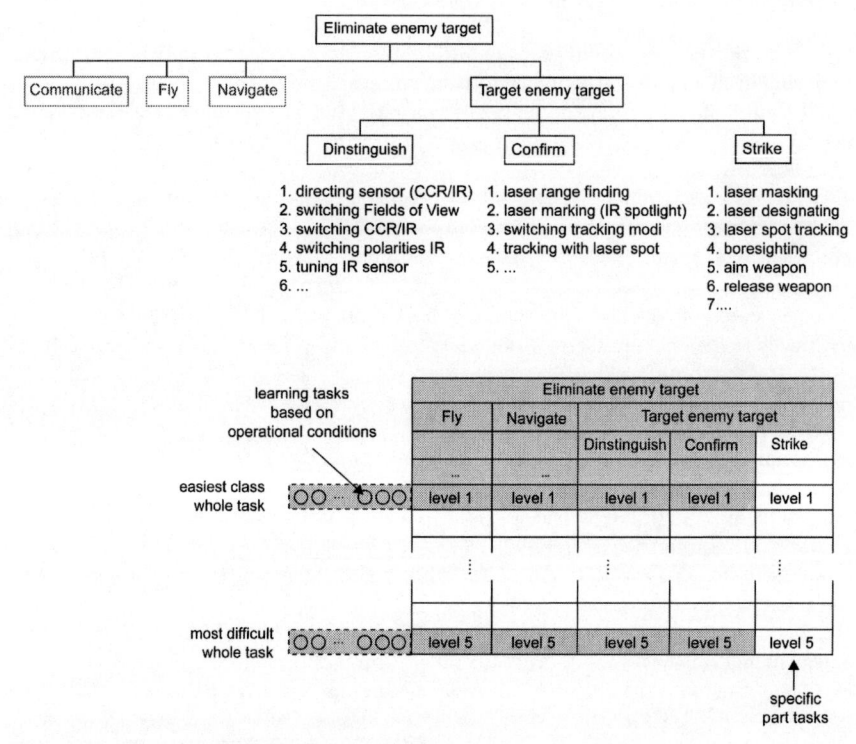

```
                          Eliminate enemy target
      ┌──────────┬─────┬────────┬──────────────────┐
  Communicate   Fly  Navigate        Target enemy target
                                ┌──────────┬──────────┬──────────┐
                            Dinstinguish  Confirm    Strike
```

Dinstinguish:
1. directing sensor (CCR/IR)
2. switching Fields of View
3. switching CCR/IR
4. switching polarities IR
5. tuning IR sensor
6. ...

Confirm:
1. laser range finding
2. laser marking (IR spotlight)
3. switching tracking modi
4. tracking with laser spot
5. ...

Strike:
1. laser masking
2. laser designating
3. laser spot tracking
4. boresighting
5. aim weapon
6. release weapon
7. ...

learning tasks based on operational conditions		Eliminate enemy target			
		Fly	Navigate	Target enemy target		
				Dinstinguish	Confirm	Strike
easiest class whole task	OO...OOO	level 1	level 1	level 1	level 1	level 1
		⋮	⋮	⋮	⋮	⋮
most difficult whole task	OO...OOO	level 5	level 5	level 5	level 5	level 5

→ specific part tasks

Figure 4. Skills analysis and proposed combined actions of the "eliminate enemy"-task

Operational conditions analysis for defining task difficulties

The actions/skills analysis is used to determine which actions have to be carried out for the assigned task and which of them have to be carried out concurrently. Given the systems (aircraft, TGP etc), the operational conditions determine the number of concurrent actions and their preciseness. Those operational conditions that require more concurrent actions and more preciseness make the task more difficult.

The operational conditions that influence task difficulty are divided into three main groups: conditions that relate to the target, to the surface and to the atmosphere. Target conditions influencing the task difficulty are for example its mobility (none/extreme), geometry (size, form, outline), its colour and temperature difference relative to its environment, location (known/approximately know/unknown). Surface conditions are for example the hilliness of the area or the occurrence of other or false targets. Atmospheric conditions are for example light conditions and the presence of moisture (fog, rain).

The operational conditions which provide the most difficult targeting task are first determined, followed by the determination of the operational conditions which provide the easiest targeting task. Finally the difficulty levels in-between are defined.

Each difficulty level represents a task class. For each task class a set of operational conditions have to be designated, which result in learning tasks that approximately have the same difficulty level. The operational conditions should be designated such that they produce a sufficient variability between the learning tasks in the same class. The learning tasks should vary just like the tasks in the real operational situations so as to enhance a successful transfer of the mastered skills to real situations.

An example of a set of operational conditions that generate a task at the most difficult level is a well camouflaged small extremely movable vaguely outlined target in a highly cluttered hilly environment of which the location is not know at dusk in foggy weather. This set of conditions requires a maximum number of concurrent actions of which some have to be carried out with a delicate touch because the target is small and extremely movable. Because the electro-optical range between target and environment is not globally discriminating the pilot has to switch repeatedly between the CCTV camera and the IR, possibly switching hot-black and hot-white sensor polarities. Meanwhile, the pilot has to switch between the different fields of view because the location is unknown and a large area has to be scanned. In addition, the pilot has to fly and navigate within the boundaries of justified operation while avoiding exposure to potential threats.

An example of a set of operational conditions that generates a task at the easiest level is a large purple immobile cube in a plain yellow environment at a given location at daytime in clear weather. Actions required by the pilot to locate the target is limited as much as possible, allowing focussing on the targeting task.

The number of intermediate difficulty levels can be vast due to the infinite possible combinations of operational conditions. To limit the infinite number of possible difficulty levels, the task situations that can be encountered in real life have to be limited at importance and frequency of occurrence. The choice for a sophisticated set of task classes that represent the majority of the important task classes draws heavily on the expertise of the instructor.

Structuring difficulty progression

The flexibility of the 4C/ID method can now be illustrated. Depending on the entry level of the trainee, the level of difficulty of the part-tasks flying and navigating can be adjusted. For example, if the trainee is very experienced in flying the aircraft, the level of difficulty of these part tasks can be set to a maximum level whilst keeping the difficulty of the targeting task at the easiest level. When the trainee is less experienced, the level of the flying task is made easier to allow sufficient focus on the targeting task.

Depending on the performance progression of the pilot, the levels of the targeting task can be adjusted and varied by the instructor to optimise the learning progress.

Further work

The analysis of TGP training tasks is not yet completed. How and to which extent the whole-task is decomposed in part-tasks should be weighed by the designer in consultation with other experts and instructors. Factors that may be taken into account are the means that are available for training, and the skilfulness of the trainee, and the time that is available for training. In order to allow the instructor for such flexibility, the database of training tasks has to be sufficiently large and tasks should be easily selectable. This will set specific requirements to the structure and interface of the task database. Adaptive training development will follow. This will start with guidelines for instructors and a database of training tasks. Based on the results of adaptive TGP training, task selector algorithms for automated adaptive training may be developed.

Conclusions

Adaptive training programmes are a means to realise a desired effect at an optimal expense. The 4C/ID method ensures an effective training programme but is not adaptive yet. To make this method adaptive requires a systematic and sufficient differentiation of difficulty levels in combination with sufficient variability within a given difficulty level. This way the level of difficulty can be optimized to the trainee's performance progression so as to ensure optimal training effectiveness and efficiency. Task difficulty is related to the number of actions that have to be carried out concurrently with a given precision. Each real life task requires a separate action/skills analysis to specify the required actions and their concurrence. Task difficulty can be manipulated by the operational conditions. Those conditions that require more concurrent actions and more precision are designated to a higher level of difficulty. Using 4C/ID as a basis, this paper discussed how to analyse systematically the fighter pilot task of targeting of an enemy target.

References

De Croock, M.B.G., Van Merriënboer J.J.G., Van der Pal, J., Abma, H.J., Paas, F., & Eseryel, D. (2002). *Advanced design approach for personalised training - interactive tools: The ADAPT Method.* ADAPT[IT] Deliverable 3.2 prepared for the European Commission DGXIII under contract no. IST-1999-11740. NLR-CR-2002-195 (downloadable from www.adaptit.org).

Kelley, C.R. (1969). What is adaptive training? *Human Factors 11*, 547-556.

Farmer, E., Van Rooij, J., Jorna, P., & Moraal, J. (1999). *Handbook of Simulator-based Training.* Aldershot, England: Ashgate Publishing Ltd.

Sweller, J., Van Merriënboer, J.J.G., & Paas, F.G.W.C. (1998). Cognitive architecture and instructional design. *Educational Psychology Review, 10*, 251-196.

Salden, R.J.C.M. (2005). *Dynamic Task Selection in aviation training.* PhD thesis. Heerlen, The Netherlands: Open University.

Romalina, E., Ramachandran, S., Fu, D., Stottler, R., & Howse, W.R. (2004). Intelligent Simulation-Based Tutor for Flight Training. Paper presented at the Interservice/Industry Training, Simulation, and Education Conference (I/ITSEC) (pp 1-13). Paper no 1743. Orlando, FL: I/ITSEC.

Van der Pal, J. (2003). *ADAPT^{IT} Final Report – Scientific Version*. Deliverable 9.3 prepared for the European Commission INFSO under contract no. IST-1999-11740. NLR-TR-2003-496 (downloadable from www.adaptit.org).

Van Merriënboer J.J.G. (1997). *Training Complex Cognitive Skills, a four component instructional design method for technical training*. Englewood Cliffs NJ: Educational Technology Publications.

Van Merriënboer, J.J.G., Luursema, J.J., Kingma, H., Houweling, F., & de Vries, A. P. (1995). Fuzzy logic instructional models: The dynamic construction of programming assignments in CASCO. In R.D. Tennyson and A.E. Barron (Eds.), *Automating instructional design: Computerbased development and delivery tools* (pp. 184-206). Berlin, Germany: Springer Verlag.

Cognitive requirements analysis to derive training models for controlling complex systems

Dina Burkolter[1], Annette Kluge[1], Kerstin Schüler[1],
Jürgen Sauer[2], & Sandrina Ritzmann[1]
[1]University of St. Gallen
[2]University of Fribourg
Switzerland

Abstract

Although simulators are widely used for training of process control tasks, simulator trainings are conducted with little consideration of research results on cognition, training design or effectiveness (Salas et al., 2006). Therefore, a hierarchical task analysis described through the sub-goal templates method, a cognitive reliability and error analysis method and a protocol analysis were applied to the Cabin Air Management System (CAMS), a process control simulation. Thirty-nine apprentices participated in a CAMS training and a test session a week later. System stabilisation and fault diagnosis as criteria as well as person-related variables such as general mental abilities, cognitive style, self-efficacy and personality traits were measured and think aloud protocols collected. Main results of the first study of the research project are presented. Each of the task analysis methods separately contributed to describe cognitive requirements. There were qualitative differences between good and poor performers, particularly with respect to decision errors, errors in sequencing and timing as well as explaining, forming rules and planning. Furthermore, person-related variables explained an additional proportion of variance. Based on these findings and the results of training research, methods of drill and practice, overlearning and error training are recommended.

Introduction

While simulator training is popular in varying work environments such as aviation or navigation as well as process control (e.g. nuclear power plants, oil refineries) the training method is applied with little consideration of research regarding training design, cognition or effectiveness (Salas et al., 2006). For this reason, Salas et al. encourage the integration of scientific findings on training with simulator application, design, and practice. With respect to training design, task analysis is an essential first step, yet Ryder and Redding (1993) consider it to be "the most crucial and resource-intensive phase in the development of any training program" (p. 77). Task analysis provides the information on which decisions about training design are based (Ryder & Redding, 1993). Furthermore, learning objectives and criteria can be derived through training needs analysis (Salas et al., 2006). There is mostly agreement on the significance of training needs analyses in training literature. However, Tannenbaum and Yukl (1992) found only a limited amount of empirical work on training needs analysis in an earlier literature review, which still seems to be the case. Therefore, in order to collect information on which the training development can be based, a task analysis was applied to a process control task. The focus was on cognitive requirements since in process control operators have to deal with complex systems which is a cognitive oriented task.

To assess and describe the task as well as the cognitive requirements, traditional and cognitive task analysis approaches are combined. The combination of different methods is recommended in literature (e.g. Cooke, 1994; Kirwan & Ainsworth, 1992; Stanton et al., 2005; Wei & Salvendy, 2004). Cooke (1994) states that combining different methods is "the best way to minimize potential measurement errors and to maximize the scope of domain coverage" and that it helps to "ensure that knowledge elicitation is thorough and accurate" (p. 838). Wei and Salvendy (2004) distinguish between traditional task analysis and cognitive task analysis (CTA) approaches. Traditional task analysis focuses on behavior, manual task procedures, and observable processes, while CTA addresses cognition and mental models. Chipman et al. (2000) defined CTA as "the extension of traditional task analysis techniques to yield information about the knowledge, thought processes, and goal structures that underlie observable task performance" (p. 3).

There are a few publications that mention data on validity and reliability of the task analysis methods used or described (Annett, 2002; Annett & Stanton, 2006). However, as Annett (2002) suggests, different considerations apply to analytic and evaluative ergonomics methods with respect to validity and reliability. While the primary purpose of analytic methods (e.g. task analysis, training needs analysis) is the understanding of the system, the primary purpose of evaluative methods (e.g. workload measurement) is to measure a parameter. The analogy with psychometrics applies to the latter, but as Annett states, is less appropriate to analytic methods. The validity of task analysis methods depends on underlying theoretical constructs, and the reliability on the data collection that has to correspond to the underlying model (Annett, 2002). In this study, analytic and evaluative methods are combined. In a first step, the goal is to gain an understanding about the task and its requirements which is done by applying task analysis methods and in a second step, the goal is to assess the predictive quality of person-related variables for the performance of process control. So, to enhance validity and reliability different approaches are applied, firstly, by combining different task analysis methods to – as stated above – enlarge the coverage of the analysis and secondly, performance is measured. In addition to validity and reliability, usability has to be considered (Annett & Stanton, 2006).

Method

To derive cognitive requirements of process control for training development, several task analysis approaches were applied to CAMS (Cabin Air Management System; e.g. Sauer, Wastell & Hockey, 2000; see Figure 1). CAMS is a micro-world that simulates a spacecraft's automated life support system. Its underlying principles correspond to a process control task. CAMS consists of five subsystems that maintain the five main system variables (O_2, pressure, CO_2, temperature and humidity) within a predefined range. The operator has to accomplish two primary tasks, system stabilisation and fault diagnosis as well as two secondary tasks, acknowledgement of alarms and tank level recordings at a regular interval (Sauer, Wastell & Hockey, 2000). Fault diagnosis refers to the number of correct repair actions in case of system faults, whereas system stabilisation is measured as the time (in seconds) that any of the parameter is out of the predefined range. Actions taken by participants and system states are automatically recorded in a log file (Sauer, Wastell & Hockey, 2000).

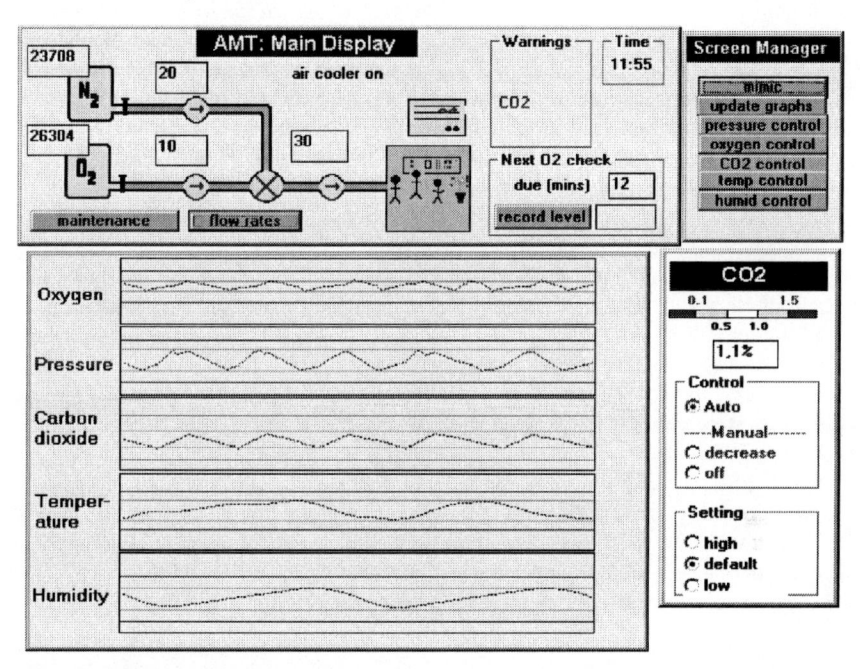

Figure 1. Main interface of CAMS

The task analysis is based on several sources of information, such as a literature review, the analysis of CAMS and its documentation, experimental data from CAMS and data from a protocol analysis with CAMS. As a first step, a hierarchical task analysis (HTA; Annett & Duncan, 1967) was conducted. The HTA served as a basis or rather framework (Shepherd, 1998) for further analysis, the cognitive task analysis (CTA; e.g. Wei & Salvendy, 2004). A helpful tool to describe the HTA is the subgoal templates method (SGT; Ormerod, Richardson & Shepherd, 1998; Ormerod & Shepherd, 2004) because it provides a nomenclature and classification for tasks that operators in process control have to accomplish (Ormerod & Shepherd, 2004). To assess possible human errors while controlling complex systems, an error analysis based on the cognitive reliability and error analysis method (CREAM; Hollnagel, 1998) was carried out. CREAM contains a method, a classification scheme and a model which had been developed from the analysis of existing human reliability approaches. Its main goal is to provide a practical approach to performance analysis as well as performance prediction (Hollnagel, 1998). With respect to performance prediction, experimental results support "the notion that error modes can be predicted in a qualitative sense" (Hollnagel et al., 1999). Since CREAM is not a hierarchical classification scheme, but rather flexibly connects classification groups (Hollnagel, 1998), it can be adapted to CAMS and its data. The last step was to conduct a protocol analysis. The think aloud protocols were transcribed, bundled to statements and then categorised.

In the experiment, 39 chemical laboratory apprentices, 20 female and 19 male (18 years on average), participated in a five-hour training on CAMS. There were no significant differences in the test score (0-50 points) for general mental abilities between female ($M = 25.3$ points, $SD = 5.4$) and male participants ($M = 26.1$ points, $SD = 4.8$; $t = -.46$, $df = 37$, $p > .05$). A test session was held one week later which included the recording of think aloud protocols ($n = 31$) while controlling CAMS and diagnosing a novel fault for a duration of five minutes. Performance measures were system stabilisation and fault diagnosis. The sample which is used for the analyses is smaller than 39 due to missing data and the exclusion of two outliers regarding system stabilisation, which were more than 1.5 or 3 interquartile ranges away from the interquartile range. For a post-hoc comparison of extreme-groups, a group of each 25% of good as well as poor performers (each $n = 7$) were formed according to the two criteria of performance in system stabilisation and fault diagnosis. The selection of the sub-samples was in accordance with the standard deviations of the CAMS performance measures, but to ensure a sufficient sample size, 25% were chosen. Knowledge about the system and the relationships between the parameters was assessed through a questionnaire (see also Sauer, Hockey & Wastell, 2000). In addition, person-related variables such as general mental abilities, cognitive style (Cognitive Flexibility Inventory; Spiro, Feltovich & Coulson, 1996; Cronbach's Alpha = .61), pre-training self-efficacy (Schyns & Collani, 2002; Cronbach's Alpha = .82) and personality traits were controlled for (Big Five Markers; Saucier, 1994; conscientiousness/openness/emotional stability; Cronbach's Alpha = .76/.74/.91).

Results

In the following section main results of the first study are presented. The process control task CAMS was analysed, the differences between good and poor performers in CAMS were explored and interrelations between CAMS performance measures and cognitive aspects were examined.

The HTA (see Figure 2) could provide a framework for further analysis of process control. By means of SGTs the tasks which are required to be accomplished in CAMS were described. There are two main tasks in process control: On the one hand, to monitor the system state and on the other hand to intervene, if there is a departure from a safe system state, that is diagnosis and repair (see also Wickens, 1992). The latter includes immediate system stabilisation and manual control. Presented in a tabular format, the HTA allows assigning types of knowledge to the tasks which provides further information for the design of training. Regarding the two main tasks of process control, monitoring requires mainly declarative knowledge whereas diagnosis and repair require mostly procedural knowledge. Based on the HTA with SGTs it was not only possible to group the system faults of CAMS according to type of fault and parameter, but also according to the steps that have to be accomplished for diagnosis and repair. In training design, this classification helps choosing system faults to use in the training and the test session.

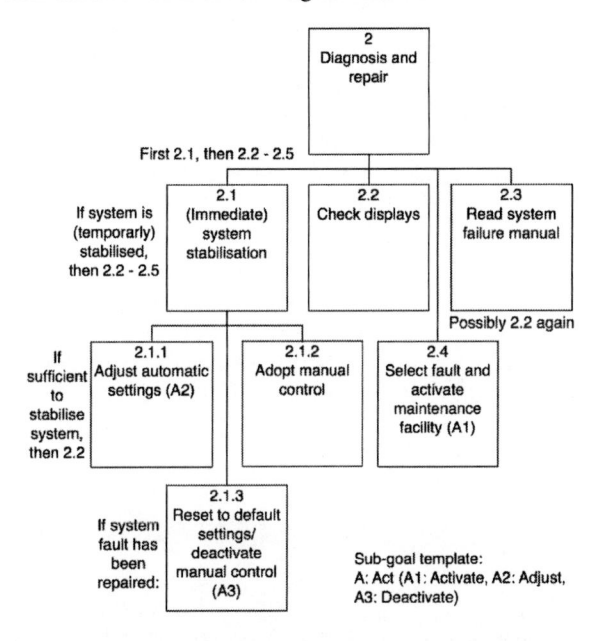

Figure 2. Extract of the hierarchical task analysis described through sub-goal templates (Ormerod et al., 1998; Ormerod & Shepherd, 2004)

Based on the log files (collected during the verbal protocols), errors made by participants diagnosing a novel fault were analysed. In general, errror modes (basic phenotypes) and person related genotypes (Hollnagel, 1998) were surveyed. However, categories such as actions of wrong type (force, distance, speed and direction), wrong reasoning, categories for temporary and permanent person related functions either did not apply to CAMS or could not be deduced from the available data. Thus, those categories were not included in the analysis.

Participants committed most errors concerning decision, sequencing and timing. Decision errors refer to making the wrong decisions, typically when there are action alternatives. In CAMS this would be the case, when the automatic controllers have to be adjusted and/or manual control has to be adopted. Furthermore, there were errors concerning actions at the wrong time and sequencing. The specific effects for actions at the wrong time are errors of timing and errors of duration. While participants started actions too late or did not execute required actions at all, no actions were conducted too early. With respect to sequencing, participants omitted actions, jumped forward or did wrong actions. There were qualitative differences between participants with good and poor performance in system stabilisation and fault finding. Poor performers committed one and a half to two times as many errors as good performers depending on the performance measure. Besides, poor performers made about twice as many wrong decisions as good performers.

Table 1. Frequencies of task management activities for the performance measures of CAMS for different groups and corresponding sub-goal templates (SGTs)

Task management activities	SGTs[1]	System stabilisation Good performers	System stabilisation Poor performers	Fault finding Good performers	Fault finding Poor performers	Total
System Monitoring	M1, M2, M3, C4	34.0%	40.5%	33.2%	42.0%	39.6%
Diagnosis and repair of system fault	A1, C4, C7, D1, E2	2.0%	3.6%	2.7%	2.2%	2.3%
Explain, form rules, plan		10.2%	7.7%	11.4%	7.2%	8.5%
Evaluate action	D4	12.2%	9.2%	13.6%	12.3%	11.6%
Call up control panels	C4, C7, E2	9.6%	10.3%	6.5%	10.9%	11.1%
Adjust control panels	A2, A3	8.6%	10.8%	9.2%	8.7%	8.9%
Consult/read manual	C1, D1	3.0%	2.6%	2.2%	5.1%	3.0%
Secondary task 1: Notice warning	C4	7.6%	6.2%	8.2%	2.2%	6.0%
Secondary task 1: Acknowledge warning	A3	7.6%	6.2%	6.5%	5.1%	4.7%
Secondary task 2: Check system clock	C3, C6	1.5%	1.0%	2.7%	0.7%	1.4%
Secondary task 2: Record tank level	C1, C2, E2	2.5%	1.5%	2.7%	2.9%	2.0%
Secondary task 2: Failed recording of system time	C6	1.0%	0.5%	1.1%	0.7%	0.9%
Total		100%	100%	100%	100%	100%

Note. Total: n = 29, good and poor performers: each n = 7. [1]According to Ormerod et al. (1998) as well as Ormerod and Shepherd (2004)

The think aloud protocols of the participants diagnosing a novel fault were categorised corresponding to the SGTs. However, the analysis showed that the SGTs needed to be grouped and adapted to CAMS (see Table 1). Besides, an additional category was introduced: To explain causes, relations or actions with regard to the CAMS task, to form a rule or to plan an action. This modification of the actions and thought processes to the CAMS task also helped enhance the inter-rater agreement between two independent raters. The inter-rater reliability coefficient (Cohen's Kappa) indicates an acceptable agreement (mean Kappa = 0.78).

System monitoring (39.6%), evaluating actions (11.6%) and to call up control panels (11.1%) were the most frequent task management activities, followed by adjusting control panels (8.9%) together with explaining, forming rules and planning (8.5%). The categories linked to the secondary task, which is tank level recording, are the least frequent (check system clock, record tank level and record system time, 0.9% to 2.0%). The largest difference between good and poor performers both in system stabilisation performance as well as in fault finding performance was found in explaining, forming rules and planning. Good performers explained, formed rules and planned up to one and a half times as much as poor performers (10.2% vs. 7.7%, 11.4% vs. 7.2% respectively). On the other hand, poor performers in both performance measures monitored the system more frequently (40.5% vs. 34.0%, 42.0% vs. 33.2% respectively). There were also differences between good and poor performance in task management activities regarding the secondary tasks (notice warning, check system clock, record system time), but they were less significant concerning their total frequency.

Person-related variables explained additional variance in CAMS performance (see Table 2). General mental abilities correlated significantly with system stabilisation ($r = -.31, p < .05$), that is, the higher the score in general mental abilities, the better the performance in system stabilisation. General mental abilities were also correlated significantly with system knowledge ($r = .41, p < .01$). So, the higher the performance in general mental abilities, the better the performance in system stabilisation as well as in system knowledge.

Table 2. *Intercorrelations between performance measures of CAMS and person-related variables*

	1	2	3	4	5	6	7	8
1. System stabilisation	–							
2. Fault finding	-.06	–						
3. System knowledge	-.43**	.13	–					
4. GMA	-.31*	.17	.41**	–				
5. Cognitive style	.34*	.31*	.06	.17	–			
6. Self-efficacy	-.18	.24	.15	.10	.09	–		
7. Conscientiousness	-.15	.22	-.05	-.04	.07	.43**	–	
8. Openness	-.04	.14	.14	-.05	.18	.24	.61**	–
9. Emotional stability	-.02	-.00	-.27	.09	.09	.07	.03	-.05

Note. n = 36. Spearman-Correlations. System stabilisation: The lower the score, the better the performance. GMA = General Mental Abilities. * $p < .05$, ** $p < .01$ (one-tailed)

Furthermore, cognitive style was significantly correlated with system stabilisation ($r = .34, p < .05$) and fault finding ($r = .31, p < .05$). Cognitive style refers to a reductive or an expansive world-view (Spiro et al., 1996). Participants who had a reductive world-view, i.e. prefer rigid prescriptions from memory and have an intolerance for ambiguity, tended to perform better in system stabilisation. On the other hand, participants with an expansive and flexible world-view who have a preference for complexity, performed better in fault finding. Other person-related variables such as self-efficacy and personality traits were not significantly correlated with the CAMS performance measures. The intercorrelations between the performance measures showed that while system knowledge and system stabilisation were significantly correlated ($r = -.43$, $p < .01$), system knowledge and fault finding were not ($r = .13$, $p > .05$). That is, the better the score in system knowledge, the better the performance in system stabilisation. System stabilisation and fault finding were not significantly correlated either ($r = -.06$, $p > .05$).

Discussion

The applied task analysis approaches contributed each in different ways to describe the task and its cognitive requirements and each revealed different aspects. This finding supports the notion to combine different task analysis methods in order to reduce potential measurement errors and to ensure a thorough analysis (Cooke, 1994). HTA and SGTs helped describe tasks and subtasks and gave an overview; but only the error analysis with CREAM could point out which aspects to emphasise in training design. With respect to usability and practical purposes CREAM in comparison with HTA, SGT and protocol analysis appears to give the opportunity to identify concrete training needs or possible performance failure for users who are not familiar with the analysis method. The findings implicate that intermediate steps between the task analysis and training design may be necessary, because deriving conclusions for training design directly from the task analysis does not always seem possible. Some potential limitations to the findings have to be considered due to the circumstance that there is little data available on validity and reliability, consequently the question of validity and reliability remains. However, as Annett (2002) states, different aspects have to be taken into account regarding analytic and evaluative methods.

To summarise, the following aspects and cognitive requirements seem to relate to performance in CAMS. To be able to control the process control task CAMS as successfully as possible, the findings indicate that decision errors, as well as errors in sequencing and timing along with giving explanations, forming rules and planning one's actions in CAMS have to be considered. Thus, the learning objectives derived from these findings are to instruct trainees to avoid decision, sequencing and timing errors and further, to enhance the ability of the trainees to explain, form rules and plan one's actions while controlling a complex system.

Additionally, characteristics of the task have to be taken into account in training design. The performance measures system stabilisation and fault finding are not significantly correlated. Additionally, knowledge about the system is significantly correlated with system stabilisation, but not with fault finding. These results correspond to Wickens' notion (1992) that the control aspects and the diagnosing aspects of process control differ from one another. In system control the focus is on the forward flow of events ("what causes what"), whereas in diagnosis and repair the events have to be reversed ("what was caused by what"; Landeweerd, 1979; Wickens, 1992, p. 509). This difference has to be considered in training design, thus different training methods for system control and diagnosis should be applied to enhance training outcomes.

Apart from learning objectives, preconditions, that is person-related aspects of the trainees, have to be taken into account for training design. As the findings showed, person-related variables help to explain performance in controlling a complex system. General mental abilities are correlated with system stabilisation and knowledge of the system. Additionally, cognitive style, that is a preference for a reductive or an expansive world-view, is related to system stabilisation and fault finding. Thus, training has to be designed according to these requirements. Furthermore, the present findings and research in training indicate methods of drill and practice, overlearning and error training have to be considered for the successful learning of the skills and requirements of process control. In order to plan an error training (e.g. Salas et al., 2006), the findings of the CREAM analysis are helpful to decide which errors to train primarily. Drill and practice as well as overlearning (e.g. Driskell et al., 1992) can be especially helpful to learn tasks with an emphasis on sequencing.

Acknowledgement

This project is funded by the Swiss National Science Foundation.

References

Annett, J. (2002). A note on the validity and reliability of ergonomics methods. *Theoretical Issues in Ergonomics Science, 3*, 229-232.
Annett, J. & Duncan, K. (1967). Task analysis and Training Design. *Occupational Psychology, 41*, 211-221.
Annett, J. & Stanton, N. (2006). Task Analysis. *International Review of Industrial and Organizational Psychology, 21*, 45-78.
Chipman, S., Schraagen, J., & Shalin, V. (2000). Introduction to cognitive task analysis. In S. Chipman, J. Schraagen and V. Shalin (Eds.), *Cognitive task analysis* (pp. 3-24). Mahwah, NJ, US: Lawrence Erlbaum Associates.
Cooke, N. (1994). Varieties of knowledge elicitation techniques. *International Journal of Human Computer Studies, 41*, 801-849.
Driskell, J.E., Willis, R.P. & Copper, C. (1992). Effect of overlearning on retention. *Journal of Applied Psychology, 77*, 615-622.
Hollnagel, E. (1998). *Cognitive reliability and error analysis method.* Oxford: Elsevier Science Ltd.
Hollnagel, E., Kaarstad, M., & Lee, H.-C. (1999). Error mode prediction. *Ergonomics, 42*, 1457-1471.
Kirwan, B. & Ainsworth, L. (1992). *A guide to task analysis.* London: Taylor & Francis.
Landeweerd, J.A. (1979). Internal representation of a process, fault diagnosis and fault correction. *Ergonomics, 22*, 1343-1351.

Ormerod, T.C., Richardson, J., & Shepherd, A. (1998). Enhancing the usability of a task analysis method: a notation and environment for requirements specification. *Ergonomics, 41*, 1642-1663.

Ormerod, T.C. & Shepherd, A. (2004). Using task analysis for information requirements specification: The sub-goal template (SGT) method. In D. Diaper and N.A. Stanton (Eds.), *The handbook of task analysis for human-computer interaction* (pp. 347-365). Mahwah: Lawrence Erlbaum Associates.

Ryder, J. & Redding, R. (1993). Integrating cognitive task analysis into instructional systems development. *Educational Technology Research and Development, 41*, 75-96.

Salas, E., Wilson, K.A., Priest, A., & Guthrie, J.W. (2006). Design, delivery, and evaluation of training systems. In G. Salvendy (Ed.), *Handbook of Human Factors and Ergonomics* (pp. 472-512). Hoboken, NJ: Wiley & Sons.

Saucier, G. (1994). Mini-Markers: A brief version of Goldbergs unipolar big-five markers. *Journal of Personality Assessment, 63*, 506-516.

Sauer, J., Wastell, D., & Hockey, G.R.J. (2000). A conceptual framework for designing microworlds for complex work domains: a case study of the Cabin Air Management System. *Computers and Human Behavior, 16*, 45-58.

Sauer, J., Hockey, G.R.J., & Wastell, D.G. (2000). Effects of training on short- and long-term skill retention in a complex multiple-task environment. *Ergonomics, 43*, 12, 2043-2064.

Schyns, B. & Collani, G. (2002). A new occupational self-efficacy scale and its relation to personality constructs and organizational variables. *European Journal of Work and Organizational Psychology, 11*, 219–241.

Shepherd, A. (1998). HTA as a framework for task analysis. *Ergonomics, 41*, 1537-1552.

Spiro, R. J., Feltovich, P.J., & Coulson, R.L. (1996). Two epistemic world-view: prefigurative schemas and learning in complex domains. *Applied Cognitive Psychology, 10*, 51-61.

Stanton, N., Salmon, P., Walker, G., Baber, C., & Jenkins, D. (2005). *Human factors methods: A practical guide for engineering and design.* Aldershot: Ashgate.

Tannenbaum, S.I. & Yukl, G. (1992). Training and development in work organizations. *Annual Review of Psychology, 43*, 399-441.

Wei, J. & Salvendy, G. (2004). The cognitive task analysis methods for job and task design: review and reappraisal. *Behaviour & Information Technology, 23*, 273-299.

Wickens, C.D. (1992). *Engineering psychology and human performance* (2nd ed.). New York: HarperCollins Publishers Inc.

How should causal knowledge about complex technical systems be trained?

Anne Klostermann
Centre of Human-Machine Systems, TU Berlin
Berlin, Germany

Abstract

A theoretical approach is presented for the support of causal knowledge acquisition in interaction with complex technical systems through training. De Kleer and Brown's theory of mechanistic mental models serves as the basis for a framework for both causal knowledge acquisition and application. Issues for operator training in complex systems are deduced. Three training modules are presented that attempt to impart knowledge about how the system works at different levels of system simulation and interaction. A pilot study explored a first operationalisation of the training modules and the applicability of a selected microworld for the investigation of causal model acquisition. Results showed that training according to the framework leads to appropriate causal knowledge acquisition. Results further revealed that the simulation in use is not complex enough. Future work will address more complex simulation environments and the operationalisation and implementation of all three training modules.

Introduction

Operators in safety critical systems rely on their internal representations of the causal functioning of the system when performing process control tasks. These causal models can be understood as a special form of mental models (Thüring, 1991; Einhorn & Hogarth, 1986) that describe knowledge about causes and effects. They enable operators to perform various tasks such as prediction of future system states, search for system abnormalities and breakdowns, and select appropriate system interventions (Hollnagel, 1998). Thus operator training strategies have to consider theories about causal knowledge acquisition. Various theories describe how users develop mental models during interaction with complex systems (e.g. Rasmussen, 1979; Moray, 1996). An approach to describe how causal models of technical devices are acquired is presented by de Kleer and Brown (1983). They identify four relevant aspects for the development of a causal model. The first aspect is the device topology (1), which is basically the representation of the components and the structure of a given device. Device topology forms the input for a qualitative simulation process, the envisioning (2). To determine the overall functioning of the device, every single component has to be represented, and associated components have to be connected. The output of this deduction process is the causal model (3). It represents the functioning of the device. This causal model can also be mentally simulated in a higher order qualitative simulation (4), "running of the causal model", e.g. to predict specific behaviour of the device.

Causal models of complex systems

The approach of de Kleer and Brown is concerned with the acquisition of a mental representation of a simple technical device, but it does not extend to the acquisition of causal models in complex human-machine interaction. Two aspects have to be considered: (1) in a dynamic and complex work system, in particular the interplay of process components and system components has to be represented, and (2) mere mental simulation of a process and its components does not suffice; direct and active interaction with the system is required for causal model acquisition. The structure of the proposed framework is closely linked to de Kleer and Brown's theoretical assumptions. However, it also refers to the two aforementioned aspects.

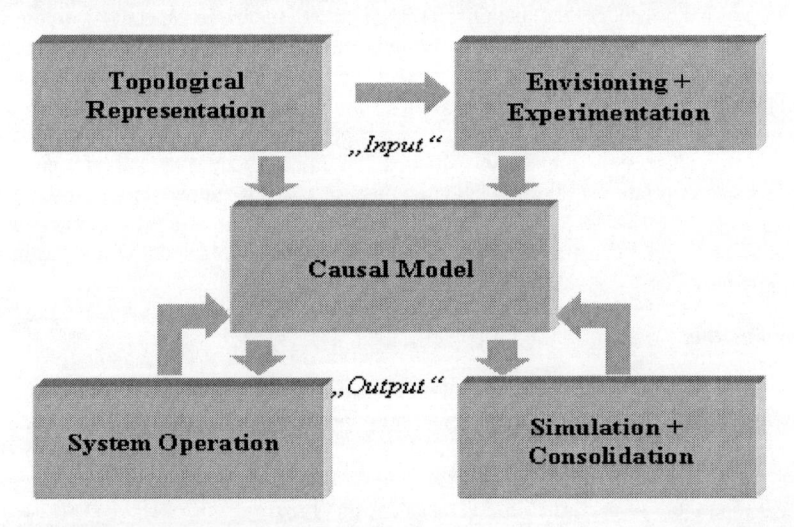

Figure 1. Causal knowledge of complex systems

Topological representation

De Kleer and Brown argue that the operator has to develop a topological representation of each system component. This does not suffice for complex systems; two aspects are required for the creation of a topological representation: the operator has to represent component models of the underlying process, and build up a representation of the system components and the interaction options.

Envisioning and experimentation

The envisioning process is a stepwise adjustment and differentiation process, where assumptions are set up and rejected. Yet De Kleer and Brown do not say how false assumptions can be detected or rejected through mere mental simulation. Within the proposed framework, it is suggested that assumptions about cause and effect have to be verified during direct interaction with the system. In order to develop a cause and effect model of the system operation, the operator also has to actively interact with the system and test hypotheses about potential system behaviour.

Causal model

The causal model represents the functioning of the system. The question here is whether this knowledge is conditional or causal. In the proposed framework, it is assumed that causal knowledge is more than knowing "if A..., then B", it is more than knowing *how* a system works. Having a causal model of a complex system makes it possible to argue *why* components are related in a cause and effect manner.

Simulation and consolidation

De Kleer and Brown assume that learners relate solely to their causal model, and that this model does not need to be reviewed again. The framework proposed here differs in that it is assumed that learning to handle a complex system requires steps of iteration during the learning process, and that mental simulation alters, consolidates or corrects the causal model.

System operation

On the basis of existing knowledge and new environmental information, causal models need to be continually reconstructed, adjusted or extended. In the proposed model, the feedback loop between system operation and causal model reflects this assumption.

Training requirements

A training strategy closely related to the presented framework assumptions should result in effective causal knowledge acquisition. Three training modules were derived from the above presented framework.

Module 1: Visualisation

Topological representations of the process and the system have to be trained in a way that prepares for the subsequent envisioning process. This includes the visualisation of process components and the structured preparation of components models (e.g. through rule-based presentation).

Module 2: Structuring support

In this module, both envisioning and interaction with the system will be supported using structured guidance, to support the "gluing together" (De Kleer & Brown, 1983) of component models to build a causal model of the system.

Module 3: Modification and consolidation

The aim of this module is to support learners in consolidating their causal model. Learners will be instructed to qualitatively simulate and interact with the process and system on a more sophisticated level. Qualitative simulation will be triggered through presetting probe questions and error scenarios. System interaction will take place both under normal operation condition and under breakdowns.

Current and future work

It is assumed that a training closely related to the above discussed modules will result in an appropriate causal model of the system to be controlled. In human-machine interaction research, simulations of complex systems are commonly applied for experimental purposes. However, for the purpose of investigating training strategies, the experimental task has to be sensitive enough to allow differentiating between the performances of well-trained and of untrained or poorly trained subjects.

Pilot study

The PESSE micro-world (Urbas, 1999) is a simulation of a distillation process where the operator's task is to maintain a tank level in a given range. An empirical pilot study was conducted to test whether the selected micro-world was sensitive for investigating training tools according to the three training modules presented above.

Design

A 2x10 factorial design with repeated measures on one factor was implemented with the between factor training (training and exploration) and the within factor trial (repeated measures for trial 1-10) as independent variables. Dependent variables were the quality of performance in system interaction and the quality of subject's system knowledge.

Procedure

Ten subjects were instructed in performing a process control task. Subjects of the training group received a training according to module one. The training consisted of a topological visualisation and of rule-based information about the interplay of the distillation process components. Subjects of the exploration group received a short description of the main components of the process control system without a description of the interrelations. Subsequent to the training session, subjects had to perform the process control task with the simulated distillation process. They had to carry out ten trials of approximately two minutes length each. Performance in system interaction was indicated by the percentage of time a subject maintained the tank level within the given range. After finishing all ten trials, subjects had to fill out a knowledge questionnaire with multiple choice and open questions.

Results

Results regarding subject's performance revealed no significant differences for the factor training (F(1,10) = 2.54, NS), pointing out that trained and untrained subjects did not differ with respect to their performance(F(1,8) = 2.54, NS). However, there was a significant main effect for the factor trial (F (9,10) = 4.41, p<.05), meaning that performance for initial trials was poorer compared to performance in later trials(F (9,72) = 4.41, p < .05), and furthermore indicating a ceiling effect for both groups after four trials.

Results regarding the quality of system knowledge revealed no significant differences between trained and untrained subjects, both regarding the multiple choice questions (T=1.823, NS) and the open questions (T= 1.213, NS).

Conclusions

Since no differences both in performance and in system knowledge between trained and untrained subjects could be found, it can be assumed that the applied simulation of a distillation process is not complex enough to investigate different training strategies. Thus, subsequent studies have to apply a more complex simulation of a technical system. Future experiments concerning the operationalisation and implementation of training modules will provide information about how causal models of complex systems should be imparted.

Acknowledgement

This research project is part of the research training group prometei programme and financed by the German Research Foundation (DFG, project number 1013).

References

De Kleer, J. & Brown, J.S. (1983). Assumptions and Ambiguities in Mechanistic Mental Models. In D. Gentner and A.L. Stevens (Eds.): *Mental Models* (pp. 150-190). Hillsdale, N.J.: Lawrence Erlbaum Associates.

Einhorn, H. & Hogarth, R.M. (1986). Judging Probable Cause. *Psychological Bulletin, 99-1,* 3-19.

Hollnagel, E. (1998). *Cognitive Reliability and Error Analysis Method (CREAM).* Oxford: Elsevier Science Ltd.

Moray, N. (1996). *A taxonomy and theory of mental models.* Proceedings of the Human Factors and Ergonomics Society 40th Annual Meeting. Santa Monica, CA: HFES.

Rasmussen, J. (1979). *On the structure of knowledge – A morphology of mental models in a man-machine system context.* Riso Report M 2192. Roskilde, Denmark: Risø National Laboratory.

Thüring, M. (1991). *Probabilistisches Denken in kausalen Modellen.* Weinheim, Germany: Psychologie-Verl.-Union.

Urbas, L. (1999). *Entwicklung und Realisierung einer Trainings- und Ausbildungsumgebung zur Schulung der Prozessdynamik und des Anlagenbetriebs im Internet.* (Progress report VDI Reihe 19, No.614). Dissertation. Düsseldorf, Germany: VDI-Verlag.

Training operators in Micro-World simulations

Michael H. Roberts, Adam C. Roberts, Peter Nickel, & G. Robert J. Hockey
The University of Sheffield
Sheffield, United Kingdom

Abstract

Highly complex simulations of work environments allow controllable, repeatable experiments, while retaining the opacity and dynamic events that occur in real world situations. However, such tasks require considerable training to ensure the high levels of skill assumed by their use as analogues of real world tasks. We studied the acquisition of operator skill in using AUTOCAMS, a process control task based on a cabin air management system, using a training programme that emphasised both knowledge-based and rule-based instruction, and both practical and knowledge-based assessments of task skill. The results showed evidence of differential acquisition rates for procedural skill and both rule- and system-based knowledge, with slower learning for system knowledge than for the other two components. The findings have implications for training of operators in complex micro-world simulations.

Introduction

There can be little doubt that extensive practice on a complex task is critical for dealing with system disturbances. However, there is some uncertainty about what should be practiced. The traditional practice specificity argument suggests that training will be more effective under conditions that mimic real-world situations, whilst other studies have found that practising a number of different task variations results in better generalisation over task conditions (e.g., Schmidt, 1975; Hall & Magill, 1995), because of the development of (more flexible) schema or mental models. A separate issue relates to the separation of procedural skills (task performance) and task knowledge, or implicit and explicit learning (e.g., Berry & Broadbent, 1988), typically accompanied by differential acquisition rates (Rasmussen, 1983).

Our approach was informed by Rasmussen's (1983) classification of operator behaviour during the control of complex systems; skill-based behaviour (SBB), based on automated responses to highly familiar events; rule-based behaviour (RBB), associated with diagnosing routine situations where routine procedures are available; and knowledge-based behaviour (KBB), where high level reasoning must be used to deal with unfamiliar problems, or those where there are no existing procedures. To study acquisition patterns we trained participants on autoCAMS, a semi-automatic complex process control simulation (e.g., Sauer et al., 2000). Using an earlier version of this simulation Hockey et al. (2007) found that system knowledge transferred better than rule-based knowledge to managing unfamiliar and complex faults, though it was less robust under conditions of noise stress. The present training regime was designed to emphasise both RBB and KBB strategies, and acquisition assessed by a series of tests designed to assess RBB and KBB skill, and both procedural and system knowledge.

Method

Participants

Eighteen postgraduate participants were recruited from computer science and engineering departments of The University of Sheffield, in order to ensure a high level of basic task competence and technical literacy. After the training and assessment, eleven participants displayed sufficient skill in the control task (and were willing) to progress to the experimental phase.

Task and training

An automation-enhanced modification (autoCAMS; Lorenz et al., 2002) of the Cabin Air Management System (CAMS; Hockey et al., 1998; Sauer et al., 2000) served as the process control environment. This task requires operators to monitor and control a semi-automatic system that controls the atmospheric environment of a closed-air system (e.g. a space capsule or submersible). Operators interact with a visual display that provides data on system variables (pressure, temperature etc.) and controllable functions (for a more detailed description, see Nickel et al., 2007).

Training involved an extensive six-week course (6 sessions, 2 hours each), including three assessment sessions, interactive tutorials, lectures on system dynamics and printed rule-based fault fixing guides, as well as lab tasks and take-away tests throughout. Skill acquisition was measured by standardised assessments at the beginning, middle and end of the programme, involving procedural and declarative knowledge, and system and rule based skills. Training began with an introduction to the CAMS onscreen mimic interface, and the subsystem diagram. Theoretical discussions about the subsystems involved reasoning the functions and effects of each subsystem and the direct and indirect interactions between each subsystem. This was supplemented with a detailed manual, before being linked to the CAMS interface.

The operators were required to maintain the system under both fault-free (FF) and fault scenarios. They encountered each fault type in practical tasks, and were required to identify that the system was in error, describe what part of the system was in error, and then discuss the possible causes for such a problem and what possible methods could be used to restore system stability through manual control. They were then required to discuss methods for determining which subsystem could be causing the error and what fault may have occurred, using knowledge of previously encountered fault types. In this way, operators created their own rule-based strategies. When the training was completed, this was supplemented with an addition to the manual including fault management strategies and a fault-finding guide. To facilitate a high level of system familiarity, a home version of the simulation was supplied, and operators were given assessed "take-away tests" after each training session as well as being encouraged to practice in their spare time

Practical assessment

Each practical assessment included three fault states involving differing levels of monitoring, maintenance of parameters and diagnostic behaviour. The fault-free (FF) condition required only monitoring activity; the simple fault (SF) condition required diagnosis of an oxygen valve leak, repair and maintenance of oxygen levels; and the complex fault (CF) condition involved two separate faults that needed to be diagnosed, repaired and normal levels maintained. As a separate test of acquisition of primary task procedural skill, they also carried out a supplementary alarm reaction time (ART) task, responding to false alarms by clicking the mouse button. As a secondary task, this is likely to reveal continued learning even when control performance is stable (Anderson, 1981).

Knowledge assessment

Knowledge was assessed by means of a specially devised questionnaire, consisting of three sections: a rule-based (R) set of questions; and two system-based sets – prompted closed questions (SK1), and more general open-ended questions (SK2).

Results

The results are summarised in Figure 1, which shows changes over the learning period in procedural skill on the primary task, secondary task alarm RT, and knowledge.

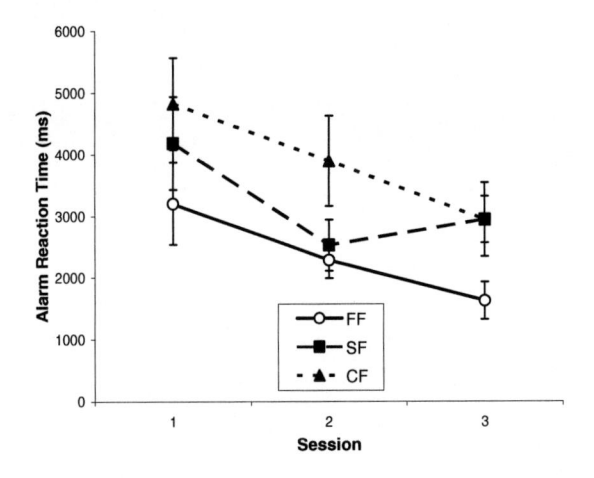

Figure 1. Effects of practice on acquisition of system control performance (FF = fault free, SF = simple fault, CF = complex fault)

Procedural learning

As can be seen from Figure 1, control error (the time that the system is out of range) falls across sessions (F(2,18)=24.95, p<.001), though shows no improvement between sessions 2 and 3, except for the CF condition, in which it takes longer for a ceiling effect to be attained. Evidence for continued leaning in the baseline (FF) condition is provided by Figure 2, which shows a monotonic fall in ART over the three sessions (F(2,18)=5.67, p <.05), as the demands of the primary task fall with further practice (Anderson, 1993). Predictably, the data also reveal a strong effect of fault difficulty on ART (F(2,18)=9.49, p<0.01), as found in other autoCAMS studies (Hockey et al., 1998, 2007; Sauer et al., 2000). The time taken to respond to alarms increases with more demanding fault states.

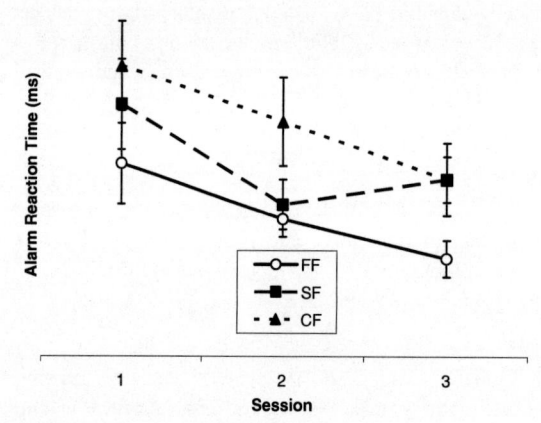

Figure 2. Effects of practice on acquisition of alarm reaction time (FF = fault free, SF = simple fault, CF = complex fault).

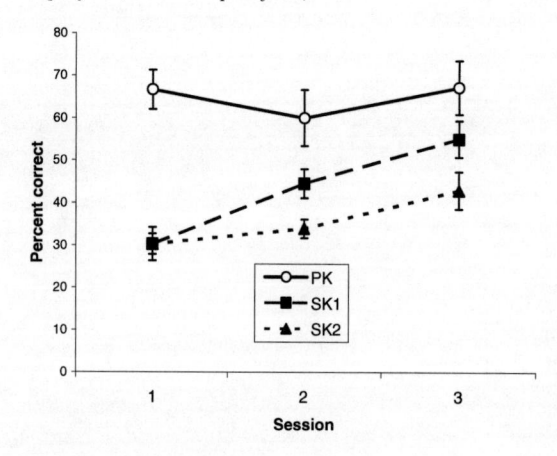

Figure 3. Effects of practice on acquisition of procedural and system knowledge (PK = procedural knowledge, SK1 = system knowledge/prompted questions, SK2 = system knowledge/open questions).

Knowledge learning

Figure 3 shows changes in rule-based and system-based knowledge over the three sessions. While there is an overall improvement in knowledge scores (main effect of time; F(2,18)=7.99, p<.01), this applies primarily to system based knowledge (both SK1 and SK2), whereas rule-based knowledge (PK) appears relatively stable. This is confirmed by the significant interaction (F(4,36)=4.26, p<.01).

Discussion

In general, the results show that acquisition of practical skill and knowledge may occur at different rates during the course of a protracted training programme. While both show obvious improvements, procedural skill appears to reach an asymptote earlier (by the second testing period), while knowledge continues to develop over the full assessment period. The data also show two further detailed patterns of learning: (1) RT to alarms continues to fall, reflecting the continued reduction in primary task demands with practice beyond the point of error reduction (Anderson, 1981) (2) The more gradual development of knowledge acquisition is confined to understanding about system relationships, while knowledge about the use of rules and procedures is established very early. At one level, such findings are consistent with widely accepted distinctions between procedural and declarative knowledge in the training/learning literature (Anderson, 1993). At another level, however, they show that such differences may also be observed within the learning of a complex task such as autoCAMS.

The goal of the training program was to provide intensive training at all levels of learning: procedural skill; problem solving skill; procedural knowledge; and system knowledge. Although the two kinds of knowledge appear to have different roles in the execution of control performance and fault management each learning component contributes to the competence expected of operators of complex systems (Hockey et al., 2007). The literature and research in this area demonstrates that training based on an understanding of system knowledge leads to more flexible learning, allowing more effective transfer to unfamiliar or complex task demands. Procedural training, on the other hand, by making fewer demands on the use of limited capacity knowledge-based problem solving strategies, is regarded as more generally useful for everyday operational performance (Moray, 1999).

We would have expected that operators who demonstrated sound system knowledge would be more successful in managing the system under the demands of novel and complex fault scenarios. This is not borne out by the correlation data, though the small sample size and non-normality for several variables makes such an analysis inappropriate. In addition, from Figure 3, it is clear that learning is still proceeding, even after six training sessions, so that the link between knowledge and performance may not yet be clearly established. In general, it is fair to say that, at least during the formative stages of acquisition, performance is not strongly determined by either kind of task knowledge, and also that rule and system knowledge contribute rather separately to performance. With more extensive training and task practice we would expect that system knowledge would help much more in dealing with complex fault states, while procedural knowledge may be more useful in managing the system under routine control conditions (Moray, 1999). We plan to test these expectations in future assessments with this sample of participants.

References

Anderson, J.R. (1981). Cognitive skills and their acquisition. Hillsdale, NJ: Erlbaum.
Anderson, J.R. (1993). Problem solving and learning. *American Psychologist, 48*, 35-44.
Berry, D.C., & Broadbent, D.E. (1988). Interactive tasks and the implicit-explicit distinction. *British Journal of Psychology, 79*, 251-272.
Hall, K.G., & Magill, R.A. (1995). Variability of practice and contextual interference in motor skill learning. *Journal of Motor Behavior, 27*, 299-309.
Hockey G.R.J., Wastell D., & Sauer J. (1998). Effects of sleep deprivation and user interface on complex performance: a multilevel analysis of compensatory control. *Human Factors, 40*, 233-253.
Hockey, G.R.J., Sauer, J., & Wastell, D.G. (2007, in press). Adaptability of training in simulated process control: knowledge- versus rule-based guidance under task changes and environmental Stress. *Human Factors, 49*.
Lorenz, B., Di Nocera, F., Röttger, S., & Parasuraman, R. (2002). Automated fault-management in a simulated spaceflight micro-world. *Aviation Space & Environmental Medicine, 73*, 886-897.
Moray, N. (1999). The cognitive psychology and cognitive engineering of industrial systems. In F.T. Durso (Ed.), *Handbook of Applied Cognition* (pp. 209–246). Chichester, UK: Wiley.
Nickel, P., Roberts, A.C., Roberts, M.H., & Hockey, G.R.J. (2007). Development of a cyclic loading method for the study of patterns of breakdown in complex performance under high load. In D. de Waard, G.R.J. Hockey, P. Nickel, and K.A. Brookhuis (Eds.) (2007), *Human Factors Issues in Complex System Performance* (pp. 325-338). Maastricht, the Netherlands: Shaker Publishing.
Rasmussen, J. (1983). Skills, rules, and knowledge: Signals, signs, and symbols, and other distinctions in human performance models. *IEEE Transactions on Systems, Man, and Cybernetics, 13*, 257-266.
Rissland, E.L. (2006). AI and Similarity. *IEEE Intelligent Systems 21(3)*, 39-49.
Sauer, J., Hockey, G., & Wastell, D. (2000). Effects of training on short and long term skill retention in a complex multiple-task environment, *Ergonomics, 43*, 2043-2064.
Schmidt, R.A. (1975). A schema theory of discrete motor skill learning. *Psychological Review, 82*, 225-260.

Introducing "medarbetarskap" as a concept facilitating work related relationships: theoretical considerations in an airport change process

Johan Jönsson, Curt R. Johansson, Marcus Arvidsson, Roland Akselsson
Lund University
Sweden

Abstract

The Swedish Air Navigation Service Provider, Luftfartsverket, together with Stockholm-Arlanda airport are implementing a new socio-technical concept called collaborative decision making. New technology and work procedures in collaborative decision making are directly affecting all organizations in an airplane turn-round process, and indirectly affecting legislators, authorities, suppliers, and passengers. A change of this magnitude needs a holistic approach covering the relationships among affected stakeholders. *Medarbetarskap* is introduced as a theoretical, ideological, and practical concept focusing on relationships based on democratic values, free and open communication, and experiential learning processes. Furthermore, medarbetarskap favours an intra-, and inter-organizational structure to align management/leadership, staff/workers, and work tasks at different systematic levels and different organizations to reach a common understanding of what is important in any given situation. From a psychological perspective, medarbetarskap facilitates learning via communication and reflection to develop knowledge about human behaviour and relationships from an individual to a societal level. The introduction of collaborative decision making will be examined from the starting-point that medarbetarskap facilitates the change process and daily operations at Stockholm-Arlanda airport by increasing horizontal and vertical collaboration, commitment, ability to influence, buy-in, empowerment, and by decreasing the gap between the technical and socio-organizational implementation process.

Introduction

The air transportation system is struggling with extensive delays. Airports are responsible for more than half of these, partially due to fragmented airport information flows, lack of accurate information, and low predictability of operations at airports (EUROCONTROL, no date). Airport delays are caused by a complex socio-technical system coordinating several airport actors' operations in and round the aircraft, at the apron, and in the vicinity of the airport. The national Air Navigation Service Provider in Sweden, Luftfartsverket (LFV), has together with Stockholm-Arlanda airport identified several shortages in the system. A new socio-technical concept, airport collaborative decision making – CDM – will therefore be introduced to bring about efficient cooperation and coordination among the different airport actors/stakeholders. CDM is a systematic and well structured way of handling information about flight operations and the turn-round process at airports. The turn-round process encompasses all events and operations concerning aircrafts' approach and arrival to, operations at (fuelling, baggage handling, catering, ground control, maintenance, etc.), and departure from an airport (Jönsson, Johansson, & Akselsson, 2006).

The Stockholm-Arlanda airport CDM project

It is planned that the CDM implementation at Stockholm-Arlanda airport will start in 2007. Most of the technical solutions are ready for use and a socio-organizational implementation process is about to start. The CDM concept contains new technology and new work procedures/tasks affecting in different ways a lot of organizations at socio-technical system levels from operators to coordinators, from work, personnel, and resource planners to management, from employers to authorities (LFV and Swedish Civil Aviation Authority) and legislators besides safety functions.

Jönsson et al. (2006) conducted a pilot study at Stockholm-Arlanda airport where the results showed that the planning and development phase of the new socio-technical concept, i.e. the introduction of CDM, was characterized by low participation of affected stakeholders, lack of information, and ineffective communication among stakeholders. In turn, that led to low knowledge and awareness about CDM, negative experiences, attitudes, and emotions towards the pre-implementation phase. A conclusion was that there should be better commitment from management and employees enhancing their communication and relationships both vertically and horizontally within as well as between organizations at the airport and beyond to customers, suppliers, competitors, and authorities.

Researchers from Lund University together with LFV and organizations operating at Stockholm-Arlanda airport will study the implementation process over approximately two years. Based on a literature review, case studies, and results from the pilot study the aim is to examine how the CDM implementation process affects management and leadership, employees and their relationships to each other and to management, and finally the safety culture as aviation is a high reliability domain. Leadership will be studied including the counterpart – the employees, as leadership seen as an isolated aspect in a change process can be misguiding without attention devoted to the employees. It will be studied with Hersey and Blanchard's (1977) situational leadership theory, even though leadership will not be treated in this paper. Safety culture will be handled in later phases of the two year project in order to further develop Ek's safety culture questionnaire (Ek, 2006) and therefore safety culture will not be treated in this paper. The focus will be on the psycho-social relationships involving and affecting the employees in a complex-dynamic setting.

Medarbetarskap and empowerment

Medarbetarskap is a Scandinavian concept based on democratic organizational values. Internationally it is a rather new concept with no particular research history and no equivalent English word according to the Cambridge or the Merriam-Webster dictionaries 2006. Medarbetarskap has similarities with empowerment but the main difference is that medarbetarskap focuses psycho-social and co-operative relations between people (Hällstén & Tengblad, 2006) instead of psycho-organizational processes and decision making characterizing empowerment (Kinlaw, 1995). Both medarbetarskap and empowerment are about roles and responsibilities, role training, and accountability. Medarbetarskap heeds how all employees support and relate to other people at different hierarchical levels, to the organization as a whole, and significant parties outside the organization in an empathic, ethical, communicative, and learning manner. The relationship part in medarbetarskap depends on leadership, commitment, influence, communication, learning, and the ability to listen.

Social and psycho-organizational aspects in a change process

Most organizations today agree on the need for a clear and wide-spread vision and strategy to successfully navigate through fierce competition. Leadership commitment and employee involvement with the ability to influence are crucial parts in development change processes (Greenbaum, Jackson, & McKeon, 1998). Leaders' leadership style and employees' interaction styles depend on their work and the job situation (Hersey & Blanchard, 1977). Organizational change needs a "change communication" strategy to be established to align all staff with the change (Greenbaum et al., 1998).

A survey of 12,000 communication professionals world-wide plus a sample survey of senior executives from U.S. Fortune 200 companies executed by Greenbaum et el. (1998), indicated that leadership and employee involvement are key drivers for change. According to their study the four best practices to succeed with a change process are: 1) effective communication, 2) employee involvement, 3) leadership and commitment from senior management, and 4) evidence that management is leading the change. Some to all of these practices are supported by other researchers and practitioners, e.g. Drucker (2002), Kinlaw (1995), Margulies and Kleiner (1995), and Waddell and Sohal (1998). These practices are all focusing on management, employees, and dialogue – three important social aspects. From a psycho-organizational perspective this can be studied, understood, and explained as leadership on the one hand, medarbetarskap on the other, and communication as the integrative link between the two psycho-organizational aspects. From a relationship perspective, the three aspects should not be studied separately. The aspects are so closely interrelated that communication should be studied as an essential function with bearing on medarbetarskap.

Working with change processes can not be done without considering possible short and long term effects on other system levels, i.e. the relationships between legislators, managers and work planners to system operators (Rasmussen, 1997). Ekstedt and Wirdenius (1996) illustrate four important levels that need to be considered when conducting a change process: 1) the physical-structural level (technology, equipment, environment), 2) the institutional level (rules, traditions, culture), 3) the work organizational level (delegation and coordination of work/team spirit), and 4) the individual level.

Purpose

The purpose of this paper is twofold. The first is exploring the literature from a theoretical and empirical perspective as well as from other theoretical considerations. It aims at introducing the Scandinavian concept of medarbetarskap, and how it relates to leadership and communication. The introduction is historical, ideological and theoretical from a psychological perspective. The second purpose is to discuss medarbetarskap in relation to the implementation of the large-scale, dynamic, and complex socio-technical concept – CDM – at Stockholm-Arlanda airport.

Medarbetarskap – two different perspectives

Medarbetarskap will first be described briefly from an "ethical connection perspective" including roles and responsibilities, abilities and authorities. As a second step medarbetarskap will be more in depth described and discussed from a "psychological perspective" adding communication and trust, development and learning to the former perspective.

Ethical connection perspective

Definition

The ethical connection perspective is mainly taken from Hällstén and Tengblad (2006), in which the concept and definition are described and discussed in length. These authors define medarbetarskap as (free translation): "Medarbetarskap concerns how a co-worker manages the relationship toward its employer and the own work" (Hällstén and Tengblad, 2006, p. 10). "Manages the relationship" stresses the employee's ability to act responsible and balance on the one hand rights and authorities, and on the other obligations and responsibilities. Medarbetarskap integrates an individual and a collective perspective with regard to the job situation. "The own work" includes responsibility, self-leadership, and demarcation of work life and private life (Hällstén & Tengblad, ibid).

Theoretical background

The theoretical background of Hällstén and Tengblad's (2006) definition of medarbetarskap refers to the stewardship theory, ability based ethics, the citizen concept, and virtue ethics.

The stewardship theory is about the individual's driving forces that are not related to motives of self-interest. Employers must be convinced that the employees will perform well under all circumstances. It is about the ambition to do the right thing, and the value of strengthening confidence and loyalty in a state of dependence favouring all participating parties. *Ability based ethics* are about the employees' abilities to maintain a worthy work life together with superiors and co-workers. *The citizen concept* (from Immanuel Kant) concerns the connection between the employees' authority and their will and ability to use their intellect. A guiding principle is to treat others as you want to be treated yourself. *Virtue ethics* emphasize the establishment of good habits. It is not the values per se that are important but how they are expressed in behaviour. Thus, medarbetarskap is about *who* I am as a person in the organization I work. Taken together Hällstén and Tengblad (2006) summarize the four theoretical perspectives related to medarbetarskap as (free translation):

> The authoritative medarbetarskap is based on a great appreciation of trustful and responsibility-taking relationships between superiors and co-workers (stewardship theory), which can create a sound foundation for the essential task and strengthen the co-worker's abilities (ability based ethics) to act as a responsible subject with moral integrity (citizen concept) and that together with superiors and other co-workers develop good habits and acting patterns (virtue ethics). (p. 14)

Psychological perspective

Theoretical background

From a psychological perspective medarbetarskap is about creating and maintaining relationships, trust, and personal development among all members within an organization, but also between collaborating or competing organizations (customers, suppliers, consultants, clients, etc.), and between organizations and society (authorities, environmental organizations, etc.). According to the medarbetarskap concept that is to be done through free and open communication – horizontally at the same or equivalent organizational level and vertically across different organizational levels – of available information and through reflection on all acts in a given situation (Argyris, Putnam, & Smith, 1985). Argyris et al. (1985) emphasize that one's own and others' assumptions concerning how and why oneself and other people act as they do, should be tested unprejudiced. Johansson (2003) argues that a reflecting discussion is a prerequisite to gain a deeper understanding of how people act, to consciously change one's own behaviour in a responsible way, and to help others to further develop. For this to be possible, all members in such a medarbetarskap-related discussion need to verbalize and openly test observable facts to gain insight in group processes and to minimize the risk to create misunderstandings and conflicts. Argyris et al. (1985) proved it to work in group settings even though free and open communication was not easily established. Conservative and hierarchical organizational levels often work as communication barriers letting information flow downwards in the organization but seldom upwards. The telling technique (one-way communication) characterizing many leaders is more common than the dialogue technique (two-way communication) characterizing medarbetarskap.

Through informal contracts employees learn from each other as equals in medarbetarskap settings. The person best suited takes the lead and creates what Risling and Risling (1996) call a learning dialogue. The primary purpose of a learning dialogue is to increase knowledge and awareness, facilitate the possibilities to have a free and open communication, and to decrease control and counterproductive behaviour. According to Kolb (1984) learning is described as a cyclical knowledge-generating process based on reflection and theorizing over concrete experiences and experimentally testing one's own ideas and hypotheses. The learner works as an active creator of knowledge and know-how in medarbetarskap situations. Concrete experiences are the foundation for learning. The learning outcome is dependent on how much time and attention is devoted to understanding the experiences. Reflection and considerations lead to general patterns from which hypotheses and theories are formulated around the experiences. Learning is transformations of what is personally experienced to a higher cognitive level. The hypotheses derived are tested in new situations through experimental variation of former experiences. Learning has two sides. The learner constructs and reconstructs meaning (knowledge) mentally, and behaviourally tests new ways of acting, talking, and performing tasks (competence).

The prerequisites for free and open communication characterizing medarbetarskap are described by what Argyris and Schön call Model II (Argyris, 1990, 1993, 1999; Argyris & Schön, 1996). Model II that is presented in table 1 opens up for rethinking a problem, i.e. to change variables governing our behaviour and apply double-loop learning, and to be aware of one's own and other people's psychological processes. For Model II and medarbetarskap to be successful a person's *espoused theory* and *theory-in-use* must be congruent. The espoused theory is a program of explicit values and attitudes affecting a person's behaviour very little, while the theory-in-use is made up of the governing variables that often unconsciously control and affect people's behaviour. In practice it means you must "walk the talk". Even though the actor usually is unaware of the discrepancy between what is said, espoused theory, and what is done, theory-in-use, work mates and other people are aware. Model I is not the opposite of Model II, but it is consciously or unconsciously the general model behind most theory-in-use independent of cultural belonging. The process and results of using Model I are hampering the process or results that could be attained by using Model II (see table 1).

Table 1. Model II theory-in-use characterizing medarbetarskap and leading to increased effectiveness (Argyris, 1999; Argyris & Schön, 1996).

Governing variables	Action strategies	Consequences for the behavioural world	Consequences for learning
Valid information	Design situations where participants can be origins and experience personal causation	Actor experienced as minimally defensive (facilitator and choice creator)	Disconfirmable process
Free and informed choice	Tasks are controlled jointly	Minimally defensive group dynamics	Double-loop learning
Internal commitment to the choice and constant monitoring of implementation	Protection of self is a joint enterprise and oriented towards growth (speak in directly observable categories) Bilateral protection of others	Learning-oriented norms (trust, open confrontation on difficult issues)	Public testing of theories

Definition

Given the theoretical background and based on a psychological perspective *medarbetarskap is defined as how an employee, be it a top level manager, a supervisor, a clerk or a blue colour worker, manages the relationships to the organization, the employer and other people inside the organization, and to the own tasks as well as the relationships to people outside the organization such as customers, suppliers, competitors or authorities through an open and reflective horizontal and vertical communication with the aim to establish mutual understanding between people, and facilitate learning about important organizational aspects such as values, attitudes, collaboration around work tasks affecting human behaviour and human relationships at individual, group, organizational, and societal levels leading people to treat each other and be treated as individuals.*

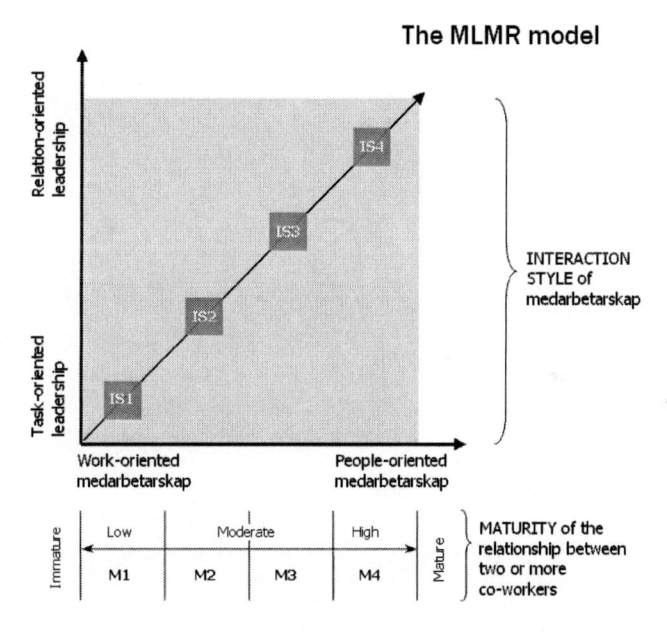

Figure 1. The Medarbetarskap-Leadership-Maturity Relationship model (MLMR)

The effects of medarbetarskap are that the co-workers have the prerequisites to feel, understand, and act with empathy (interaction style) towards other people. As figure 1 illustrates, medarbetarskap is a continuum ranging from a work-orientation focusing on the work to be performed to a people-orientation focusing on interpersonal job relations to other people inside or outside the organization. Integrated with managers' and supervisors' leadership orientation and the relationship maturity of the organizational members, the medarbetarskap influences the interaction style at different levels in the organization. The interaction style vector in figure 1 illustrates how a structural focus on work procedures, equipment and materials can be developed to encompass a dynamic focus on relationships between employees, between employees and management and between other people within and outside the company. The medarbetarskap-leadership-maturity relationship model (MLMR) offers interesting possibilities to investigate what are the most productive and efficient interaction styles in different work settings. Work-oriented medarbetarskap and task-oriented leadership can for instance be expected to be favourable in a newly established company with rather low maturity of the staff – interaction style IS1. However, it has to be empirically examined whether people-oriented medarbetarskap and relationship-oriented leadership with high maturity of the staff – interaction style IS4 – is a better combination of medarbetarskap and leadership than people-oriented medarbetarskap and task-oriented leadership, where medarbetarskap and leadership complement rather than match each other. Other combinations of medarbetarskap, leadership and staff maturity have to be carefully studied. The MLMR model is partially influenced by Hersey and Blanchard's (1977) situational leadership model – Leader Effectiveness and Adaptability Description (LEAD). In LEAD the leader adapt the leadership style (task behaviour and relationship behaviour) dependent of four different levels of follower maturity.

Medarbetarskap is seen at four levels. Maturity 1 (M1) stands for low relationship maturity between co-workers. M1 denotes a maturity level that is rather developed compared to relationships that has not reached medarbetarskap. Dependent on the maturity level of the relationship a co-worker has the will and ability to act in specific interaction styles (IS). As the relationship maturity increases from M1 to M4, the employees have the ability to change their interaction style from IS1 to IS4. At a more mature relationship the possibilities to use different interaction styles increase and therefore more diverse needs can be handled at any given situation. At M1, IS1 can be used; at M2, IS1 and IS2 can be used; at M3, IS1 to IS3 can be used; and at level M4, all IS can be used. The interaction styles are defined as:

- *IS1: Task-professional medarbetarskap and leadership*
  A co-worker has support and the will and ability to communicate, and learn when the situation relates to operative tasks.
- *IS2: Collegial-professional medarbetarskap and leadership*
  A co-worker has support and the will and ability to communicate, and learn when the situation relates to collegial relationships important to the operative tasks.
- *IS3: Socio-professional medarbetarskap and leadership*
  A co-worker has support and the will and ability to communicate, and learn when the situation relates to all types of social relationships at work. Tasks and relations are permeated with positive values, attitudes, and emotions influencing the professional self.
- *IS4: Socio-emotional medarbetarskap and leadership*
  A co-worker has support and the will and ability to communicate, and learn when the situation relates to all types of social

Communication and change

According to Pastor (1996) any organization going through a change must constantly communicate with all its employees. When employees feel included and informed about the organizational change and how it will impact them, there is greater chance they will see themselves as part of the whole team and pull together for the good of the organization. Greenbaum et al. (1998) say that leadership commitment and employee involvement are essential to gain employee buy-in. Employee involvement and influence is more than building commitment. It is a mechanism to create an effective, specific, and actionable implementation plan based on real behaviour changes.

In the Greenbaum's et al. (1998) study only 30 per cent of the surveyed employees agreed that they had "an opportunity to contribute ideas before changes are made to affect me" (p. 9). This proved a large gap between management's intention to involve employees and employees' perception about their level of involvement. Kappelman and Richards (1996) studied influence in the decision process affecting their individual sphere in the bank branch during the implementation of a data system. The more empowered employees showed 88 per cent more motivation, 146 per cent more satisfaction with their training and 99 per cent more satisfied with the change process.

Communication must have an impact on social behaviour to be effective in a change process such as the implementation of new technology like CDM. Mass communication is important in spreading awareness of new possibilities and practices. However, at the stage where decisions are to be made about whether to adopt or not, personal communication is far more likely to be influential (Servaes, 1996). Communication structures in organizations as in networks can both be horizontal and vertical. The information and cooperation in vertical structures have less probability to be reliable due to barriers between the levels. These are hard for subordinates to penetrate and lacking trust can develop into conflicts obstructing collective action. The prerequisites in horizontal communication structures make it easier to solve conflicts. Better communication possibilities and greater openness facilitates trust among equal partners. Collective understandings are easier to penetrate (Putnam, Leonardi, & Nanetti, 1992).

Likert's (1961) linking pin theory describes how an organization is represented as a number of overlapping *work units* in which members of one unit are leaders of another. These individuals are the *linking pins* in the organization forming a social network. The linking pins can at the same time be subordinates in one group setting and superiors in another, creating vertical linking. They can also be members at the same level in different groups creating horizontal linking. According to Likert (1961) this scheme is an effective way to make decisions and perform work tasks. Linking pins do not only facilitate information, communication, and decision making, but also dissemination of knowledge and competence development. This is of importance for the CDM implementation at Stockholm-Arlanda airport.

Margulies and Kleiner (1995) mention how self-managed project or product work groups facilitate change communication due to their ability to make decisions regarding the project. They also mention that working as a close team develops bounds between the members and employee motivation rises as a result of job satisfaction and self actualization. Linked to medarbetarskap organizational communication benefits since project teams stimulate lateral exchange of information as a strong complement to vertical communication. Brower (1995) develops this theory further when he describes how empowered teams (also applicable for medarbetarskap) are aligned along three dimensions: internally within the team; horizontally with customers, suppliers and other teams in their own organization; and vertically with all the hierarchy levels in the organization. Within the aligned team, members share the mission, vision, values and goals. But for that to become an intra- or even an inter-organizational culture, those aspects must be spread as a common understanding over the boundaries for just one team.

Lateral information does not necessarily have to be intra-organizational. With "boundary spanners" (compare with Likert's linking pin theory) this can be facilitated into an inter-organizational co-ordination (Mulford, in (Granot, 1999)). Boundary spanning could be ad hoc and informally operated by people with similar interests exchanging ideas and information. But until spanning becomes routinised, policy-making personnel need to be actively involved and call for activity beyond the boundary of one organization (Granot, 1999).

Discussion

Stockholm-Arlanda airport is a dynamic and complex system. The complexity of the system is one reason to implement the CDM concept for coordinating all processes in the turn-round process. However, the complexity and all the uncontrolled factors make the implementation of CDM difficult. Therefore it is necessary to have an approach like medarbetarskap in the implementation process to manage the complexity when individuals, organizations, and society simultaneous interact. The optimal implementation and use of the CDM concept is believed to bring financial profit as well as advantages in planning, leading, and executing the turn-round process.

The pilot study at Stockholm-Arlanda airport (Jönsson et al., 2006) shows that participation, empowerment, and ability to influence the CDM implementation process are low. This leads to negative emotions and lack of understanding towards the implementation process (psycho-organizational aspects). Lack of information and ineffective communication (social aspects) in the planning and development phase of the CDM concept seems to be one of the causes to that. Intra- and inter-organizational relationships are halting as both hierarchical and organizational boundaries hamper communication, learning, and collaboration. Results in the pilot study made it explicit that upper management held back information to their employees, employees did not actively search for information, and organizations did not share information with other organizations as a matter of winning or losing business advantages and financial profits. The ineffective social aspects and insufficient psycho-organizational and psycho-social aspects are believed to be the major causes for delaying the CDM implementation when most technical solutions are developed. Medarbetarskap pays attention to the relationships in general and to an open and free communication (Argyris, 1990, 1993; Argyris et al., 1985), experiential learning (Kolb, 1984), cross-boundary relationships (Brower, 1995; Granot, 1999; Likert, 1961), and interpersonal psychological processes in particular.

Following this discussion, medarbetarskap can be an important concept facilitating the implementation and operation of new technologies such as CDM at airports. It can favour more functional organizations and better understanding within and between organizations. To optimize effectiveness, medarbetarskap and leadership need to work in symbiosis. An example of developing medarbetarskap at Stockholm-Arlanda airport is the creating of organizational (vertical) and professional (horizontal) groups. These groups will have the ability, internally and externally, to communicate and learn from each other's diversities, creating a shared understanding of the CDM concept. The magnitude of the changes will involve the relationships between authorities that perform a controlling function, employers, safety managers and engineers, suppliers, unions, airplane operators, and passengers.

The theoretical background is mostly based on theories that take time to implement, to work with, and to understand. Never the less, medarbetarskap is a concept integrating the counterparts in consideration, i.e. leaders – communication – employees. The ideology behind medarbetarskap is the same ideologies that most people take for granted in their every day life, namely democracy. It is a matter of course that we enjoy societal democracy, and it is the same thoughts behind organizational democracy and union democracy. It is not the meaning that medarbetarskap shall lead to large-scale meetings where all have the same possibility to influence or make decisions. It is still an organization where management and the president have the legal and economical responsibility to create strategy and tactics, and to lead the organization. But medarbetarskap is about the fact that all employees in an organization have the same value, and the possibility to influence, affect decisions, and be empowered. What it comes down to in practice is that if the employees cannot cooperate (on a daily basis or in a change process) with each other, they will find it hard to cooperate with their supervisors or managers. Furthermore, it must be considered to be of utmost importance for an organization to utilize the commercial potential of a well developed medarbetarskap.

The plan for the forthcoming two-year project between Lund University and Stockholm-Arlanda airport is to study medarbetarskap; the function of medarbetarskap, and how medarbetarskap is affected by and affects the implementation of CDM (new technology, procedures, and tasks). The authors believe that the groups/organizations with a more developed medarbetarskap can more efficient cope, adopt, and manage the new working conditions in a competitive, dynamic and complex socio-technical system.

References

Argyris, C. (1990). *Overcoming organizational defenses: Facilitating organizational learning.* Boston: Allyn and Bacon.

Argyris, C. (1993). *Knowledge for action: A guide to overcoming barriers to organizational change*. San Francisco: Jossey-Bass.
Argyris, C. (1999). *On organizational learning*. Oxford; Malden, MA: Blackwell Business.
Argyris, C., Putnam, R., & Smith, D.M. (1985). *Action science: Concepts, methods, and skills for research and intervention*). San Francisco: Jossey-Bass.
Argyris, C., & Schön, D.A. (1996). *Organizational learning II: Theory, method and practice*. Reading, MA: Addison-Wesley.
Brower, M.J. (1995). Empowering teams: What, why, and how. *Empowerment in Organizations, 3*, 13-25.
Drucker, P.F. (2002). *Management challenges for the 21 st century*. Oxford: Butterworth-Heinemann.
Ek, Å. (2006). *Safety culture in sea and aviation transport*. Lund University, Lund.
Ekstedt, E., & Wirdenius, H. (1996). Struktur, institution och individ: Kunskapens bindning och organisationers förnyelse [Structure, institution and individual: The binding of knowledge and the renewal of organizations]. In G. Ekvall (Ed.), *Navigatör och inspiratör: Om chefer, ledarskap och förändring [Navigator and inspirer: About managers, leadership and change]* (pp. 161-189). Lund: Studentlitteratur.
EUROCONTROL. (no date). *An interactive CDM project presentation*. Retrieved October 20, 2005, from http://www.euro-cdm.org/
Granot, H. (1999). Emergency inter-organizational relationships. *Disaster Prevention and Management, 8*, 21-26.
Greenbaum, K.B., Jackson, D.H., & McKeon, N.I. (1998). Communicating for change. *The Marsh and McLennan Companies Quarterly, 28(1)*, 8.
Hersey, P., & Blanchard, K. H. (1977). *Management of organizational behavior: Utilizing human resources*. Englewood Cliffs, N.J.: Prentice-Hall.
Hällstén, F., & Tengblad, S. (2006). Medarbetarskap i praktiken [Medarbetarskap in practice]. In F. Hällstén & S. Tengblad (Eds.), *Medarbetarskap i praktiken [Medarbetarskap in practice]* (pp. 9-32). Lund: Studentlitteratur.
Johansson, C.R. (2003). *Personal, och organisationsutveckling genom personalsamverkan [Personnel and organizational development through personnel cooperation]*.Unpublished manuscript, Lund.
Jönsson, J., Johansson, C.R., & Akselsson, R. (2006). Collaborative decision making (CDM): A pilot study exploring participation and empowerment before implementing new technology and work procedures. In D. de Waard, K.A. Brookhuis, and A. Toffetti (Eds.), *Developments in human factors: In transportation, design, and evaluation* (pp. 237-248). Maastricht: Shaker Publishing.
Kappelman, L.A., & Richards, T.C. (1996). Training, empowerment, and creating a culture for change. *Empowerment in Organizations, 4(3)*, 26-29.
Kinlaw, D.C. (1995). *Medarbetarskap: Att på bästa sätt använda och utveckla de anställdas kompetens* (C. G. Liungman, Trans.). Lund: Studentlitteratur.
Kolb, D.A. (1984). *Experiential learning: Experience as the source of learning and development*. Englewood Cliffs, NJ: Prentice-Hall.
Likert, R. (1961). *New patterns of management*. New York: McGraw-Hill.

Margulies, J.S., & Kleiner, B.H. (1995). New designs of work groups: Applications of empowerment. *Empowerment in Organizations, 3(2)*, 12-18.

Pastor, J. (1996). Empowerment: What it is and what it is not. *Empowerment in Organizations, 4(2)*, 5-7.

Putnam, R.D., Leonardi, R., & Nanetti, R.Y. (1992). *Making democracy work: Civic traditions in modern Italy*. Princeton, NJ: Princeton University Press.

Rasmussen, J. (1997). Risk management in a dynamic society: A *modelling problem. Safety Science, 27*, 183-213.

Risling, U., & Risling, A. (1996). V*attentrappan: Att utveckla kommunikation och organisatorisk kompetens [The water step: To develop communication and organizational competence]*. Solna, Sweden: Arbetslivsinstitutet.

Servaes, J. (1996). Linking theoretical perspectives to policy. In J. Servaes, T.L. Jacobson, and S.A. White (Eds.), *Participatory communication for social change* (pp. 29-43). Thousand Oaks, CA: Sage Publications Inc.

Waddell, D., & Sohal, A. S. (1998). Resistance: A constructive tool for change management. *Management Decision, 36*, 543-548.

Acknowledgement to reviewers

The editors owe debt to the following colleagues who helped to review the manuscripts for this book:

Henrik Artman, Royal Institute of Technology (KTH), Sweden
Chris Baber, University of Birmingham, Birmingham, UK
Richard Backs, Central Michigan University, USA
Susanne Build, Würzburger Institut für Verkehrswissenschaften, Veithochheim, Germany
Richard Bye, Network Rail, London, UK
Jeff Caird, University of Calgary, Calgary, Canada
Nick Dickety, Health and Safety Executive, Gas & Pipelines Unit, Norfolk, UK
Judy Edworthy, University of Plymouth, Plymouth, UK
Stéphane Espié, INRETS, Arcueil, France
Stephen Fairclough, Liverpool John Moores University, Liverpool, UK
Frank Flemisch, DLR German Aerospace Centre, Braunschweig, Germany
Peter Hancock, University of Central Florida, Orlando, FL, USA
Per Henriksson, VTI, Linköping, Sweden
Piet Hoogeboom, NLR National Aerospace Laboratory, Amsterdam, The Netherlands
Jettie Hoonhout, Philips Research, Eindhoven, the Netherlands
Addie Johnson, University of Groningen, Groningen, the Netherlands
Bodil Jönsson, Lunds Tekniska Högskola, Lund, Sweden
Micky Kerr, Leeds University Business School, Leeds, UK
Josef Krems, TU Chemnitz, Chemnitz, Germany
Dietrich Manzey, TU Berlin, Berlin, Germany
Nicolas Marmaras, National Technical University of Athens, Zografos, Greece
Stefan Röttger, TU Berlin, Berlin, Germany
Leif Rydstedt, Högskolan Väst, Vänersborg, Sweden
Jürgen Sauer, Universität Freiburg, Freiburg, Switzerland
Harald Schaub, IABG, Ottobrunn, Germany
Frank Steyvers, University of Groningen, the Netherlands
John Stoop, Delft University of Technology, Delft, the Netherlands
Oliver Straeter, Eurocontrol, Brussels, Belgium
Andy Tattersall, Liverpool John Moores University, Liverpool, UK
Pieter Unema, University of Utah, Salt Lake City, US
Hendrik-Jan van Veen, TNO Defence, Security, and Safety, Soesterberg, the Netherlands
Colete Weeda, Intergo BV, Utrecht, the Netherlands
Steve Westerman, University of Leeds, Leeds, UK
Heino Widdel, FGAN – FKIE, Wachtberg, Germany

In D. de Waard, G.R.J. Hockey, P. Nickel, and K.A. Brookhuis (Eds.) (2007), *Human Factors Issues in Complex System Performance* (pp. 511). Maastricht, the Netherlands: Shaker Publishing.